CW01671760

LAKELAND FROM THE AIR

In memory of my mother, who never quite believed
that photography could be a proper job.

LAKELAND FROM THE AIR

Peter Thornton
LBIPP, MMPA

Dalesman Books • 1985

The Dalesman Publishing Company Ltd,
Clapham, via Lancaster, LA2 8EB

First published 1985

© Peter Thornton 1985 (photographs, and text on pages 9-14)
© Dalesman Publishing Company Ltd 1985 (text on pages 25-78)

ISBN 0 85206 850 6 (hardback)
0 85206 901 4 (paperback)

Copies of the photographs in this book may be purchased from
Lakeland Photographic, Blackhall Yard, Kendal, Cumbria, LA9 4BW

Printed in Great Britain by Fretwell & Cox Limited,
Goulbourne Street, Keighley, West Yorkshire BD21 1PZ

Contents

"Mountain Lakeland" text by Tom Bowker

Cover photograph: Derwentwater and Skiddaw from above Borrowdale

Original photographs printed by Diane Law

Foreword
by A. Wainwright

FOR nearly sixty years I have been walking the fells of Lakeland, surveying the topography of the district and looking down on the valleys and lakes from the ridges and summits — always from a height of six feet above the ground.

Now, in this unique book, I see these well-loved places in a new dimension, with fresh eyes. Here are familiar subjects as I have never seen them before, presented in a collection of magnificent colour pictures by an expert photographer. Far below in these wonderful aerial scenes are the roads we have so often travelled, the paths and the mountain tops we know so well, all viewed in a new perspective and providing a rare opportunity to study, at leisure, their fascinating detail. They give renewed life to our tattered maps.

For anyone intimately acquainted with the Lake District this book will be a source of endless pleasure. Many, like myself, will prefer to look up at mountains, not down on them, and choose to have beauty around them, not far below, but all will rejoice greatly at seeing, for the first time, this lovely corner of England as the birds see it.

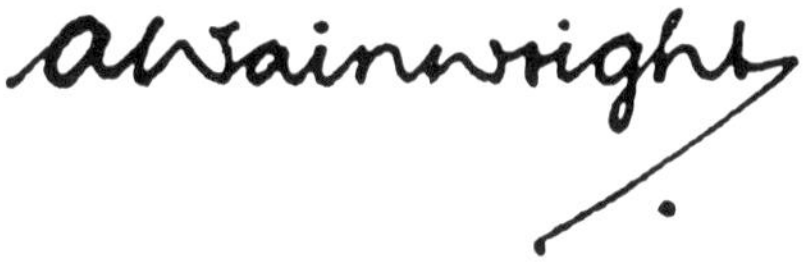

Lakeland from the Air

MY first flight was a birthday present at the age of twelve. It was from a small airfield near Ascona in Switzerland. I took my first aerial photograph on that flight and can remember my surprise on finding that it had come out. Was it really as simple as this? Just point the camera out of the window and press the button?

The Air Training Corp was next, with what were rather quaintly termed "Air Experience Flights". We were taken up in RAF Chipmunks, then the standard trainer. The Chipmunk can be transformed into a Spitfire by any cadet with the slightest imagination. The flights were magic, especially when we were able to take the controls and could then boast of having actually flown an aircraft, if not solo then very nearly so. Upon reflection, I don't suppose the instructors used to fight for the privilege. There was always at least one cadet willing to attempt to fill the small greaseproof bag that was tucked away in the back.

I joined the British Aircraft Corporation upon leaving school. The following two years were hardly packed with rich aviation experience but I did see Concorde 002 make its maiden flight. Teacher Training College followed, leading to a job at Longlands Boys School in Kendal. Not a lot of aviation opportunities here. A fellow teacher did once hire a Dart Herald 50-seater aircraft for an hour — it made a science lesson with a difference.

Then came photography. And at last the chance to climb aboard an aircraft and actually be in charge. We would take off and head for the Lakes. Upon arriving there we would look for pictures. Around Great Gable, past Scafell, then back to Keswick. In minutes. This was landscape photography without all the hard work! No picture was out of reach, and the amount of work that could be done in an afternoon was amazing.

This was the freedom of flying that no scheduled passenger can experience. The freedom of looking as far as you can see and saying "go there". With no roads to follow or maps to read. Just keep above 3,500 feet and watch out for the RAF flying beneath (rather pointless really for if they haven't seen you then there's not a lot that you can do!).

If you haven't experienced it then why not hire an aircraft for an hour or so. Get two friends and ring up Carlisle or Blackpol airport for a quote. It's not as expensive as you might think, and well worth the trip. (Is that worth 10% off my next trip?).

The Art of the Aerial Photographer

All photography is a blend of art and science. Aerial photography is no exception. The science, or perhaps craft would be a better term, lies in the choice of equipment and materials and in the mechanics of their use. The art is in how they are used.

A photographer will normally have control over viewpoint, lighting, arrangement of the subject and the lens in use. The aerial photographer is, in common with the landscape photographer, more limited. The lens is often the camera's standard lens. A wide-angle lens cannot be used in an aeroplane as wings and fuselage will intrude into the picture. A telephoto lens will emphasize any haze, an all too common problem. Arrangement of the subject is not usually possible, although industrial clients occasionally ask to be warned as to when photography is taking place, to give them a chance to arrange a site.

Lighting can be varied by choosing the time of day carefully. This, of course, only applies to the main target of the flight. Other jobs on the same flight then have to be shot in the same conditions, which may not then be the most suitable. The "safe" light is the midday sun. An evening or late afternoon sun can be very effective but many Lake District valleys will then be in deep shadow and impossible to photograph.

The main variable is the position of the aircraft in the sky. This is where the aerial photographer applies his art. There are three parameters which can be adjusted — height, angle and position. Maximum height (within the aircrafts limits) is usually limited by visibility. Minimum height is limited by law! Most of the photographs in this book have been taken at a height of between 500ft and 2,500ft which, if you think about it, is the height at which many landscape photographs are taken.

The angle at which the camera is pointed will vary between about 5 to 45 degrees to the ground. A flatter angle will be used when taking a landscape type of photograph, a steeper angle when photographing buildings and the like. A common mistake by beginners is to get too far overhead of the target and then to shoot almost vertically downwards. The most pleasing views are usually the ones that you would see if there had been a conveniently placed mountain on whch to stand! The position of the aircraft can then be varied to get precisely the view that is wanted, taking into account the position of the sun and also of the inevitable unsightly nearby rubbish tip!

The photographer develops a natural instinct for the picture that simply "looks right". The real problem is to convey this to the pilot, who is faced with an entirely different set of priorities. There is a limited amount of space out of which to shoot and the aircraft must be moved around rather than the camera. They cannot fly backwards and can take a surprisingly long time to turn round, especially if over a populated area where spectacular aerobatics are best avoided.

Once the photographer begins to work out the cost of each mistake then the end of creativity is in sight! Persistence is the key. A bad shot does not become a good one just because the aircraft is on its fourteenth pass and the job started to lose money four minutes ago. The final reward is a photograph of a view which few people have ever seen, and which cannot easily be copied!

Dambusters

Good pilots have two qualities — skill, allied to a keen instinct for self preservation. An aerial photographer needs to be single minded in pursuit of a picture. If getting a certain picture necessitates flying the aircraft up a blind valley at 300 feet then he will ask the pilot to do so. If the manoevre is potentially dangerous then it's his job to refuse. He must set the limits beyond which he will not go. After all he knows the aircraft's capabilities better than the photographer.

There are pilots who regard every tricky situation as a challenge. They are the ones to avoid! There are the occasional frustrated Biggles types whose big regret is that they missed out on the Battle of Britain.

I remember flying over Helvellyn towards Haweswater. The pilot saw the dam. His eyes narrowed, the nose dipped and, above the noise of the engine, I heard a familiar tune being whistled. The Dambusters march! There is a button on the control column which is used in connection with the radio. I got a strange feeling that it had been transformed into a bomb release switch!

Thankfully the majority of pilots are highly competent, especially if they hold a commercial licence. (It is, in fact, illegal for a pilot with a simple Private Pilot's Licence to undertake commercial work such as professional aerial photography). There is a popular line with flying instructors. "There are old pilots and there are bold pilots but there aren't many who are old *and* bold!"

Alternatives

Aircraft are not too expensive if they are being used on a well planned series of photographs. If, however, the weather turns bad and only half of the targets are reached or perhaps there is just one urgent job to be done, possibly a hotel say five miles away from our Studio, then costs can mount up alarmingly.

A hired aircraft is, in many ways, a real bargain. Over £1 per minute sounds expensive (it is!) but there is nothing else to pay. No maintenance charges, no petrol to buy, no pilot's wages. None of the worries of having to look afer an expensive piece of equipment. But it takes an hour to set the job up. There's a fifty mile drive to the airport, after which you have to fly back to where you've just come from and hope the weather hasn't changed. So what are the alternatives? The new generation of microlight aircraft are very tempting of course. £5,000, or less, to buy, strap it onto the roof-rack, put the engine in the boot and look for a green field near the site. I've seen pictures taken from microlights and they can be very impressive. Besides which, the opportunity to buy your own aircraft and set it against tax . . . ?

There are two main problems. Firstly I feel that flying and photography both demand full attention. I get very involved in the picture I'm taking. I can afford to do so because I've nothing else to concentrate on. If I had to contend with the possibility of flying into the ground then it all might become a bit too much — and no picture is that important. Secondly, most of my flights last about three hours and tour the complete Lake District. That's seven hours in a microlight!

Model aircraft, kites and balloons

What about model aircraft? Cheap and easy and convenient. Launch it from the back of the car and zoom around the target (radio controlled of course), then land on the pavement and home in time for tea.

Everyone who has never flown one is convinced that they must be the answer. Anyone who has, knows that they are not. Any model aircraft big and stable enough to carry a decent-sized camera is hardly a model at all! They are large, heavy, expensive and, in the wrong hands, dangerous. Even an expert would never fly one in a built-up area. And there's the problem of aiming the thing at the target when it's just a buzzing dot in the sky!

Kites have been used with some success but most of the pictures taken by kites have not been really planned beforehand. Send the camera up, press the shutter with some kind of remote release and see what turns out. Try to take a specific picture and it's not very easy at all. And then the wind drops!

A balloon could do the job. Or a radio-controlled airship. A video camera would have to be mounted with the still camera in order to allow manoeuvring to take place from the ground. Such equipment is technically feasible but expensive.

All of these alternatives involve expense and hard work. Compared with which a phone call to the airport and a 50 mile drive suddenly seem very easy. There is, as yet, no real alternative to a human eye behind the camera and personally I can't see that I look forward to the day when there will be. Who would subsidise my flying then?

Lakeland Aviation

Lakeland is not normally thought of as being in at the birth of aviation. The first flight in the Lake District is believed to have been a balloon ascent from Kendal in 1825 by a Mr Charles Green who went on to make many flights in the Cumbria area. The man-carrying kite was next, making its appearance in 1899 when its inventor, Samuel Cody, was appearing in "The Klondyke Nuggett" at Carlisle. Aerial photography was in existence in 1902 — as shown by an aerial shot of Cockermouth in the town library.

The first powered aircraft to be constructed in this area was built by the remarkable Rev Sidney Swann, vicar of Crosby Ravensworth. Unfortunately it never really flew although in 1910 it managed a 30 yard hop. The same year saw the commencement of Britain's first airship project, at Cavendish Dock, Barrow in Furness. Involved in this project was Barnes Wallis, later to design the famous "Bouncing Bomb" of Dambuster fame.

Perhaps the most famous aviation pioneer in Cumbria (or Westmorland as it then was) was Captain E.W. Wakefield. He developed the first seaplane successfully to take off from water in Britain. The first flight took place just south of Bowness Bay in 1911. The well-known Bowness photographer, Frank Herbert, was soon to take a series of aerial photographs of Bowness and the surrounding area, being piloted in the famous Waterhen, another Wakefield craft. Passenger flights began in 1912, costing from two guineas upwards. No complicated C.A.A. regulations then!

Much later, during World War Two, White Cross Bay near Bowness was used to construct Sunderland flying boats, thus keeping alive the tradition started those thirty odd years ago.

A Reflection upon Town Planning

Did you ever wonder why so much of our civic architecture is so, what shall we say, uninspiring? The aerial photographer knows the reason why. You would be amazed at how impressive Kendal Bus Station is from 1,000 feet in the air. Likewise many other structures which are not exactly universally loved for their appearance at ground level.

Have you ever been lucky enough to fly over a town? If so, then I wonder what your first thought was when you first looked down at the landscape below. Could it have been that the buildings looked just like models? And how are these modern concrete monstrosities visualised by the people who approve them?

You're there before me!

Winter Conditions

There are some spectacular aerial views to be had in the winter. A crisp clear day, a deep blue sky and a thick covering of snow transform the whole Lakeland area. The mountains take on a hostile and other worldly appearance. Gone are those friendly summer slopes, to be replaced by a land of snow, ice and treacherous cornices.

Opening the aircraft window lets in an icy blast which freezes the hands in seconds. Take the picture, close the window and try to warm the hands enough to be able to change the film. There are pictures everywhere. Half frozen lakes, icy mountain tops and villages buried under a blanket of snow.

Winter Lakeland is magical, but there is a problem. Nobody wants to buy the pictures! The occasional sale to a newspaper will possibly pay for the petrol driving to the airport and members of the public will buy some of the mountain shots. My industrial customers and the hotels will look at the pictures, admire them and then ask for "the same thing without the snow please".

So it's not really profitable but I'll always find some excuse — after all I don't smoke and I don't drink a lot!

High Flying

There is one picture that I didn't manage to get. I once saw an aerial photograph that took in the whole of Lakeland. It's a picture that has stayed in my mind since and it's one that I would give a lot to take. There are two components to such a picture — height and clear air.

Clear air (really clear air) happens about three or four times a year, the

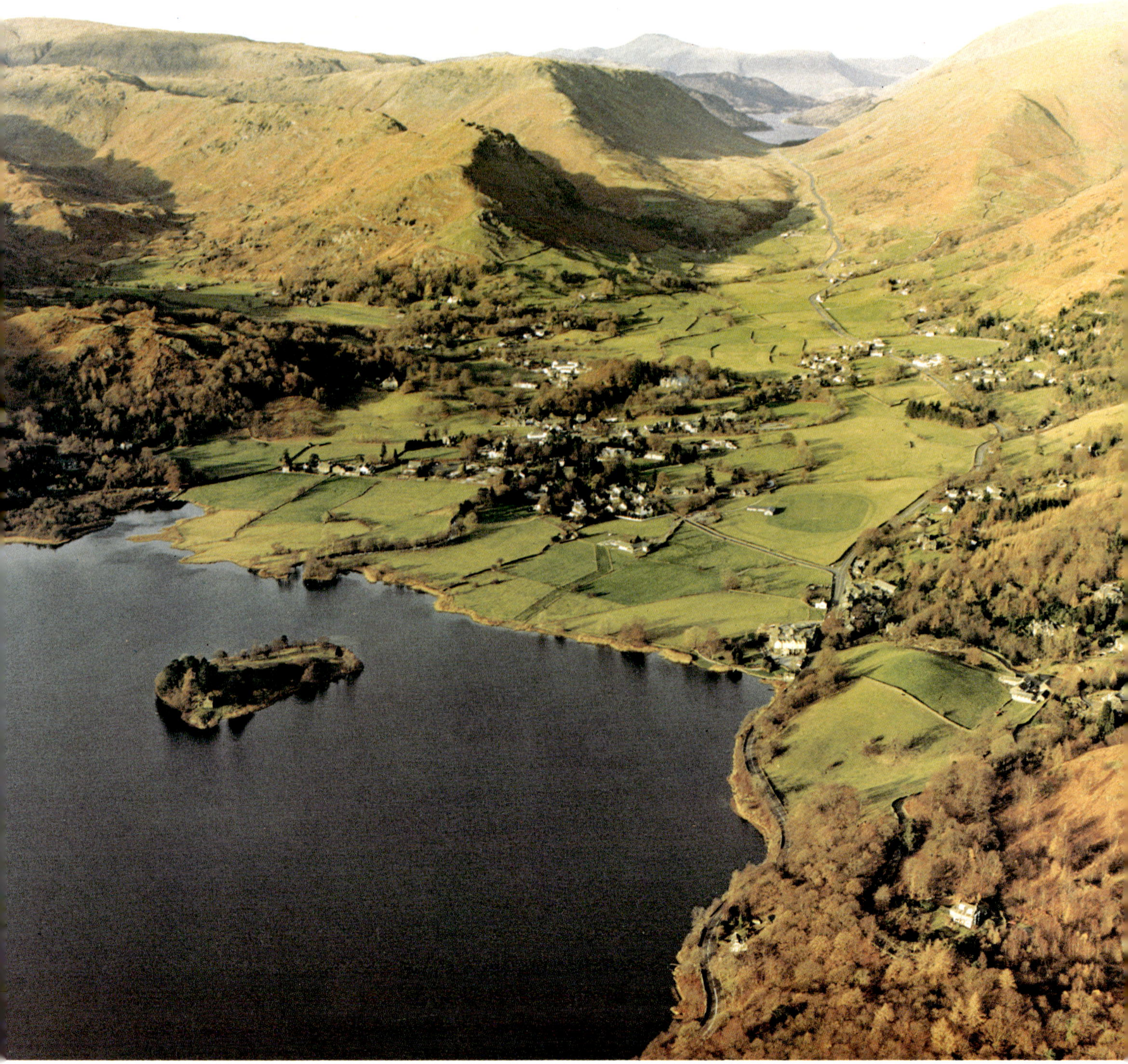

1. GRASMERE AND THIRLMERE. The A591 Kendal to Keswick main road can easily be picked out, running first alongside Grasmere lake, past the Prince of Wales Hotel and then climbing over Dunmail Raise to Thirlmere. Immediately beyond Grasmere village is Helm Crag, while the dominant peak in the far distance is Skiddaw.

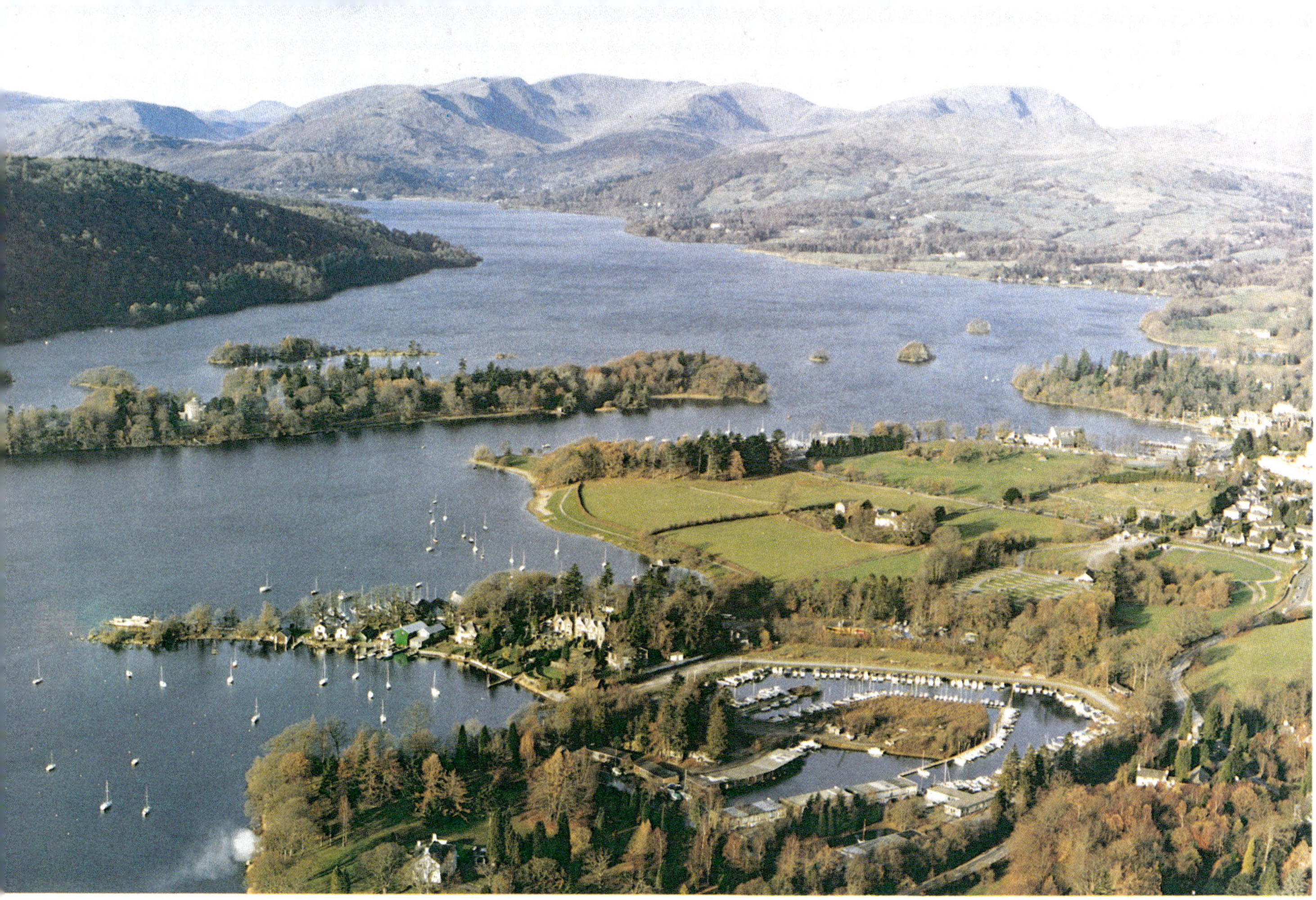

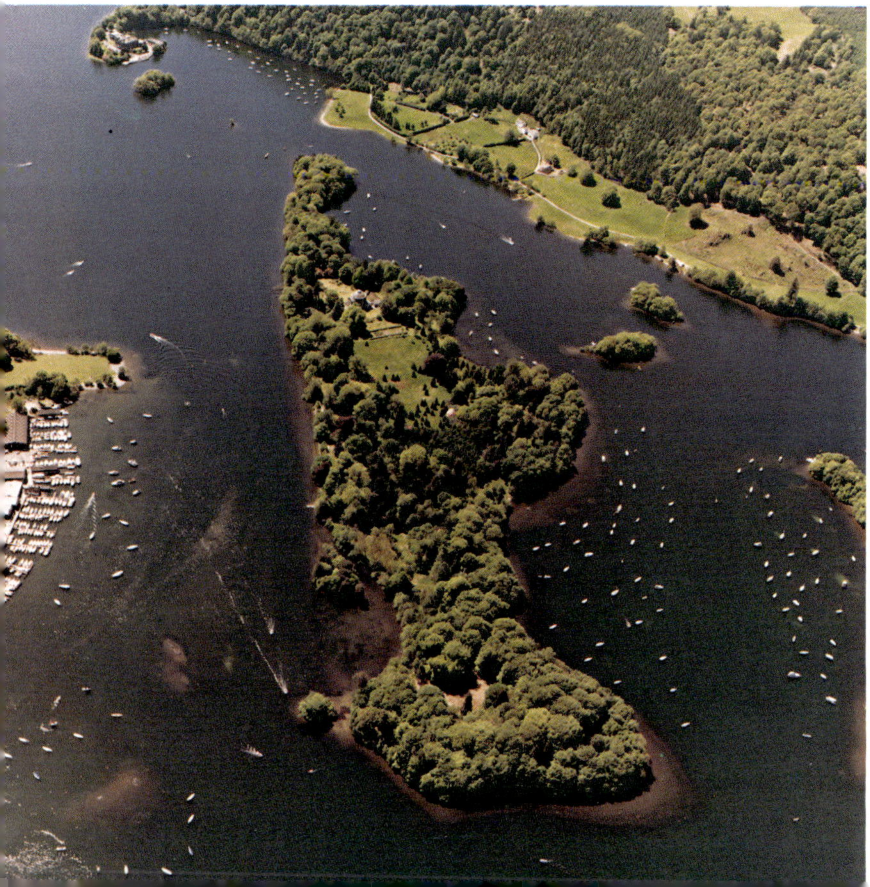

2. *Above* WINDERMERE. The camera looks north-west up the lake towards Ambleside and the high peaks, which from left to right include distant Skiddaw, the Helvellyn and Fairfield range, and Red Screes. Bowness and its bay are on the extreme right of the picture. At the tip of the long promontory to the left of the marina is the landing stage for the Windermere ferry.

3. *Left* BELLE ISLE, WINDERMERE. The largest of the Windermere islands is densely wooded — apart from the area at the south end where stands the famous round house. This picture gives a vivid impression of the amount of boating activity on the lake in the summer months, and also — bottom left — the rocks breaking the surface of the water which form a navigational hazard. Holidays Afloat are on the left of the photograph just to the north of Cockshott Point.

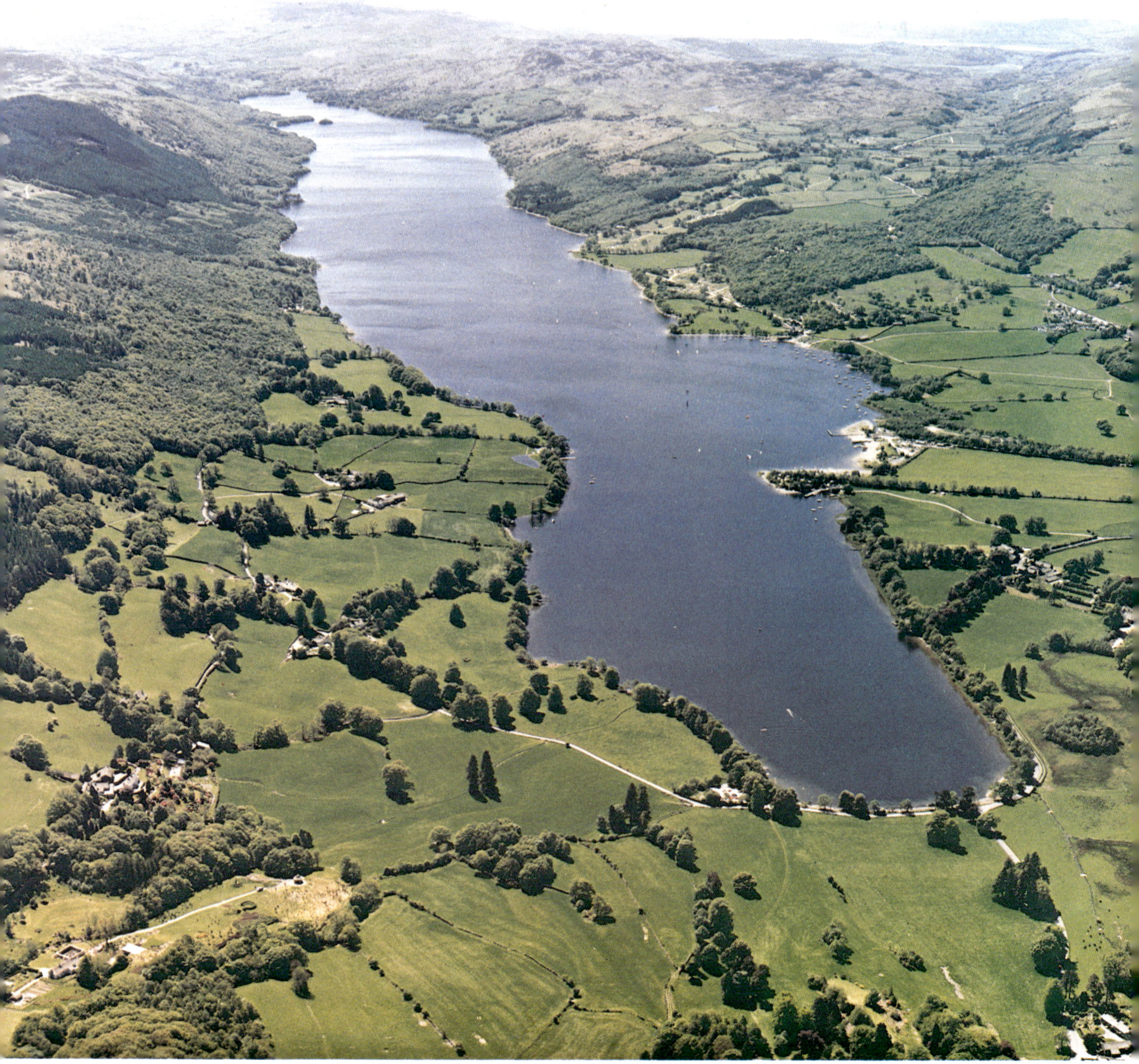

4. CONISTON WATER. The sweeping panorama from the head of the lake shows the Duddon estuary in the far distance. The promontory on the right-hand side of the lake has on it Waterhead Pier, beyond which yachts cluster close to the public launching site.

5. ***Below*** **ENNERDALE WATER. The least frequented of the major lakes has a rugged character all of its own. Broad at the base, it narrows between the twin hills of Bowness Knott (left) and Anglers' Crag (right). Beyond, the harsh lines of some of the worst Lake District afforestation lead the eye to distant Pillar.**

6. ***Right*** **WASTWATER. Utterly unmistakable with at its head Great Gable and, on either side, Kirk Fell and the Scafell range. The renowned screes on the right-hand side of the lake look much less ferocious from the air.**

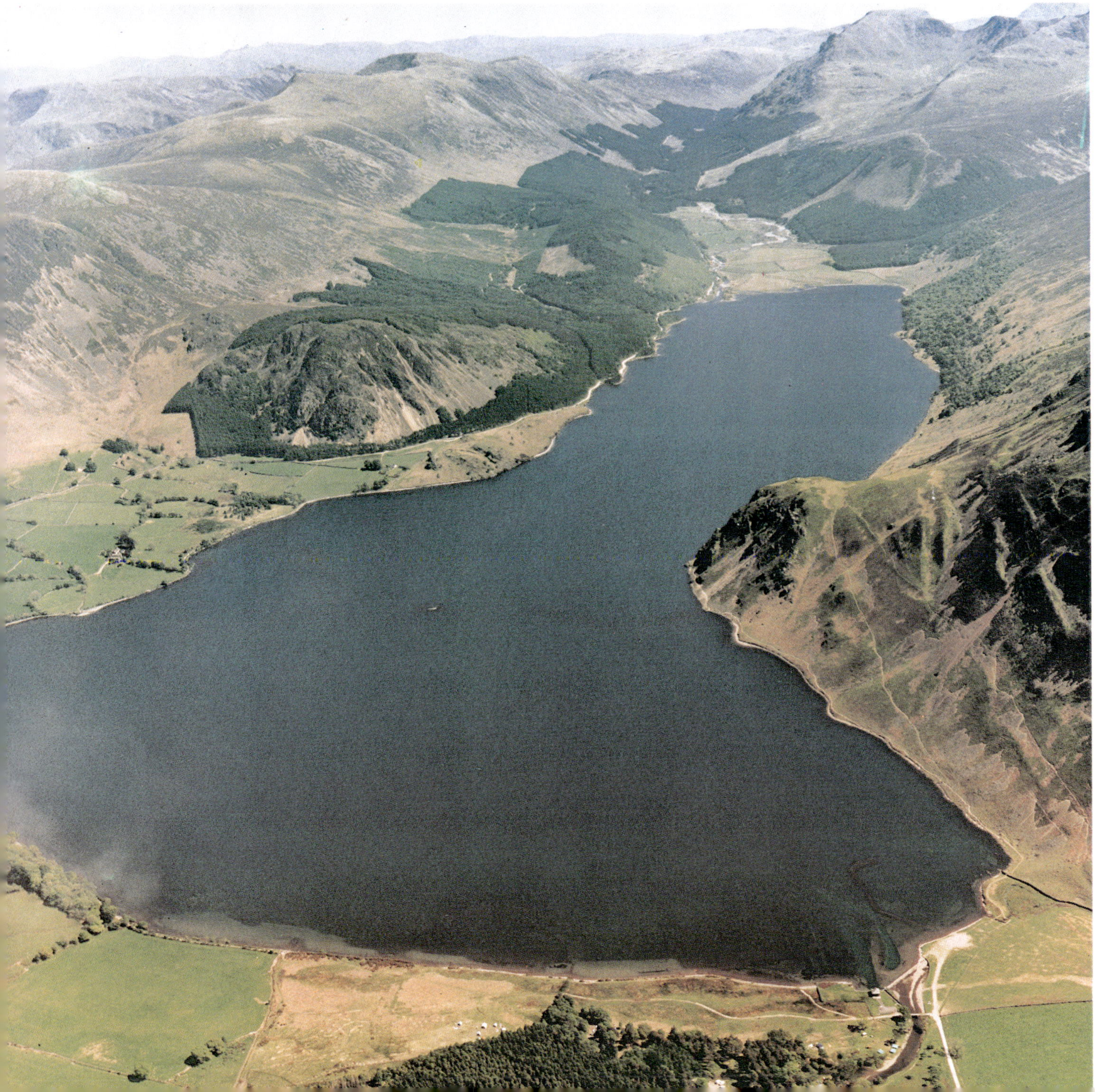

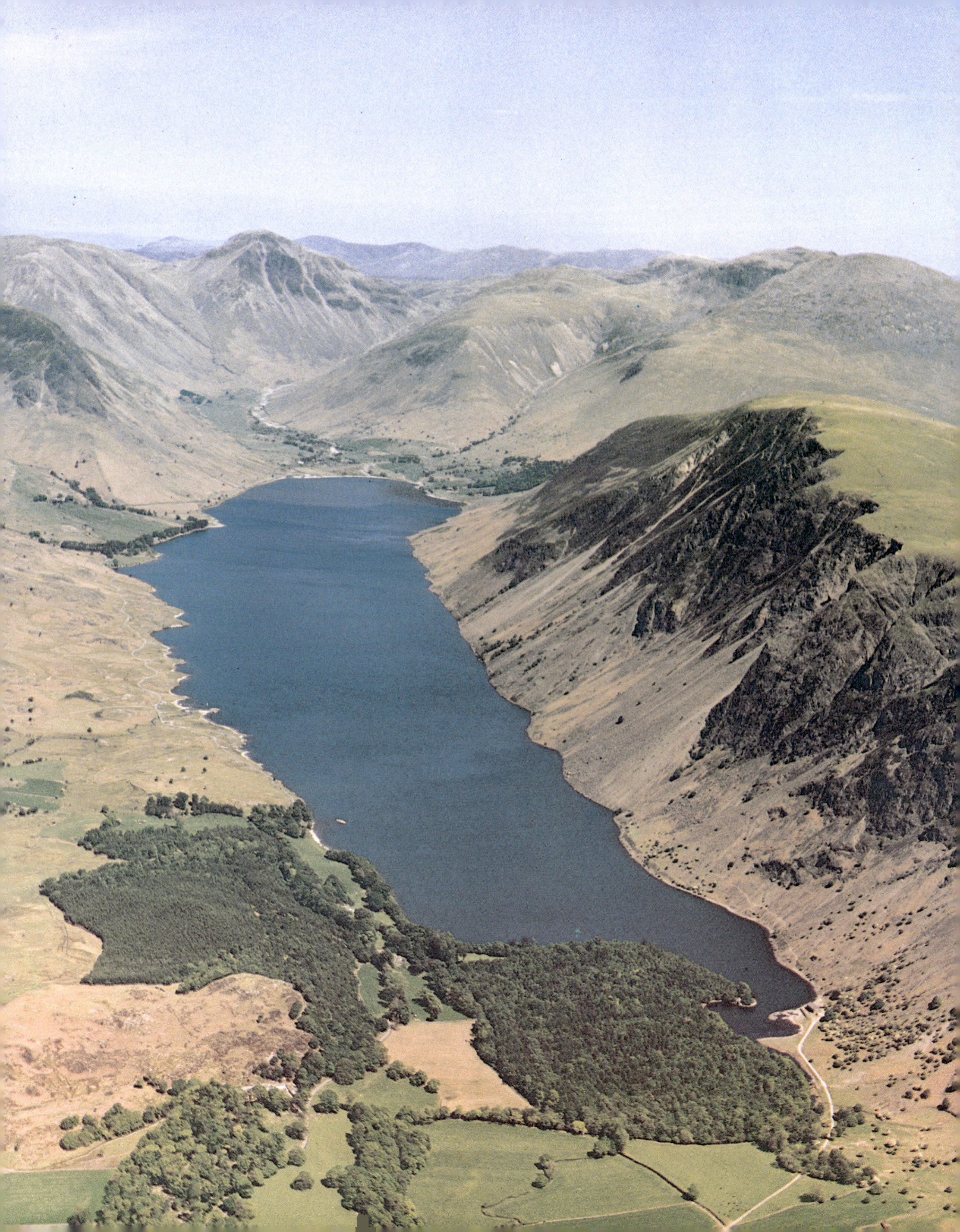

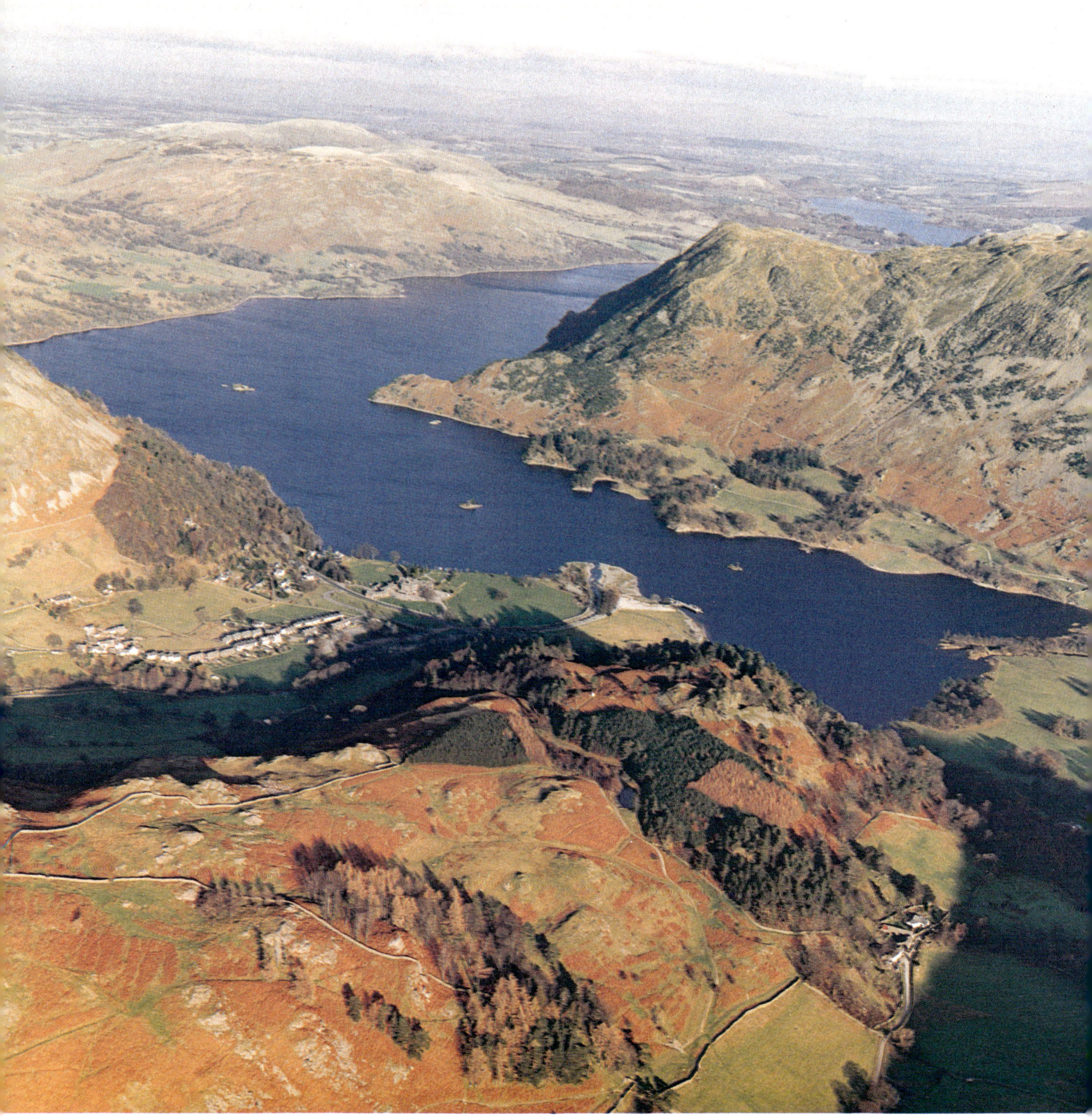

7. **ULLSWATER.** The plane has just flown over Helvellyn prior to taking this view from above Glenridding. It dramatically shows the "dog's leg" nature of the lake with the final reach pointing towards distant Penrith and the Pennine fells on the far side of the Eden valley. Geographers will note the rock detritus dumped by Glenridding Beck at the point it enters the lake — to the left of which is the Ullswater Hotel and to the right the steamer landing stage. Birk Fell is the dominant peak directly opposite.

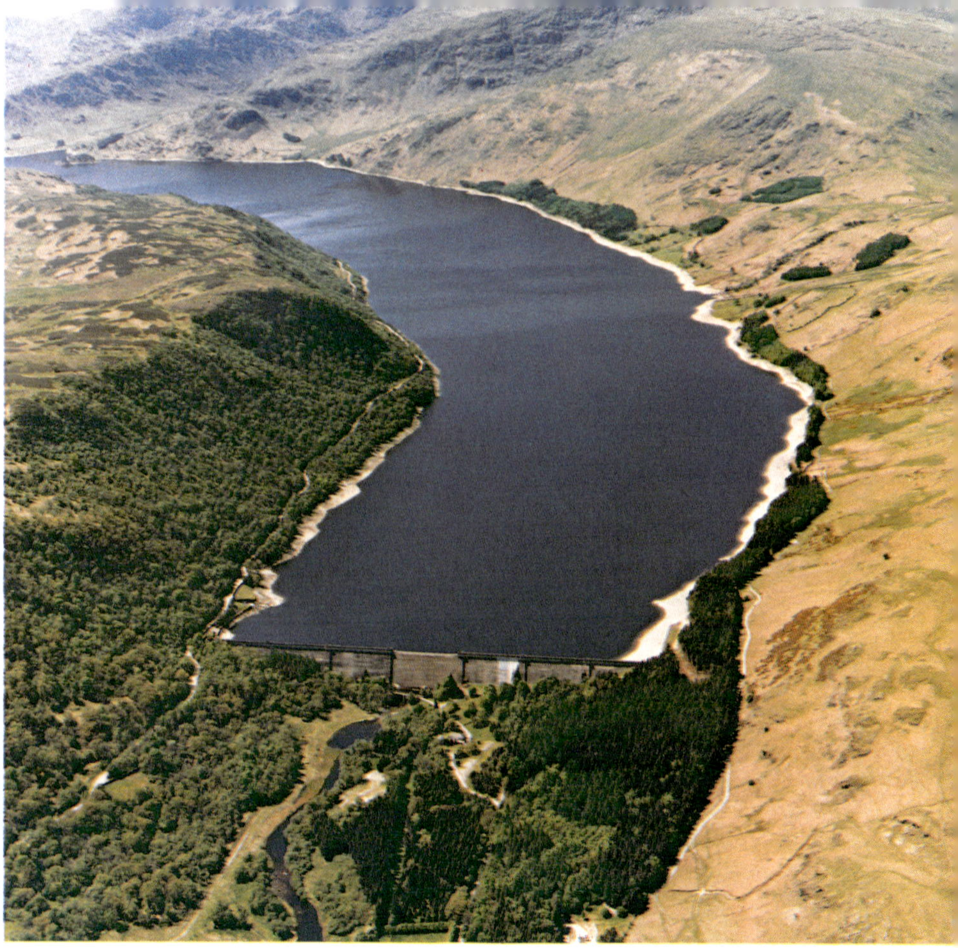

8. HAWESWATER. Paradise lost — in the sense that this huge sterile reservoir replaced one of the most intimate and secluded of lakes. The scars created by the "draw-down" of water look if anything worse from the air than from ground level.

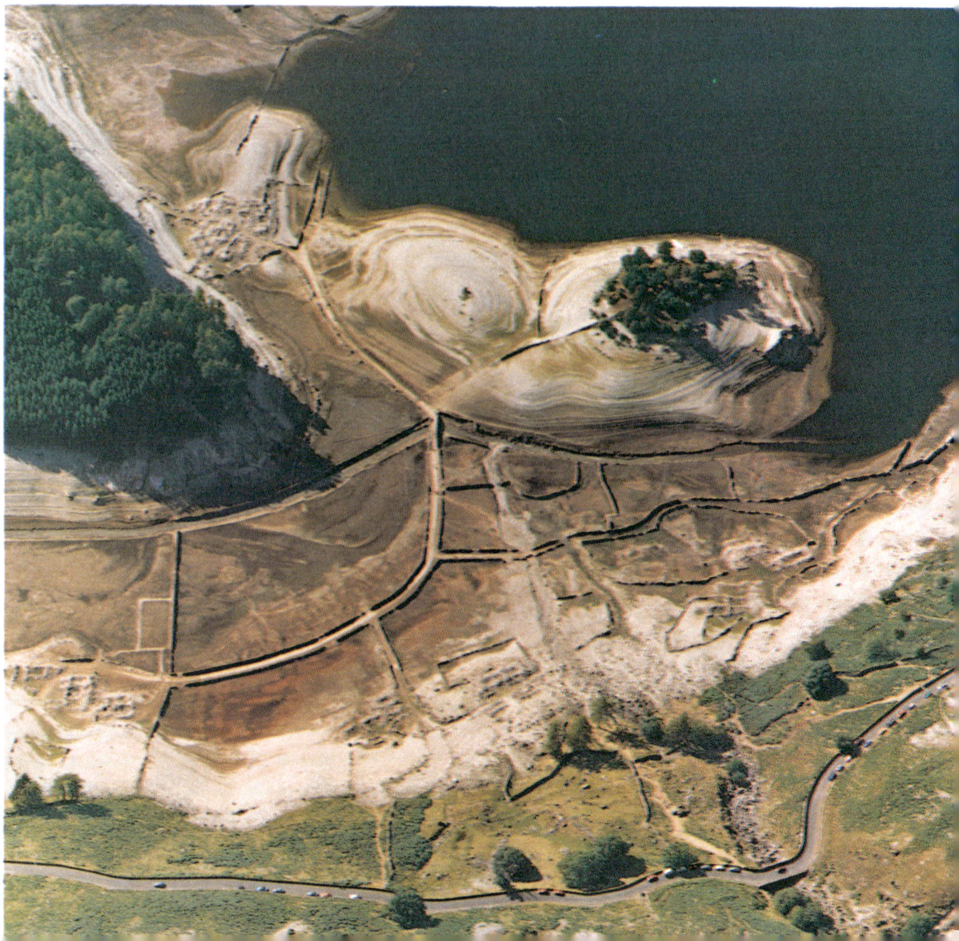

9. HAWESWATER. The photograph above was taken on May 31st, 1984 when the reservoir was almost full. Only weeks later the drought of that year caused the water level to drop to no less than 60 feet below normal, exposing many remains of the former Mardale village at the head of the lake and creating a major tourist attraction. On the extreme left of the photograph are the ruins of the Dun Bull Hotel — with the rectangular outline of the tennis court still clearly discernible. The road from the hotel leads to a junction, where one arm heads down-valley past the site of Goosemire Farm. The other arm crosses the packhorse bridge to where a cluster of buildings (top left, next to the wood) included the church.

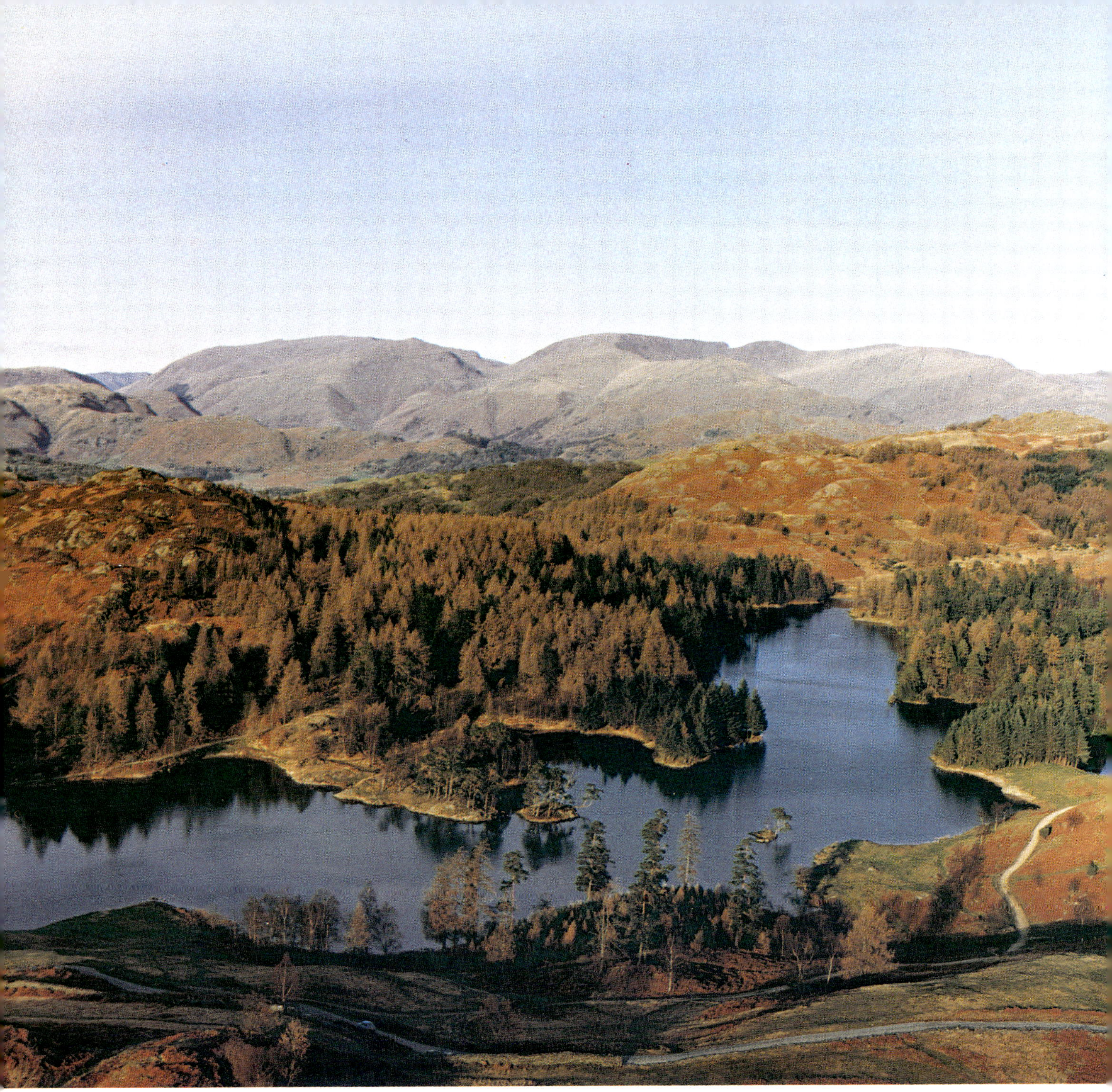

10. TARN HOWS. One of the best-known places in the Lake District visited by some three-quarters of a million people a year. This view looks almost due north across the foot of the Langdale valleys towards Helvellyn.

The Lakes

IT is generally agreed that there are sixteen lakes in the Lake District. The preceding photographs give a fascinating bird's-eye view of eight of them — and one tarn. Two more — Derwentwater and Bassenthwaite Lake — appear as part of the picture in several of the later photographs in this book.

Grasmere

photo 1 Grasmere would be an attractive and popular tourist area without its Wordsworthian associations. It lies in a pleasant green vale, almost ringed by mountains. Its river, the Rothay, is joined by a beck from Easedale before flowing into a mile-long lake. The most shapely of the local peaks, which is best seen with the still lake in the foreground, is Helm Crag. Grasmere's strong links with the Wordsworths, William and Dorothy, means that it enjoys a remarkable popularity. It has been estimated that between 70,000 and 80,000 tourists annually tramp through the churchyard to inspect the grave of William. About 50,000 people a year visit Dove Cottage, his first Grasmere home, and the nearby museum. The Wordsworths moved to Grasmere in 1799. This village was already very old. Oswald, king of the Northumbrians, is said to have named a local well and to have founded the church, which bears his name. In Norman times, the Conqueror gave the barony of Kendal to Iva de Talebois, and then the settlement was Grismere, which is taken to mean "lake of pigs".

For centuries the people lived their quiet, pastoral lives, watched packhorse trains lumbering on the high tracks and sad little processions on the corpse road from the Langdales as the dead were carried to St. Oswald's Church for burial. A few years before the Wordsworths arrived a turnpike road had been made through Grasmere (it passed Dove Cottage) and wheeled traffic was beginning to develop. Two years after William Wordsworth's death in 1850 the first of a long line of Grasmere Sports was held on the Moss and it lasted for two days. Today Grasmere Sports is a highlight in the Lakeland calendar, with its guides races and wrestling in the Cumberland and Westmorland styles. The Sports are attended by over 15,000 people.

Thirlmere

photo 1 Once a modest lake of 300 acres, Thirlmere was transformed by Manchester Corporation into a vast reservoir. The city obtained its Parliamentary Bill in 1879, and engineers constructed a stone dam which at its greatest height is 104 feet. Today the lake is three and two-thirds miles in length, with a top water level of 587 feet above the level of the sea. The average rainfall here is 90 inches, and every day over four and a half million gallons of water are discharged into St. John's Beck. The broom and hawthorn which in days gone by were such a delightful feature of the banks of Thirlmere have now vanished to be replaced by an artificial landscape of serried ranks of conifers. There are over 2,000 acres of such species as Norway and Sitka spruce, Douglas fir, European and Japanese larch, Scots pine and Mountain pine, and each Christmas between 35,000 and 40,000 young trees are sold for household decoration.

The main road keeps to the east of the lake, but for motorists not in a hurry there is a minor road which twists and turns along the western shore. It passes close to the site of Armboth House, reputed to be haunted at Halloween by the ghost of a bride who was pushed into the lake and drowned immediately before her wedding breakfast was to be held at the house. W. T. Palmer mentions in *The English Lakes* "that on a certain night all the fugitive spirits whose bodies were destroyed in unavenged crime assembled at Armboth House — bodies without heads, the skulls of Calgarth with no bodies, a phantom arm, and many weird shapes; the windows were alight with corpse candles, chains clank in corridors and there are eternal shriekings".

When Manchester took over Thirlmere the old coach road and the "city" of Wythburn — just a few cottages at the southern end of the lake! — were inundated. Wythburn church, at the very base of Helvellyn, was high enough above water level to be safe from interference. The building seen today, its white walls contrasting vividly with the greens and browns of the forest, is the same as that known and commented upon by the Lake Poets.

Windermere

Windermere is the largest lake in England. It was formed about 15,000 years ago when a glacier occupied an old river valley, grinding it deeper. The maximum depth of Windermere is 219 feet. When the ice melted, water remained in the valley because it had been dammed by a moraine. Windermere is replenished by lively fell streams — Brathay, Rothay, Trout, Cunsey and the overflow from Blelham Tarn among them — and it overflows as the river Leven, which joins the sea near Greenodd. The Lake is long but relatively narrow (averaging a mile). It is canal-like in its general appearance but quite unlike a canal in its ever-varied shoreline and the beauty of its wooded islets. In summer the lake is warm on top and cold lower down; the layers do not mix until autumn, when the surface water cools down. Fish abound in the water and include char, perch, eels, pike and brown trout. *photos 2, 3*

The head of Windermere has the attraction of broad water and decorative reed beds. Waterhead's most conspicuous object is the pier where the Sealink craft call regularly. They were steamers once, but have now been converted to diesel propulsion. The first steamer service began on Windermere in 1845 with a steam yacht called "Lady of the Lake"; the Furness Railway bought the steamer service in 1871, and it was nationalised after the last war. Waterhead has a variety of facilities for water sports, such as power boating and water ski-ing.

Bathing in such a deep stretch of water is not encouraged, though Windermere attracts marathon swimmers from all over the country. By map measurement the length of the lake is 9¾ miles, but the shortest practical distance — allowing for a sufficient depth of water in which swimmers can move — is about 10 miles.

Windermere has had its moments, and not least among them was a voyage made by the Queen and Duke of Edinburgh. Queen Adelaide, wife of William IV, was on the lake in 1840, and the point at which she landed, near Bowness, is still known as Queen Adelaide's Hill.

Rising mid-lake, opposite Bowness, is the 38-acre wooded Belle Isle (formerly named Long Holm), which is inhabited and open to the public. A boat service operates from the end of Bowness Promenade. Long ago the Philipsons were here, progenitors of "Robin the Devil" who was besieged during the Civil War and afterwards behaved disgracefully in Kendal church. After them, the Braithwaites, Floyers and Barlows owned the island, but a new-comer, named English, commissioned John Plaw, an obscure architect, to design the present elegant house in circular style. When foundations were dug in 1774 traces of Roman activity were uncovered, and as the house rose, Mr. English was criticised for destroying the natural life of the island. He sold out in 1781 to Isabella, the teenage heiress of the Workington Hall Curwens, for £1,720, having sunk £6,000 into the project. The spirited Isabella eloped to Edinburgh and married her cousin John Christian who adopted the name Curwen. He declined a peerage on two occasions. Their grand-daughter, another Isabella, married Wordsworth's clergyman son in 1832. Dora Wordsworth often came to Belle Isle which now belongs to Mr. and Mrs. Edward Curwen.

Coniston Water

photo 4 (see Coniston village, page 57)

Ennerdale Water

photo 5 Iron ore and bilberries, conifers and trout, deer and honey bees are but some of the contrasting elements of a valley which contains one of Cumbria's largest yet least-visited lakes. If it is accepted that there are lake and town partnerships, Derwentwater belonging to Keswick and Ullswater to Penrith, then Ennerdale Water undoubtedly belongs to Whitehaven. For this reason it tends to be regarded as an outcast of the Lake District, being dismissed as part of industrial West Cumbria rather than revered as a relatively unspoilt section of the National Park.

Ennerdale is a walker's valley, with motor roads fighting shy of the water's edge. From the west end Angler's Crag and Bowness Knott, the two bluffs forming the "narrows", make a fine foreground to the lofty heights of Steeple, Windy Gap, Pillar and Haycock. On the lake itself an island — little more than a cairn of stones sticking up from an underwater ridge — looks like a full stop on a clean sheet of blue notepaper.

There is a delightful ledge-like path alongside the lake by the foot of

Angler's Crag. It passes close to a rift on Crag Fell, known for totally obscure reasons as Robin Hood's Chair, and a scene of pioneer desecration in the form of carved initials dating back to 1700. Crag Fell is where Whitehaven and Egrement folk in their hundreds used to pick bilberries on a commercial scale, using "combs", "picks" and biscuit tins to harvest as many as eight pounds in a single afternoon.

Wastwater

photo 6

Wastwater is perhaps the most awe-inspiring of all the English lakes. It is hemmed in by the great mountains of Red Pike (2,269 ft.), Kirk Fell (2,630 ft.), Great Gable (2,949 ft.) and Scafell Pike (3,210 ft.). Its waters can look decidedly ominous for this is also the deepest of the English lakes. It takes the form of a fissure which plunges beneath the surface of the water for more than 250 feet — the bottom of the lake is below sea level.

Adding an extra element of grandeur are the famous screes on the south-east side of Wastwater. These extend the whole length of the lake and have been formed by gradual erosion. They are "streaked with brilliant hues of red and brown, like the changing colours of a pigeon's neck".

Wastwater and Wasdale have been described as "as grand a combination as can be found in the British Isles". It was an American who said to Nancy Price "that it was the last place God made, and He has lost His touch". Nancy herself said, "Imagine a black mass of rock hollowed out by a great cheese scoop into the shape of a cradle; that was something like the effect the mountains and dales have to me".

Ullswater

photo 7

Ullswater is seven and a half miles long, averaging three quarters of a mile wide, and with a maximum depth (near Howtown) of 205 feet. It has three distinct bends, giving it a dog's leg appearance. The first reach is from the head of the lake, about Glenridding, to Silver Point (so named, perhaps, from the birches which grew here and were regularly felled by clog-makers). Place Fell (2,154 feet) dominates this part of the lake. The second reach extends from Silver Point to Howtown, and again the lake is mountain-dominated, the highspots including High Dod (1,640 feet) and Hallin Fell (1,271 feet). Howtown Bay, a bold indentation in the shoreline, is matched up across the water by the bold promontory of Skelly Nab. The remaining reach has a gentle shoreline, ending with the bold flourish of Dunmallet (775 feet) near Pooley Bridge.

Seven valleys converge on Ullswater, each of them terminating with triangles of low ground extending into the lake like flaps of loose skin. Westerly winds are broken up by the mountains; the blasts, funnelled by the different valleys, come down to the lake from different angles so that a boatman, setting off from Glenridding in a calm, might encounter a 30 miles an hour wind in the next reach of the lake.

Ullswater has a few small islands, one of which features in old Arthurian legends. Scale House Falls impress voyagers on the lake if the weather has been wet and white water is tumbling down the fellside like milk. Another feature best seen from the water is a simple plaque set on the steep face of a crag to commemorate Norman William Birkett, the champion in the House of Lords over a battle with Manchester Corporation over the right to take water from Ullswater.

Ullswater is clear but deep. A skin-diver who knows it well refers to its "eerie-green". In the depths of the lake, beyond an angler's range with rod and line, a curious fish known as the skelly swims and feeds. Skelly was described as "a sort of fresh water herring" and so little was seen of it in recent years that it was feared to be extinct, poisoned by pollution from lead mines in Glenridding valley. It was common in Wordsworth's day, and he wrote in 1805 that "fishermen drew their nets ashore and hundreds of fish were leaping in their prison". Happily, the skelly is still present in Ullswater.

Two diesel craft — *Raven* and *Lady of the Lake* — operate a summertime service on Ullswater.

Haweswater

photos 8, 9

In recent times, Manchester Corporation set a concrete dam in the mouth of old Mardale. A pleasant mere was extended into an all-embracing reservoir. The scenery remains sublime, especially a horseshoe shape of fells at the dalehead.

Bampton church (like that of Patterdale, eight miles to the west) is dedicated to St. Patrick. A pleasant road runs south-westwards to where the dam of the Manchester reservoir is seen, partly shielded by trees. (The dam is actually best seen from a distance, as during the descent to Bampton from Shap).

The community in Mardale had to leave as the water was impounded. Demolished were the little church and the *Dun Bull Inn,* formerly a wellknown gathering place for fox-hunters and fell-walkers. Crowds flocked to the valley during the drought of 1984 when many of the remains became visible. From the terrace of the *Haweswater Hotel,* about mid-way along the shore of the reservoir, there is an uninterrupted view of the western fells. Red squirrels frolic on the trees behind the hotel.

Hotel patrons are amongst the limited number of people who are allowed to fish in the lake, its tributaries and the dam in the neighbouring Wet Sleddale. The fish are brown trout and char, the latter staying in the depths, except at spawning time. The old technique of trolling for char is not allowed.

From the car park at the end of the road are several attractive footways, one (by Blea Water) leading up on to High Street (2,663 feet).

Tarn Hows

photo 10

Tarn Hows, to which one can motor from Hawkshead Hill, a point midway between Hawkshead and Coniston, is frequently cited as an example of all that is scenically of the best in Lakeland. The National Trust has provided well-screened parks for vehicles close to the open water, the conifers and the mountains which collectively make up one of the best-known views in England. The Tarns are artificial in the sense that they have formed behind a man-made dam. The conifers are not typical of the Lake District. They combine magnificently to form a stimulating sight. The National Trust received them from Sir S. H. Scott in 1930.

MOUNTAIN LAKELAND

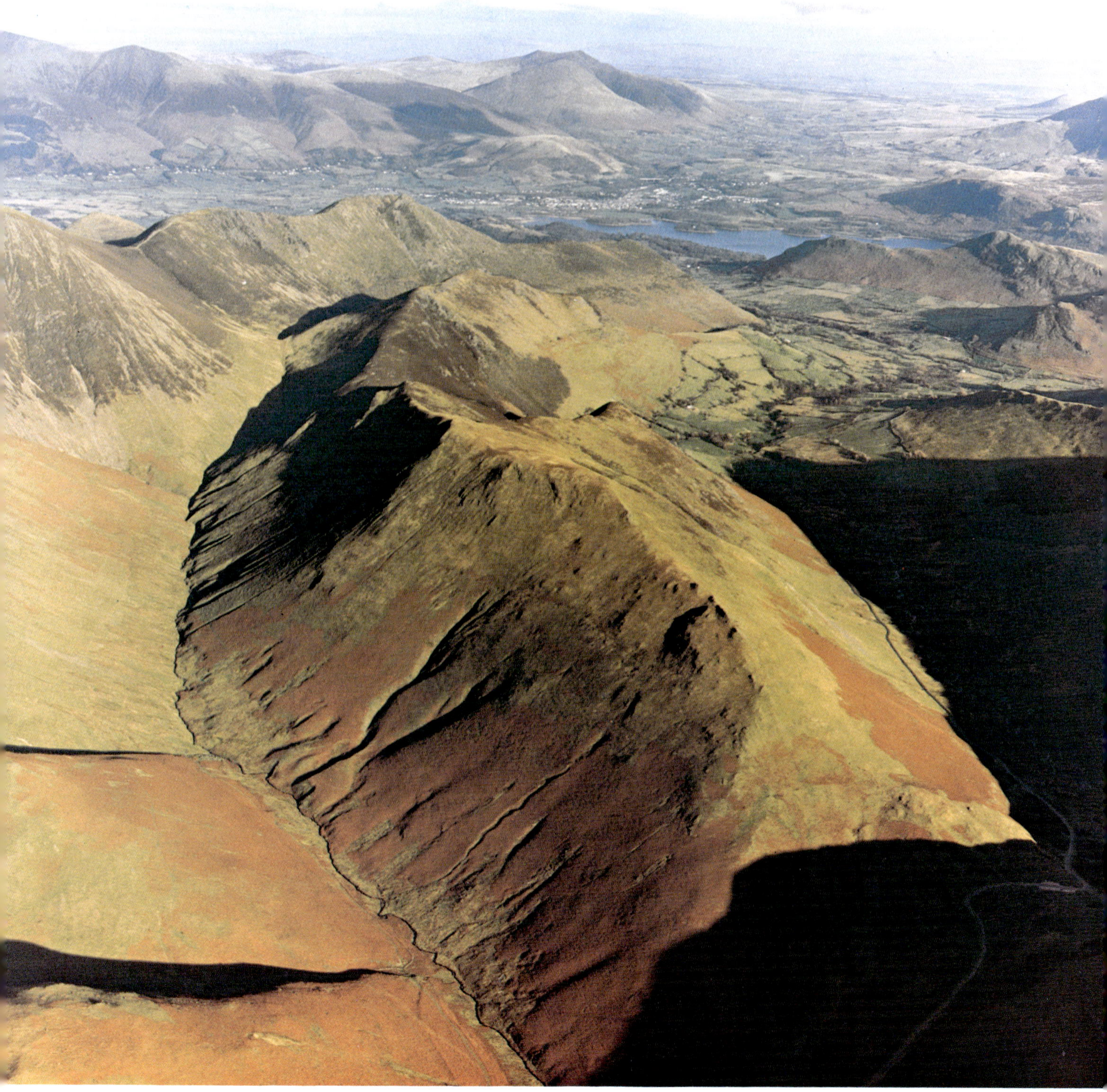

11. KNOTT RIGG — and beyond. Many of the best-known fells of northern Lakeland appear in this mountain panorama. Knott Rigg occupies the centre of the picture, with at its right the Newlands valley, at the foot of which is Catbells. To the left of Derwentwater is Causey Pike. Beyond Keswick are, first, the shapely slopes of Latrigg and then the huge mass of Blencathra with the "scooped" summit that gives rise to the alternative names of Saddleback.

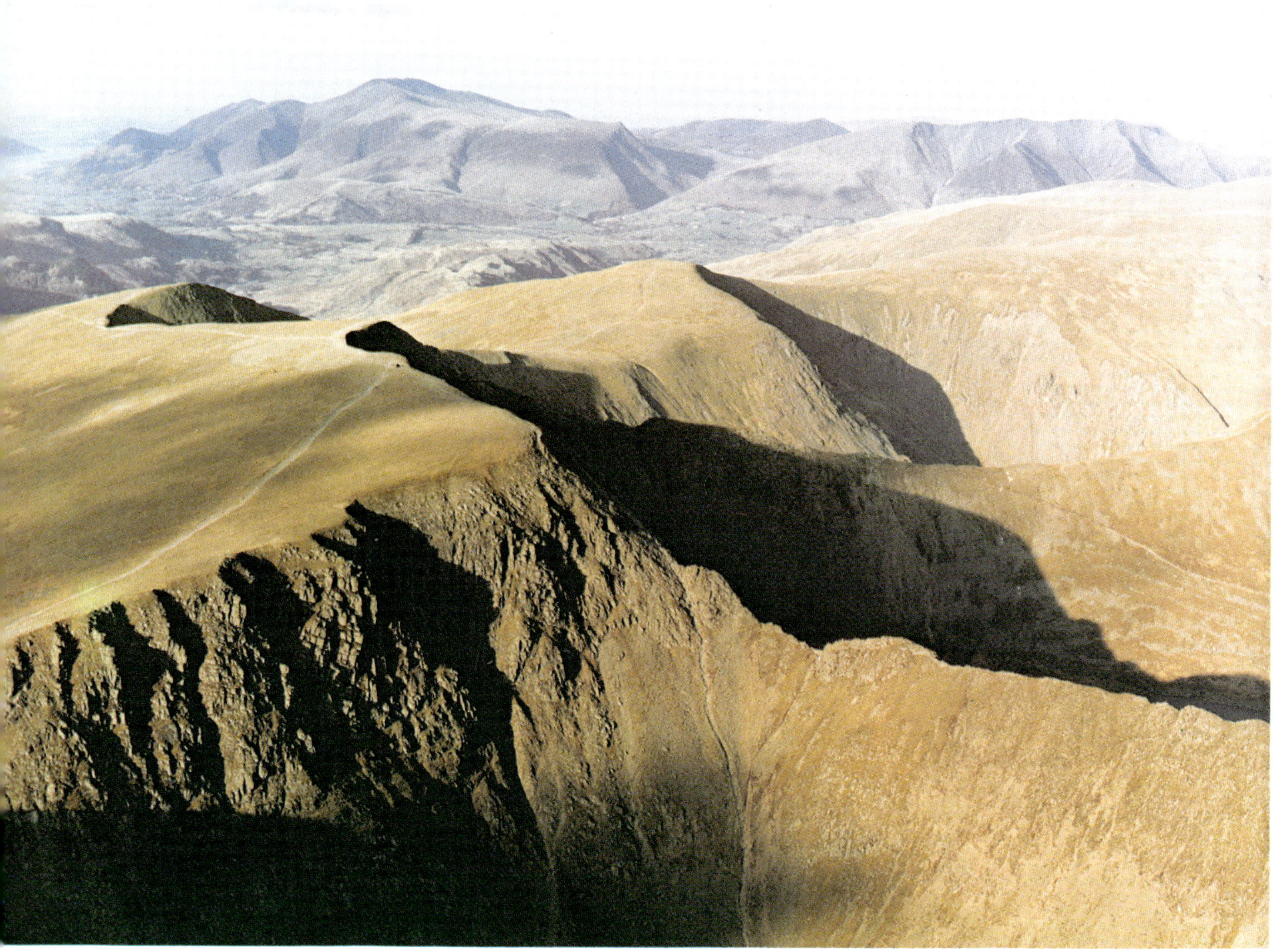

12. *Above* HELVELLYN. The two faces of Lakeland's most popular peak, with smooth grassy slopes to the west and dramatic ice-scarred ridges to the east — including Striding Edge (foreground) and then Swirral Edge. Skiddaw and Blencathra rise proudly in the background, while just discernible beyond Bassenthwaite Lake (top left) is Criffell in far-distant Kirkcudbright.

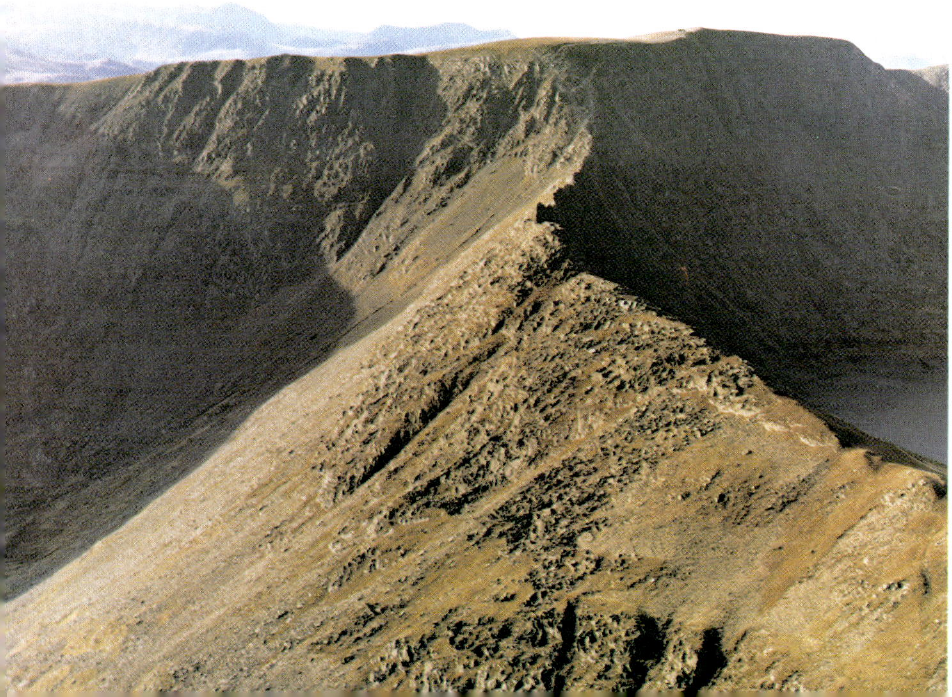

13. *Left* STRIDING EDGE, HELVELLYN. Profile of England's most famous mountain ridge, looking directly towards the peak's 3,118ft summit. Almost lost in the shadows on the right is Red Tarn, a text-book example of a corrie lake.

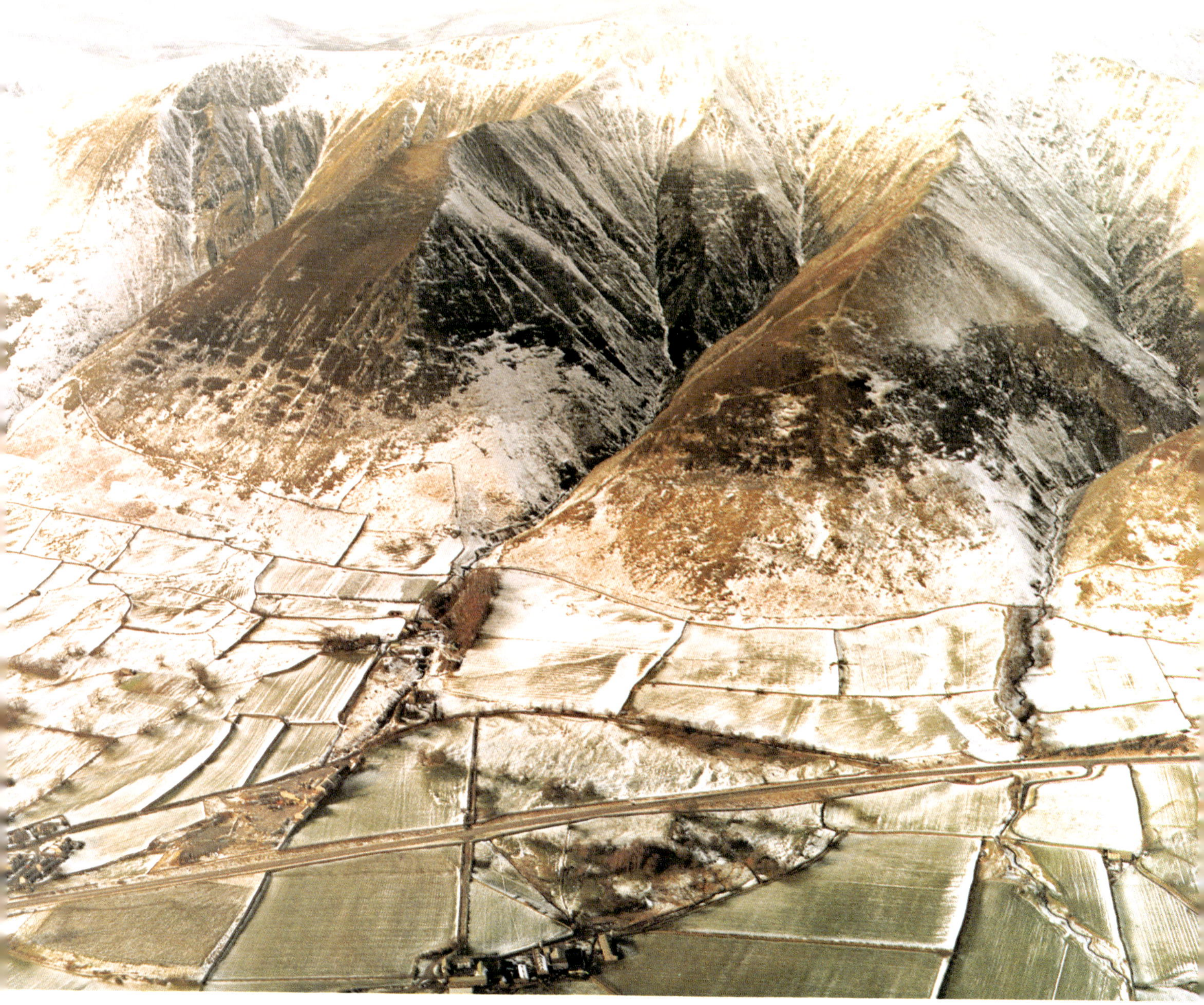

14. BLENCATHRA. A combination of snow and low winter light throws into sharp relief every nook and cranny of this magnificent mountain. Viewed from near Threlkeld, on the left is Gategill Fell and on the right Hallsfell Ridge.

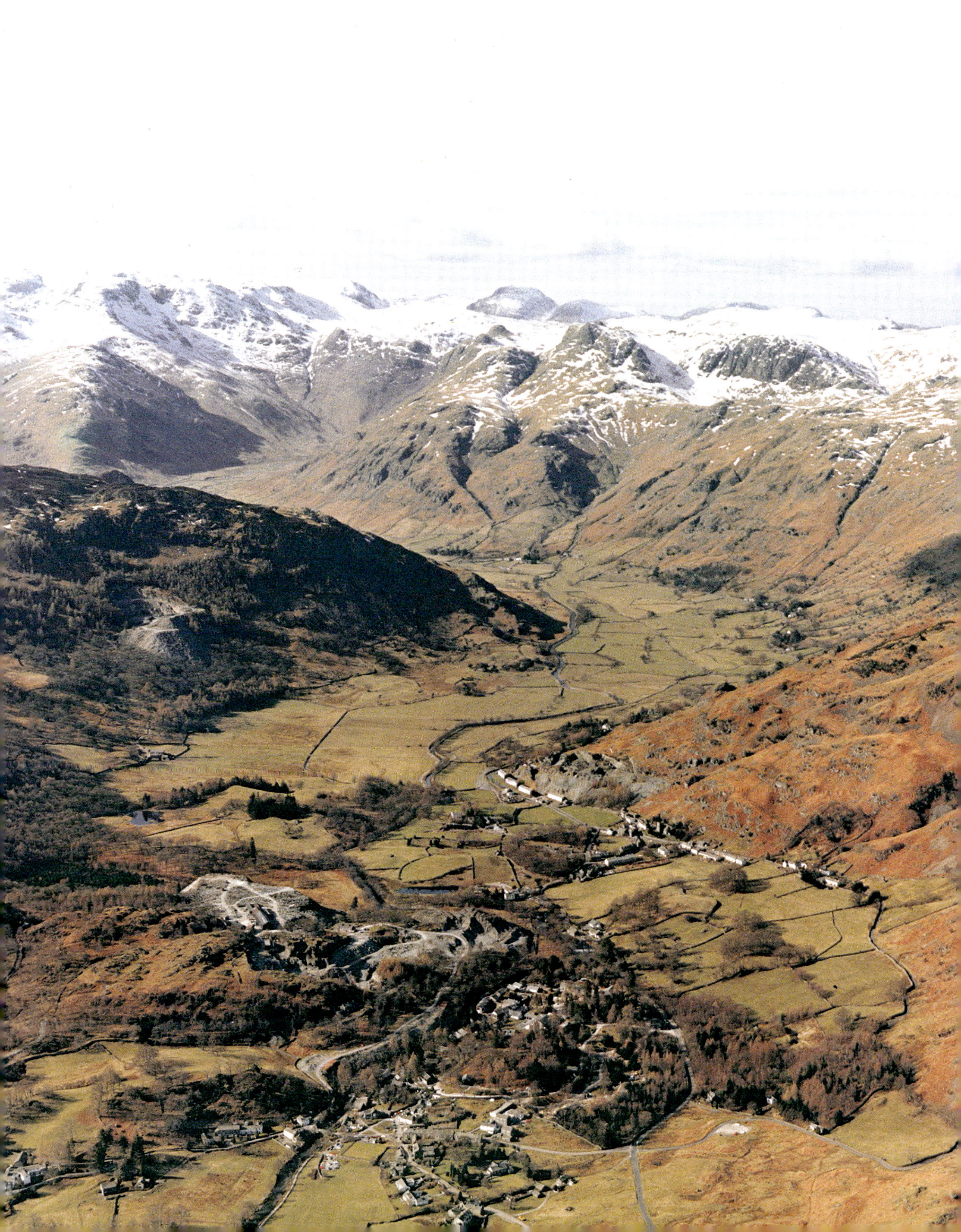

15. *Left* THE LANGDALE FELLS. A peep into the heart of mountain Lakeland. Looking up Great Langdale from above Elterwater village, the instantly recognisable Langdale Pikes almost shout to be noticed. They precede the great core of high peaks which begins with Bow Fell on the left and extends round by way of Hanging Knotts to Allen Crags.

16. *Below* THE LANGDALE PIKES. From directly above the distinctive relief of the Pikes is lost. Harrison Stickle is the brown lump between Stickle Tarn and the headwaters of Dungeon Ghyll, to the left of which is Gimmer Crag. Above the tarn is Pavey Ark, while in the background the snow-covered fells give way to Derwentwater and Bassenthwaite Lake.

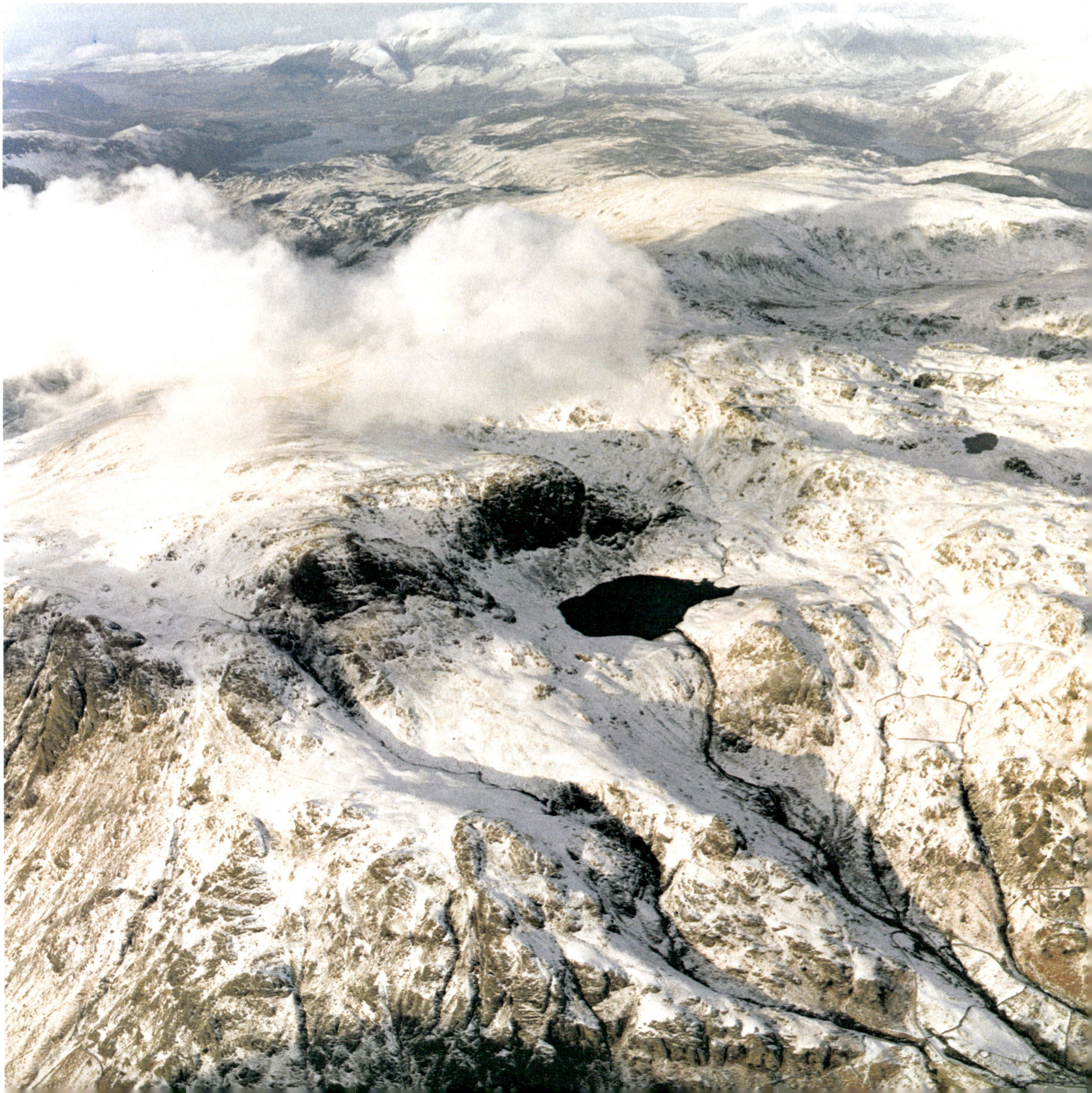

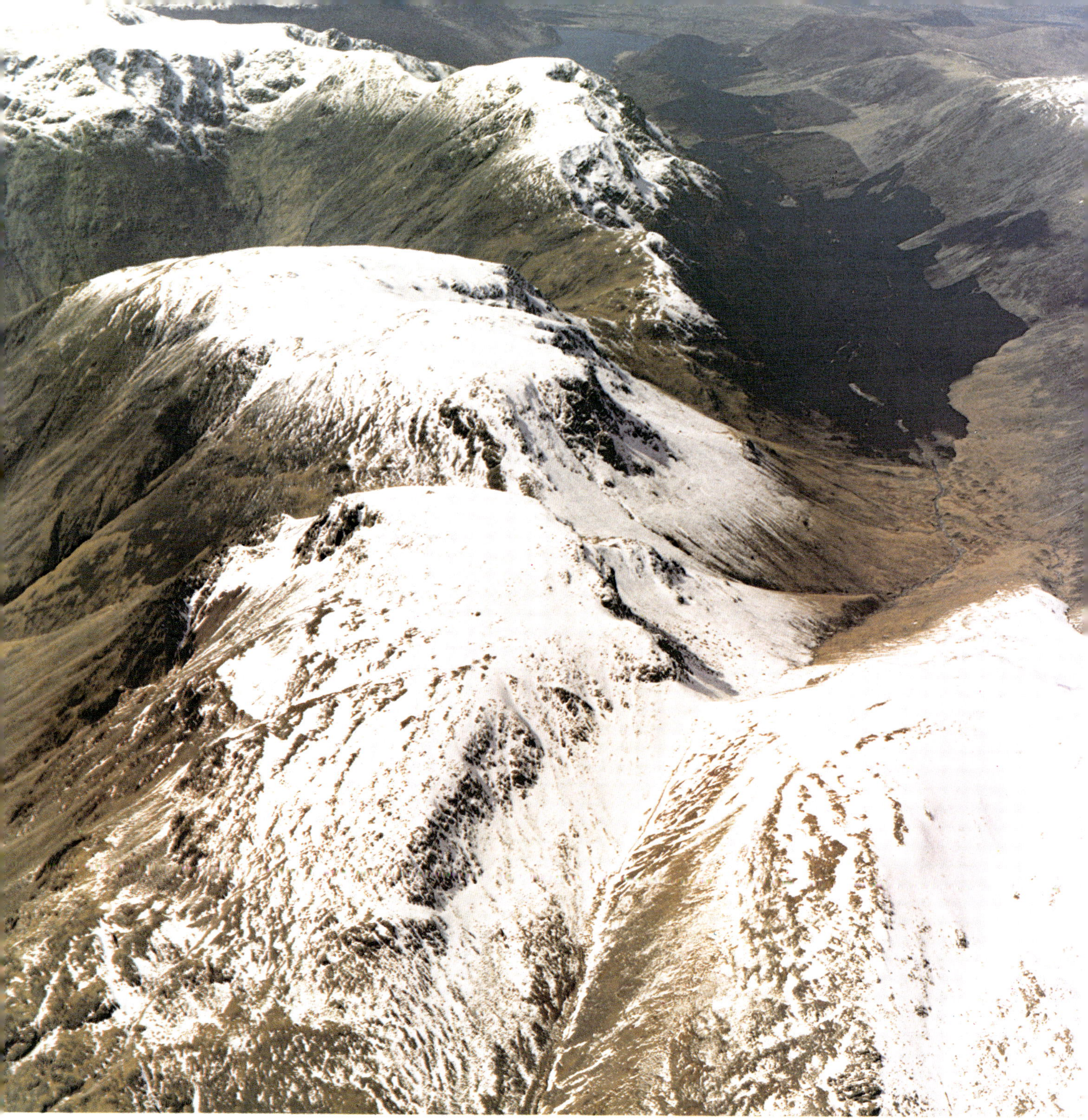

17. **PILLAR AND GREAT GABLE.** Pillar is the most distant of the major snow-covered peaks with Ennerdale Water directly behind it. Working back towards the camera comes the dip of Black Sail Pass, then Kirk Fell and finally Great Gable, separated from Green Gable by Windy Gap. It is interesting to compare this picture with photo No. 5, looking up Ennderdale in the opposite direction.

18. *Right* NAPES RIDGES, GREAT GABLE. The south face of the mountain showing some of the most famous chunks of rock in Lakeland which provide the classic climbing grounds of Napes Needle, Gable Traverse and Needle Ridge. This is an awe-inspiring, elemental landscape complete with all the most chilling shades of grey, brown and off-white.

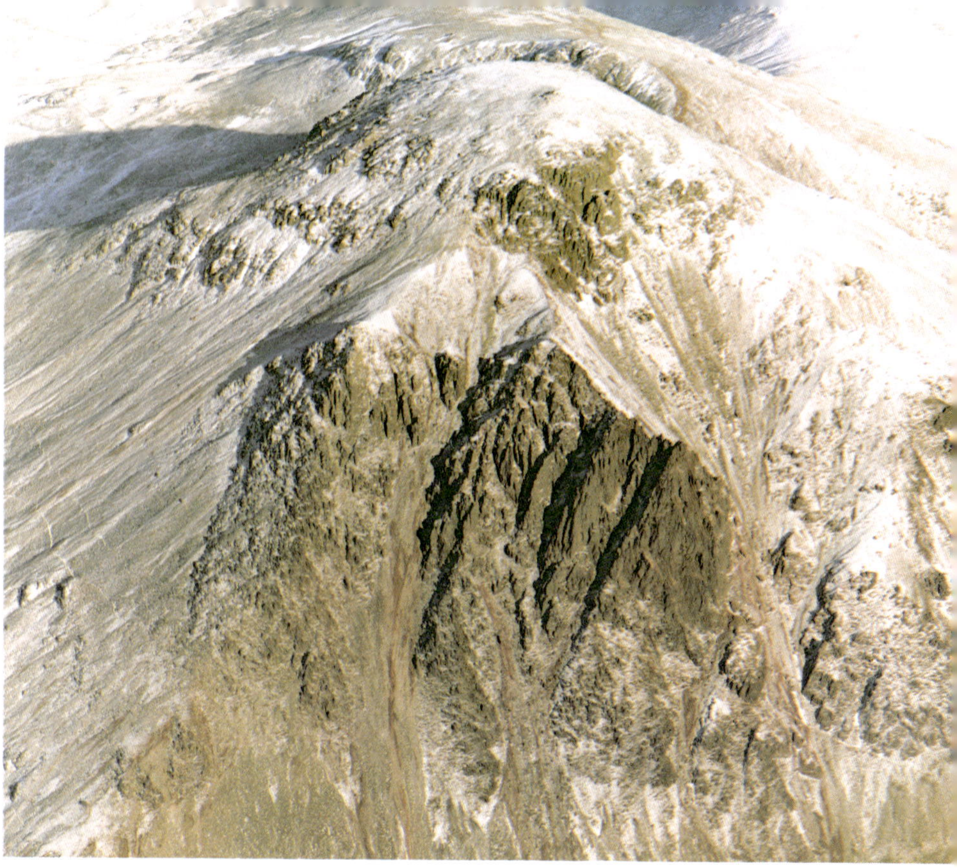

19. *Below* GREAT GABLE. The thrusting dome of this revered peak, seen broadside on looking towards Styhead Pass (far right). Observe the thin line of Moses' Sledgate, descending from the shadowy area on the left of the summit down to the bottom right of the picture.

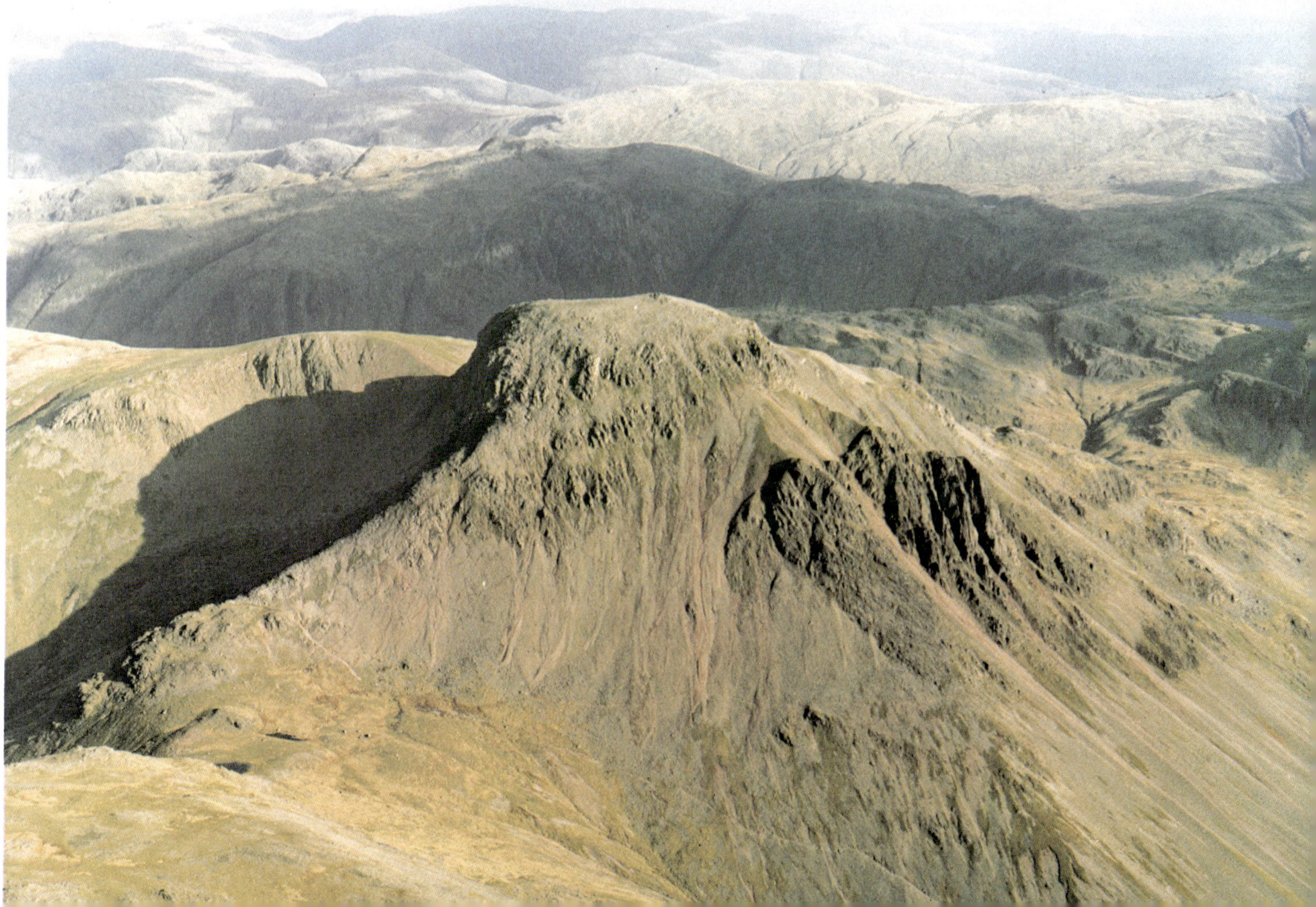

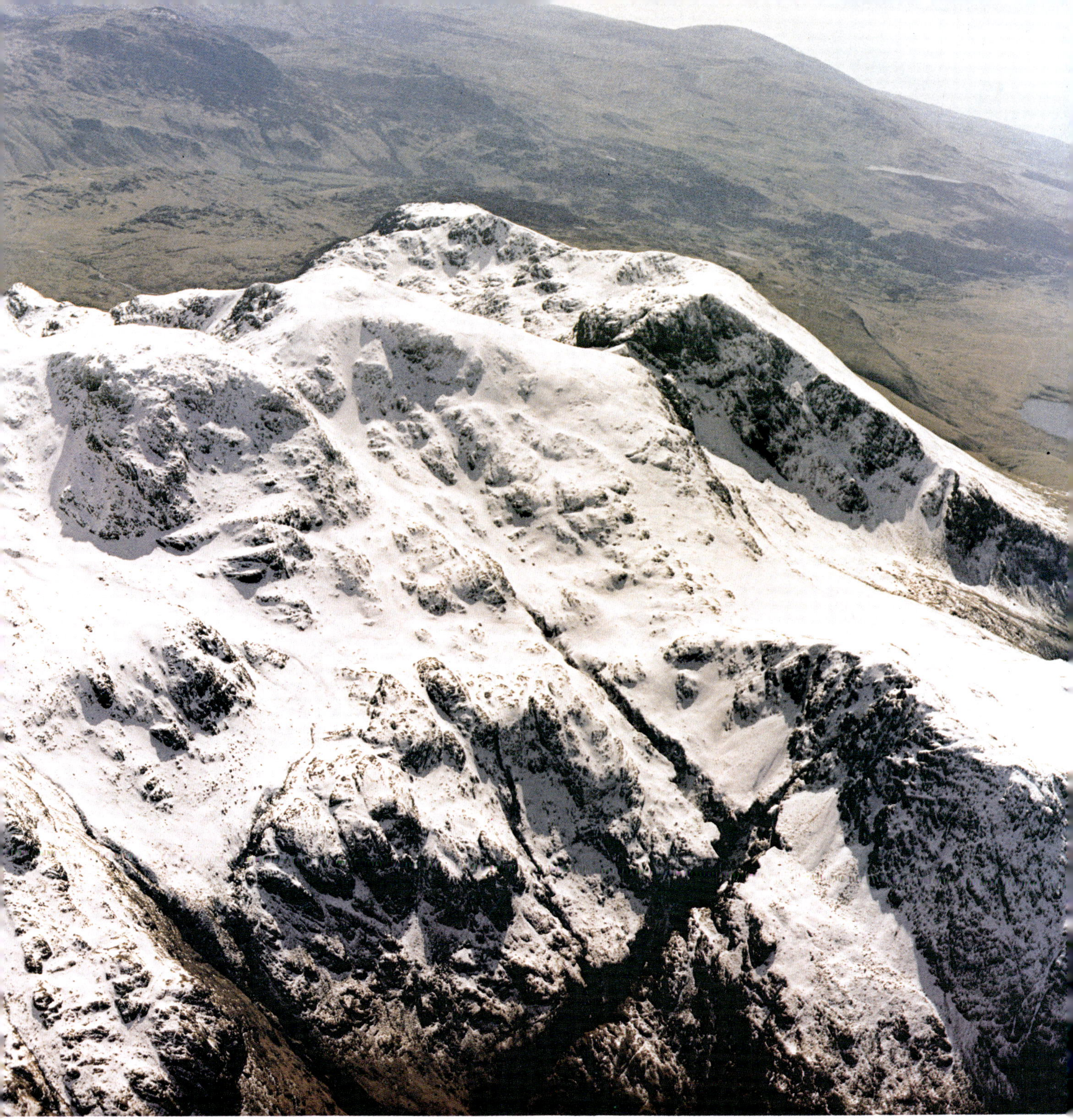

20. THE SCAFELLS. A confusion of separate peaks, most easily identified by following the forked-lightning gash of Piers Gill up from the foot of the picture. This points initially towards Lingmell before turning to follow an alignment that runs between Broad Crag (left) and the dome of Scafell Pike — at 3,210ft England's highest mountain. Beyond the Pike — and from this angle looking higher — is Scafell itself.

Mountain Lakeland

THE concept of mountains as a playground came late. Mountain pasture was hard won. Early dwellers in the shadow of the fells could hardly be indifferent to their surroundings but probably eyed them with some apprehension. The network of walls that pins down the cramped fields of Wasdale Head is the result of a herculean harvesting of stones. The men who wrought this feat may have paused in their labours to appreciate the play of cloud shadow across the sanguine pinnacles and scree chutes of Gable, but more likely wondered if they heralded a rainstorm that mountains would channel down to sluice away their hard won topsoil and sow a fresh crop of boulders.

Neolithic axe-makers, Roman legionaries, miners, shepherds, packmen, quarrymen, "colliers", ironmasters, Cistercian and Premonstratension monks knew mountain Lakeland as a workplace. Scots raiders, smugglers, forgers, proscribed Jacobites and "Moonshiners" knew mountain Lakeland as a place of refuge. All, as they went about their business, helped blaze the high paths which thousands walk for fun today. If any scrambled to the tops just for the hell of it they left no record.

When it came to mountain Lakeland the early tourists were by and large a wimpish crew, their knapsacks packed with hyperboles. From Skiddaw top they saw "chasms of enormous depth in the bowels of the mountain, forming steeps of slaty shiver, yawn upwards with frightful grin". The Coniston fells were described as "stupendous mountains, whose airy summits the straining eye can scarcely reach and which all but deny access to the human foot". There were men of sterner stuff around, however, like Budworth and Coleridge, whose packs were filled with sensible things, like sandwiches, brandy, spare shirts, portable inkhorns, and "natty green oilskins" — men whose calmer gaze saw a rugged, adventurous, oftimes heartachingly lovely, playground whose dangers were more apparent than real.

The leisured and professional Victorian middle-class, ostensibly using the area as a training ground for their Alpine expeditions, were the first to seriously explore the mountaineering possibilities of the crags and fells. The recent ITV series "Lakeland Rock" vividly illustrated how the seeds of this pioneer sowing have flowered. Men who have learnt their skills on Lakeland's crags and fells have gone out to create legends on the highest mountains and the fiercest mountain faces of the world.

Although only truly "mountains" when garbed in winter gear, the Lakeland fells are sufficient unto themselves for many of us lesser mortals, the magnificent walking and climbing they provide being played out against an often breathtakingly lovely backcloth — the view. Graham Sutton maintained that "a view is like bootlaces; its proper function is to provide excuses for a lot of halts, going up".

Knott Rigg, Causey Pike, Catbells and Newlands.

photo 11

The Newlands valley is surrounded by some of the shapeliest Lakeland fells. Coleridge, ever perceptive in his descriptions of mountain Lakeland, called them "a great Camp of Mountains — each Mountain is a Giant's Tent".

The Cistercians of the fourteenth century created their "Neulandes" by draining Husaker Tarn. The name and site linger on in Uzzicar Farm, under Barrow. In Elizabethan times German miners were imported to work Newlands copper and lead, christening their find *Gottesgab* or "God's Gift". Highly skilled and paid they imported spices, wines, and feather beds to beguile local girls. Their memory lingers in the defunct Goldscope Mine and the local and anglicized German names, like Moser, Calvert, Raisley and Caryus.

Newlands was the Klondike of Lakeland during the bonanza mining decades and fortunes were made and lost in this valley once echoing to the clack of giant water-wheels and hazy with the smelts' reek. Now Newlands is a scene of lush pastoral beauty, with farms scattered like fat dice in the crinkles of a crumpled baize.

Many shapely and deservedly popular minor fells adorn the valley, Barrow, Causey Pike, Catbells, and the Knott Rigg-Ard Crags ridge so gloriously predominant in photo 11. Elegant walking all, they are ideal for introducing children to the hills or for a leisurely half day or evening stroll, often giving an unusual and intimate viewpoint on their loftier neighbours.

Curving behind Knott Rigg is the deep defile formed by the Rigg and Sail becks. It provides a delightful pedestrian link between Newlands and Buttermere that avoids the grinding gears, fumes and sole-searing tarmac of the road over Newlands Hause. Sail Beck on a summer evening can be magnificent with the crests haloed in a blaze of gold and a silent silver thread of beck spilling over the high rim of Addacombe Hole.

The patch of paler brown under the summit of Ard Crags, and overlooking Newlands, is the Keskadale Oaks, one of the surviving remnants of original or "relict" woodland that has survived the axe of farmer, miner or "collier".

Helvellyn and Striding Edge

photos 12, 13

It is a safe bet that there will be more people on Helvellyn top, on any given day, than on any other Lakeland high fell. In the late sixties a Brathay Hall Expedition Group survey counted, on one specific day, 150 people on Scafell Pike, 192 on Gable and 614 on Helvellyn.

Photo 12 dramatically highlights why Helvellyn's west approaches are dull plods and all the magic lies under the eastern rims. Here the growling ice has sculpted elegant ridges and craggy combes which time and weather have honed to a rare finish.

Photo 13, truly a picture that makes one's feet itch, portrays what draws many to Helvellyn — Striding Edge. The circuit of Red Tarn Cove over Striding Edge and Swirrel Edge is a Lakeland classic. Under snow and ice it's superb, often quite "hairy", requiring the comfort of ice-axe, crampons and possibly a rope.

Helvellyn is rich in memorials. They mark the death of an unfortunate, perhaps over enthusiastic, follower of foxhounds who plunged off Striding Edge; two magnificent men in their flying machine who mistook Helvellyn for an aircraft-carrier; and a Victorian doggy who for months guarded his master's corpse, earning poetic praise from both Wordsworth and Sir Walter Scott. There is a school of thought, admittedly largely composed of cat lovers, who believe Faithful Fido fortified himself with bits of Master.

Captain Joseph Budworth, a one-armed veteran of the Siege of Gibraltar, made perhaps the first recorded ascent in 1793. He celebrated his success by gleefully "trundling" boulders off the top — an enjoyable pursuit and acceptable in those days when at the worst it might only frighten a few sheep. Not a sport to be advocated nowadays, however, especially on a Bank Holiday. Coleridge made a moonlit climb in 1802, a bold venture for the time. He exulted in the view, describing Striding Edge as "that prodigious precipice of grey stone with deep Wrinkles, facing me".

Crowded mountains Helvellyn and its clutch of attendant peaks might be but tucked into their rough folds are many lovely quiet corners. Cupped in a slabby fold of Ruthwaite Cove is Hard Tarn, a mountain gem. Nethermost Edge gives a taste of Striding Edge, minus the queues. Shapely Catstycam, "the Cat's Ladder", throws a nice ridge down into lonely Keppel Cove. Even the plebian western flanks have creamy cascades and derelict lead mines tucked away.

Helvellyn tries hard to be all things to allcomers, and invariably delights.

Blencathra

photo 14

A lovely name for a magnificent mountain, certain to be included in any Lakeland team versus a World Mountain XI. Saddleback is the peak's prosaic alternative and when approached from Penrith it is easy to see why. Blencathra has the good sense to turn its tame flank towards Skiddaw House, from where it is only likely to be seen by the Faithful, who will undoubtedly forgive it.

Blencathra is seen at its best when approached up the Vale of St. John. It fills the sky ahead — a mountain wall 2,500 feet high and almost three miles long, buttressed by flying ridges and cleft with deep shadowy hollows. Photo 14 does eloquent justice to this magnificent mountain wall towering above the village of Threlkeld.

From Threlkeld's streets one particular curving and castellated ridge captures the eye. This is Hallsfell (the right-hand of the two principal ridges in the photograph). The estimable Mr. Wainwright describes this ridge as "positively the finest way to any mountain top in the district." With Sharp Edge just around the corner not everyone will agree. Hallsfell is undoubtedly an entertaining route, particularly the succession of rocky tors known as "Narrow Edge", and especially under the conditions portrayed in the illustration. It also has the added merit that it lands you slap-bang up against the summit cairn.

Sharp Edge, however, is something else again. Tucked out of sight, you have to sweat a little for your reward, which is proper. It is the "edgiest" of Lakeland's "edges". Although shorter than its rival, Striding Edge, its problems cannot be as easily avoided. Up Sharp Edge and down Hallsfell, or vice versa — now you are really talking about a great Lakeland day, especially under snow.

Gategill Fell (left of Hallsfell) and Doddick Fell (to the right and out of the picture) would be raved about if they were stuck onto a lump like Loadpot Hill. On Blencathra they play a supporting role. Even Scales Fell and Blease Fell, the broad ridges that make book-ends to the Threlkeld flank, the poor relations of the Blencathra ridges, provide interesting ascents, such is the quality of the mountain.

In 1793 a Mr. Hutchinson led a party up Blencathra. The expedition foundered somewhere on Scales Fell with all the wimps pleading to "let blood and return". Now Blencathra is very, very good, but it's not that good.

Langdale Pikes

photos 15, 16

It is easy to see from photo 15 why Langdale was christened "the long valley". Man has long dwelt in it too. The Neolithic axe-makers worked their "rough-outs" close to the summits of Harrison Stickle and Thunacar Knott and in "Stone Axe Gully", under Pike O' Stickle, before transportng them to the coast for polishing and export. Baysbrown — "Bruni's Cowshed" — Farm, under Lingmoor, is the oldest farmstead in the valley and may have been worked in the tenth century. Iron was once worked in Langdale, slate still is, and the Elterwater Gunpowder Mill, now the site of luxury time-share chalets, produced until the 1930s.

Many of the fells hide their finest treasures from the tourist, reserving them for the fellwalker and climber. The Pikes, however, are right little show-offs, putting on a display as soon as the motorist tops the hill above Windermere. To a certain extent it is all bluff and bluster. They have a skeleton in their craggy cupboard which photo 16 clearly displays. The exciting facade hides a dreary plateau of bog and grass.

Poseurs the Pikes may be but the facade is magnificent, providing a splendid mix of crags, climbs, ravines, scrambles, cascades and a fine high tarn. Enough to keep a couple of battalions of climbers, walkers, scramblers, photographers, painters, or whatever, happy for months. Photo 16 certainly does it justice. To the left and central are the clean, steep, slabs and walls of Gimmer Crag. Above the dark waters of Stickle Tarn, dammed in 1824 to provide power for the gunpowder mill, tower the vegetated and uncompromising buttresses of Pavey Ark. The frail filament of snow slantingly draped across this crag indicates the line of Jakes Rake, a popular scramble. Bathed in shadow and slanting across the lower half of the illustration, its upper gorge tucked under the summit crag of Harrison Stickle, is Dungeon Ghyll. Followed as close as the cascades allow, it gives one of the best "becking" expeditions in Lakeland. Dungeon Ghyll Force was reputedly the model for the "deep, romantic chasm" of Coleridge's famously rudely interrupted and curtailed poem "Kubla Khan". Visible along the bottom of the illustration are Raven Crag and the line of small fierce crags overlooking the "ODG" (Old Dungeon Ghyll Hotel), a famous mountain hostelry.

Budworth "bagged" the first recorded ascent of the Pikes. On the descent the old sweat was overcome by a touch of the hyperboles when he came to "a large bulging part of the mountain, across a sward nearly perpendicular and of immoderate height". Before he would allow his guide to lead him across this "mauvais pas" he insisted upon bandaging his offside eye with his handkerchief. This on top of having only one arm!

Great Gable

photos 17, 18, 19

Gable, as it is more commonly and affectionately known to the Faithful, looks good from all angles. A fact not necessarily true of many popular Lakeland peaks, as already noted with the Langdale Pikes.

Gable's most photographed profile is the classic rugged pyramid it presents towards Wasdale Head, fittingly chosen as the centre-piece of the emblem of the Lake District National Park. Broadside on Gable is a thrusting dome, as seen in photo 19. Clearly visible on this picture emerging out of the shadow of Gable Crag, crossing the grassy saddle of Beckhead, and slanting down onto Gavel Neese, is Moses Sledgate. This path was reputedly named after Moses Rigg, a "moonshiner" who had his still, or "worm", nearby, and was his pipeline to his customers.

In the 1890s climbers discovered a roofless man-made structure high on the face of Gable Crag, which has traditionally become christened the Smugglers' Hut. Of the many theories advanced as to its purpose, a favourite is that it was a prepared bolt-hole for the Jacobite Earl of Derwentwater. He was captured at Preston in 1715, however, and executed shortly afterwards. Perhaps his last thought, as the axe descended, was a regretful vision of a safe eyrie above the green hills of home.

Photo 18 shows a bizarre view of Gable that can be seen to similar effect from Lingmell. The first thought is that Gable was once a green and pleasant hill over which some celestial tipper had poured millions of tons of ash and clinker. This has spilled down the fell undeterred by the bandolier of crag slung diagonally from the crest of Gavel Neese to the saddle of Styhead. Grey is predominant and the paths are like old fight scars slashed across a dinosaur's hide. All colour has not been expunged by the grey torrent. Fingers of green claw out of the detritus and the deep runnels of Great and Little Hell Gates are smudged with rouge, as if Gable has been attempting to repair the ravages of time. In the photograph winter has hopefully added a puff or two of powder.

Napes Needle is perhaps the most famous chunk of Lakeland rock and probably the only British rock-climb to which the man in the street could put a name. (It is visible in photo 18 at the foot of Needle Ridge, the right-hand of the three sharp shadow-etched ridges). The most exciting way up Gable for the fellwalker cum scrambler is the Gable (or Climbers') Traverse. In the picture it can be spotted as a fine scar running towards the Napes Ridges, through which it weaves a delightful thread of airy slab, "Fat Man's Agony", and spiky ridge.

Photo 17 shows a snow draped Gable accompanied by Kirkfell and Pillar. This splendid trio form the "make or break" section of the classic Ennerdale Horseshoe. Starting from the foot of Ennerdale Water, with its turning and high point Gable's bouldery dome, this mountain walk, twenty-one miles and around 9,000 feet of climbing, is a "cracker".

The Scafells

photo 20

With its tilted background of grassy lowland apparently higher than the snow peaks, photo 20 could puzzle if you are not an active fell spotter. The key is the forked-lightning gash of Piers Gill ripping deep into the craggy heart of Scafell Pike. In the 1880s a climber was badly injured whilst exploring this ravine. Mountain rescue was spur-of-the-moment stuff in those days. Whilst one man rendered first-aid, others went for the nearest farm gate to serve as a stretcher and a third found himself galloping down Wasdale on a borrowed horse for the nearest doctor.

Above and to the right of Piers Gill are the ramshackle crags of Lingmell. The obvious snowy shelf curving above the craggy left flank of the gill marks the line of the Corridor Route, an interesting way to the summit of England. It was formerly referred to as the Guides Route, probably as a result of the Victorian practice of climbing the mountain on the back of led ponies. Wordsworth made such an ascent, with Dorothy, in 1818.

Scafell Pike top is the central snow dome, superimposed on the rugged flanks of the apparently higher Scafell. Not the first time, Scafell Pike has suffered by comparison to its elegant mate across Mickledore — the "Great Door". Early surveyors dismissed it as merely an encumbrance, the "Pikes of Scafell". The sun-splashed snow arete of Mickledore, christened "that Hyphen" by Coleridge, is clearly visible abutting the grim buttress of Scafell Crag. Undoubtedly this is the finest crag in Lakeland and upon its stark walls daring men have long breathed life into their dreams. Foxes Tarn, Lord's Rake and Broad Stand offer lesser mortals exciting ways to Scafell top.

The sunlit breach in the crags above Mickledore marks the line of Broad Stand. In 1802 Coleridge slithered down it to make the first descent, a daring and hazardous undertaking for the time. He arrived at the bottom with an eruption of "great red heat-lumps" and a "Palsy of the Limbs".

To the left of Scafell Pike is Broad Crag. The eroded "tourist" route from Esk Hause passes across its bouldery summit dome. Beyond Broad Crag rises the elegant outlier of Pen, which overlooks the Great Moss, the heart of the Cumbrian Badlands. To climb Scafell Pike by way of Pen, or Little Narrowcove, pays proper tribute to England's summit.

The foremost impression of Scafell Pike, reinforced when you gaze at photo 20, is one of brute strength rather than elegance. Capped by a dome of man-trap boulders, mailed in rock and scree, its topography complicated and offering no easy escape route, it is potentially, and especially under the conditions portrayed, the most dangerous mountain in Lakeland.

TOWNS AND VILLAGES

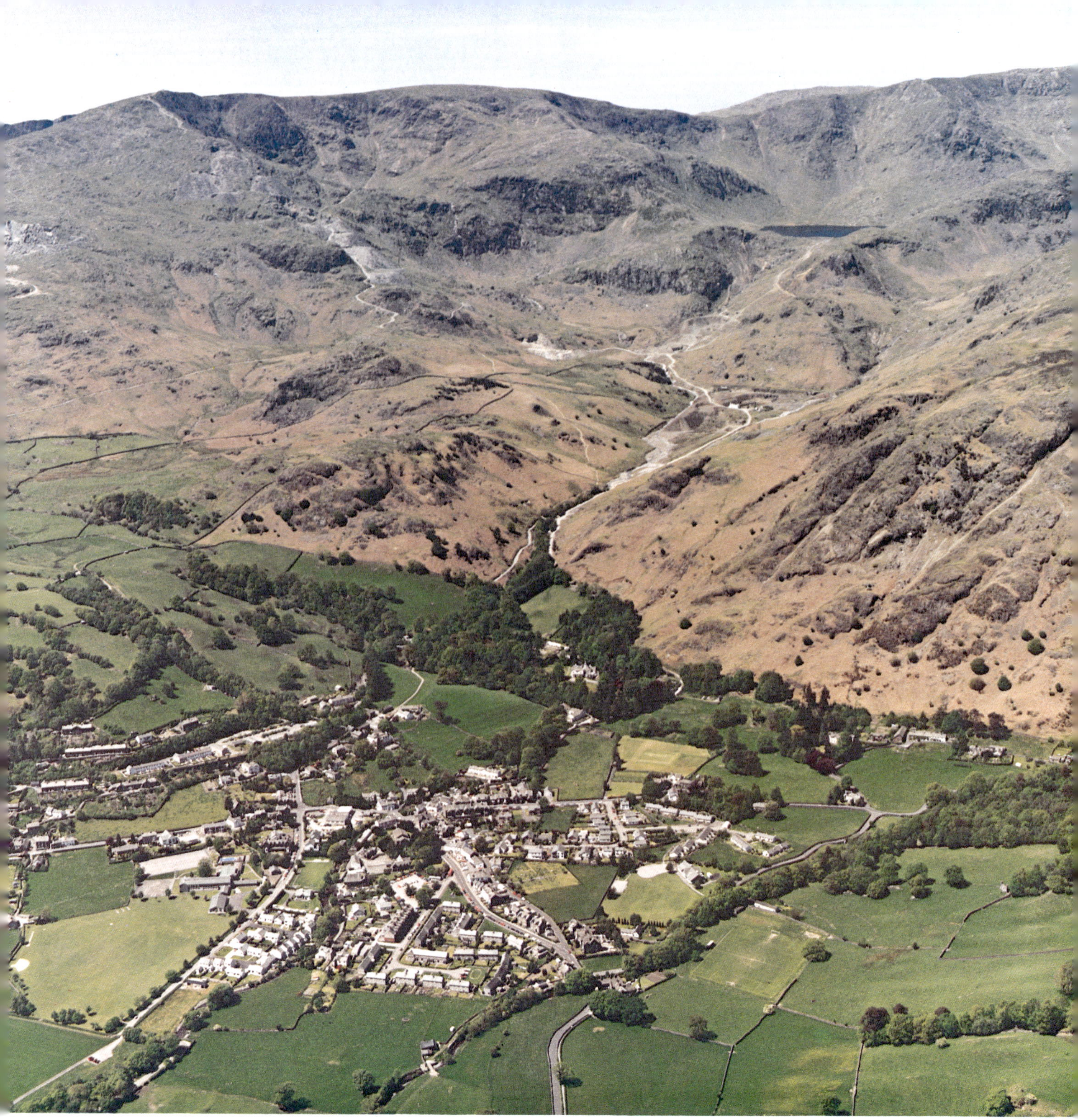

21. CONISTON. Looking west towards Coniston Old Man (left) and Swirl How on the far right, below and left of which is the blue-black blob of Levers Water. Clearly visible as a thin white line is the track from the village up the valley of Church Beck to the spoil heaps which mark the site of Coniston's once flourishing copper mines. Leading out of the bottom of the picture is the road to Hawkshead.

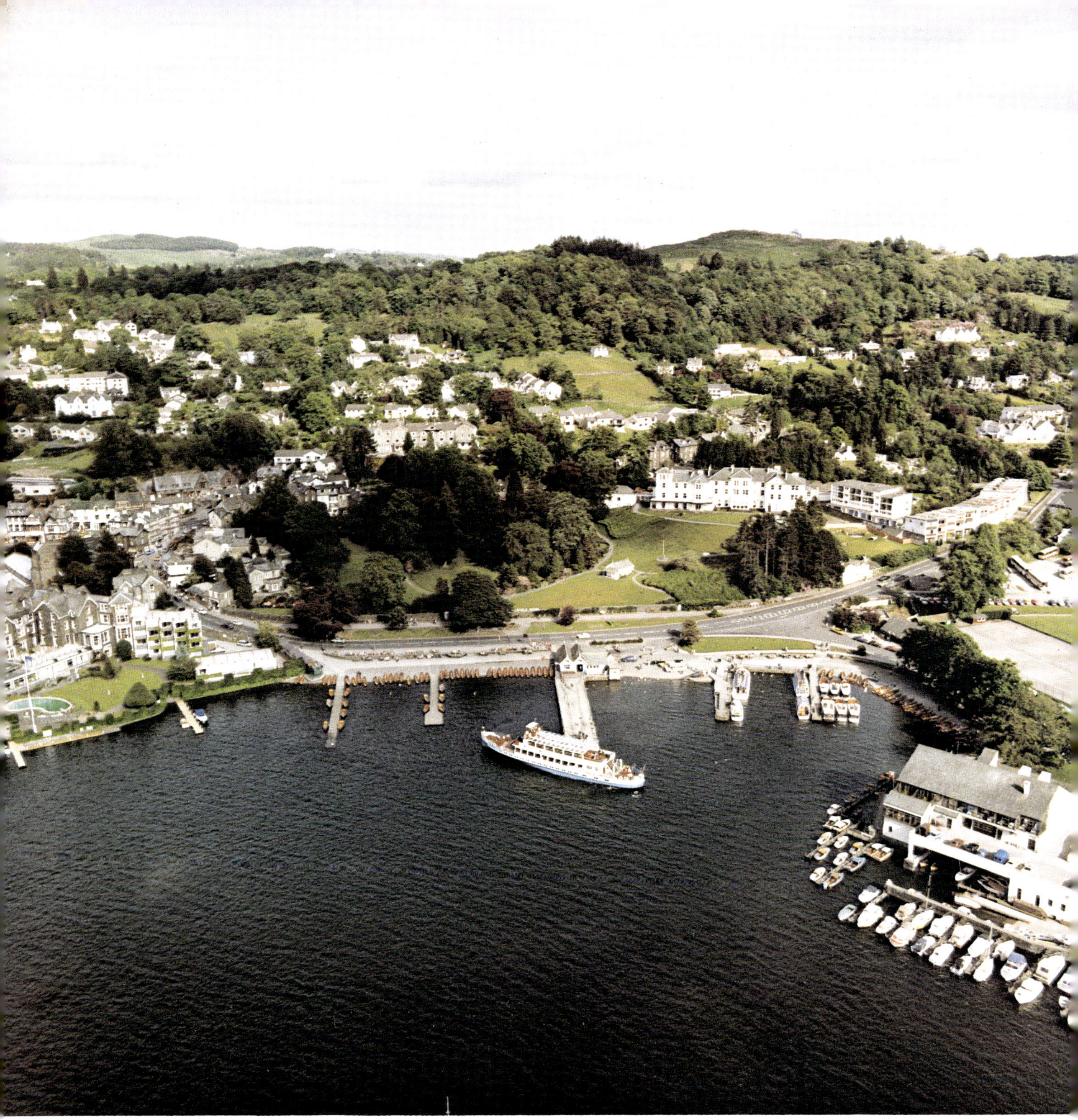

22. **BOWNESS — in high summer.** **Boats a-plenty stand at the various moorings and one of the Windermere steamers is at the main pier. The large all-white building in the centre right of the picture is the Belsfield Hotel, once a private mansion occupied in the 19th century by Furness industrialist H.W. Schneider. Each day he travelled down the lake en route to Barrow in his own private steam-yacht, reputedly preceded from the house by his butler carrying breakfast to be served on board.**

23. BOWNESS — the town centre. As indicated by the church and some of the older houses, this is a former village settlement of considerable antiquity. In recent times it has virtually merged with Windermere town, a much newer creation of the railway age. Prominent in the foreground is the Old England Hotel with its grounds right on the water's edge.

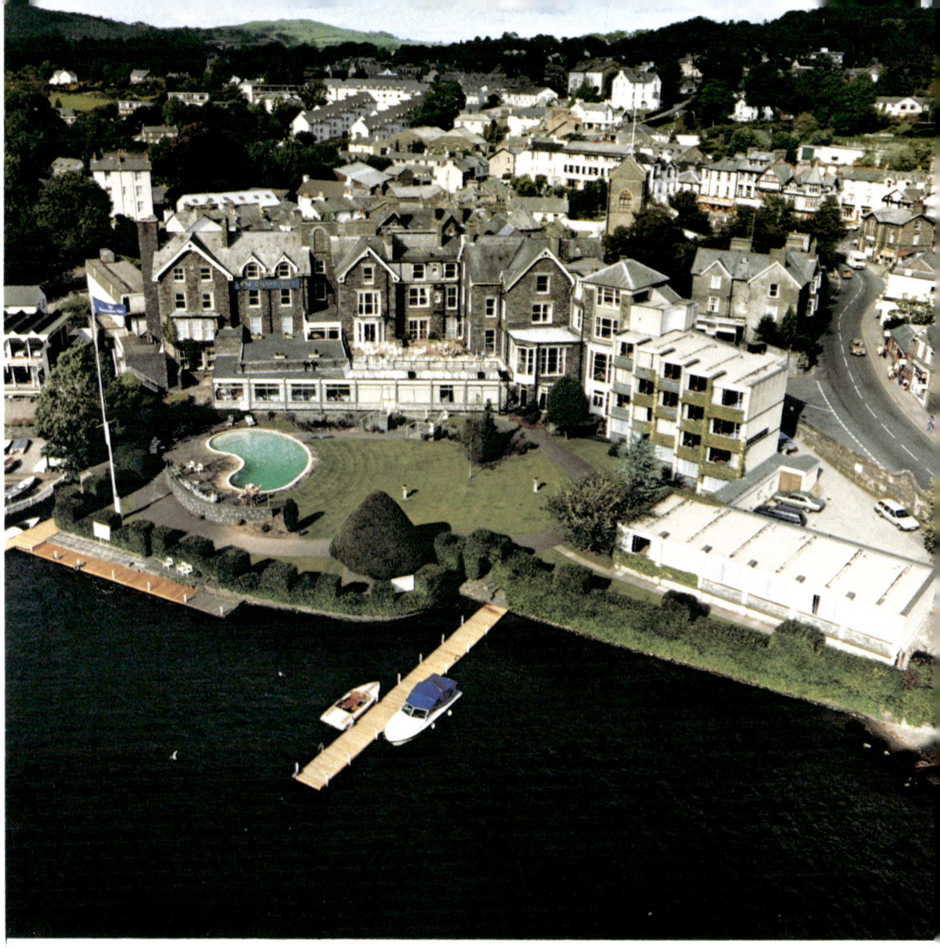

24. BOWNESS — in mid-winter. Gone are all the boats and waterfront bustle and all is hushed under a covering of snow.

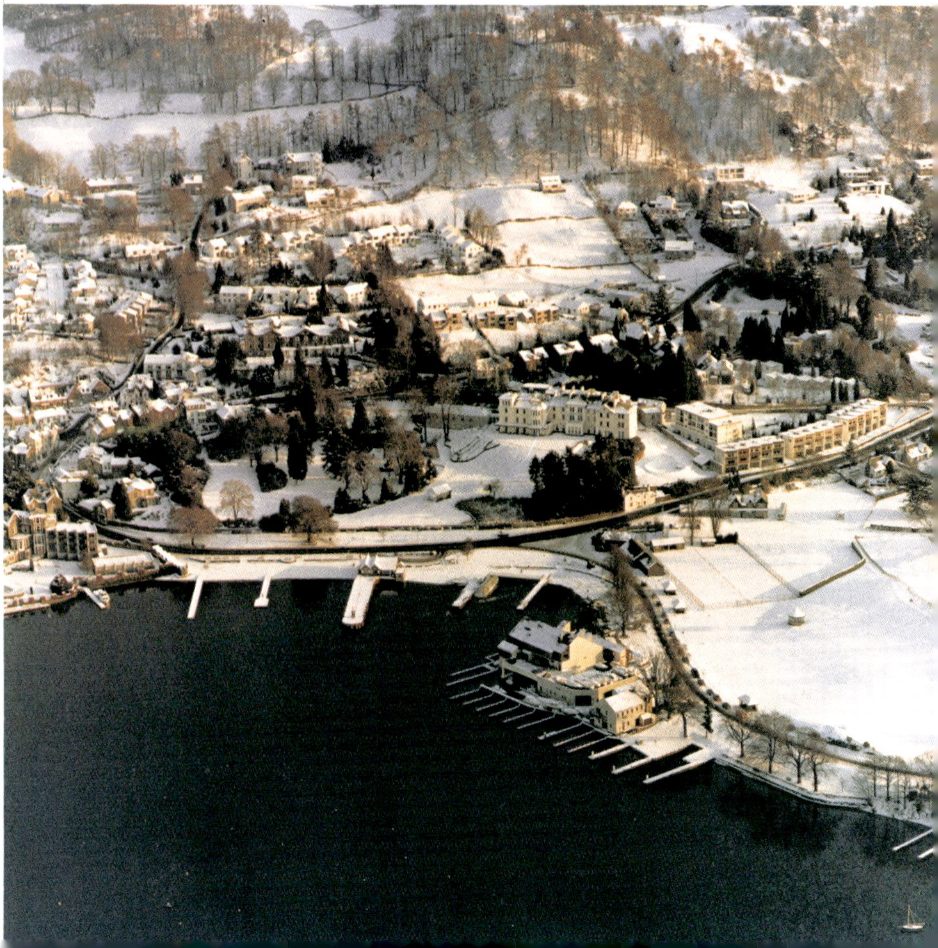

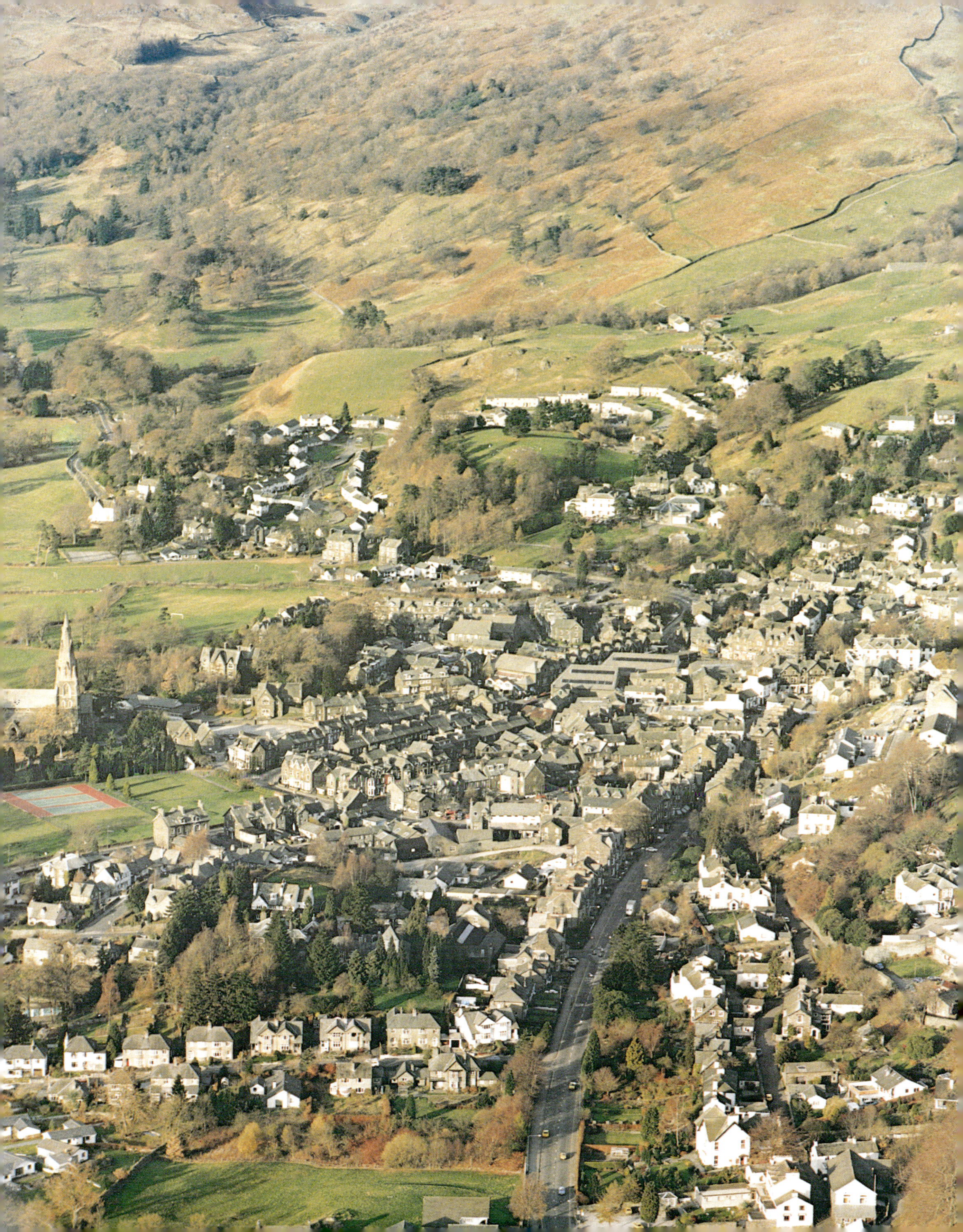

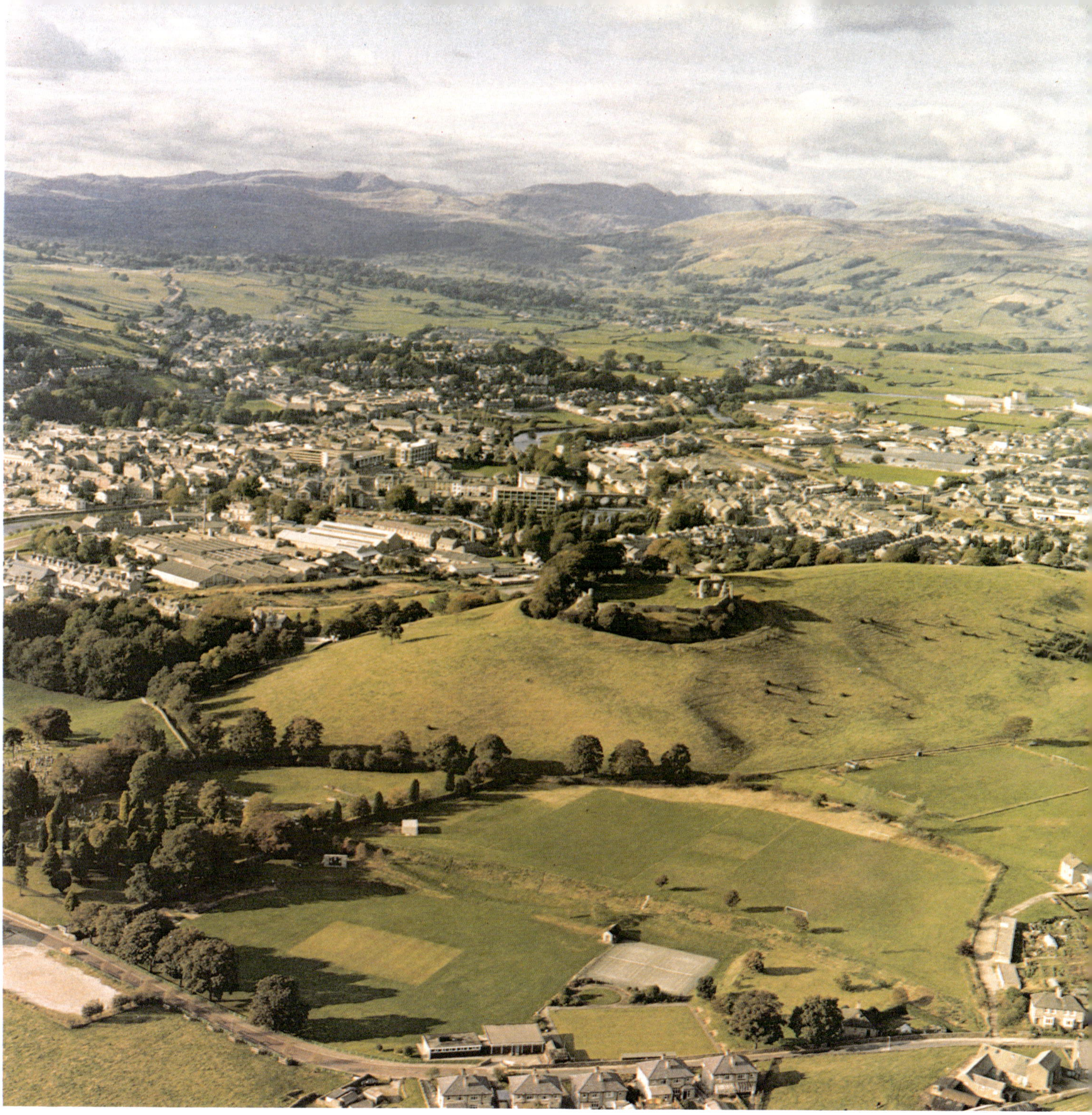

25. *Left* AMBLESIDE. The camera looks along the main southern approach road, which twists and turns through the town and can then be picked up again as it heads north-west towards Rydal (top left). The long line of trees running across the top of the picture marks the valley of Scandale Beck. The church, setting for an annual rush-bearing ceremony, dominates the west side of the town.

26. *Above* KENDAL. The great green hump in the middle of the picture is the town's most historic landmark — Castle Hill, crowned by the ruins of the castle itself (see photo 33). Beyond, the river Kent snakes its way through the centre of Kendal — note the "artificial" banks erected in recent years to prevent devastating flooding. In the distance is the rolling countryside which provides the town with such an attractive setting.

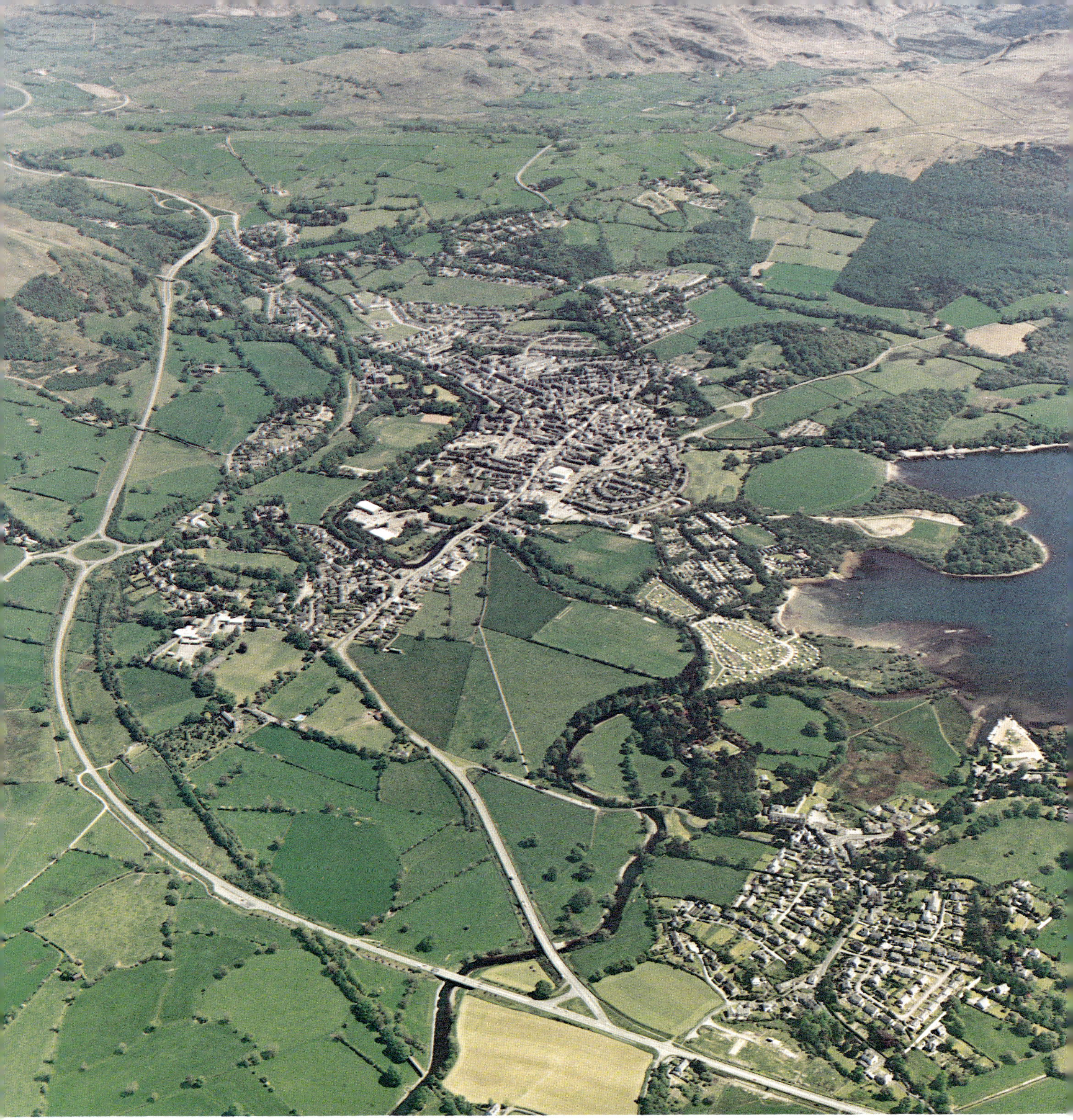

27. **KESWICK.** A picture for those opposed to major road development in National Parks! This view shows better than any ground-level photograph how the controversial A66 "improvement" created a Keswick by-pass completely out-of-scale with the surrounding landscape and settlement. The unobtrusive Cockermouth–Penrith railway which it displaced can be picked out as a long line of trees, running from the centre bottom of the picture across the river Derwent and the "new" A66, then past Crosthwaite church and into the town before curving round into the Greta gorge. Portinscale is at bottom right, while above it Friar's Crag juts out into Derwentwater.

28. WHITEHAVEN. What was once a major port serving the third largest town in the north of England is today comparatively deserted. One has to look carefully for signs of former glory in this picture, although the "grid-iron" pattern of the town centre is a reminder of the spacious days when it was laid out by the Lowther family, later the Earls of Lonsdale. They spearheaded the development of coal mining under the sea, a reminder of which is the ornamental "candlestick" chimney between the inner harbour and the start of the cliffs. The distant skyline includes many of Lakeland's highest peaks — in the centre is Pillar, just to the right of Ennerdale Water.

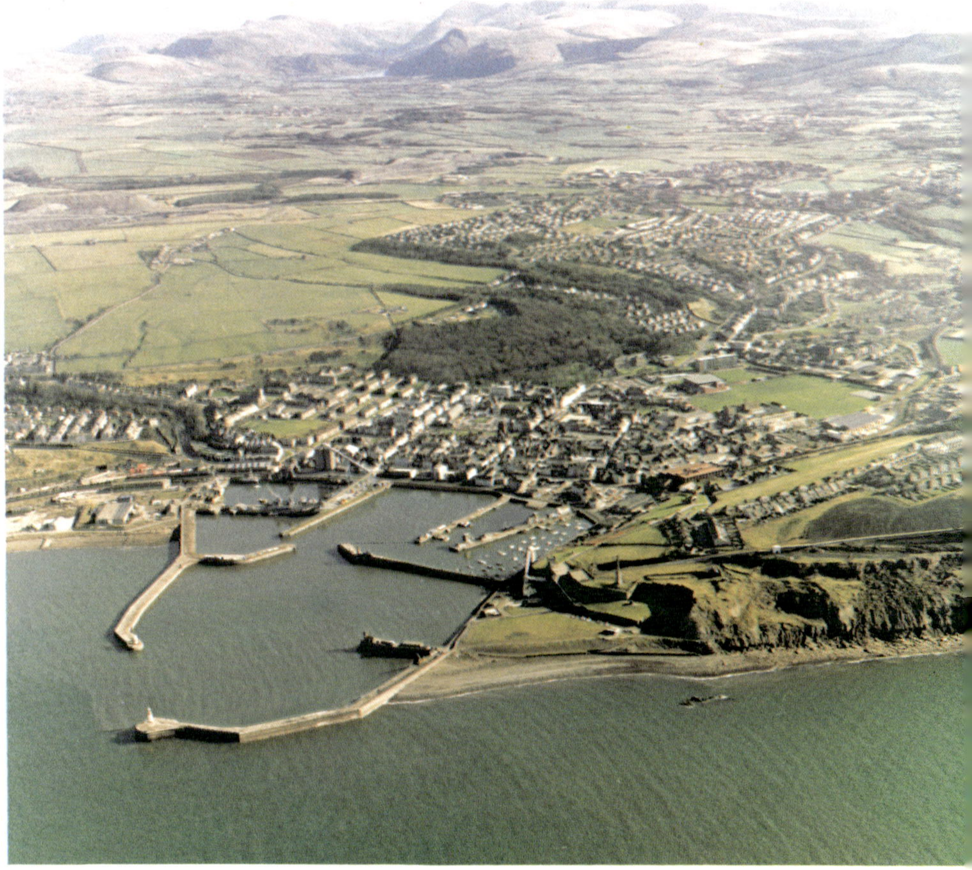

29. MILLOM. The plane is directly above the site of the once vast Hodbarrow iron-ore workings, with the large white area in the centre of the picture marking the site of the now totally demolished Millom iron works. On the left is the edge of the town, which until the discovery of haematite deposits in the 1860s was simply the tiny village of Holborn Hill. The deep inlet of the Duddon estuary stretches inland towards Broughton-in-Furness at its head, with the Duddon valley curving away towards the Scafell range (top left).

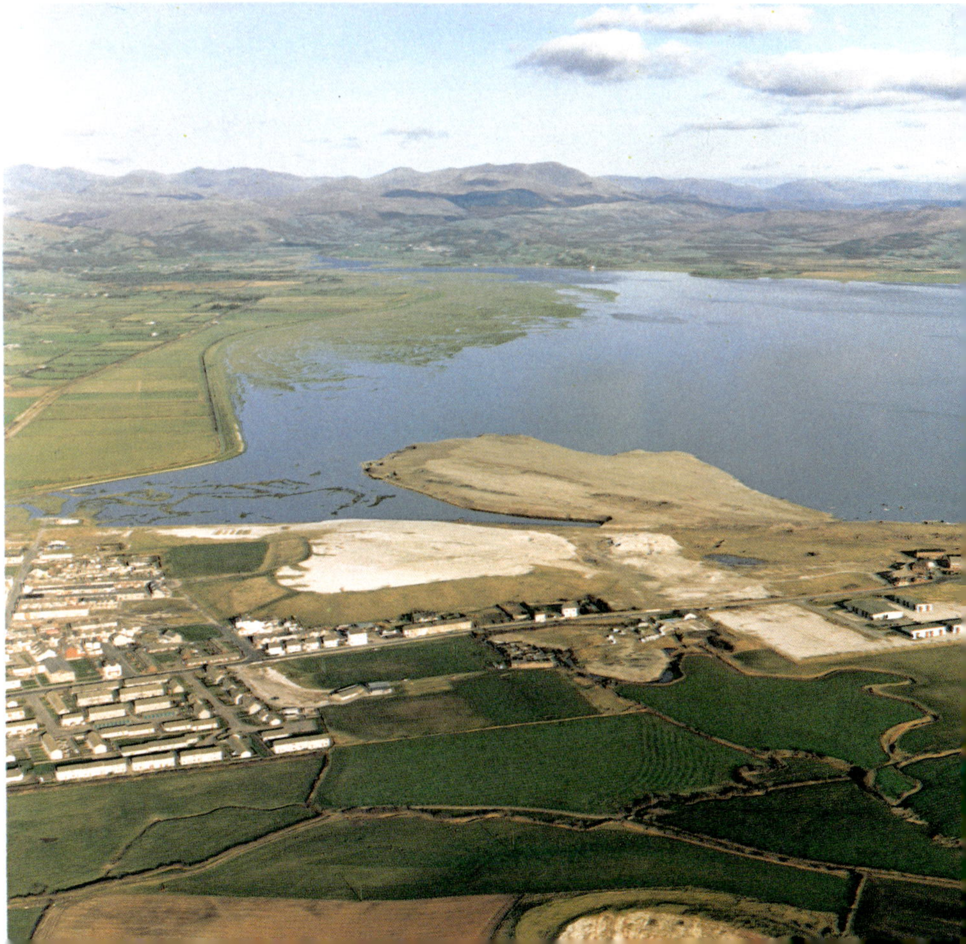

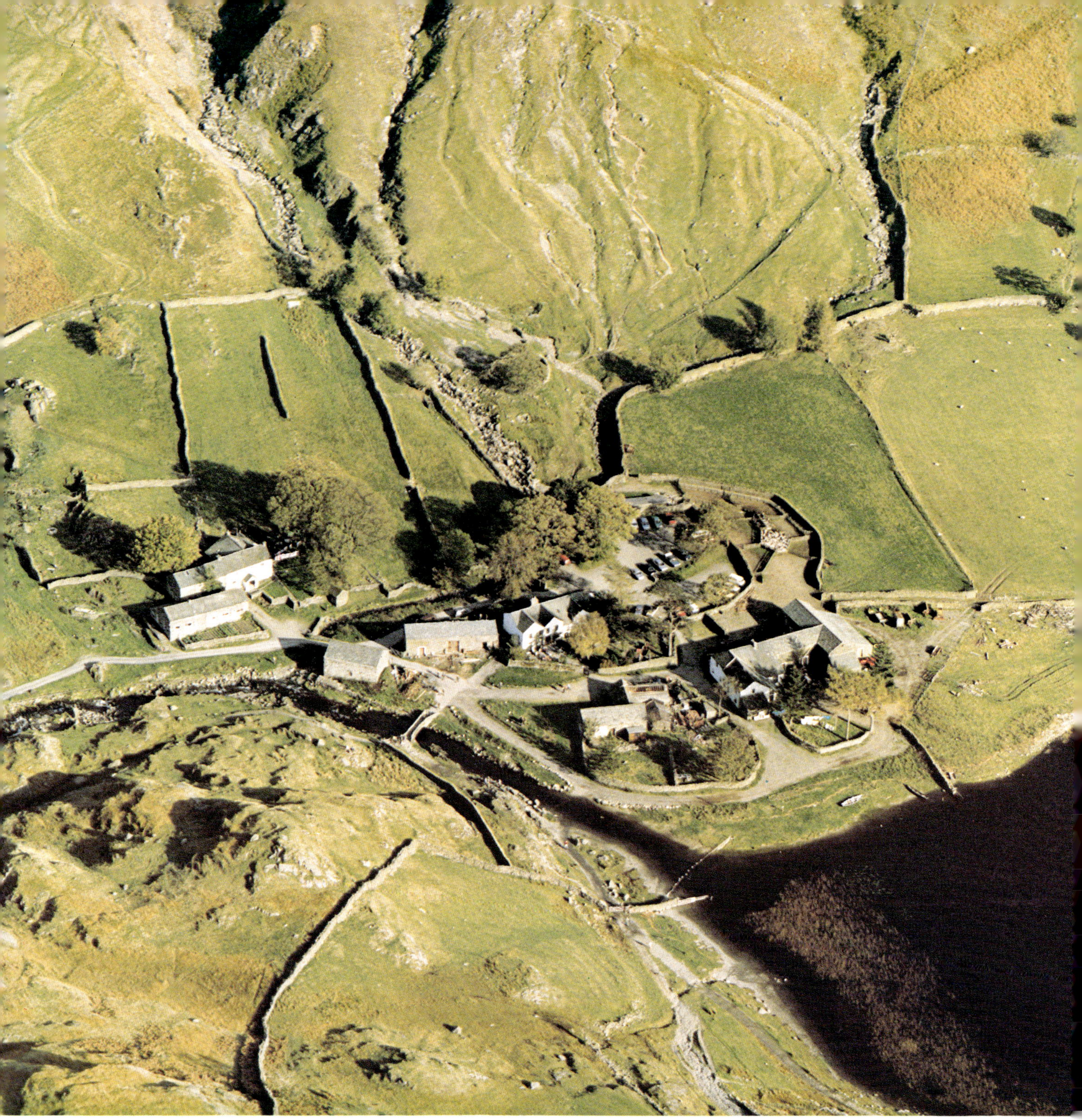

30. WATENDLATH. More of a hamlet than a village but in a jewel of a setting complete with its own tarn (bottom right). It is reached by a narrow and at times extremely congested road climbing from the east side of Derwentwater across Ashness Bridge. This view shows rugged Raise Gill descending towards the small car park, to the right of which sheep-dipping is in progress in the farm yard. Watendlath Beck leads out of the left of the picture, eventually to descend spectacularly down the famed Lodore Falls.

Towns and Villages

THE main settlements lie at the edge of the Lake District, where the valleys broaden into the low country. Until the transport revolution last century, a Lakeland dalesman was parochial in his outlook, his vision restricted by the high hills, his gossip coming from the packhorse men, or from chance encounters with friends at the weekly market. He might be born, live, love and die in a single valley, in which his home occupied one end, and the market town lay at the other.

With its discovery by the tourist, the Lake District's historic isolation was at an end. The 19th century saw the transformation of the way of life. The Lake District we know today is largely the creation of visitors. Wordsworth was a Cumbrian who returned to the area after years spent well away from it; his poetic friends were truly off-comers. In the wake of the first intrepid tourists, who had the habit of writing their experiences — and thus commending the Lake District — came the new settlers.

What we see most readily today in the main towns and villages is a concept of Victorian and Edwardian times. The social life of Lakeland changed quickly and dramatically. Fine new houses appeared beside Windermere; they included a mock castle at Wray. A building boom created houses, hotels looking like palaces and shops catering for visitors. Steam yachts appeared on the major lakes, and steam-hauled trains chugged along lines extending from the peripheral areas to places among the fell ranges.

To the new settlers, among whom — in the latter days — was Hugh Walpole, the Lake District offered escape from areas desecrated by industry. He arrived at Brackenburn, near Keswick, in 1923, and wrote of his "little paradise", with its "running stream, garden, lawn, daffodils, squirrels, music-room, garage, four bedrooms, bath — and all. Entranced and excited".

Coniston

photo 21

Most visitors reach Coniston with a sense of discovery, for although the main road connects Ambleside and Broughton-in-Furness, with a branch to Greenodd, the best tourist approach is from the east. It is an immensely satisfying journey if it begins with a ferry crossing of Windermere, continues through the Sawreys and Hawkshead and then takes in Tarn Hows. As the road dips towards Coniston, with coppice on either side, this village and its setting are wonderfully revealed.

Coniston Water, over five miles long, is set in fairly gentle countryside, though the rising ground to the east has changed its character because of the Forst of Grizedale. Westwards are fertile fields and then the craggy Coniston Fells loom spectacularly. They are presided over by the Old Man, which reaches an altitude of 2,635 feet but looks much higher. The boundary of Coniston parish runs along the top.

Coniston village is typical of a small Lakeland community, with its buildings of native stone, jostling together beside the church beck and then spreading along the main road. Norsemen knew Coniston well, as place-names testify. Here, too, came monks from Furness, who were able to keep a boat and 20 nets at the lake in the 13th century. Iron was smelted in "bloomeries". Over 250 years ago German miners disturbed some of the crags as they quested for copper.

Flemings occupied Coniston Hall and built the original church (1586). Ruskin took over a mean dwelling, Brantwood, in 1871, and extended it radically during the following 29 years. He was buried in Coniston churchyard. Coniston has an informative Ruskin Museum. Another literary giant. Alfred Tennyson, honeymooned at Tent Lodge.

A gondola, recently restored, sails on Coniston Water. There are smaller rowing craft for hire. Donald Campbell used the lake for world water speed records, and he died here when his craft *Bluebird* left the water, somersaulted and sank in January, 1967. The railway to Coniston is closed but the slate quarries thrive, as they have done for over 300 years, producing green slate for the facings and roofs of buildings.

Bowness

photos 22, 23, 24

Visitors to Bowness usually approach from the direction of Windermere town. They follow Lake Road, descend Crag Brow and, passing close to St. Martin's Church, bear left to behold Bowness Bay, which in summer is one of Lakeland's most popular areas for mass recreation.

There is a temptation to think that because the settlement of Windermere took its name from the lake it is the most ancient village in these parts. There was virtually no Windermere until the coming of the railway in 1847. Railway money led to the transformation of the tiny hamlet of Birthwaite (the name means "clearing among the birch trees") into a town. Bowness, lower down the hill and at the edge of the lake, is by far the older place. Its rectory was built in 1416 and partly rebuilt in the 17th century; the church of St. Martin's existed before 1483. That was the year when rebuilding took place after a fire.

The money of wealthy off-comers financed a building boom which brought hotels, shops and large houses to the Bowness district. Outsiders with means were also able to indulge in costly sports, such as racing with large yachts. Sailing yachts were raced regularly on Windermere as early as 1849, and a club was formed in 1860. It came under Royal patronage in 1887. The age of gracious living by comparatively few wealthy people reached its peak in the latter part of the 19th century. H. W. Schneider, the Furness industrialist, settled at Belsfield in 1869, and he had a small steamer built for the regular journey from Bowness to Lakeside, where he entrained for his office in Barrow. The steamer was called the "Esperance," and a special pier for it was constructed in Bowness Bay. Early in the morning, Schneider would leave Belsfield, preceded by a butler who carried breakfast on a tray. The industrialist would enjoy the meal during a sail down the lake, and he did not have to wait for a train at Lakeside for a "special" was laid on for him.

The main tourist area, beside the lake, was radically altered in 1912 when a promenade was constructed. During this century new ideas have become established — and some old customs have quietly faded. For many years a depth-loving fish called the char was caught commercially, but in 1922 netting on Windermere was prohibited. The char caught today have been lured by hook and long line. It is a specialist's job, but there are still men at Bowness who excel at it. The lake is the main attraction at Bowness. At the time of peak usage in high summer, 1,600 boats have been counted. In the coldest winters sports can be held on the overlying crust of ice. An estimated 100,000 people stood on ice nine inches thick during a cold snap in 1894.

Ambleside

photo 25

Ambleside may be derived from the shieling of Amal, or Hamel. It was Amelsate in the 13th century, set fairly high up beside Stock Beck, a village of consequence which became a prosperous town when market charters were awarded to it in the 17th century. It was soon an important tourist centre favoured by some of the first "seekers after the pictuesque" and by the armies of visitors who followed the newly-blazed trails into the Lakeland valleys.

Climb the hill to the most ancient part of Ambleside and you see the church of St. Anne, built in 1812 on the site of an earlier place of worship. There is 15th and 16th century work in the old mill by the beck, but a mill stood here in the 12th century, its simple machines powered by the force of water rushing down Stock Ghyll. A 16 feet overshot wheel was removed, but the fabric of the building is in "good heart".

Old Ambleside was the home of the Braithwaites. They built a hall near the beck. This building was demolished, but their curious summer house, set on a bridge, survives in remarkably fine condition. A hoary old story which may still be heard tells that Bridge House was built by a Scotsman who wanted to avoid paying ground rent! People lived in the house until 1901. Bridge House is still occupied in summer, when it has a useful role as an information centre. Its owners are The National Trust.

Most of the old churches of the Lake District (particularly those at the daleheads) are modest in size and unpretentious in character. It is almost as though the builders did not have the heart to compete with the magnificence of the mountains. Nine years before Ambleside became a parish a new church, dedicated to St. Mary, was opened in the town, and even the most unobservant visitor cannot fail to see it, with a spire extending its height to 180 feet. Inside there is seating for 550 worshippers. In some respects the church of St. Mary is untypical of the old Lakeland building style. In other ways the church mirrors the district it serves. Ambleside is very proud of its rushbearing festival. The custom began when earthen church floors were sweetened by the strewing out of freshly-cut rush. On rushbearing day the young folk of Ambleside carry rushes and flowers through the town. Everyone gathers on the Market Place to sing a special hymn composed by Owen Lloyd.

Kendal

Kendal, by the Kent, is an "auld grey town",light grey in tone, from the native limestone used in the construction of most of the buildings. Four famous old streets, connecting, give Kendal its main traffic artery. Kirkland, Highgate, Stramongate and Stricklandgate enfold between individualistic properties, many of them pubs. A medieval settlement stood at the oldest section, Kirkland. *photo 26*

Speed's map of Kendal, in the middle of the 17th century, shows that the houses then formed a narrow band north and south of the three streets. Areas nearer the river, which are now fully built up, were then only orchards, gardens or fields. It might be said, therefore, that most of the Kendal yards — there were once nearly 100 — came into being during the industrial revolution, and were not built, as popular legend has it, as a form of protection when the Scots were raiding. Kendal was an early home of the woollen industry.

Old Kirkbie in Kentdale was known for years as the Gateway to the Lakes. The gateway became clogged with traffic. Now most of the northbound vehicles use the M6, which lies to the east, or the western by-pass to the Lakes. Kendal, though not in the National Park, holds the Park's administrative office.

Holy Trinity Church impresses by its size. Here is a square tower 80 feet high, and it makes the rest of the huge building look squat. Holy Trinity is 140 feet long by 103 feet wide, with stonework of 13th, 15th and 19th centuries. Within are the chapels of the Parrs, Bellinghams and Stricklands. In 1970, a corona was hung over the high altar in memory of Bernard Gilpin (1517-1583); this native of Kentmere became known as the "Apostle of the North".

Keswick

Keswick, capital of northern Lakeland and one of the most exquisitely situated towns in Britain, was originally Ketel's Wyke — the landing place on Derwentwater where the Viking, Ketel, ran his boat ashore. This was in the 9th century, but over 300 years earlier St. Kentigern had been in Carlisle when he heard of the paganism of the folk in the mountain region to the south-west. Turning aside into the forest, he preached and then erected a cross, signifying the faith. The site was Crosthwaite where the parish church of Keswick now stands — it is one of the most interesting buildings in the whole of the town and lies on the north side of the Portinscale road. *photo 27*

The church is traditionally said to have been built by Alice de Romille in the 12th century, and in 1306 it was noted that the parishioners "to the detriment of the market of Cockermouth, come in a great concourse to Crosthwaite Church every Sunday to buy and sell corn, flour, beans, peas, linen and cloth, fish and flesh". The present church was built in 1553, and today is chiefly visited for its associations with Robert Southey who was buried here in 1843. His table tomb is inscribed with his own words: "Not to the grave, not to the grave my soul descend to contemplate the form that once was dear". At the base of the tomb is the inscription: "Restored by the generosity of the Brazilian Government, 1961" — Southey had a history of Brazil published in 1813. Inside the church is a life size marble effigy of the poet with a long inscription composed by William Wordsworth; the baptistry is a memorial to Canon H. D. Rawnsley, vicar here for 34 years and founder of the National Trust. Keswick is very much a religious centre, the annual Convention for the "promotion of practical holiness" held in mid-July attracting several thousand visitors from all over the world.

Southey lived at Greta Hall, now part of Keswick School, for forty years. Prior to this it was occupied for four years by Samuel Taylor Coleridge, a slave to opium, who wrote: "I question if there be a room in England which commands a view of mountains and lakes and woods superior to that in which I am now sitting". Many of the literary lions of the 19th century visited Greta Hall. William and Dorothy Wordsworth came frequently, no doubt admiring Southey's collection of 14,000 books. John Ruskin spent his honeymoon in the town, and described it as "a place almost too beautiful to live in". Shelley lived in Keswick with his runaway bride, Harriet Wesbrook, in a cottage on Chestnut Hill. Other visitors included Keats, Scott, Hazlitt, De Quincey, and Charles Lamb who remarked: "We thought we had got into fairyland".

Whitehaven

photo 28

There is nowhere else in England quite like West Cumberland. Cut off from the rest of the country by the great barrier of the Lake mountains, it would have remained isolated and insignificant had it not been for its rich mineral resources. These, coupled with the resourcefulness of a people noted for their independence, enabled the region to overcome its geographical handicaps and develop strong maritime trading links with Ireland and the Americas.

Outcrop coal mining around Whitehaven began as early as the thirteenth century, but was not systematically developed until some 400 years later when the area came into possession of the Lowthers, later the Earls of Lonsdale. Successive members of the family built a harbour, expanded the mines and initiated development of what Nikolaus Pevsner has described as "the earliest post-mediaeval planned town in England". These changes gathered momentum at the beginning of the eighteenth century when Whitehaven already had over 2,000 inhabitants and was the third largest town in the north of England after Newcastle and York. It entered a golden age as shipping, initially developed to take coal to the Isle of Man and Ireland, brought in its wake the growth of a Continental and American trade in wines, spirits, tobacco and timber. In 1725 Daniel Defoe noted that the settlement had "grown up from a small place to be very considerable by the coal trade, which is increased so considerably of late, that it is now the most eminent port in England for shipping of coals except Newcastle and Sunderland". By 1762 its population had soared to 9,063.

Under the guidance of the Lowthers' celebrated mining engineer, Carlisle Spedding, the mines spread under the sea and were soon to be described as "perhaps the most extraordinary of any in the known world".

Millom

photo 29

A "new town" owing its origins to the discovery in 1856 of a deposit of haematite iron ore which was to prove the largest in the world until the opening up of the Lake Superior workings in Canada later in the century. It was situated at Hodbarrow on the north side of the Duddon estuary, the find leading to the development of rail facilities at the then village of Holborn Hill, erection of an ironworks and creation of an ore port at nearby Borwick Rails. Production of ore rose from 32,521 tons in 1863 to 117,329 tons in 1865. The associated building of "a sort of model town" named Millom soon transformed Holborn Hill from a village of less than 200 inhabitants into the largest settlement in the district, housing close on 4,000 people by 1876.

Millom ironworks survived tenaciously in its remote location, but its days were numbered when Hodbarrow mines closed in 1968 after raising the colossal total of over 25 million tons of haematite. In fact it closed later the same year, after an offer to sell the works for £1 had apparently found no takers. Millom has never been quite the same since.

Watendlath

photo 30

This remote and once rarely visited hamlet, with its tarn and fells, stone houses and aged packhorse bridge, inspired a series of books based on old Cumbrian life. The Herries stories were an immediate success, attracted crowds of Walpole devotees, and every property in Watendlath claimed to be the home of the convincing fictional character, Judith Paris. But, once discovered, Watendlath came to be loved for its own sake.

Watendlath Beck leaves its upland valley by way of Lodore Falls which, in a wet season, can be relied upon to come "thundering . . . and thumping . . . roaring . . . leaping . . . with a dreadful uproar". Near the foot of the falls stands the modernised Old Lodore Hotel where Southey stayed in 1802. It was a small public house in those days where they kept a canon which was discharged, on payment of 4s., to demonstrate the echoes from the fells. Southey was disgusted at the price but revelled in the thunderous rolls reverberating round the hills.

NEW VISIONS

Fresh Angles on Familiar Landmarks

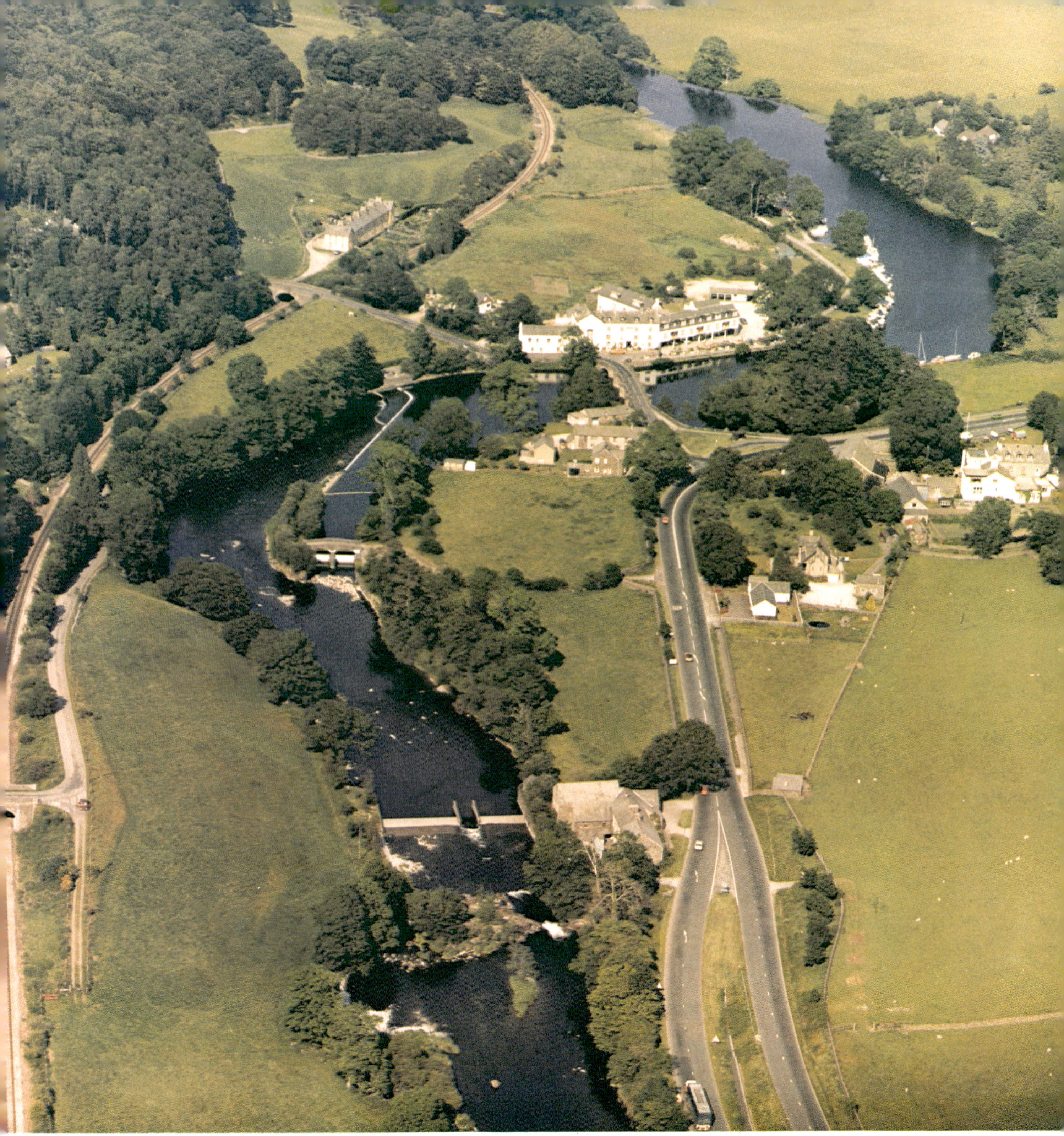

31. NEWBY BRIDGE. Rail, river and road parallel one another in the form of the preserved Lakeside & Haverthwaite Railway, the river Leven forming the outlet from Windermere and the main A590 Barrow–Levens Bridge highway. The Old Swan Hotel can hardly be missed in the centre of the picture.

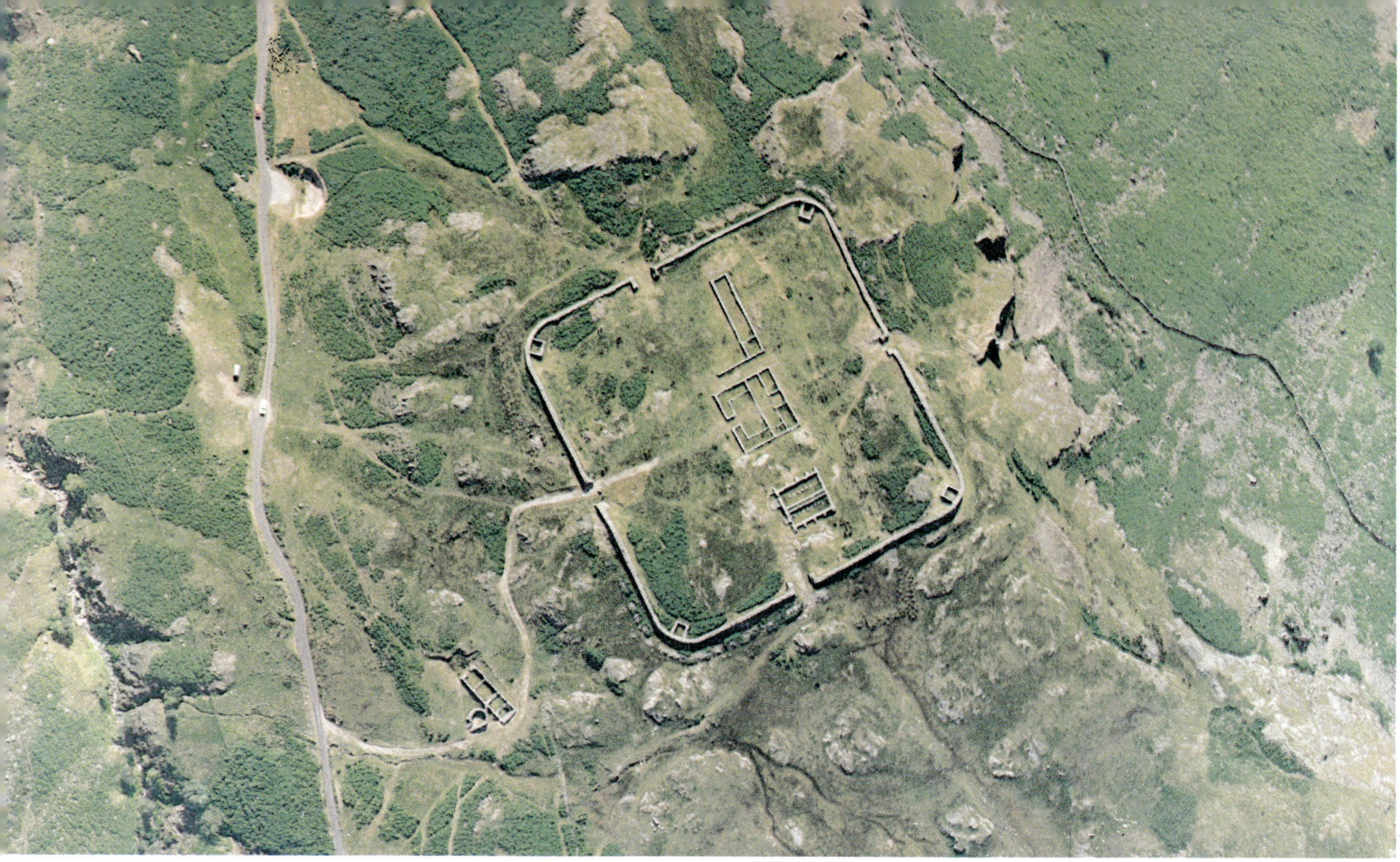

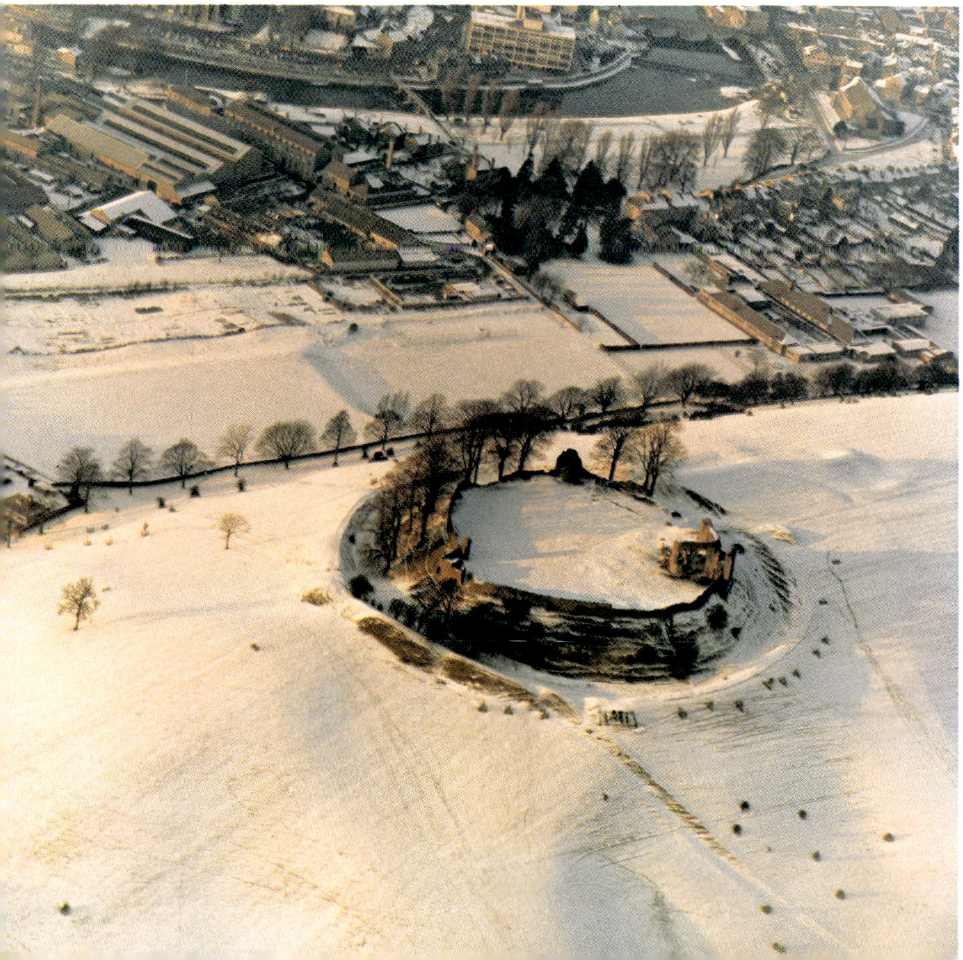

32. *Above* HARDKNOTT ROMAN FORT. A view from almost directly overhead gives a remarkable impression of one of the most evocative Roman military sites in Britain. The rampart wall with its gateways and turrets encloses the three principal remains — from top to bottom the Commander's House, Headquarters and Granaries. To the left of the main fort complex is the separate Bath House with its circular hot room. The road is the western side of Hardknott Pass — at 1-in-3 one of the steepest climbs in England but looking comparatively innocuous from this angle.

33. *Left* KENDAL CASTLE. Snow cloaks all that remains of the birthplace and home of Katherine Parr, who became the sixth wife of Henry VIII in 1543. Compare this picture with the summer view from a similar angle (photo 26).

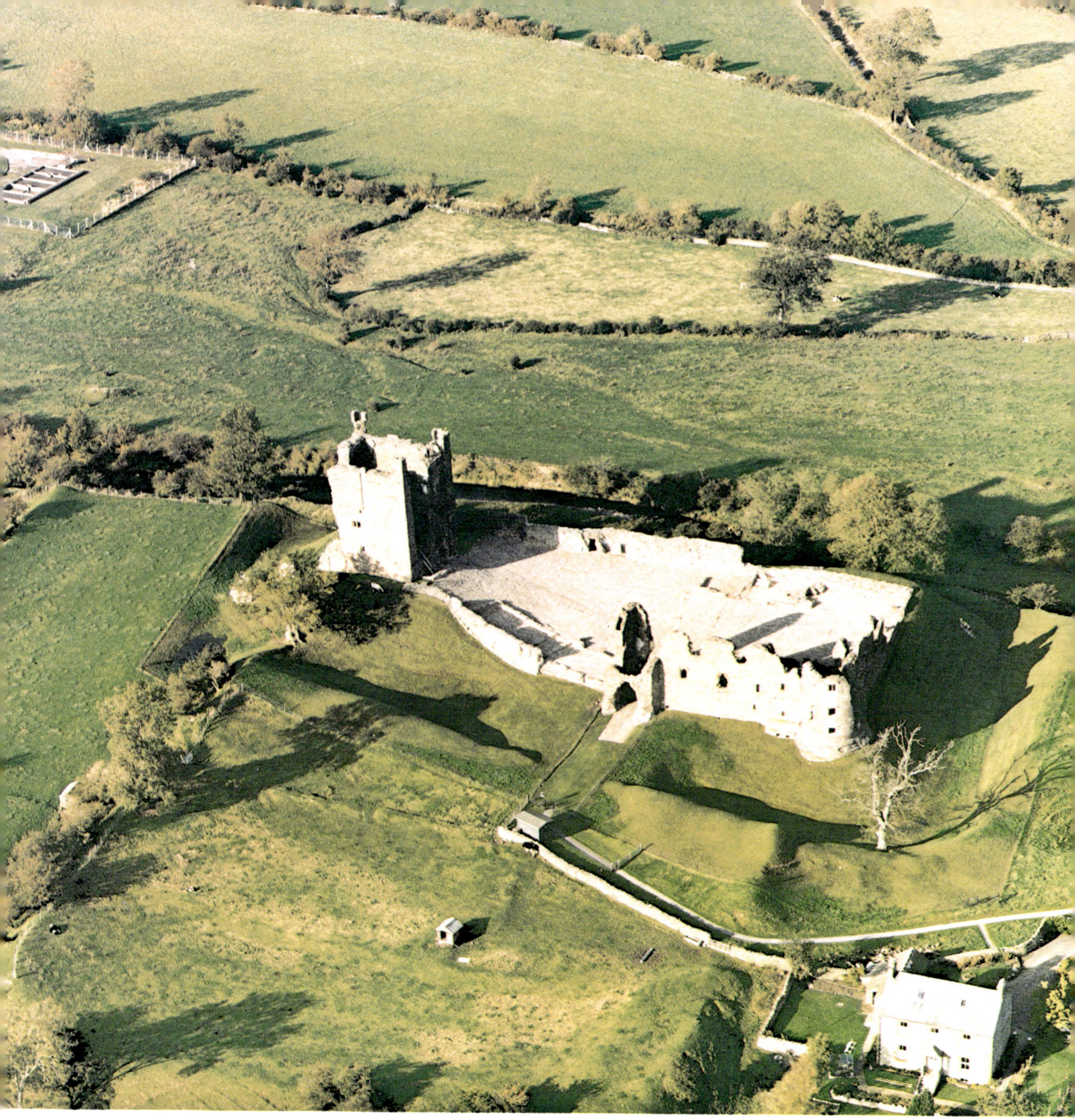

34. BROUGH CASTLE. One of several castles in the Eden Valley, Brough was built in the 11th century by William II and restored some 600 years later by Lady Anne Clifford before again falling into ruin. It stands on the site of Veterae, a Roman fort.

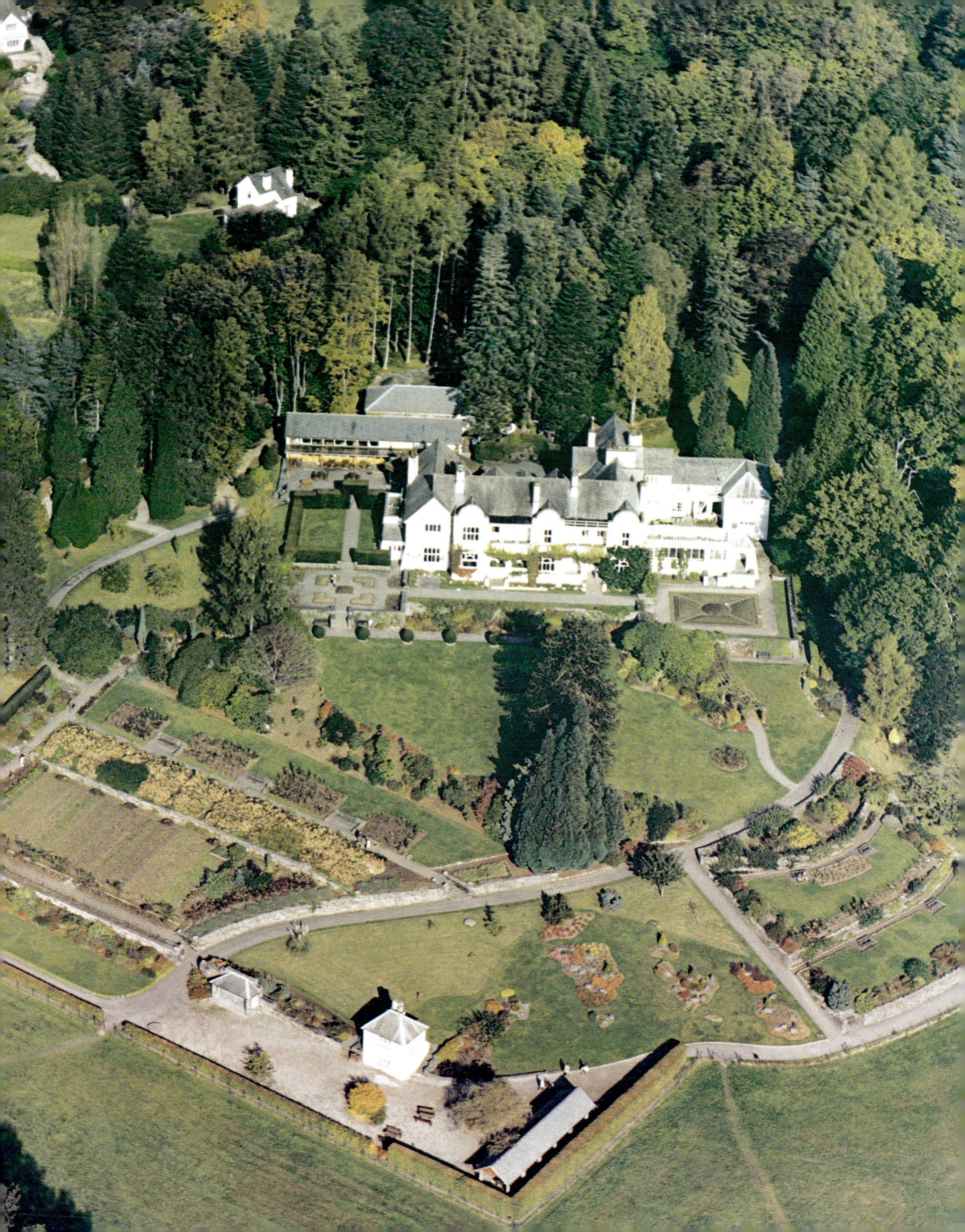

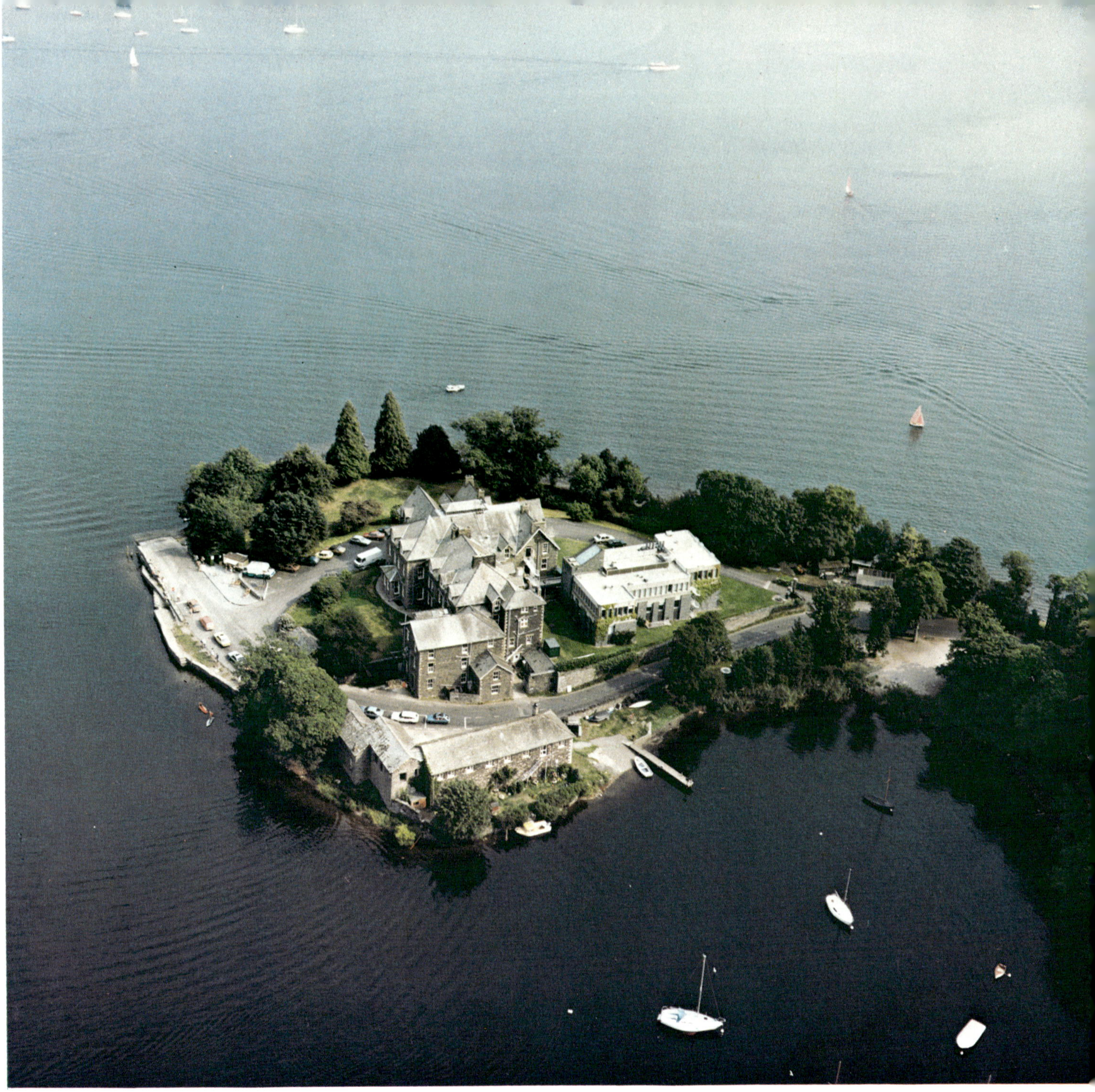

35. *Left* BROCKHOLE, WINDERMERE. The former home of the Gaddums, Lancashire cotton magnates, is now the Lake District National Park Centre — and the single most visited building in the area. This photograph shows to good effect some of the magnificent woodland surrounding the house.

36. *Above* FERRY HOUSE, WINDERMERE. From this angle the narrow-necked peninsula which forms the western landing point for the Windermere Ferry looks deceptively like an island in the middle of the lake. A queue of cars waits alongside the Ferry Hotel for the arrival of their transport — the good ship "Drake".

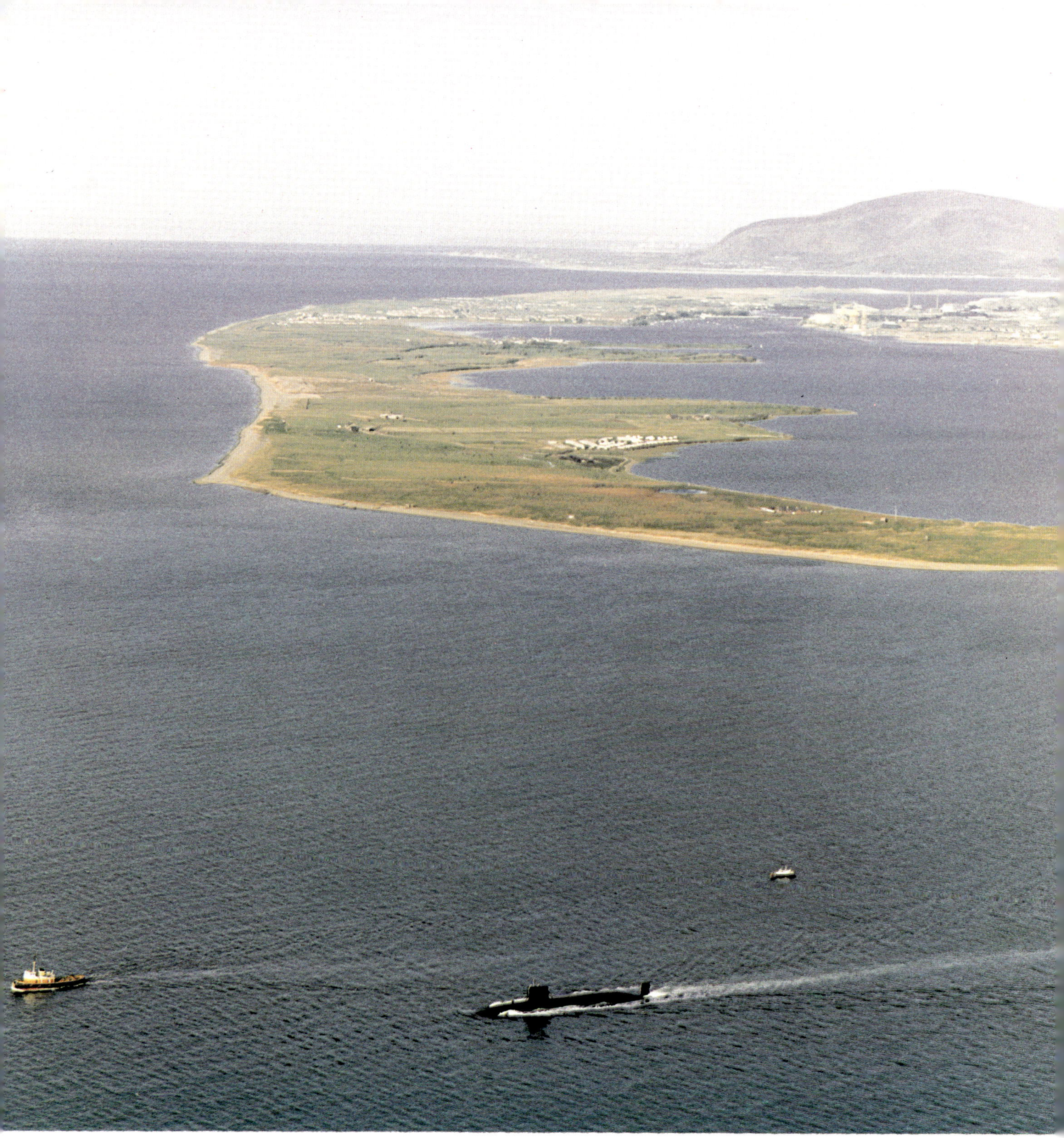

37. WALNEY ISLAND. Like a teardrop rolling off the face of Lakeland, Walney reaches out into the Irish Sea. The southern end nearest the camera remains undeveloped; to the north is Vickerstown, the 19th century overspill suburb of Barrow, to which it is connected by a bridge across Walney Channel. As always, Black Combe in the right background looks considerably higher than its actual 1,969 feet. At sea, a nuclear-powered submarine is just out from the Barrow dockyard.

38. ST. BEES HEAD. The most westerly point in Cumbria also boasts the county's only sea cliffs of any real significance, towering a maximum of around 300 feet above the often savage Irish Sea. The land is cultivated right to the cliff edge — apart from the small area occupied by the lonely lighthouse.

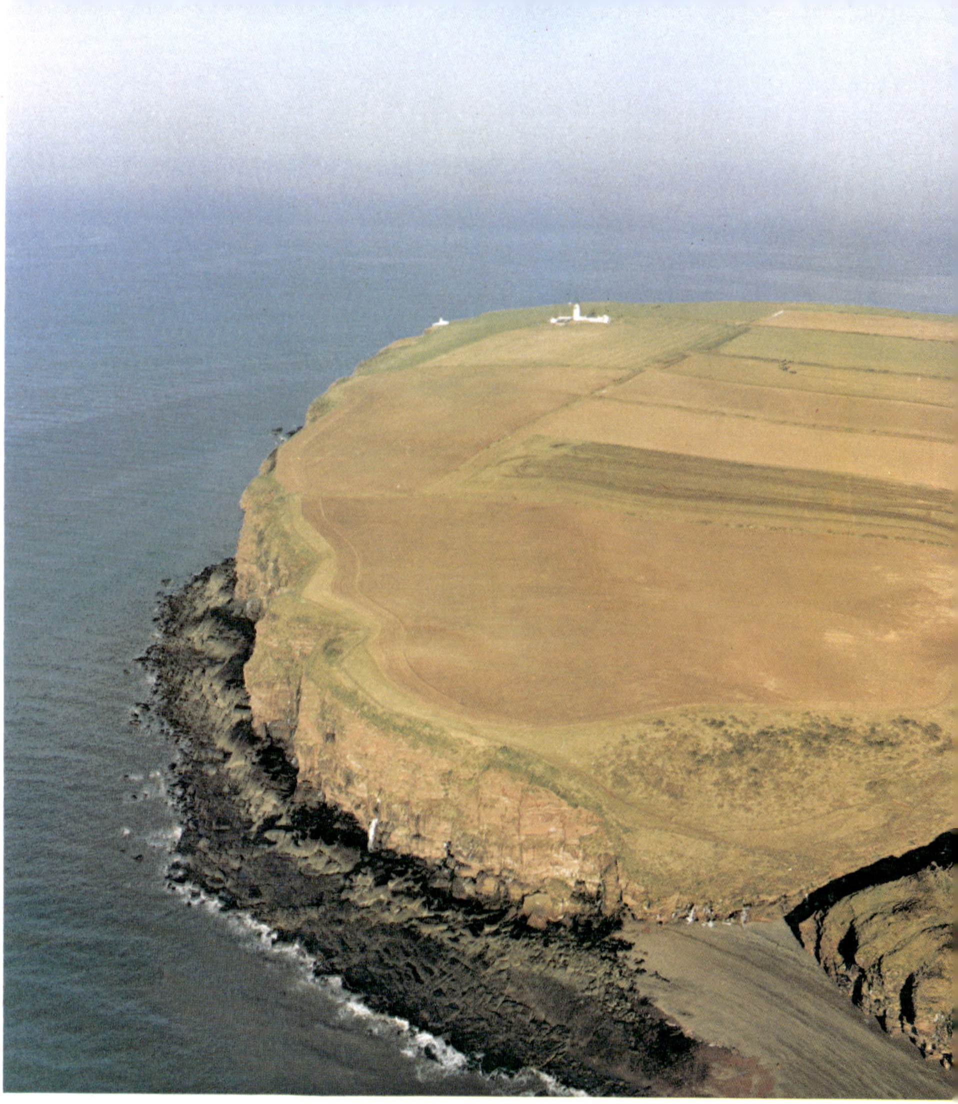

39. RAVENGLASS & ESKDALE RAILWAY. The Ravenglass terminus of this delightful 15-inch gauge railway, much developed and visually improved since it came under the auspices of a preservation society in 1960. Note the two Pullman cars to the right of the station and, beyond the car park, the full-size line linking Barrow with Whitehaven.

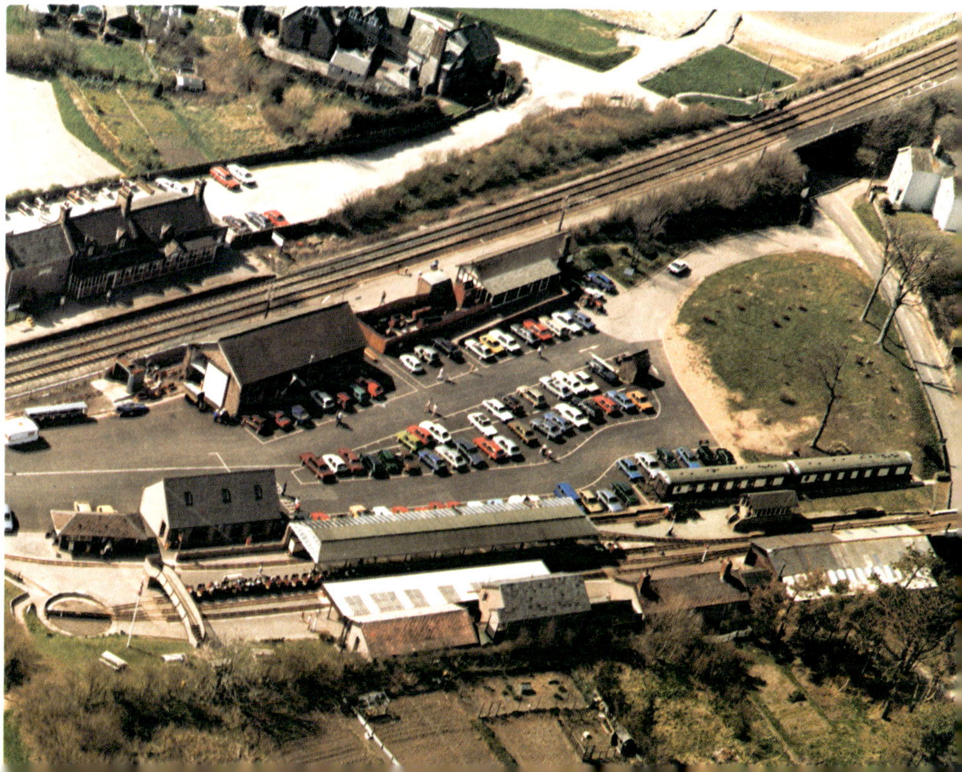

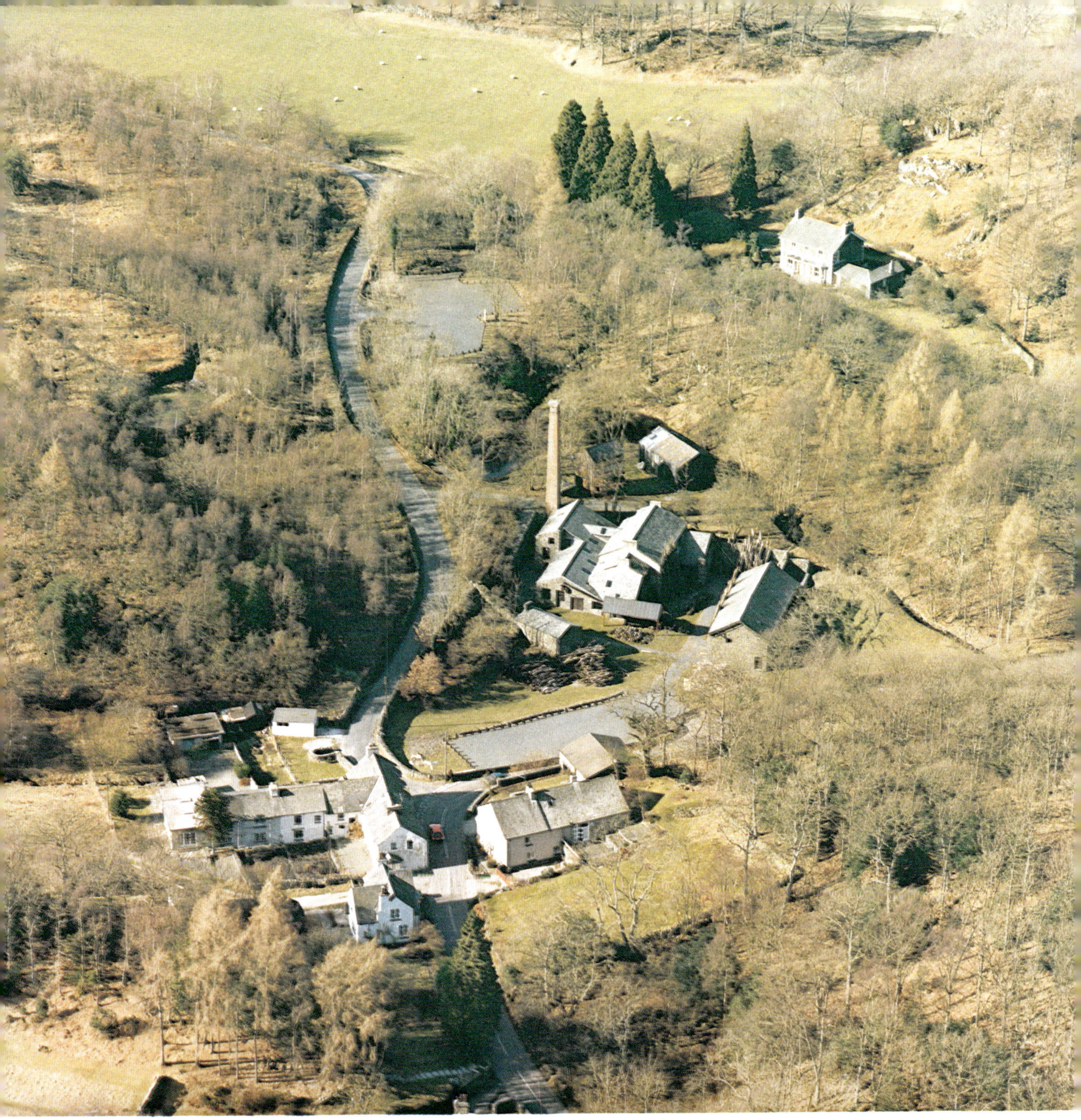

40. **STOTT PARK BOBBIN MILL.** At the foot of the picture is the road from Newby Bridge which curves right and runs roughly parallel to nearby Windermere as it heads towards Hawkshead. Going off to the left of the bobbin mill — now a working museum — is the minor road to Finsthwaite. As might be expected, the area is surrounded by extensive woodland.

New Visions

Fresh Angles on Familiar Landmarks

ONE of the most remarkable aspects of aerial photographs is the way they give a totally new perspective — for better or worse — of familiar features of the landscape. This is why they can so often bear examination again and again. The photographs on the preceding pages illustrate the point by looking at a varied range of buildings, landmarks and features — most of them well-known — both within Lakeland and on its fringes.

Newby Bridge

photo 31 The river surging under Newby Bridge is the Leven, outflow of Windermere, heading for Morecambe Bay, which it joins near Ulverston. Fell Foot, on the east shore of the lake (and immediately opposite Lakeside) is a Country Park of the National Trust. About 18 acres are open to the public.

From Newby Bridge, a road leads to the west of Windermere lake, with Hawkshead as the destination. Lakeside, beside this road, is the terminus for the white-hulled lake vessels. Here, too, is the end of a branch railway which has been reopened to passengers from Haverthwaite. A preservation society keeps the railway spirit alive, and old rolling stock has been assembled.

Hardknott Roman Fort

photo 32 Hardknott Castle, nine miles north-east of Ravenglass at the western end of Hardknott Pass, is the best preserved Roman fort in Cumberland south of Hadrian's Wall and one of the outstanding remains of the Roman army surviving in Britain. It is an isolated fort, 800 ft. above sea level and relatively difficult of access.

The remains today consist of a small three acre stone Roman auxiliary fort designed for 500 infantry, an external military bath-house and an adjacent uphill exercise or parade ground. The fort stands beside and was connected to the passing Roman road, originally built from the coast via Hardknott and Wrynose passes to Windermere and beyond. The Romans built three forts along this route at Ravenglass, Hardknott and Ambleside. Hardknott, the centre fort of the triad, is now under the custody of the Department of the Environment, and it can be reached by road from Ambleside or Ravenglass. Eskdale is ideal walking country and at the fort site two car parking areas have been provided for visitors. A pleasurable way of visiting the fort is to use the Ravenglass and Eskdale miniature railway to Dalegarth and then walk up the valley towards the pass.

Whichever method is employed the visit is well worth the effort, for Hardknott is one of the classic Roman military sites of North Britain both for its romantic atmosphere and the superbness of its natural position, perched on a ledge beneath Hardknott Fell and hemmed in by mountains.

The fort was built in the reign of the Emperor Hadrian (117-138), whose name and titles occur on a fragmentary gateway inscription found near the fort's south-east gateway in 1964. The fort seems to have been destroyed by the local tribesmen in the troubles of 196-7 and never re-occupied by the Roman Imperial Army. It thus had a brief military life when compared to its neighbouring forts at Ravenglass and Ambleside where Roman occupation is attested until the end of the 4th century AD.

Hardknott Castle lies in some of the finest unspoilt scenery in Cumbria. It affords an excellent excursion for all students of Roman Britain ranging from archaeological societies to school parties studying Roman history. Nor can the casual visitor with a minimum interest in the Romans fail to be astonished and impressed by the remains. It constitutes for all lovers of the Lake District a precious and unique monument in that area's history.

Kendal Castle

photo 33

The earliest keep "on the brow of a green hill" was probably constructed of timber. The date of the first stone castle is unknown, but great families were here — Taillebois, de Lancaster, le Brus and de Roos. Then in the late 14th century Sir William Parr acquired it by marriage. From his line in 1513 sprang Katherine Parr who survived three years of marriage to Henry VIII. Thrice widowed, she took a fourth husband, Lord Seymour, and died of her first childbirth, leaving an infant daughter, Mary. This "matronly, learned, discreet" and honoured little lady was buried beneath her husband's chapel at Sudeley and her tomb was desecrated in the 1780s. Her remains, still beautiful and richly attired, were dragged into rude public gaze, a sacrilege that would not have happened at Kendal. By the 1580s, Kendal Castle was likely to collapse under its weight of years and decay ravaged the birthplace of an English Queen-Consort.

Brough Castle

photo 34

Standing on the site of the Roman fort of Verterae, Brough Castle was built in the 11th century by William II. Its purpose was to defend Stainmore Pass against Scots raiders heading for the lower Tees valley and North Yorkshire. The home of the 13th Baron Clifford (1435-61), nicknamed "The Butcher" for his cruelty in the Wars of the Roses, it was restored in the 17th century by Lady Anne Clifford but again fell into ruins.

Architecturally, it resembles other castles in the north of England at Appleby, Brougham, Prudhoe, Barnard Castle, Richmond and Middleham. Though all different in detail, they belong to the same group of early keep and curtain wall type, with many later additions, mainly domestic, made within the original wall enclosure.

Brockhole, Windermere

photo 35

Brockhole, the Lake District National Park Centre, attracts tens of thousands of visitors each season, most of whom have crisp memories of the Englishness of its style, its setting with gardens giving way to lawns, and views of the rocky lake shore. Cars are driven into a park with space for 300 vehicles. Covered with mono-blocks, much of the parking area is, in effect, a hard grass surface rather than giving the impression — as do many parks — of being a bleak section of the high Cairngorms. Visitors may arrive by water, in boats from Bowness that call at the jetty; they stride along a path between trees to open ground (part of the 32 acre estate) and see the old home of the Gaddums, white, elegant, above terraces where, in spring, azaleas and rhdodendrons bloom.

In the house the Gaddums built are exciting exhibitions telling the story of the Lake District from the earliest times to the daily life of the present day. There is a café in which 100 people can be comfortably seated under a roof that is timber-lined, topped off with local slate.

The whole of the ground floor of Brockhole is devoted to the main exhibition, telling the Lakeland story in models, pictures and with full use of audio-visuals. There are twice weekly guided tours of the gardens from May to September. There, too, is a Poet's Corner, set in an alcove, with a broad window leading the eye across the Brockhole estate to the lake and, beyond, to the turreted hills of Langdale. Voices recorded on tape give readings from writers associated with the area, including William Wordsworth, Arthur Ransome and Beatrix Potter. The World of Beatrix Potter Exhibition recreates the tales of this immortal children's writer.

The farmer, so often overlooked by those writing about Lakeland, is seen as the man who sustains the basic industry, agriculture. One section of the main exhibition relates to the construction and maintenance of drystone walls. In the lecture theatre, films and slide sequences on various aspects of the Lake District are shown throughout the day. In addition, throughout each season there is a daily list of special events: day courses, film shows, "Meet the Author" sessions, and events for children such as "Young Explorers" and "Young Birdwatchers" which make use of the Centre's grounds and wooded lake-shore. Teddy Bear's Picnics are arranged in the summer.

Ferry House, Windermere

photo 36

A ferry which can accommodate 10 vehicles operates from a point just below Bowness to Ferry House. The present ferry, which has been converted to diesel-propulsion, is named *Drake*. It crosses 700 yards of water eight times an hour, saving traffic a 15-mile journey around the lake shore. The lake is 50 feet deep at the ferry, and the boat keeps to a precise course because of cables stretching from shore to shore. There have been few ferryboat mishaps, but ĭn 1635 about 50 people and several horses were drowned. Tradition has it that the victims were a wedding party returning from Hawkshead and the cause of the mishap was probably a sudden violent storm.

Ferry House is the headquarters of the Freshwater Biological Association, having been converted from the old *Ferry Hotel*. Here scientists study Windermere intently. Because of its great depth, it has little rooted vegetation and the important plants are planktonic, which give the water a greenish hue in summer. Large numbers of perch and pike have been taken from the water as part of a scheme for correcting the fish population by permitting other species to gain strength. One pike recovered weighed 33½ lb and was 42 inches long. The Association was at Wray Castle (now used as a Merchant Navy training school) before moving to Ferry House.

Perch abound in Windermere, and average three to the pound. Eels, too, are common. The average size of a silver female eel (caught when running to sea) is 14 oz, and such fish have seen from 10 to 12 years in fresh water since they entered the lake as elvers. The male eel is only 3½ oz after it has been seven to nine years in fresh water.

Walney Island

Walney — anciently Waghany and Woney — is by far the largest of the Furness islands. Long and slender, it curves in at the ends as though giving special protection to Barrow. The size and shape of Walney are roughly those of Windermere lake, which came into being when a glacier moved down an old river valley, broadening and deepening it. The earth moved at Windermere might have been piled up off the Furness coast! In fact Walney consists of the New Red Sandstone, covered by glacial deposits which have been overblown by sand. The length of the island is ten miles, and it has rather more than 3,000 acres. *photo 37*

Walney's age-old fight has been against the sea, which yearly erodes the low sandy cliffs of the western parts. Some 500 yards of land have gone from one part of it during the past 40 years. The highest point of the island, Beacon Hill, is a mere 78 feet above sea level. The sea threatens to split Walney into two, and it has become perilously slim at the waist.

Walney, in the old parish of Dalton, had a chapel in 1568. The main settlements were the hamlets of Biggar and North Scale, the latter being burnt down by the Royalists during the Civil War. Walney's old island flavour vanished in 1908. In the earliest days, men could cross the channel at low tide. It was dredged for shipping, and a steam ferry was introduced. Then Vickers, owners of the Naval Construction Works at Barrow, built a bridge to replace the steam ferry. Vickerstown developed on the Walney side as a dormitory and pleasure ground for Barrovians.

Travel north from Vickerstown, and you see farmland on which many sheep are wintered. The remains of a wartime air station stand in this area. To the south of Vickerstown the old Walney reasserts itself. At Biggar hamlet, old houses look at each other across cobblestones, and you are told that when the houses were built none of the windows faced the west, in case of war, when foreign ships could be guided by lights on shore. Beams of black Spanish oak are to be found in the *Queen's Arms* at Biggar. They are so tough today that it is almost impossible to drive a nail into them. Local people believe they came from a galleon of the Armada, wrecked on the Walney coast.

St. Bees Head

photo 38

Old Red-head, as the headland at St. Bees was known, lifts itself to a height of over 200 feet, and the tides encounter the red rock with a resounding thwack. From St. Bees, you may see the loom of Irish lighthouses. This, indeed, was a beacon coast, with fires kindled at St. Bees, Newton Knott above Muncaster and Black Combe. St. Bees has two heads, in fact; the division between them occurs at Flenswick Bay, in which the beach is composed of granulated shingle. The headland is Cumbria's most westerly point.

St. Bees is flamboyant. The red cliffs obrude between the summer greens of the land and the bluey-greens of a sunlit sea. Cushions of thrift can be seen shimmering in the westerly winds. Bloody cranesbill stains part of the cliff-top in an area where the plant life is of two distinctive types: open country and woodland. The sea cliffs, with their generous ledges, appeal to some 15,000 nesting seabirds. Guillemot, razorbill, kittiwake, herring gull are most prominent at England's most important seabird station. The auks perch like two-tone skittles on the highest cliffs, near the lighthouse; the headland is, elsewhere, in rather ragged decline.

Ravenglass & Eskdale Railway

photo 39

Since it was opened in 1875 the Ravenglass and Eskdale Railway has twice had the threat of abandonment hanging over its head. Today it is supported by a preservation society, and is again thriving. Some 200,000 people a year enjoy the thrill of a journey from the shore of the Irish Sea to the foot of Scafell behind a miniature steam locomotive.

Always known locally as "Ratty", the railway was initially built as a 3ft. gauge line to tap iron ore deposits in the valley. The mineral workings soon failed, but the line managed to struggle on by catering for the tourists which even then were flocking to Lakeland in considerable numbers. The railway closed in 1912, but was taken over by Mr. W. J. Bassett-Lowke, the famous model-maker, and relaid to a gauge of 15 inches. The work was completed by 1917, and additional prosperity came in 1922 with the opening of a granite quarry alongside the line.

By the 1950s "Ratty" was in trouble again. Increasing competition had made the quarry uneconomical and in 1953 it closed. Once more it was found that the line could not survive on passenger traffic alone, and in September 1960 it was offered for sale by auction. Over the years scores of people had come to love the little railway, and were not prepared to see it go without a struggle. The Ravenglass and Eskdale Railway Preservation Society was formed and subscriptions and donations started to pour in. At the auction held at Gosforth Village Hall a successful bid of £12,000 cheated the scrap merchants. Today "Ratty" is more healthy than ever before, but still needs all the help it can get.

Stott Park Bobbin Mill

photo 40

The mill at Stott Park was converted to bobbin manufacture in 1841 from an older corn mill. Soon afterwards it acquired some revolutionary bobbin machinery invented by John Braithwaite of Ellerbeck Mill, Crook

— just a few miles away on the east side of Windermere. At first the mill was powered by water from High Dam on Finsthwaite Heights, a huge wheel of 32 feet diameter turning the complex machinery. In later years this was replaced in turn by the turbine engine, the steam engine and electricity.

In the peak years a labour force of around fifty produced some quarter of a million bobbins each week. The coming of plastics caused production to turn over to making brush handles and shafts for carpenters' and garden tools, as well as tourist souvenirs, but eventually the mill closed in 1971.

CW01671741

OXFORD MEDICAL PUBLICATIONS

Pickard's Manual of Operative Dentistry

SINCE - 1968
Kansara
Medical Book Distributors
4, Nandanvan Chambers, 1st Floor,
Opp. Town Hall, Ellisbridge, Ahmedabad-380 006.
Phone : (O) 079-26587570
Tel.Fax : 079-26576885 • M : 98250 10970
E-mail : medibooks_2000@yahoo.com
NO OTHER BRANCH

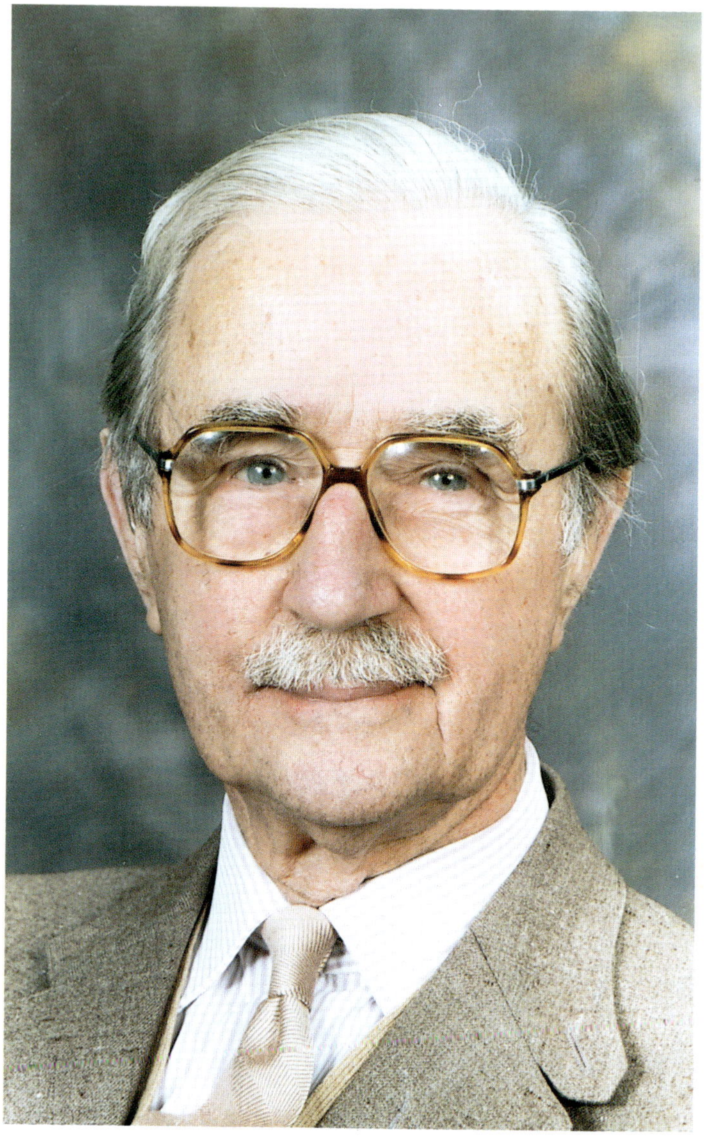

Professor HM Pickard 1909–2002

Pickard's Manual of Operative Dentistry Eighth edition

Edwina A. M. Kidd
Professor of Cariology
Guy's, King's, and St Thomas' Dental Institute
King's College
London

Bernard G. N. Smith
Professor of Conservative Dentistry
Guy's, King's, and St Thomas' Dental Institute
King's College
London

Timothy F. Watson
Professor of Microscopy in Relation to Restorative Dentistry
Guy's, King's, and St Thomas' Dental Institute
King's College
London

Based on the first five editions of *A manual of operative dentistry*

H. M. Pickard
Emeritus Professor in Conservative Dentistry
University of London
Formerly of the Royal Dental Hospital of London School of Dental Surgery

OXFORD
UNIVERSITY PRESS

OXFORD
UNIVERSITY PRESS

YMCA Library Building, Jai Singh Road, New Delhi 110 001

Oxford University Press is a department of the University of Oxford. It furthers the University's objective of excellence in research, scholarship, and education by publishing worldwide in

Oxford New York
Auckland Bangkok Buenos Aires Cape Town Chennai
Dar es Salaam Delhi Hong Kong Istanbul Karachi Kolkata
Kuala Lumpur Madrid Melbourne Mexico City Mumbai Nairobi
Sao Paulo Shanghai Taipei Tokyo Toronto

Oxford is a registered trademark of Oxford University Press in the UK and in certain other countries

Published in India
by Oxford University Press, New Delhi

© Oxford University Press 2003

The moral rights of the author have been asserted
Database right Oxford University Press (maker)

First edition published 1961
Published in India by Oxford University Press, New Delhi, 2004

All rights reserved. No part of this publication may be reproduced, stored in a retrieval system, or transmitted, in any form or by any means, without the prior permission in writing of Oxford University Press, or as expressly permitted by law, or under terms agreed with the appropriate reprographics rights organization. Enquiries concerning reproduction outside the scope of the above should be sent to the Rights Department, Oxford University Press, at the address above

You must not circulate this book in any other binding or cover and you must impose this same condition on any acquirer

ISBN 0 19 566927 4

Reprinted by arrangement with Oxford University Press, Oxford, for sale in India, Bangladesh, Nepal, Bhutan, Sri Lanka, and Myanmar only, and not for export therefrom

Printed at Ajanta Offset and Packagings Ltd, Delhi 110 052
Published by Manzar Khan, Oxford University Press
YMCA Library Building, Jai Singh Road, New Delhi 110 001

Preface to the eighth edition

It is 41 years since the first edition of this book was published. In that time there have been so many developments in our understanding of dental disease, in materials, and in techniques so that there is now very little of that first edition remaining except the basic philosophy for managing patients with dental disease. This philosophy has several parallel threads which weave together.

- Dentists primarily look after people with dental problems – not just mouths or teeth.
- An understanding of the disease processes is fundamental to their management.
- The diseases should be managed – not just treated.
- Prevention is the keystone of management. The effectiveness of the prevention of dental caries in a selected group is shown by the fact that about three-quarters of undergraduate dental students at our dental institute now have no caries or restorations. Sadly, this is not yet the case with all people of that generation.
- When treatment is needed, the development of excellent operative skills is still of paramount importance. This can only be achieved by extensive supervised clinical practice and chairside teaching which remain as important as ever in the crowded undergraduate curriculum. If students do not develop sufficient skill during their undergraduate course there is little opportunity for most dentists to develop basic skills in a supervised setting after qualification.
- When active treatment is needed, the choice of materials and techniques should be based on a thorough understanding of them and the advantages and disadvantages of the alternatives. This choice is getting more difficult as the range of materials and techniques increases so that an even greater understanding of the properties of dental materials is now necessary.

One of the major developments since the seventh edition has been the increased use of bonding techniques which in turn allow much less destructive tooth preparation. For example, in the seventh edition the use of amalgam for the management of smooth surface lesions was deleted, and we now feel that the evidence to support the use of composite materials for occlusal lesions is sufficient for us to recommend that amalgam should no longer be used for occlusal restorations. These developments justify a new chapter (Chapter 6) which brings together parts of other chapters from the last edition and adds substantial new material.

The intention is that this book contains the material a student needs to know (except endodontic and periodontal treatment) up to the point that crowns become necessary. In other words, students can provide long-term stabilization, including permanent intracoronal restorations and cores for crowns, until they have learnt about crowns and then can continue treating the same patients if that is the policy of their undergraduate school. An increasing number of schools adopt policies of 'whole patient care' and 'continuity of care' so that students can manage their own patients and all their dental needs from an early introduction through to the end of the undergraduate course. In some schools this gives the students three or more years of contact with some patients at regular recalls after the initial course of treatment. During that time they can move on to other procedures, as necessary, with the same patient, for example crowns, bridges, and partial dentures. They also have an opportunity to see the short-term (one or two years) success or failure of their restorations.

Previous editions have included a brief list of 'further reading' at the end of each chapter. This has been brought up to date and retained but we suggest that readers use the list of topics at the beginning of each chapter as 'keywords' to initiate their own computer search of the literature.

There are two significant, current educational and clinical concepts which we believe we have developed further in this edition. The first is 'problem solving' and the emphasis on *managing* disease rather than *treating* it as an example of real problem solving. The second concept is 'evidence-based practice'. This is a manual of operative dentistry, not an authoritative textbook, however many of the changes in this edition are based on recent research evidence. If evidence is considered as not just research-based scientific evidence but includes the evidence of experience, then we believe that this edition reflects the current state of play in operative dentistry.

We are considerably indebted to many colleagues who have allowed us to use their illustrations. They are acknowledged in the captions to the relevant figures together with a source of the original publication where applicable.

E. A. M. K.
B. G. N. S.
T. F. W.

March 2003

Contents

PART 1

DISEASES, DISORDERS, DIAGNOSIS, DECISIONS, AND DESIGN

1

Why restore teeth?

Dental caries

- The carious process and the carious lesion
- Plaque retention and susceptible sites
- Severity or rapidity of attack
- The carious process in enamel
- The carious process in dentine
- Root caries
- Secondary or recurrent caries
- Residual caries

Diagnosis of dental caries

- The diagnostic procedure
- Assessment of caries risk
- Symptoms of caries
- The relevance of the diagnostic information to the management of caries

Preventive, non-operative treatment

- Patient involvement
- Why is the patient a caries risk?
- Mechanical plaque control
- Use of fluoride
- Dietary advice
- Salivary flow

Operative treatment

- Caries in pits and fissures
- Approximal lesions
- Smooth surfaces and root caries

Tooth wear

- Erosion
- Attrition
- Abrasion
- Summary of the causes of tooth wear
- Acceptable and pathological levels of tooth wear
- Consequences of pathological tooth wear
- Diagnosing and monitoring tooth wear
- Preventing tooth wear
- The management of tooth wear

Trauma

- Aetiology of trauma
- Examination and diagnosis of dental injury
- Management of trauma to the teeth

Developmental defects

- Acquired developmental conditions
- Treatment of developmental defects
- Hereditary conditions

Why restore teeth?

The four conditions which result in defective tooth structure, sometimes requiring repair, are dental caries, tooth wear, trauma and developmental defects. This chapter discusses the causes, diagnosis, and management of these conditions.

A clear understanding of the conditions is essential if the dentist is to plan and execute treatment logically, effectively, and in the patient's best interests. Indeed, unless the dentist understands the processes it will not be possible to decide whether treatment is necessary at all.

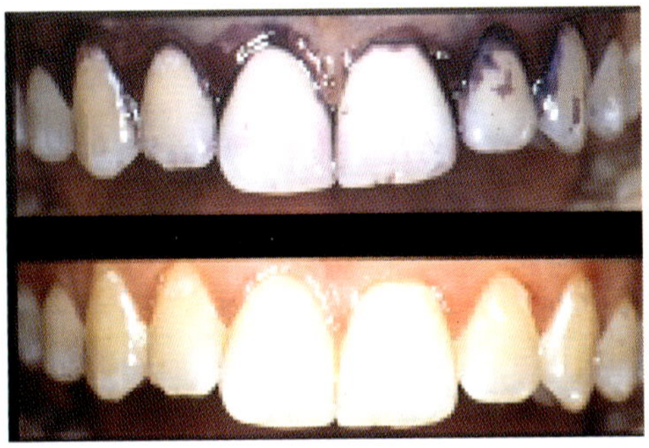

Fig. 1.1 The upper anterior teeth of a young adult. In the upper picture a disclosing agent reveals the plaque or biofilm while in the lower picture this has been brushed off by the patient. White spot lesions are visible on the canines and lateral incisors but not on other tooth surfaces although plaque was present.

Dental caries

Dental caries is a process which may take place on any tooth surface in the oral cavity where a microbial biofilm (dental plaque) is allowed to develop for a period of time. Although there are some 300 bacterial species in dental plaque, it is not a haphazard collection of micro-organisms. It is an ordered accumulation forming a community with a collective physiology.

The bacteria in the biofilm are always metabolically active, causing minute fluctuations in pH. These may cause a net loss of mineral from the tooth when the pH is dropping. This is called demineralization. Alternatively there may be a net gain of mineral when the pH is increasing. This is called remineralization. The cumulative result of these de- and remineralization processes may be a net loss of mineral and a carious lesion which can be seen. Alternatively the changes may be so slight that a carious lesion never becomes apparent (Fig. 1.1).

The carious process is the metabolic activity in the biofilm. This is an ubiquitous, natural process because the formation of the biofilm and its metabolic activity cannot be prevented. However, disease progression can be controlled so that a clinically visible enamel lesion never forms. The de- and remineralization processes can be modified particularly by regular disturbance of the biofilm with a toothbrush and fluoride toothpaste. If the biofilm is partially or totally removed mineral loss may be stopped or even reversed towards mineral gain. The fluoride in the toothpaste delays lesion progression by inhibiting demineralization and encouraging remineralization.

Diet plays a significant role in the carious process because the bacteria in the biofilm are capable of fermenting a suitable dietary carbohydrate substrate (such as the sugars sucrose and glucose) to produce acid, causing the plaque pH to fall within 1–3 minutes. Unfortunately the plaque remains acid for some time, taking 30–60 minutes to return to its normal pH in the region of 7. The buffering capacity of saliva is important in this return to neutrality and this means that anyone with a dry mouth is very susceptible to caries. These

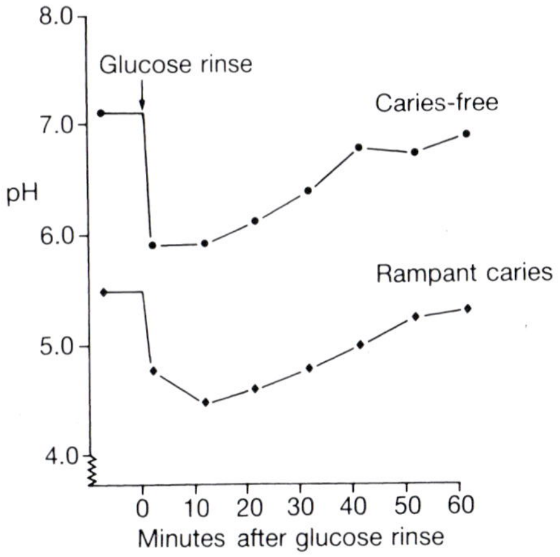

Fig. 1.2 Changes in plaque pH following a glucose rinse ('Stephan curve').

changes in pH can be represented graphically over a period of time following a glucose rinse (Fig. 1.2).

The carious process and the carious lesion

Carious lesions can form on any tooth surface exposed to the mouth; thus they can form on enamel, cementum, or dentine. It is perhaps unfortunate that the word 'caries' is used to denote both the carious *process* that occurs in the biofilm at the tooth or cavity surface and the carious *lesion* that forms on the tooth tissue.

The carious lesion forms as a direct consequence of the activity in the biofilm but this activity cannot be seen; it is the consequence of the carious process that the dentist sees and describes as a carious lesion.

Plaque retention and susceptible sites

Any site on the tooth surface that favours plaque retention and stagnation is prone to decay. The following sites particularly favour plaque retention:

- enamel pits and fissures on occlusal surfaces of molar and premolar teeth (Fig. 1.3); buccal pits of molars and palatal pits of maxillary incisors
- approximal enamel smooth surfaces just cervical to the contact area (Fig. 1.4)
- the enamel at the cervical margin of the tooth at the gingival margin (Fig. 1.5). In patients with gingival recession, the area of plaque stagnation is on the exposed root surface (Fig.1.6)
- the margins of restorations, particularly where there is a wide gap between the restoration and the tooth or those where the restoration overhangs the margin of the cavity (Fig.1.7).

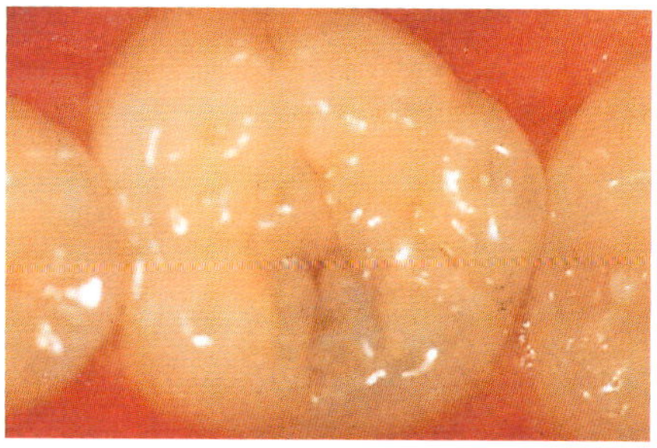

Fig. 1.3 Occlusal caries in a lower first molar tooth.

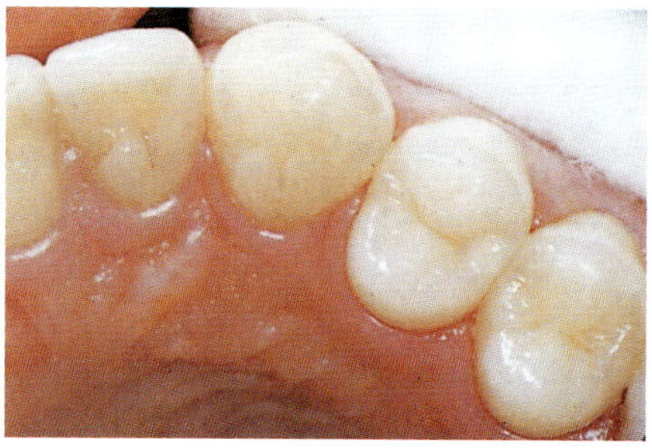

Fig. 1.4 A carious lesion is present on the distal aspect of the first premolar tooth. The lesion is shining through the marginal ridge which shows a pinkish grey discoloration.

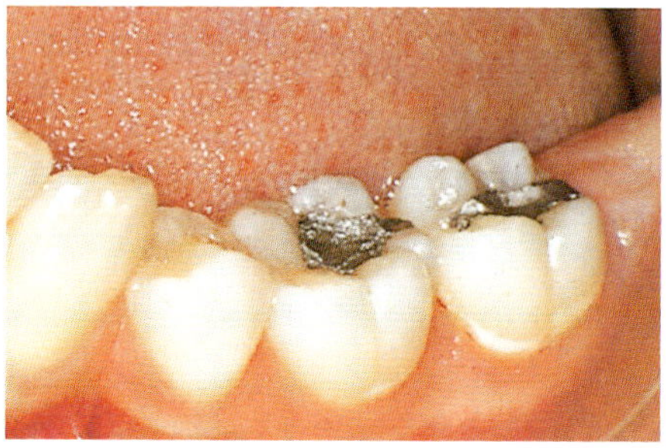

Fig. 1.5 White spot enamel lesions at the cervical margins of both molar teeth.

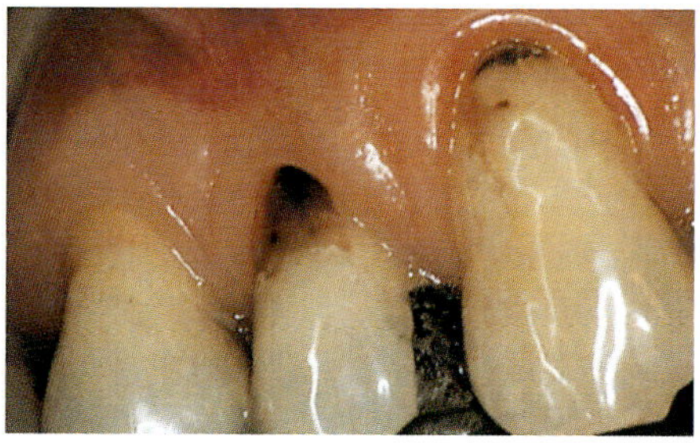

Fig. 1.6 Caries on the exposed buccal root surface of the first premolar tooth.

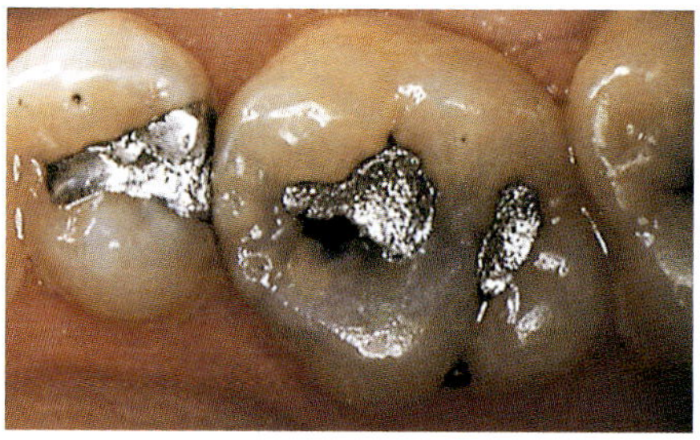

Fig. 1.7 Caries at the margin of the occlusal restoration in the first molar tooth.

In younger age groups pit and fissure caries is more common than approximal caries and buccal and lingual caries; posterior approximal caries is more common than anterior approximal caries. However, in older patients root surfaces exposed by gingival recession may be the predominant site for caries to occur.

Caries at the margins of a restoration should be, in a perfect world, the least common lesion. However, while placing a filling may make it easier for a patient to clean because the 'hole' is now restored, the filling will not prevent the biofilm forming on the tooth tissue next to it. Unless this is regularly disturbed by the patient, a new lesion will develop. It is all too easy to forget that the 'action' is in the biofilm and the lesion, which may have been removed and replaced by a filling, merely reflected the activity of the biofilm – unless restoration of the tooth has needlessly enlarged the cavity.

Severity or rapidity of attack

Under normal conditions the tooth is continually bathed in saliva which is capable of remineralizing the early carious lesion because it is supersaturated with calcium and phosphate ions.

Dental caries may be classified according to the severity or rapidity of the attack, and different teeth and surfaces are involved depending on the severity. Thus in a mild case only the most vulnerable teeth and surfaces are attacked, such as occlusal pits and fissures. A moderate attack may involve occlusal and approximal surfaces of posterior teeth and in a severe attack buccal and lingual surfaces close to the gingival margin and anterior teeth, which otherwise remain caries-free, also become carious.

Rampant caries

Rampant caries is the term used to describe a sudden rapid destruction of many teeth, frequently involving surfaces of teeth that are ordinarily relatively caries-free. Rampant caries is most commonly observed in the primary dentition of infants who continually suck a bottle or comforter containing, or dipped into, a sugar solution (Fig. 1.8). Rampant caries may also be seen in the permanent dentition of teenagers and is usually due to frequent cariogenic snacks and sweet drinks between meals (Fig. 1.9). It is also seen in mouths where there is a sudden marked reduction in salivary flow (xerostomia). Radiation in the region of the salivary glands, used in the treatment of a malignant growth, and Sjögren's syndrome, an autoimmune condition which may involve the salivary glands, are the most common causes of severe xerostomia. In addition, a large number of therapeutic drugs, such as antidepressants, tranquillizers, antihypertensives, and diuretics, retard salivary flow.

The management of rampant caries is more difficult than the management of caries which has progressed at a slower pace because of the extent of the caries and the rate at which it progresses. However, the treatment is the same in principle. The disease is managed by preventing further disease progression and stabilizing existing lesions before restoring teeth permanently. If caries is not managed by preventive, non-operative treatment the restorative treatment will be doomed to a cycle of disease, repair, new disease and further repair, and, before too long, extraction.

Arrested caries

Arrested caries is in distinct contrast to rampant caries, and the term describes carious lesions which do not progress. It is seen when the oral environment has changed from conditions predisposing to caries to conditions that tend to slow the lesion down. Figure 1.10 shows an arrested lesion on the mesial aspect of a lower second molar. The lesion probably stopped after extraction of the first molar. The environment changed, becoming less plaque retentive, easier to clean, and more accessible to saliva. Operative treatment is clearly not necessary.

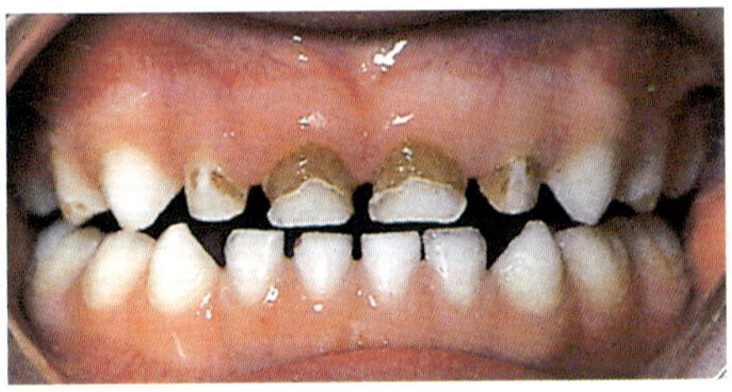

Fig. 1.8 Rampant caries of the deciduous teeth. This child continuously sucked a bottle of sweet drink.

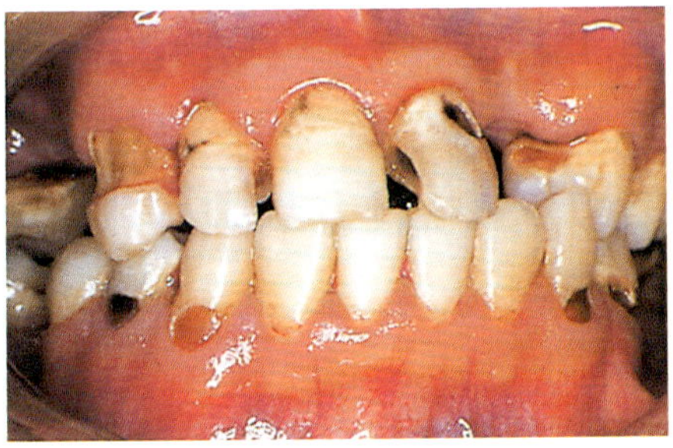

Fig. 1.9 Rampant caries in a 19-year-old man.

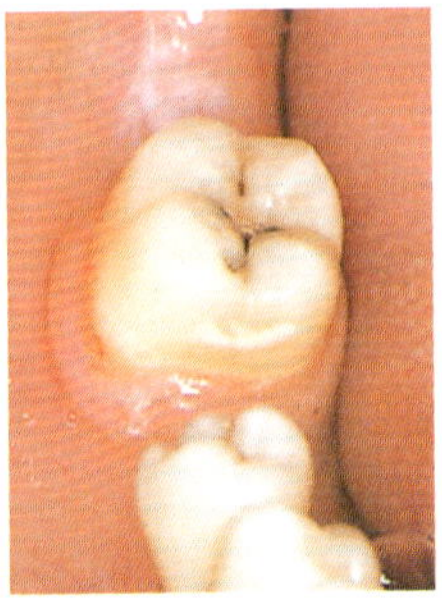

Fig. 1.10 Arrested caries on the mesial aspect of the second molar tooth. This lesion probably stopped progressing after extraction of the first molar tooth.

The carious process in enamel

The earliest clinically visible evidence of enamel caries is the white spot lesion, for example at the cervical margin of the tooth (Fig. 1.5). This may also be seen on extracted teeth as a small opaque white area just cervical to where the approximal contact area was. The colour of the lesion distinguishes it from the adjacent sound enamel, but at this stage there is no cavity and the enamel overlying the white spot is hard. In the active lesion it may have a matt surface because there has been direct dissolution of the outer enamel surface. Sometimes the lesion is shiny and this would indicate that good plaque control has been re-established and the outer demineralized enamel has been worn away. This lesion is arrested and sometimes it may appear brown due to exogenous stains absorbed by this porous region. Both white and brown spot lesions may have been present in the mouth for some years, as it is not inevitable for a carious lesion to progress.

If this smooth surface lesion is examined histologically in a thin ground section with transmitted light, it is usually seen to be cone-shaped, with the apex of the cone pointing towards the enamel–dentine junction (Fig. 1.11). The shape of the white spot lesion is determined by the distribution of the biofilm and the direction of the enamel prisms. Thus on an approximal surface the lesion formed beneath the biofilm is a kidney-shaped area between the contact facet and the gingival margin. Within the enamel, spread of dissolution takes place along the enamel prisms. The conical shape of the smooth surface lesion is the result of systematic variations in dissolution along the enamel prisms. The oldest or most active part of the lesion is centrally where the lesion is deepest. The conical shape represents increasing stages of lesion progression beginning with dissolution that would only be seen at the ultrastructural level at the edge of the lesion. This emphasizes that the lesion is driven by, and reflects, the specific environmental conditions in the overlying biofilm. One important feature of the histological picture is that the early enamel lesion is a subsurface demineralization beneath a relatively intact surface zone.

If the early enamel lesion progresses, the intact surface breaks down, forming a physical defect in the surface (cavitation). Plaque formation continues within the cavity and this may not be accessible to cleaning aids such as a toothbrush or dental floss. For this reason a cavitated lesion is more likely to progress, although it can still become arrested if the patient is able to clean.

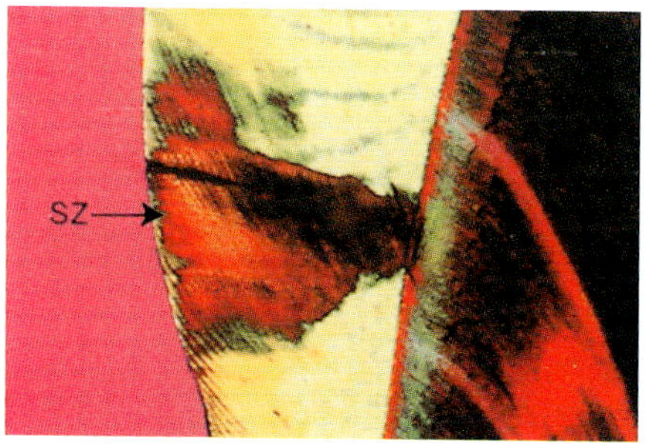

Fig. 1.11 Longitudinal ground section through a carious lesion on a smooth surface examined in water with polarized light. The lesion is cone-shaped. Note the relatively intact surface zone (SZ).

Fissures and pits are obvious stagnation areas where plaque can form and mature. The lesion forms at the entrance to the fissure (Figs. 1.12 and 1.13), and the erupting tooth is particularly susceptible to plaque stagnation. There are two reasons for this. The first is that children, especially young children, are not adept at removing plaque. Secondly the erupting tooth is below the line of the arch and tooth-brushing misses it unless the brush is brought in at right angles to clean the surface specifically (Fig. 1.14).

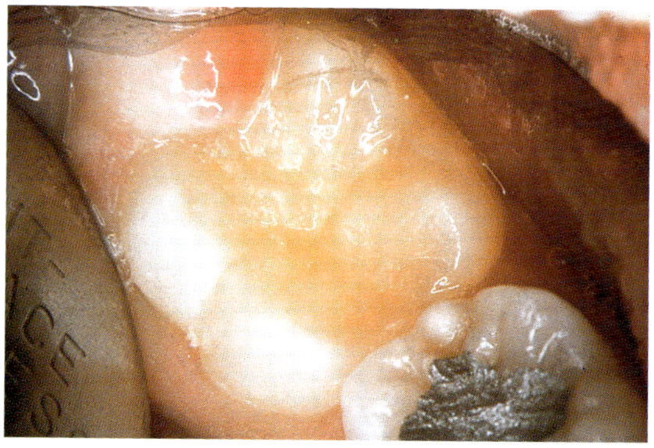

Fig. 1.12 This erupting molar appears caries-free but it is not. (By courtesy of Dental Update.)

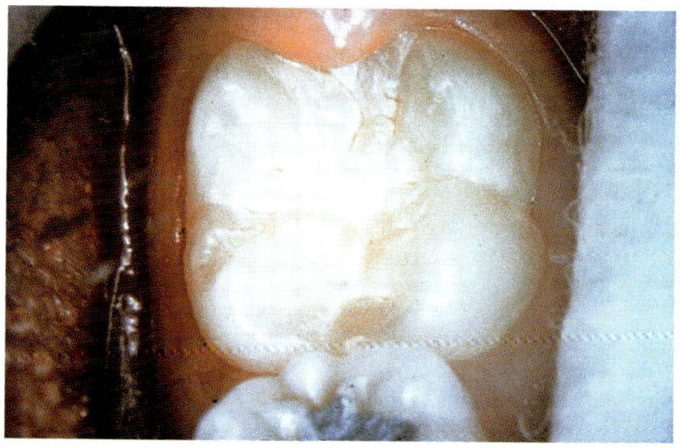

Fig. 1.13 The surface of the tooth seen in Fig. 1.12 has now been brushed to remove all plaque and thoroughly dried. A white spot lesion is now obvious at the entrance to the fissures. (By courtesy of Dental Update.)

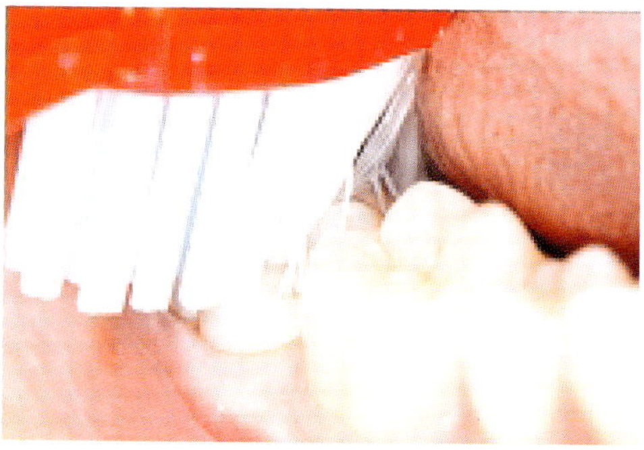

Fig. 1.14 The correct position of the toothbrush on an erupting second permanent molar. (By courtesy of Dental Update.)

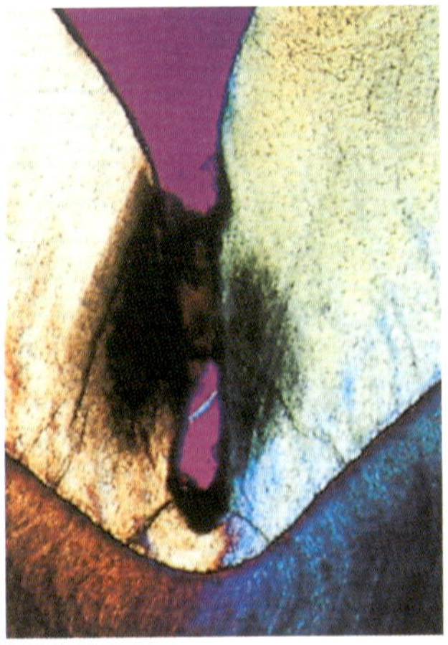

Fig. 1.15 A longitudinal ground section through an occlusal fissure showing a small carious lesion in enamel. The section is in water and viewed in polarized light. The lesion forms on the fissure walls, giving the appearance of two smooth surface lesions.

The histological features of fissure caries are similar to those already described for smooth surfaces. The lesion forms around the fissure walls and gives the appearance in section of two small smooth surface lesions (Fig. 1.15). The lesions again follow the direction of the enamel prisms and this anatomy gives the lesion the shape of a cone with its base at the enamel–dentine junction (Fig. 1.16).

The carious process in dentine

Histologically, the carious process may be in dentine before an enamel cavity forms. On an occlusal surface the lesion widens as it approaches the enamel–dentine junction, guided by prism direction. Eventually a cavity forms and now the hole is filled with plaque and the biofilm sits directly on the exposed dentine. At this stage demineralization spreads laterally along the enamel -dentine junction, undermining the enamel (Fig. 1.17).

Undermined enamel is brittle and will in due course fracture if subjected to occlusal forces, producing a large cavity. Undermined enamel is of particular relevance in cavity preparation because superficially sound but undermined enamel

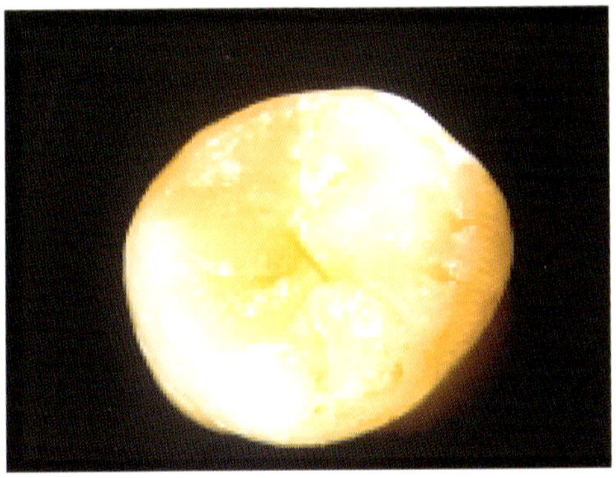

(a)

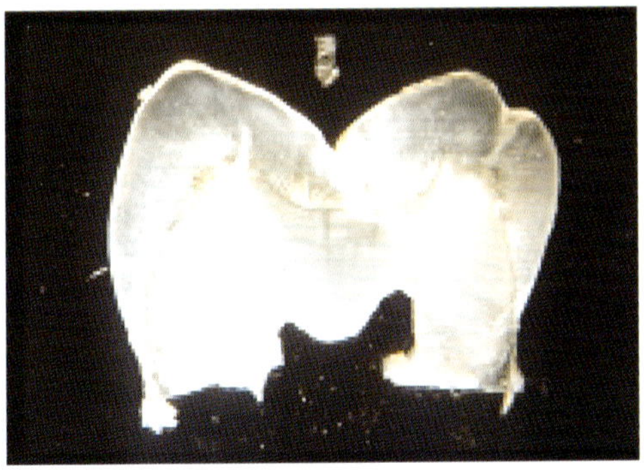

(b)

Fig. 1.16 (a) A molar tooth with a white spot lesion formed in an area of plaque stagnation at the fissure entrance.
(b) A hemisection of this tooth showing a larger lesion than would be expected from examination of the outer enamel surface. This is purely a function of the direction of the enamel prisms in this region. (By courtesy of Dental Update.)

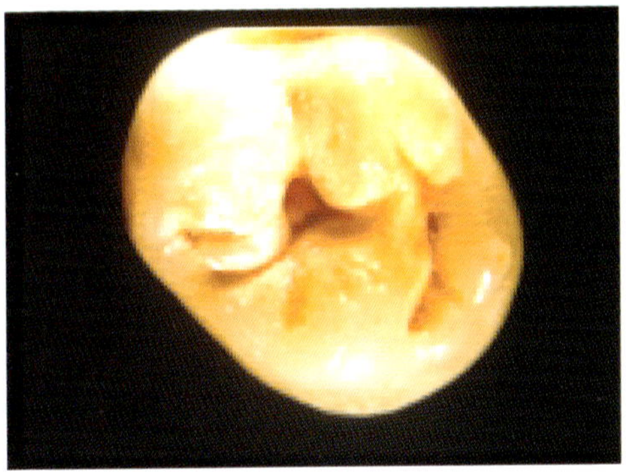

(a)

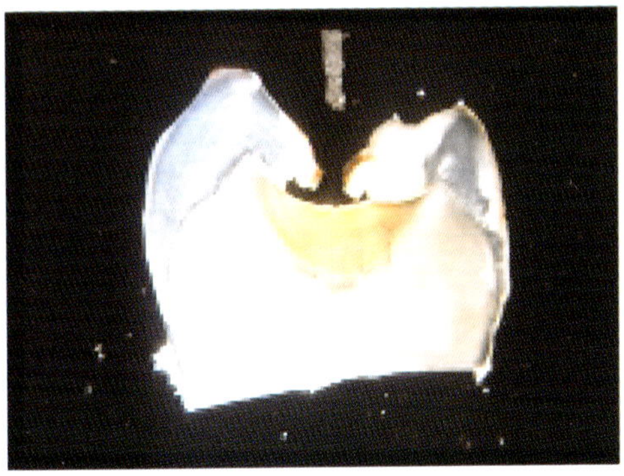

(b)

Fig. 1.17 (a) A molar tooth with a cavity whose base is in dentine.
(b) A hemisection of this tooth showing the cavity and lateral spread of the lesion at the enamel–dentine junction. There is extensive demineralization of the dentine. This wide undermining of the enamel on an occlusal surface is a factor of the anatomy of the area. (By courtesy of Dental Update.)

must often be removed to gain access to demineralized dentine beneath it. In addition, it is probably unwise to leave undermined enamel occlusally unless it is supported by an adhesive restorative material.

Pulp–dentine defence reactions

Dentine is a vital tissue containing the cytoplasmic extensions of the odontoblasts and must be considered together with the pulp since the two tissues are so intimately connected. The pulp–dentine complex, like any other vital tissue in the body, is capable of defending itself. The state of the tissue at any time will depend on the balance between the attacking forces and the defence reactions. The important defence reactions are tubular sclerosis within the dentine, reactionary dentine at the interface between dentine and pulp, and inflammation of the pulp.

Tubular sclerosis occurs through precipitation of minerals in the tubular space and is protective in that it reduces the permeability of the dentine, inhibiting the penetration of acids and bacterial toxins. Reactionary dentine is formed by the odontoblasts beneath the carious stimulus. A slowly progressing lesion may give time for a considerable reparative dentine response, whereas with more acute larger lesions the response may be disorganized or even non-existent. Regular removal of the biofilm from the surface of any lesion encourages lesion arrest and these defense reactions then predominate. This retreat of the pulp from injury has important implications in the operative management of caries (see p. 64).

Inflammation is the fundamental response of all vascular connective tissues to injury. Inflammation of the pulp (pulpitis) may, as in any other tissue, be acute or chronic. In a slowly progressing carious lesion, toxins reaching the pulp may provoke chronic inflammation. However, once the organisms actually reach the pulp (a carious exposure), acute inflammation may supervene.

Inflammatory reactions have vascular and cellular components. In chronic inflammation the cellular components predominate and there may be increased collagen production, leading to fibrosis but without immediately endangering the vitality of the tooth. However, in acute inflammation the vascular changes predominate.

Infection is the most common cause of pulpal inflammation and caries is the most common microbial source. Caries of peripheral dentine will result in pulpal inflammation and chronic inflammatory cells (macrophages, lymphocytes, and plasma cells) will infiltrate the pulp near the odontoblast layer. Indeed, this infiltration may even be seen in initial enamel caries. This chronic inflammatory reaction is mainly due to the movement of bacterial toxins through the dentinal tubules. With increasing carious involvement of enamel and dentine, the area of chronic inflammation increases in size but it is believed to remain localized until pulp exposure. After exposure, bacteria may enter the pulp. Polymorphonuclear leucocytes may now predominate, and acute inflammation can supervene and spread throughout the pulp, resulting in pulpal necrosis.

One objective of the preparation of a carious cavity for a filling is to remove the bacterial biofilm that drives the carious process before carious exposure occurs. Once the bacterial irritant is removed, the local inflammation it has caused has an inherent potential to heal provided that the cavity is restored with a non-irritating material that seals the margin of the filling and the pulp still has an adequate blood supply. The age of the tooth will have some bearing on this: a young tooth with a good blood supply is more likely to recover from inflammation than an old tooth with more fibrous tissue within the pulp chamber and a constricted blood supply. The cavity seal prevents further bacterial ingress and assault on the pulp–dentine complex.

However, if the operative procedure is performed in a manner that is harmful to the pulp or the restorative material is a poor cavity seal, irritating or defective, a local necrosis in the pulp can result. The area of necrosis may harbour bacteria and the inflammation may move apically until the entire pulp is necrotic. This is followed either by spread of toxins into the periapical tissues at the root apex, producing the chronic inflammatory response of chronic apical periodontitis, or, if organisms pass into the periapical tissues, an acute apical abscess develops (see p. 47, 48).

Degenerative or destructive changes in dentine

These include demineralization of dentine, destruction of the organic matrix, and damage and death of odontoblasts. Since carious enamel is porous, acids, enzymes, and other chemical stimuli from the tooth surface will reach the outer dentine, evoking a response in the pulp–dentine complex. Thus, both reparative and degenerative changes begin before cavitation of the enamel occurs and while the microorganisms are still confined to the tooth surface. With cavitation of enamel, bacteria have direct access to dentine and the tissue becomes infected.

Demineralization of dentine precedes bacterial penetration, and this is of importance in operative dentistry since an objective is to remove the infected and necrotic dentine, although uninfected but demineralized dentine may be left.

Of course, this is easier said than done because it is difficult to differentiate between the two layers. Thus, where the pulp is not at risk or the strength of the tooth is not jeopardized, all the soft, infected dentine is removed. However, if the carious dentine is close to the pulp, it is often left if it is reasonably hard, even though it may contain a few organisms. These remaining organisms are then sealed within the tooth. This encourages tubular sclerosis and reparative dentine formation. This is discussed further in Chapters 3 and 7.

It is important to realize that the rate of progress of caries in dentine is highly variable and provided the biofilm is removed from the tooth or cavity surface the progress of the disease can be arrested. Clinically, the dentine in actively progressing lesions is soft and wet, and, because of the speed at which some lesions develop, the defence reactions may not have time to be effective. In contrast, the dentine in arrested or slowly progressing lesions has a hard, leathery, or dry consistency. The defence reactions are well marked and the carious lesion accumulates minerals from the oral fluids and from pulpal blood flow.

Root caries

Dentine caries beneath enamel has been considered in the preceding section. However, root surfaces become exposed in many mouths and these surfaces are susceptible to root caries and also appear more vulnerable than enamel to mechanical wear and chemical damage (Figs. 1.18 and 1.19).

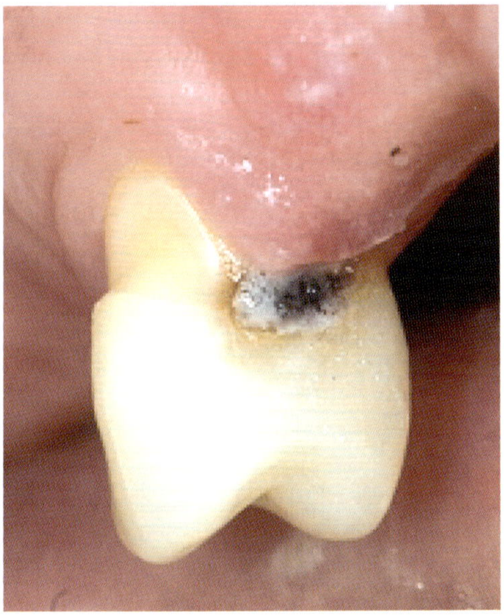

Fig. 1.18 An active root carious lesion on the mesial aspect of a premolar. Notice there is no lesion on the buccal surface of the tooth. Indeed, this has been so well brushed, it has been partly worn away. The lesion has formed in an area of plaque stagnation next to a removable partial denture. Plaque can be seen in the cavity.

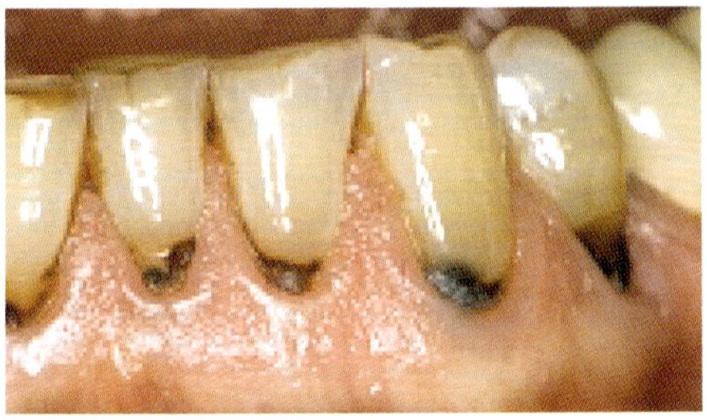

Fig. 1.19 These lesions are on the root surface, close to the gingival margin. They are darkly coloured and leathery in texture. These are slowly progressing lesions. This woman is in her 70's. She has a dry mouth and rheumatoid arthritis (secondary Sjögren's syndrome). It is not easy for her to clean.

Exposed root surfaces occur following gingival recession, which is usually associated with periodontal disease, and so it is hardly surprising that root caries is more commonly seen in older people. Not all patients with exposed root surfaces will automatically develop root caries. If the biofilm is regularly disturbed with a toothbrush and a fluoride-containing toothpaste, the root surface will not develop a clinically detectable lesion.

Histologically, in the early lesion demineralization appears to take place beneath a well-mineralized surface layer. Deep to the lesion there are often areas of tubular sclerosis and reactionary dentine. Bacteria seem to penetrate the tissues at an earlier stage in root caries than in coronal caries, although lesions are often rather superficial.

Despite the presence of these bacteria, active, soft root carious lesions can be converted into arrested lesions by regular tooth brushing with a fluoride-containing dentifrice. The soft surface is worn away to leave a hard and shiny root surface which is minimally infected (Fig. 1.20).

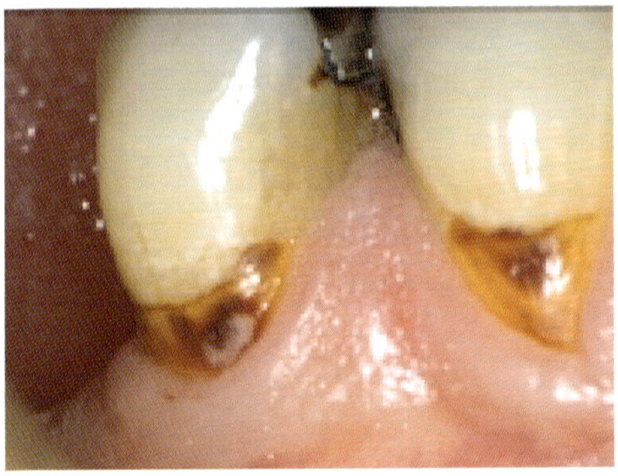

Fig. 1.20 An arrested lesion is present on the canine. It is hard and shiny. Part of the lesion of the first premolar is active. It is soft and covered with plaque. The remainder of the lesion is arrested. Tooth brushing alone will arrest the active part of this lesion.

Secondary or recurrent caries

Placing a restoration does not confer immunity on the tooth, and secondary or recurrent caries may occur in the tooth tissue adjacent to the filling material. Secondary caries is the same as primary caries except that it is located at the margin of a restoration. Like primary caries, it is caused by the metabolic activity in the biofilm at the tooth or cavity surface. Thus it is most often localized gingivally where plaque is most likely to stagnate (Fig. 1.21). It can be arrested by regular disturbance of the biofilm with a fluoride-containing dentifrice.

This emphasizes the point that the best way of managing caries is by preventing lesion progression and not by filling holes in teeth. Even the very best operative dentistry is a poor substitute for unblemished enamel and dentine, and opera-

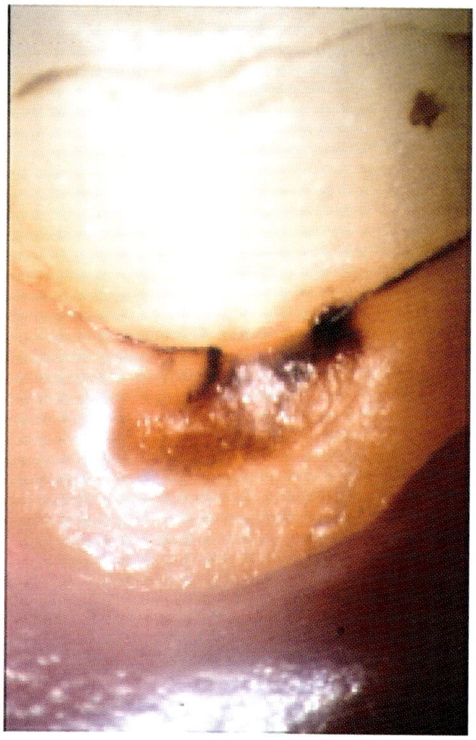

Fig. 1.21 Secondary caries at the margin of a tooth-coloured restoration. This can be arrested by plaque control alone.

tive dentistry must be seen as making good a failure to prevent disease from progressing in the first place. Operative dentistry also enables the patient to resume effective plaque control by filling the hole where plaque may stagnate.

Residual caries

When preparing a carious tooth to receive a restoration the dentist removes soft, infected dentine. This is part of the carious lesion, but not all of it. Demineralization of dentine precedes bacterial infection and beyond the demineralized area is the region of tubular sclerosis. The parts of the carious lesion that remain after cavity preparation are called residual caries. The nature of this tissue will depend on where the dentist has decided to stop removing tissue. This will be discussed further on pp. 63 and 64.

Diagnosis of dental caries

It is important to recognize active carious lesions as soon as possible so that preventive treatment has a chance to arrest lesion progression. The prerequisites for caries diagnosis are:

- good lighting
- clean teeth
- a three-in-one syringe so that teeth can be viewed both wet and dry
- sharp eyes with vision aided by magnification. This is particularly necessary for older dentists who are unlikely to be able to see as well as they did in their youth (see Chapter 4)
- reproducible bitewing radiographs.

It is also important to realize that all lesions, irrespective of their stage of progression, are arrestable if the biofilm that drives their progress can be removed. Thus two important questions for the practitioner to answer are:

- is the lesion active or arrested?
- if it is active, is a restoration needed so that the patient can clean effectively?

The diagnostic procedure

The white spot lesion, although caused by plaque, is also obscured by it. A logical way to proceed is for the dentist to examine the teeth both before and after removal of plaque. Many experienced practitioners choose to carry out their examination immediately after the patient has seen the hygienist.

The three-in-one syringe is invaluable in the diagnosis of the depth of penetration of the white spot lesion. A white spot lesion that is visible only once the enamel has been throughly dried has penetrated about halfway through the enamel. A white or brown spot lesion that is visible on a wet tooth surface has penetrated all the way through the enamel and the demineralization may be in the dentine. Demineralization may be in dentine before cavitation occurs, but the lesion can still be arrested if plaque control can be established.

On no account should a white spot lesion be jabbed with a sharp probe to see if the probe sticks in the tissue. The probe is likely to break the relatively intact surface zone of the enamel lesion and cause a cavity (Fig. 1.22).

Finally, good bitewing radiographs are essential for the diagnosis of approximal lesions where a contact point is present. A film-holder and beam-aiming device should always be used to ensure the correct angulation of the beam and as an aid in

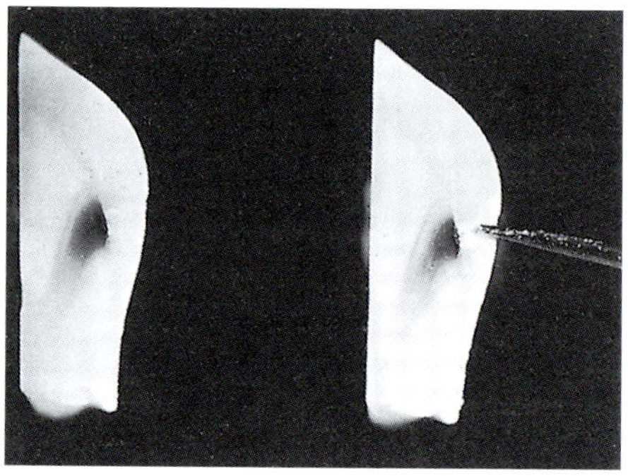

Fig. 1.22 A smooth surface lesion before and after probing. Note the damage that can be caused by a sharp probe.

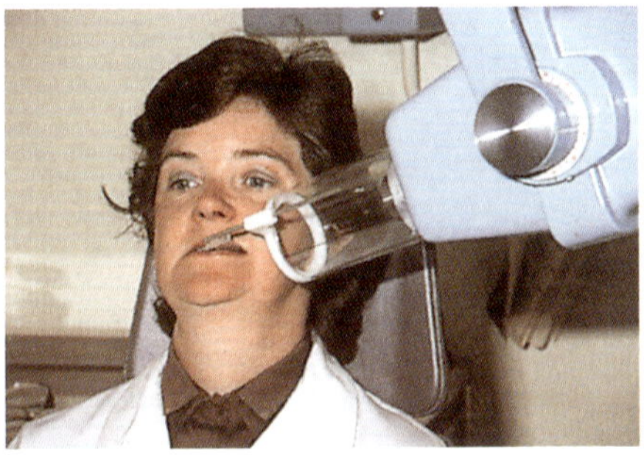

Fig. 1.23 A film-holder and beam-aiming device in use to take a bitewing radiograph.

reproducing the same geometry in any subsequent radiograph (Fig. 1.23). Where a lesion is to be monitored for progression or arrest, this reproducibility of view is essential; otherwise an apparent change in the lesion may simply be an artefact of geometry.

Diagnosis of caries on occlusal surfaces

Visual examination and examination of the bitewing radiograph are both important. Before attempting an accurate visual diagnosis, clean the occlusal surface with a rotating bristle brush in the handpiece. Unless this is done the lesion may not be seen (Fig.1.12). The active, uncavitated lesion is white, often with a matt surface (Fig. 1.13). The corresponding inactive lesion may be brown. These enamel lesions are *not visible on a bitewing radiograph*. The enamel lesion that is only visible on a dry tooth surface is in the outer enamel. The lesion visible on a wet surface is all the way through the enamel and may be into dentine.

Cavitated lesions may present as microcavities with or without a greyish discoloration of the enamel (Figs. 1.24 and 1.25). The microcavity is easily missed on visual examination unless the surface is perfectly clean and dry. Careful examination of bitewing radiographs is important and serves as a useful safety net to avoid missing microcavities. A lesion that has been missed on visual examination but found on radiograph is called *hidden caries* (Fig. 1.26). More advanced lesions may present as cavities exposing dentine (Fig. 1.27). Cavitated lesions are usually

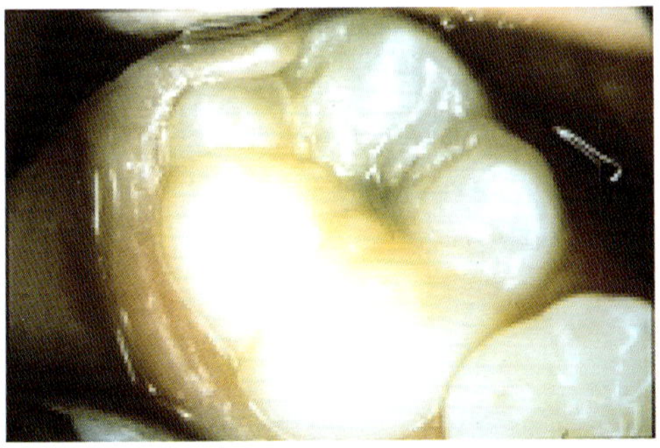

Fig. 1.24 The grey discoloration of this occlusal surface is caused by demineralized, discoloured dentine shining through relatively intact enamel. This lesion was visible in dentine on bitewing radiograph. (By courtesy of Dental Update.)

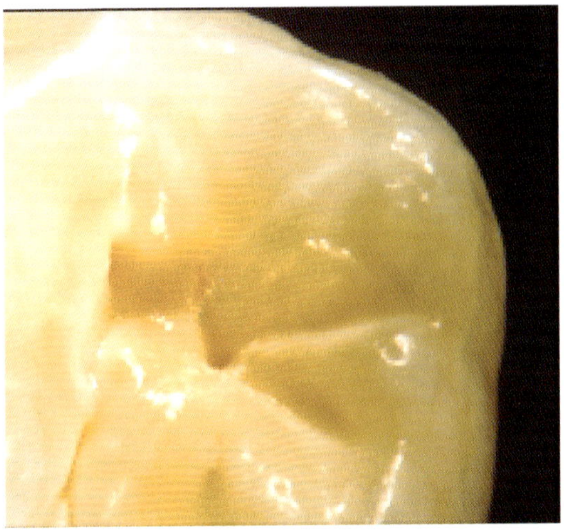

Fig. 1.25 There is a microcavity in the white spot lesion in this occlusal surface. It looks like a slightly widened fissure or a hole left by a woodworm. Histologically, this lesion is well into dentine and it may be visible in dentine on a bitewing radiograph.

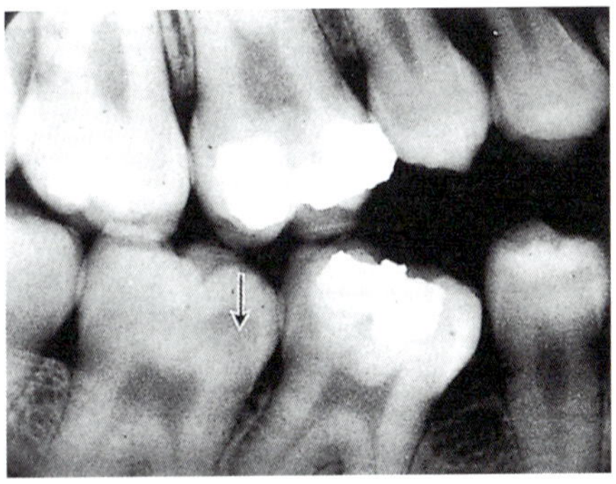

Fig. 1.26 A bitewing radiograph showing occlusal caries in the lower second molar (arrow). Clinically there was no detectable cavity in this tooth, although the fissure was stained and the enamel discoloured. (By courtesy of Dental Update.)

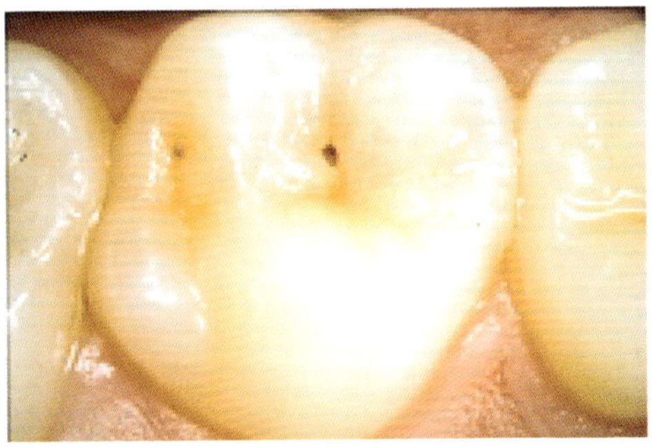

Fig. 1.27 A cavitated lesion exposing dentine. The lesion is visible in dentine on a bitewing radiograph. (By courtesy of Dental Update.)

visible in dentine on a bitewing radiograph. Cavitated occlusal lesions, whether microcavities or cavities that clinically expose dentine, are usually active because the patient cannot clean plaque out of the cavity.

Diagnosis of caries on approximal surfaces

It is difficult to see a carious enamel lesion on an approximal surface because the lesion forms just cervical to the contact area and vision is obscured by the adjacent tooth. If the lesion is discovered clinically, it is usually at a relatively late stage when it has already progressed well into dentine and is seen as a pinkish grey area shining up through the marginal ridge (Fig.1.4). It must be emphasized again that teeth should be isolated, clean, and dry to pick up this appearance.

Bitewing radiographs are of paramount importance in diagnosing approximal caries *in both enamel and dentine* (Fig. 1.28). However, it should be remembered that the technique is relatively insensitive, and once a lesion is visible in enamel on a bitewing radiograph it is usually in dentine when examined histologically.

The approximal enamel lesion appears as a dark triangular area in the enamel on a bitewing radiograph. The lesion may be seen just in the outer enamel, throughout the depth of the enamel, in the enamel and outer dentine, or reaching right through the dentine (Figs. 1.28 and 1.29). The pulp is often exposed by the carious process in the latter appearance.

It is not possible to judge the activity of a lesion from a single bitewing radiograph. A series of radiographs, perhaps taken at yearly intervals, is required to judge lesion progression or arrest. It is essential to use film-holders and beam-aiming devices (Fig. 1.23) so that views are reproducible. Slight alterations in the beam angle will affect the radiographic view.

It is also not possible to know whether a lesion is cavitated from its appearance on a radiograph. The radiographic appearances 0, 1, and 2 in Fig. 1.29 are not usually cavitated. Radiographic appearance 4 would be cavitated.

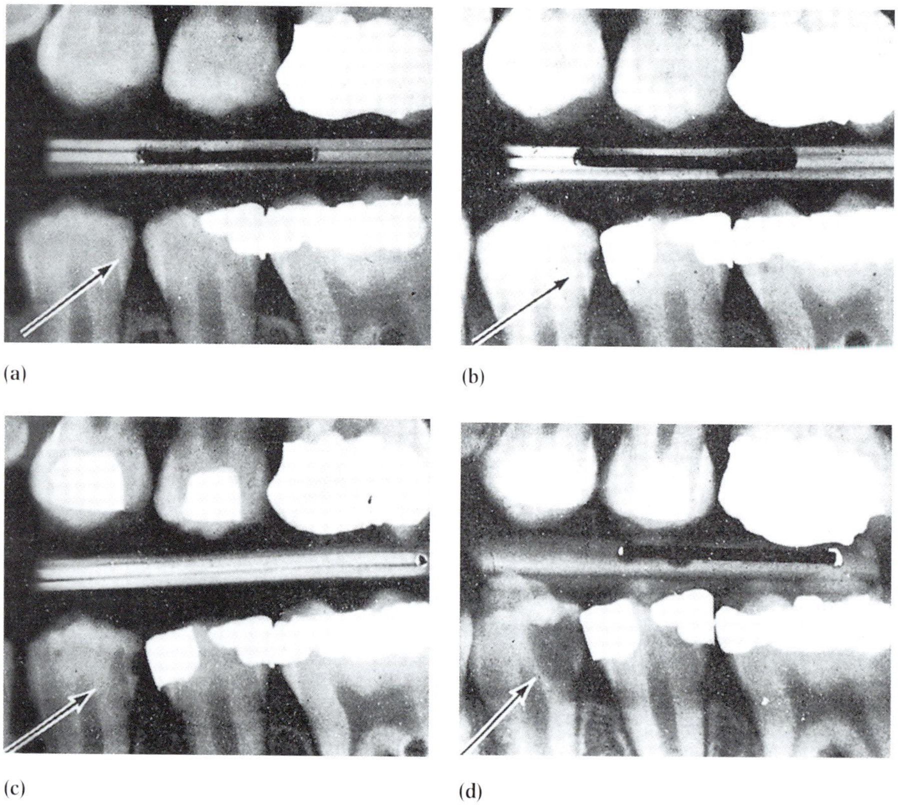

Fig. 1.28 The radiographs record the progress of approximal caries on the distal aspect of a mandibular first premolar over a period of 18 months in a patient aged 15–16 years. This picture has some historical interest. It appears in the first edition of this book, published in 1961. Speed of progression is rapid. There was no fluoride in toothpaste at this time.
(a) Early enamel lesion
(b) Nine months later – late enamel lesion
(c) Twelve months later – marked dentinal spread
(d) Eighteen months later – approaching carious exposure.

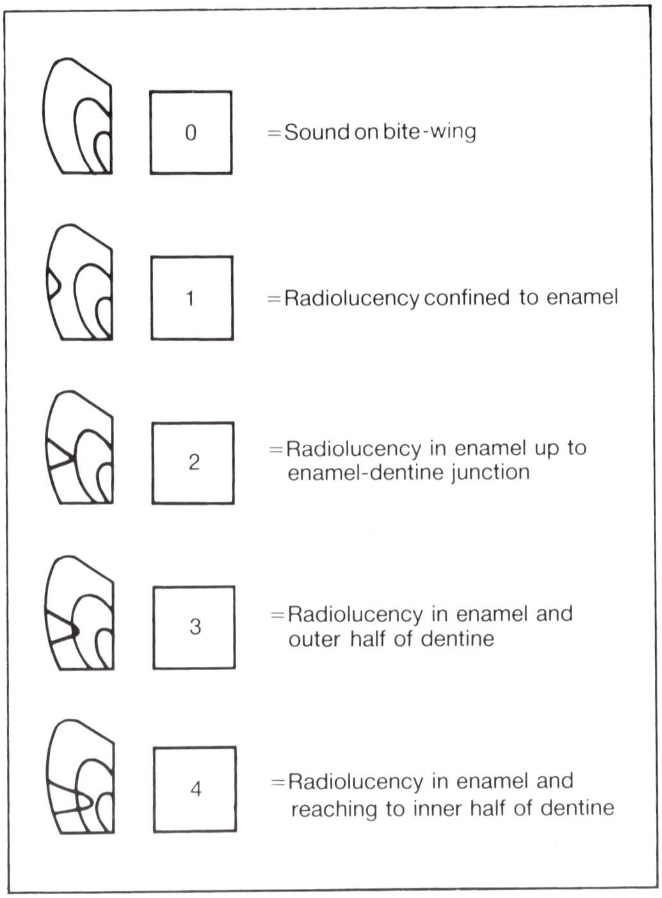

Fig. 1.29 Diagrammatic representations of caries on bitewing radiographs.

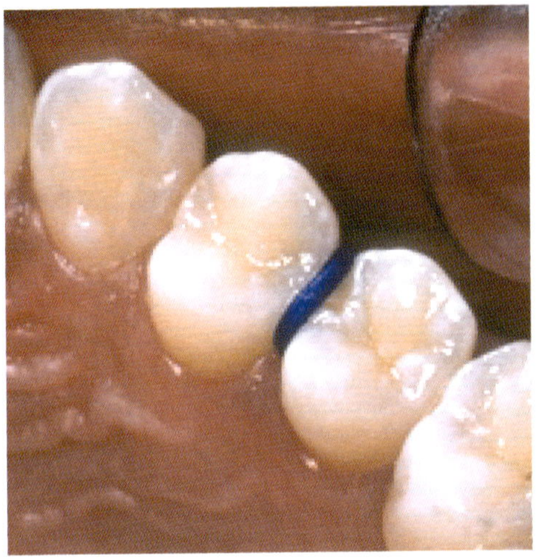

(a)

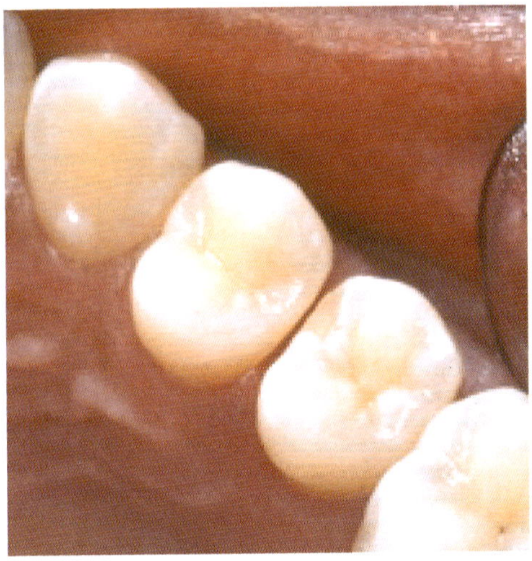

(b)

Fig. 1.30 (a) An orthodontic elastic separator has been placed between two premolars.
(b) After 5 days the separator is removed and now a probe can be used gently to feel whether a cavity is present. (By courtesy of Dr D. Ratledge.)

Appearance 3 is the problem. In contemporary European populations about 60% of these lesions are not cavitated, although the higher the caries risk of the patient the more likely it is the lesion is cavitated. Fortunately, it is possible to use an elastic separator to create a small space between the teeth (Fig. 1.30). Now a probe may be used gently to feel for a cavity.

In contrast to the enamel surface, an approximal lesion on the root surface may be diagnosed visually if the gingival health is good. If the gingivae are red, swollen, and tend to bleed, detailed caries diagnosis in these areas should be deferred until the teeth have been scaled and cleaned and improved oral hygiene has been achieved.

Caries on the approximal root surface is visible on a bitewing radiograph (Fig. 1.31), although its appearance is sometimes confused with a cervical radiolucency – or 'burnout'. The latter is a perfectly normal appearance at the gap between the dense enamel over the crown of the tooth and the crest of the alveolar ridge where the X-rays pass tangentially through the dentine of the root (not through enamel or bone), giving a relatively radiolucent appearance (Fig. 1.31).

Transmitted light can also be of considerable assistance in the diagnosis of approximal caries, particularly in anterior teeth. The operating light is reflected through the contact point with the dental mirror, and a carious lesion appears as a dark shadow following the outline of the decay (Fig. 1.32).

In posterior teeth (Fig. 1.33) a stronger light source is required, and fibre-optic lights, with the beam reduced to 0.5 mm diameter, have been used. It is important that the diameter of the light source is small so that glare and loss of surface detail are eliminated. The light should be used with dry teeth. The technique has particular advantages in patients with posterior crowding, where bitewing radiographs will produce overlapping images, and in pregnant women, where unnecessary radiation should be avoided.

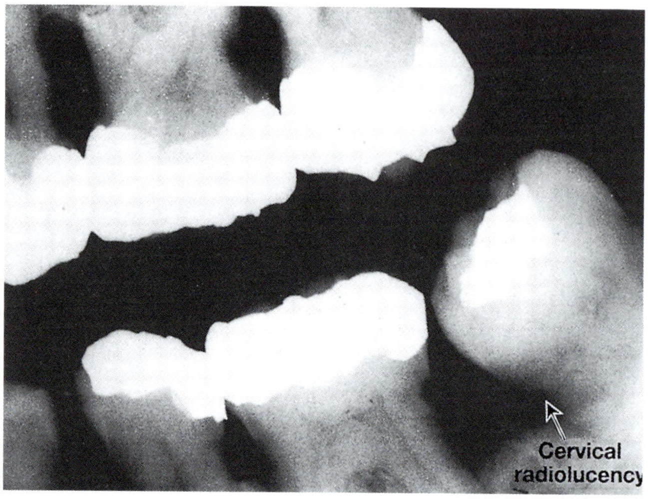

Fig. 1.31 A bitewing radiograph showing root caries on the distal aspect of the upper second premolar, upper first molar, and lower first molar. The arrow points to the cervical radiolucency on the lower third molar. This is a normal appearance but it can sometimes be confused with root caries.

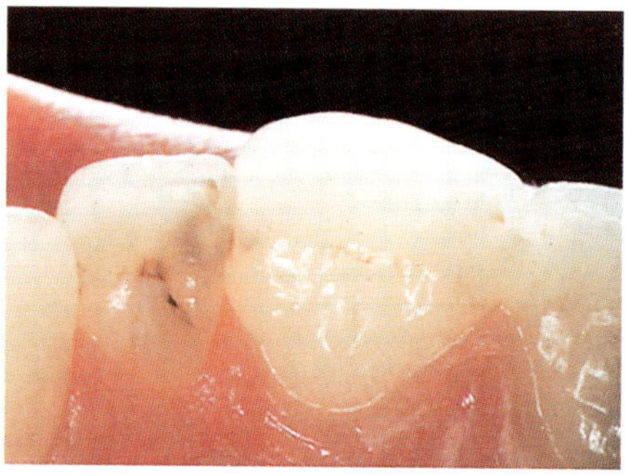

Fig. 1.32 A mirror view of the palatal aspect of the upper anterior teeth. A small lesion is visible on the distal aspect of the central incisor and a larger lesion is present on the mesial aspect of the lateral incisor.

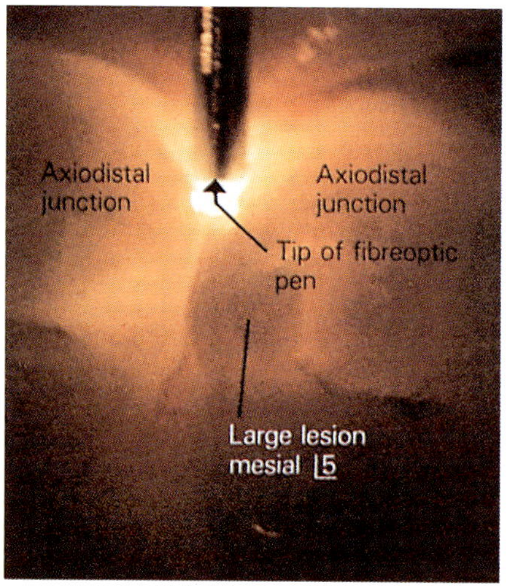

Fig. 1.33 A fibre-optic light in use to assist in the diagnosis of approximal caries. Shadowing indicates a lesion. (Reproduced by courtesy of Dental Update.)

Diagnosis of caries on exposed smooth surfaces

Caries on smooth surfaces can be seen at the stage of the white or brown spot lesion before cavitation has occurred, provided that the teeth are clean, dry, and well lit. Uncavitated, active lesions are close to the gingival margin and have a matt surface (Fig. 1.5). Inactive lesions may be further from the gingival margin, white or brown in colour with a shiny surface.

Root surface caries, in its early stages, appears as one or more small well-defined discoloured areas located along the gingival margin. Active lesions are soft, plaque-covered, and close to the gingival margin (Fig. 1.18). Arrested lesions are hard and shiny, plaque-free, and some distance from the gingival margin (Figs. 1.20 and 1.34). As with enamel caries, great care should be taken when using a probe on these lesions; otherwise, healing tissue may be damaged. However, it is essential to feel these lesions to determine their activity.

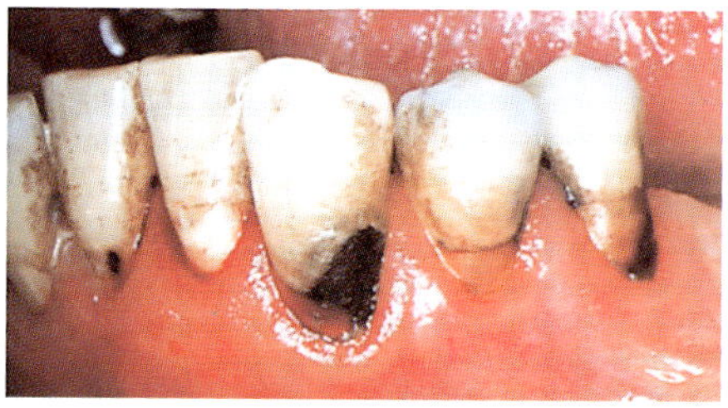

Fig. 1.34 Arrested or slowly progressing root surface caries. This lesion felt hard when an excavator was scraped across it.

Assessment of caries risk

The previous sections concentrated on individual lesions but these lesions are clustered in individuals. It is important to assess an individual patient's susceptibility to carious lesion formation and progression. This is an important part of contemporary practice for the following reasons:

- It makes economic sense to target preventive treatments in practice at the appropriate risk group.
- Dental care neither begins nor ends with a single course of treatment but is ongoing. When a course of dental treatment is complete, dentist and patient decide when it would be wise to check that all is well. This recall interval is based partly on an assessment of the risk of disease progression and should not be standardized at six months or any other period.
- Patients should be made aware of their risk status. This knowledge encourages them to keep appropriate recall appointments and to become involved in their own preventive care and, if they pay for this, may help them budget for dental bills.

Figure 1.35 lists some of the many factors relevant to the assessment of caries risk. *Social factors* will be assessed,

CARIES RISK ASSESSMENT	
HIGH RISK	LOW RISK
SOCIAL HISTORY	
Socially deprived	Middle class
High caries in siblings	Low caries in siblings
Lower knowledge of dental disease	Dentally aware
Irregular attendence	Regular attendance
Ready availability of snacks	Work does not allow regular snacks
Low dental aspirations	High dental aspirations
MEDICAL HISTORY	
Medically compromised	No medical problem
Handicapped	No physical problem
Xerostomia	Normal salivary flow
Long-term cariogenic medicine	No long-term medication
DIETARY HABITS	
Frequent sugar intake	Infrequent sugar intake
FLUORIDE USE	
Non-fluoride area	Fluoridation area
No fluoride toothpaste	Fluoride toothpaste used
PLAQUE CONTROL	
Infrequent, ineffective cleaning	Frequent, effective cleaning
Poor manual control	Good manual control
SALIVA	
Low flow rate	Normal flow rate
CLINICAL EVIDENCE	
New lesions	No new lesions
Premature extractions	Nil extractions for caries
Anterior caries or restorations	Sound anterior teeth
Multiple restorations	No or few restorations
History of repeated restorations	Restorations inserted years ago
Multiband orthodontics Partial dentures	No appliances

Fig. 1.35 Caries risk assessment.

often unconsciously, as the patient enters the room. Dress, demeanour, and ethnic background will be apparent for subjective appraisal but must not be allowed to prejudice more objective observations. Questions on employment, attendance patterns, and disease pattern of other family members elicit valuable information. During history taking the patient's dental aspirations become apparent and wise treatment planning will encompass these aspirations. Sadly, dental caries is now principally a problem of the socially deprived, although there are many exceptions.

The *medical history* is always important in dental practice and some illnesses specifically predispose to a high risk of dental caries. The most important of these are medical problems causing xerostomia, such as radiotherapy in the region of the salivary glands, Sjögren's syndrome, and long-term use of some medications such as tranquillizers, antihypertensives, and diuretics. Frequent medication may itself pose a problem if the medication is sugar-based.

Dietary habits and the patient's attitude to them are of prime importance since diet is one of the main factors in the development of dental caries. For this reason a dietary history is an important part of the assessment in patients with a high caries activity. A diet sheet, on which the patient is asked to record everything taken by mouth for a four-day period, can be a useful record. Figure 1.36 shows such a diet sheet where it seems obvious that frequent sweet drinks, sweets, and other sugar-containing snacks taken before bed are a potential cause of caries in this mouth.

Fluoride history is also of importance since the fluoride ion delays lesion progression. It is always wise to check that a fluoride toothpaste is used. Sometimes patients with multiple carious lesions select a particular brand of toothpaste, manufactured for sensitive teeth, which does not contain fluoride.

Clinical examination is the most useful indicator of caries risk. A history of repeated restoration and re-restoration, together with multiple new lesions on clinical and/or radiographic examination, is an obvious caries risk. Stagnation areas such as unsealed deep fissures, multiband orthodontic appliances, partial dentures, and poor restorative dentistry encourage plaque accumulation and increase caries risk. *Plaque control* itself is very relevant, and removal of smooth surface plaque may uncover multiple cervical white spot lesions or cavities in caries-prone mouths.

Saliva is essential to tooth integrity and for this reason its examination is a logical step in a caries risk assessment. The most important factor is flow rate and it is easy to measure stimulated salivary flow at the chairside. The patient chews paraffin wax to stimulate saliva and spits it into a measuring cylinder. The stimulated salivary flow rate can then be expressed in millilitres (ml) per minute.

The normal stimulated secretion rate in adults is 1–2 ml per minute. An individual with severe salivary gland malfunction may produce less than 0.1 ml per minute. In less severe cases of hyposalivation the stimulated secretion rate is between 0.7 and 0.1 ml per minute. The term xerostomia (dry mouth) is used to describe this condition.

Where the dentist suspects from clinical examination that the mouth is dry, or where it is difficult to explain a high caries activity, salivary flow should be measured. Sometimes both dentist and patient will be surprised because the patient is not always aware the mouth is dry.

Symptoms of caries

Thus far the signs of caries – that is, what the clinician can detect – have been considered. However, patients often seek treatment for the *symptoms* of caries. What are these symptoms?

Unfortunately, caries presents symptomatically at a relatively late stage. The patient may feel a 'hole in a tooth' with the tongue, brown or black discoloration or cavities may be seen, or frank pain may be suffered.

Caries, even in dentine, is not painful *per se*, but cavitation may occasionally present as mild pain with sweet things or with heat or cold. Normally, the enamel and the necrotic dentine insulate the sensitive dentine and pulp from these stimuli. However, a much more common cause of pain, which may be intense, is pulpitis (the commonest 'toothache') which occurs late in the development of a carious lesion when the caries is very close to the pulp or actually exposing it (see p. 10).

A chronically inflamed pulp may be symptomless or produce only mild symptoms. In contrast, acute pulpitis is very painful, with the pain often being initiated by hot and cold stimuli. Unfortunately, the pain is not well localized to the offending tooth, and the patient may only be able to indicate which quadrant, or even which side, of the mouth is involved. (See Chapter 2 for further details on the diagnosis and management of toothache.)

The relevance of the diagnostic information to the management of caries

There are three approaches to the management of active caries:

- attempt to arrest the disease by preventive, non-operative treatment
- remove and replace the carious tissues (operative dentistry) and prevent recurrence by preventive, non-operative treatment
- extract the tooth.

Preventive, non-operative treatment

The management of active caries always requires preventive treatment and in cases where cavities preclude plaque control, operative treatment is also needed. Notice the use of the term *preventive treatment*. This implies active intervention by the dental team that is skilful, time-consuming, and worthy of payment. It is not an 'observe' or 'wait and watch' approach.

All patients should be put into a caries risk category, either high or low, with all others designated as medium risks.

Patient involvement

The carious process can be arrested by meticulous plaque control, dietary modification, judicious use of fluoride, and salivary stimulation. Each of these approaches requires the active cooperation of the patient. The patient is in control of his or her own dental destiny because it is the patient, not the dentist, who influences the carious process. For this reason it is absolutely essential to involve the patient from the outset, and the patient must acknowledge the problem and have some sense of control over it.

One of the best ways to ensure active patient cooperation is to turn the patient into their own personal dentist so that the patient could, in theory, check their own mouth. The dentist should give the patient a mirror and show the patient their own carious lesions. The dentist should show the patient the white spot and a red and swollen gingival margin that bleeds on probing. Disclosing solution should be applied to demonstrate the plaque in that specific position. The dentist should explain how plaque causes caries and show the patient their own radiographs. The dentist should explain that the patient is looking at decay and that the cause must be found so that the process can be arrested. It should be explained that only the patient can carry out this part of the treatment. The ability of the patient to understand their essential role in disease control greatly influences the prognosis.

Above all, the dentist must begin to determine the patient's wishes with respect to the caries problem. What efforts is the patient prepared to make in caries control? Fillings have an important role to play in restoring cavities and thus facilitating the patient's plaque control, but they are only part of the treatment. Direct questioning on attitudes may not be helpful, how-ever, because a patient may tend to answer a question in a way that 'pleases' the dentist. It can take a long time before the patient's attitudes are revealed. These attitudes are important in assessing prognosis and in logical and realistic treatment planning.

Why is the patient a caries risk?

The dentist needs to determine the relative importance of the various caries-promoting factors for the individual patient. Unless practitioner and patient can work together to find the cause of the problem, relevant solutions cannot be found. The involved patient begins to understand the relevance of the partnership approach and often enters into the detective work of determining the cause with admirable gusto.

The following should always be checked for their relative importance in the high risk patient:

- *Plaque control*: A disclosing agent should be used so that the patient can see the relationship between plaque and carious lesions.
- *Diet*: All patients designated as high risk should keep a diet sheet.
- *Fluoride history*: The fluoride content of the water, toothpaste, and any mouthwash the patient uses should be checked.
- *Salivary flow*: Stimulated salivary flow should be measured.

Some risk factors such as plaque control, diet, and fluoride use are amenable to alteration by the patient. Other risk factors, such as a dry mouth, are less amenable to alteration. For instance, a patient with Sjögren's syndrome will always be at high risk and will always have to make strenuous preventive efforts.

A dental practitioner is also unlikely to be able to modify or alleviate social deprivation in a particular patient but may be able to observe social factors change over time, sometimes for better and sometimes for worse.

Mechanical plaque control

Regular disturbance of the biofilm with a toothbrush and toothpaste containing fluoride will prevent the formation of visible lesions and will arrest lesions that have already formed. The dentist should check that the patient's toothpaste contains fluoride.

The dentist should show the patient the carious lesions and then disclose the teeth. This will demonstrate the relationship of the biofilm to the lesion. Now watch the patient in action with a toothbrush to remove the plaque, helping improve technique where necessary.

The patient should be encouraged to feel the shiny, plaque-free surface with their tongue with the aim of achieving this feel at home. The dentist should note whether the patient *can* remove plaque. If the patient *can* but *does not*, the problem is motivation, not manual dexterity.

With children, pay particular attention to the occlusal surface of erupting teeth. The erupting tooth is below the line of the arch and will be missed by the brush unless it is brought in at right angles to the arch. Remember an occlusal surface is most susceptible to plaque stagnation during eruption and teeth can take months or years to erupt. There is huge individual variation in eruption times. Molars take longer to erupt than premolars but within a specific tooth type there is great variation from person to person. The prevention programme must therefore be tailored to the needs of the individual. The patient and parent should be seen on regular recall until they are able to attend with the surface plaque-free after home cleaning. If this is consistently not achieved, consideration should be given to fissure sealing the surface with a resin to obliterate the groove fossa system, thus aiding plaque control.

Where a bitewing radiograph shows an approximal lesion in the outer enamel, the patient should be shown how to use dental floss.

Root surface lesions are just as amenable to control by mechanical plaque control as coronal lesions. Pay particular attention to the approximal surfaces of teeth next to a denture. Patients need to be shown how to angle the toothbrush to reach these areas or, alternatively, use strips of cotton gauze or cloth in a similar manner to flossing to remove the gross plaque from these hard-to-reach areas (Fig. 1.18).

Use of fluoride

The dentist should check that the patient is using a fluoride toothpaste. Some products formulated for sensitive teeth and some herbal toothpastes do not contain fluoride. The paste should be used twice daily and cleared from the mouth by spitting rather than vigorously rinsing. A fluoride mouthrinse (0.05% sodium fluoride) used every day is a useful fluoride supplement in a high risk patient, although the cost of the product may preclude its use by some patients.

Surgery application of fluoride varnish is a sensible preventive measure and particularly valuable in those unlikely to comply with a daily mouthwash regime.

Dietary advice

Dietary advice should be given based on a diet sheet. Figure 1.36 shows a diet sheet completed by a middle-aged patient with a high incidence of caries. The sugar attacks have been highlighted. Note the frequency of sugar intake. This gives the dentist the opportunity to explain the Stephan curve (Fig. 1.2) and the importance of decreasing the frequency of sugar intake. The dentist should try to get the patient to suggest changes. This approach helps the patient to set realistic goals and enables the dentist to see whether the relationship between diet and caries has been understood by the patient. The dentist should check that the main meals are adequate, and a list of foods that are safe for teeth may be helpful here. The negotiated dietary change should be recorded on paper so that the patient can take this away and ponder at leisure. The dentist should record the goals agreed in the notes so that specific enquiry can be made at the next visit. A reasonable aim for this patient would be to try to confine sugar to mealtimes.

Salivary flow

Salivary flow should be measured because a feeling of a dry mouth may be subjective rather than actual.

When the salivary glands are capable of secreting, chewing gum stimulates salivary flow. A chewing gum with an artificial sweetener (sorbitol or xylitol) should be chosen in preference to a sugar-containing gum. Of the two artificial sweeteners, xylitol seems the better as this product may suppress counts of some acidogenic micro-organisms.

Sometimes patients with a dry mouth suck sweets or sip sweet drinks to alleviate the problem. This is obviously very unwise in patients who are already at high risk to caries because they are short of saliva.

Operative treatment

The role of operative dentistry in the management of dental caries is to facilitate plaque control. Tooth restoration also restores:

- appearance
- form
- function.

Caries in pits and fissures

Uncavitated lesions can be controlled by mechanical plaque control with a fluoride-containing toothpaste. Where a patient cannot or will not remove plaque, a fissure sealant is a wise intervention to prevent plaque stagnation.

Cavitated lesions should be visible in dentine on a bitewing radiograph and should be treated operatively because the patient will be unable to clean plaque out of the hole in the tooth.

Approximal lesions

The diagnosis of cavitation was discussed on p. 14. Cavitated lesions need operative treatment because even the most fastidious of flossers cannot clean plaque out of the hole – the floss simply skates over the top.

In anterior teeth, approximal lesions may be unsightly because the demineralized dentine appears black or brown. This would be a reason to restore, even if no cavity was present.

Smooth surfaces and root caries

Many smooth surface lesions, including cavitated ones, can be arrested by preventive, non-operative treatment. Lesions which are plaque traps or unsightly should be restored.

Tooth wear

Tooth wear is defined as the surface loss of dental hard tissues other than by caries or trauma, and is sometimes called 'tooth surface loss' (TSL). This distinguishes it from early enamel caries that is characterized by *subsurface* loss of minerals beneath a relatively intact surface zone. The term 'tooth wear' is preferred to 'tooth surface loss' because it is easily understood by patients and because the extensively

	Thursday		Friday		Saturday		Sunday	
	Time	Item (8)	Time	Item (8)	Time	Item (8)	Time	Item (8)
Before breakfast	7.30	Tea*	7.0	Tea*	7.30	Tea*	7.05	Tea*
Breakfast	8.00	2 Wheat slices 2 Crispbread 1 Apple Coffee*	8.00	2 Wheat slices 2 Crisp bread 1 Apple Coffee*	8.30	2 Wheat slices 2 Crispbread 1 Apple Coffee*	8.05	2 Wheat slices 2 Crispbread 1 Apple Coffee*
Morning	9.00	Polo	10.00 11.30	Murray mint Tea* Biscuit	11.15	Tea*	10.00 12.30	Lemon Barley Tea*
Mid-day Meal	12.30	Meat roll Tea*	2.00	Steamed fish Parsley sauce Boiled potatoes	1.45	Sausage, onion, Boiled potatoes Ice Cream, tinned fruit	1.40	Roast lamb, potatoes, cabbage carrots
Afternoon	2.00 5.30	2 Cream crackers 1 Dairy Lea Tea* 2 Shortbread biscuits Tea*	2.45 6.00	Tea* Tea*	2.30 5.45	Tea* Tea*	2.00 4.00	Tea* Tea*
Evening Meal	8.00	Chop, leeks, boiled potatoes Choc-ice Tea*	8.30	Bacon sandwich Tea*	7.30	Fried kipper bread and butter	8.15	Ham salad, bread and butter Tea*
Evening and night	1.00	Horlicks* Biscuits	10.00 1.30	Peanuts Horlicks* Biscuit	9.15 1.45	Chocolate Horlicks* Biscuits	1.15	Horlicks* Biscuits

Fig. 1.36 A diet sheet completed by a middle-aged patient with a high incidence of caries. The frequent sweet drinks, sweets, and the pre-bed sweet drink and snack are a potential cause of caries in this mouth. Note the frequency of sugar intake – eight times per day.

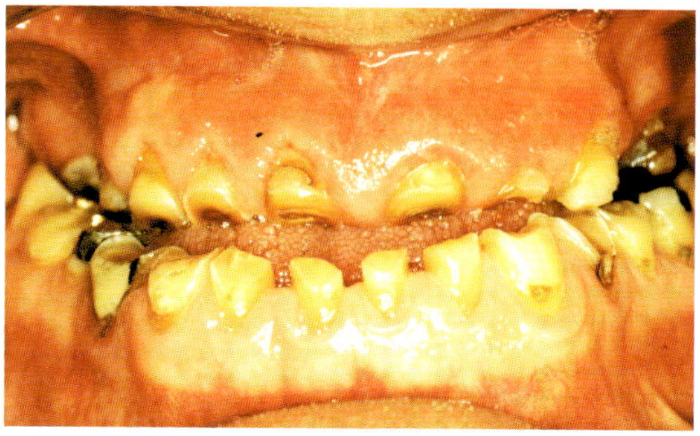

Fig. 1.37 Extensive wear.

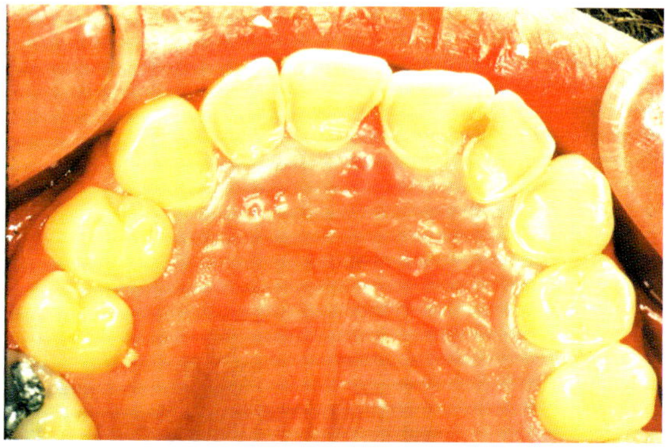

(a)

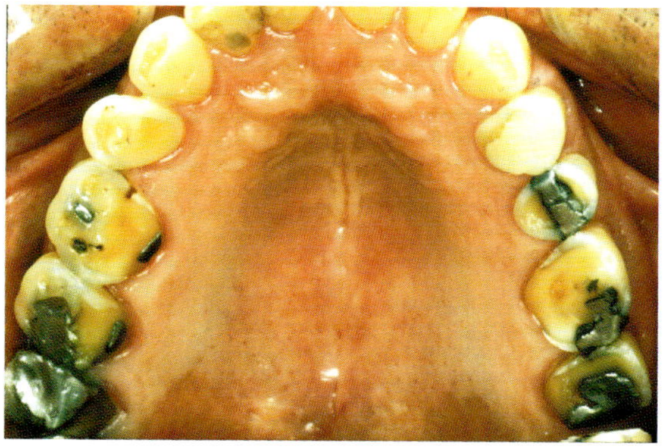

(b)

Fig. 1.38 (a) Regurgitation erosion affecting the palatal surfaces of the upper incisor and premolar teeth. This was due, in this case, to bulimia nervosa. The patients commonly overeat and then deliberately vomit in an attempt to maintain a low body weight.
(b) Posterior teeth with severe palatal erosion, particularly of the first molar teeth. The patient was a chronic alcoholic.

worn teeth lose a good deal more than just their surface (Fig. 1.37).

Tooth wear occurs naturally throughout life and so it is common to find moderate degrees of wear in older people. What is remarkable is that they do not wear more. Enamel is one of the few tissues in the body that does not regenerate or replace itself in the way that skin, blood cells, and fractured bones do. Fortunately, the dentine does show some reparative mechanisms insofar that reactionary or reparative dentine will be laid down in the pulp chamber as a response to tooth wear, even though it cannot of course replace itself once worn away from an exposed surface in the mouth. Teeth are in use every day and it is an impressive feat of nature that in most patients they do not wear out, even after several decades of use.

However, sometimes the wear becomes excessive as a result of one or more of the following causes: erosion, attrition, and abrasion.

Erosion

This is defined as the loss of dental hard tissue as a result of a chemical process not involving bacteria. The chemical is acid and the source is either regurgitated stomach acid or acid from the diet.

Regurgitated acid is the most common cause of erosion and causes the most damage. Previously dentists thought that dietary erosion was the most common. This is because it is easy to take a dietary history from a patient and they are likely to be truthful about their diet. In contrast, many of the conditions which cause regurgitation erosion are embarrassing and some patients do not readily talk about them. These include eating disorders (Fig. 1.38a), chronic alcoholism (Fig. 1.38b), and even the less polite symptoms of indigestion. Some patients suffer from gastro-oesophageal reflux disease (GORD), which can cause dental erosion, and yet they have no other symptoms other than their tooth wear. Gastroenterologists call these patients 'silent refluxers' and they can be identified by tests carried out by these specialists. There is also a group of patients who voluntarily regurgitate their stomach contents, chew, and then swallow. These ruminants may be embarrassed to admit to a habit that is natural to them but others may find strange. The dental devastation is extreme.

Although regurgitation usually first affects the palatal surfaces, it often also causes strange unexplained cupped-out lesions in molar teeth, starting with the tips of cusps (Fig. 1.39).

Dietary acid does produce erosion but it is not entirely clear that this is always the result of the acid entering the mouth and contacting the teeth. In some cases there may be a secondary effect, particularly with fizzy drinks which introduce gas into the stomach which, in turn, comes back into the mouth carrying not only the acidic fizzy drink but also the stomach acid.

In chronic alcoholic patients there is good evidence that the alcohol produces damage to the stomach lining, which in turn results in regurgitation of acid. Therefore it is the acid coming back rather than the alcohol itself which causes the erosion (Fig. 1.38b).

In the past, industrial acids in the form of vapour or droplets in the air caused dental erosion and this was investi-

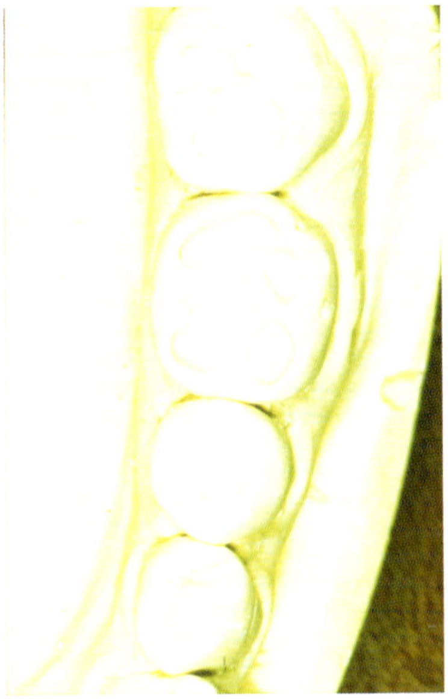

Fig. 1.39 Cupped-out erosion lesions on the occlusal surfaces of another patient with an eating disorder.

gated in car battery manufacturers and other industrial processes. As a result of these investigations, health and safety legislation to prevent exposure to industrial acid was introduced in most countries: consequently, industrial erosion is now very rarely seen.

Attrition

This is defined as mechanical wear between opposing teeth (Fig. 1.40) and commonly occurs in combination with erosion. By definition, attrition can only be present on contacting occlusal or incisal surfaces, or surfaces that were once in contact. Where erosion and attrition coexist, some areas of the worn occlusal surface may not make contact in any mandibular excursion. This pattern shows that attrition cannot be entirely responsible for the tooth wear and that an erosive element must also be present (Fig. 1.41).

The physical effect of food wearing the tooth surface is not well understood, but it is thought to have little effect in contemporary diets in Western countries. It may be of more relevance in particularly abrasive diets (e.g. some vegetarians).

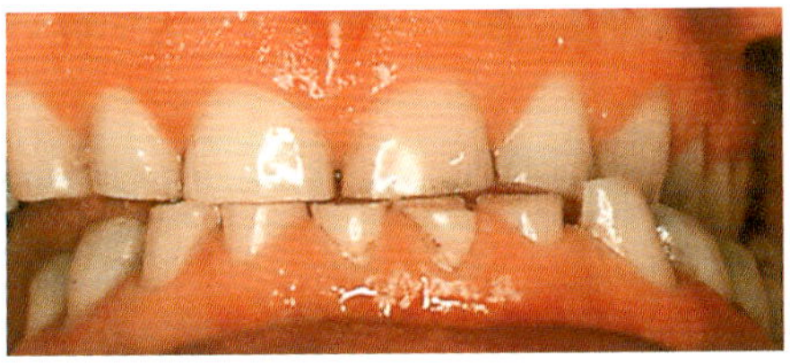

Fig. 1.40 Attrition. The patient is making a right lateral excursion of the mandible and the upper and lower teeth fit well together at this point. It is likely that the patient bruxes in this position at night. Note also that the upper and lower teeth are worn by approximately the same amount.

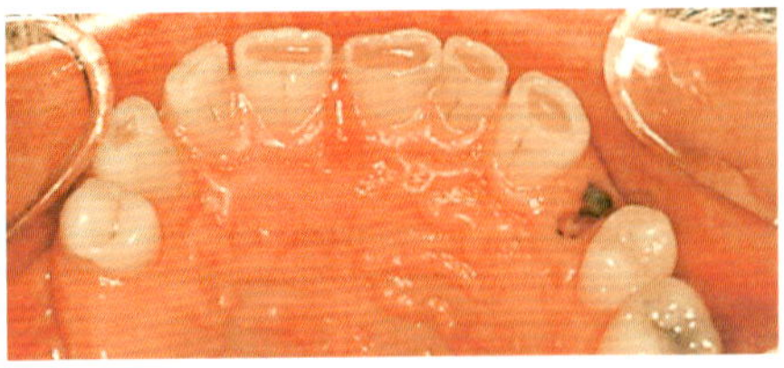

Fig. 1.41 Incisal wear which is the result of a combination of erosion and attrition. The incisal edges are cupped out and do not make contact with the opposing teeth in any excursion of the mandible.

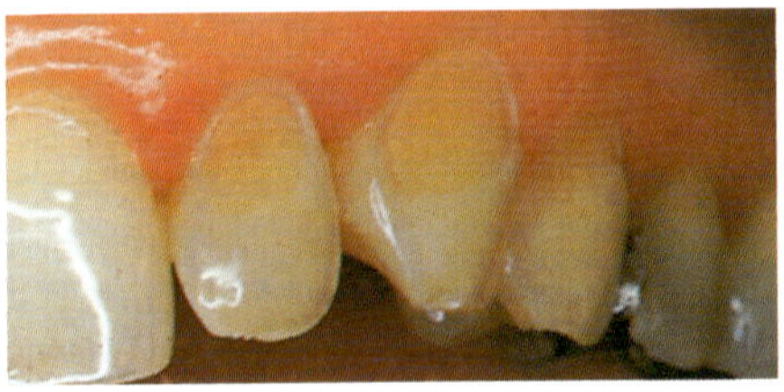

(a)

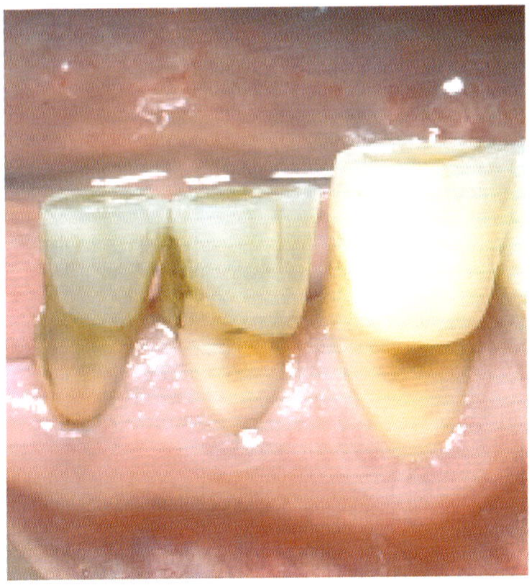

(b)

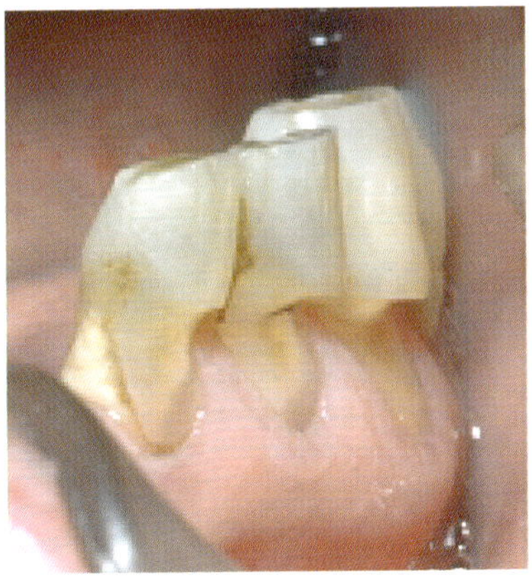

(c)

Fig. 1.42 (a) Dish-shaped abrasion–erosion lesions. Large areas of dentine are exposed at the base of saucer-shaped lesions.
(b) and (c) V-shaped notch lesions which occur at the necks of teeth. Note also that all the enamel surfaces have been worn smooth.

Abrasion

This is the wearing away of tooth substance by mechanical means other than by opposing teeth, such as holding a pipe or perhaps over-vigorous toothbrushing. It is easy to understand how tooth tissue softened by acid is particularly susceptible to such wear, and it can be difficult to make a clear distinction between erosion and abrasion. Abrasion–erosion lesions commonly present buccally at the cervical margin, and are either dish-shaped (Fig. 1.42a) or in the form of a sharp V-shaped notch (Fig. 1.42b and c). The reason for these two distinctly different presentations is not known.

The V-shaped notches of the necks of teeth involving both enamel and dentine are sometimes called 'abfraction lesions' and some dentists believe that these are caused by the tooth flexing under occlusal forces, especially in lateral excursive movements. However, there is no reliable scientific evidence of this. The aetiology remains a mystery.

Summary of the causes of tooth wear

These are set out in Fig. 1.43.

Acceptable and pathological levels of tooth wear

It is normal for teeth to wear, but the process is regarded as pathological if they become so worn that they function ineffectively or seriously mar appearance. The distinction between acceptable and pathological tooth wear at a given age is based on a prediction as to whether the tooth will survive that rate of wear in a functional and reasonable aesthetic state until the end of the patient's normal lifespan.

Consequences of pathological tooth wear

There are several important clinical features that can result from pathological tooth wear. These include the following:

- exposure of dentine on buccal or lingual surfaces normally covered by enamel (Fig. 1.38)
- notched cervical surfaces (Fig. 1.42b and c)
- exposure of dentine on incisal or occlusal surfaces – further erosion often results in preferential loss of dentine to produce a cupped surface (Fig. 1.39)
- restorations (which do not erode) left projecting above the tooth surface
- exposure of reparative dentine or pulp
- wear producing sensitivity
- pulpitis and loss of vitality attributable to tooth wear
- wear in one arch more than in the other
- inability to make contact between worn incisal or occlusal surfaces in any excursion of the mandible.

Some of these features require operative intervention to protect the pulp, reduce sensitivity, and improve appearance or function. However, restorations will not prevent further wear. Just as with dental caries, restoration can temporarily replace the lost tooth surface but wear will continue on any tooth surface exposed around the restoration if the cause is not identified and prevented.

Diagnosing and monitoring tooth wear

It is relatively easy to diagnose that teeth are worn, provided that they are viewed clean and dry. Differentiating between acceptable and pathological levels of wear can be more difficult because the decision depends on the age of the patient. Also, a single examination will not show whether the wear is static or progressing, nor the speed of any progression.

Where a pathological rate of tooth wear is suspected, study models taken at six-monthly or yearly intervals will determine the rate of progression and the effectiveness of preventive measures. If these measures are not entirely successful, the series of models will help to decide if and when to intervene operatively.

Assessing the aetiology

Finding the cause of tooth wear can be very difficult, but a careful sympathetic history is helpful. Many of these patients have conditions which they find difficult or embarrassing to discuss, such as eating disorders – bulimia nervosa and anorexia nervosa – or chronic alcoholism. Bulimia nervosa is a variation of anorexia nervosa in which the patient deliberately vomits repeatedly (often between 2 and 30 times a day) in an attempt to control body weight. Eating habits are bizarre and compulsive, and the patients tend to be secretive about them and do not regard themselves as ill. The repeated vomiting often causes very rapid erosion, occasionally so fast that vital pulps are exposed.

Chronic alcoholism causes a chronic gastritis which in turn produces dental erosion in some patients, even without recurrent frank vomiting.

The history might include questions on the following topics.

RELATING TO EROSION

- Past and present diet, including questions on a series of food and drink items known to cause dietary erosion (Fig. 1.44).
- Digestive disorders which may produce a regurgitation erosion, including pregnancy sickness.
- Past and present slimming habits, including any tendency to anorexic or bulimic behaviour.
- Weight loss and cessation of periods in women that might be indicative of anorexia nervosa.

Erosion (most common and most damaging)

Regurgitation erosion
Commonly affects the palatal surfaces of upper anterior teeth and the occlusal and buccal surfaces of lower posterior teeth. Caused by the regurgitation of hydrochloric acid from the stomach in patients with:

- various digestive disorders, including hiatus hernia and chronic indigestion
- anorexia and bulimia nervosa
- chronic alcoholism
- morning sickness associated with pregnancy
- voluntary regurgitation.

Dietary erosion
Commonly affects the labial surfaces of upper anterior teeth. Caused by an excess of food and drink with a low pH, including:

- citrus (and other) fruit and fruit juices (citric acid)
- pickles and other food and drink containing vinegar (acetic acid)
- carbonated drinks (carbonic and sometimes other acids).

Industrial erosion
Commonly affects the labial surfaces of the upper anterior teeth and may cause pitting. Caused by industrial processes which produce acid fumes or droplets. Workers should be adequately protected against this and the condition is only rarely seen nowadays.

Attrition

Physical wear of one tooth against another. Affects the incisal edges and occlusal surfaces of opposing teeth. May be accelerated by erosion or may be caused entirely by bruxism or other parafunctional activities.

Abrasion

Commonly affects the neck of the buccal surfaces of both anterior and posterior teeth. The aetiology is not clear, but some dentists believe that it is caused by physical wear from external agents such as:

- abrasive toothpastes and powders (e.g. smokers tooth powder)
- hard toothbrushes or the excessive use of other tooth-cleaning aids
- habits such as thread biting and pipe smoking that can cause wear in the form of notches in the incisal edges

Fig. 1.43 The most common causes of tooth wear.

Name .... Number .... Sex M F
Address .... Tel no ....
.... Occupation ....
.... Work place ....
Interests, hobbies, sport activities ....
Medication ....
Illness present .... Illness past ....
Has the illness been treated .... By a doctor .... In hospital ....

GASTRIC SYMPTOMS	PAST SYMPTOMS			NO	PRESENT SYMPTOMS		
	Frequency per week	Frequency per day	Duration		Frequency per week	Frequency per day	Duration
Belching							
Heartburn							
Acid taste in the mouth							
Vomiting							
Regurgitation ? chew cud							
Stomach ache							
Gastric pain on awakening							
How does the patient treat gastric pain?							
DIET	PAST CONSUMPTION			NO	PRESENT CONSUMPTION		
	Frequency per week	Frequency per day	Duration		Frequency per week	Frequency per day	Duration
Citrus fruits							
Citrus fruit juice							
Other juices							
Special juices							
Sport drinks							
Fruit berries							
Soft drinks, acidic beverages							
Yoghurt							
Vitamin-C drinks, chewable tablets							
Acid sweets							
Special diet							
Vinegar							
Herb tea							
Pickles							
Other acidic food, etc.							
Alcohol							

Fig. 1.44 An *aide-mémoire* for use when taking a history relating to erosion.

- Alcohol intake.
- Past and present medical history and medication, including vitamin C, iron preparations, and hydrochloric acid for achlorhydria.
- The patient's present and past occupation relevant to industrial erosion.

Figure 1.44 provides a useful *aide-mémoire* for the inexperienced clinician who finds the variety and complexity of the questions a lot to remember.

RELATING TO ATTRITION

- Clenching and grinding habits. Has a sleeping partner heard grinding noises?
- Periods of stress or anxiety.
- Other habits, including pipe smoking, opening hair-grips, and biting thread.
- Has the patient a 'square jaw' with over-developed muscles?

RELATING TO ABRASION

- Oral hygiene techniques, including past and present use of abrasive tooth-cleaning techniques and materials.
- Habits which might abrade teeth, such as pipe smoking.

On the basis of the answers to these questions it may be possible to define the aetiology as one of the following:

- dietary erosion
- regurgitation erosion
- industrial erosion
- attrition
- abrasion
- combined aetiology (try to assess the importance of each aetiological factor)
- aetiology not determined.

Preventing tooth wear

Prevention clearly depends primarily on making an accurate diagnosis of the cause. Some erosive causes, once identified, are easy to prevent, others are more difficult.

When the problem is gastro-oesophageal reflux disease or a milder form of indigestion then the condition can sometimes be controlled by prescribed medication or over-the-counter remedies. Patients with eating disorders are more difficult to treat successfully. Often the condition lasts for a few years and then burns itself out. The dental management should be to monitor and maintain and preferably not to provide too much interventive treatment unless there are strong indications, until after the condition has resolved: e.g. the cupped-out lesions shown in Fig. 1.39 do not usually cause sensitivity or problems with function or appearance. If they are filled without preventing the cause then further erosion will often continue around the margins of the fillings or elsewhere on the tooth. Some patients may have 30 or 40 such lesions affecting all their occlusal surfaces and maintaining the restorations involves extensive treatment for which there is very little justification. An exception to this principle might be the use of adhesive composite restorations to support fragile enamel margins, especially where these have an impact on the patient's appearance.

Attrition due to nocturnal bruxism may be helped by occlusal adjustment to remove interferences which trigger the grinding, and in other cases an acrylic bite plane is provided for use at night. This may reduce the grinding habit and will absorb the wear, with the acrylic being replaced periodically.

Abrasion may be prevented by changing the abrasive activity, for instance:

- the brushing method
- the brushing frequency (no more than twice per day)
- the toothpaste used.

The management of tooth wear

Unlike early caries, tooth wear is an irreversible process. Management should have the objective of maintaining a functional comfortable dentition of good appearance for life, so the emphasis should be on prevention and monitoring in the early stages, avoiding the temptation of placing restorations until they are necessary. They become necessary only when the patient becomes concerned about the appearance, or the teeth become sensitive, or the dentist becomes concerned about physical changes such as changes in occlusal vertical dimension or pulp exposure. If restorations are placed while the wear is progressing, particularly with erosion, they may accelerate rather than slow down the rate of wear in the surrounding tooth tissue. In advanced cases, crowns are required.

Trauma

While caries and tooth wear are diseases of slow onset, traumatic injuries are acquired suddenly, and when these involve the hard dental tissues and the pulp they usually require immediate operative management. Trauma to the mouth can produce these local injuries:

- lacerations to the lips, tongue, and gingival tissue
- alveolar fractures, so that a number of teeth become mobile within a block of bone
- complete or partial subluxation of a tooth
- root fracture
- damage to the apical blood vessels without fracture
- fracture of the crown of the tooth involving enamel alone, enamel and dentine, or exposure of the pulp.

These injuries can, of course, occur in combination. Only the last one listed will be discussed in detail here.

Aetiology of trauma

Trauma is commonly caused by the following:

- falls

- sports or athletics
- blows from foreign bodies
- fights
- car or bicycle accidents
- injuries during convulsive seizures (e.g. epilepsy)
- battered child syndrome (the most difficult and yet the most important to diagnose).

Examination and diagnosis of dental injury

When other injuries have also been sustained, particularly head injuries, these must be investigated and dealt with before detailed examination and treatment of the dental injury. When this has been done a careful history of the accident as it relates to the teeth must be recorded, together with any symptoms such as pain, fracture, or loosening of teeth.

An examination must be made for any extra-oral wounds and injuries to the mucosa and gingivae. The crowns of the teeth are examined for fractures, pulp exposure, and colour changes. Displacement or looseness of teeth should be noted, together with abnormalities of the occlusion.

The vitality of the injured and adjacent (and usually the opposing) teeth must be tested (see Chapter 2) and periapical radiographs must always be taken to look for root fracture. Where fractures of the maxilla or mandible are suspected, further radiographs of the facial skeleton will be required. Where teeth are fractured and the inside of the lips is lacerated, radiographs should be taken of the soft tissues to check that fragments of teeth are not present.

At subsequent recall visits the colour of the tooth and further vitality tests and periapical radiographs will show whether the pulp has remained vital or not. If the tooth begins to discolour (Fig. 1.45), this is a sign that the pulp has died and it should be removed immediately to prevent the risk of acute infection and further discoloration.

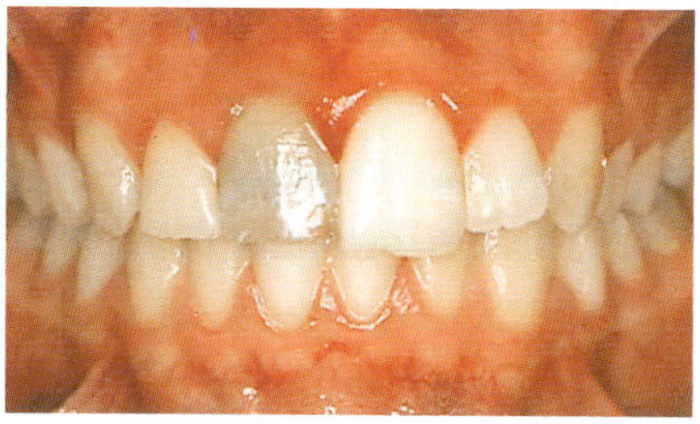

Fig. 1.45 A discoloured upper right central incisor resulting from a necrotic untreated pulp.

Management of trauma to the teeth

Where enamel is crazed or slightly chipped either no treatment or simply smoothing the enamel may be all that is required. However, the vitality of such teeth should be checked periodically and new periapical radiographs taken to look for signs of pulp death.

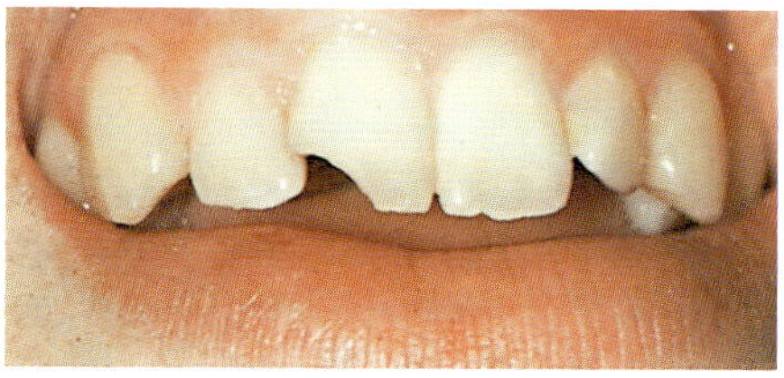

Fig. 1.46 A fractured incisor involving enamel and dentine, but not the pulp. (By courtesy of Mr P. Longhurst.)

Where fracture of enamel and dentine has occurred (Fig. 1.46) the exposed dentine is often very sensitive to hot, cold, and sweet stimuli, and the patient's appearance may be affected. Usually, a tooth-coloured composite restoration is required at once (with a suitable lining to protect the pulp) to restore appearance (see Chapter 10). Again, the tooth must be checked for vitality and periapical radiographs taken periodically.

Where the fracture has exposed the pulp it is often necessary to remove the pulp tissue, as pulp necrosis is likely to occur. In young teeth with incompletely formed apices only the coronal pulp tissue is removed (pulpotomy) and a calcium hydroxide dressing is placed on the remaining pulpal tissue so that the apex can continue to form. The crown of the tooth is restored with tooth-coloured composite. Radiographs are taken to monitor the formation of the apex and a root canal filling is placed when the apex is complete.

Teeth which have become discoloured following trauma can be bleached after root filling (see Chapter 10). If this is not successful, the buccal surface can be veneered with composite or porcelain (see Chapter 10), or a crown can be made.

The management of root fractures, tooth extrusions, avulsions, and intrusions is beyond the scope of this book.

Developmental defects

Teeth do not always develop normally, and there are a number of defects in tooth structure or shape which occur during development and become apparent on eruption. Such teeth are often unsightly or prone to excessive tooth wear, and thus they may require restoration to improve appearance or function or to protect the underlying tooth structure.

Acquired developmental conditions

Enamel hypoplasia and hypomineralization

Ameloblasts are specialized cells that are vulnerable to the effects of generalized systemic conditions such as the infectious diseases of childhood. Alternatively, they may be damaged by adverse local conditions such as trauma to, or infection of, a deciduous predecessor.

The usual consequence of damage to the ameloblasts is the formation of either hypoplastic or hypomineralized enamel.

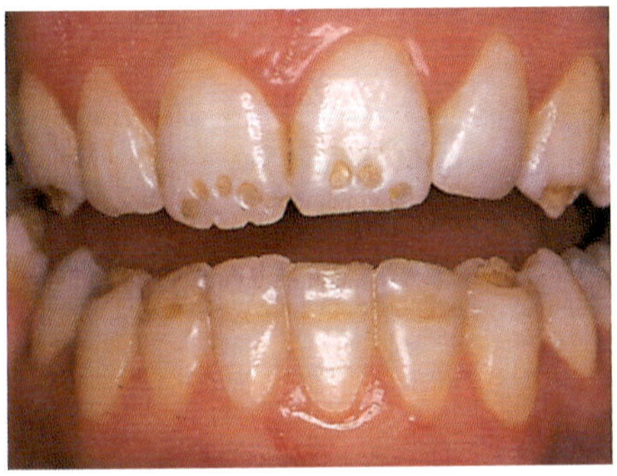

Fig. 1.47 Hypoplastic enamel in a patient who had a severe childhood illness. The pitted enamel is symmetrically distributed and occurs at the point on the tooth which was developing at the time of the illness.

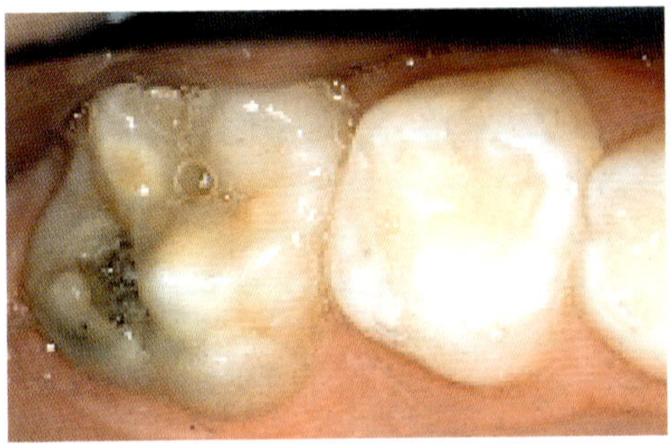

Fig. 1.49 A yellow–brown area of opaque hypomineralized enamel on a first molar. The disto-palatal fissure shows severely hypomineralized, broken enamel with demarcated opacities at the cavity border (by courtesy of Dr K. Weerheijm).

Hypoplastic enamel results from the production of a reduced amount of matrix which matures normally; thus, the enamel is pitted or thin but of normal hardness (Fig. 1.47).

Hypomineralized enamel results when a normal amount of matrix fails to achieve full mineralization. The affected enamel has a normal shape and thickness but has an opaque chalky-white appearance (Fig. 1.48).

The degree of hypoplasia or hypomineralization that results from a systemic disturbance reflects its severity, timing, and duration. Consequently, systemic disturbances usually affect multiple teeth, and the position of the enamel defect corresponds to the enamel formed at the time of the disturbance. The majority of systemic disturbances last only a few weeks and for this reason the defect takes the form of a narrow horizontal band around the affected crown or crowns. Since all the developing crowns are affected, the resulting lesions are bilaterally symmetrical.

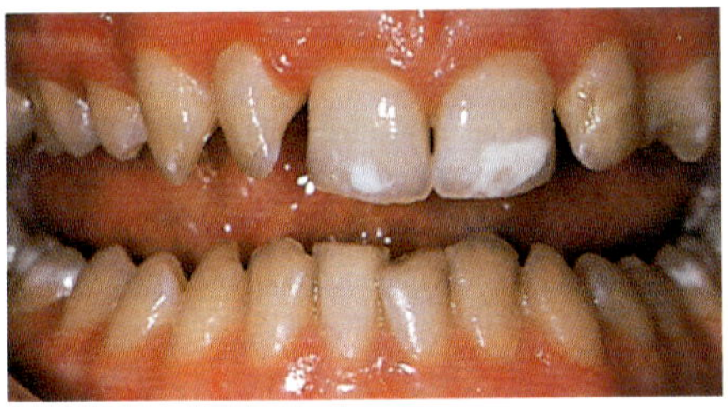

Fig. 1.48 Hypomineralized enamel on the labial surfaces of upper central incisors.

Molar–incisor hypomineralization

This is a specific and rather prevalent hypomineralization defect affecting the occlusal surface of first permanent molars. Between one and four molars may be affected and the defects range from white–yellow or yellow–brown demarcated opacities to severely hypomineralized, broken enamel (Fig. 1.49). The hypomineralized enamel can be chipped off easily leading to unprotected dentine, plaque stagnation, and rapid caries development. This loss of enamel can occur immediately after eruption or under masticatory forces. The affected teeth can be very sensitive to drying, and hot and cold stimulae and mechanical stimulae, such as toothbrushing, may cause toothache.

Lesions may also occur in the upper incisors and, more rarely, the lower incisors. The more molars affected, the more likely the incisors will also show opacities. This particular localization of defects indicates that a systemic defect is responsible. The upset would occur during the first years of the child's life, when the crowns of the first molars and incisors are mineralizing. The precise cause of the defect is not known but several causes may be responsible, including:

- breast-feeding (milk dioxin)
- respiratory diseases
- oxygen shortage of ameloblasts
- high-fever diseases.

Generalized intrinsic enamel stain

Two substances which may be ingested during tooth formation are of particular importance; these are the fluoride ion and the drug tetracycline.

DENTAL FLUOROSIS

Dental fluorosis may occur when the total daily intake of the fluoride ion from sources such as water, toothpaste, drops, and tablets is high while the enamel is undergoing pre-eruption formation and maturation. It may be seen as a number of chalky-white flecks or confluent blotches and brown discoloration sometimes accompanied by pitting of the enamel (Fig. 1.50). Most severe cases are seen in areas

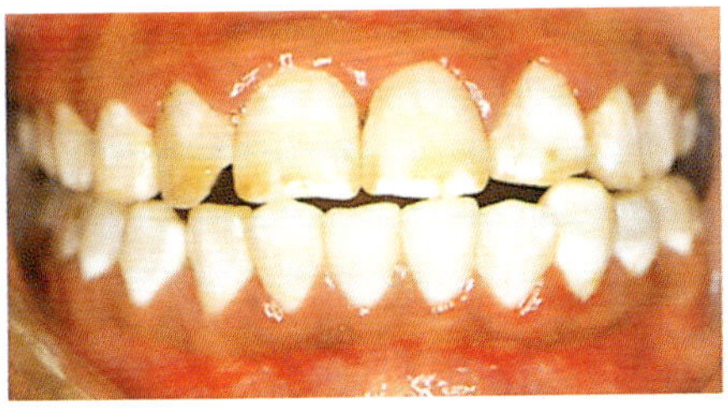

Fig. 1.50 Enamel fluorosis resulting in white mottling of all the teeth and brown discoloration of the upper incisor teeth.

where the fluoride content of the natural water supply is high, such as parts of Africa and India.

TETRACYCLINE STAINING

Tetracycline staining is a cause of tooth discoloration which should never happen. This group of broad-spectrum antibiotics has an affinity for calcified tissue. It can cross the placental barrier to affect the deciduous teeth. If the drug is taken by infants and young children the developing permanent teeth will usually be discoloured (Fig. 1.51). If tetracycline staining is to be avoided, this group of drugs should not be administered in pregnancy or to children under 12 years. There are effective alternatives to tetracycline and the medical profession has been informed for many years about the dental consequences of prescribing tetracycline. So there should no longer be this problem, but, sadly, cases do still occur occasionally, especially from parts of the world where antibiotics are freely available without prescription.

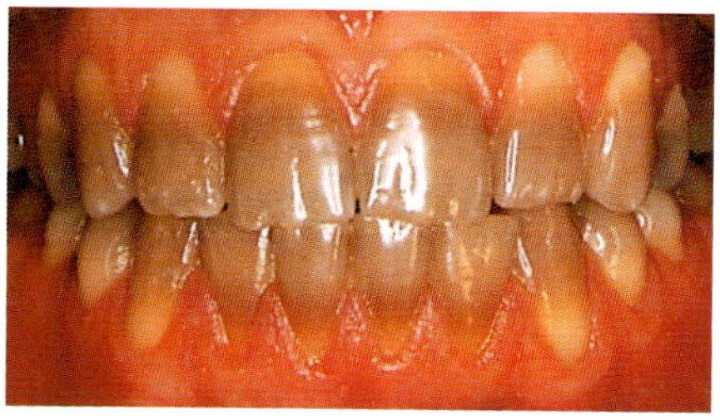

Fig. 1.51 Severe tetracycline stain. Note the horizontal banding which does not appear to be related to the stage of development of the tooth at which the drug was administered.

Treatment of developmental defects

Because many of these conditions do not progress, the treatment can often be deferred until the patient is concerned about the appearance. The aim of treatment is almost entirely cosmetic, but no less important for that. Where molar hypomineralization results in chipping of the enamel and plaque stagnation, a restoration may be needed so that the patient can clean.

Bleaching may be effective in some cases of tetracycline stain, but in most cases composite restorations or veneers of composite or porcelain, often with little or no tooth preparation, are the treatment of choice. Crowns may be necessary in the most severe cases.

Hereditary conditions

The inherited conditions which may result in defects in tooth number, shape, size, or structure are hypodontia, microdontia, amelogenesis imperfecta, and dentinogenesis imperfecta. Fortunately the two last conditions are rare.

Hypodontia, microdontia

Hypodontia (sometimes known as oligodontia) is a condition, usually with a strong family history, in which some teeth do not form at all. It may be associated with microdontia, where some teeth are abnormal in shape or size (Fig. 1.52). However, the enamel is normal in texture and colour. Third molars, upper and lower second premolars, and upper lateral incisor teeth are the most commonly affected. Of the three, the upper lateral incisor teeth, and other incisors and canines where they are affected, are the most important to the operative dentist. In hypodontia it may be necessary to alter the shape of adjacent teeth by restorations or crowns, with or without preparatory orthodontic treatment, to improve the patient's appearance. In microdontia it is often possible to alter the shape of the affected teeth.

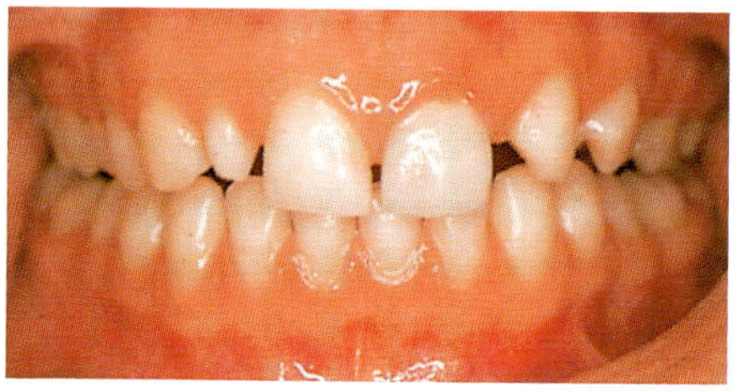

Fig. 1.52 Microdontia of the upper right lateral incisor (a peg-shaped lateral). The upper left lateral incisor tooth is missing (hypodontia). This peg-shaped lateral incisor could be built up using composite (Chapter 10) or a porcelain veneer (Chapter 11).

Amelogenesis imperfecta

This is a condition associated with extensive abnormalities of enamel formation. At least two different clinical patterns are recognized.

Generalized hypoplasia of the enamel involves a defect of matrix formation, although the matrix present appears normally mineralized. In its severe form the defect results in thin enamel with teeth appearing yellow because the underlying dentine shows through. Another form of the defect presents as a granular or pitted enamel surface which may pick up stain (Fig. 1.53).

In contrast, *generalized hypomineralization* of the enamel involves a normal amount of matrix formation, but its subsequent maturation is faulty and incomplete. The quantity

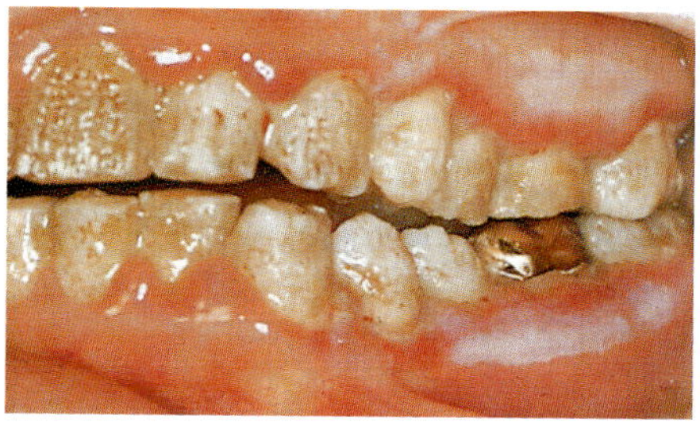

Fig. 1.53 Amelogenesis imperfecta. Not only is the enamel deeply pitted and stained in this 16-year-old girl but there is considerable gingival inflammation resulting from very poor oral hygiene. There are two reasons for the poor oral hygiene: the pitted teeth are very difficult to clean, but, perhaps more importantly, because the patient was so unhappy about her dental appearance it was very difficult to persuade her to take trouble over cleaning them. Nevertheless crowns were provided and her appearance and oral hygiene both improved dramatically.

of the enamel is normal but the tissue is frequently soft, friable, and easily lost. This enamel may appear stained and darkened or dull and chalky-white.

Dentinogenesis imperfecta

There is deficient formation of dentine and the condition is characterized by a brown opalescent discoloration of the teeth, which are prone to early fracture and excessive wear (Fig. 1.54). Radiographs typically show pulpal obliteration and shortened roots with small bulbous crowns. The treatment of this condition is beyond the scope of this book.

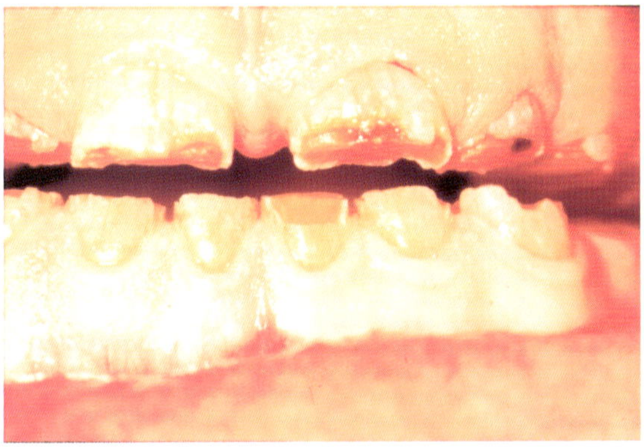

Fig. 1.54 Dentinogenesis imperfecta.

Further reading

Andreasen, J. O. and Andreasen, F. M. (1990). *Essentials of traumatic injuries to the teeth.* Munksgaard, Copenhagen.

Bartlett, D. W. and Smith, B. G. N. (1996). The dental relevance of gastro-oesophageal reflux. *Dent. Update.* **23**, 205–8, 250–3.

Fejerskov, O. and Kidd, E.A.M. (2003) *Dental caries.* Blackwell Munksgcard, Oxford.

Kidd, E. A. M. and Joyston-Bechal, S. (1996). *Essentials of dental caries.* Oxford Medical Publications, Oxford.

Kidd, E. A. M. and Smith, B. G. N. (1993). Toothwear histories: a sensitive issue. *Dent. Update.* **20**, 174–8.

Smith, B. G. N. (1991). Some facets of tooth wear. *Ann. R. Aust. Coll. Dent. Surg.* **11**, 37–51.

Smith, B. G. N. and Knight, J. K. (1984). A comparison of patterns of tooth wear. *Br. Dent. J.* **157**, 16–19.

Smith, B. G. N. and Knight, J. K. (1984). An index for measuring the wear of teeth. *Br. Dent. J.* **156**, 435–8.

Weerheijm, K. L., Jälevik, B. and Alaluusua, S. (2001). Molar–incisal hypomineralization. *Caries Res.* **35**, 390–1.

Winter, G. B. and Rapp, R. (1979). *A colour atlas of clinical conditions in paedodontics,* pp. 147–94. Wolfe Medical Publications, London.

2

Making clinical decisions

Who makes the decisions?
- Professionalism
- Large and small decisions

The four main decisions
- Diagnosis
- Prognosis
- Treatment options
- Further preventive measures

The information needed to make decisions and how it is collected and recorded
- History
- Examination
- Examination of specific areas of the mouth
- Detailed charts
- Special tests

The history and examination process

Planning the treatment

Some common decisions which have to be made
- Diagnosing toothache
- Whether to restore or attempt to arrest a moderate-size carious lesion and whether to restore or monitor an erosive lesion
- Whether to extract or root treat a tooth
- Which restorative material to use

Making clinical decisions

Who makes the decisions?

Gone are the days when most patients attended their dentist or other professional adviser, sought and accepted their advice without question, and felt almost detached from the process. Although patients used to do things 'under doctor's orders', many now take a much more lively interest in the management of their own health. Indeed, without this involvement by the patient, the preventive measures described in Chapter 1 would be impossible. Along with this involvement, which many patients seek and which should be encouraged in those who do not, comes a responsibility for participating in decisions about their own welfare. In the final analysis, it is patients who will decide whether they will attend for treatment, whether they will clean their teeth effectively, and what sacrifices of time, effort, and finance they are prepared to make.

A dentist's role is to offer advice and, if the advice is accepted, provide treatment. This advice can usually be classified as follows:

- diagnosis
- prognosis
- treatment options
- prevention of further disease.

These matters will be dealt with in more detail shortly, but first it is necessary to understand the nature and status of this professional advice.

Professionalism

The professional–client relationship is special in that professional people take upon themselves the duty of setting their clients' interests above their own. It is this aspect of professionalism which engenders trust in patients and explains why they so often accept the advice of the dentist. Once this professional relationship begins to break down, as it does if the dentist puts their own interests before that of the patient, then the patient's confidence is lost and they begin to mistrust the dentist's advice. This is quite different from the shared involvement in the management of a condition such as dental caries or tooth wear as described in Chapter 1.

Dental patients, along with many other sectors of society, are becoming more inclined to complain when things go wrong. There is an increasing tendency to believe that when problems arise it must be someone's 'fault', and when the person (in this case the dentist) can be identified they are not only likely to receive a complaint but increasingly the patient will initiate legal action against the dentist to recover financial damages and costs. In the decade 1992 to 2001, claims against dentists in the UK, dealt with by a large protection organization, increased by an average of 13.6% per annum (225% over the 10-year period) and the cost of settling the successful claims increased by 7.7% per annum.

Students starting work on patients should pay attention to what they are being taught on the ethical and legal relationships between clinicians and patients and should learn from the examples of their teachers. This is not the place to elaborate on this teaching but students should start by understanding two important terms used by lawyers. These are 'a duty of care' and 'informed consent'.

The dentist has not only the general duty of care to everybody they come into contact with but also a professional duty of care as outlined above. Many legal cases hinge on whether the dentist has complied with this professional duty.

'Informed consent' means that the patients must be given sufficient information to understand what is being proposed, the probable outcome, and their own responsibilities for prevention and maintenance before they can properly agree to the treatment. Again, 'informed consent' or lack of it is a common issue in legal cases.

However, as a dental student, do not be unduly frightened by this. Your dental school is responsible for the patients you treat and will deal with the legal aspects of any complaints and litigation, although you do have an ethical responsibility for the care of your patients. Once you qualify, the professional indemnity organizations will help you with these matters. Despite this help, complaints and legal cases are very upsetting and time-consuming: dentists should do all they can to avoid them, not only in the patients' interests but also in their own.

In order to give advice the dentist will need information, and a large part of this chapter is taken up with describing what this information might be and how it should be collected and collated. In some cases this information alone will be enough to enable the dentist to give advice and take a decision. However, in many cases another element – *judgement* – will need to be applied. If all diagnosis and treatment planning were straightforward, so that a given set of facts always resulted in the same treatment plan, the process could, and by now probably would, be undertaken by computers. Judgement is based on the evidence available from research as well as the clinician's own experience and that of others. Using the terminology of British law, some of these judgements can be made 'beyond reasonable doubt' but others have to be made 'on the balance of probability'. It is the skill and care with which these judgements are made that distinguishes the really good dentist from the merely good dentist. In difficult cases many experienced clinicians seek second or even third opinions, discussing the case with colleagues before reaching a final decision as to the best advice to offer the patient.

Large and small decisions

Many decisions are rather routine in their nature and become automatic with practice, rather like the subconscious decision to press the accelerator to drive the car faster. While learning to drive, this decision, like many similar decisions in dentistry, has to be considered consciously. Other decisions may be slightly more difficult, such as whether all the dentine caries in a tooth must be removed and whether fissure caries has extended to the point where it should be restored or not (see Chapters 1 and 7); these decisions are always made at the conscious level. Then there are the much more substantial decisions which sometimes have to be made – for example, whether to advise a patient to have all his or her teeth extracted, or to have them all crowned or extensively restored, or to adopt some middle course of a few extractions with a simpler level of restorations and perhaps a partial denture.

The four main decisions

Diagnosis

Diagnosis is the recognition of a disease. Sometimes a bald statement of the diagnosis is sufficient; for example, amelogenesis imperfecta. In most cases, however, the diagnosis should include the extent, location, and other characteristics of the disease. For example, a diagnosis of caries or periodontal disease is not enough without describing where it occurs, how extensive it is, and whether it is currently active or arrested.

Techniques for diagnosing dental caries, tooth wear, tooth trauma, and developmental defects were described in Chapter 1.

Prognosis

The prognosis of a condition is the estimate of what will happen in the future both with and without treatment. Therefore the prognosis for an early enamel carious legion is good if appropriate preventive measures are taken, whereas the prognosis for maintaining the vitality of the pulp if caries is so extensive that symptoms of pulpitis arise, is poor. However, in the latter case, if other conditions are favourable, the prognosis for keeping the tooth if root canal treatment is carried out is good.

Treatment options

This often seems to be the most important decision, particularly for the patient, in that it affects what will be done. However, it is based so fundamentally on the first two decisions, diagnosis and prognosis, that it is, in reality, no more important, and often less so, than they are. Chapters 6–12 clarify the options available in given situations together with the reasons for choosing between them.

Further preventive measures

As was shown in Chapter 1, the long-term success of treatment is dependent in many cases on the patient's willingness and ability to cooperate in preventing further disease. A decision about the likelihood of this being effective should be attempted before the definitive treatment plan is decided, in particular if extensive treatment is contemplated. Thus the aim of an initial treatment plan may be to stabilize active disease, assess its cause, and start preventive measures. The patient's response to this initial treatment will be an important factor when planning subsequent care.

The information needed to make decisions and how it is collected and recorded

Part of the skill of an experienced clinician is to decide what information is needed, and to acquire it accurately and rapidly so that they are in the best position to give good advice without undue delay. Some clinicians adopt a 'data gathering' approach in which, using check-lists, they try to accumulate all the information which would conceivably be of some relevance about a patient. To do this comprehensively requires several hours of discussion and examination, and this is clearly impractical and unnecessary in most cases. An example of a questionnaire used to gather information about a patient with dental erosion was shown in Fig. 1.44. Some clinicians find this systematic approach useful, and it is particularly valuable to the inexperienced. Others find that a more discursive approach helps the patient to open up and discuss matters which are sometimes embarrassing or difficult to talk about. These two approaches, which are not mutually exclusive and thus may be combined, are discussed in Kidd and Smith (1993), referred to at the end of Chapter 1.

Some information is essential for all patients, some is useful for most, and in others a very detailed investigation of a narrow field of interest is necessary in order to reach a diagnosis or make one of the other decisions outlined above. Figure. 2.1 shows a list of information which may be helpful to a student when first meeting patients. It is not meant to be followed slavishly but it is a useful *aide-mémoire* for the inexperienced. However, it is dangerous to begin the examination of a patient without first ensuring that it will pose no risk to either the patient or the dentist. For this reason a full medical history should be taken before the examination, irrespective of any other history.

Lists such as the one in Fig. 2.1 are an oversimplification and suggest that the entire history should be taken first, followed by the examination of the patient. Some dentists even do this in two separate areas of the surgery, attempting to separate the conversational and clinical aspects of the process. This is often not practical and indeed may be undesirable. It is much better to mix the two processes together and maintain a steady conversation with the patient before, during, and after the examination, pausing to take notes or, better still, dictating them to the dental nurse or onto a tape as the process continues.

The reason for this is that until the dentist has made an initial examination of the mouth it is often not possible to tell what detailed line of questioning to pursue. For example, if the patient complains of discoloured teeth, a quick examination will show whether this is surface or intrinsic stain. If it is surface stain there is no need for questioning on the administration of tetracycline in childhood or the ingestion of excessive fluoride. Another common example is the patient who complains about his teeth 'crumbling away'. This may be the result of caries and failing restorations, tooth wear, or a developmental defect. Again, a quick examination will show which approach to the dietary history is likely to be most helpful – to pursue a detailed history relating to sugar or a detailed history relating to erosive materials – or whether, if it is a developmental disturbance, diet has no bearing on the matter at all. It is necessary here to describe the history and examination process in some sort of order, even if this order will seldom be followed comprehensively in practice. An example of a typical sequence of events mixing the aspects of the history and examination into an order for a given patient is given on p. 45.

History

The following information is usually needed.

About the patient

NAME, ADDRESS, TELEPHONE AND FAX NUMBERS, AND E-MAIL ADDRESS

This information is essential and it should always be checked for accuracy. It is quite possible to have two people with the same first or surname in the waiting room or the practice, and only careful and routine checking will prevent serious mistakes being made.

AGE, GENDER, AND OCCUPATION

Age will have considerable bearing on the state of dental development in younger patients and is important for a variety of reasons at other ages. The patient's gender usually has no bearing on the treatment advised, although it is usually recorded to avoid confusion. It should not be assumed that female patients are more concerned with their appearance than male patients. The patient's occupation may have a bearing on the condition itself (for example, wine tasters appear to be prone to dental erosion) and may affect availability for treatment.

ATTITUDE AND MOTIVATION TO DENTAL HEALTH AND TREATMENT

Whereas information about age and occupation is easily obtained by direct questioning, assessment of attitude to dental health and motivation is more difficult. Direct questioning is usually unhelpful because the patient will tend to answer the questions in a way which will 'please' the dentist. However, attitudes may become apparent during conversation, particularly when past dental treatment and experience are discussed.

DIET

Since diet plays a major role in dental caries and can be of importance in tooth wear, a discussion about diet is often useful. A question such as 'Do you think you have a sweet or a sour tooth?' can often elicit valuable information about attitudes as well as facts. For instance, the way that the patient answers such questions may reveal whether they appreciate the relevance of diet to dental disease and whether modification of diet has been tried in the past. However, a detailed examination of diet is reserved for those with specific caries or tooth wear problems which will only become obvious after clinical examination. This is an example of how history and clinical examination go together to produce information relevant to the *particular patient*.

HABITS

It is useful to enquire about tooth-cleaning habits and the toothpaste used, but other habits may also be relevant; for example, smoking will increase the likelihood of surface stain on teeth. Following clinical examination further questions may be needed; for example, a particular pattern of tooth wear may suggest questions about grinding habits, an erosive diet, or alcohol consumption. Any apparent discrepancy between what patients say that they do when they clean their teeth and the clinical condition may be cleared up by asking them to bring brush and paste to the surgery.

History

C/O
HPC
- Commencement
- Location
- Type
- Incidence
- Duration
- Initiating factors
- Relieving factors

PDH
- Current treatment
- Regularity of visits
- Treatment received
  - *Ortho*
  - *Perio*
  - *Cons*
  - *Surgical and why*
  - *Prosth*
- Advice on prevention
- ?Fluoride

GMH
- Heart disease
- Rheumatic fever
- Chest disease
- Jaundice or hepatitis
- Medication and drugs
- Allergies
- Abnormal bleeding
- Hospital admissions
- Operations
- Other serious illnesses
- Abnormal reaction to anaesthetic
- Pregnancy
- Contact with HIV or AIDS

SH
- Work
- Time to travel
- Availability for treatment

HABITS
- Oral hygiene
- Diet
- Smoking
- Alcohol
- Bruxing, clenching

Examination

Extra-oral
- Symmetry
- Lips
- Nodes
- TMJ

Intraoral

Mucosa
- cheeks
- palate
- tongue
- floor of mouth
- edentulous ridges
- sulci

Periodontium
- gingivae
- oral hygiene
- calculus
- pockets
- mobility
- periodontal charts

Teeth
- overall assessment, caries, tooth wear and restoration status.
- comments specific to one tooth
- caries chart

Occlusion
- intercuspal position
- retruded contact position
- lateral excursions
- protrusion
- fremitus
- faceting

Prosthesis
- type, material, support
- teeth replaced
- appearance
- tooth wear
- retention, stability

Special tests

Vitality
Radiographs
Study models
Diet analysis

KEY

C/O	Complaining of
HPC	History of present complaint
PDH	Past dental history
GMH	General medical history
SH	Social history

Fig. 2.1 *Aide-mémoire* for the history and examination of the new patient.

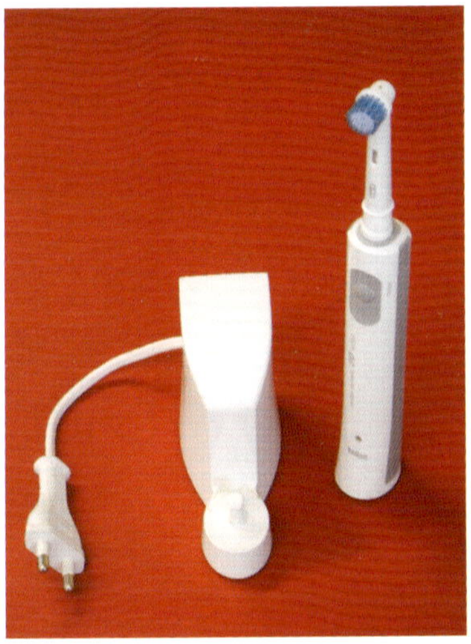

Fig. 2.2 An oscillating, round-head electric toothbrush.

Electric toothbrushes have been available for some time but have had a mixed reception from the dental profession. The newer, oscillating rotatory brushes (Fig. 2.2) are more successful than hand brushing with some patients. Patients who appear to be trying with a hand brush but are not being successful should be encouraged to try this type of electric brush.

WILLINGNESS TO MEET FEES AND OTHER EXPENSES

Most dental treatment involves the patient in some expense. This will be the full professional fee in some cases, while in third-party payment schemes (e.g. the UK National Health Service) there is often a partial fee to be paid. Even in 'free' systems (e.g. treatment by students in UK dental schools) the patient may have to take time off work and lose income. Usually, it is not possible to estimate the fee or the amount of time involved until an outline treatment plan is established. Sometimes this 'ideal' outline plan will be too costly for the patient and an alternative might have to be sought. It is important to establish this at an early stage before too much time is spent in detailed planning.

About the patient's general condition and health

Here a check-list is useful and questions are usually asked, and followed up when necessary, about the following:

- history of heart or chest disease
- current (or recent) medication
- allergies
- any difficulty in the arrest of haemorrhage after extraction or injury
- previous hospital admissions
- other diseases
- pregnancy
- contact with HIV or AIDS.

When these questions are answered positively it may be necessary to refer to the patient's general medical practitioner or to arrange further investigations (for example, blood tests) before proceeding with treatment. It may also be advisable to write directly to a hospital consultant asking for advice; for example, asking a cardiologist whether antibiotic prophylaxis is necessary for specific dental procedures.

Relevance of these questions and their answers

For a full understanding a textbook on human disease should be consulted and a specific reference is given at the end of this chapter. It is written for dentists and describes medical problems and their specific dental relevance. Whenever your patient has a medical problem, look it up in this book. Gradually you will learn a great deal, and more importantly it will give you the knowledge and confidence to care for the patient appropriately. Some examples of the importance of medical history follow.

Briefly, the type of heart disease which is relevant are the conditions which affect the smooth flow of blood through the heart, such as valve replacements or valve damage. In some cases a definite history of rheumatic fever producing a heart murmur is also relevant. However, a vague history of rheumatic fever without evidence of heart pathology is less relevant. The danger to the patient from internal heart disturbances is that bacteria entering the bloodstream from the mouth can lodge on the heart valves and produce an endocarditis. For this reason in established, clear cases prophylactic antibiotics are given for those dental procedures where the introduction of bacteria into the bloodstream is likely; for example, extractions. However, in the past this preventive measure has been taken too frequently and there is now evidence that over-prescription of antibiotics for vague prophylactic reasons is more dangerous than the problem itself. This is for two reasons: the increasing risk of patients becoming allergic to antibiotics and because the bacteria become resistant to them.

Over-prescription of antibiotics may be regarded as defending the dentist against accusations of neglect rather than truly defending the patient. It has been claimed that, in children at least, there is a greater risk of death from an anaphylactic shock resulting from antibiotic allergy than from endocarditis if prophylactic antibiotics are not given. (Many patients with poor oral hygiene and bleeding gums will be introducing bacteria into the bloodsteam, in any case, each time they eat or brush their teeth.)

Other heart conditions which do not affect the internal surface of the heart, for example coronary bypass operations, do not require antibiotic prophylaxis.

The history of chest disease or respiratory problems is more important in relation to the administration of general anaesthetics, which are no longer given within dental surgeries but only in hospitals and similar environments with proper resuscitation equipment, drugs, and trained staff.

The main relevance of chest problems is that some patients do not like the chair fully reclined as it affects their breathing. An asthmatic patient will find dental treatment impossible during an attack.

The current or recent medication is relevant if it is likely to produce a degree of dry mouth (xerostomia). This may in turn affect caries, periodontal disease, and tooth wear. It is increasingly important in older dentate patients. However, all medications should be recorded and the student should look up the medication in the *British National Formulary*. This will explain its mode of action and list complications, such as dry mouth, or relevant drug interactions. Some medications should be carried by the patient and it may be wise to check this. For instance, an asthmatic who uses an inhaler should bring this to the surgery in case an asthma attack starts during treatment. Similarly, patients who take glyceryl trinitrate for angina should carry this medication in case they need it.

Many patients are now concerned about allergies. Some patients claim to be allergic to local anaesthetics and restorative materials such as nickel-containing alloys. When these appear to be genuine problems the patients should be sent for appropriate allergy testing. However, the greatest concern is to do with mercury allergy and toxicity and this is dealt with on p. 61. Patients with severe difficulty in the arrest of haemorrhage will usually know about this, particularly if they have a bleeding dyscrasia such as haemophilia. Minor degrees of prolonged bleeding do not affect operative dentistry significantly.

Previous hospital admissions are more of general interest than specifically relating to operative dentistry unless they are as a result of trauma, which affected the teeth as well as other parts of the body.

One of the most important diseases which affects patient management is diabetes, particularly if it is poorly controlled. It increases the risk of progressive periodontal disease, which is difficult to control. In addition, a dental appointment must not interfere with a diabetic patient's eating pattern. This should be discussed when appointments are scheduled.

The relevance of pregnancy in the past is that some patients, particularly multiple pregnancies with morning sickness, are at risk of dental erosion. If this was the major factor in the erosion and there are no further pregnancies expected then often the erosion has reached a stable condition and will only progress at the normal rate of wear. A second consideration is that in the later stages of pregnancy patients find it difficult to sit or lie in the dental chair for prolonged periods and if possible extensive treatment should be deferred until after the birth. Similarly, it is wise not to take radiographs during pregnancy unless they are needed for the diagnosis of acute pain. There is little evidence that the amount of ionising radiation from a dental radiograph actually affects the fetus but it is nevertheless a wise precaution. Babies are born with defects and you do not want any mother to look back and wish she had never allowed you to take a radiograph.

The patient's reason for attendance

Some patients have an urgent problem such as pain or trauma, while others attend for a routine examination without particular symptoms. When symptoms are present the patient should be encouraged (without the use of leading questions) to describe these as clearly and in as much detail as possible. Some indication of the relevance of painful symptoms was given in Chapter 1 and will be expanded under the heading 'Diagnosing toothache' on p. 47.

Past dental history

A patient's past dental history can be of considerable assistance. Previous treatment indicates susceptibility to disease as well as attitudes towards dental care. For instance, the question 'Have you had many fillings done?' may lead the patient to explain that most teeth, have been restored. If this question is then followed up by asking whether most of the fillings are old or whether they have to be replaced regularly, the information obtained may indicate whether the patient is currently a high caries risk. It is thus possible to build up a picture of past dental history which may include caries experience, restorative treatment received, susceptibility to periodontal disease, periodontal treatment received, extractions and the reason for the loss of the teeth, and information about prosthetic replacements.

Family and social background

Where an inherited condition is suspected, clearly the distribution within the family is important. In other cases attitudes to dental health, either positive or negative, engendered within the family may have an important bearing on the condition with which the patient presents or upon acceptance of treatment. The same is true of the patient's social background. Other aspects of the social history – for example, availability for long appointments – will also determine the type of treatment.

Examination

General appearance

The patient may appear nervous or relaxed, fit and well or elderly or ill, clean and tidy or dirty and dishevelled. These or similar observations will guide but should not dictate treatment. It takes time to get to know people and instant judgements are unwise. For instance, a neglected general appearance does not necessarily mean that the person does not care about their dental health.

Factors which predispose to particularly hazardous cross-infection

Some people – for example, drug addicts, homosexuals, or heavily tattooed patients – are more likely to be carriers of

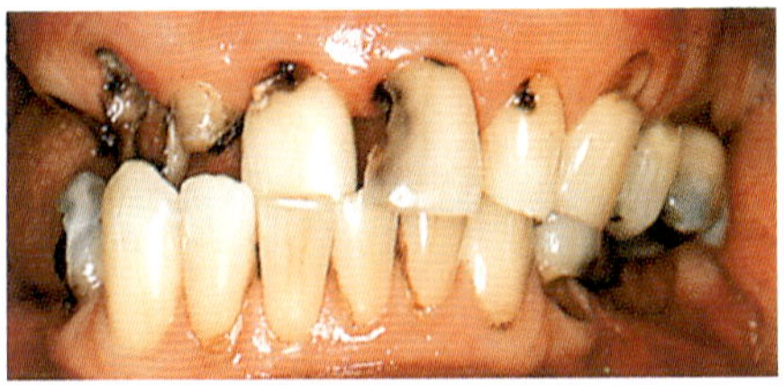

(a)

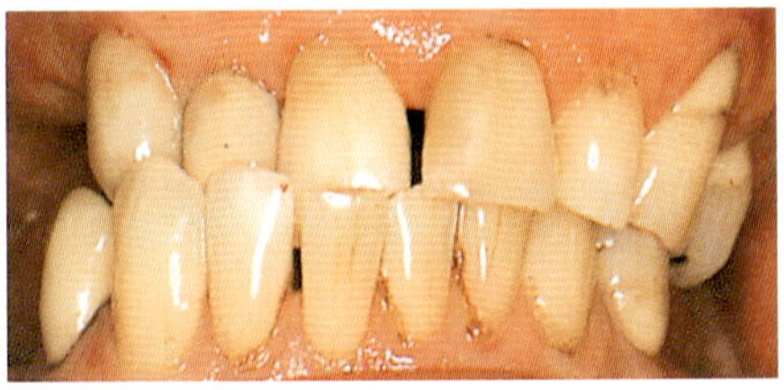

(b)

Fig. 2.3 (a) Before and (b) after a course of treatment by an undergraduate dental student. This patient presented with a very neglected mouth and with poor motivation and low expectations of treatment. However, he not only benefited from the student's treatment but also heeded the advice and encouragement given. He is now highly motivated towards maintaining his remaining teeth and his whole attitude to dentistry has been changed by this experience.

the hepatitis B virus and HIV (human immunodeficiency virus).

The extra-oral facial appearance

The temporomandibular joint and lymph nodes should be palpated. Any obvious asymmetry is noted and the lips are examined. Such things as injuries or scars on the lips may be accompanied by dental injuries. Where the patient's problem involves appearance, the dentist will make their own assessment of this while listening to the patient.

The mouth in general

Oral hygiene is relevant in both periodontal disease and caries. A general impression of whether the mouth is well cared for by both the patient and previous dentists is useful, but patients do sometimes increase their dental awareness considerably and previous neglect need not imply future neglect (Fig. 2.3).

Examination of specific areas of the mouth

The soft tissues

A routine examination of the inner aspects of the lips, the tongue, and *all* the lining mucosa of the oral cavity should be made at *all* examinations since, amongst other things, early neoplastic change can be detected and early treatment can be life-saving (Fig. 2.4).

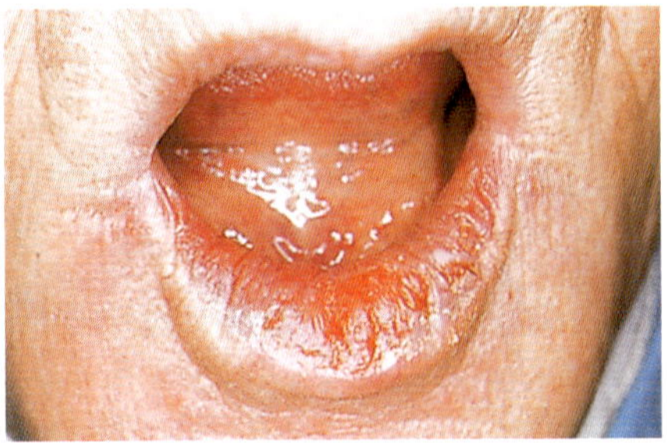

Fig. 2.4 Early neoplastic change in the lower lip. The lip was hard and a biopsy showed squamous cell carcinoma. Without careful observations this lesion could have been mistaken for other less serious conditions. (Courtesy of Professor P. R. Morgan.)

The periodontal tissues

A general assessment of the state of periodontal health is always necessary. This will include oral hygiene, the presence of both supra- and subgingival calculus, the health and position of the gingival tissues, the presence of pockets, and whether there is bleeding on probing and mobility of teeth. In many cases a more detailed periodontal examination (see later) needs to be undertaken.

Caries experience past and present

Again, a general impression can be gained of the extent of the carious lesions and previous restorations. It is reasonable to assume that restorations are most commonly the result of caries but, of course, other conditions (see Chapter 1) may also have been responsible.

Other conditions affecting the teeth

These include trauma, tooth wear, dental defects, missing teeth, and malpositioned teeth.

The general state of the restorations

See Chapter 12.

The occlusion

First, the static relationship of the teeth in *intercuspal position* (ICP) should be examined to determine the horizontal and vertical overlap of the anterior teeth (overjet and overbite), together with the relationship of the posterior teeth. Next, and perhaps more importantly, the way in which the teeth function against each other in forwards, backwards, and lateral movements of the mandible should be examined. This is often relevant to the decision as to how to restore a tooth. If a cusp functions vigorously against an opposing tooth when the jaw moves, then it may need protecting in some way by the restoration, but if it immediately discludes in all movements of the mandible, it may not (Fig. 2.5).

Dentures

The presence and nature of dentures should be noted. It is important to decide whether dentures are satisfactory or in need of replacement. If abutment teeth for satisfactory dentures need to be restored, a decision must be made as to whether these teeth can be restored to fit the denture and, if so, how this can be done. Alternatively, if new dentures are

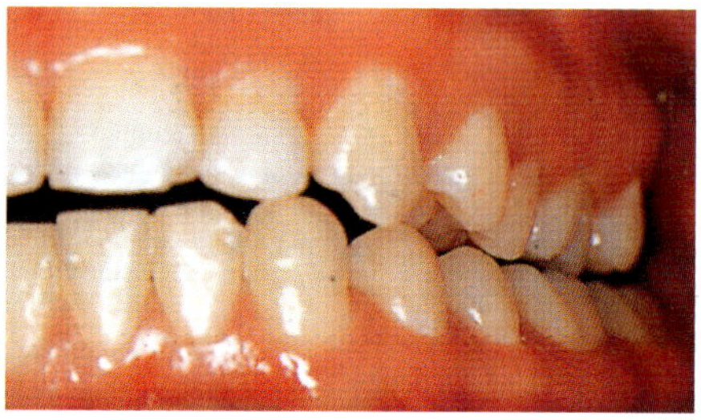

Fig. 2.5 The patient is making a left lateral excursion of the mandible. The buccal cusp of the upper first premolar is not in contact with the opposing teeth, but the buccal cusps of the upper second premolar and first molar teeth are in contact. Therefore these cusps are at greater risk if they are weakened by caries undermining them than in the case of the upper first premolar tooth.

necessary, they must be designed before planning any restorations required in the abutment teeth. This is important because design features relevant to the dentures (for example, guide planes, rest seats, undercuts for clasps) should be incorporated into the abutment restoration.

Detailed charts

In some cases much more detailed information is required.

Periodontal charting

This may include plaque indices, probing depths, bleeding points, gingival level, and tooth mobility.

Conservation charting

This will include caries and existing restorations. The recognition of caries was described in some detail in Chapter 1 and so it is only necessary here to describe how dental caries and restorations are recorded. Caries, restorations, and other details are commonly recorded on a chart (Fig. 2.6). This represents the dentition when viewed from in front of the patient, so that the teeth on the right side of the page are on the patient's left and vice versa. The convention is that the horizontal line between the upper and lower teeth represents the tongue, so that the lingual or palatal surfaces are those nearest to this line, and the buccal or labial surfaces are those at the top of the top row and the bottom of the bottom row. The marks on the posterior teeth divide the tooth into occlusal, mesial, distal, buccal, and lingual surfaces, and the same applies to the anterior teeth except that there is no occlusal surface.

For reference to individual teeth, other than by using this chart, there are four systems of tooth notation in use (Fig. 2.7).

The first two are in common use in the UK; they are the Palmer system and the system using two letters to distinguish the quadrant. In both these systems the teeth are numbered 1 to 8 starting at the mid-line. In the Palmer system the quadrant is designated by a vertical line at the midline and a horizontal line separating the upper and lower teeth. This is convenient when hand-writing notes and remains in common use for this purpose. However, it is difficult to record these lines in the computer and so for computer records the second system using two letters to designate the quadrant is in more common use. The letters are UR for upper right, UL for upper left, LR for lower right, and LL for lower left.

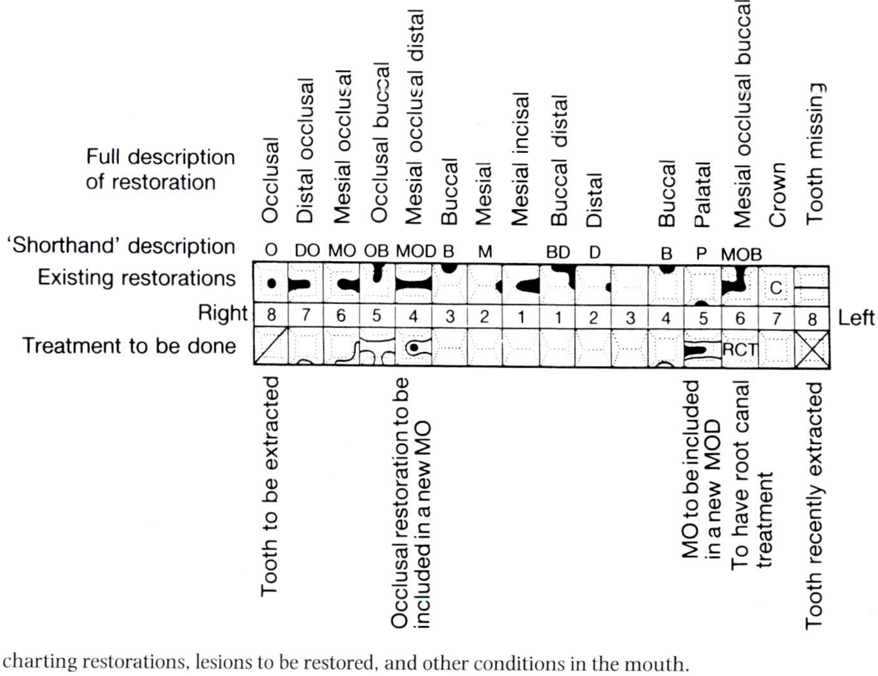

Fig. 2.6 Conventions for charting restorations, lesions to be restored, and other conditions in the mouth.

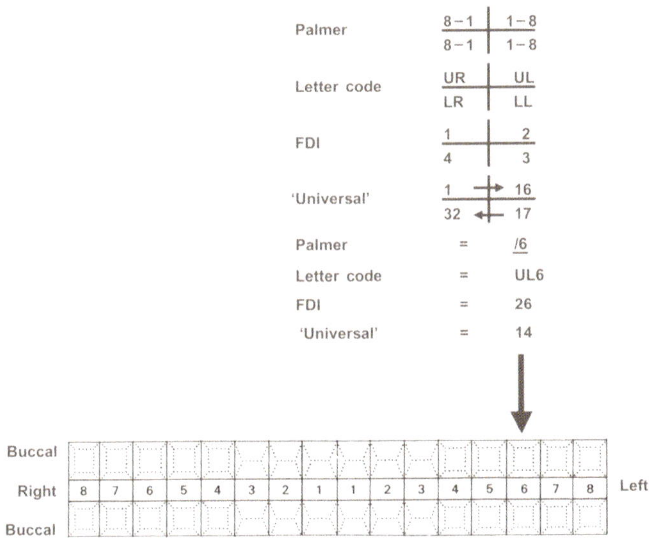

Fig. 2.7 The four different tooth notation systems – see text.

In both systems the deciduous teeth are lettered a–e from the mid-line.

The other two systems both use two digits and because of this there is a great risk of confusion between them. The first system, commonly used in Europe, is the Federation Dentaire International (FDI), which numbers each quadrant in a clockwise direction so that the upper right is 1, upper left 2, lower left 3, and lower right 4. This is not particularly logical as many people would read across the page and thereby reverse quadrants 3 and 4. This has being done on a number of occasions and has sadly resulted in the extraction of the wrong tooth or the wrong treatment. The second two-digits system is known as the 'Universal system' and is in common use in the United States. In this system the teeth are given individual numbers from 1 to 32, starting with the upper right third molar and moving clockwise round to the lower right third molar. This means that tooth 1 6 (one six) in the FDI notation is quadrant one, tooth number 6: i.e. the upper right first molar, whereas tooth 16 (sixteen) in the Universal system is the upper left third molar tooth.

With the increasing internationalisation of dental journals, conferences, and other forms of communication, having two separate two-digits systems clearly opens a minefield of confusion and error. Dental students should know about all four systems because they will see them referred to in journals and other publications, but it is the firm recommendation of the authors of this book that they should only use the first two systems which cannot be confused. The proponents of the FDI system claim that the two letters system is language dependent but the almost universal language used in international publications and computers is English. A notation system has no value unless it is surrounded by text and if this text is in a language other than English then the appropriate two letters in that language could be substituted.

There are a number of widely used conventions for charting caries, restorations, and other changes, and some of these are shown in Fig. 2.6. Because these charts are commonly dictated to dental surgery assistants, no attempt should be made to represent the size of the lesion or restoration on the chart. They are simply a shorthand notation and are not meant to be pictorially representative.

Special tests

A number of special tests may be required to supplement the information obtained from the history and examination.

Radiographs

Radiographic diagnosis of caries was dealt with in Chapter 1. If radiographs are being prescribed to be taken by a radiographer, then the provisional diagnosis and/or reason for taking the film(s) should be noted. Once taken, other radiographic findings relating to alveolar bone levels, periapical and other pathology, unerupted teeth, etc. should be recorded in the notes. Radiographs should not just be taken: what they show should be clearly recorded by writing a radiographic report in the notes.

Vitality tests

COLOUR

A non-vital tooth commonly becomes darker and less translucent than the corresponding vital tooth if it is not promptly treated by removing the necrotic pulp and root filling with an inert non-staining material. If the change is slight, particularly when the tooth is heavily filled, the difference in colour may be difficult to detect. Transillumination will help to detect slight changes in colour and particularly translucency.

PRESENCE OF A SINUS

A sinus over the apical region is strong evidence that there may be a necrotic pulp in a nearby tooth. Usually, but not always, the sinus discharges close to the apex of the affected tooth. If there is any doubt, and in particular when several teeth possibly have necrotic pulps, a useful investigation is to insert a gutta-percha point into the sinus (Fig. 2.8a) and take a radiograph (Fig. 2.8b). This also helps to distinguish between periapical changes arising from a necrotic pulp and pathology elsewhere, such as a lateral root canal or lateral perforation of the root by instrumentation.

RADIOGRAPHS

Periapical radiographs give no direct evidence of pulp vitality. However, a periapical radiolucency usually represents a granuloma which in turn is the result of pulp necrosis. The less common periapical (radicular) cyst is also a sign of a non-vital pulp. It is not usually possible to differentiate between these two conditions from the radiographic appearance alone. However, mistakes can be made when normal

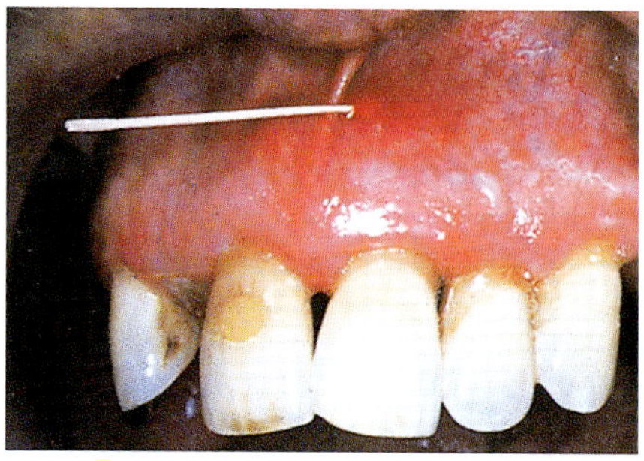

(a)

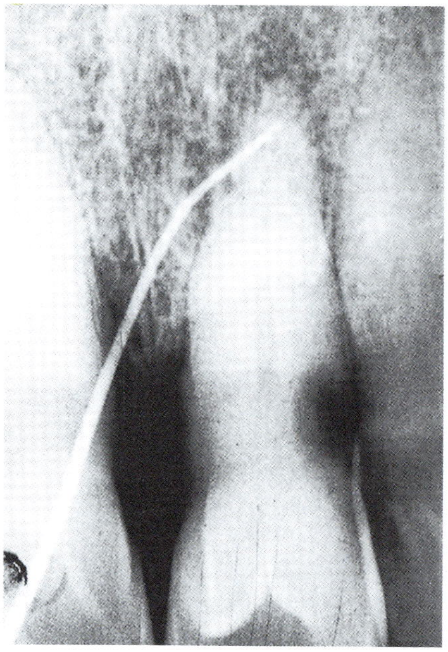

(b)

Fig. 2.8 (a) A sinus is present over the upper left central incisor and a gutta-percha point has been gently inserted into it.
(b) The radiograph of the tooth shown in (a) shows that a sinus comes from the apex of the tooth. It is possible that it might have come from a deep pocket. Extensive alveolar bone loss can be seen. The distal root caries can also be seen and this is the reason for the pulp dying.

structures such as the mental foramen, the incisal canal, or the maxillary antrum are superimposed on the root. In these cases it should be possible to trace an intact lamina dura around the normal apex. Another rare cause of periapical radiolucency, which may be associated with a tooth with a *vital* pulp, is the osteolytic phase of hypercementosis.

THERMAL AND ELECTRICAL STIMULI

The definition of pulp vitality is that the pulp retains a blood supply. Unfortunately, as yet there are no reliable, economically available methods of testing the integrity of the blood supply without damaging the pulp.

There are methods using the Doppler effect measured by a laser which will record blood flow in the pulp. However, because of the currently high cost of the equipment and the skill needed for its effective use, it is only being used for research at the present time. However, it is possible to test whether there is an intact nerve supply by thermal or electrical stimuli. Care must be taken in interpreting these indirect results. If there is a reliable positive response to a stimulus, it can be assumed that the nerve supply is intact and therefore the blood supply must be. However, the reverse is not true; there are a number of conditions in which the nerve supply is interrupted or degenerates without losing the blood supply. This occurs after a blow, particularly in young patients, and it also occurs with extensive reparative dentine formation in teeth which have been extensively restored and in older patients. Also, to complicate matters further, a number of patients will give false positive responses. This may be a result of anxiety about the test, fearing that it will hurt, or it may be that the test is badly performed so that the gingival tissues or the adjacent teeth are stimulated. In some cases it is thought that a necrotic pulp may conduct an electrical stimulus to the apical tissues, thus producing another explanation of a false positive result.

Despite these difficulties, the results of thermal and electrical stimuli are very valuable, but only when taken in conjunction with other observations.

A cold stimulus can be applied by soaking a small pledget of cotton wool in ethyl chloride which cools by rapid evaporation, and then applying this to the tooth. Alternatively, ice sticks can be made by freezing water in suitable containers. Heat can be applied by warming a stick of gutta-percha, although care should be taken with this test not to damage other structures or overheat and damage a normal pulp. Occasionally, a non-vital tooth may give a false positive response, possibly because the heat is conducted through the dentine to the periodontal membrane. However, a vital tooth usually responds quickly but a false positive response is slow. When carrying out electrical or thermal tests, a normal tooth is first tested to demonstrate the sensation to the patient and also to act as a basis for comparison.

An electric pulp tester (Fig. 2.9) has the advantage that initially it can be applied to the tooth with no electrical stimulus, and the current can be switched on and increased. This allows the patient to distinguish between the sensation of the tooth being touched and a stimulus being applied. It also allows the test to be curtailed as soon as any sensation is felt rather than (if the pulp is already hypersensitive) suffering the application of hot or cold stimuli. Electric pulp testers give a numerical value which, although not particularly accurate, can be compared with subsequent readings. For all these reasons electric pulp tests are preferred to thermal tests in most situations.

There are several types of electric pulp tester. The one shown in Fig. 2.9 consists of a metal handpiece which is held by the operator with gloved hands and is therefore insulated and not part of the electrical circuit. The patient also

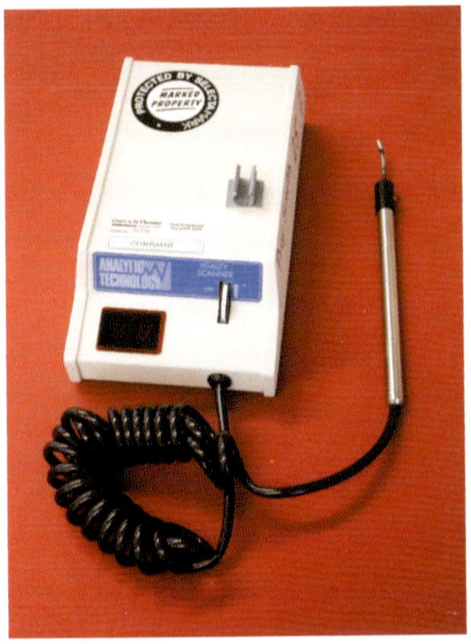

Fig. 2.9 An electronic battery-operated pulp tester (see text).

holds the metal part of the handpiece while the current automatically increases and is instructed to let go the moment they feel a sensation in the tooth. This breaks the electrical circuit and the sensation stops. In this way the patient is more in control of the process and once used to it gives more reliable responses than with other systems. The reading is given electronically on a scale from 1 to 80 and there are a range of normal readings for different teeth in the mouth.

PERCUSSION

Percussion tests are performed by gently tapping the crown of the tooth with a light instrument, for example the end of a mouth mirror handle. The crown should be tapped first in an axial direction and then obliquely on the buccal or lingual surfaces. This yields *no direct evidence* of the pulpal condition. What it detects is inflammation in the periodontal membrane. In this situation, the tooth will act as a piston in its socket and be uncomfortable.

The periapical tissues may be inflamed as a result of toxins originating in a necrotic pulp. The periodontal membrane may be inflamed by recent trauma or by a periodontal abscess. In each of these cases the tooth is tender to percussion (TTP) but only in the case of the necrotic pulp being the source of infection is it also non-vital.

INSTRUMENTATION

As a last resort, a test cavity can be cut into an area of dentine that is normally sensitive. This is rarely done with an intact sound tooth, but with heavily restored, crowned, or grossly carious teeth where the vitality of the pulp is in doubt, it is common practice to start cavity preparation, or the removal of an old restoration, before giving a local anaesthetic. As soon as a sensation is felt a local anaesthetic is given; the absence of sensation increases the likelihood of the pulp being non-vital.

Finally, with all pulp testing it is important to realize that a positive response from the dental pulp does not necessarily mean that it is normal. There are no methods for detecting whether part of the pulp is damaged or necrotic, and this is particularly important in multirooted teeth.

Occlusal analysis

Sometimes a more detailed analysis of the occlusion, using articulated study casts, is useful in planning treatment. However, such analyses are expensive and time-consuming to produce, so they are not used as a routine but only when there are clear questions which are important and which can only be assessed in this way. Articulated study casts are usually required when partial dentures are designed, and, it is important that this is done at the treatment planning stage before any teeth are restored. A more detailed description of functional occlusion is given by Smith (1998; Chapter 4).

Diet analysis

The past and present diet can be investigated by questioning and by completing a *diet sheet* (Fig. 1.36).

Salivary analysis

In patients with a high caries incidence, the salivary flow rate should be measured (see p. 21).

The history and examination process

As stressed earlier, the full history is *not* usually completed before the examination starts. Although there are many variations, a common pattern of history and examination would proceed as follows:

- reason for attendance
- medical history
- initial preliminary examination
- initial assessment of the patient's general oral and dental condition and the specific problem, if there is one
- further conversation to elicit more details of the symptoms (if there are any), and the background to the problem which is likely to be relevant – for example diet, social history, etc.
- further detailed examination
- general assessment of the patient's dental awareness and expectations
- special tests
- diagnosis and prognosis
- start the treatment planning process (see later).

Whatever sequence is used for a particular patient, it is helpful if the findings are recorded in a systematic way. The record must always be made while the patient is present, and the need for a contemporaneous record cannot be overstressed both in the interests of accuracy and also for dento-legal reasons (see later).

Planning the treatment

Treatment should follow a planned course in all cases. This is not to say that the plan is unalterable, and the temptation to write down a treatment plan as a prescription and then follow it without further thought or revision should be avoided. It is necessary to maintain constant vigilance for changes in the clinical circumstances, the patient's response to treatment, and the success of earlier stages in the treatment.

The general approach to treatment planning should be one of *problem solving*. This seems obvious, but is not always as simple as it sounds. One set of circumstances – for example, mild disturbance in the appearance of a tooth – might be a real problem to one patient, causing great distress, and yet go unnoticed by another.

Cosmetic problems like this can be regarded as the *patient's* problem and they will ultimately decide whether they want treatment or not. Other problems are more the *dentist's*. To continue with the same example, the dentist must decide between recommending a composite restoration, a veneer of composite or porcelain, or a crown. The final decision is taken jointly between patient and dentist and illustrates the important principle of treatment planning referred to earlier. The patient must be properly *informed* about treatment alternatives and must give *informed consent* to the treatment.

Treatment plans can conveniently be divided into 'simple' and 'complex'. A simple treatment plan is by far the most common and is all that is usually required for patients at recall visits, sometimes over many years of maintenance of a good standard of dental health. In such cases the dentist is monitoring health. However, there is a danger of both dentist and patient being lulled into a false sense of security, and it is important that at each re-examination relevant questions are asked and a proper examination made so that slow and steady development of periodontal disease or secondary caries is recognized.

A typical 'simple' treatment plan would be:

1. Reinforce oral hygiene procedures lingual to lower molars.
2. Scale and polish.
3. Replace stained composites as charted (and the dental chart might show two or three anterior composites to be replaced).

A more complex treatment plan is often required for patients who have not attended for some time or where there is a need for a major reassessment of a declining state of dental health. In these cases it is helpful to divide the treatment into stages:

1. Urgent treatment for the relief of pain or other symptoms.
2. Treatment for the stabilization of progressive disease or conditions which may become acute (e.g. temporarily restore very carious teeth, remove necrotic pulps, or extract teeth even if they are symptomless at the time).
3. Assess the cause of the dental disease and begin initial preventive measures.
4. Reassess the patient's response to this initial treatment and decide the broad outline of the future plan. At this stage it may be necessary to decide between a number of alternative solutions of different complexity and cost. For example, the same clinical condition (a badly broken-down mouth with many failing restorations and unsatisfactory partial dentures) may be treated in different patients by one of the following:
   - extracting all the remaining teeth and providing complete dentures
   - providing extensive restorative treatment with multiple crowns and fixed bridges to replace the partial denture
   - a midway position between these extremes with some extractions, some restorations and new partial dentures.

   The basis of this broad decision will be the patient's motivation, their response to initial treatment and preventive measures, and the cost. It is a crucial decision and one of the most difficult to make. It there is any doubt, it should be deferred or, better still, a second opinion should be sought from a colleague who may be a member of the practice or clinic, a local consultant, or recognized specialist. In some cases, for example hypodontia, decisions may need to be made about orthodontic treatment before providing veneers or crowns and bridges.
5. Provide the initial stage of definitive treatment which may be further preventive measures, periodontal treatment, orthodontic treatment, extractions, or other surgical treatment.
6. A further reassessment to evaluate the success of the first stage of treatment and revise the treatment plan as necessary.
7. Provide the final stages of the active course of treatment.
8. Reassessment, maintenance, and reinforcement of preventive measures.

The importance of making plans, both simple and complex, and of recording the decisions in the patient's record can be summarized as follows.

- It ensures that the clinician reviews the treatment in the light of all available evidence at the start of treatment and at stages throughout it.
- It is a record for later reference, particularly in complicated cases and after a lapse of time. This is available mostly for the benefit of the patient, but on occasions, when patients complain, it may have dento-legal importance and may protect the dentist against unjustified complaints. In this context, when the treatment plan is complex and expensive, it may be wise to put the advice in the form of a letter to the patient so that they have time to consider it and its implications before acceptance or rejection. The letter is also a written record, of which the patient has a copy, in cases where there is a dento-legal problem later.
- It avoids the risk of disorderly and ill-advised management which may arise if treatment is undertaken piecemeal. Unfortunately, this is a danger in clinics which are organized on a rigid departmental basis, so that a logical course of treatment is interrupted by different lengths of waiting lists in each department or by the student's inability to carry out certain items of treatment. In a learning environment some restrictions may be necessary, but it is important that the guiding principal is comprehensive 'whole patient care' and this should be emphasized throughout the undergraduate course. The older systems of compartmentalized teaching (often based on medical courses without recognizing the considerable differences between medical and dental education) have largely disappeared from dental schools, being replaced by a rounded approach to dental care. This is what happens in general dental practice and should be encouraged as early as possible in the undergraduate curriculum.

Some common decisions which have to be made

Clearly, it is not possible to give guidance on every decision which may have to be made, but the following set of examples illustrates the nature of the decision-making process. The examples to be described are:

- diagnosing toothache
- whether to restore or attempt to arrest a moderately-sized carious lesion and whether to restore or monitor an erosive lesion
- whether to extract or root treat a tooth
- which restorative material to use.

Other major decisions are discussed elsewhere; for example, whether caries is present or not (Chapter 1) and whether existing restorations should be replaced or not (Chapter 12).

Diagnosing toothache

This diagnosis is made almost entirely by the dentist, and although as much information as possible should be obtained, there is frequently a substantial element of judgement involved. Having made the diagnosis, again it is the dentist's job to give a prognosis, but the decision on treatment is usually shared much more equally between dentist and patient.

The patient complaining of 'toothache' is most likely to be suffering from one of the following conditions:

- acute pulpitis
- acute apical periodontitis
- acute apical abscess
- acute periodontal abscess
- chronic pulpitis
- chronic apical periodontitis (apical granuloma)
- exposed sensitive dentine
- food packing
- cracked cusps.

This list of conditions is in approximate order of the severity of the pain and also of the frequency in which pain is the presenting symptom, although there are considerable individual variations in this. It is worth remembering that 'common diseases occur commonly' and that pulpitis resulting from caries is the most common cause of toothache.

There are several other painful conditions of the mouth and face which may be confused with toothache, but are not usually described by the patient as toothache, for example maxillary sinusitis, pericoronitis, trigeminal neuralgia, mandibular dysfunction, atypical facial pain, and lesions of the salivary glands and soft tissues. However, patients with maxillary sinusitis and pericoronitis do sometimes complain of toothache, and textbooks on oral pathology and oral medicine should be consulted for descriptions of these conditions.

The features of the nine conditions listed above are as follows.

Acute pulpitis

There is severe pain, poorly localized to the tooth, and it may not even be possible for the patient to tell whether the source of the pain is in the upper or lower jaw; however, the pain is always localized to one side or the other. To aid the clinical diagnosis and provide a basis for rational treatment planning, two clinical presentations of acute pulpitis are recognized: *reversible pulpitis* and *irreversible pulpitis*.

Unfortunately, the clinical signs and symptoms of pulpitis are poorly correlated with the histological appearance of the pulp and so this is a clinical rather than a histological distinction. If the dentist considers it likely that the vitality of the pulp during treatment can be maintained the 'reversible' label will be given, whereas if they think that the pulp is damaged beyond repair the pulpitis will be considered irreversible and either root canal treatment or extraction will be the procedure of choice.

Reversible pulpitis is characterized by pain initiated by hot and cold stimuli lasting for a few seconds and disappearing when the stimulus is removed. In distinction to this, irreversible pulpitis is characterized by pain of several minutes or hours duration, also initiated and exacerbated by hot and cold stimuli but persisting long after the stimulus is removed. Alternatively, irreversible pulpitis may present as sudden *unprovoked* attacks of toothache which increase in frequency and severity but are poorly localized. In both reversible and irreversible pulpitis vitality tests may show an exaggerated response from the affected tooth, but this is not always the case. At this stage the tooth is not tender to percussion because the periapical tissues are not yet inflamed. There may be some evidence of the cause of the pulpitis, such as caries or a heavily restored tooth, but this is not a reliable way of diagnosing the affected tooth. Sometimes the tooth in the quadrant with the most obvious gross caries has been non-vital for some time and is symptomless, but another tooth with less obvious caries, perhaps gingival to an existing restoration, is the source of the pulpitis.

Acute apical periodontitis

This is very much better localized, and the classic presenting sign is that the patient presents indicating which tooth is causing pain by gingerly pointing to it, whereas the patient with acute irreversible pulpitis holds their hand to the side of their face. The tooth will be very tender to touch, let alone percuss, and there may be some tenderness over the apex in the buccal sulcus. The pulp may retain some vitality as the periapical tissues become inflamed before the pulp finally becomes necrotic. Again, there may be caries in the crown of the tooth.

The physiological basis for this accurate localization of the pain by the patient compared with poor localization with pulpitis is that the pulp contains *pain* nerve endings only, but the periodontal ligament contains both *pain and pressure-sensitive* nerve endings. Therefore in acute pulpitis, only poorly localized pain is felt, whereas in acute apical periodontitis pain is felt *and* movement of the tooth stimulates the pressure-sensitive nerve endings and identifies the affected tooth.

Acute apical abscess

The patient will usually present with a large tender swelling, either intra-orally or on the face, although sometimes the patient presents before the swelling has appeared or after it has spontaneously burst or subsided. The spread of infection from the apices of teeth follows well-defined patterns which are described in textbooks of oral surgery. For example, an acute apical abscess on an upper lateral incisor commonly points onto the palate, whereas on the upper canine tooth it points facially and causes swelling of the cheek and may close the eye. The tooth will be very tender to touch and the patient will often not be prepared to close his teeth together. The patient may also feel unwell and have a temperature. By this stage the pulp will usually give a non-vital response, although pulp tests are unreliable in view of the patient's distress.

Acute periodontal abscess

An acute periodontal (or lateral) abscess forms at the base of a deep periodontal pocket. The presentation is similar to that for acute apical periodontitis or acute apical abscess but the tooth may still be vital. This is because the inflammation is not the consequence of spread of infection from a necrotic pulp.

However, in some cases infection arising from a deep periodontal pocket meets up with infection arising from a necrotic pulp. The jargon term for this condition is a 'perio-endo' lesion. It is often not possible to say which came first. Either the periodontal lesion reached the apex, cutting off the blood supply to the pulp which consequently became necrotic or periapical infection from a necrotic pulp spread to join the infection at the base of the periodontal pocket. Either way the tooth will have a very poor prognosis but can sometimes be saved by effective endodontic and periodontal treatment.

Chronic pulpitis

This produces mild, poorly localized pain which sometimes comes and goes over a period of weeks or months. Eventually, if untreated, the pulp usually dies and the symptoms of chronic pulpitis disappear, although symptoms of periapical changes may take over. The tooth will usually respond to vitality tests and will not be tender to percussion. With poor localization and the absence of positive signs, this is one of the most difficult conditions to diagnose. However, it is often possible to reach the general conclusion that chronic pulpitis is the most likely cause of the symptoms. If the pain is not too severe, no treatment should be given initially other than reviewing the patient frequently and waiting for the chronic pulpitis to recover, which it may well do if it is the result of caries which has been treated. Alternatively the pulp may die, in which case regular vitality tests may localize the condition to one tooth and the pulp remnants can be removed. If the pain is more severe, the causative tooth can be found only by removing restorations from the teeth one at a time and dressing the teeth with sedative materials until the symptoms disappear (see Chapter 3). Sometimes, on removing the restorations, previously unrecognized caries or a cracked cusp is revealed and this is the cause of the chronic pulpitis.

Chronic apical periodontitis

This is usually a symptomless condition, although the patient may feel a very mild pain on biting. Vitality tests will be negative, and the tooth may be slightly tender to vigorous percussion and may emit a slightly duller sound. The patient may present with a sinus. However, the main diagnostic test is a periapical radiograph on which a periapical radiolucency is seen. When a sinus is present a gutta-percha point may be gently inserted into it before the radiograph is taken and the resulting film will show this point approaching the apex of the relevant tooth (see Fig. 2.8). In all the other conditions listed so far, there is no radiographic change in the periapical tissues except a slight thickening of the apical periodontal space with an acute apical abscess owing to the intense pressure in the area which extrudes the tooth slightly from its socket.

In its chronic state, an apical granuloma is not infected with bacterial organisms but is a chronic inflammatory response to toxins leaching from the apex of a tooth with a necrotic pulp. These toxins percolate through the granulation tissue and become diluted and absorbed, so that there is a natural limit to the size of a chronic periapical granuloma. Beyond this size the toxins become too dilute to stimulate the formation of osteoclasts and the removal of bone.

A periapical granuloma is highly vascular because granulation tissue is essentially a repair tissue. If the necrotic pulp is removed and the tooth root filled, the granuloma will be replaced by normal bone (Fig. 2.10).

Two changes can occur within a chronic apical granuloma: it may become infected and flare up into an acute apical abscess, or it may become cystic. The clinical signs of acute change are those of an acute apical abscess, although the radiograph will show a periapical radiolucency. Similarly, the cyst may become infected and flare up into an acute apical abscess. These changes are described in textbooks of oral pathology, and the management is described in textbooks of endodontics and oral surgery.

Exposed sensitive dentine

This may result from gingival recession or surgery producing exposed root surfaces, or it may result from a failing restoration or caries exposing dentine to oral fluids. The patient will usually complain of sensitivity to hot, cold, and *sweet* food and drink, but the sensitivity (rather than pain) is often poorly localized. It may indeed be generalized in several areas of the mouth. Pulp tests applied to enamel surfaces will produce a normal response, but if the exposed dentine surface is stimulated either thermally or electrically, or is scratched with a probe, there may be an increased response. The teeth are not tender to percussion.

Food packing

When the contact point between adjacent teeth is not tight, either as a result of the teeth drifting apart or because of a poorly contoured restoration, food wedges between the teeth and causes periodontal pain. Meat fibres are the most troublesome.

Cracked cusps

Cusps may crack either superficially or deep into the tooth, whether the tooth is restored or not. The crack may involve the pulp or pass only through enamel and dentine. The symptoms are often poorly localized and may occur only periodically. Sometimes there is a sharp pain on biting hard on tough food, and occasionally with thermal stimuli. Thermal and electrical pulp tests are often inconclusive and the tooth may not be tender to percussion although pressure laterally on individual cusps may produce pain. Transillumination may help to show the crack, or applying disclosing solution or other stain to the tooth may reveal it. Unfortunately, many teeth show multiple cracks which do not cause symptoms (perhaps because these cracks only involve enamel), and thus it is difficult to be sure that any crack that is seen is actually the cause of the pain (Fig. 2.11). A useful diagnostic test is to ask the patient to

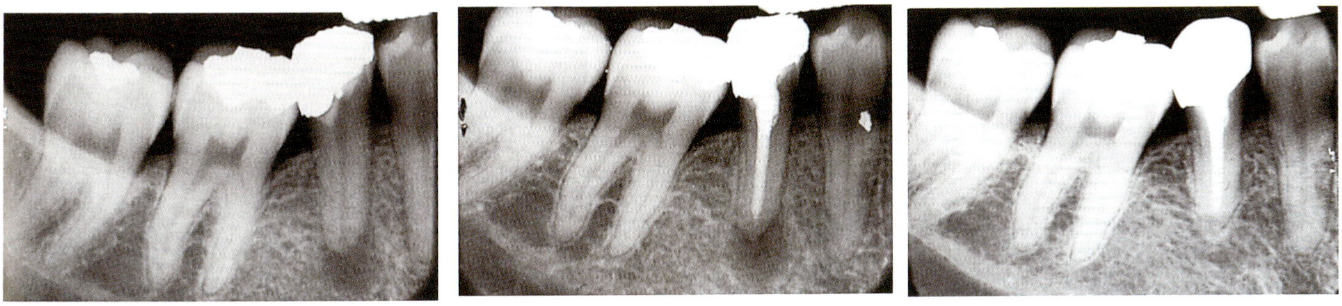

(a) (b) (c)

Fig. 2.10 (a) The pulp of the second premolar tooth has become necrotic and a periapical granuloma has formed.
(b) Immediately after root filling.
(c) Three years later periapical bone has reformed. (Reproduced by courtesy of Professor T. R. Pitt Ford.)

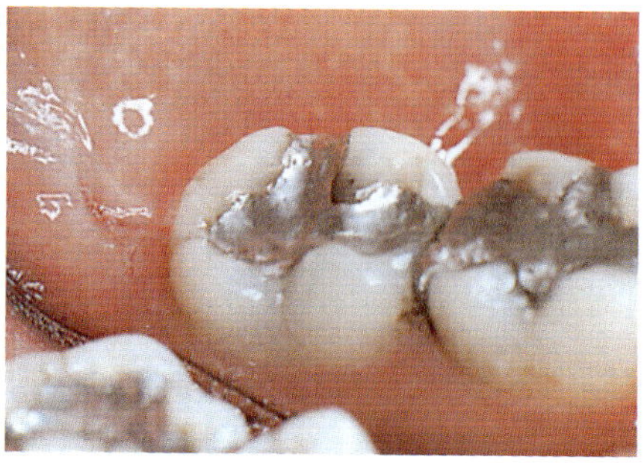

Fig. 2.11 Cracks are obvious in the distal and lingual walls. Lateral pressure on the disto-lingual cusp caused pain but pressure on the other cusps did not. (Reproduced by courtesy of Dr D. W. Bartlett.)

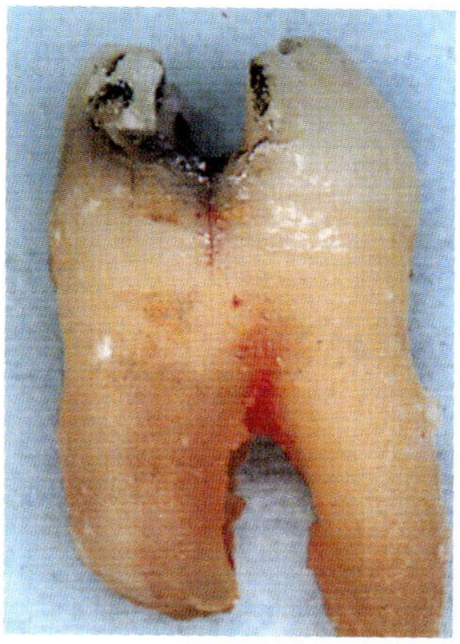

Fig. 2.12 A cracked tooth. The restoration was removed and the base of the cavity stained with disclosing solution before the tooth was extracted. The disclosing solution demonstrated the presence of this deep crack which inevitably involves the pulp. (Reproduced by courtesy of Professor A. H. R. Rowe.)

bite on a cotton-wool roll. Pain is often felt when the pressure is *released* rather than when it is *applied*. Sometimes, when the restoration is removed from a suspect tooth, the crack is seen at the base of the cavity and these deep cracks are more likely to cause symptoms (Fig. 2.12).

Making the diagnosis

Although it is necessary to know the characteristic symptoms and signs of each of the conditions listed above, it is also necessary to have a systematic method of diagnosing the cause of symptoms in a patient with toothache.

The history should concentrate on the nature of the pain, its duration, and initiating stimuli. Clues should be followed; for example, chronic sensitivity to sweet foods may suggest exposed dentine rather than any of the other conditions, and chronic tenderness to biting will suggest either a cracked cusp or perhaps chronic apical periodontitis. The past dental history may be of interest in cases where trauma or recent restorations may be the cause.

On examining the patient, the dentist should look for possible causes such as caries, leaking restorations, cracked cusps, or evidence of trauma. Radiographs, vitality tests, and percussion tests are all required in order to be confident of a diagnosis in almost every case. Radiographs may show periapical radiolucencies, failed root fillings, internal or external root resorption, fractured roots, and other possible reasons for the toothache. The value of vitality and percussion tests is clear from the earlier descriptions.

Figure 2.13 shows the typical interpretation of signs and symptoms in toothache.

Finally, despite having completed a full investigation, there are occasions when the cause of the pain is still not clear. At this point it is wise to reconsider other causes of pain, such as trigeminal neuralgia, but if these can safely be eliminated then, and only then, the dentist should start to remove previous restorations.

A simplistic maxim, but one well worth remembering, is 'diagnosis should precede treatment'. Far too often busy dentists, pressed for time, feel an obligation to start treating teeth without having made a thorough diagnosis of the cause of the toothache.

Whether to restore or attempt to arrest a moderate-size carious lesion and whether to restore or monitor an erosive lesion

With caries this decision will primarily be the dentist's, but with an erosive lesion the patient will often be much more involved in the decision.

Guidance is given in Chapter 1 as to when, in general, caries should be removed and the tooth restored, and when measures should be taken to arrest lesion progression. These general guidelines must now be applied to the individual patient. The factors to be considered will include the age and previous caries experience of the patient. The social history may also be important in that if the patient is able (and likely) to come for regular examinations then it is better to give even reasonably advanced lesions the chance to arrest, whereas with a patient who is going away for a year or two the opposite decision is likely to be made.

With a carious lesion the main problem in making this decision is to decide the *prognosis*. This is also the problem in deciding what to do about an erosive lesion, but in this case the consequences of not treating the lesion are likely to be less rapid if the wrong decision is made. It is possible to see the full extent of the erosive lesion, and pulp exposure arising from dental erosion is very uncommon. With caries the extent of the lesion within the tooth is less clear, and if the wrong decision is made and the caries develops rapidly then pulpitis may ensue. This is part of the reason why the patient can be more involved in the decision as to whether to restore an erosive lesion. The primary reasons for restoring these lesions are as follows:

- they spoil the patient's appearance (this is the patient's decision not the dentist's)

	Acute pulpitis	Acute apical periodontitis	Acute apical abscess	Acute periodontal abscess	Exposed sensitive dentine	Food packing	Cracked cusp	Chronic pulpitis	Chronic apical periodontitis (apical granuloma)
History	Recent pain with hot and cold. May be very severe. Poorly localized.	Tender to bite. Well localized.	Pain and swelling. Very well localized.	Localized swelling. Some pain.	Generalised pain to hot, cold and sweet.	Pain after eating fibrous food, e.g. meat.	Vague intermittent pain usually on biting. May be poorly localized.	Vague, unprovoked intermittent but increasing pain. Poorly localized.	May have had pain in the past. Now not sensitive to hot and cold.
Clinical examination	Possibly caries or recent large restoration.	Possibly caries.	May be extraoral or intraoral swelling over apex of tooth.	Intraoral swelling nearer to gingival margin. Tooth may be mobile.	Gingival recession. Exposed dentine at the gingival margin. Sensitive to probe or cold air.	Open contact points. Gingival inflammation. Food usually present.	Often nothing, but crack may be seen. May be painful with occlusal contact only.	May have large restoration or caries.	May have large restoration or caries.
Vitality test	Hypersensitive.	May still be vital, but usually non-vital.	Non-vital.	Often vital.	Vital.	May be vital or non-vital.	May be hypersensitive.	Often normal but may be hypersensitive.	Non-vital.
Percussion	Not tender.	Tender.	Tender to touch. Too tender to percuss.	Slight tenderness, more to lateral than axial pressure.	Not tender.	Not tender to percussion. May be sore with lateral percussion.	Usually not tender but may be.	Not tender.	Slightly. May give dull sound on percussion.
Other clinical tests			Raised temperature. Looks ill.	Deep pockets. Pus may be released on probing pocket.		Floss passes the contact easily.	Sometimes tender to lateral pressure on an individual cusp.		
Radiographic findings	Probably caries close to pulp. No periapical change.	Usually no periapical change in the early stage.	Usually no periapical change except slight thickening of apical periodontal membrane.	Alveolar bone loss. Usually no periapical change.	May be some alveolar bone loss.	None.	None.	None.	Periapical radiolucency.
Findings on further investigations	Carious exposure of pulp.	Necrotic pulp.	Pus may be drained via access cavity to root canal without local anaesthetic, giving immediate relief of pain and confirming the diagnosis.				Crack sometimes visible at base of cavity when old restoration removed. If left, cuspal fracture will eventually occur.	Symptoms may settle if restoration removed and tooth dressed with calcium hydroxide, but pulp often dies eventually.	Necrotic pulp.

Fig. 2.13 Typical signs and symptoms in toothache. Unfortunately, not all symptoms fall precisely into this pattern and clinical judgement and experience is often needed for their interpretation.

- they are sensitive in a way that cannot be controlled by topical agents (again, only the patient knows how sensitive they are and how much he or she can tolerate)
- the dentist may be concerned about the weakening or other mechanical effects of allowing the lesion to progress.

Whether to extract or root treat a tooth

Again, the patient is often very much involved with this decision. Some patients (a rapidly declining number) will opt to have a painful or broken-down tooth extracted on the grounds of time involved in treatment, fear of treatment, lack of confidence that root treatment is likely to be successful, or cost. This is particularly likely with a tooth which does not show and which may appear to the patient not to have any great value. In this case, if the tooth is painful or grossly carious or has a necrotic pulp, the dentist should comply with the patient's wish for an extraction even though they may feel sure that the tooth can be saved with a good prognosis and that this is the treatment they would strongly advise. It would not be ethical to leave the patient in pain when a simple form of treatment, such as extraction, would reliably relieve it and the patient will not accept other forms of treatment.

However, most patients are willing to accept the dentist's advice. Advice should be based on the general long-term interest of the patient rather than on an oversimplified wish to retain all teeth at all costs. For example, pulpitis in a first molar tooth in a child with crowded arches may well be best treated by extraction followed by balancing extractions or by orthodontic treatment to close the space and relieve the crowding, even if this is not the ideal tooth to extract for orthodontic purposes. In contrast, posterior teeth, notably second and third molars, are particularly valuable if a partial denture may have to be worn. This is because a denture is much more stable if it has a posterior abutment tooth to retain and support it.

Finally, it must be remembered that some teeth cannot be saved because of gross caries and even though root canal treatment may be possible, it is not advisable because it will not be possible to restore a healthy functional crown.

Which restorative material to use

Much of the answer to this will become apparent in later chapters. However, decisions made now with the current state of development of restorative materials will alter, probably quite rapidly in the next few years. This has certainly been the case to a very considerable extent since the first edition of this book, and so it is important that the decisions made in a given set of circumstances do not become fossilized in the dentist's mind so that they continue to use the same materials and the same techniques long after these have been replaced by improved materials and techniques. There is a happy medium between seizing on every new material which comes onto the market and assuming that it will outperform all its predecessors, and retaining too conservative a view, being unprepared to use new materials until they have survived long-term clinical trials.

Further reading

Faculty of General Dental Practitioners (2000). *Adult antimicrobial prescribing in primary dental care for general dental practitioners*. Royal College of Surgeons of England, London.

Longman, L. P. and Martin, M. V. (1999). A practical guide to antibiotic prophylaxis and restorative dentistry. *Dent. Update*. **26**, 7–14.

Martin, M. V., Gosney, M. A., Longman, L. P., and Figure, K. H. (2001). Murmurs infective endocarditis and dentistry. *Dent. Update*. **28**, 76–82.

Scully, C. and Cawson, R. A. (1998). *Medical problems in dentistry* (4th edn). John Wright, Bristol.

Smith, B. G. N. (1998). *Planning and making crowns and bridges*, Chapter 4. Martin Dunitz, London.

3

Principles of cavity design and preparation

G. V. Black

Why restore teeth?

What determines cavity design?

- The dental tissues
- The diseases
- The properties of restorative materials

Resin composites

- Composition of composites
- Polymerisation of composites

Glass ionomer cements

- Conventional, autocuring, glass ionomer cements
- Resin-modified glass ionomer cements (RMGIC)
- Polyacid-modified resin composites (PAMRC)
- Fluoride-releasing materials

Dental amalgam

- Composition of amalgam alloys and their relevance to clinical practice
- The safety aspects of amalgam

Cast gold and other alloys

Principles of cavity design

- When is a restoration needed?
- Gaining access to the caries
- Removing the caries
- How should soft infected dentine be removed?
- Stepwise excavation
- Put the instruments down: look, think and design
- The final choice of restorative material
- Making the restoration retentive
- Design features to protect the remaining tooth tissue
- Design features to optimize the strength of the restoration
- 'Resistance form'
- The shape and position of the cavity margin

Possible future developments in cavity design

The control of pain and trauma in operative dentistry

- Pre-operative precautions
- Pain and trauma control during tooth preparation
- Avoiding postoperative pain

Cavity lining and chemical preparation

- Objectives and materials

Principles of cavity design and preparation

G. V. Black

In the first decade of the twentieth century an American dentist and teacher, G. V. Black, established principles governing the design of cavities and suggested steps in their preparation. He based these principles on what was known at the time about the natural history of caries and the restorative materials available. The wisdom of his work was such that it remained virtually unchallenged for more than half a century. Now, with new materials, a better understanding of caries, and research findings into the success or otherwise of various restorative procedures, the principles have been largely revised.

G. V. Black was a far-sighted scientist who would surely have expected that his ideas would have been taken up, researched, and revised by successive generations of clinicians and scientists. It would perhaps have been a disappointment to him that this was not done until relatively recently, but he would undoubtedly have been the first to applaud these developments. In 1908 Dr Black wrote: 'the complete divorcement of dental practice from studies of the pathology of dental caries, that existed in the past, is an anomaly in science that should not continue. It has the apparent tendency plainly to make dentists mechanics only.'

Since his principles have now been so extensively modified, and since many conditions in addition to caries are treated operatively (see Chapter 1), no further reference will be made to Black's principles.

Black also described a classification of carious lesions which is still widely used in dental schools. However, this classification is now regarded as incomplete in that it does not include root caries and secondary caries. Also, it does not include non-carious lesions, which are treated in the same way as carious lesions. Therefore this classification is not used in this book but it is useful clinical shorthand and is as follows:

- Class I. Caries affecting pits and fissures.
- Class II. Caries affecting the approximal surfaces of posterior teeth.
- Class III. Caries affecting the approximal surfaces of anterior teeth.
- Class IV. Caries affecting the approximal surfaces of anterior teeth and involving the incisal angle.
- Class V. Caries affecting the cervical surfaces.

Why restore teeth?

The objectives of restoring teeth are as follows:

- to restore the integrity of the tooth surface
- to restore the function of the tooth
- to restore the appearance of the tooth
- to remove diseased tissue as necessary.

What determines cavity design?

The general principles of cavity design are related to the following:

- the structure and properties of the dental tissues
- the diseases (e.g. caries, pathological tooth wear, periodontal disease)
- the properties of the restorative materials.

The dental tissues

Enamel, the hardest tissue in the body, is relatively inelastic and rather brittle. Its structure consists of interlinked prisms or rods and it has a greater tendency to split along the line of the prisms than in other directions. For this reason grossly unsupported enamel to which occlusal forces are applied directly should usually be removed so that it does not fracture and leave a gap between the restoration and the tooth. This weakness can be determined by placing a hand instrument, such as an excavator or chisel, with moderate force on the weak margin. This loading will cause fracture – or not – depending on the strength of the enamel. Elsewhere, unsupported enamel may be left, particularly when the restoration is to be made with a composite or glass ionomer material since these materials bond to the dental tissues and thus give them some support. The risk to unsupported enamel where there are no direct occlusal forces is from the restorative procedure itself; for example, tightening a matrix band (see

p. 136) may damage unsupported enamel at a cervical margin.

Dentine is softer, more porous, and more elastic than enamel; it is also sensitive. The elasticity of dentine allows the use of pins, which may help to retain a restoration and which can be screwed into a slightly undersized hole. If this were attempted in enamel it would split; compare putting a wood screw into a pre-drilled hole in wood or china. The enamel–dentine complex that forms a functioning tooth is unique in that the brittle ceramic-like enamel is mutually supported by the elastic dentine, joined at the immensely strong enamel–dentine junction.

In a vital tooth dentine is intimately connected with the pulp, being permeated by tubules which contain the cytoplasmic extensions of the odontoblasts at their pulpal ends. For this reason dentine and pulp are often considered together. This intimate connection between the two tissues means that diseases or operative procedures that affect the dentine may also affect the pulp.

The shape, size, and condition of the pulp will affect cavity design. In a slowly progressing carious lesion, reparative dentine within the pulp chamber will have reduced the size of the pulp so that in some cases the cavity will extend into the contours of the original pulp chamber (Fig. 3.1). However, in most cases the preparation is designed to avoid the pulp. In all cases, precautions are taken to avoid physical, thermal, or chemical damage to the pulp during cavity preparation and placing the restoration.

The gingival tissues become inflamed in the presence of plaque, and so cavities are designed and restorations placed in such a way that minimal encroachment upon the gingival attachment occurs, and also so that the margins of restorations are as easy to clean as possible. This also helps to reduce the likelihood of recurrent (sometimes called secondary) caries.

The diseases

The effect of caries, tooth wear, trauma, and defects in tooth structure have been described in Chapter 1. The implications of these must be considered in designing cavities. For example, the spread of caries along the enamel–dentine junction undermines the enamel and has an important influence over cavity design. Near the pulp the distinction between infected carious dentine and dentine which has been affected by caries, but which does not yet contain bacteria, is important in deciding how much to remove. Of particular importance is the fact that restorations can only repair the cavities cut to remove carious lesions, and preventive measures such as good plaque control with a fluoride toothpaste and dietary advice are essential if restorations are to last.

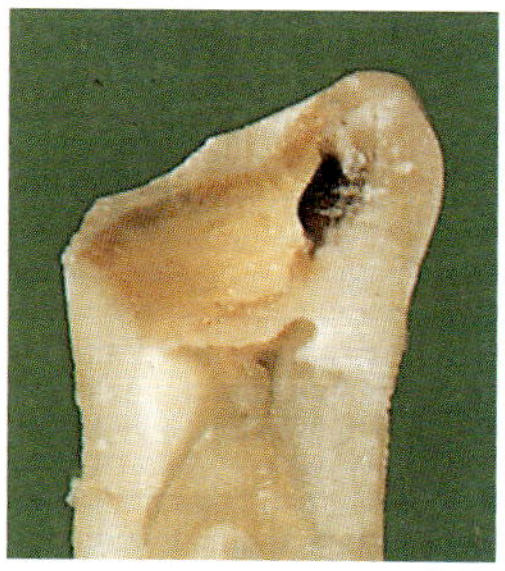

Fig. 3.1 A hemisection of an extracted tooth to show reparative dentine reducing the size of the pulp chamber. However, the caries has now progressed into this reparative dentine.

Similarly, in cases of extensive tooth wear the proportions of erosion, attrition, and abrasion contributing to the tooth wear must be diagnosed, if possible, and the success of preventive measures assessed before the teeth are restored. If further tooth wear cannot be prevented, the rate at which the condition is likely to progress will affect the choice of restoration and its design. As an example, if the main cause of tooth wear is acid regurgitation which cannot be prevented medically or surgically, the dentist may need to consider crowning the teeth so that they last as long as possible in these adverse circumstances.

The properties of restorative materials

The materials currently used to restore teeth which will be described in this book are as follows:

- resin composites
- glass ionomer cements
- hybrid materials of composite and glass ionomer cement
- dental amalgam
- cast gold and other alloys
- porcelain.

Other materials used for crowns and bridges are not described in this book.

When considering dental materials it is useful to have some concept of an ideal material. Unfortunately, this dental paragon does not exist, but scientists are continually striving to improve dental materials and enormous strides have been made since the first edition of this book.

The ideal material would have these properties:

- be easy to use
- be tooth-coloured
- be adhesive to tooth substance
- have no change of volume on setting
- provide protection from recurrent caries
- have adequate strength
- be insoluble and non-corrodible in the mouth
- be non-toxic and non-irritant to pulp and gingival tissues
- be easy to trim and polish
- resist the formation of dental plaque

- have a rate of wear similar to enamel
- have a coefficient of thermal expansion similar to enamel and dentine
- have a thermal diffusivity similar to enamel and dentine
- have a low water absorption
- be radiopaque
- have a good shelf life
- be inexpensive.

While the relevance of some of these ideal properties is obvious, others need a word of explanation. Adhesion to tooth substance is desirable, so that the filling may give some support to the tooth and be retained within it. In addition, any adhesive material should minimize the gap between restoration and tooth. Leakage of bacteria between a filling and a tooth is potentially irritating to the pulp. In addition, bonding of the restorative material may make it unnecessary to produce retentive features in a cavity. A volume change in a material as it sets is a problem because expansion may fracture the tooth and contraction may either open up a gap between the filling and the cavity wall or impart significant stresses to the tooth. Since recurrent caries may occur around restorations, a material which exerts some cariostatic or bactericidal effect is potentially useful.

The mouth is a highly hostile environment for any material, being warm, wet, and full of bacteria which potentially may cause disease. In addition, the temperature of the mouth is not constant, since hot and cold food and drinks transiently pass through it. This means that the cavity seal of a material may be lost unless it has a thermal diffusivity and coefficient of thermal expansion that are similar to enamel and dentine.

The ideal material would resist plaque formation and would be capable of accurate finishing to a smooth lustrous surface which is easily cleaned and which would not dissolve, corrode, or wear excessively in service. Radiopacity is important in the diagnosis of recurrent caries on radiographs (see p. 195).

A textbook of dental materials should be consulted to study the composition, setting reactions, and properties of the materials described in this book. Advances in materials science have had a profound effect on operative techniques, making the study of dental materials particularly relevant and important to today's graduate. The following brief description of some of the relevant clinical properties of materials is given to illustrate the effect they have on cavity preparation.

Resin composites

There are several groups of resin composite materials, often simply shortened to 'composites'. Although most composites are tooth-coloured, some have been designed for use in anterior teeth, where appearance is most important, while others have been designed for posterior teeth where strength and abrasion resistance are of prime importance. In both cases the material is capable of being attached physically to the enamel by means of the acid-etch technique. Composite is strong in thin sections when attached to enamel and so the enamel margins can be bevelled, prepared with a cavo-surface angle of 90 degrees, or undercut (Fig. 3.2).

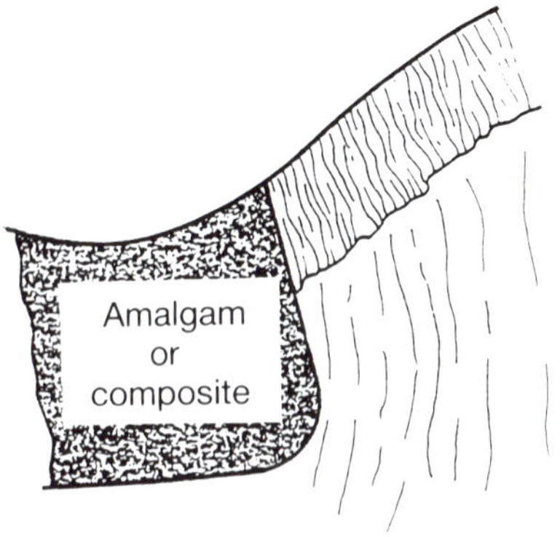

(a)

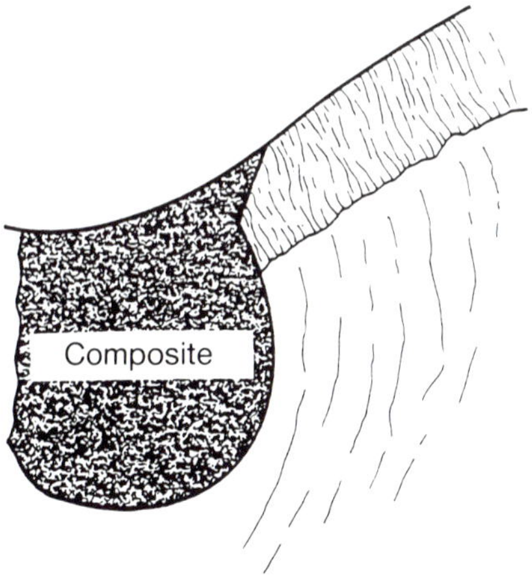

(b)

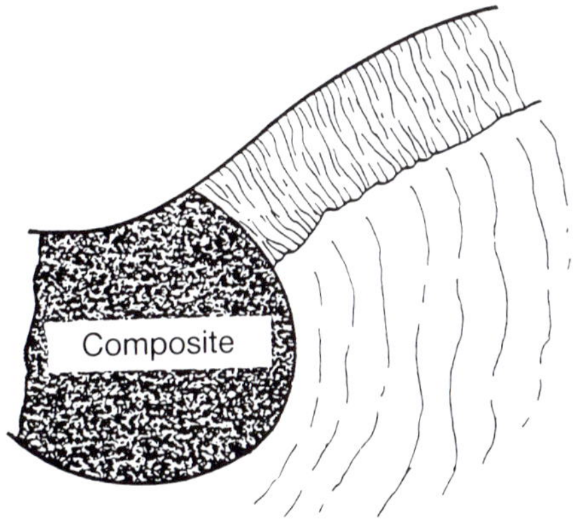

(c)

Fig. 3.2 (a) The margin angle of the cavity and the restoration is such that there is sufficient bulk-strength in each.
(b) The enamel margin is sometimes bevelled when composite is used.
(c) Alternatively, when dentine caries undermines the enamel, the enamel may be left undercut provided that it is not subjected to direct occlusal forces.

Composites can be attached to dentine using layers of adhesive materials. Unfortunately, the bond to dentine, historically, has not been as strong as the bond to enamel. Since all the currently available composites shrink as they polymerize, there is a danger that the material will move away from the dentine towards the enamel in cavities bounded by enamel on one side and dentine on the other, as commonly occurs with cervical cavities. This invites recurrent caries on the dentine side of the cavity. This problem is reduced by packing the material into the cavity in special ways (see Chapters 6–9).

Composition of composites

All composites are a mixture of a resin and filler. The two commonly used *resins* are either BIS GMA or urethane dimethacrylate. BIS GMA resin is made by a reaction between bisphenol A and glycidylmethacrylate, but this resin has the consistency of thick treacle at room temperature. Therefore, the manufacturers use a diluent monomer (triethylene glycol dimethacrylate (TEGMA) to reduce the viscosity and allow the filler particles to be added to the resin.

In order to maintain good physical properties, all of the resins currently used in the manufacture of composites have a very *hydrophobic* (water-hating) nature. They resist water uptake, and indeed show reduction in their physical properties after long-term exposure to water. This means that it is difficult to bond these materials directly to wet tooth tissue without the use of a *hydrophilic* (water-liking) intermediate adhesive layer (see Chapter 6).

The type, concentration, particle size, and particle-size distribution of the *filler* used in a commercial composite material are major factors controlling the properties and handling characteristics of the material. Fillers include quartz, fused silicon, and various types of glass including aluminosilicates and borosilicates. All contain radio-opacifiers such as barium oxide. Radiopaque materials must always be chosen for posterior teeth so that the material can be distinguished from dental caries on radiographs.

Conventional composites contain 60–80 per cent by weight of quartz or glass particles of sizes ranging from 1 to 50 μm. Manufacturers coat the filler particles with a silane *coupling agent* to enhance bonding between the filler and the resin matrix. Particle-size distribution may vary within the range given above from one composite to another. The more modern materials contain larger quantities of smaller particles (1–5 μm), making the material easier to smooth and polish.

The search for a polishable material led to the introduction of a group of materials called *micro-filled composites* which contained silica particles with a mean diameter of only 0.04 μm. Initially it proved impossible to incorporate high filler loadings in these materials and this led to inadequate physical properties. The manufacturers solved this problem by making prepolymerized blocks of resin containing a high filler loading of silica. These blocks were ground up to give particles of resin-silica which were then mixed into more resin to form pastes of appropriate viscosity for clinical use.

Derivatives of this type of polishable material are the composites with filler particles not exceeding 0.6–1 μm size. The use of a filler size below that of visible light wavelength enables the material to maintain a better shine, as the exposed filler edges will not readily reflect light. The larger filler particle size will also give better strength and mechanical properties than the micro-filled materials.

A third series of composite materials contain a blend of both conventional glass or quartz particles together with some submicron particulate silica. These products are referred to as *hybrid* composites and a total filler content of 80–90 per cent by weight can be achieved.

There is considerable ongoing research work to develop new fillers and resins for use in composites. The main aim of this is to reduce the shrinkage of the resin materials. The first manufacturer to produce a reliable 'no shrink' material will deserve to do well.

Polymerization of composites

Polymerization can be activated *chemically* by mixing two components (usually two pastes), one of which contains an initiator and the other an activator. Alternatively, polymerization can be activated by exposure to blue *visible light* at 470 nm wavelength. These light-cured materials are supplied as a single paste and require the use of a specialist light source. Care must be taken to protect the dispensed material by a light-proof cover, since exposure to sunlight, or the surgery operating light, may initiate polymerization, causing the paste to thicken and become unworkable. Light-cured materials give the clinician a longer working time but great care must be taken to build the material up in increments that are not too thick. If too thick an increment is placed, the material at the base of the cavity will not set because the light cannot reach it. This leaves the clinician in a fool's paradise thinking that a restoration is satisfactory because it has a hard surface concealing a 'soggy bottom'!

Glass ionomer cements

Glass ionomer cement is the most recently developed restorative material is general use. It adheres chemically to enamel and dentine. Since it links to calcium ions in the dental tissues, the bond to enamel is stronger than the bond to dentine because enamel is more highly mineralized. The adhesion mechanisms are covered in more detail in Chapter 6.

Conventional, autocuring, glass ionomer cements

Glass ionomer cements (or glass polyalkenoate cements) are *water-based* and hence obviously *hydrophilic*. They consist of an *alumino-silicate glass* with a high fluoride content which reacts with a *poly (alkenoic) acid*. The resulting cement consists of glass particles surrounded and supported by a matrix arising from the dissolution of the surface of the glass particles in the acid. *Calcium* polyacrylate chains form quite rapidly when the cement is mixed and this develops a matrix that holds the particles together. Now *aluminium* ions begin to form aluminium polyacrylate chains which are less soluble and stronger, and the final matrix formation takes place. *Fluoride*, which is used as a flux in the manufacture of the glass particles, is released from those particles and lies free within the matrix but plays no part in its physical make-up. Thus, the fluoride is able to leach out of the restoration and return to it, so that the restoration can be regarded as a *fluoride reservoir*.

Approximately 24 per cent of the set cement is water, some of which is 'loosely bound' and easily removed by dehydration. The rest is 'tightly bound' water which cannot be removed and remains an important part of the setting reaction. In the early stages after mixing, the calcium polyacrylate chains remain highly soluble in water so that further water can be taken up. Conversely, the loosely bound water can be lost by evaporation if the cement is exposed to air. This problem of initial water loss or water uptake is critical to the cement and explains why it is essential to protect the surface of the newly set material with a layer of resin. A careful matrix technique should be used because finishing techniques, other than minimal carving with sharp instruments, must be delayed to a subsequent appointment by which time the material will have fully matured.

The properties of glass ionomer cements – adhesion to tooth structure, initial high levels of fluoride release, and fluoride uptake – make them ideal restorative materials for the restoration of non-load-bearing surfaces and erosion lesions, and materials of choice for the stabilization of carious lesions. However, they may not be strong enough to resist occlusal forces.

New 'posterior restorative grade' glass ionomer cements have been developed which are radio-opaque, reasonably tooth-coloured, and very fast setting. These mature very quickly and so can be used as provisional restorations during the 'caries control' phase of treatment. In fact, they were originally made for the *atraumatic restorative treatment (ART)* technique. This technique was instigated by the World Health Organization for use in the developing world by semi-skilled personnel working in difficult environments – with no electricity or normal facilities. Tooth decay is managed by simple hand excavation of the gross caries and then sealing the cavity with an adhesive material – normally glass ionomer cement. In this way, populations can receive restorative dental treatment where previously there was none.

Resin-modified glass ionomer cements (RMGIC)

These cements are another type of material which forms part of the continuum between conventional glass ionomer cements and composites. They contain resin chains – capable of light activation – mixed as an *interconnected polymer network* with the powder/matrix of the conventional cement. These materials show the fluoride release and fluoride uptake of a conventional glass ionomer cement. The set of the resin component is light-initiated, but the set and maturation of the glass ionomer components continue after light exposure. These materials will set in the dark and do not give unlimited working time. It is not correct to describe them as light-cured glass ionomer cements; *resin-modified glass ionomer cements* is a more accurate term.

The resin addition is said to make these materials more user-friendly than the traditional glass ionomer cements. The resin in the material will bind chemically to resin composite which would appear to make these materials ideal for some of the layered glass ionomer–composite restorations described later in this text.

All light-cured materials shrink on setting, but the shrinkage stresses in these materials are relieved by water uptake. There is some evidence that the hydrophilic resins in these materials take up water and this may cause colour change over time.

Polyacid-modified resin composites (PAMRC)

These materials are incorrectly – but commonly – known as *compomers* and contain much reduced amounts of glass ionomer components such as alumino-silicate glass and pendant carboxyl groups attached to the resin backbone chain. However, they are principally composites. These materials do not set in the dark, and this simple test will enable a practitioner to differentiate a resin-modified glass ionomer material from one which is principally a composite. They are designed to absorb water to allow the glass ionomer setting reaction to proceed, once the restoration has been placed and polymerized. All of these materials are therefore packaged in airtight foil packs to prevent ingress of water vapour. The materials are more tolerant of moisture than the conventional composites. However, they can be considered as hydrophobic materials for the purposes of making a bond to wet tooth tissue, needing an intermediate hydrophilic bonding system.

Fluoride-releasing materials

There has been much debate about the benefits of restorative materials with fluoride. Clearly there is an advantage to be had by having fluoride release from a material into the adjacent tooth tissues. Unfortunately, there is great difficulty in determining how much fluoride is going to be useful. Conventional glass ionomer cements release massive amounts of fluoride when newly placed and immature, whilst polyacid-modified composites produce very little to start with and have a low release thereafter. Eventually, the fluoride output from the conventional cement falls to quite low levels, unless *recharged* by fluoride mouth rinses, and so the long-term benefit may be questionable. It is perhaps unfortunate that so much reliance has been placed on the benefit of fluoride release. There are many other reasons why materials such as conventional glass ionomer cements can work so effectively: they seal well, buffer acidic conditions in their vicinity, and place little stress on the tooth when setting. In summary, fluoride release from materials is beneficial, but is probably more related to the marketing of dental materials than dental science.

Dental amalgam

Amalgam is an alloy of mercury with silver and other metals such as tin and copper to give a set material which does not adhere to tooth structure and therefore needs to be retained within the cavity by mechanical means. It has adequate strength in bulk but is brittle in small sections and so it is necessary to design cavities so that amalgam margins are in excess of 70 degrees (Fig. 3.3). This has been shown to be a critical measurement with amalgam since amalgam margin angles less than this tend to break in clinical service, resulting in ditched margins (see Fig. 12.12a on p. 196). It is not tooth-coloured and therefore is used only in posterior teeth where its strength, abrasion resistance, and ability to retain a good polish still make it a popular material.

Although amalgam does not adhere to the tooth surface, it has been shown that there is a reduction in micro-leakage around amalgam restorations over a period of time, and this is attributed to corrosion products forming at the tooth–amalgam interface.

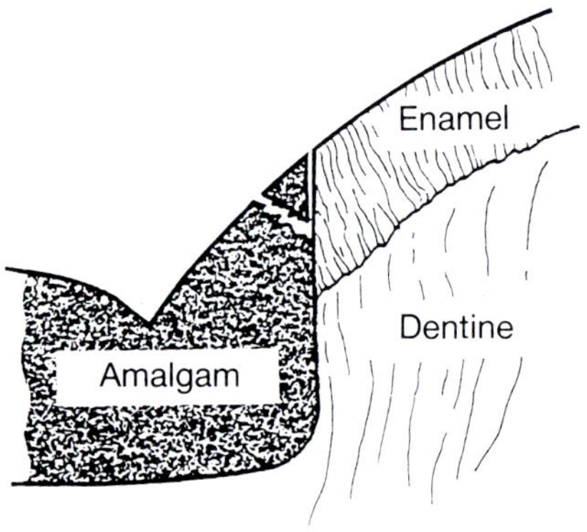

Fig. 3.3 An amalgam restoration prepared and carved so that the amalgam margin angle is too acute. This increases the likelihood of fracture of the amalgam margin. Modification to the angles shown in Fig. 3.2a is required for sufficient strength of the amalgam.

Amalgam is condensed into a cavity with more force than other materials and this must be resisted by the design of the cavity preparation.

Composition of amalgam alloys and their relevance to clinical practice

When the alloy was originally formulated the major components were silver (65 per cent), tin (29 per cent), and copper (6 per cent). Thus a silver–tin intermetallic compound (Ag_3Sn), known as the gamma (γ) phase, predominated which was strengthened by a small amount of copper. However, modern amalgam alloys now contain more copper (10–30 per cent instead of 6 per cent). These *copper-enriched* alloys also contain small quantities of other metals such as palladium. The high copper alloys have two important advantages over the original formulation and both affect the marginal adaptation of the set material. Set amalgams undergo a certain amount of plastic deformation or *creep* when subjected to stress such as occlusal stress. Creep causes the set amalgam to flow over the margins of the cavity to give an unsupported edge, which may be further weakened by *corrosion* of the alloy. Fracture of this edge may form a *ditch* around the margin of the filling (see p. 196). Copper-enriched alloys exhibit less creep and less corrosion that the original alloys, and clinical trials show that they are less prone to ditching. Since an objective of operative dentistry is to produce a smooth and therefore easily cleaned junction between the filling and the tooth, this is an important advantage and explains why the earlier alloys have been replaced by the copper-enriched type.

Sometimes a small amount of zinc is used as a scavenger for oxygen during the production of an alloy. If a zinc-containing alloy is contaminated with moisture during condensation, the zinc reacts with water, producing hydrogen. This causes a delayed expansion of the alloy which may produce pain. For this reason moisture control is important when placing these materials.

The shape and size of alloy particles vary from one product to another because two different methods are used to manufacture the particles. They may be cut from a pre-homogenized ingot of alloy; this produces *lathe-cut* alloy powders with particles of irregular shape that are then graded according to size. Alternatively, the particles may be produced by atomization, where the molten alloy is sprayed into a column filled with inert gas. The droplets of alloy solidify in a *spherical* form as they fall down the column. The shape of the alloy particles (lathe-cut or spherical) is relevant to the dentist using the material. Spherical alloys require less force (condensation pressure) to push them into position, but slip away from the condensing instrument. Some alloys use a combination of shapes and sizes of particle.

High copper levels in alloy powders are produced by the manufacturer in a number of ways. The ratio of metals may be adjusted at the melting stage and either lathe-cut or spherical powders produced. These are called *single-composition copper-enriched alloys*. Another approach is to blend particles of a conventional alloy with those of a silver–copper alloy to achieve a higher overall copper content. These blends are called *dispersion-modified copper-enriched alloys*. One widely used product contains two parts by weight of a lathe-cut alloy containing less than 6 per cent copper and one part by weight of spherical silver–copper eutectic particles (28 per cent copper). The final copper content in the blended alloys is 12 per cent. Since the alloy is a mixture of lathe-cut and spherical particles it will handle more like the former than the latter, requiring considerable packing pressure for condensation.

It can be seen that practitioners have a number of alloys to choose from but should always know which alloy they are using. The choice of alloy will have a bearing on both the clinical handling and the long-term performance of the restorative material.

The safety aspects of amalgam

The controversy over the safety of amalgam restorations is an important subject that has received much attention in the news media. The topic is raised at regular intervals, and all dentists should be conversant with the latest scientific literature so that the matter can be discussed with patients in an informed manner. Details of a review article by Eley and Cox (1993) are given at the end of the chapter.

There is concern over the safety of amalgam because of the mercury it contains which could be released when a filling is placed, during the functional life of a restoration, or during its removal. Scientific groups throughout the world have investigated the safety of amalgam, and there is no evidence that the *minute amount* of mercury released from dental amalgams contributes to systemic disease or has any systemic toxological effects. There is no justification for discontinuing the use of dental amalgam as a filling material or recommending replacement of existing amalgam fillings. Specifically, there is no proven relationship between amalgam and multiple sclerosis, Alzheimer's disease, myalgic encephalitis, or migraine.

There has also been concern about the possible effects of mercury from amalgam restorations in pregnancy. Human studies show no correlation between the surface area of amalgam restorations and mercury levels in maternal blood, amniotic fluid, milk, or neonatal blood. However, there is no doubt that *high* levels of mercury are toxic and dental practitioners must handle it with care so that the local and general environment is not contaminated with either mercury or waste amalgam. Entrapment filters should be fitted to drainage systems to prevent amalgam waste reaching the sewage system, and waste amalgam should be collected and kept under reducing agents such as photographic fixer. Strict mercury and amalgam hygiene procedures should be observed in amalgam preparation, placement, removal, and polishing to minimize the mercury exposure of staff and patients.

Nevertheless it is important to put the role of dental amalgam in environmental mercury pollution into context. A report in 1992 by the United States Environmental Protection Agency showed that in 1989 discarded household batteries accounted for 86 per cent of waste mercury while dental amalgam represented only 0.56 per cent. This amount is tiny when compared with other sources of pollution and has actually decreased by 75 per cent in the last 20 years, demonstrating the awareness and response of the profession to the possible hazard. The preceding paragraphs all deal with the *toxicity* of mercury. Everybody – patients, ancillary staff, and dentists – is susceptible to the toxic effects of mercury. In addition, a very small number of people are genuinely *allergic* to mercury. The number of reported cases which have been confirmed by properly controlled allergy testing is only a few dozen worldwide. However, some patients consider that a very wide range of symptoms of which they complain should be attributed to mercury allergy. In many cases no allergy is confirmed when these patients are tested. However, the possibility must be taken seriously, and if the patient is sufficiently concerned and the symptoms are such that it is conceivable that they may be due to mercury allergy, he or she should be referred for proper allergy testing.

Following each round of media attention to this subject, many dentists are asked by patients to remove all their amalgam fillings and replace them with alternative materials. These requests should usually be kindly and gently resisted, with a full explanation of the difference between toxicity and allergy which many patients find difficult to understand.

Cast gold and other alloys

The advantage of cast metal is that it is strong in thin sections and can be used to protect weakened tooth structure. This property is the major reason for using cast metal restorations, and so cavities are designed so that weakened cusps are protected by a layer of metal. The cavity is prepared in such a way that the restoration (an inlay) is made outside the mouth and then cemented into the cavity.

At one time the small gold inlay was a popular restoration and innumerable inlays have served well for many decades. However, they cannot now be regarded as cost-effective by comparison with improved amalgam and other restorative materials and so are seldom made by most dentists. In the United Kingdom National Health Service less than one in a thousand restorations is a gold inlay, and most of these are to provide protection for weakened tooth structure. Therefore the cavity design for small gold inlays is of only limited practical importance, but inlays still have a role to play for larger restorations protecting the tooth.

Principles of cavity design

When is a restoration needed?

One of the most important reasons for placing a restoration is to aid plaque control.

Occlusal surfaces

When an occlusal surface is cavitated the dentine is always involved. The lesion is usually detectable in dentine on a radiograph. The dentine is soft, it contains many micro-organisms, and the lesion is active. A toothbrush cannot get into the undermined cavity to remove the plaque (Figs. 1.17a and 1.27).

Approximal surfaces

When an adjacent tooth is present, approximal cavitated lesions are difficult to reach. Dental floss will skim the surface, but not access the cavity. Remember that in contemporary populations some 60 per cent of approximal lesions, just visible in dentine on bitewing radiographs, are *not* cavitated. When in doubt, the teeth may be separated with an orthodontic elastic and gently *feel* to see if a cavity is present (Fig. 1.30). If it is, operative dentistry is needed as part of caries management.

Free smooth enamel surfaces

Where a cavity is on a free smooth surface the area can be reached with a toothbrush, although sometimes undermined enamel has to be removed. In this case, twice-daily cleaning with a fluoride-containing toothpaste will arrest lesion progression (Fig. 1.5).

Root surfaces

The active lesion is soft and heavily infected with micro-organisms (Fig. 1.18), but with thorough cleaning with fluoride-containing toothpaste these lesions can be arrested. The soft dentine is gradually worn away, leaving a hard shiny surface from which few bacteria can be cultivated (Fig. 1.20). Smooth surface lesions only require restoration as part of caries management if this will aid plaque control.

Other reasons

Other reasons where a restoration may be needed include:

- the tooth is sensitive to hot, cold, and sweet
- the pulp is endangered
- previous attempts to arrest the lesion have failed and there is evidence that the lesion is progressing
- function is impaired
- drifting is likely through loss of contact point
- the carious lesion is unsightly.

A number of stages are suggested for designing cavities. These are a sequence of practical steps and thought processes. Part of the clinician's role is to make judgements (see Chapter 2), and this must be done throughout the procedure rather than making a single decision at the beginning and then following it slavishly. In the case of a carious tooth the stages will often be as follows:

- gain access to the caries
- remove the caries
- put the instruments down, look, think, and design
- complete the preparation.

Gaining access to the caries

The relatively small carious lesion, which nevertheless needs to be restored, presents a problem of access when it is on the occlusal surface, the approximal surface, or around and beneath existing restorations. Access is not usually a problem with initial lesions on the buccal and lingual surfaces of teeth.

Access to caries in the occlusal dentine is made by cutting through the overlying enamel. With more advanced lesions this undermined enamel will already have caved in, opening up immediate access to the carious dentine.

There are at least four ways of gaining access to caries on the approximal surface of a posterior tooth (Fig. 3.4). When the lesion is sufficiently large that it is inevitable that the marginal ridge will have to be removed, access is gained just inside the marginal ridge and the remainder of the marginal ridge is broken away shortly afterwards. The marginal ridge is not cut directly, as this would almost inevitably cause dam-

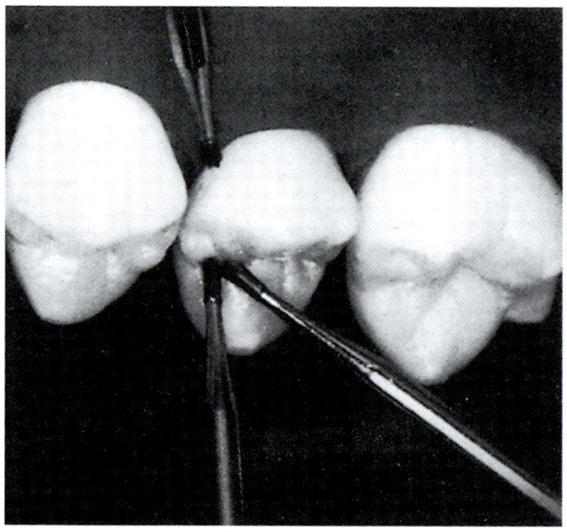

Fig. 3.4 Access can be gained to approximal caries in one of four ways (see text).

age to the adjacent tooth. The second method is to gain access via buccal or lingual surfaces. This is more appropriate where there is a distorted contact point producing caries towards the gingival end of the approximal surface, leaving a sound marginal ridge. It is more practical where there has been a degree of gingival recession. The third method is to approach from the occlusal surface, leaving the marginal ridge intact. Fourthly, when the adjacent tooth has been extracted for other reasons, direct access is possible. However, in many cases removing the adjacent tooth will improve access for cleaning, and even relatively large enamel lesions will arrest so that restoration may not be necessary.

Access to the approximal surfaces of anterior teeth with minimal lesions is usually from the lingual or palatal surface, leaving as much of the intact buccal enamel as possible, even though it may be unsupported by dentine. On occasions, for example with overlapping teeth, buccal or even incisal access is more sensible (see Fig. 10.2).

Gaining access to caries around existing restorations can be the most difficult of these procedures. When the whole restoration has to be removed then the problem is relatively straightforward, but increasingly the virtues of repairing existing amalgam or composite restorations are being acknowledged. For this reason access to caries is usually at the expense of part of the restoration, rather than sound enamel, but without destroying the retention and other characteristics of the restoration. If the operator is not confident that all the caries has been reached, it is safer to remove the whole of the old restoration. Chapter 12 describes why it is sometimes better to leave part of the old restoration in place.

Removing the caries

Once sufficient access is available, caries is removed from the enamel–dentine junction. Caries should not be left at the enamel–dentine junction because no restorative material forms a perfect cavity seal and the disease may progress more readily if caries is left in this area. In addition, enamel undermined by caries is vulnerable to fracture in areas of occlusal stress.

It is not always easy to judge when the enamel–dentine junction is caries-free. Traditionally, the aim has been to remove all *demineralized* tissue in this area. To this end cavity preparation continues until the enamel–dentine junction looks stain-free and feels hard to a sharp probe. However, it has been shown that areas of hard but stained dentine at the enamel–dentine junction may be as minimally infected as adjacent stain-free areas. Thus, it is not obligatory to make the enamel–dentine junction stain-free as well as hard. Certainly, where tooth tissue is at a premium, the authors leave stained but hard tissue at the enamel–dentine junction. Staining at the enamel–dentine junction would, however, be removed if it were likely to show through the enamel when placing an anterior restoration.

The final stage in caries removal is to deal with the dentine over the pulp. Since demineralization precedes bacterial penetration, the interface between the dentine that is demineralized and that which is infected would be an ideal place to stop tissue removal. This is the rationale behind the technique of *indirect pulp capping*, when stained but firm dentine is left in the base of a cavity in a symptomless vital tooth to avoid exposure. The demineralized dentine which remains in the deepest parts of the cavity is then covered with a therapeutic material (usually calcium hydroxide) to encourage reparative dentine formation and remineralization of residual dentine, and to kill any remaining micro-organisms.

The problem for the clinician is to distinguish between the dentine which should be removed and that which may be left. Currently, clinical judgement is used to make this decision and the best rule of thumb is that the soft dentine is heavily infected and should therefore be removed.

Research indicates that it may be important to isolate a deep cavity from saliva, since it has been shown that micro-exposures (a pulpal exposure that is too small to see) will often heal by reparative dentine formation provided that bacterial contamination is minimized. For this reason, a rubber dam (see p. 81) is helpful when restoring very carious teeth.

Where excavation of pulpal caries results in an obvious carious exposure, removal of the pulp and root canal therapy are usually necessary if the tooth is to be saved. Occasionally, a small carious exposure in an otherwise symptomless and vital tooth may be dressed with calcium hydroxide. This *direct pulp cap* aims to preserve a healthy vital pulp by encouraging dentine bridge formation to wall off the exposure. There is considerable controversy over whether or not it is better to use a dentine adhesive applied directly to such exposures rather than calcium hydroxide-based lining materials. One of the reasons for failure in such treatments is postoperative marginal leakage leading to pulp death, a problem that is significantly reduced by the use of adhesive materials. Much of the work cited for both arguments stems from animal experiments which may not accurately model the clinical situation. At present, the authors would favour the use of *small amounts* of calcium hydroxide liners used directly over an exposure as this has a long record of clinical success, but also taking care to ensure that the restoration/tooth margins are well sealed.

How should soft, infected dentine be removed?

At the enamel–dentine junction a slowly rotating bur is the most convenient instrument. The bur may also be used over the pulpal surface of the cavity, but a hand excavator is preferred because this allows the best vision and tactile sensation.

Recently, a chemo-mechanical caries removal system (Carisolv™) has been used to facilitate the removal of carious dentine. The method consists of the application of a mixture of sodium hypochlorite and three amino acids (lysine, leucine, glutamic acid) in a gel preparation to the carious lesion. The product also contains carboxymethyl cellulose to increase the viscosity, and a dye, erythrosin, so that the dentist can see the gel easily. The agent is claimed to soften carious dentine by chemically disrupting the denatured collagen which is then scraped away with specially-designed hand instruments. The technique is more time consuming than the use of burs and excavators, but it is self-limiting and it is not possible to take away too much as is possible with a bur. This means that the technique can often be used without a local anaesthetic and it may have particular merit in the management of patients who fear either an injection or the use of 'the drill', or both.

Stepwise excavation

Stepwise excavation differs from the classical excavation of caries described above. Only the necrotic layer of dentine is removed at the first visit and the remaining soft, infected dentine is covered with calcium hydroxide or zinc oxide and eugenol before placing a temporary restoration.

After a period of weeks, cavities are reopened and further excavation carried out prior to a definitive restoration. The logic of this approach is that sealing the infected dentine from the mouth allows the pulp–dentine complex to lay down reparative dentine and tubular sclerosis to occur. On re-entry and further excavation, exposure is less likely. Where the stepwise approach has been compared to conventional complete excavation, controlled trials have shown more pulpal exposure in the latter group.

This procedure should be considered where a tooth is vital, has no symptoms of irreversible pulpitis, and a pulp exposure seems likely after examination of the radiograph.

Put the instruments down: look, think, and design

This is the most important stage in the preparation. Poor decisions lead to as many failures as poor technique. The main decisions to be made are as follows:

- the final choice of restorative material
- how to retain the restorative material in the cavity
- design features to protect the remaining tooth tissue
- design features to optimize the strength of the restoration
- the shape and position of the cavity margin.

The final choice of restorative material

In most cases the cavity will be started with the expectation of using a particular material, and in most cases this decision is obvious from the outset and is not altered at this stage. However, in other cavities the extent of the caries will be greater or less than was anticipated and a change of plan may be necessary. For instance, if the caries was more extensive than anticipated, a decision to restore with amalgam may be altered to the choice of an inlay with cuspal protection. Alternatively, the adhesive materials, glass ionomer cement, and resin composite may be used to reinforce weakened dentine and enamel. Similarly, with occlusal caries, a decision may be made at this stage between a composite restoration, or a combined composite restoration and fissure sealant.

Making the preparation retentive

Retention can be defined as the features of a preparation which prevent the restoration falling out in any direction. Retention for any restoration should be visualized as preventing loss of the restoration in five directions (Fig. 3.5):

- occlusally
- buccally
- lingually/palatally
- mesially
- distally

or at angles between these directions.

Composite restorations are attached to enamel and dentine by acid etching, which produces a large number of small retentive pores into which the resin flows (see Chapter 6). It is still a mechanical form of retention relying on these miniature undercut cavities and is sometimes referred to as micromechanical retention. Glass ionomer cement bonds adequately to enamel and dentine by both mechanical and chemical means and does not require mechanical undercuts unless subjected to occlusal forces (see Chapter 6).

Amalgam is not adhesive, thus in an amalgam restoration which restores two surfaces of the tooth, say the occlusal and buccal surfaces, features will be required which prevent the loss of the restoration occlusally and buccally. With a large restoration, retention will be required in three, four, or even all five directions.

The means by which the restorative material will be retained permanently within the cavity vary according to the material. Amalgam needs to be retained by physical means,

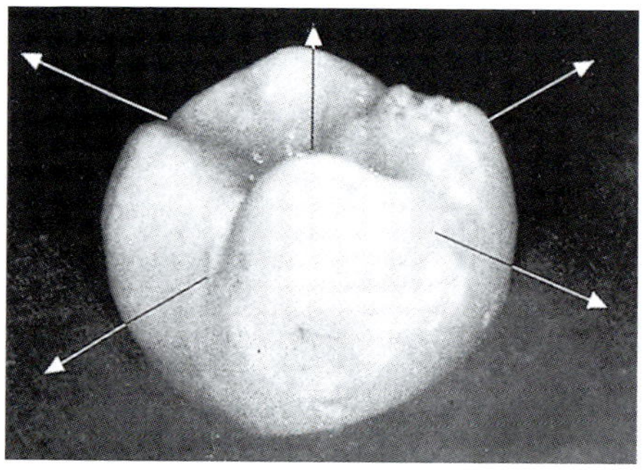

Fig. 3.5 Cavities should be designed with retentive features which prevent the restoration being lost in all five directions and at any angle between them.

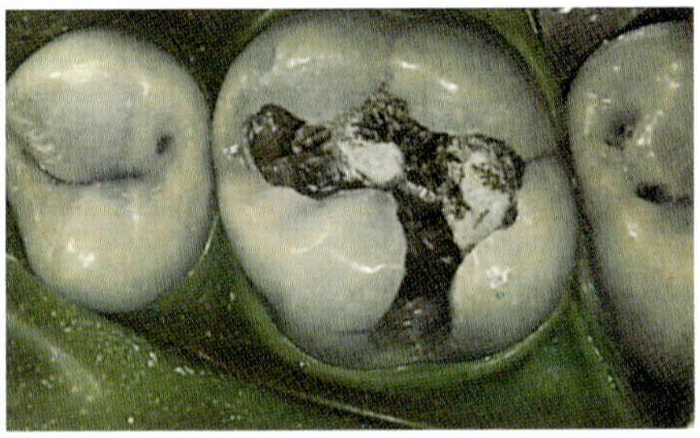

Fig. 3.6 An occlusal–palatal cavity, both parts of which are independently retentive.

such as undercuts in the preparation, retention grooves, and pins. Each part of the amalgam cavity should be independently retentive. Thus, with the occlusal–buccal or palatal restoration, it is ideal if both the occlusal and buccal or palatal parts are retentive independently of each other (Fig. 3.6).

Cast gold and other alloy restorations are retained by means of a different type of micromechanical retention with the gold surface and the prepared tooth surface interlocked with rigid cement (Fig. 3.7), which may also be adhesive to both components. For this reason the path of insertion of the restoration should be within the angle shown in Fig. 3.7 and is described in more detail in Chapter 11.

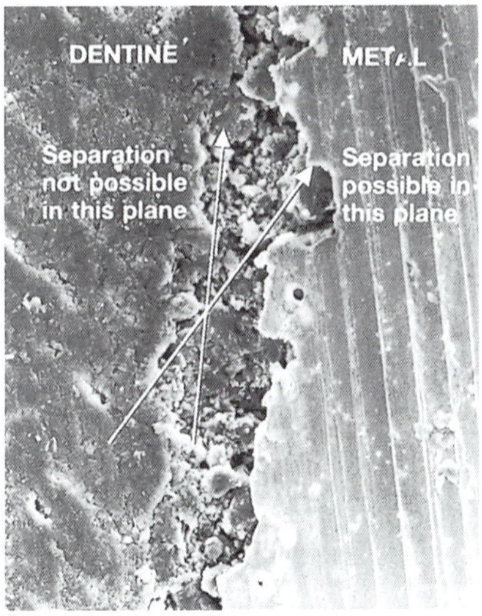

Fig. 3.7 A scanning electron micrograph of a dentine–cement–cast metal interface. The cement, in this case, is not adhesive and so the surfaces can separate at the angle shown. However, if they are to separate at angles less than this, the areas of cement within the irregularities of the metal or dentine surface would need to shear and crumble away. Field width, 100 μm. (Reproduced by courtesy of Dr M. O. Atta.)

Design features to protect the remaining tooth tissue

The remaining tooth tissue, particularly the enamel, may be vulnerable to fracture as a result of either occlusal forces or the insertion of a restoration.

With amalgam restorations, unsupported enamel on the occlusal surface should be removed, as should sharp edges of enamel elsewhere. Although these latter edges are not vulnerable to occlusal forces, they may be damaged in tightening a metal matrix band or while condensing the amalgam (see Chapter 8).

It is less important to remove undermined enamel when adhesively-retained restorations are used because the restorative material, such as composite or glass ionomer cement, will support the enamel except in areas subjected to direct occlusal forces. Articulating paper should be used to check the exact contact areas between opposing teeth to help with the decision as to whether or not to remove unsupported occlusal enamel.

When the cavity is large and the remaining cusps are weak, the choice is to remove the weak cusp altogether, to protect it from occlusal forces by covering its occlusal surface by means of a cast metal inlay/onlay (see Chapter 11), or to support it by bonding it to other parts of the tooth with glass ionomer cement, composite resin, or a combination of the two materials (see Chapter 8).

Design features to optimize the strength of the restoration

Some restorative materials, particularly amalgam and porcelain, are weak in thin sections and when they have sharp angles. This means that sufficient tooth tissue should be removed to allow adequate thickness of the material. In addition, cavo-surface angles of amalgam and porcelain preparations should approximate to 90 degrees to allow sufficient bulk of material at the margin.

A good example of this design feature is in the occlusal–proximal amalgam restoration, in which the angle between the occlusal floor and axial wall of the preparation is rounded over or bevelled. This is done because the amalgam in this region is shallow, since there is usually an occlusal fossa immediately above it. This area coincides with the narrowest

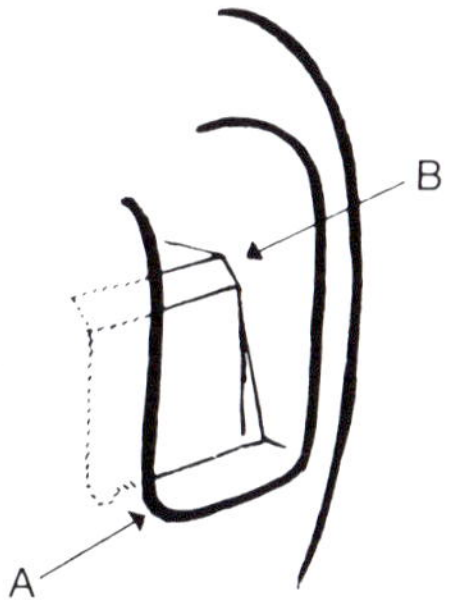

Fig. 3.8 The proximal box of an occlusal–proximal amalgam cavity. The angle between the occlusal floor and axial wall of the box has been bevelled (B) for the reasons described in the text. Note also that the corners of the box are also rounded (A) to reduce the risk of voids in the amalgam here, resulting from the difficulty in packing amalgam into sharp angles.

part of the occlusal preparation and a cavity with a sharp internal angle would concentrate stresses, increasing the likelihood of the amalgam fracturing here (Fig. 3.8).

'Resistance form'

In older terminology relating to stylized cavity shapes and originating with G. V. Black, 'retention form' was a term used to describe the design features of a cavity which prevented loss of the restoration axially. 'Resistance form' was used to describe design features which resisted loss in other directions. This distinction is no longer useful, in particular in relation to the retention mechanisms of adhesive materials. Therefore the term 'retention' should be used as it is described on p. 64, and the term 'resistance', if it is needed at all, should now be applied to the design features described in the two previous paragraphs.

The shape and position of the cavity margin

The shape of the cavity margin will largely be determined by the choice of material. Amalgam and porcelain cavity margins should be finished at approximately 90 degrees, as described earlier. Cast metal restorations can be finished to acute angles, and so the cavity margin can be a very oblique bevel. The shape of the margin for composite restorations may be bevelled in some cases to improve retention and appearance (see Chapters 6 and 9).

The position of the cavity margin is largely determined by the caries but cavity margins should be supragingival wherever possible to improve access for cleaning. In posterior restorations involving the approximal surface, a decision must be made as to whether or not the margin of the preparations should be extended beyond the contact area to improve access for cleaning. Traditionally, it has always been cut clear of the contact area, but this should no longer be an automatic decision. Cutting the cavity free of the contact area may well be more destructive than is necessary in a number of cases (see Chapter 8). The important consideration is how the patient can clean the margin so that further caries may be prevented.

With anterior approximal restorations the cavity margin is commonly left in contact with the adjacent teeth for aesthetic reasons and because access for cleaning is good anteriorly.

Possible future developments in cavity design

Looking back at the changes which have occurred in the approach to cavity design in the last 30 years, it is inevitable that further changes will occur in the future. Therefore the principles outlined above should be regarded as the current 'state of play' and not set in concrete in the dentist's mind.

It is possible that we are at the threshold of a major development in thinking about restoring teeth. Until now the concept has been to remove diseased hard tissue and replace it with little more than a plug in a hole. (Fillings used to be known as 'stoppings'.) The only materials available until fairly recently had very little resemblance – structurally, chemically, aesthetically, or functionally – to dental tissues. They did not bond adequately to the dental tissues and did not have therapeutic properties such as resisting recurrent caries (with the exception of silicate cement). Despite these drawbacks they served their purpose adequately. However, new objectives are emerging. In the future the emphasis will be more on genuinely *restoring* teeth rather than just repairing them. One example of this approach is the arrest of early enamel lesions rather than cutting out the diseased tissue. Another example is the 'layered' or 'combination' restoration, in which a large cavity is filled with glass ionomer cement to replace the dentine and then is 'topped off' with a layer of composite to replace the enamel. The properties of glass ionomer cement are nearer to those of dentine than they are to enamel, and the material bonds to dentine and leaches fluoride. The composite, which can be attached micromechanically to the surface of the glass ionomer cement and the etched enamel walls, replaces the enamel and has a similar appearance. Its properties resemble enamel more than glass ionomer cement does. This 'layered' restoration is not yet a true reconstruction of the tooth, but it is closer than a restoration in amalgam.

In the future, these attempts may be seen as a crude start to a new era in which cavity design may be drastically altered or indeed become unnecessary, either because new techniques or new materials become available. Many anterior restorations needed for reasons of trauma, tooth wear, or hypoplasia already require little cavity preparation because of the conservative use of adhesive materials.

The control of pain and trauma in operative dentistry

Some operative procedures are painless, some are uncomfortable, and many are potentially painful. It is not sufficient simply to give a local anaesthetic; many procedures can still be uncomfortable, for example heavy-handed lip retraction, trapping the lip between the teeth and an instrument, and requiring a tense patient to keep their mouth open for long periods without relaxing. All these are sufficiently uncomfortable to deter many patients from visiting the dentist even when pulpal anaesthesia is effective. Patients should not be expected to submit to anything more than minor discomfort of short duration, unless the measures required to avoid it would require greater discomfort or risk to their general well-being.

Pre-operative precautions

Proper diagnosis of the condition of the pulp before administering local anaesthesia is necessary. Sometimes local anaesthesia has been provided without establishing the condition of the pulp, only to find later that the tooth was root-filled or contained a necrotic pulp.

Some patients, particularly later in life, have formed sufficient secondary dentine for their teeth to be insensitive to all but the most extensive preparation. These patients may not need local anaesthesia. However, for the majority of patients local anaesthesia is required once it is established that the pulp is vital. It is bad practice to leave administration of a local anaesthetic until it is essential because the patient is experiencing pain. This is unpleasant for the patient and destroys confidence.

Alternative or additional methods of controlling pain and apprehension are relative analgesia with nitrous oxide–oxygen mixtures in conjunction with local anaesthetics, oral or intravenous sedation with midazolam or diazepam, or in rare cases full general anaesthesia. These methods are only very rarely required if the patient is handled sympathetically and gently. Some patients who have had a traumatic dental experience or need a difficult form of treatment may be offered one of these approaches but, where possible, they should be weaned off it again as soon as possible in their own interest. There are two reasons for this. First, if elaborate precautions such as these need to be taken, dental treatment tends to be deferred until batches of treatment are necessary and this is not the best way to maintain a healthy dentition. Second, as was stressed in Chapter 1, effective communication between operator and patient is necessary if the patient is to cooperate in all the preventive measures necessary for long-term dental health. This is not possible with a sedated or unconscious patient. General anaesthesia is only given in the UK in hospitals with full recovery and emergency services and is limited to patients who are classified as having 'special needs', many of whom have some learning difficulties or behavioural problems.

Pain and trauma control during tooth preparation

Patients usually prefer the air turbine to preparation of teeth at low speed because of the vibration felt at low speed (see Chapter 5). This vibration can be minimized by ensuring that the handpiece bearings are in good condition and by deadening the vibration by pressure on the tooth with a finger whilst it is being prepared. This vibration should not deter the operator from completing the removal of caries at low speed because using the air turbine will almost inevitably result in unnecessary tooth destruction.

With an anaesthetized tooth there is a danger of causing thermal damage to the pulp by inadequate cooling of the bur. Figure 3.9a shows the pulp immediately below a very deep cavity cut at low speed under a continuous stream of water; the tooth was extracted shortly afterwards. Here the pulp shows no detectable signs of injury. Figure 3.9b, in contrast, shows the pulp condition 11 days after using a high-speed handpiece without water spray. The destruction of the odontoblast layer is clearly seen, with all the cellular and vascular changes of inflammation.

Direct trauma to the pulp should of course be avoided, although probably all dentists have occasionally exposed pulp at the base of a deep cavity when they were not expecting to. This may be because the pulp is unusually large or has not formed reparative dentine at the rate which would normally be expected. The terms 'carious exposure' and 'traumatic expo-

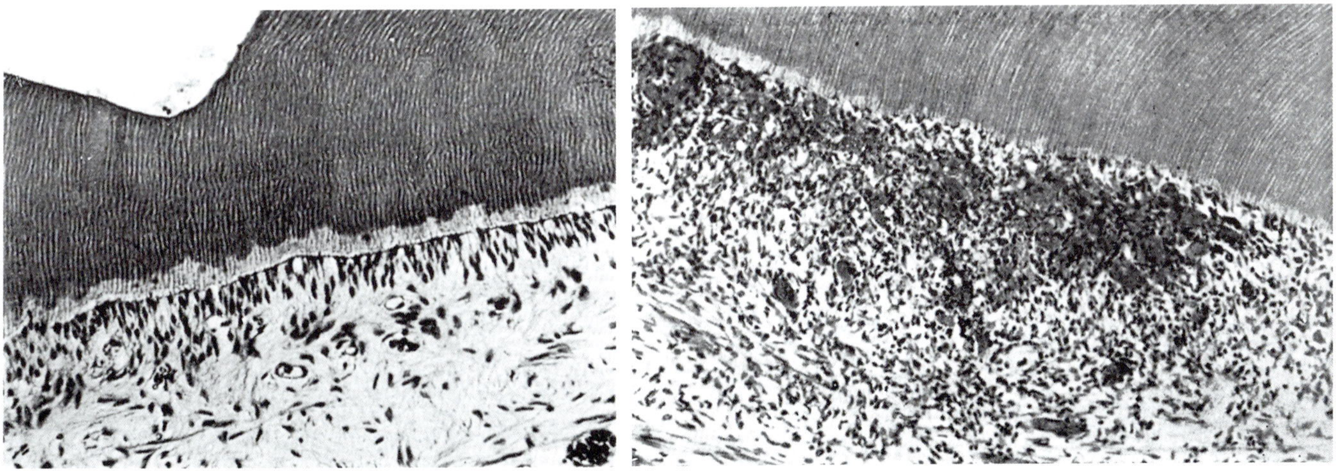

(a) (b)

Fig. 3.9 (a) Pulp below the deepest part of a cavity prepared at 5000 rev/minute under a constant stream of water.
(b) Localized destructive lesion of the pulp adjacent to a cavity prepared with an airotor without water spray. (Reproduced by courtesy of Professor D. S. Shovelton.)

sure' are used to describe exposure of a vital bleeding pulp. The distinction between the two is not always clear, but in the former the dentist feels that exposure is inevitable if all the soft dentine is removed whereas in the latter it is not.

Direct trauma to the gingival tissues should be avoided and careful selection of the size of bur to be used, adequate support of the handpiece, and a gentle technique will usually prevent this. Occasionally, with cavities that extend well below the gingival margin, it is necessary to retract the gingival tissues with a rubber dam or to remove gingival tissue surgically.

Avoiding postoperative pain

Postoperative pain may arise from the lips and soft tissues if they have been stretched or damaged. It may also arise from the pulp if it has been damaged or the cavity has been inadequately lined or sealed. Finally, pain may come from the periapical periodontal tissues if the restoration is left high so that the tooth is in traumatic occlusion. These circumstances should all be avoided.

Cavity lining and chemical preparation

A whole battery of materials are now available for the treatment of a prepared cavity surface in order to promote adhesion or a good cavity seal; these are detailed in Chapter 6. Other materials, such as calcium hydroxide-based linings and glass ionomer cement, are placed on a cavity floor for protective, therapeutic, or structural reasons. Varnishes, which are natural or synthetic resins in a solvent, are no longer considered appropriate for improving the marginal seal of an amalgam restoration.

Objectives and materials

The objectives in preparing a cavity to receive a restorative material can be considered under the following headings:

- cleaning the cavity
- therapeutic
- protective
- structural
- attaining cavity seal and promoting adhesion.

These objectives will be discussed below, together with the materials currently available. The clinical techniques for handling the materials will be found in Part II of this book.

Cleaning the cavity

Cavity preparation, without water spray, produces grinding debris and it is important to wash the cavity thoroughly to remove this. Before placing the restorative material the cavity should be dried with air.

Therapeutic

Cavity preparation is usually carried out to remove dental caries. Details of the management of carious dentine have been given on p. 63. A therapeutic lining material may be placed on the partly demineralized dentine in the base of the cavity for the following reasons:

- to stimulate the odontoblasts to lay down reparative dentine
- to encourage remineralization of the dentine
- to provide a hostile environment for any bacteria that may remain in the base of the cavity.

The preferred material in these circumstances is a setting cement containing calcium hydroxide, which is believed to achieve each of these objectives. It is believed that, to be effective, the calcium hydroxide must be released from the cement. The material should be used as a thin layer for its therapeutic effect and then covered with glass ionomer cement if further thermal insulation is required.

Antibiotic–corticosteroid preparations have also been used as therapeutic lining materials. These preparations are unrivalled in their ability to suppress the pain of pulpitis when placed on carious exposures. Unfortunately, their use is a temporary expedient since pulp death also invariably occurs some time later. For this reason they should only be used where root canal treatment is planned and insufficient time or inadequate anaesthesia prevents pulp extirpation at that visit.

Protective: thermal

If the cavity is to be filled with amalgam or cast metal, an insulating layer may be required between the metal filling and the pulp–dentine complex. Fortunately, dentine itself is a good insulator and thus there is no justification for removing it to make room for an insulating layer. However, in a deep or moderately deep cavity there may be insufficient thickness of dentine remaining and the cavity will then require a lining. Glass ionomer cement is a good choice but should be sublined with calcium hydroxide in deep cavities. However, it bonds to the dentine walls and releases fluoride, and it can be used in much thicker layers than other lining materials. If the restoration is to be amalgam, the glass ionomer lining should be designed so that the amalgam is thick enough for strength. If composite is to be used, the glass ionomer cement lining is usually built up to the enamel–dentine junction (or overbuilt and cut back to this level when set). In other words, the glass ionomer cement replaces all the dentine and the composite replaces the enamel. No lining should be so thick that it causes the structural integrity of the overlying restoration to be compromised. Clearly, if there is insufficient room then the lining is unnecessary anyway.

Protective: chemical

Whilst many of the materials that we use will be cytotoxic to the pulp cells, especially the odontoblasts, much evidence suggests that so long as the cavity is well sealed the pulp–dentine complex is capable of repair. There will be far more pulpal injury arising from bacterial toxins percolating along a defective marginal gap than from the materials themselves. Lining materials may help to protect the pulp from chemical insults, but their benefits may be more of an illusion than fact.

Structural

It is possible to use a lining material to restore the internal form of a cavity (see p. 126) to produce a flat pulpal floor and a smooth axial wall. This means that less filling material will be required and the internal shape of the cavity may be less complex. Both these factors are of considerable advantage when using cast metal as an intracoronal restoration. Glass ionomer cement is an ideal material for this purpose because it is adhesive to dentine and thus may afford some support to the weakened tooth tissue.

Attaining cavity seal and promoting adhesion

If a filling does not seal a cavity, leakage of bacteria and fluids carrying molecules and ions in solution can occur between the restoration and the cavity wall. Such leakage may result in tooth discoloration under amalgams, hypersensitivity, pulpal damage, and a rapid breakdown of certain filling materials. All restorative materials leak to some extent but there is much that can be done to improve cavity seal. Details of how this is achieved are given in Chapter 6.

Further reading

Bjørndal, L. (2002). Dentine caries: progression and clinical management. *Oper. Dent.* **27**, 211–17.

Eley, B. M. and Cox, S. W. (1993). The release, absorption and possible health effects of mercury from dental amalgam: a review of recent findings. *Br. Dent. J.* **175**, 355–62.

Ericson, D. and Bornstein, R. (2001). Development of a tissue-preserving agent for caries removal. In: *Tissue preservation in caries treatment* (ed. xxx), Chapter 19, pp. 153–66. Quintessence Books.

Frenken, J. E. and Holmgren, C. J. (1999). *Atraumatic restorative treatment for dental caries*. STI Book b.v., Nimegen.

Kidd, E. A. M. (2000). Caries removal and the pulpo–dentinal complex. *Dent. Update.* **27**, 476–82.

Kidd, E. A. M., Joyston-Bechal, S., and Beighton, D. (1993). Microbiological validation of assessment of caries activity during cavity preparation. *Caries Res.* **27**, 402–8.

Mertz-Fairhurst, E., Cootes, J. W., Ergle, J. W., and Reuggenberg, F. A. (1998). Ultraconservative and cariostatic sealed restorations: results at year 10. *J. Am. Dent. Assoc.* **129**, 55–66.

Rickets, D. N. J. (2001). Management of the deep carious lesion and the vital pulp–dentine complex. *Brit. Dent. J.* **191**, 606–10.

Van Noort, (2002). *An introduction to dental materials* (2nd edn). Mosby Wolfe.

PART 11

TREATMENT TECHNIQUES

4

The operator and the environment

The dental team

The dental school and practice environment

The surgery

- Positioning the patient, the dentist, and the dental nurse
- Lighting
- Siting of work-surfaces and instruments
- Aspirating equipment; cavity washing and drying
- Hand and instrument cleaning

Close-support dentistry

- Maintaining a clear working field for the dentist
- Instrument transfer

Moisture control

- Reasons for moisture control
- Techniques for moisture control

Magnification

Protection, safety, and management of minor emergencies

- Eye protection
- Airway protection
- Soft tissue protection
- Avoiding surgical emphysema
- Dealing with accidents and accident reporting
- Protection from infection

The operator and the environment

The dental team

Dentists are leaders of a group of individuals whose combined efforts are devoted to the prevention of dental diseases and the restoration and preservation of dental health. The dentist is assisted at the chairside by a dental nurse, sometimes called a dental surgery assistant (DSA). Many dentists employ hygienists to whom they delegate some of the preventive aspects of dental care such as oral hygiene instruction, scaling and polishing, dietary advice, and fluoride application. Technical work, such as making crowns, bridges, and dentures, is carried out to the dentist's prescription by a dental technician who may, increasingly rarely, work in a laboratory attached to the practice or in a separate commercial laboratory. These members of the team, who are all directly or indirectly involved in providing dental care, will usually have appropriate qualifications (in the case of hygienists they *must* be qualified). In addition, most dentists employ receptionists, secretaries, practice managers, or some combination of such team members who do not need a special dental qualification.

Since the seventh edition of this book in 1996, substantial changes in the dental team have been proposed and some implemented in the UK. These are the greater recognition of professionals complementary to dentistry (PCD) and the introduction of recognized specialists who are registered with the UK General Dental Council. Dental hygienists and operating therapists have been enrolled with the GDC for many years but new groups, such as clinical dental technicians and orthodontic assistants, are being introduced. Qualified dental nurses can take additional certificates in oral health education, dental radiology, and the care of sedated patients. It is policy within the UK National Health Service to increase the roles and numbers of all these professionals complementary to dentistry, thus expanding the dental team.

At the specialist level there are now registered specialists in periodontics, endodontics, and prosthodontics as well as consultants in restorative dentistry. General dental practitioners can refer patients to these specialists and consultants either for advice or for treatment within their specialities.

This means that increasingly the general dental practitioner, being the first point of contact for patients, is the central hub of the team allocating work to and supervising the PCDs and referring individual patients to specialists and consultants. He or she will then receive them back either to carry out the treatment advised or to monitor and maintain the treatment provided by the specialist or consultant.

The dental student should meet and work with all these groups from the beginning of clinical training if at all possible. Such contact is an important part of training because it develops effective communication with them and a proper understanding of their roles, which is essential to the smooth running of the dental team. Where possible these teams should train together as well as interacting from an early stage.

The dental school and practice environment

The dental school environment is obviously very different from general practice, although many features are common to both. There is an entrance, which should be well signposted so that the patient knows where to go and is not embarrassed by finding themselves in the doctor's surgery next door or in the wrong hospital department. Other information, such as hours of opening and arrangements for out-of-hours emergency treatment, should be clearly shown.

Everyone concerned with dental care should appreciate that the hospital or practice, which seems so commonplace when one works in it every day, is a new and possibly frightening environment for patients. Dentists and staff should look critically at the surroundings to see that they are as attractive and welcoming as possible. Design, decor, and cleanliness are important; plants and magazines in a waiting area are a welcoming sight. Even more important is the personal touch: a friendly smile from the receptionist and the prompt attention of the dentist or student, or a genuine apology for unavoidable delay, all help to transform what is often a worrying experience for patients into a warm and welcoming one.

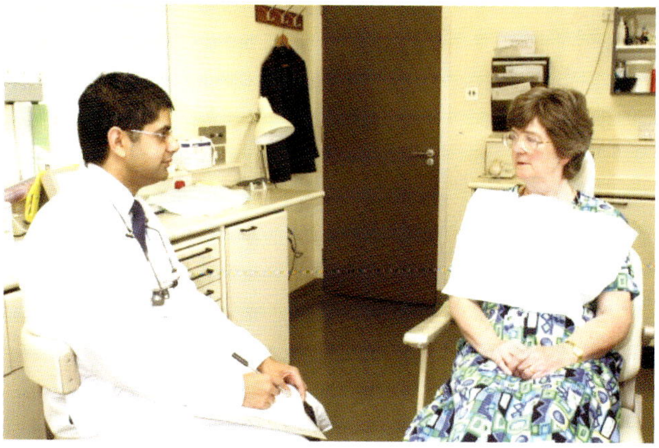

Fig. 4.1 Dentist and patient talking. They are sitting at the same level and facing each other with eye-to-eye contact. At this stage, gloves should not be worn.

The surgery

Positioning the patient, the dentist, and the dental nurse

Patient, dentist, and dental nurse must all be positioned for maximum comfort and visibility, with minimum distortion of backs and necks. Initially, the dentist and patient need to talk to each other, and this should be with both seated face to face on the same level (Fig. 4.1). If the dentist stands towering over the patient or talks to the back of their head, communication is poor and the patient feels even more at a disadvantage.

When the time comes to examine the patient, or perform operative treatment, the dental chair is tilted back and raised so that the patient is horizontal (Fig. 4.2). The chair should be designed to support the patient's head, back, and arms.

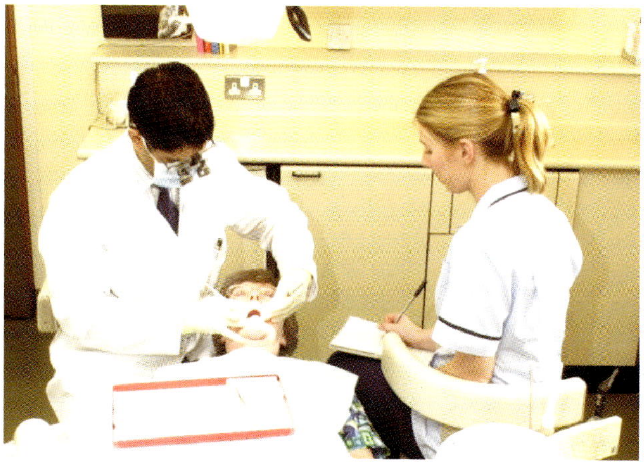

Fig. 4.2 Dentist, dental nurse, and patient positioned to carry out an intraoral examination. Note that the patient has now been provided with eye protection. The nurse is charting and so is not wearing gloves. Once the dentist starts to operate, the dental nurse should also wear protective spectacles.

The patient's head should be at the top of the headrest, so that the dentist does not have to bend forward excessively to see into the mouth, and at the dentist's mid-sternum level, bringing the mouth to the correct focal range of the eyes. The dentist's knees will now fit under the headrest.

The dentist sits, usually behind the patient, on a stool with castor feet which enable it to be moved easily by the operator while seated. The dentist's back is supported, feet flat on the floor, and the top of the thighs parallel with the floor. The long axis of the dentist's upper arm should be vertical and the elbows close to the rib cage, while the head is tilted forward so that the eyes can see the fingertips.

For a right-handed dentist, the dental nurse sits on the patient's left-hand side, facing the patient. Her stool should also have a backrest, but for her to be able to see clearly into the mouth she should be seated some 10 cm (4 inches) higher than the dentist; thus her stool may require a bar on which she can rest her feet and may have a backrest which can be swung round to the front to support the dental nurse when she leans forward towards the patient (Fig. 4.2).

So far, the vertical positioning of the dentist's stool, the dental chair, and the dental nurse's stool have been considered. Positioning must also be considered in a horizontal plane. If the patient's head in the dental chair is represented by a clock-face, the right-handed dentist usually sits slightly to the right-hand side of the patient, at 11 o'clock, but with the facility to move between 1 and 8 o'clock. The dental nurse is usually positioned at 4 o'clock, but may also take up a position anywhere between 1 o'clock and 4 o'clock (Fig. 4.2).

The patient may also be asked to turn their head towards or away from the dentist. For example, when examining the buccal surfaces of teeth in the upper left quadrant the patient's head should be turned to the right so that this area can be seen clearly by direct vision. When examining lower teeth the patient should tip the chin down. Conversely, when examining upper teeth the patient should tip their head back.

Although the dentist usually sits at 11 o'clock, some operators move round to the 8 o'clock position and readjust the patient's chair when working on the lower right quadrant by direct vision. The base of the chair should be lowered and the backrest raised slightly, the patient's head turned towards the dentist (Fig. 4.3).

Unfortunately, much dental equipment is designed for right-handed dentists and is not readily adapted for left-handed use. Much of this advice on positioning will not apply to left-handed dentists, and their position will not simply be the reverse of the right-handed dentist's position because of the inflexibility of the equipment. Left-handed dentists usually need to experiment with positions until they are able to equip a surgery for their own use.

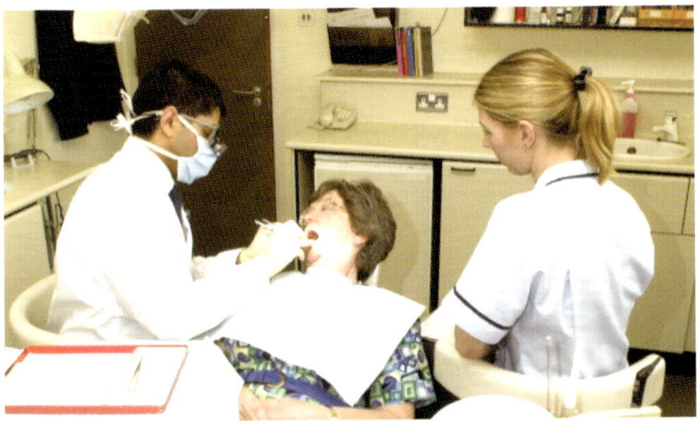

Fig. 4.3 Dentist in the 8 o'clock position examining the lower right quadrant by direct vision.

Lighting

If the dentist is to see well, the small operating field must be lit adequately. The level of illumination of the surgery as a whole, whether by natural or artificial light, should be bright and is usually above that needed for normal purposes so that there is not too much contrast with the higher level of illumination of the operating field. This reduces the extent to which the dentist's and dental nurse's eyes have to adapt. The operating light is situated above the patient's head and its direction is varied with the arch being examined.

Siting of work-surfaces and instruments

The dentist and dental nurse need work-surfaces around them on which to place instruments and materials. The dental nurse needs facilities for mixing materials, and the dentist needs an area for the patient's notes and a viewing box for radiographs.

The dentist requires easy access to the handpieces and hand instruments. These may be situated on the dentist's side of the chair, over the patient, or on the nurse's side (Fig. 4.4). Each of these positions has disadvantages. The dental nurse cannot reach the instruments if they are on the dentist's side and therefore has to walk around the chair at least once between each patient. Many patients feel claustrophobic with instruments and trays positioned over their chest. When handpieces and instruments are on the dental nurse's side this layout also presupposes that she will always be present to pass them to the dentist. A fourth possibility – the instruments placed behind the head of the chair – has the major disadvantage that it increases the risk that instruments will be passed over the patient's face and dropped, causing injury. This possibility, together with the awkwardness of the instruments being behind the dentist's back, makes this the least popular arrangement.

It is obvious that surgery design, even for a single dentist, is open to considerable variation. In a dental school, where operating areas must be designed for right- and left-handed students working with and without dental nurses, the prob-

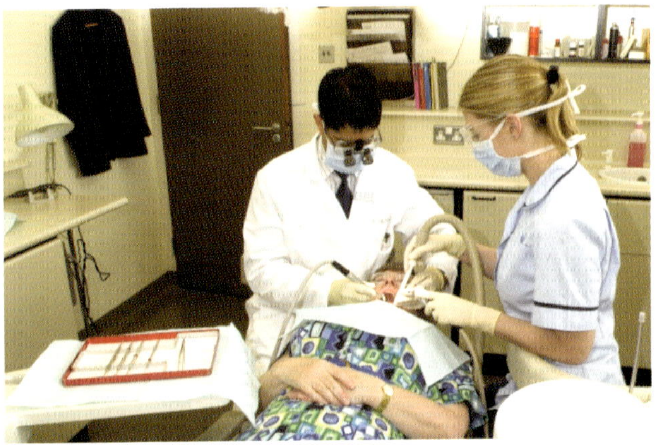

(a)

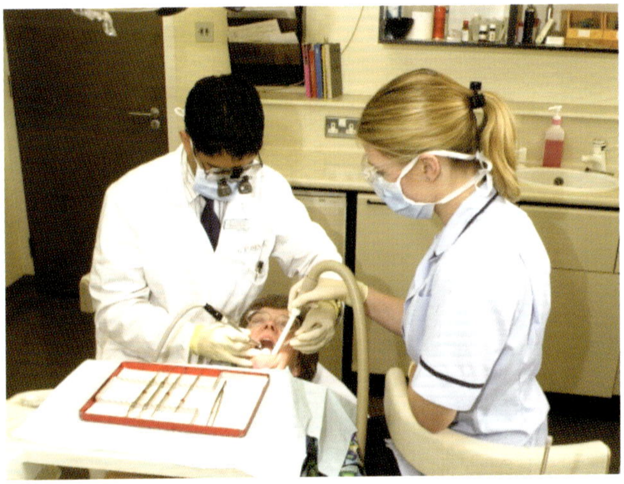

(b)

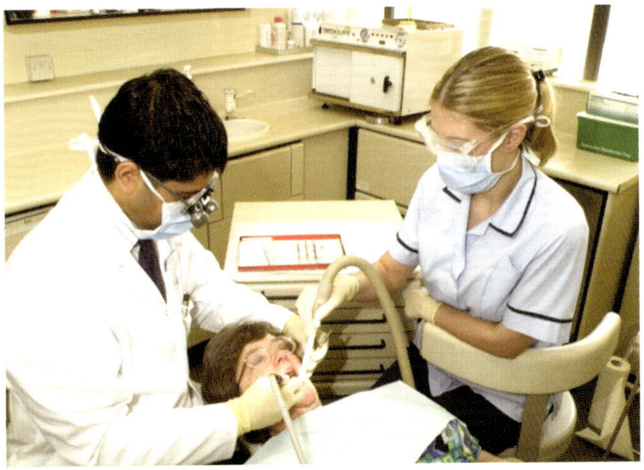

(c)

Fig. 4.4 (a) Instruments on the dentist's side of the chair. (b) Instruments on the cervical tray over the patient's chest. (c) Instruments on the dental nurse's side of the chair.

lems are virtually insoluble. Maximum flexibility must be allowed with work-surfaces provided on both sides, and this is also important in a dental practice where the dentist may have to work unaided for limited periods.

Aspirating equipment; cavity washing and drying

High-speed cutting instruments require water cooling, and cavities must be washed, dried, and isolated from saliva. Thus, suction equipment to remove liquids from the mouth is essential, as is a syringe which will deliver a jet of water or air, or a spray mixture of the two – a three-in-one syringe. Aspiration of liquids and cavity washing and drying should be a principal responsibility of the dental nurse and so the equipment must be available on her side of the chair. In addition, a three-in-one syringe should also be available on the dentist's side. At the end of treatment patients like to rinse their mouths, and a spittoon is commonly available on the dental nurse's side of the chair.

Hand and instrument cleaning

Hand basins should be available to both dentist and dental nurse. Instrument cleaning and sterilizing facilities should be on the dental nurse's side of the surgery, when not provided centrally in a hospital. It is the dentist's responsibility to ensure sterility and clean working practices (see Chapter 5).

Close-support dentistry

Close-support or four-handed dentistry are the terms used to describe systems of close cooperation between dentist and dental nurse in the actual dental treatment of patients. Such cooperation is essential for maximum operating effectiveness. Unfortunately, many dental students have spent a major part of their course operating alone, and acquire time-wasting and inefficient operating habits which then have to be corrected if their clinical standards are not to fall when they enter the hurly-burly of general practice. Fortunately, some four-handed dentistry is now taught in dental schools, and it is important that students learn how a trained and efficient dental nurse works so that they can subsequently train an assistant to work with them happily and efficiently.

Maintaining a clear working field for the dentist

A principal role of the dental nurse in close-support dentistry is to maintain a clear working field so that the patient is comfortable and the dentist can see the working area. This involves aspiration of water and coolant spray, retraction of soft tissues, keeping the mirror free of spray, and keeping the cavity clear of debris.

When aspirating, the dental nurse should place the aspirator in the mouth before the dentist positions the mirror and handpiece. She first retracts the lip with her finger or the tip of the three-in-one syringe and then places the aspirator tip in position (Fig. 4.5a). The dentist may then position the mirror and handpiece (Fig. 4.5b). If this order is reversed the dentist's view is likely to be obstructed by the aspirator tip. The tip of the aspirator should never contact the patient's soft palate as this might cause retching.

The orifice of the aspirator tip may be positioned either 'on site' (Fig. 4.5a) or behind the last tooth (Fig. 4.5c). In either position the aspirator tip also retracts soft tissue. When 'on site' it is placed next to the tooth being prepared, level with its occlusal plane on the side of the arch nearest to the dental nurse. The bevel of the aspirator tip is parallel to the arch and about 1 cm away from the tooth so that the coolant spray is not diverted away from the tooth. Alternatively, the aspirator tip can be placed 'retromolar', just distal to the last molar, which is where water will naturally collect with the patient supine.

The dental nurse also assists with soft tissue retraction in other ways, mainly with tissues on her side of the arch. Thus, when working on the left side of the mouth, the cheek and lips on the patient's left side are the responsibility of the dental nurse, whilst tongue retraction is the responsibility of the den-

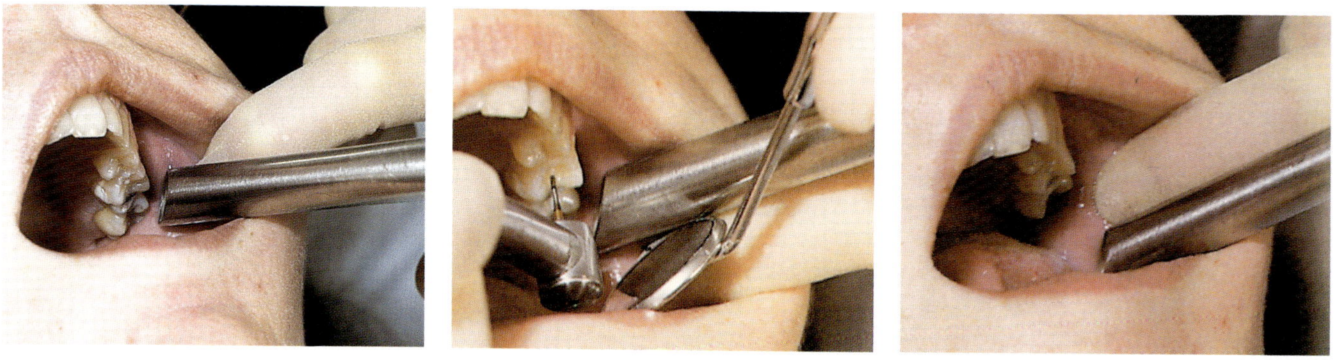

(a) (b) (c)

Fig. 4.5 (a) Dental nurse retracting the patient's lip and placing the aspirator tip next to the tooth to be prepared.
(b) Once the aspirator tip is in position, the dentist may position the mirror and the handpiece.
(c) An alternative position for the aspirator tip is just distal to the last molar, which is where water will naturally collect with the patient supine.

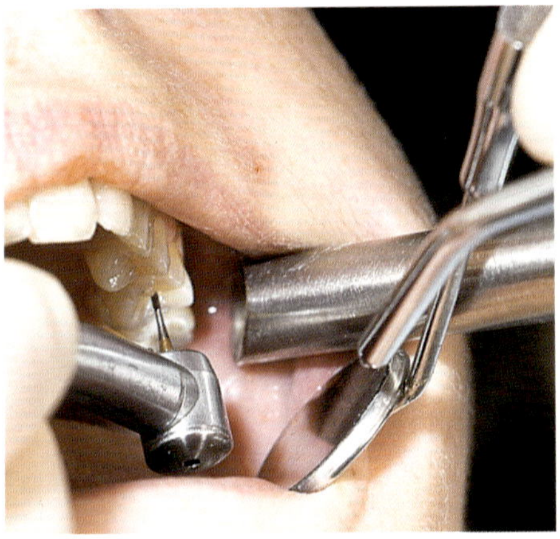

Fig. 4.6 The dental nurse is using a three-in-one syringe to wash and dry the mirror while the dentist uses the air turbine.

tist. Conversely, when working on the right-hand side, tongue retraction is the responsibility of the dental nurse while the dentist retracts lips and cheeks.

When cutting with the air turbine, the mirror surface quickly becomes obscured by spray. The dental nurse should keep the mirror clear by washing it with spray and blowing air over it (Fig. 4.6). Each time the cutting stops, the dental nurse should wash and dry the cavity and the mirror so that the dentist can see clearly.

Instrument transfer

In efficient close-support dentistry all hand instruments are on a work-surface in front of the dental nurse, who hands them to the dentist. This means that the dentist can concentrate on the mouth at all times without having repeatedly to look away to pick up and replace instruments. However, if dentist and dental nurse are going to work efficiently, the dentist must use a fixed sequence of instruments for any

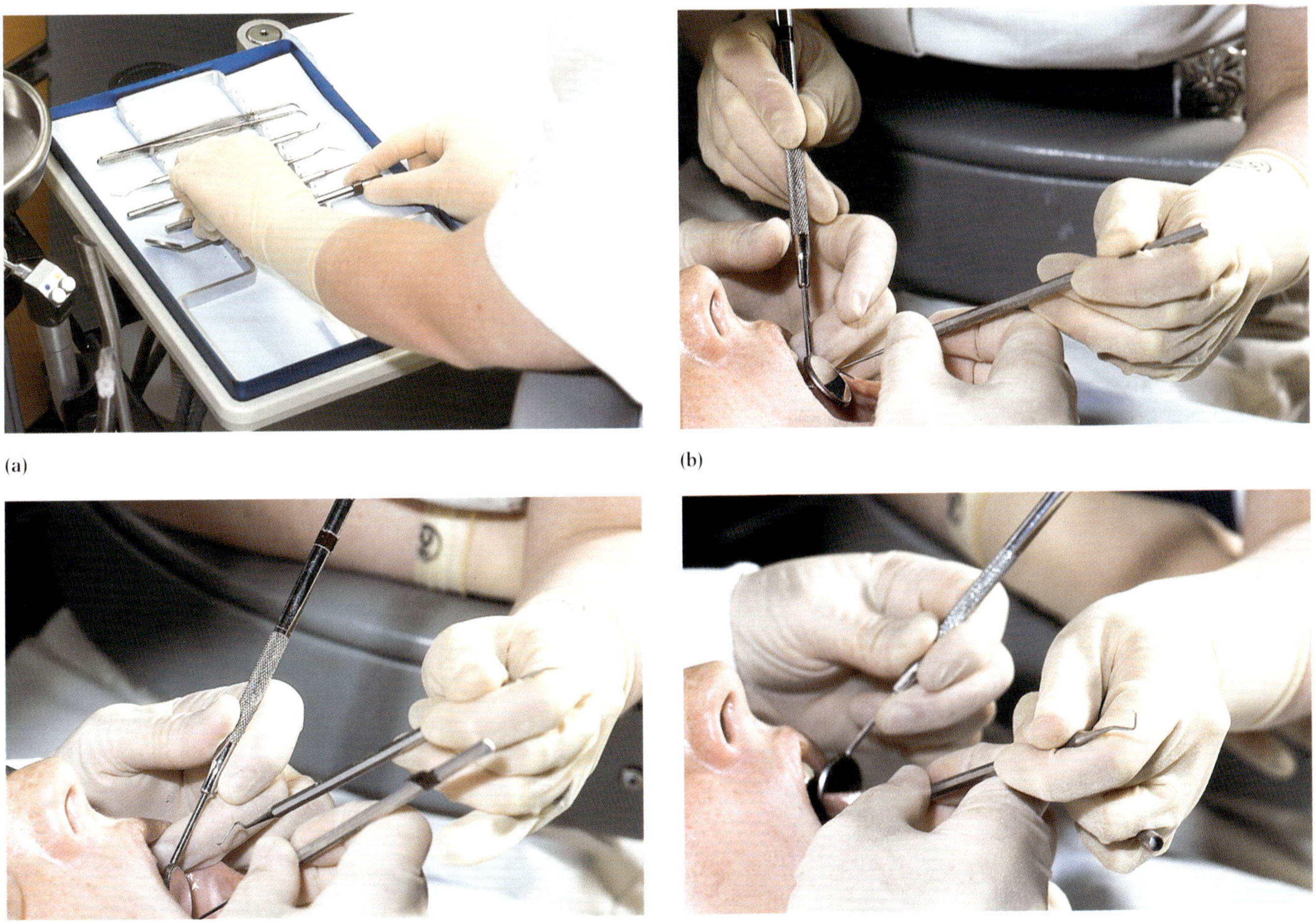

(a) (b) (c) (d)

Fig. 4.7 (a) The dental nurse is picking up a mirror and probe. Note that she grasps the non-working ends.
(b) The mirror and probe are placed firmly into the dentist's hands. They are immediately ready for use.
(c) To exchange an instrument the dental nurse brings in the new instrument (a Briault probe in this picture) parallel with the instrument that the dentist is using.
(d) Exchange is completed by the dental nurse taking away the old instrument with the little finger of her left hand while placing the new instrument into the dentist's hand.

procedure and the dental nurse must anticipate which instrument the dentist will require next.

When passing an instrument the dental nurse picks it up at its non-working end (Fig. 4.7a), leaving sufficient length of instrument shaft for the dentist. Instruments to be passed to the dentist's right hand are picked up with the dental nurse's left hand. The dental nurse would only pass a mouth mirror to a dentist's left hand with her right hand. All instruments are passed with their working ends pointing in the direction of use. The dentist simply keeps his or her hands in the operating position and the instruments are presented so that they are immediately ready for use (Fig. 4.7b).

It is often necessary for the dental nurse to exchange one hand instrument for another. She picks up the new instrument from the tray with the thumb and first two fingers of her left hand. She rotates her hand anticlockwise so that the instrument is resting between the thumb and first two fingers with her palm uppermost. The instrument is now brought in parallel with the instrument that the dentist is using (Fig. 4.7c). Next she takes away the old instrument with the little finger of her left hand (Fig. 4.7d) and at the same time places the new instrument into the dentist's hand.

It is important that instruments are exchanged in front of the patient in the 'instrument transfer zone'. This is an area around the sides and to the front of the patient's face (Fig. 4.7b). *Instruments should never be passed over the patient's face, and in particular not over the eyes.*

Moisture control

Reasons for moisture control

Fluids need to be removed from the mouth for the patient's comfort and to improve the dentist's vision. Large amounts of water from handpieces and the three-in-one syringe accumulate in the mouth, and in addition salivary flow is stimulated by dental treatment. Saliva is teeming with micro-organisms and it is preferable to exclude this extraneous infection from all cavities. In addition, salivary contamination must be avoided in certain techniques, for example pulp capping and root canal treatment.

Contamination by moisture has a detrimental effect on all filling materials and it is essential that cavities are kept dry to produce a good restoration. In this respect saliva is not the only possible contaminating fluid; crevicular exudate and bleeding from gingival margins must also be considered.

Techniques for moisture control

Aspiration

The role of the dental nurse in aspiration and cavity washing and drying has already been discussed. Since dental students will frequently have to work alone, a few comments on aspiration of water without the help of a dental nurse are relevant.

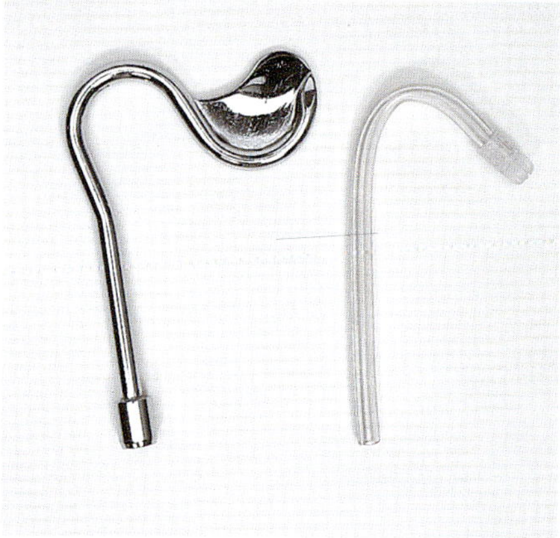

Fig. 4.8 Two endpieces for a saliva ejector. The design on the right is made of disposable plastic. The metal saliva ejector on the left has a flange to retract and protect the tongue and the floor of the mouth.

Fluids can be evacuated from the mouth with a *saliva ejector*, which may be held by the patient. This is connected to a curved endpiece (Fig. 4.8). There are several designs to this endpiece, some of which incorporate a flange to retract and protect the tongue and the floor of the mouth. This is particularly valuable for the clinician working alone.

It is very difficult for the dentist working alone to see clearly when using an air turbine in the upper arch since the water spray continually obscures the mirror, although a little detergent on the mirror helps. Attempts can be made to move the mirror away from the spray, but the temptation to bend your back or neck and work by direct vision should be resisted as far as possible.

Cotton-wool rolls and cellulose pads

Cotton-wool rolls are used to absorb saliva and other fluid and to particularly retract the cheeks, lips, and tongue. They are not sufficient to deal with the large volume of airotor spray but are used when restorations are being placed. They are

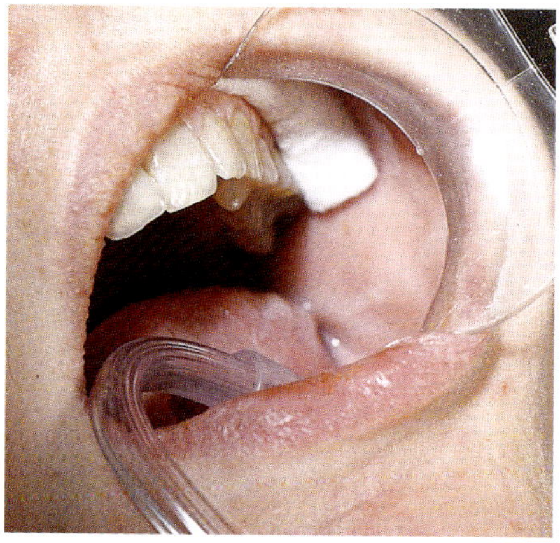

Fig. 4.9 A cotton-wool roll and saliva ejector in place so that the dentist can keep the upper left quadrant dry. The retractor is being used to hold back the lip so that the cotton-wool roll shows in this photograph.

placed in the upper buccal sulcus close to the orifice of the parotid duct (Fig. 4.9), in the lingual sulcus close to the orifices of the submandibular and sublingual ducts, and in the lower buccal sulcus. Alternatively, triangular cellulose pads can be used in the buccal sulcus.

Rubber dam

The method which gives the most complete control over moisture in the mouth is the rubber dam. The tooth or teeth to be treated, together with adjacent teeth, are placed through holes in a rubber sheet, leaving the crowns of the teeth on one side and the mouth with its moisture and infection on the other (Fig. 4.10).

The advantages of the rubber dam are as follows:

- Complete isolation of the teeth from saliva, blood, or gingival fluid exudate is possible. This is important with all restorations but particularly so in 'bonded' restorations.
- The rubber dam aids isolation from bacteria in saliva and so is indicated when infection for the rest of the month must be excluded, for example in direct and indirect pulp capping and endodontic treatment.
- The rubber dam protects the patient from swallowing or inhaling instruments. Dentine pins, fractured burs, pieces of amalgam, wedges, crowns, inlays, endodontic instruments, flanges from saliva ejectors, and even handpiece heads have all found their way into the trachea or oesophagus.
- The rubber dam protects the dentist from infection from the patient. Its use is indicated in all patients whose blood and saliva may potentially transmit disease to the dentist or their staff (e.g. carriers of hepatitis B).
- The rubber dam has the effect of psychologically, as well as physically, separating the dentist from the patient. Not only are water, air spray, dust, debris, and the high-velocity sucker on the dentist's side of the rubber, but patients will frequently remark, with some surprise, that they feel safer with the rubber in position, or that they feel detached from what is going on, almost as if the dentist were not working on them. It is not unusual for a patient to fall asleep with a rubber dam in place.
- Once the rubber dam is in place, operative dentistry is quicker and more efficient. Wet mouths, writhing tongues, contracting lips, and garrulous patients disappear behind the rubber dam.

However, the technique has its disadvantages:

- The patient can no longer speak easily. Conversations thus become one-sided and cease.
- A few patients dislike the rubber dam intensely, feeling claustrophobic when it is in position.
- The rubber is held on posterior teeth with clamps, and a tooth which has been clamped may be sensitive for some hours after the clamp has been removed.
- The rubber dam takes time to apply and remove, although the more experienced the dentist is in its use, the less time is taken. Once the rubber is in position, however, operating conditions are improved and therefore time is saved.

RUBBER DAM EQUIPMENT

This is shown in Fig. 4.11 and consists of the following items:

1. **Rubber dam.** It is supplied in ready-cut 15 cm (6 inches) square sheets. The rubber is resistant to tearing and it grips the teeth well and retracts gingival tissue. A dark colour (green, blue, or black) is preferred because it contrasts well with the teeth, and fragments torn off and left behind are easily seen and removed.

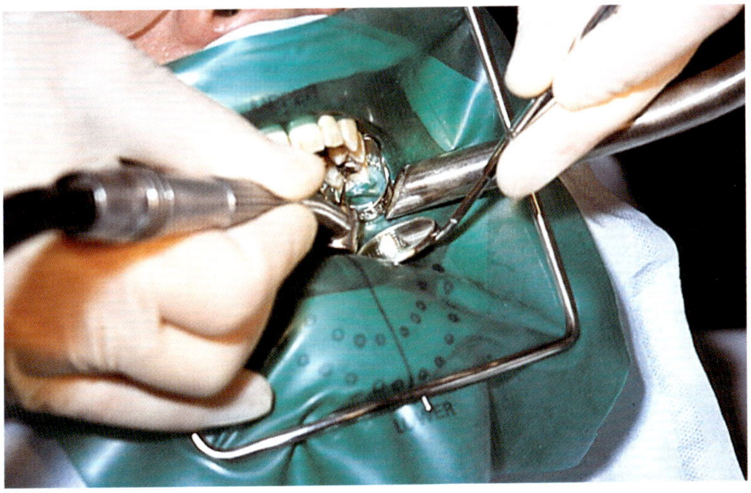

Fig. 4.10 A rubber dam in position.

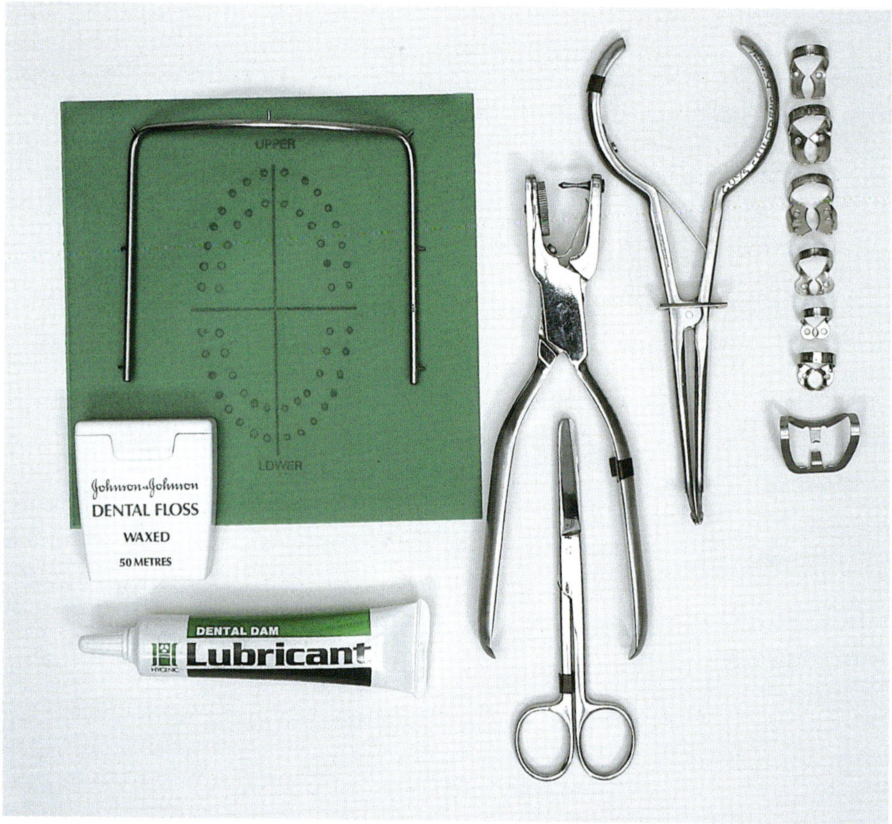

Fig. 4.11 Rubber dam equipment.

2. **Rubber dam punch.** The punch must give a clean cut otherwise there will be a weak point at the edge of the hole from which a tear may arise (Fig. 4.12). Some punches have holes of varying diameters: the larger the hole, the easier it is to stretch over a tooth; the smaller the hole, the tighter the grip. It is useful to punch a hole in one corner of the rubber dam – near the edge – to check that the hole is being punched cleanly. A ragged hole in the centre of the sheet wastes a whole sheet. Assuming that you always punch it in the same position, this hole also helps to orientate the rubber dam when it is being stretched over the rubber dam frame.

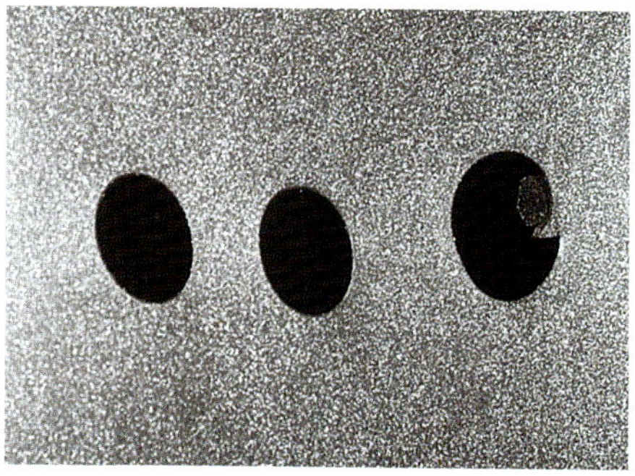

Fig. 4.12 Three holes have been punched in the rubber. The one on the right-hand side has not been cleanly cut and is likely to tear when the rubber is stretched.

3. **Rubber dam stamp for marking the positions of the holes.** This inked rubber stamp produces a series of dots on the rubber corresponding to the average positions of the teeth. When the dam is in position it should reach up to a point just below the patient's nose, thus covering the mouth but not the nose (Fig. 4.10). To achieve this when applying the rubber to the maxillary teeth or mandibular third molars, the position of the upper central incisors should be stamped about 2.5 cm (1 inch) from the top edge of the rubber sheet. For mandibular teeth the holes should be placed further up the sheet so that the rubber does not cover the nose.
4. **Rubber dam clamps.** These are metal clips which fit the neck of the tooth and hold the rubber dam in position. In addition, they may occasionally help to provide gingival retraction. The following clamps make a good basic set (Fig. 4.13):
   - BW, JW molar clamps, wingless; used when the clamp is positioned on the tooth before the rubber.
   - K molar clamp, winged; the wings allow the clamp and rubber to be placed simultaneously.

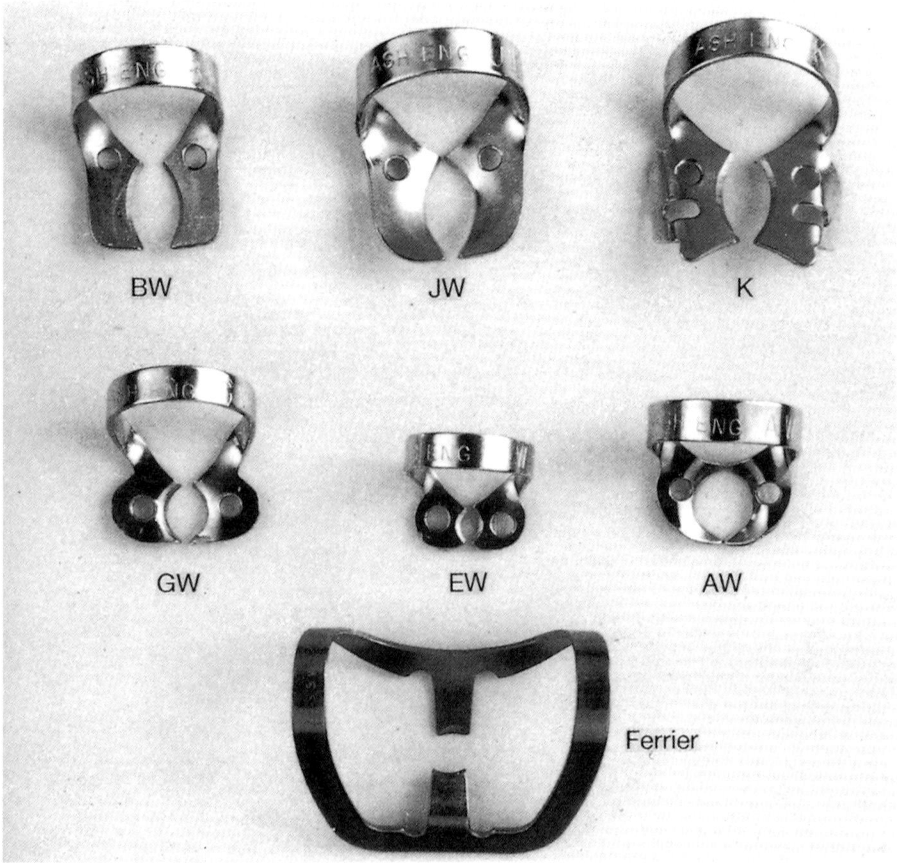

Fig. 4.13 A set of rubber dam clamps. BW, JW, wingless molar clamps. K, winged molar clamp. GW, premolar clamp. EW, clamp for small tooth. AW, wingless molar clamp, retentive design. Ferrier, cervical clamp, Ferrier pattern.

- GW premolar clamp.
- EW clamp used on any small tooth.
- AW molar clamp, wingless; used on partially erupted teeth only. The jaws of this clamp are retentive and point gingivally, thus aiding retention on a tooth whose maximum bulbosity is subgingival.
- Cervical clamp, Ferrier pattern, for use on anterior teeth where retraction of rubber or gingivae is required to allow access to a cervical cavity.

5. **Rubber dam clamp forceps.** An instrument for placing, adjusting, and removing clamps.
6. **Rubber dam lubricant.** A water-based gel is supplied for this purpose but brushless shaving cream is equally suitable. A little lubricant should be applied around the holes in the rubber before sliding it over the teeth.
7. **Waxed dental floss or tape.** This can be used to carry the rubber past a tight contact point (see Fig. 4.17).
8. **Rubber dam holder or frame.** This holds the free edges of the rubber and prevents them from falling into the mouth or back against the patient's face. Several designs are available and one device is shown in Fig. 4.10.

EXAMPLES OF RUBBER DAM APPLICATIONS

1. **Rubber dam application for occlusal restorations in molar and premolar teeth.**

Only the tooth to be treated needs to be isolated, although access is improved if more teeth are included. Since a rubber dam clamp will be required, and these can be uncomfortable, local or topical analgesia may be used even if the operative procedure itself does not require it. A clamp of suitable size is selected and tried on the tooth, placing it just coronal to the gingival margin. The clamp should be expanded using the forceps so that it just passes over the bulbosity of the tooth: it is unwise to open the clamp too widely as it is more likely to fracture and there is also a greater risk of the gingival tissues being 'nipped' by the jaws of the clamp. Floss should be attached to the holes of the clamp so that it can be retrieved should the clamp fracture across the bow (Fig. 4.14a).

If the dentist prefers to position the clamp before applying the rubber, a wingless clamp is selected. Having placed the clamp on the tooth, the floss is threaded through the punched and lubricated hole in the rubber dam (Fig. 4.14b) and the dental nurse gently pulls on the floss as the dentist slides the rubber over the bow of the clamp, first one side and

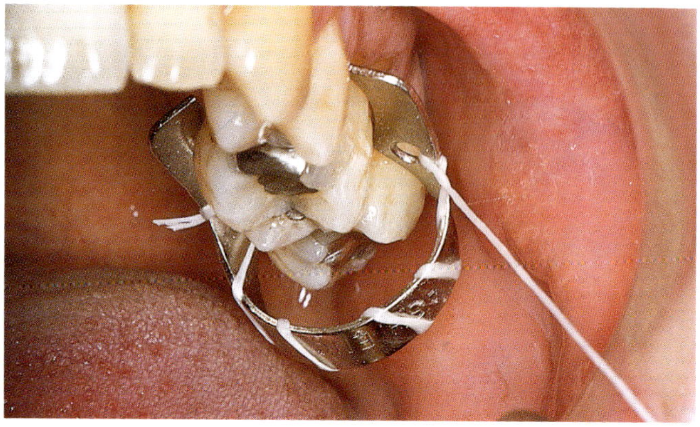

(a)

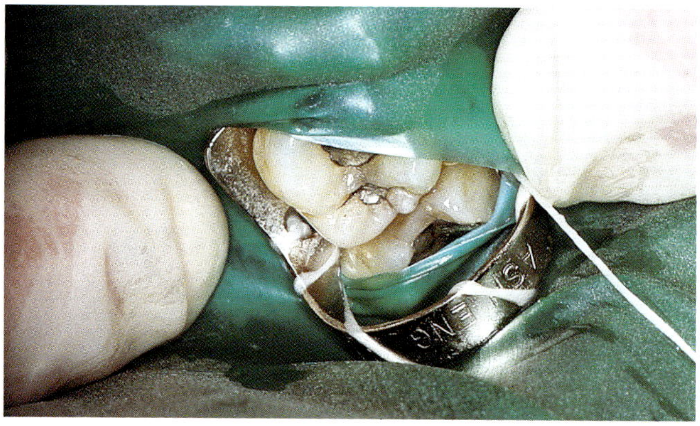

(b)

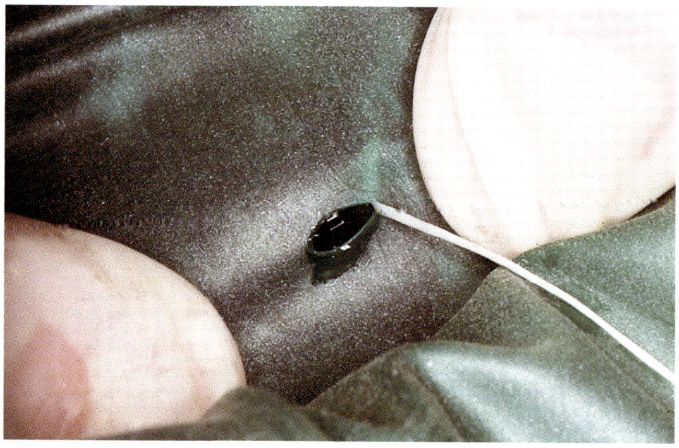

(c)

Fig. 4.14 (a) A wingless clamp in position on the upper second molar. Floss has been attached to the clamp so that the dentist can retrieve it should the clamp fracture across the bow.
(b) The floss is now threaded through the punched and lubricated hole in the rubber dam.
(c) The dentist now slides the rubber over the bow of the clamp, first one side and then the other. The dental nurse gently pulls on the floss as the rubber is placed.

then the other (Fig. 4.14c). A variation on this technique is to insinuate the bow of the clamp through the punched rubber dam hole before placing the clamp on the tooth. The forceps are then positioned for expanding the clamp over the tooth, with the rubber bunched up, but not obscuring the view of the clamp as it is placed. Once the clamp is stable on the tooth, the dam is stretched over the rest of the clamp and the tooth as before.

Another method of applying the clamp and rubber simultaneously is to use a winged clamp with the wings engaged in the lubricated hole (Fig. 4.15a). The dental nurse should gently retract the rubber so that the dentist can see the tooth clearly (Fig. 4.15b). If only one tooth is being isolated – for instance in an endodontic procedure – then the rubber sheet can be pre-stretched over the frame, so improving visibility. A disadvantage of this method is that the gingival margin cannot be seen while the clamp is being placed. Once the clamp is in position, a flat plastic instrument is used to disengage the rubber from the wings of the clamp (Fig. 4.15c).

A piece of absorbent soft material, such as a paper towel in which a hole has been cut, is now placed between the rubber and the patient's face to prevent the uncomfortable feeling of rubber against the face (Fig. 4.10). Finally, the frame is positioned.

2. **Rubber dam application for proximal cavities in posterior teeth.**

The dentist must first decide which teeth are to be isolated. The more teeth that are passed through the rubber, the better will be the access. If a molar, premolar, or distal surface of a canine is to be restored, the major part of that quadrant is usually isolated; a clamp retains the rubber on the most distal tooth and a contact point holds the rubber anteriorly. Dental floss is passed through the contact points to discover what difficulties may be experienced when applying the rubber. If dental floss cannot be passed or tears, the rubber will not pass or will tear unless the cavity is partly prepared or the restoration smoothed.

Once the clamp and rubber have been placed on the most posterior tooth the rubber should be 'knifed' through each contact area (Fig. 4.16), sawing it from side to side while pressing its leading edge apically to carry it through the contact point. When a tight contact is encountered, the dentist should not spend too long on it but move to the next tooth. Once most of the teeth are through the rubber, the paper towel and the frame are applied. This improves access to deal with any remaining difficult contacts. With these the rubber should be positioned so that a leading edge of the hole is just over the contact area (Fig. 4.17). The dental nurse should hold the rubber in this position while the dentist passes floss through the contact, carrying the rubber with it. Once the floss has passed the contact it should be removed buccally and the procedure repeated until all the rubber has also passed the contact.

Finally, wooden wedges should be inserted interproximally if a bur is to be used in this area, as wedges help to reduce the risk of tearing the rubber or injuring the gingivae (Fig. 4.18).

When a matrix band has to be placed on a clamped tooth, the clamp may prevent the band from seating and therefore

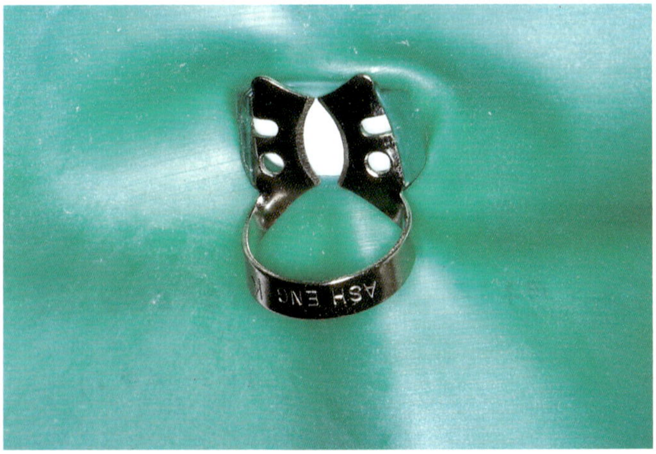

(a)

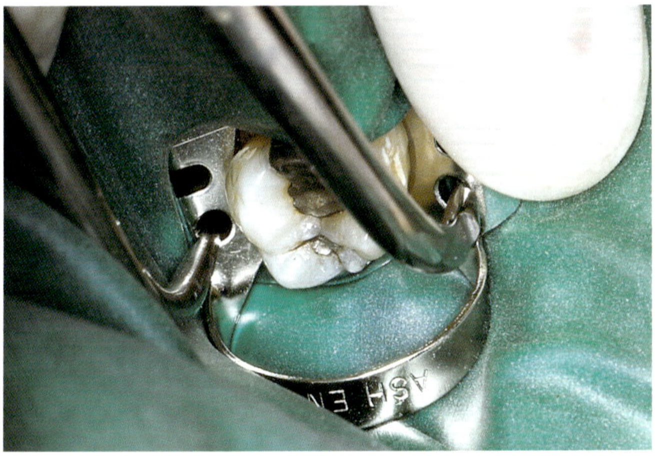

(b)

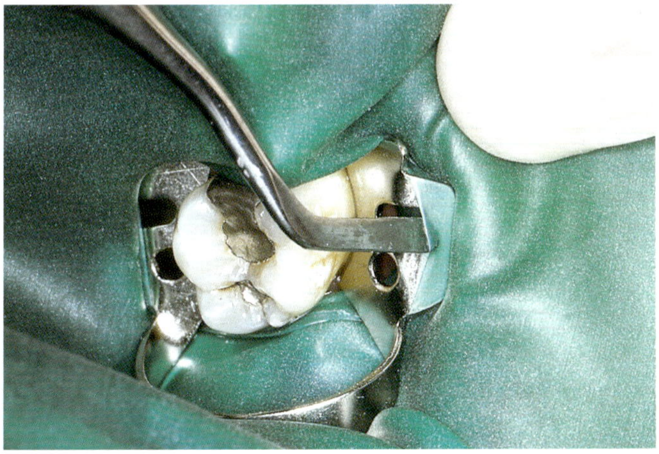

(c)

Fig. 4.15 (a) A winged rubber dam clamp engaged in the lubricated hole in the rubber.
(b) Clamp and rubber are being placed on the tooth simultaneously. The dental nurse should gently retract the rubber so that the dentist can see the tooth clearly.
(c) A flat plastic instrument is used to disengage the rubber from the wings of the clamp.

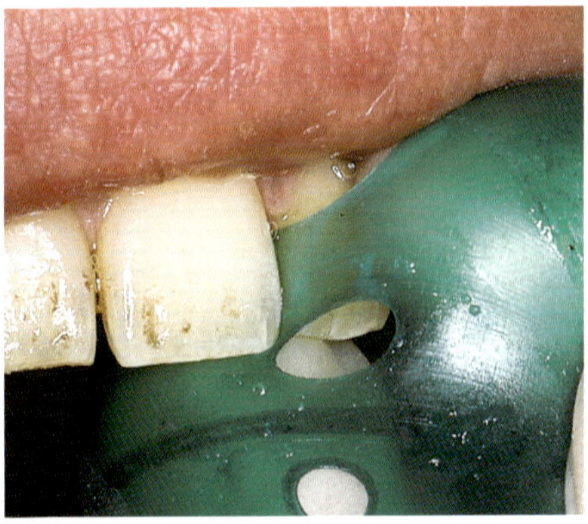

Fig. 4.16 The rubber is 'knifed' through the contact area.

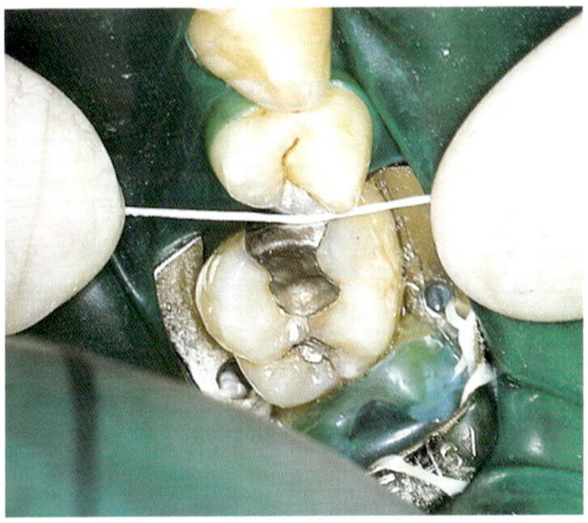

Fig. 4.17 The dentist flosses the rubber down through the contact point.

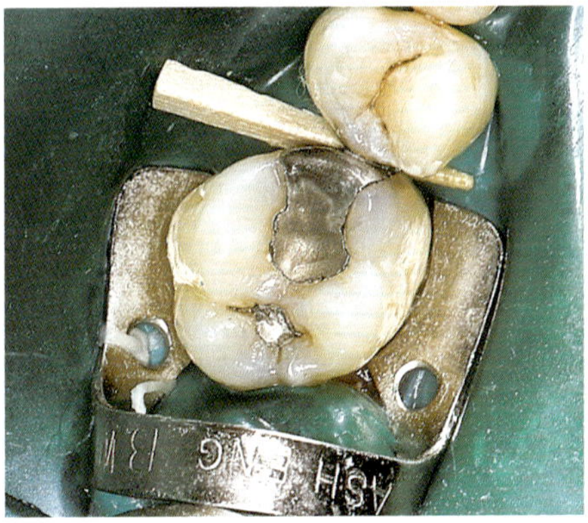

Fig. 4.18 A wedge is inserted to reduce the possibility of tearing the rubber or injuring the gingivae during cavity preparation.

must be removed before the band is positioned. The band then performs the function of the clamp.

3. **Rubber dam application for anterior teeth.**
Clamps are used less often in this situation. A sufficient number of teeth should protrude through the rubber for its stability and for good access. Instead of using clamps, the dam can be stabilized on the most posterior teeth to be

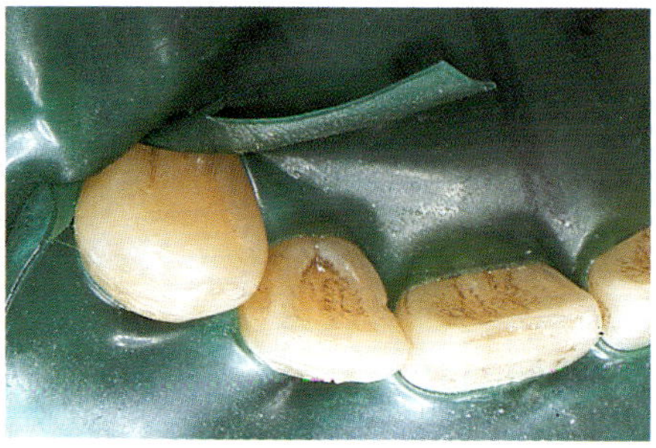

Fig. 4.19 A strip of rubber has been placed between the upper canine and premolar to hold the rubber dam in position.

isolated (often the canines or premolar teeth) in one of three ways:

- If there is a tight contact between the canine and premolar teeth, this will hold the rubber in position.
- The retention of the rubber dam in a contact area may be improved by passing an extra strip of rubber dam through the contact (Fig. 4.19).
- Floss ligatures may be used to hold the rubber in position. Waxed dental floss is placed around the tooth and, while pulling on the ends of the floss from the buccal side, the lingual floss is pushed firmly apical to the maximum bulbosity of the tooth using a flat plastic instrument (Fig. 4.20). Finally, the floss is tied tightly in a surgical knot on the buccal side (i.e. a double throw on the first bight). It is important that the rubber is not stretched too tightly when the frame is applied since this may both restrict access and pull the rubber away from the teeth, allowing leakage.

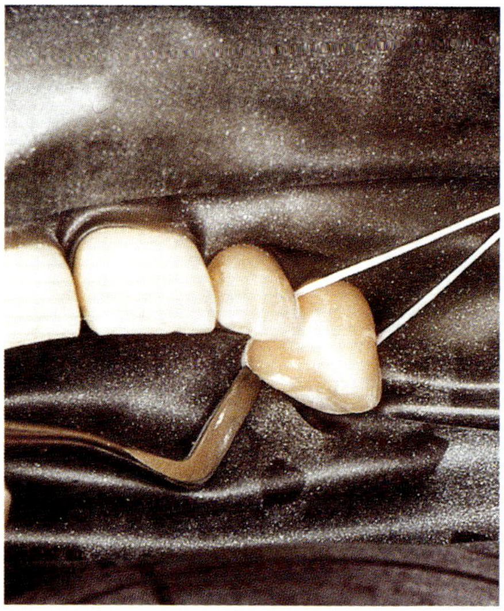

Fig. 4.20 A floss ligature is being placed around the upper canine to hold the rubber dam in position. A flat plastic instrument is used to push the floss on the palatal side of the tooth apical to the maximum bulbosity while the floss is pulled firmly from the buccal side.

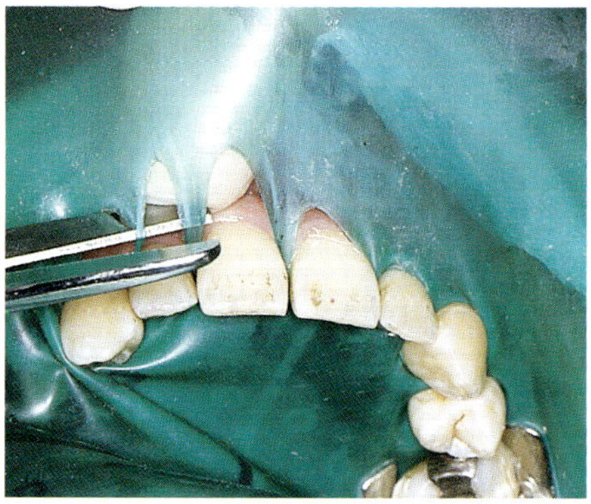

Fig. 4.21 When removing the dam the rubber is pulled buccally and cut interdentally with scissors. Note the dentist's finger protecting the anaesthetized lip.

Several problems can arise when trying to apply a rubber dam for cervical cavity preparations. Where a cervical cavity is to be prepared, the hole in the rubber should be placed either further buccally or lingually to the adjacent teeth, as dictated by the position of the cavity.

Retraction of the rubber is often required, and the cervical clamp should be used. If the jaws of the manufacturer's clamp are not in the optimum position, the clamp may be modified by heating it in a Bunsen burner flame and bending the labial jaw apically and the lingual jaw coronally.

While the cervical clamp will provide a small amount of gingival retraction, grossly subgingival caries should be uncovered by periodontal surgery at least three weeks before definitive cavity preparation. This produces a supragingival cavity with good access, and better plaque removal is possible.

REMOVING THE RUBBER DAM

Once the restoration is completed the dental nurse washes and aspirates any debris from the area, and then the dentist retracts the dam buccally and cuts it interdentally with scissors. The anaesthetized lip should be protected with a finger (Fig. 4.21). Finally, the clamp, rubber dam frame, and paper towel are removed. At this stage the dentist should check the rubber to see it is 'all there'. Any little piece left in the mouth must be removed.

Magnification

A rubber dam aids visibility and magnification improves it still further. Older dentists often find, with a decline in focusing adaptability of the eye and general visual deterioration, that magnification is essential. However, it is helpful in more delicate procedures at any age, and dental students should try to gain some experience of magnification to see how much it helps them. Several different magnification systems are available, varying in price by several orders of magni-

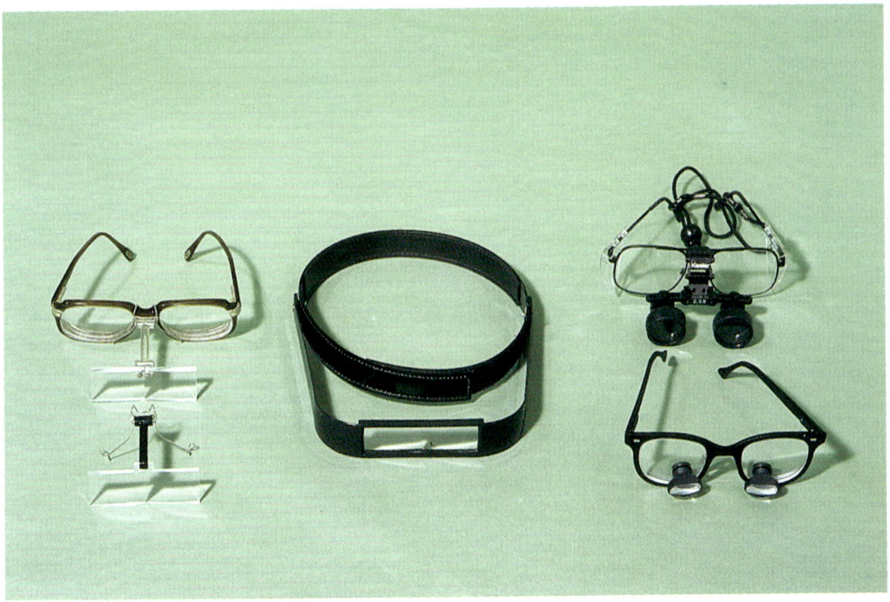

Fig. 4.22 *A selection of magnifiers.* The two on the left are the least expensive and attached to the user's own spectacles. The examples are clipped on to the dentist's prescription spectacles, but they can also be attached to safety spectacles. The magnifiers in the middle are held by a head loop, and these were popular at one time, although they are less popular now that dentists routinely wear safety spectacles to which similar, lighter magnifiers can be attached. The two magnifiers on the right are more expensive. The upper one is adjustable and so, because it can be produced in larger numbers, it is not so expensive as the lower one but is relatively heavy and the spectacles need to be held in place by a cord round the back of the head. The magnifiers at the bottom right are made specifically for the dentist with the correct inter-pupil distance, and with both the magnifiers and the surrounding lens made with the dentist's prescription built into them. The magnifiers are cemented through the main lens so that they are closer to the eye and this gives a better width of field and depth to focus. However they are very expensive.

tude. The simpler, less expensive systems are effective and, with experience, simple to use. The more expensive, sophisticated magnifiers are less cumbersome and should have a greater depth of focus and width of field. The higher the magnification, the narrower the field of view and the greater the effect of tremor. A magnification of 2.5 times is satisfactory for most purposes, but in endodontics, for example, up to 4 times magnification is used. Good visual discrimination in dental procedures requires good depth perception, which in turn requires good binocular function. If you have difficulty with this, with or without prescription spectacles, you should ask your optician for a STEREOPSIS test for binocular function. A selection of different types of magnifier (sometimes called loupes) is shown in Fig. 4.22. Many systems are now marketed with integral lighting systems, which are particularly valuable as the strong light is always focused where the operator is looking. This speeds up many procedures as there is no need to keep adjusting the surgery operating light.

Try to read the print in Fig. 4.23. If you have difficulty reading the text above line A, with spectacles if you wear them, then you should have your eyes tested. If you have difficulty with the text between lines A and B, magnification will help. Most dentists would need magnification to read the text below line B. The lowest line of text is 0.075 mm high (75 microns) and this compares with a stainless steel matrix band which is 50 microns thick. The printed lines are from 50 to 15 microns thick. When making inlays and crowns, the aim is to achieve a cement line at the margin of less than 20 microns.

This typeface is used throughout this book. It is Photina and the lower case letters are 1.5 mm high (9 point)

This typeface is Univers Medium (a non-serif, i.e. unembellished font) which may be easier to read at this size—1 mm high (5 point)

This font is the smallest which is usually used in opticians reading tests. It is 0.66 mm high (4.5 point)

A

Magnification may help with this 0.5 mm high font

And with this 0.33 high font

And even more so with this 0.25 mm high font

B

These lines are:
50 microns thick
25 microns thick
20 microns thick
15 microns thick

Fig. 4.23 An eye test. Acknowledgement: This figure has been produced with the assistance of Dr John Butler.

Protection, safety, and management of minor emergencies

There are inevitable risks in all operations and dentistry is no exception. The dentist works in the limited space of the mouth, a cavity covered by soft and mobile tissues, and at the origins of the respiratory and alimentary tracts. Sharp hand instruments, high-speed rotary instruments, and the manipulation of small objects in awkward positions provide opportunities for possible injury and mishap. However, care and forethought will greatly reduce these inherent risks.

Eye protection

An important example of such forethought is the use of plastic eye-protection spectacles for supine patients who are not already wearing their own spectacles. If the current fashion is for small lenses, larger safety spectacles should be used instead of the patient's own. Eyes are vulnerable to dropped instruments and materials. These accidents should never happen because nothing should ever be passed over the patient's face. However, an inexperienced dentist or dental nurse might momentarily forget the correct position of the instrument transfer zone, and cutting debris or calculus can fly out of the mouth.

Dentists and dental nurses should also wear protective spectacles, even if their vision is normal. This is particularly important, for both dentist and dental nurse, when cast metal or amalgam is being cut in the mouth.

Airway protection

Another major consideration with a supine patient is preventing the inhalation of small objects such as metal restorations, pins, and small hand-held files used for cleaning root canals.

Complete protection against this type of accident is provided by a rubber dam, and for this reason its use is highly desirable for many procedures, in particular endodontic treatment. It may be necessary to restore a tooth before endodontic treatment to allow a rubber dam to be placed. If the use of a rubber dam is impossible, then files and other endodontic instruments must be secured by means of a clip and chain (a 'parachute') or by tying dental floss to them and wrapping the other end of the floss around the operator's fingers.

When fitting a restoration, such as an inlay or crown, which may also be dropped, a rubber dam is not appropriate because occlusion must be checked and the rubber dam precludes this.

If a small object, such as an inlay, is lost in the mouth, the first action is to lean the patient forward and ask them to rinse and cough. Then the fauces and the sublingual and vestibular sulci should be examined thoroughly in that order. The tongue and palate should not be disturbed too much because the object may be retained in the oropharynx for a short time before ingestion.

Then the patient should be got out of the chair, as far as possible without remaining in the upright position for too long, bent sharply at the hips and given one or two firm slaps on the back to help dislodge the object from the oropharynx. If a high-volume aspirator is in use, the possibility of the object having been sucked up must be checked. If all this fails to recover the object, the possibility of inhalation or ingestion must be considered. Sometimes the patient knows that they felt 'something going backwards' and may even know that they have swallowed it. However, the patient may be completely unaware of anything untoward. Quite large objects, such as a full molar crown, can fall straight through the glottis into the bifurcation of the trachea without the patient being aware of it.

The next step is a thoracic radiograph to localize the foreign body in the oesophagus or stomach (Fig. 4.24) or, more seriously, in a bronchus. In the latter case, reference to an accident and emergency department or a thoracic surgeon is required because bronchoscopy and early removal are necessary to avoid pulmonary collapse.

Most objects of dental origin inadvertently swallowed can be relied upon to pass through the alimentary tract without incident. Exceptions are sharp objects such as endodontic files, which may become lodged and require surgical removal. Progress should be monitored by abdominal radiographs if necessary, and by faecal examination using a sieve under running water.

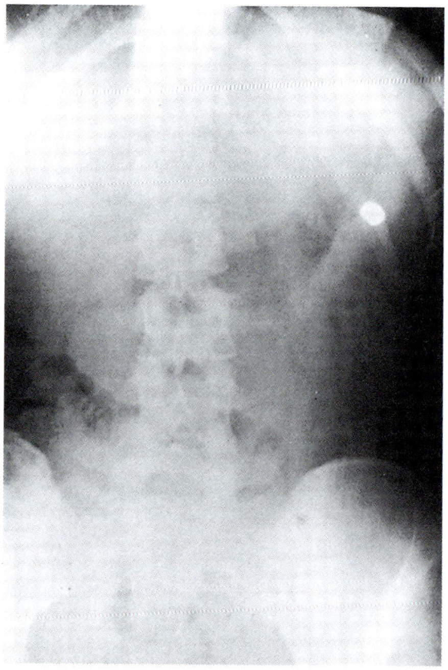

Fig. 4.24 Radiograph showing a gold crown in the stomach. (Reproduced by courtesy of Professor A. H. R. Rowe.)

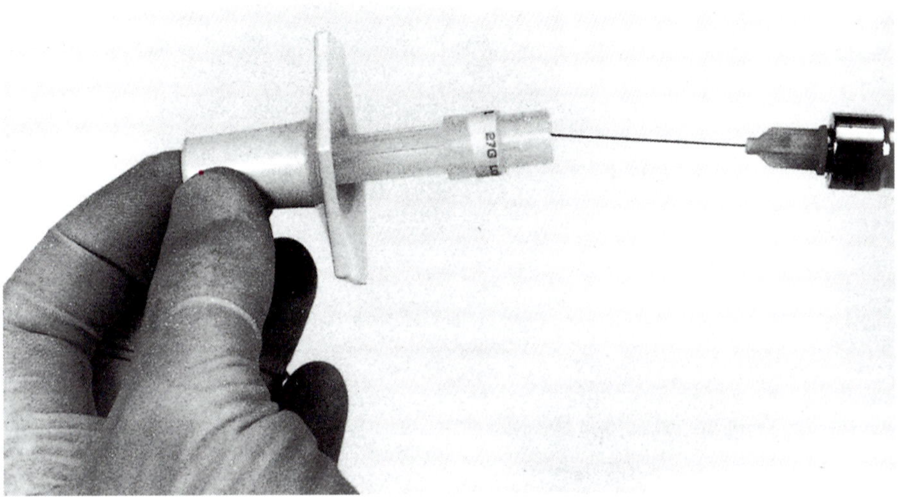

Fig. 4.25 A needle guard to prevent needlestick injuries.

Soft tissue protection

Care must be taken to avoid injury from local anaesthetic (or other) needles. Not only can they cause physical injury but they risk transmitting infection. Dental staff, cleaners, and waste disposal personnel are all at risk unless all needles and other sharp disposable instruments are properly disposed of in a rigid, sealable 'sharps container'. Needlestick injuries can occur when re-sheathing a local anaesthetic needle after giving the injection. There are various designs of needle guards to help avoid this (Fig. 4.25). However, it is much safer to re-sheath the needle by chasing the sheath with one hand holding the syringe – and the other tucked well away – thus avoiding the possibility of a needlestick injury because the sheath is not hand-held.

Obviously, skilful operating is of primary importance. The insertion of sharp instruments to the correct point of application and their withdrawal without touching lips, cheek, or tongue is a basic requirement. The use of finger or thumb rests at all times and insistence upon sharp instruments are essential to good practice; blunt instruments require more force and are likely to slip. A trivial injury to soft tissue may upset a patient to an extent out of all proportion to its severity, undermining their confidence in the dentist.

Rotary instruments are another potential source of trauma to soft tissues. The tongue, lips, and cheeks should be retracted gently but firmly with mirrors, flanged saliva ejectors, or the flattened end of the aspirator tip, taking care to avoid pressure on the alveolar mucosa or excessive retraction of labial and buccal fraena. A rubber dam is a reliable way of retracting soft tissue. Cuts on the mucosa, should they occur, may need one or more fine sutures to bring their margins together and speed healing.

High-speed instruments are a source of risk, especially if they are bent or rotating eccentrically. The rules are as follows:

- The shank must be firmly held in the chuck and be incapable of working loose.
- Bent instruments must be discarded immediately.
- Never attempt to restraighten a bent instrument because this leads to sudden fracture and a high-speed projectile is produced.
- Long-tapered diamond instruments are particularly prone to bending and therefore should be examined before use. This is best done by holding the handpiece away from the patient and giving a short tap on the foot control so that the concentricity of the tip can be checked visually.

Occasionally the head of a tungsten carbide bur breaks at the neck while cutting. It should be recovered to prevent the patient swallowing or inhaling it.

Soft tissues may also be injured by careless use of caustic agents, such as the acid used to etch enamel, or hot instruments which are used occasionally to remove excess gutta-percha root canal points for example. These injuries may pass unnoticed until the local anaesthetic has worn off.

When operating on the lower teeth, inferior dental or mental anaesthesia may leave the lower lip numb for some time after the patient has left the surgery. Patients should be warned to avoid biting the anaesthetized lower lip.

Avoiding surgical emphysema

When using an air turbine or a three-in-one syringe near a breach in the mucosa or the orifice of an empty root canal, surgical emphysema may be caused by the compressed air.

This is important because of the possible spread of infection into deeper tissue planes. The risk can be minimized by avoiding directing jets of air into these areas.

Dealing with accidents and accident reporting

The aphorism that 'prevention is better than cure' is nowhere more true than in the field of accident and misadventure. However, accidents will happen occasionally and there are some rules that should be followed:

- A student should inform the teacher immediately.
- Provide whatever immediate treatment is needed (for example, sutures) or arrange other investigations such as a thoracic radiograph.
- Show the patient by your attitude and sympathy that you care for their welfare.
- Explain what has happened but do not be defensive or offer financial compensation.
- Make a careful record of the incident, at the time, in the patient's notes. The dental nurse should be asked to record the event as well. Retain any evidence such as broken burs.
- If the accident is serious, a qualified dentist should inform their protection organization. A telephone call to the dental secretary of the appropriate society is an immediate source of sound advice.
- Continue to follow up the incident carefully until it is clear that all is well.

Protection from infection

It is very important that patients and staff are protected from infection. Infection can potentially be transmitted from the dental personnel to the patient or vice versa, or from patient to patient (cross-infection). Decontamination and sterilization are rapidly changing fields with concerns about bacteria, viruses, and prions: you should consult the current advice from your National Dental Association. In the UK, this is the British Dental Association's advice leaflet number 12.

Further reading

British Dental Association (2000). Advice sheet 12. (Frequently revised – ask for latest edition.) BDA, London.

Paul, E. (1980). *A manual of four-handed dentistry*. Quintessence, Chicago, IL.

5

Instruments and handpieces

Hand instruments
- Instruments used for examining the mouth and teeth
- Instruments used for removing caries and cutting teeth
- Instruments used for placing and condensing restorative materials

Hand instrument design

Using hand instruments

Maintaining hand instruments
- Sharpening hand instruments
- Decontaminating and sterilizing hand instruments

Rotary instruments
- The air turbine
- Low-speed handpieces
- Maintaining and sterilizing handpieces
- Burs and stones
- Finishing instruments
- Maintaining and sterilizing burs and stones

Tooth preparation with rotary instruments
- Speed, torque, and 'feel'
- Heat generation and dissipation
- Effects on the patient
- Choosing the bur for the job

- Surface finish
- Finishing and polishing restorations

Air abrasion

Auxiliary instruments and equipment

Instruments and handpieces

Instruments are used to examine, clean, cut, and restore teeth. The main types are either hand-held or rotary instruments driven in a handpiece. Falling somewhere between these and the larger items of equipment dealt with in Chapter 4 are a group of auxiliary instruments which are used in operative dentistry and which will be described briefly in this chapter. These include fibre-optic lights for illumination, lights used for polymerization of certain materials, and ultrasonic scalers.

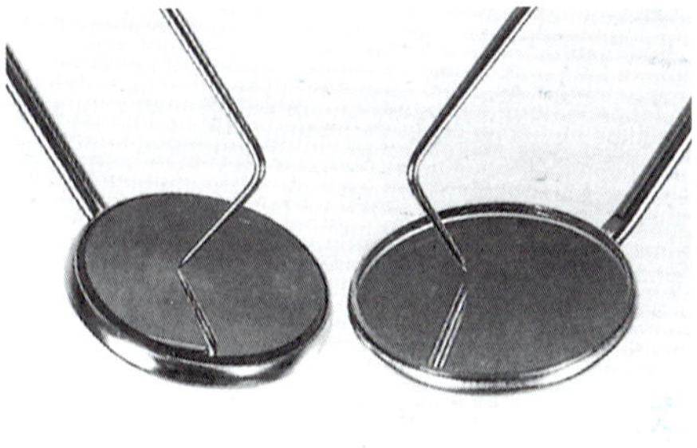

Fig. 5.1 The two types of mouth mirror: left, front-surface reflecting; right, rear-surface reflecting. Note the double image in the rear-surface reflecting mirror.

Hand instruments

These may be divided into instruments used for the following purposes:

- examining the mouth and teeth
- scaling
- cutting teeth and removing caries
- placing and condensing restorative materials
- carving and finishing restorations
- miscellaneous.

Instruments used for examining the mouth and teeth

Mouth mirrors

These vary in size, and although flat mirrors are most commonly used and preferred for most procedures, concave (magnifying) mirrors are also available. However, the two main types are rear-surface and front-surface reflecting mirrors (Fig. 5.1). The former has the reflective surface beneath the glass so that the image is actually seen through the thickness of the glass twice. This can produce a double image when it is necessary to look at the mirror from an angle, but the glass surface means that it is resistant to damage. Front-surface mirrors produce a clearer image, particularly at angles, and for this reason have become much more widely used in recent years. However, they are easily scratched and so care should be taken, particularly during cleaning and sterilization. It is perhaps worth having both types in a standard examination kit, with the rear-surface mirror being used for general purposes and for retracting the tongue and cheeks, reserving the front-surface mirror for detailed examination.

Probes

A large variety of probes have been suggested, but many of these were designed to enable the operator to probe enamel surfaces with some vigour in diagnosing whether or not they were carious. For reasons described in Chapter 1 this is now known to be undesirable, and a basic set of three probes is all that is usually needed (Fig. 5.2). The straight probe (actually bent, but called straight in contrast to the many curved varieties) is used for a number of purposes including checking the margins of restorations and examining caries in dentine during cavity preparation; for most of these purposes it is helpful if it is sharp. The Briault probe is another

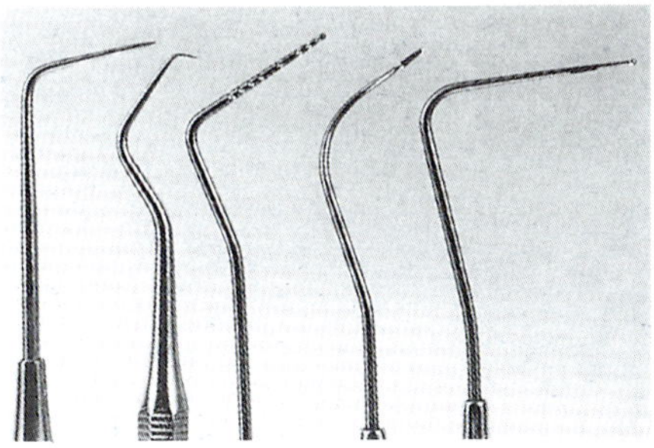

Fig. 5.2 Probes. From the left: straight, Briault, graduated periodontal, furcation, and CPITN periodontal probe.

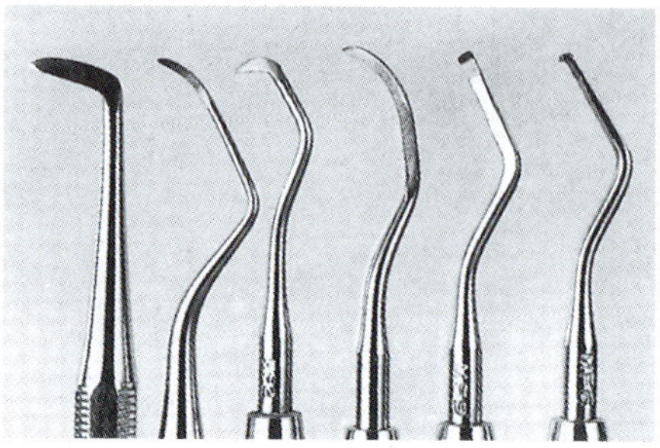

Fig. 5.3 A selection of scalers. Note the angulation of the head and the extent to which some of the cutting blades are offset from the long axis of the handle.

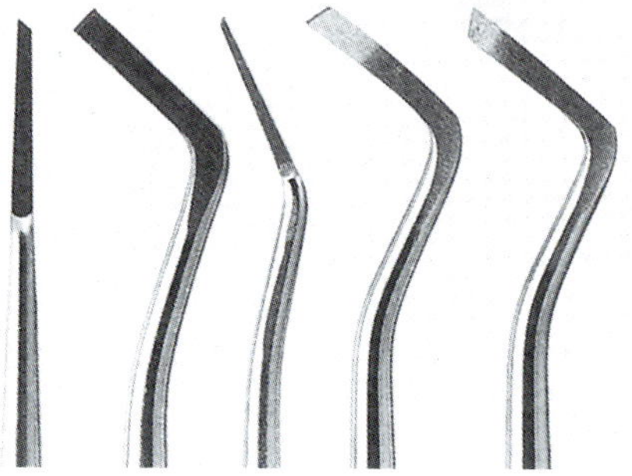

Fig. 5.5 A selection of straight and angled chisels. From the left: straight, hatchet, hoe, and a pair of gingival margin trimmers for trimming mesial and distal boxes in posterior teeth.

sharp probe; the design improves access to the enamel–dentine junction during cavity preparation. Many operators use this probe for the detection of subgingival calculus. The periodontal probe is blunt or has a small ball at the end; it is marked with graduations to measure the depth of periodontal pockets. These marks are also useful for a number of other measuring purposes, such as measuring the width of a tooth when a temporary crown is to be fitted. Two other types of periodontal probe are also shown in Fig. 5.2.

Scalers

A selection of scalers is shown in Fig. 5.3. These are used for removing supra- and subgingival calculus and other deposits from teeth. They are also useful for removing temporary crowns. A periodontal textbook should be consulted for more details of the types and uses of scalers.

Instruments used for removing caries and cutting teeth

Excavators

These are used for removing softened dentine and temporary fillings. The back of the blade can also be used for placing linings, and they are sometimes used for carving amalgam. They have a discoid or ovoid blade, the margin of which is bevelled to a sharp cutting edge (Fig. 5.4).

Chisels, hatchets, and hoes

Straight and angled chisels are used for splitting off unsupported enamel. Perhaps the most useful chisel is the gingival margin trimmer (Fig. 5.5), which is a double-ended instrument with curved blades and a sloping cutting edge. It is used to trim the margins of small cavities adjacent to other teeth where access for rotary instruments is limited.

Hatchets and hoes are similar to chisels in having a straight bevelled cutting edge, and their purpose is similar. In design they are always angled or contra-angled. They differ from one another in that the cutting edge of the hatchet is in the plane of the shank (like an axe), whereas the cutting edge of the hoe lies in an axis at right angles to this plane (as in the gardener's hoe) (Fig. 5.5).

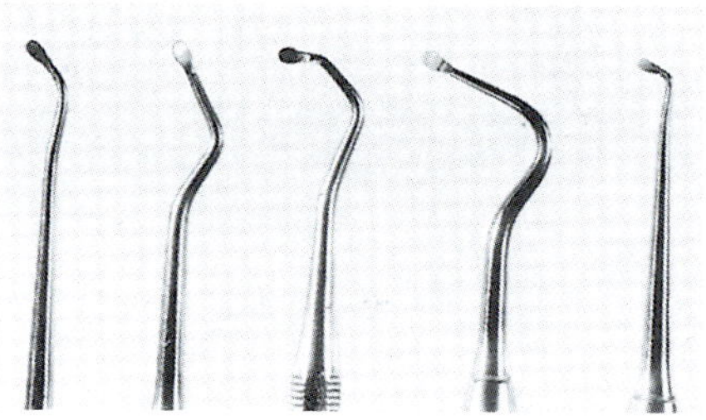

Fig. 5.4 A selection of excavators.

Instruments used for placing and condensing restorative materials

Plastic instruments

Some of these have flat blades and are used for conveying and shaping materials which do not involve the use of particularly heavy pressure. Some have rounded ends and are used for pushing the materials into cavities and for shaping and burnishing them. For some materials (e.g. wax) it is necessary to heat the instrument, and it is wise to set aside two or three plastic instruments which can be heated, as regular heating tends to spoil the surface and damages the temper of the metal.

Flat plastic instruments for general use are made of stainless steel, but composite restorative materials are best placed and shaped by thin Teflon-coated or titanium nitride instruments to which the composite does not stick (Fig. 5.6a). Some manufacturers produce instruments with colour-coded handles for ease of identification.

Condensers or pluggers

These are used for compressing and forming filling materials, particularly amalgam. They are used with heavy pressure. A variety of shapes and sizes are available to suit different circumstances and the end may be smooth or indented. Smooth versions are preferred as the indented type becomes clogged with old amalgam (Fig. 5.6b).

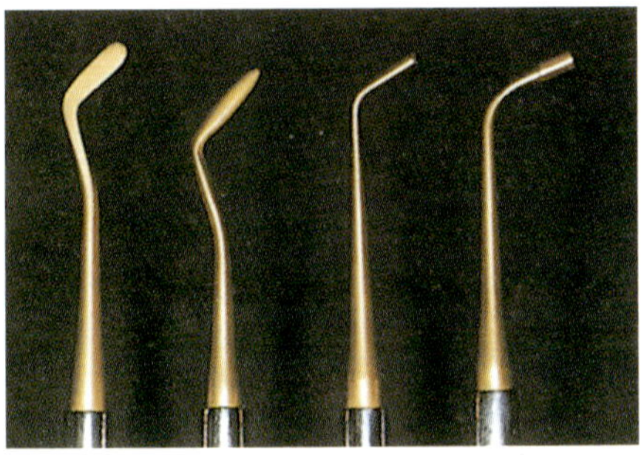

(a)

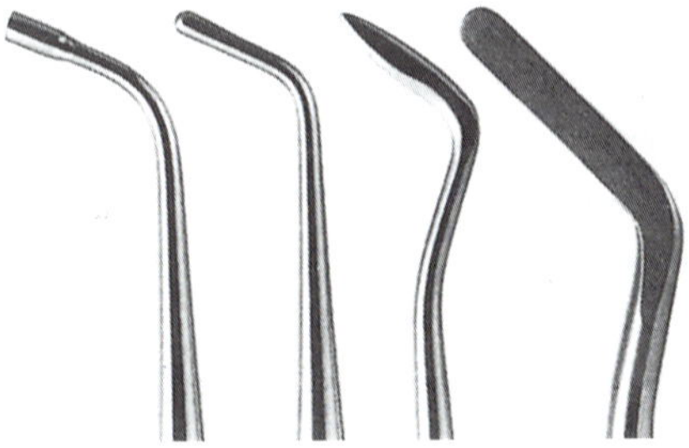

(b)

Fig. 5.6 (a) A set of four titanium nitride instruments used for placing and shaping composite. The surface of the instrument is very hard and is not scratched by the composite filler particles. It also resists the composite sticking to it. From the left: flat-plastic, carving instrument, burnisher, plugger.
(b) Stainless steel 'plastic' instruments. From the left: amalgam condenser, burnisher, carving instrument (a half Hollenback), flat-plastic.

Carving and finishing instruments

These have sharp or semi-sharp blades of various shapes and are used to carve materials by cutting or scraping. Their smoothness is important, and so is the correct degree of sharpness. Instruments used for carving amalgam should be kept separate from those for carving wax as the latter will need to be heated and thus eventually become damaged.

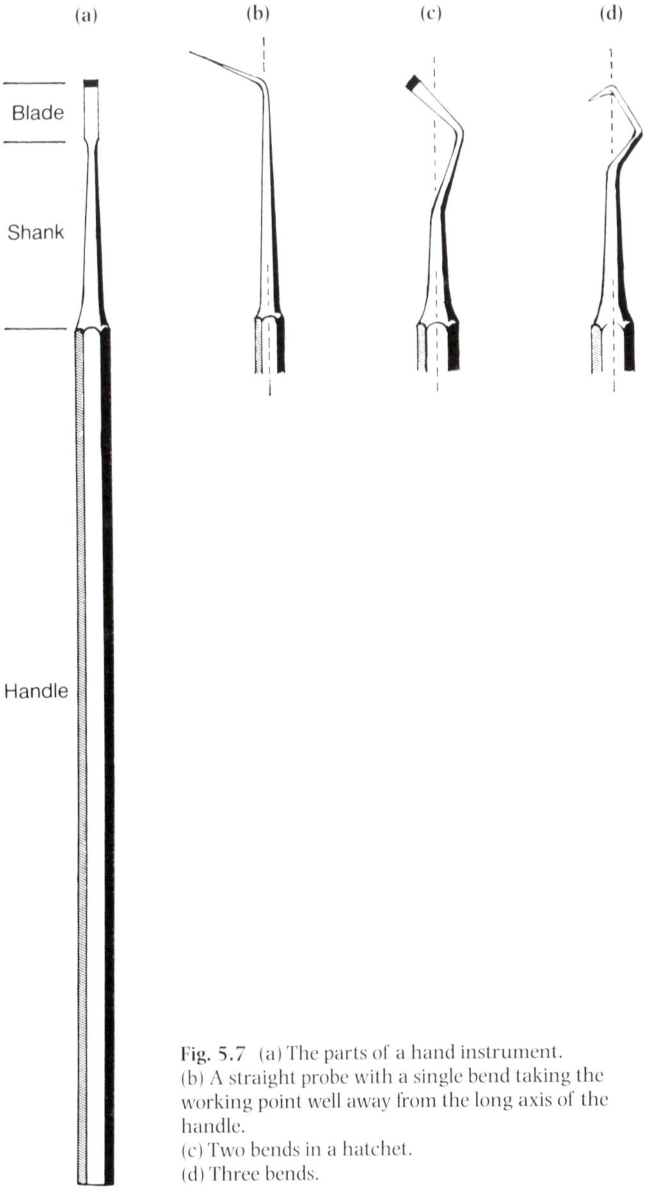

Fig. 5.7 (a) The parts of a hand instrument.
(b) A straight probe with a single bend taking the working point well away from the long axis of the handle.
(c) Two bends in a hatchet.
(d) Three bends.

Hand instrument design

Most hand instruments are made of stainless steel or, in the case of some cutting instruments, carbon steel. Some chisels and scalers have tungsten carbide tips brazed to the cutting edge, and these retain their sharpness for much longer.

The majority of hand instruments have three parts (Fig. 5.7): the blade, the shank, and the handle. To be effective the working surface of the instrument (e.g. a chisel or scaler) must meet the surface at an angle. In some instances this angle is critical; in others it may vary over a wide range. There are many areas in the oral cavity where direct access is impossible with a straight instrument and so instruments commonly have one, two, or three bends in their shank to facilitate access to awkward places. Sometimes these angles bring the working end of the instrument back into line with the shank; sometimes it is offset (see Fig. 5.7). In general, instruments with the working tip in line with the handle are the most stable and easiest to use, but access is improved by offsetting the working tip.

The design of the handle is related to the purpose of the instrument. Instruments used primarily for tactile and exploratory purposes, for example probes, have small-diameter, light-weight handles. Instruments designed to transmit heavier pressure and which will be held for long periods of time, for example scalers, have larger-diameter, heavier handles.

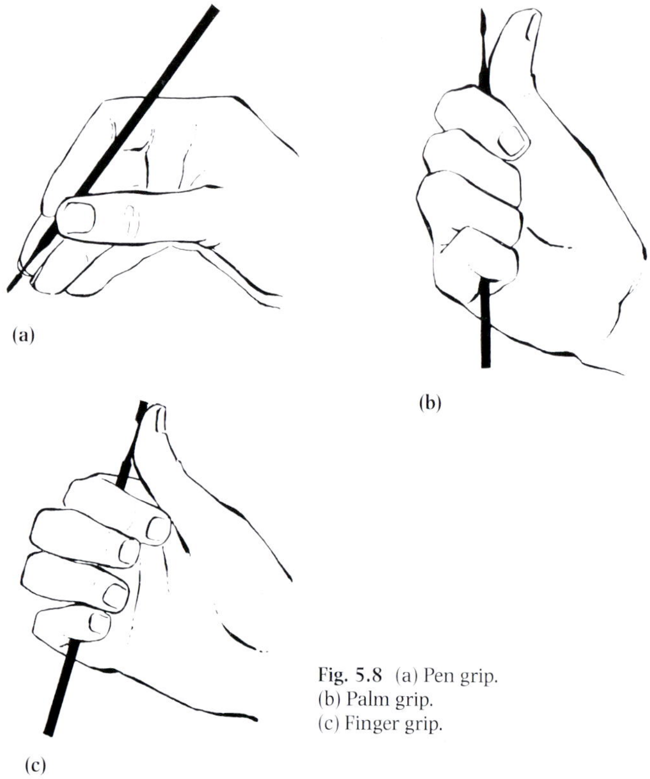

Fig. 5.8 (a) Pen grip.
(b) Palm grip.
(c) Finger grip.

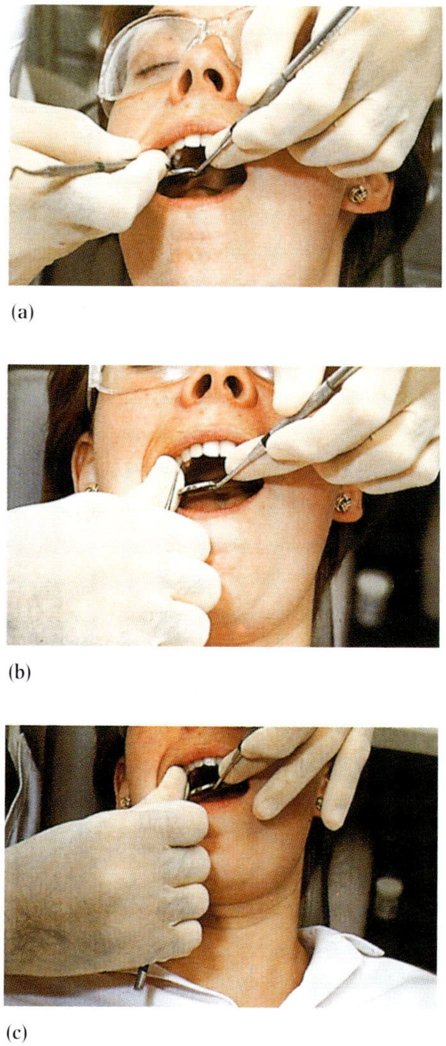

Fig. 5.9 (a) Pen grip.
(b) Palm grip.
(c) Finger grip.

Using hand instruments

A hand instrument may be grasped in one of two ways:

- The pen grip (Figs. 5.8a and 5.9a) is self-descriptive and is most frequently used. It allows a light or a heavy touch and finely controlled movements over a wide range. The middle and ring fingers are used for support.
- In the palm grip (Figs. 5.8b and 5.9b) the instrument is held between the thumb and forefinger, and the handle lies across the palm and is clasped by the remaining fingers. The thumb is used for support. This grip, which is used when operating upon maxillary teeth, provides heavy force over a limited range of movements but with greater control than with the pen grip. The finger grip (Figs. 5.8c and 5.9c) is a modification of the palm grip. It is of limited value and is used when the palm grip fails to give the correct line of access.

The requirements of accuracy in fine movements, and of safety in forceful manipulation, demand that all instrumentation be accompanied by finger or thumb support upon adjacent firm structures, of which the firmest are the crowns of the adjacent healthy teeth. The thumb and the third or fourth fingers of the hand holding the instrument are the rests most often used. This is a rule which must be closely observed; there are very few exceptions (Fig. 5.9).

Maintaining hand instruments

Sharpening hand instruments

Instruments intended to cut will only do so if they are sharp. One of the main differences between an amateur and professional carpenter is the skill with which they identify when their instruments need sharpening and how they keep them sharp. All dentists should be professionals.

Steel instruments with bevelled edges, such as chisels, can be sharpened on a small flat sharpening stone (Fig. 5.10a) or on a mounted stone in a handpiece (Fig. 5.10b). Light machine oil is used as a lubricant and the instrument is held to produce a 30°– 45° bevel. A fine edge initially cuts better but rapidly becomes blunt.

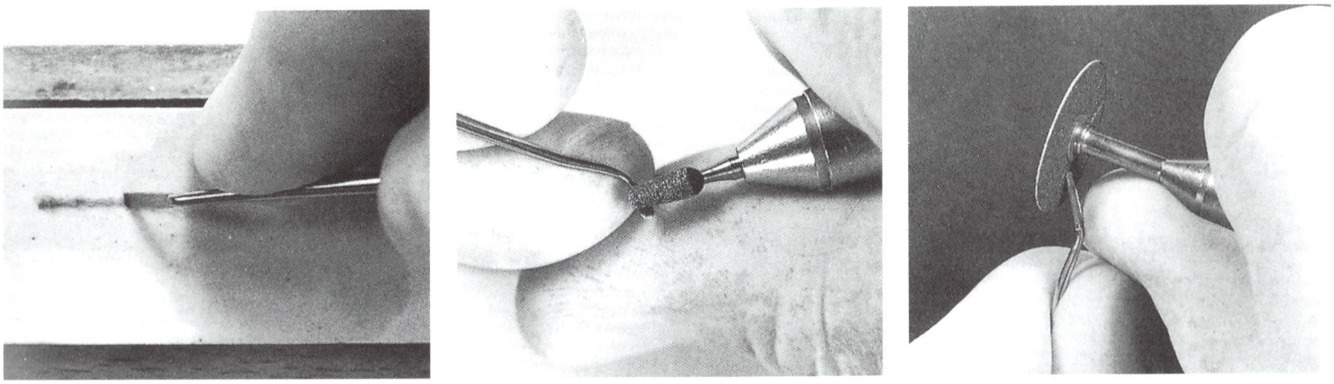

(a) (b) (c)

Fig. 5.10 (a) Sharpening a chisel on a flat oil stone.
(b) Sharpening an excavator with a mounted stone in a straight handpiece.
(c) Sharpening a chisel with a disc in a straight handpiece.

An alternative method (Fig. 5.10c), ideal for probes but also suitable for excavators and scalers, is to use a fine abrasive disc. Light pressure is used with no lubricant. Overheating must be avoided carefully. This method removes metal rapidly and gives a coarser finish to the edge, but has the advantage of speed.

Tungsten carbide-tipped instruments retain their sharpness for very much longer than steel instruments, but when they do become blunt they are best returned to the manufacturer for sharpening.

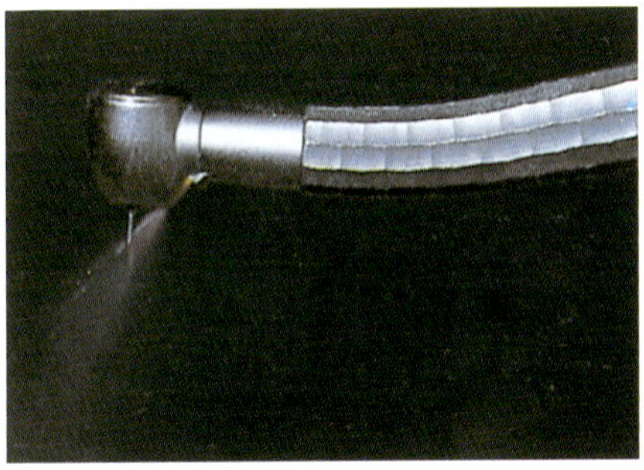

Fig. 5.11 Air turbine handpiece in operation showing the water spray and also the fibre-optic light system.

Decontaminating and sterilizing hand instruments

All instruments must be cleaned before being sterilized. Stainless steel, tungsten carbide, and Teflon-coated instruments can be autoclaved. Carbon steel instruments will corrode if autoclaved and then left in a wet condition. The ideal is to autoclave them in a post-vacuum autoclave which leaves the contents dry at the end of its cycle, but these are not generally available in dental surgeries.

Rotary instruments

Rotary instruments, consisting of burs, stones, and discs, are small instruments held in a handpiece. The instrument is rotated in the handpiece by power from an external source, either compressed air or more directly by an electric motor. There are two broad types of equipment used to provide the rotary power covering two speed ranges:

- the air turbine
- low-speed handpieces.

The air turbine

The air turbine (or airotor) (Fig. 5.11) gives the highest speeds but with rather less torque than low-speed handpieces (see later). Speeds are in the range 250 000–500 000 rev/minute. These very high speeds are achieved by a small air-driven turbine or rotor mounted in bearings in the head of a contra-angle handpiece. The shank of the bur is inserted into the rotor of the handpiece and revolves with it. The handpiece always contains a system which directs water spray at the cutting head of the bur and often also contains a fibre-optic light (Fig. 5.11).

Low-speed handpieces

Low-speed handpieces are either contra-angle or straight (Fig. 5.12). The contra-angle handpiece is used almost exclusively in the mouth, and the straight handpiece is used for trimming temporary crowns or for carrying out other similar procedures outside the mouth. The speed of these handpieces is less than that of the air turbine but the torque is greater. Most handpieces are equipped with a water spray for use in the higher speed ranges. The speed ranges are given in the caption to Fig. 5.12, and although the handpieces are called 'low-speed' to distinguish them from the air turbine, which will only operate at very high speeds, some of them operate at speeds approaching that of the air turbine.

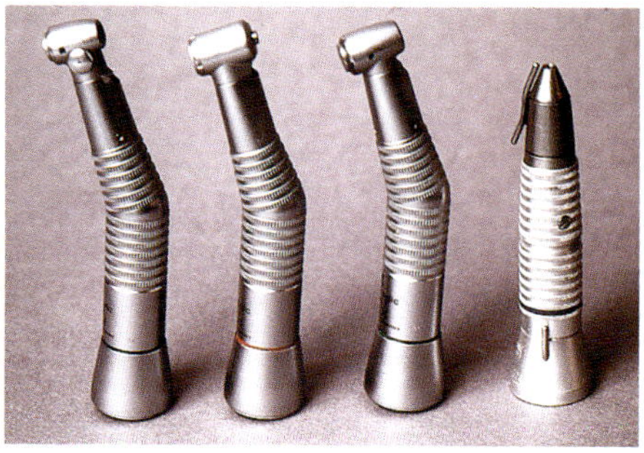

Fig. 5.12 A selection of low-speed handpieces. From the left:
1:1 ratio contra-angle handpiece used for most procedures. Latch-grip burs are used. Commonly identified with a blue-coloured band on the shank of the handpiece and a blue dot on the head. Speed in the range 400–40 000 rev/minute.
1:4 ratio speed-increasing handpiece. Takes friction-grip burs and operates in the speed range 16 000–160 000 rev/min. Commonly identified with a red band. Useful for finishing cavity preparations and also finishing restorations.
7:1 ratio speed-reducing handpiece. Takes latch-grip burs and is used for drilling pin holes and other procedures where a slow speed is indicated. Operates in the speed range 550–5500 rev/min and is commonly identified with green bands.
A straight handpiece which takes straight burs or may be modified to take latch-grip burs. A 1:1 ratio handpiece is identified with a blue band and reducing speed is identified with a green band. Used to trim temporary restorations and other similar procedures. Usually used outside the mouth.

The drive for low-speed handpieces comes from a small electric motor attached directly to the handpiece, and the speed of this is controlled by a foot control or a control on the electric motor or on the dental unit. An alternative, which is usually less expensive, is an air motor, again attached directly to the end of the handpiece. Low-speed handpieces can be rotated clockwise or anticlockwise, whereas the air turbine only rotates clockwise.

Maintaining and sterilizing handpieces

Modern handpieces are autoclavable and must be autoclaved between patients. Most handpieces should be lubricated

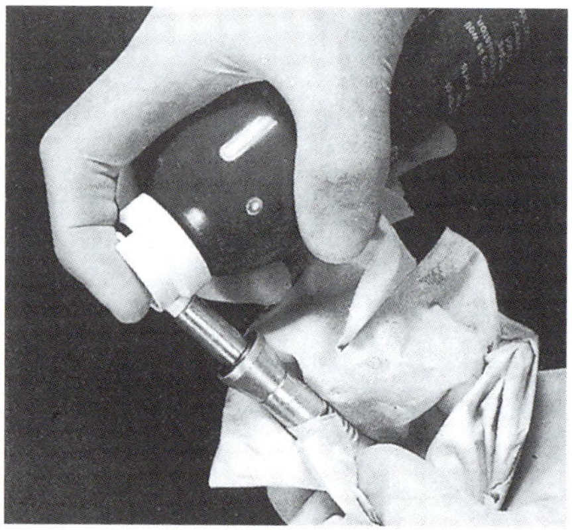

Fig. 5.13 An aerosol lubricant being used with a low-speed handpiece. Different adaptors for the nozzle of the aerosol are available for each type of handpiece. The paper towel is used to absorb excess lubricant coming though the head of the handpiece.

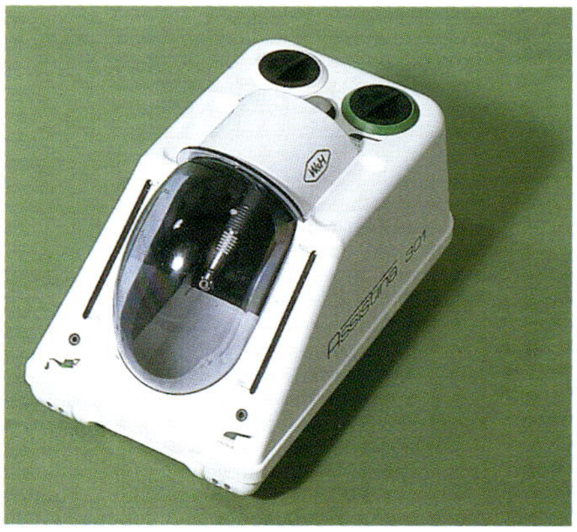

Fig. 5.14 An automatic handpiece cleaning unit which is connected to the air supply. The shield at the front is rotated out of the way and the handpiece plugged onto the connector. A detergent is then flushed through the handpiece followed by oil, both of which come from refillable containers at the back of the unit. This is a more efficient and quicker system than using aerosols.

before and after autoclaving using a lubricant delivered from an aerosol can through an adapter (Fig. 5.13) or by an air-driven cleaning and lubricating machine (Fig. 5.14).

Burs and stones

A selection of burs and stones is shown in Figs. 5.15, 5.16, and 5.17. Rotary cutting instruments are retained in the handpiece by one of three methods:

- friction – with a separate bur changer – in the older type of air turbine
- a latch grip – in the contra-angle low-speed handpiece
- a quick-release clamping chuck – in the straight handpiece and now in most contra-angle, low-speed handpieces and air turbines.

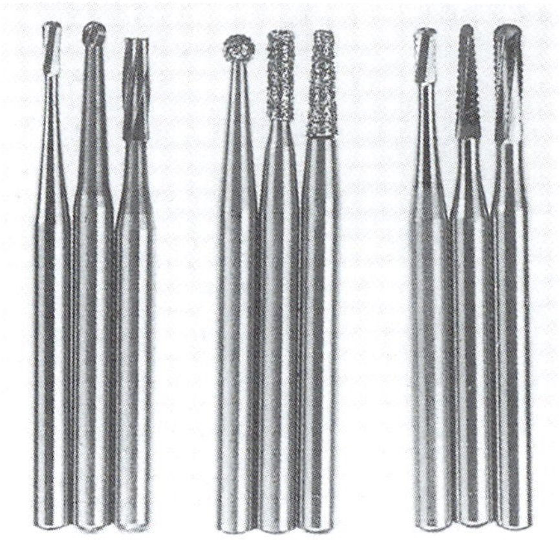

Fig. 5.15 A selection of friction-grip burs for the air turbine. From the left: three tungsten carbide burs, three diamond burs, and three metal-cutting burs. Note the very fine cross-cuts on the metal cutting blades.

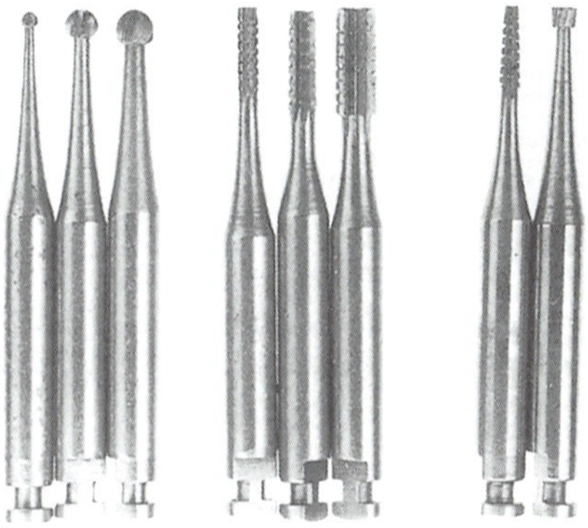

Fig. 5.16 A selection of steel latch burs for use at low speed. From the left: three round burs of different sizes, three straight cross-cut fissure burs, a tapered cross-cut fissure bur, and an inverted cone bur.

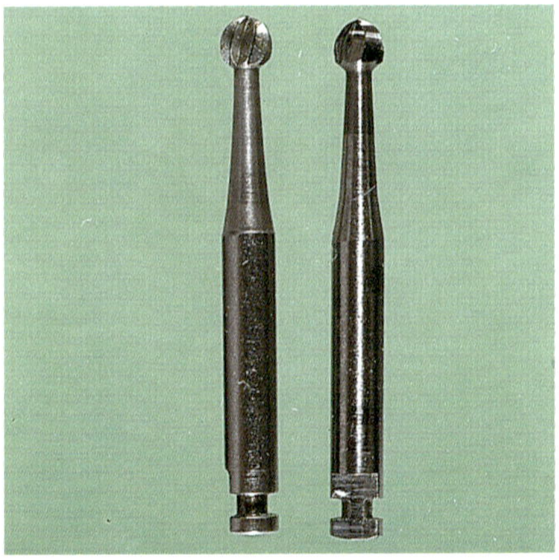

Fig. 5.17 Similar sizes of steel and tungsten carbide burs. The head of the tungsten carbide bur (right) can be seen attached to a steel shank. The head is a slightly different shape.

The cutting end of the instrument consists of either a set of blades of tungsten carbide or steel, or abrasive material, ranging in hardness from diamond to sand, embedded in a suitable medium.

Air turbine burs

Burs used in the air turbine always have friction-grip shanks and the cutting end is diamond or tungsten carbide. These hard materials are necessary because of the very high speeds (Fig. 5.15).

Air turbine burs are used to cut sound enamel and dentine and to remove existing restorations. They should not be used to remove caries because they cut too fast and the sense of 'feel' is lost (see p. 63). When cutting enamel some operators prefer diamond and some tungsten carbide burs. However, ceramic materials are best cut with diamond burs while all other restorations are best cut with tungsten carbide. Special tungsten carbide burs (Beaver burs) are produced to cut metal restorations in the mouth. Diamond instruments cut cast metal very slowly and ordinary tungsten carbide burs tend to break.

A very large selection of shapes of burs is available and advice will be given in later chapters on the choice of bur for specific procedures.

Low-speed burs

As with the air turbine burs, a large selection of shapes is available (Fig. 5.16) which include:

- round burs
- flat fissure burs which are parallel-sided and have blades which may be plain or cross-cut to increase efficiency
- tapered fissure burs which may also be plain or cross-cut
- inverted cone burs.

All these burs are available in a range of sizes which are numbered according to the diameter of the cutting tip.

Steel, diamond, and tungsten carbide low-speed burs are available. Steel burs are not expensive but have a short working life because they are rapidly blunted by enamel and will rust after autoclaving if they are not dried. Tungsten carbide burs run more smoothly than steel and they can be autoclaved; therefore they are becoming more popular than steel. Many dentists now discard steel burs after a single use (Fig. 5.17).

Round burs are used to remove soft carious dentine at slow speed. The steel bur will not cut sound dentine or enamel very quickly at low speed, and so the experienced clinician can feel their way around a cavity, removing softened dentine and leaving sound dentine behind. Round burs are used because, as caries spreads out in dentine simultaneously in all directions, carious lesions in dentine are often naturally round.

Stones

These are made of abrasives such as carborundum (green) or alundum (white or pink) which are moulded into a range of shapes and fixed directly to a bur shank (Fig. 5.18). They are commonly used for shaping, smoothing, and finishing cast metal and porcelain restorations out of the mouth. For this purpose they are usually used at medium speeds in the straight handpiece.

Finishing instruments

Burs and points

In addition to burs for every basic cavity preparation, a whole range are produced for finishing preparations and restorations. These are made of steel (for amalgam) or of very find diamond particles or multi-fluted tungsten carbide (for composite) (Figs. 5.19 and 5.20).

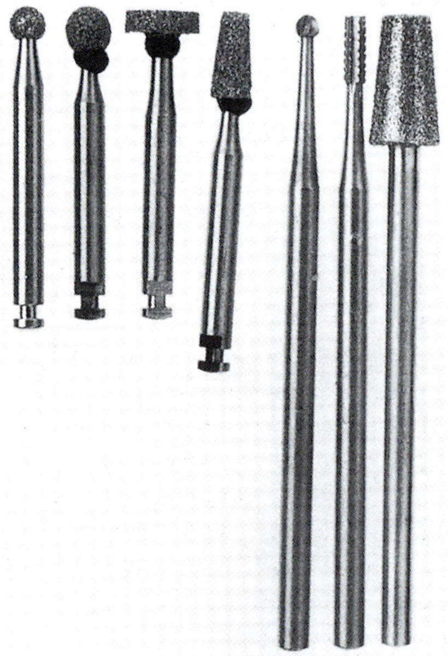

Fig. 5.18 A selection of stones mounted on latch-grip shanks and three straight-shank instruments. The instrument on the far right is a diamond-coated instrument for use in the laboratory or at the chairside for coarse adjustment of restorations and appliances.

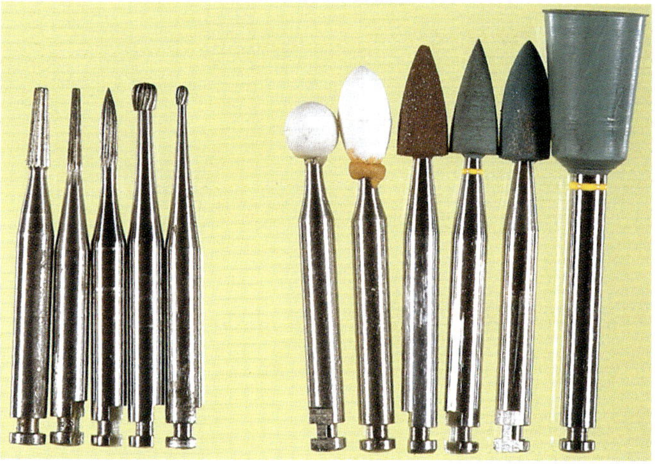

Fig. 5.19 Finishing instruments for amalgam. From the left: five plain-cut plain steel finishing burs, two mounted stones, three mounted abrasive rubber points from coarse to fine, and a mounted abrasive rubber cup.

Discs

Rigid and flexible discs are available with abrasive materials of different degrees of coarseness applied to one surface (or occasionally both). Some discs also cut at their edge. All discs are mounted on mandrels, with some flexible discs designed for clinical use snapped on to split mandrels so that they can be changed easily. Mandrels for laboratory discs are usually of a screw fixing design. Rigid discs are used in a straight handpiece outside the mouth for cutting and trimming such things as posts and temporary crowns. Flexible single-sided discs are commonly used for finishing composite and other restorations, and are available in a wide range of grits and sizes (Fig. 5.20).

Abrasive strips

Hands-held flexible strips of metal, plastic, or linen with abrasive on one side can be used to finish restorations. Metal strips are sometimes used to remove overhanging amalgam ledges on old restorations, but they are not very effective and are traumatic to the gingival papilla (see Chapter 12). Plastic strips are used to finish composite restorations on the approximal surfaces of teeth (Fig. 5.20).

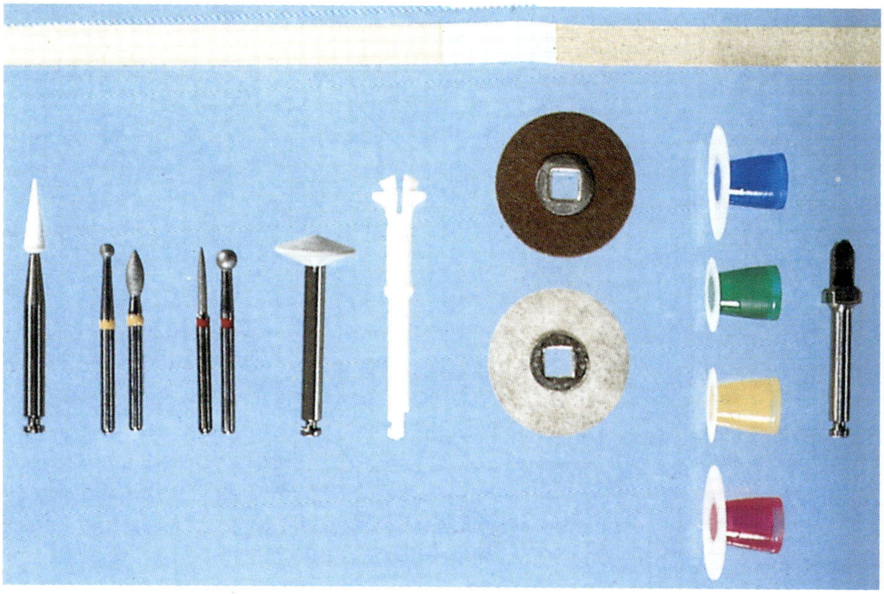

Fig. 5.20 Composite finishing instruments. Across the top is a plastic finishing strip with a blank area in the middle to facilitate passage between the teeth. On the right the abrasive is coarse and on the left it is fine. From the left: a mounted fine white stone, two medium-grit composite finishing diamonds, two fine-grit composite finishing diamonds, a mounted abrasive rubber disc, a mandrel for the two abrasive single-sided flexible discs which are snap-fit onto the mandrel, and four colour-coded flexible abrasive discs mounted on plastic stubs which fit the mandrel to the right of the picture.

Maintaining and sterilizing burs and stones

All burs and stones used in the mouth must be autoclaved. Steel burs are increasingly being regarded as disposable. Flexible discs and strips are disposable.

Tungsten carbide burs become blunt and diamond burs become clogged or the diamond particles become lost or worn. They should be assessed regularly and discarded when they have completed their useful life. Tungsten carbide burs occasionally break in use and diamond burs become bent. A bent bur should always be discarded immediately.

Tooth preparation with rotary instruments

Speed, torque, and 'feel'

The speed ranges used in tooth preparation are shown in the caption to Fig. 5.12. Torque is the turning movement of the instrument. In a high-torque cutting system, considerable pressure can be applied to the surface being cut by means of the bur with only minimal slowing of the drive, although other factors such as heat, vibration, and the amount of material removed may rise conspicuously. Broadly speaking, the higher is the speed the lower is the torque. It is more efficient to cut hard materials such as enamel, porcelain, and metal at high speeds and to cut softer materials such as carious dentine at lower speeds with higher torque.

An important characteristic of cutting systems is the 'feel' which the operator senses through the handpiece. At high speed there is very little 'feel' and the cutting must be controlled visually. This is difficult because of the water spray. At lower speeds 'feel' is useful in controlling the cutting process, particularly close to the pulp. This is the principle reason why low-speed sharp burs should be used for removing carious dentine.

Heat generation and dissipation

Heat is generated in proportion to the work done and is potentially damaging to a vital pulp. High-speed cutting always produces sufficient heat to necessitate a cooling water spray, and in most air turbine systems the water spray comes on automatically when the foot control is depressed. Prolonged slow-speed cutting also generates heat, and most low-speed handpieces now have a built-in water spray, although this may have to be switched on when it is required. In the finishing stages of preparation too much water spray can hinder vision, and at that stage very little tooth tissue is being removed and hence little heat is being produced. Therefore it is usual for the water spray not to be used and for the dental nurse to wash and dry the cavity at frequent intervals, which serves the dual purposes of improving visibility and cooling the tooth.

One of the many advantages of using natural extracted teeth in preclinical practical courses is that occasionally an inexperienced student will cut enamel and dentine without sufficient cooling and the distinctive burning smell pervades the classroom. This is a good lesson because, once recognized, the students know that they must never produce this smell in clinical work.

Effects on the patient

Tooth preparation with rotary instruments has the potential of producing pain, vibration, pressure, trauma, and long-term effects on the pulp. Provided that cooling is adequate (and the water is not too cold), superficial preparation of the enamel is not painful. However, cutting dentine in a vital tooth is painful and local analgesia is usually used. High-speed cutting of enamel produces intense localized heat, even with apparently effective cooling. As an illustration, the reader should try cutting an extracted tooth with the air turbine in a darkened room with eyes dark-adapted.

The range of perceptible vibration is limited and rotary instrumentation at speeds over 40 000 rev/minute produces high-frequency vibrations above the normal range of perception. Therefore patients usually prefer the air turbine to tooth preparation at lower speeds. An electric motor drive may produce less vibration than an air motor, particularly when the air motor, which has more moving parts, becomes worn. Therefore electric motors are preferred, although they are more expensive and the maintenance costs are usually higher. Another source of vibration is the attachment of the bur to the handpiece. Friction-grip shanks have no movement between the bur shank and the chuck, whereas conventional latch burs are a looser fit and therefore are capable of vibration. An increasing number of handpiece systems now have friction chucks which grip latch bur shanks more firmly and produce less vibration. The chuck is released by a button at the back of the handpiece head.

Very little pressure is used in cutting at high speed, as pressure would slow the bur and reduce cutting speed. Greater pressure is used at lower speeds and higher torques, and this must be carefully controlled or the patient will find it uncomfortable.

Sharp revolving instruments used at awkward angles in the restricted confines of a mouth which moves independently of the operator give rise to real risks of accidental damage. This is a principal reason why the undergraduate student must develop a high level of skill in the use of the full range of rotary instruments before starting clinical work. Even experienced dentists occasionally cause damage to tissues around the tooth. Accidental and unexpected exposure of the pulp (a traumatic exposure) sometimes results from careless cutting or from variations in, or a lack of understanding of, pulpal anatomy. Proper examination of the pre-operative radiographs, and care, should avoid these injuries. Damage to sound adjacent teeth in the preparation of approximal surfaces is commonplace and difficult to avoid. Usually the damage is minor and may not be seen. However, it does create plaque-retentive areas on the adjacent surface and increases the risk of development of a new carious lesion. Great care should be taken to avoid these injuries by using appropriately sized and shaped burs, and hand instrumentation when appropriate. Good illumination is essential and magnification helps. The adjacent teeth are sometimes physically protected with a matrix band (see Chapter 8).

It is not always possible to avoid some injury to the gingival margin adjacent to the cavity being prepared. Proper selection of bur shapes and sizes and the use of a rubber dam or gingival retraction with cord (see Chapter 10) will help, but in any case such minor injuries usually heal with no long-term ill effect.

It is difficult to disentangle the effects of caries, tooth preparation, and the restorative materials when pulp changes occur. All dentists will find that teeth which they have restored occasionally suffer acute or chronic pulpitis or degenerative or necrotic changes in the pulp. If this occurs frequently, it is because the dentist is being too optimistic about pulp prognosis, or is being traumatic in tooth preparation, or there is something wrong with the restorative materials or techniques being used. One of the things that should be checked is that water cooling is sufficient.

Choosing the bur for the job

Skilled and experienced clinicians often use a limited number of burs from the very wide variety produced for the same purpose and obtain equally satisfactory results. However, the inexperienced student needs to start somewhere, and it is better for the clinical teacher to suggest a range of burs than for this to be prescribed in a textbook. However, clinicians will experiment with new designs of bur throughout their practising lifetimes, and it is an important part of postgraduate continuing education to read catalogues, visit dental trade exhibitions, and generally seek better ways of making preparations.

The illustrations in Chapters 7–11 show a number of burs being used for specific purposes, and in some cases these are designed especially for that purpose. There is a saying 'a bad workman blames his tools', but the corollary is that a good workman knows which tool does the job best for him/her.

Surface finish

For most purposes, a relatively smooth finished enamel surface is preferable, although the faster cutting systems generally produce rough surfaces. Therefore many preparations consist of two stages, the initial rapid tooth reduction followed by more precise shaping and finishing. As a general rule, straight-cut burs provide a smoother finish than cross-cut designs and tungsten carbide burs provide a smoother finish than either steel or diamond burs.

Finishing and polishing restorations

The surfaces produced by various finishing instruments on composite are shown in Fig. 5.21. The margins and surfaces of restorations should be smoothed and polished so that plaque retention is minimized. There is a wide and increasing range of instruments to do this, in particular instruments for finishing composite materials. Ideally, any material should be shaped properly in its unset stage so that it requires minimal finishing with medium or fine abrasive instruments. If more shaping is necessary, a coarser instrument should be used first. Several finishing systems – for example disc systems – have four grades of abrasives. It is not always necessary to start with the coarsest, but one of the finest should be used at the end of the procedure.

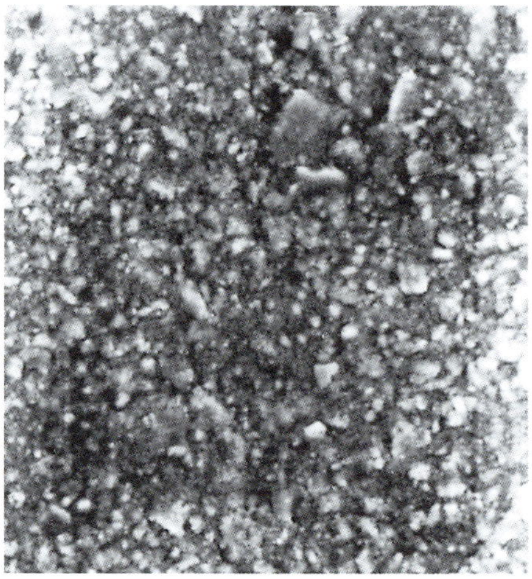

(a)

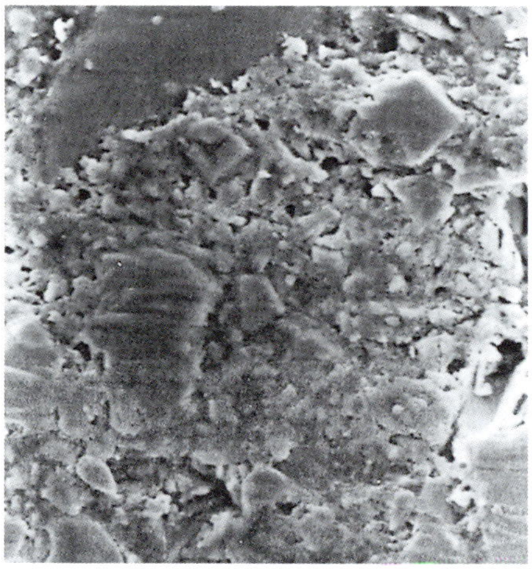

(b)

Fig. 5.21 The surface of composite (a) as left by a matrix strip and (b) finished with a coarse abrasive disc. Field width for both, 30 μm. (Reproduced by courtesy of Dr M. O. Atta.)

Air abrasion

Air abrasion is a means of cutting or preparing tooth surfaces by harnessing the transferred kinetic energy of alumina particles accelerated in a controlled compressed air stream. The technique has been shown to be particularly appropriate for minimal preparation techniques and for use in conservative repairs of existing restorations, by leaving a rough surface for bonding. This method of cutting teeth dramatically reduces the problems of heat generation, vibration, and other mechanical stimulation, resulting in relatively pain-free procedures when compared to the dental drill. The main disadvantage is the dust cloud generated. The current systems have full US Federal Drug Administration (FDA) approval for clinical use of 25 μm alumina particles or larger. Indeed, recent advances in micro-abrasion technology allow a metered flow of alumina particles and almost instantaneous initiation and termination of the abrasive stream, all helping to reduce the dust cloud produced. Further advances in the technique include the use of a shroud (or curtain) of water around the powder–air stream to limit powder spread. These factors, coupled with the judicious use of rubber dam isolation, face mask protection for the dental team, and efficient high-volume suction, all help to minimize the risks of particle inhalation further (Fig. 5.22).

Currently these methods remove *sound* and reasonably hard tooth structure and restorations effectively. Current research is investigating the use of particles with modified hardness that will be suitable for preferential removal of very soft carious tissue.

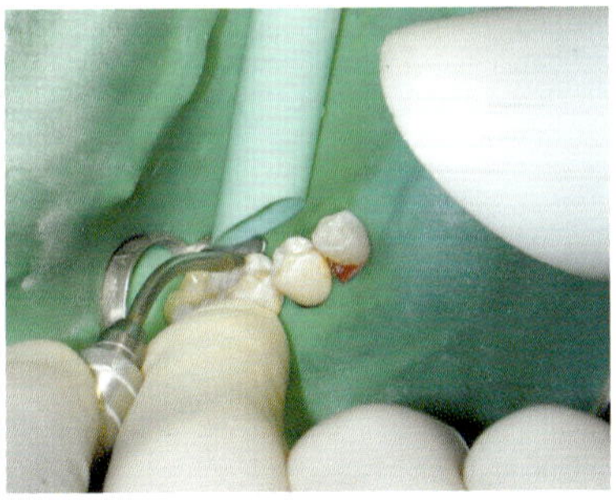

Fig 5.22 An air abrasion handpiece being used to cut an occlusal cavity. Note the suction tips used to remove the alumina powder.

Auxiliary instruments and equipment

Very good illumination for cavity preparation can be obtained with fibre-optic lighting systems producing illumination at the head of the handpiece (Fig. 5.23). These are available in both air turbine and slow-speed handpieces. Independent fibre-optic lighting, especially when used with magnifying loupes, has also been used as well as, or instead of, the normal operating light.

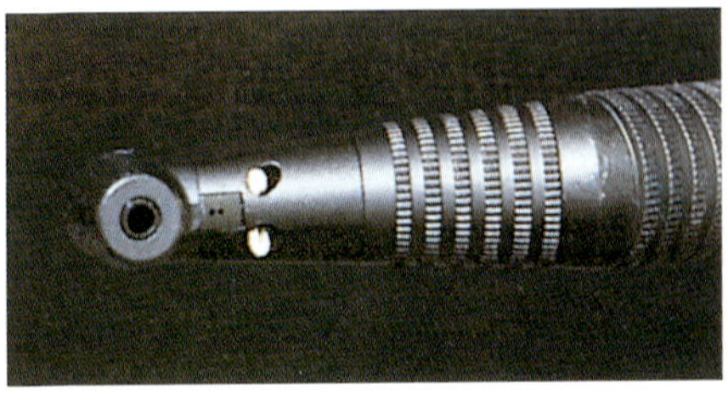

Fig. 5.23 A fibre-optic lighting system built into the head of a contra-angle low-speed handpiece.

Many resin-based restorative materials are now polymerized by the application of intense blue (470 nm wavelength) visible light. The original instruments used light transmitted from its source down a flexible light guide which is either a fibre-optic cable or a gel. The end of this is applied to the tooth. Alternatively, the light can be contained in a hand-held piece of equipment connected to the electrical supply. In this case the short light guide is rigid and more robust. Rechargeable versions, which are simply left parked in the charging unit while not in use, are now available. Earlier versions of these have tended to have poor battery life, but many of these problems are now being overcome by the development of light-emitting diode (LED) curing systems that have less power requirement (Fig. 5.24). There are other developments, such as high-intensity plasma or laser-based curing lights, which claim decreased polymerization times and speedier working. However, it is not yet known whether there may be deficiencies in the material properties arising from the use of these lights. Indeed, some curing lights are now made that have a low starting intensity of curing, increasing over time, that allows the polymerizing material to undergo a gel phase of setting prior to final hardening (Fig. 5.24). This is claimed to reduce the polymerization stresses that are transmitted to the tooth.

All systems produce light of such intensity that it can be damaging to the retina and so it must not be shone in the direction of the patient's, operator's, or dental nurse's eyes, and so protective screens or spectacles are used. One of these is shown in use in Fig. 9.8.

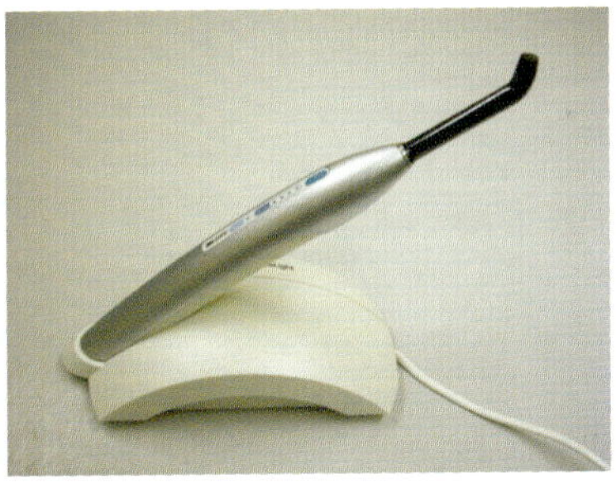

Fig. 5.24 A rechargeable, battery-powered, LED-illuminated curing light with variable initial cure rates, shown in its charging stand. Eye protection should always be used, or alternatively, both the operator and nurse should avoid looking at the light when it is on.

Many surgeries are now equipped with ultrasonic and electrosurgical equipment. Ultrasonic scalers are a quick and efficient way of removing calculus. The working tip is vibrated at ultrasonic frequency under voluminous water spray. Their use is described fully in textbooks of periodontology. Ultrasonic instruments are also used with special files in endodontics (see textbooks on endodontics) and have other uses such as loosening crowns or posts when they have to be removed (see textbooks on crowns and bridges).

Electrosurgical equipment, with a fine point or loop electrode, is occasionally used, for example to remove hyperplastic gingival tissue, to gain access to cavity margins, or to expose the margin of a tooth fractured below gingival level.

6

Bonding to tooth structure

Why bond to tooth tissue?

The substrate; enamel and dentine

- Enamel
- Dentine
- Enamel–dentine junction
- Cutting

Choice of materials for bonding techniques

- Spectrum of bonding materials
- Overall requirements for adhesion

Composites

- Bonding to enamel
- Bonding to dentine
- Bonding to wet dentine (and enamel)

Important considerations on the use of bonding agents

- Number of stages and film thickness
- Speed of application
- Good clear instructions
- Ease of dispensing and handling
- Sensitization
- Shelf-life

Glass ionomer cements

- Adhesion mechanisms: conventional glass ionomer cements
- Conditioning the dentine
- Bonding glass ionomer cements to enamel
- Bonding glass ionomer cements to dentine

The resin-modified glass ionomer cements

The polyacid-modified resin composites

Bonded amalgam restorations

Bonding to tooth structure

Why bond to tooth tissue?

The reasons for wanting to use adhesive materials in restorative dentistry can be usefully summarized as:

- prevention of leakage, reducing risk of pulpal damage
- allows more conservative tooth preparations
- bonded restorations strengthen tooth tissue.

Attaining a successful long-term bond of restorative materials to tooth tissue continues to be a significant challenge for dental biomaterials and clinical researchers. A major cause of this challenge derives from the inherent shrinkage of resin-based restorative materials transmitting great strain to the interface between tooth and adhesive. The regrettable failure of adhesive bonding systems is also partly attributable to the technical difficulties of handling materials in a confined space, followed by their subsequent exposure to one of the most hostile biological environments – the mouth. The fact that dentists can now place increasing reliance on bonding techniques, without recourse to the more destructive mechanically retentive tooth preparations, indicates that a degree of success has been achieved. Even though there is a need for improvement in handling techniques and simplicity of use, many of the advances in this field of dental research are well ahead of those in orthopaedic surgery and at the forefront of adhesives research in general.

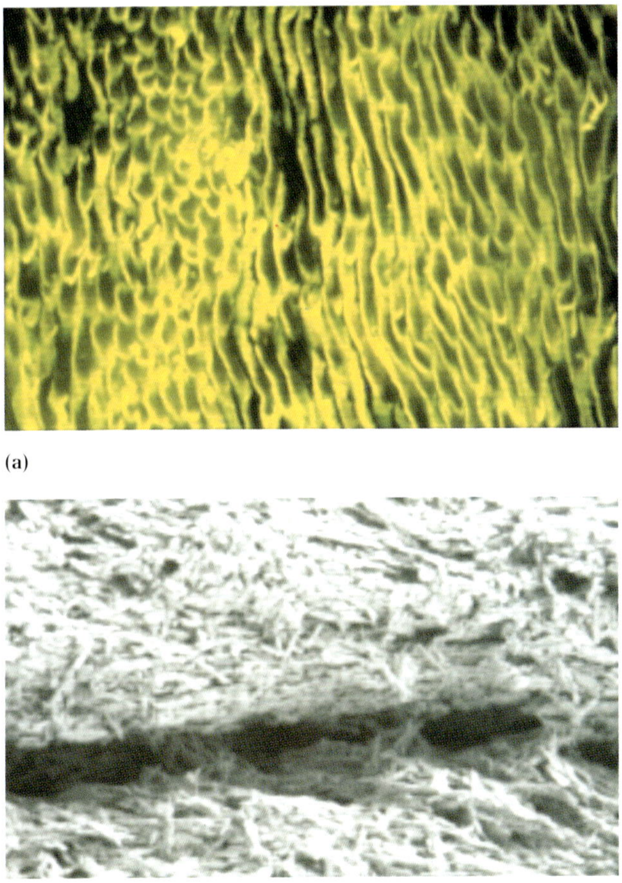

(a)

(b)

Fig. 6.1 (a) Enamel prisms imaged 'end on' using a confocal optical microscope. Notice that some of the prisms appear horseshoe-shaped whilst others have been sectioned at an oblique angle. Field width 200 μm.
(b) The boundary between the sides of two enamel prisms imaged using a field emission scanning electron microscope. The hydroxyapatite crystals and the prism boundary have been highlighted by lightly etching the enamel. Field width 2 μm.

The substrate; enamel and dentine

The physical characteristics of the dental hard tissues have been described briefly in Chapter 3, but in order to understand mechanisms of adhesion of restorative materials it is important to have a more detailed knowledge of the dental structures.

Enamel

The basic structural unit of enamel is the hydroxyapatite crystal. Approximately 10 000 of these long, slender crystals are closely packed together to form a 4–7 μm diameter prism or rod (Fig. 6.1). This unit extends from the enamel–dentine junction (EDJ) to the surface of the tooth, a distance of up to 2.5 mm. The hydroxyapatite crystals can be very long indeed in comparison to their width, behaving rather like the fibres in a rope; this, in conjunction with the complexity of the prism shape and course, leads to an extremely tough and hard-wearing material. Such strength is, however, highly directional in this

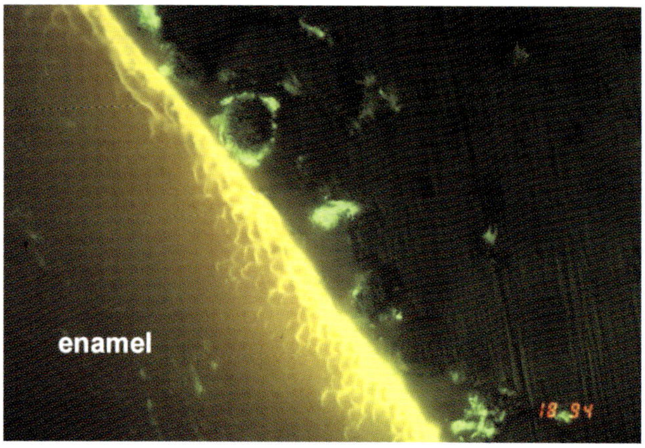

Fig. 6.2 The interface between etched and bonded enamel prisms and a restoration. The bonding agent has been labelled with a yellow fluorescent dye and its penetration around the horseshoe-shaped enamel prisms can be seen. Enamel prisms are easily separated from one another in the lateral walls of a cavity such as this, especially if the restoration shrinks. Field width 500 μm.

biomaterial. The prism unit is very difficult to pull and break in its long axis because of the crystal orientation. The most optimal enamel prism orientation for bonding is therefore in their long axis. Attachment to the sides of prisms is less satisfactory. Prisms can, however, be bent laterally and ruptured by weaker forces than are required for breakage in the long axis. Such prism orientations will be readily encountered in the lateral walls of proximal cavities (Fig. 6.2).

Dentine

The major structural unit of dentine is the dentine tubule, running from the enamel–dentine junction to the pulp. This 1–2 μm diameter tubule conveys pulpal fluid from the pulp to the enamel, so maintaining the hydration of the tooth and other physiological functions (Fig. 6.3). Dentine is wet and sticking something to a wet surface is not easy. The inherent outward flow of fluid will give a profound reduction in the penetration of bonding agents into the tubules and may have an effect on water-sensitive cements. Tubule density at the enamel–dentine junction is 19 000/mm^2 and increases towards the pulp to 45 000/mm^2. The diameter of the tubule also increases from 0.8 μm at the enamel–dentine junction to 2.5 μm at the pulp (Fig. 6.4). As a consequence, there is much more intertubular dentine in the outer dentine than near the pulp. It is therefore self-evident that deeper dentine will be much 'wetter' than that at the periphery of the tooth, so affecting the performance of water-sensitive restorative materials.

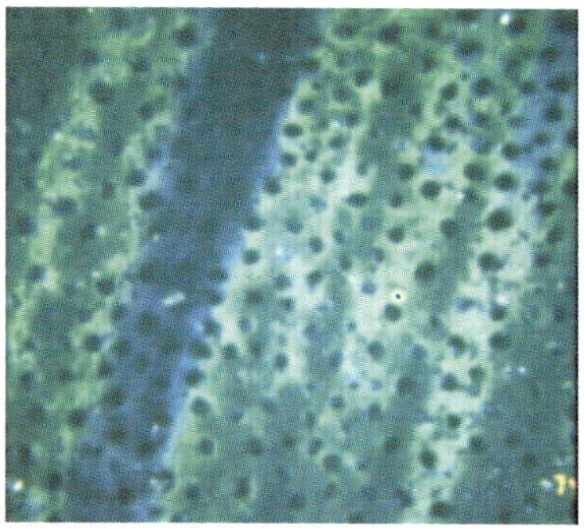

Fig. 6.3 Dentine cut with a dental bur at 90° to the dentine tubules and then acid-etched. The grooved surface arises from the use of a bur. The 1–2 μm diameter tubules are spaced well apart. Field width 150 μm.

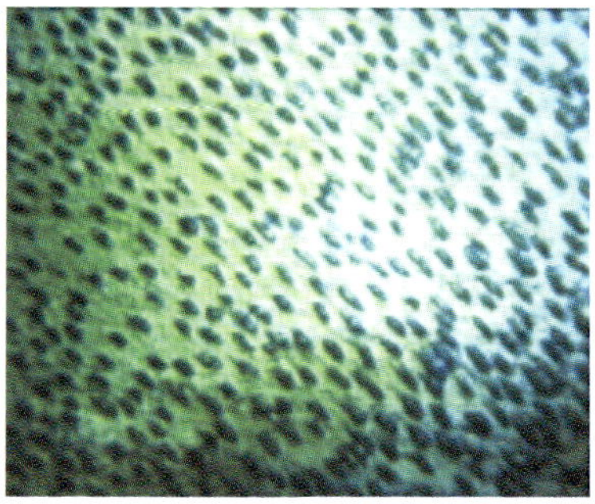

Fig. 6.4 Dentine sectioned closer to the pulp than in Fig. 6.3, showing greater packing density of tubules. Field width 150 μm.

In the outer two-thirds of the dentine, the tubule itself is surrounded by a thin coating of highly mineralized peritubular dentine. The bulk of the dentine consists of a matrix of type 1 collagen embedded in hydroxyapatite crystals, so forming the intertubular dentine. Hypermineralization of dentine will occur as a defence reaction to caries and tooth wear. This reduces permeability and confers a protective function, preventing noxious substances entering the pulp. It is important to realize that dentine affected by caries will be different to bond to than freshly-cut dentine where there have been no defence reactions. Much of the published data describing bond strengths and morphological properties of bonding materials relate to work undertaken on young teeth – often extracted third molars – that have not suffered any disease processes such as caries or tooth wear.

Dentine is neither strong nor weak in any particular direction; compared to enamel it has less obvious 'grain structure' and is resilient, hence, as ivory, the material can be beautifully carved. Due to its water content and slight flexibility, dentine is a multiphase material which presents many problems for bonding.

Enamel–dentine junction

Enamel and dentine are intimately related to each other with a scalloped interface at the enamel–dentine junction (Fig. 6.5). The enamel 'protects' the dentine from wear and the dentine 'supports' the brittle enamel. Without adequate support from the dentine the enamel shell is easily lost: examples of where this occurs are when the dentine structure is defective – as in dentinogenesis imperfecta or following dentine caries (see Chapter 1). When a tooth is loaded to

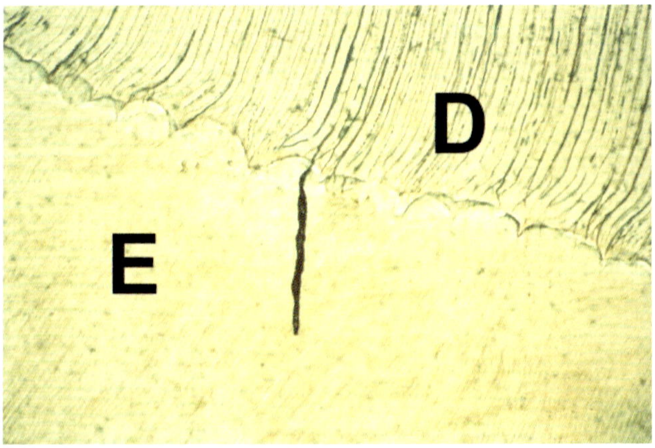

Fig. 6.5 Thin ground section of enamel–dentine junction showing scalloped appearance – concavities towards the pulp – of the complex interface. The dentine (D) is of great importance in supporting the enamel (E). If there are deficiencies in its make-up, such as in dentinogenesis imperfecta or following undermining caries, then the enamel flakes away (see Chapter 1). Field width 1 mm.

the point of failure then cracks will propagate along the parallel enamel prisms near the surface of the tooth. Reduction in crack-growth energy occurs with lateral deflection of the crack. Many of the crack-stopping features within enamel, such as the crossing of sheets of prisms relative to one another, help to distribute stresses around a tooth, without catastrophic failure.

Cutting

Cutting these hard tissues produces a new structure called the smeared layer (<20 μm thick) on both the enamel and dentine. This is variably attached to the tooth surface and consists of cutting debris which is pressure-welded to the tooth and has the effect of reducing fluid outflow from the dentine by plugging the tubular openings (Fig. 6.6). Due to its brittleness, cutting enamel introduces subsurface cracks

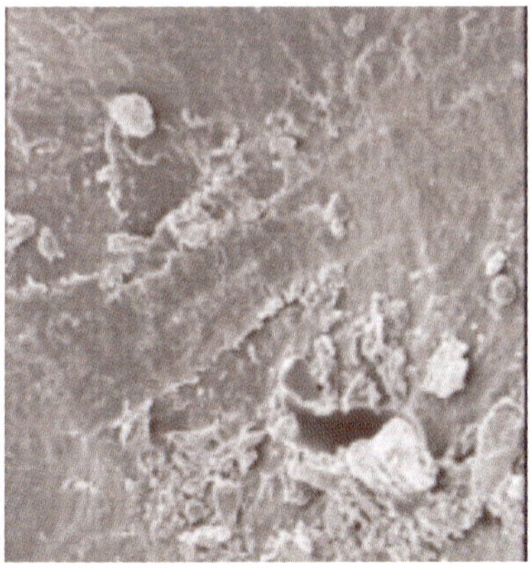

Fig. 6.6 Dentine smear layer imaged using Scanning Electron Microscopy (SEM): this is a barrier to good bonding and is normally removed using acids. Field width 500 μm. (Courtesy Dr A. Banerjee.)

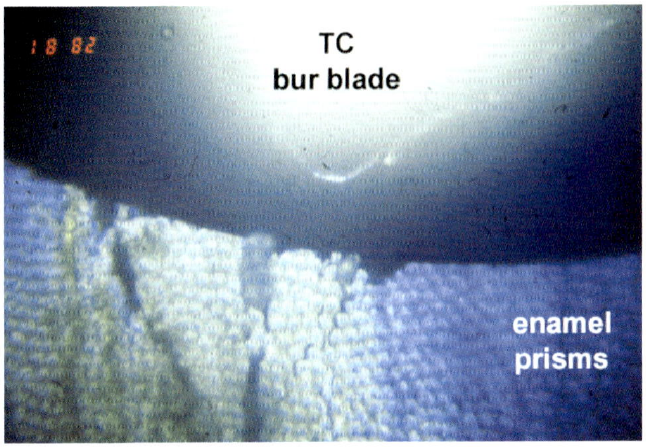

Fig. 6.7 Cracking visible in an enamel interface that has just been cut with a tungsten carbide bur. The cracks can be seen propagating around the horseshoe-shape enamel prisms. Field width 200 μm.

and fault lines, which can lead to structural weakness if materials are bonded to this damaged substrate (Fig. 6.7).

Choice of materials for bonding techniques

The range of restorative materials available to a dentist is ever-increasing, with the manufacturers making incremental changes in both formulation and presentation of materials on a regular basis, as outlined in Chapter 3. Achieving an attachment to tooth tissue for these restorative materials is obviously closely related to the major chemical reactions involved in their conversion from the plastic or fluid state to the solid. The tooth-coloured filling materials fall within a range, which on the one hand consists of the *resin composites* and on the other the *glass ionomer cements* (GICs). As may be inferred by their names the former consist of a resin and filler system, whilst the latter are water-based cements. Straddling these are the *polyacid-modified resin composites (compomers)* with mainly composite-like properties and the *resin-modified glass ionomer cements* which are more closely related to the conventional glass ionomer cements.

Spectrum of bonding materials

The general properties of these materials are covered in Chapter 3. Figure 6.8 summarizes their constituents and requirements for bonding to tooth tissue.

Overall requirements for adhesion

The general perceived requirements for adhesion are expounded in many dental materials textbooks. Good substrate wetting, a low 'contact angle', and a clean substrate are normally considered essential. The surface tension of the liquid bonding agent must always be less than the surface

Composites	– Resin/filler: not self-adhesive; hydrophobic – *adhesive essential*
Glass ionomer cement	– Acid-base cement/no resin: water-based – *self-adhesive*
Resin-modified glass ionomer	– Acid-base cement/resin: hydrophilic – *primer for adhesion of resin*
Polyacid-modified composites	– Modified resin/ionomer filler: slightly hyprophilic – *adhesive essential*

Fig. 6.8 Bonding materials: summary of their constituents and requirements for bonding to tooth tissue.

energy of the enamel or dentine. The contamination of the tooth surface by saliva, blood, or other proteinaceous substances reduces the surface energy of the substrate and impairs the wetting by the liquid adhesive: put simply, the first thing to touch a 'clean' tooth surface, whether it be saliva or bonding resin, makes the stronger bond.

The most likely mechanisms of bonding to tooth structure are:

- mechanical theories that involve the concept of interlocking of the solidified bonding agent with the irregularities of the surface of the adherend
- adsorption theories that comprise all the explanations involving chemical bonding between the adhesive and adherend. The forces involved may be primary (ionic and covalent) and secondary (hydrogen, dipole interaction, or van der Waals) valence forces
- diffusion theories that involve the concept of bonding between mobile molecules as they move across the interface.

The enamel–composite bond falls into the first category: the tooth surface is etched, dried, and free-flowing fluid resin placed and cured (Fig. 6.9). A viscous glass ionomer cement may fall into the second and third categories because even without acidic conditioning of the tooth, conventional GICs are inherently adhesive restorations when compared with the resin composites.

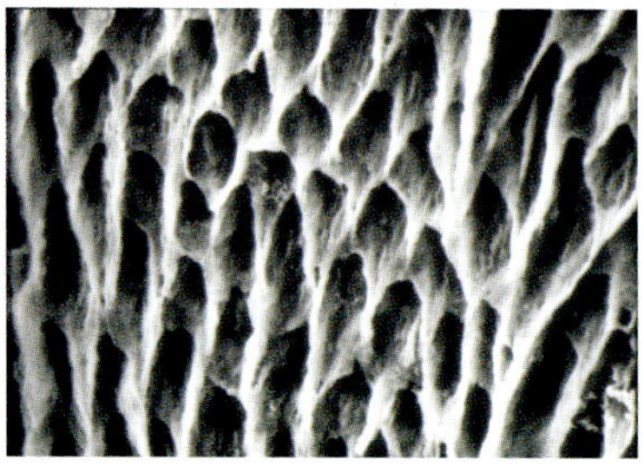

Fig. 6.9 The tooth's view of an acid-etch retained bonding resin. The enamel was etched, washed, and bonded, but then dissolved away in strong acids. The acid-resistant resin can be seen to have flowed into the prism boundary regions. Field width 80 μm. (Courtesy of Professor A. Boyde.)

Composites

The majority of resin composites are inherently hydrophobic (water-hating) materials and so some form of intermediary bonding resin needs to be applied to the tooth.

Bonding to enamel

The bonding of composites to enamel is dependent upon the mechanical retention of resin tags within the highly mineralized enamel (Figs. 6.2 and 6.9). These tags lock into pores created within and around the enamel prisms by the etching action of acids (phosphoric acid has been most widely used). The low-viscosity, unfilled resin is effectively sucked into these pores by capillary attraction. Currently, the etching times with phosphoric acid vary between 15–30 seconds depending on the state of the tooth. As an example, a tooth with fluorotic enamel would be etched for the longer period. Washing away the phosphoric acid-etchant gel is important, with a 10–20 second rinse being sufficient.

Successful enamel bonding was discovered in 1955, and it was essential that a dry-field bonding technique was meticulously implemented. Enamel is a substrate that can be dried relatively easily and the use of intermediate hydrophobic resins dictates such an approach, even though vigorous post-etch drying for 10–20 seconds will cause collapse of the exposed hydroxyapatite crystals. In this way, the ideal enamel etch pattern would show clinically as a 'frosty' appearance awaiting these resin intermediaries. Many bonding systems are now designed to work in a moist environment using hydrophilic (water-liking) resins dissolved in water-miscible solvents: these displace the water from the tooth surface. When using these materials profound drying of the tooth is contraindicated.

Bonding to dentine

Bonding to dentine presents a more difficult problem because it is a living, wet tissue and contains less mineralized tissue than enamel. Resin-based adhesives have been developed for bonding to dentine and these generally work by removing the surface smear layer and infiltrating the exposed dentine. Whilst it is possible to dry out dentine after etching, in the same way as enamel, the net result may prevent satisfactory resin penetration for some of the bonding

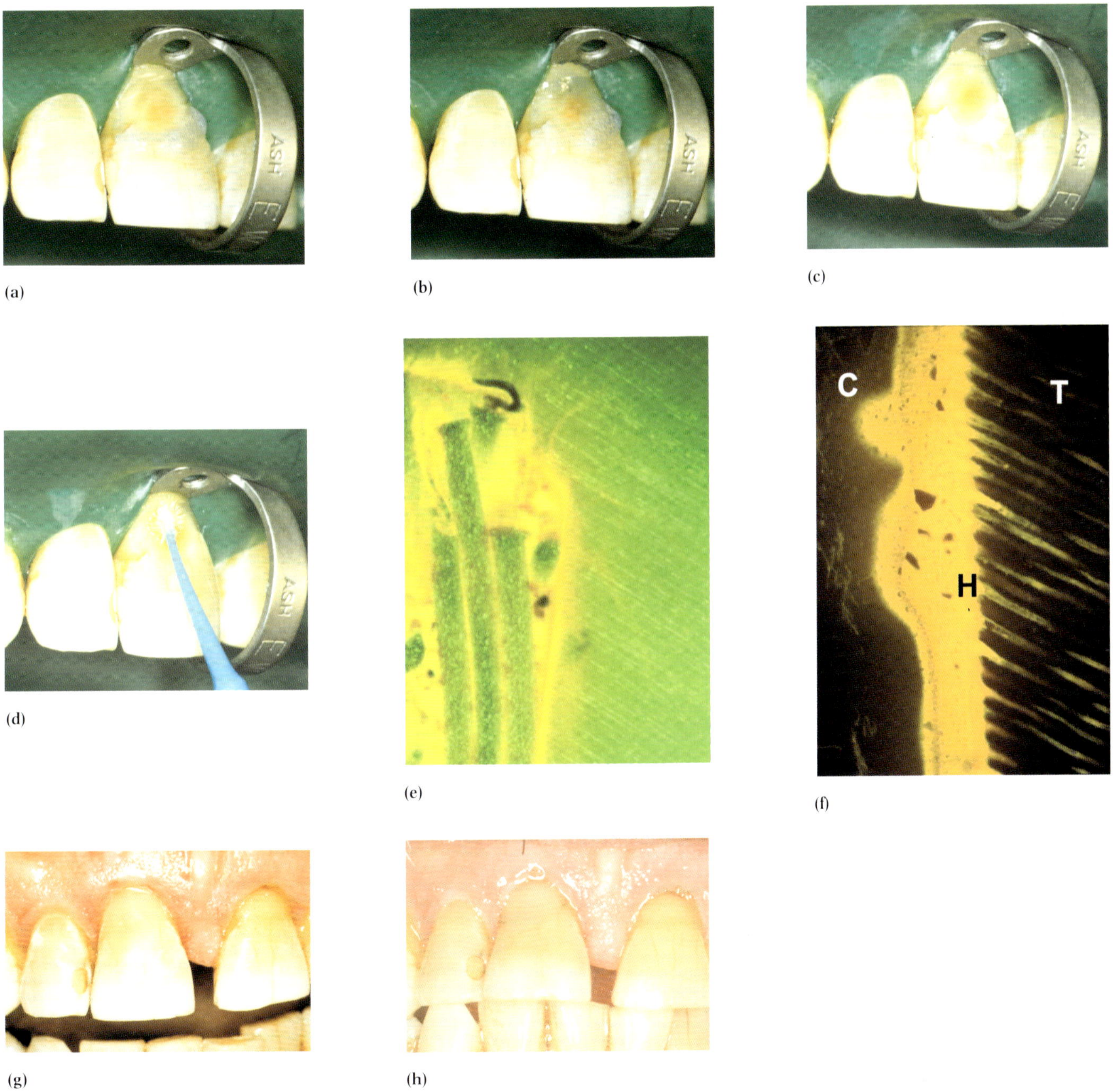

Fig. 6.10 Placement of a resin composite restoration using a total-etch system for a wear cavity. No tooth preparation was undertaken. The bonding agent was applied as a separate primer and adhesive.
(a) Application of the phosphoric acid-etchant for 10 seconds to the enamel.
(b) Continuation of etching of dentine for further 10 seconds.
(c) Etchant washed off and the tooth dried. The etched enamel appears frosty which implies that the tooth has been allowed to dry out more that would be required with modern adhesive systems. However, if the adhesive contains water- or alcohol-based solvents then over-drying is not a major concern.
(d) Application of primer to the tooth using a microbrush.
(e) Microscopic image of an equivalent brush in an *in vitro* cavity.
(f) Development of the *hybrid zone* (H) in an equivalent *in vitro* cavity. The penetration of resin into the tubules (T) and the intertubular dentine can be seen on the right. The air-inhibited zone forms a bond with the composite (C) on the left. Field width 80 μm.
(g) Final restoration.
(h) Same restoration ten years later: the margins have remained relatively stain-free.

agents in use. This is because the drying causes the fragile, exposed collagen network to collapse and the resin cannot penetrate this collapsed structure.

The main problem of dentine bonding is that a hydrophobic resin composite is required to stick to a 'watery' substrate. Resin technology has now developed such that it is possible to produce a bonding agent in a solvent that will infiltrate and stick to wet dentine (Fig. 6.10) and maintain the bond over a significant time period (Fig. 6.10h).

Bonding to wet dentine (and enamel)

Most dentine bonding agents require smear layer removal with weak acids. There are two ways of doing this. The more established systems use a separate etch stage with phosphoric acid followed by the bonding agent, whilst others combine acid and the bonding agent and are therefore called 'self-etching'.

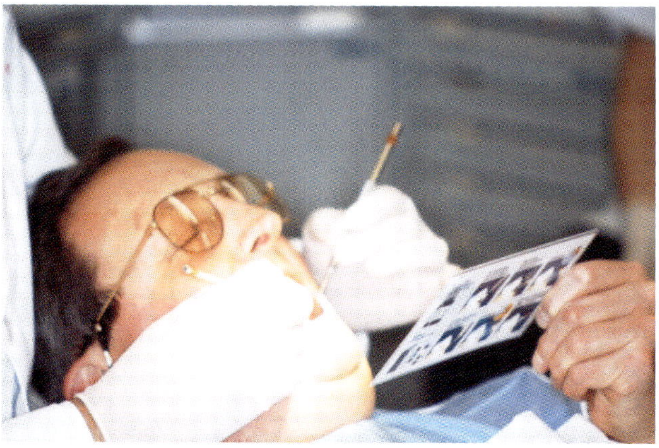

Fig. 6.11 Simplified pictorial instructions in laminated plastic are easy to follow, although it is not normal to ask the patient to hold the instructions as you work! When you are using a material that is new to you, put the instructions so that you can read them as you work, just as you would with a new recipe in the kitchen.

Separate etching stage

The smear layer is removed with acid (Fig. 6.10a–c) and then the bonding agent is applied (Fig. 6.10d and e). This dentine bonding system uses alcohol and water as the solvent base for the hydrophilic resin: these materials will be capable of re-wetting a dried collagen surface, although their penetration time into the substrate may be slightly longer than the more volatile solvent bases such as acetone.

Solvents such as acetone mix freely with water and therefore require a moist tooth surface for thorough dentine penetration in the technique described as '*wet bonding*'. This does not mean bonding through a pool of blood and saliva, but it does mean that the tooth surface should not be dried out too much as this will cause collapse of the exposed collagen network – and enamel crystallites – with grossly inadequate penetration of the bonding agent. Judging the correct degree of wetness in these situations is a problem. Some suggest that surplus water should be removed by the use of a cotton-wool pledget. For these materials, the desiccating effect of an air blast and the frosted appearance of etched enamel should be avoided (cf., Fig. 6.10c).

A low-molecular-weight hydrophilic resin (e.g. Hydroxy Ethyl MethAcrylate: HEMA), in a suitable solvent (e.g. water, alcohol, acetone), is flooded over the altered surface of the dentine (Fig. 6.10d–f). It then flows into the dentinal tubules and the porous intertubular dentine between them. The type of solvent in use is critical for the method of handling the bonding agent. The instructions indicate how the material should be handled and must be followed exactly (Fig. 6.11). Data sheets may give some indication of content or, alternatively, it is a reasonable test to smell the bonding system before use (although don't make a habit of it...) to determine the type of solvent in use.

Having acted as a good 'wetting agent' on the dentine and enamel, layers of increasingly resinous hydrophilic material are applied and the relative stiffness of the resin component is increased by gentle evaporation of solvent. The most effective way to make this resinous structure really strong is to polymerize it. Many systems therefore involve either a light-curing stage or a self-curing reaction. The dentine and patient are consequently embedded in an increasingly hydrophobic and stiff resin matrix which acts as a firm foundation on which to build a composite restoration. The region between the unaffected dentine and the restoration is a mixture of both and so is called the *hybrid zone* (Fig. 6.10f). Another name for it is the *interdiffusion zone* which also indicates the 5–10 μm penetration of the resins into the intertubular dentine.

After curing, all resin-based materials will have a thin layer of slippery, 'greasy', unpolymerized material on the surface where they are exposed to the air – the *air-inhibited layer* – and this allows increments of material to be bonded to each other. The most important consideration for achieving a sound, reliable bond is the avoidance of *any* contamination between these layers. Should salivary contamination occur at any stage during the making of a composite restoration, then the surface should be re-etched and washed to remove the instantaneously formed pellicle. The bonding agent is then wiped over the surface and light-cured before continuing.

Self-etching adhesives

A problem with bonding agents that have a separate etching stage is that successful bonds will only be achieved if the adhesive resin penetrates to the depth of demineralization caused by the acid-etching. Materials that use a self-etching combination will not suffer from this problem because the two components are already combined (Fig. 6.12). They will also not require a separate washing and drying stage before the application of the bonding agent, so helping to reduce

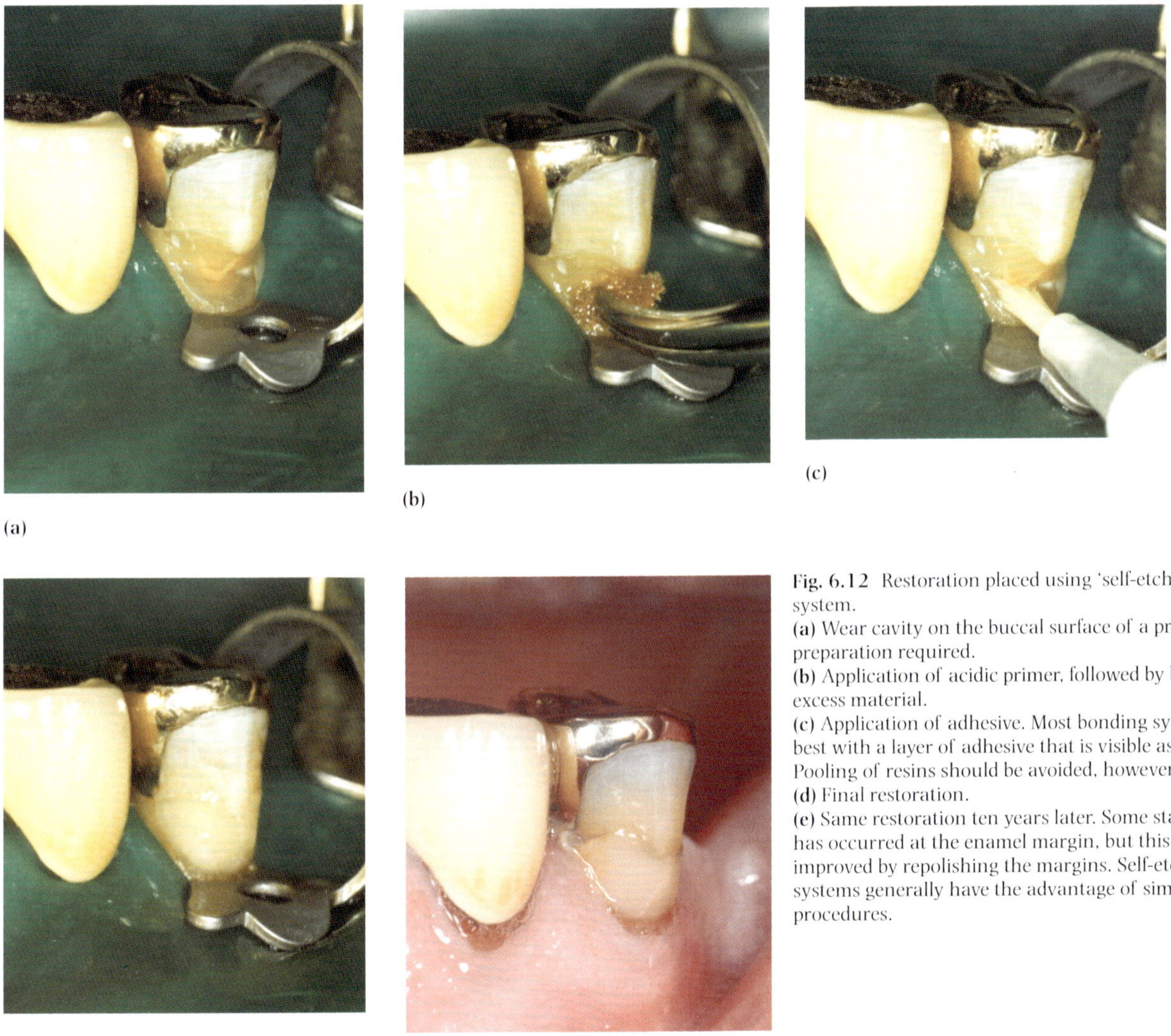

(a) (b) (c) (d) (e)

Fig. 6.12 Restoration placed using 'self-etching' bonding system.
(a) Wear cavity on the buccal surface of a premolar. No cavity preparation required.
(b) Application of acidic primer, followed by blowing away of excess material.
(c) Application of adhesive. Most bonding systems will work best with a layer of adhesive that is visible as a shiny layer. Pooling of resins should be avoided, however.
(d) Final restoration.
(e) Same restoration ten years later. Some staining or leakage has occurred at the enamel margin, but this could be improved by repolishing the margins. Self-etching bonding systems generally have the advantage of simple handling procedures.

the risk of contamination. Self-etching adhesives would therefore appear to offer the ideal solution of simple handling and technique insensitivity, giving excellent dentine bonds, but the evidence for successful enamel bonding with these materials has been less convincing (Fig. 6.12). These materials may be applied as two separate stages (Fig. 6.12) or alternatively as one component (Fig. 6.13b).

New techniques for cavity preparation and finishing will offer huge scope for the development of simpler bonding agents.

Important considerations on the use of bonding agents

Number of stages and film thickness

Over the last few years the number of components needed to make a successful dentine and enamel bond has decreased. Most systems now use a single bottle or dispensing device, but there is usually a need to apply a number of layers to get the desired result. The tooth should have a shiny surface after adhesive application. Too much resin can cause problems, especially if it shows on a radiograph as a radiolucent line under a restoration. Equally, too little resin will give an 'impoverished' bond with an inadequate distribution of physical–mechanical properties across the bonded interface. Some authors advocate the use of a semi-flexible filled bonding resin to allow stress distribution in the interface between tooth and restoration: the *elastic wall* concept. This implies relatively thick adhesive layers with the attendant problems of accurately controlling these.

Speed of application

It is a fact of life that waiting for 20 seconds can seem like a lifetime in the dental chair – both for the patient and the operator. As a result of this the dental second is like the dental millimetre – much shorter than SI units and open to abuse! It is consequently an advantage if different stages in bonding can be capable of being placed in quick succession.

Good clear instructions

These should be well presented and easy to use at the chairside. Laminated and sealed wipe-clean card systems are particularly convenient to work with close to the patient, especially if the operator is unfamiliar with the product (Fig. 6.11). It is good practice to put unfamiliar instructions in front of you and follow them exactly.

Ease of dispensing and handling

Some of the greatest advances in resin-based bonding materials are being made in their chairside presentation. Dispensing volatile solvents from bottles can be quite difficult, with potential for wastage and evaporation of material if the top is inadvertently left off. There are major advantages in the use of single-dose capsules/tips/foil bubble packs (Fig. 6.13). Such devices will cut down on wastage, ensure more consistent product composition because of the avoidance of evaporation, and reduce the risks of cross-infection.

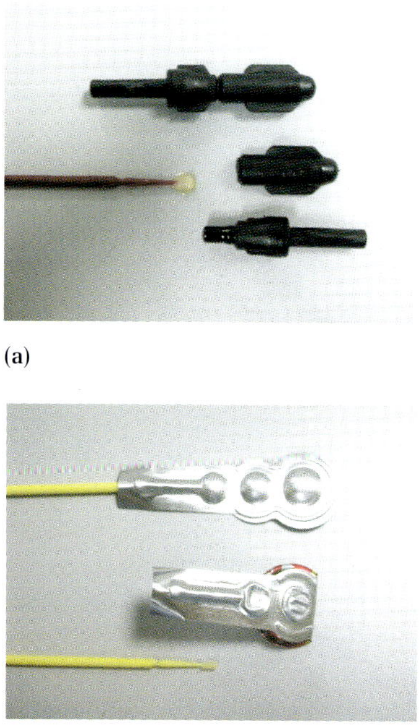

(a)

(b)

Fig. 6.13 (a) This black capsule contains only a dentine bonding agent (it is normally wrapped in a sealed foil pack). When it is broken open the disposable applicator gathers the bonding agent which can now be put on the tooth surface, following etching.
(b) This product is a self-etching adhesive. This means that it contains both the etchant and the bonding agent in one liquid. It is supplied in a foil pack with two 'blisters' containing the components. These are squeezed together and this mixes them. Another squeeze propels the mix onto the microbrush (yellow handle). The self-etching adhesive is now applied to the tooth using the microbrush. This material has a very low pH and is self-etching. Very small volumes of bonding agent are needed for each patient.

Sensitization

Many of the materials are designed to penetrate living tissue and as such are easily capable of causing skin sensitization if the individual is chronically exposed to them. Wearing latex gloves does not reduce the risk as the solvents and chemicals can easily penetrate them. It is therefore important that both the dentist and nurse avoid touching resin-based materials.

Shelf-life

Most of the materials currently available have a good shelf-life when unopened. Refrigeration will help to prolong this. Systems which contain volatile components (e.g. acetone, alcohol) must be tightly stoppered to prevent evaporation. Systems which are dispensed as a single dose (Fig. 6.13a) or mixed at the chairside (Fig. 6.13b) may be less sensitive to problems of shelf- life.

The immediate bond strengths of dentine bonding agents are now very high. Unfortunately, the technique sensitivity of many of the dentine bonding agents means that the operator has only one chance of achieving a strong bond and this bond may deteriorate over time in the hostile oral environment. Such high immediate bond strengths therefore incorporate a degree of redundancy.

Glass ionomer cements

Adhesion mechanisms: conventional glass ionomer cements

The development of the tooth–glass ionomer bond evolves over time. The setting reaction of GICs is an acid-base reaction between a basic alumino-silicate glass and a polyalkenoic or poly (acrylic) acid. Unlike the resin composites, the full strength of the material is not achieved immediately as there is no light-activated polymerization reaction. Also, unlike resin-based systems, the bond strength increases with time to become eventually limited by the cohesive–tensile strength of the cement rather than its bond strength alone.

The initial attraction between the cut tooth and freshly placed cement will be due mainly to polar attraction, with weak hydrogen bonds predominating. At this stage the acidity of the cement allows it to act as a self-etching agent and so modifies the cavity smear layer. The hydrogen ions will be rapidly buffered by the phosphate ions from the hydroxyapatite crystals, but widespread exposure of collagen will be limited because of the weakness of the acids involved. Even though the cement may be relatively viscous, the watery environment of the tooth and the free water in the cement should ensure an ionic exchange at the interface. In this way, good wetting of the substrate by the bonding agent is achieved.

The continuing development of the bond is thought to be due to further movement of ionic species in the interface, perhaps due to diffusion as the phosphate ions are displaced by the polyalkenoic acids. This theory suggests that to maintain an electrolytic balance it is necessary that each phosphate ion takes with it a calcium ion. These are taken up by the cement adjacent to the tooth, to produce an *ion-enriched layer* that is firmly bound to both enamel and dentine (Fig. 6.14). When GICs break, it often happens above this layer as a cohesive failure within the cement itself.

Maximum achievable bond strength for GICs is only reached when the cement has undergone its maturation process. On addition of the liquid to the powder, hardening occurs due to attack of the glass surface by hydronium ions (hydrated protons of the acid), causing the release of calcium and aluminium ions. The ions form salt bridges between carboxyl groups of the polyacid, resulting in a gelled matrix surrounding the intact glass particles. The maturation of GIC restorations is relatively slow and can take up to six months, although will be clinically acceptable at 24 hours. In the initial stages of the setting reaction, divalent calcium ions are rapidly released and form primarily calcium salt bridges between polyacrylate chains within the cement. Such salt bridges will also form at the interface with hydroxyapatite, i.e. the tooth. At this stage, both water uptake and water loss can occur, with the attendant clinical problems of water contamination and dehydration. The restoration must therefore be protected from excess water gain and loss by covering with resin immediately after placement. In later stages of the setting reaction, cross-linking by trivalent aluminium ions gives greater stability to the matrix structure.

At full maturation, the cement at the interface will have become very viscous and its initial reactions with the tooth substrate will have ensured a close adaptation. Minimal contraction or expansion of the cement, if it is kept fully hydrated, will also maintain the close approximation of tooth and cement to allow further ion exchange to occur over the lifetime of the restoration.

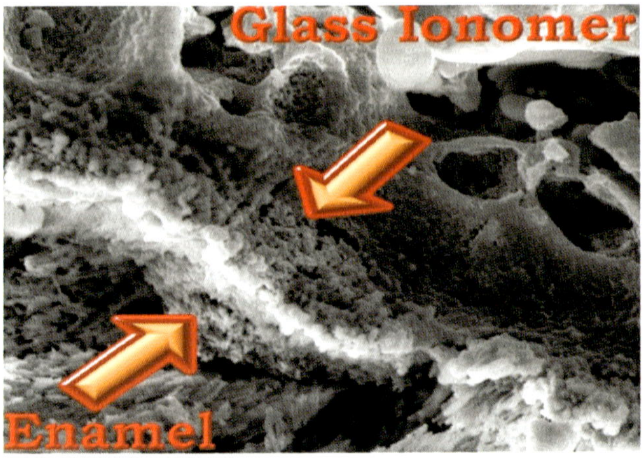

(a)

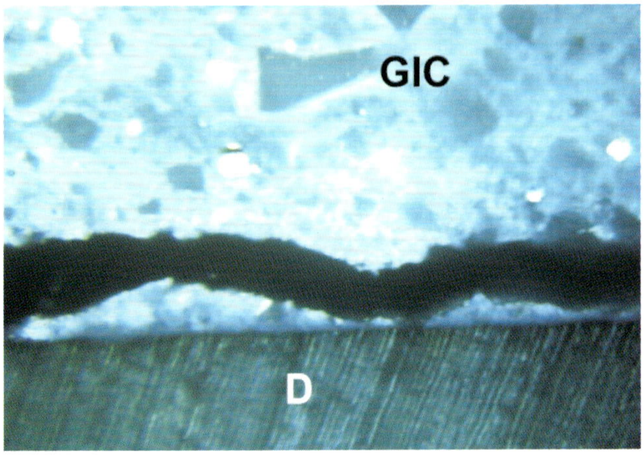

(b)

Fig. 6.14 (a) SEM image showing interface between glass ionomer and enamel. The section surface has been lightly etched and a raised area (between the arrows) shows the ion-enriched layer at the tooth–restoration interface. Field width 10 μm. (Courtesy of Dr Hien Ngo.) (b) Fractured GIC–tooth interface (D) showing the cohesive failure common to these materials. The ion-enriched layer is still attached to the tooth. Field width 300 μm.

Conditioning the dentine

Glass ionomer cements are appropriate for restoring cavities where little or no cavity preparation is undertaken. The tooth will, however, be coated with a pellicle and other surface debris and so some sort of cleaning or conditioning treatment is required. As the adhesion to tooth tissue is primarily mediated by the mineral component, the use of strong acids is contraindicated because they will cause exposure of a collagen network in the dentine and a reduced bonding potential. Poly (acrylic) acid (PAA) has a minor effect on the dentine, just removing the smear layer and surface contaminants, without opening the dentine tubules too widely: it is therefore the conditioner of choice for conventional GICs. There are two advantages in using PAA for conditioning the dentine. Firstly, since it is the acid utilized in the cement itself, any residue inadvertently left behind will not interfere with the setting reaction; and secondly, it will enhance the wettability of the tooth surface to a water-containing cement and preactivate the calcium and phosphate ions in the dentine, rendering them more available for ion exchange with the cement.

Bonding glass ionomer cements to enamel

The conventional GICs have very different interfacial characteristics with tooth tissue compared to the resin composites and dentine bonding agents. As previously outlined, their bonding mechanisms are restricted essentially to

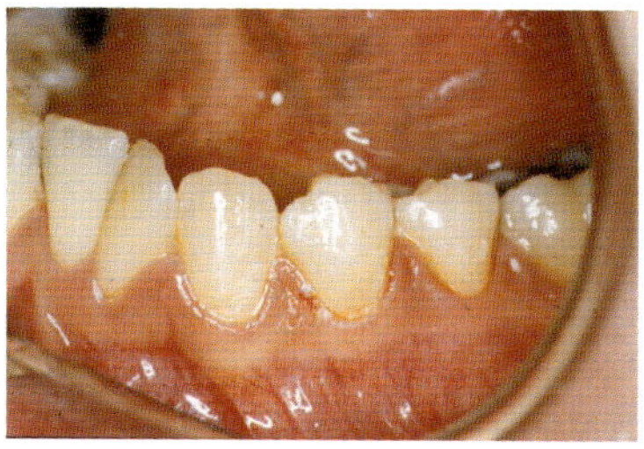

(a)

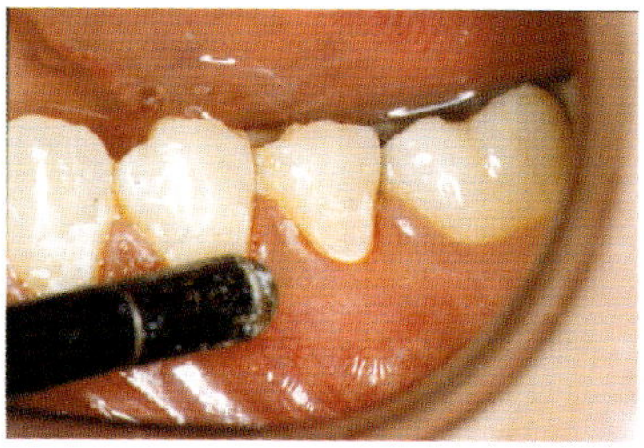

(b)

Fig. 6.15 (a) Buccal–cervical glass ionomer cement restorations in the first and second premolars.
(b) Same restorations showing desiccation and chalky appearance of the surface of these immature restorations. Surface protection with resin or varnish should be placed on all GIC restorations, especially when they are less than a few days old. (Courtesy of Dr Sharan Sidhu.)

surface attraction only. This has severe implications if the materials become dimensionally unstable, as may happen as a result of excess water uptake or desiccation. Drying problems will be most pronounced in relation to enamel, where the cement will be adherent to the surface alone and where dehydration is first going to appear clinically.

Dehydration can happen quite quickly intraorally with the placement of a rubber dam, or during impression-taking procedures: the first sign of this drying in the cement is a chalky-white appearance on its surface (Fig. 6.15). Immature GICs can be protected from dehydration by the application of petroleum jelly when working with a rubber dam. There will almost certainly be cracks below the enamel surface from previous cutting operations so that any shrinkage of the cement on drying will cause the enamel to break. The bond between glass ionomer and enamel is stronger than often realized; indeed it can be stronger than the bond between enamel prisms, especially when these are running parallel with the cavity surface.

Bonding glass ionomer cements to dentine

Correct mixing of GICs is critical for clinical success. When mixing by hand the consistency should be almost equivalent to that of a composite restoration. This stiff mix, with a high powder/liquid ratio, imparts increased strength to the cement and its adhesive interface. Reducing the amount of powder in the mix will lead to a cement that sets by 'drying out' rather than the correct chemical reaction causing reduced strength, poor appearance, and questionable dimensional stability. A more consistent mix will be produced by the use of encapsulated syringe-based dispensing systems, although their powder/liquid ratio will be lowered because of their need to flow through a nozzle. Following conditioning with PAA, the tubular openings may be exposed and so it is possible to find 2–3 μm long 'plugs' of GIC matrix occupying these openings, especially if the cement is put under pressure by the use of matrices or hand-instrument condensing as it reaches the *gel* stage during setting. These plugs may impart some mechanical interlocking to the bond interface but are in no way equivalent to the long tags seen with resin-based dentine bonding systems.

The resin-modified glass ionomer cements

The resin-modified glass ionomer cements have an interesting mixture of properties. The addition of light-curing radicals and resins does allow *command cure* of the cement but these cements also have an active acid-base reaction at work during the initial stages of mixing, so that setting from this cause may overtake the dentist's decision to light-cure. In other words, the cement may be chemically set before the dentist has had chance to light-cure it. Whilst there is some self-adhesion with these materials, more reliable bonding will be produced by the use of conditioners or primers containing HEMA. These can produce an interfacial appearance very similar to those of the resin composites when used in conjunction with a dentine bonding agent.

Dynamic interactions can still occur with these materials after the initial set. Resin-modified GICs can be porous to pulpal fluids. There is often a non-particulate, easily stained layer of solid material (<30 μm thick) between the bulk of the cement and the dentine, which forms within 24 hours and which is visible microscopically (Fig. 6.16). This layer only forms next to dentine tubules which communicate with the wet pulp cavity. Long tags of resin-infiltrating dentine tubules *are not* a characteristic feature of resin-modified glass ionomer cements. The name '*absorption layer*' has been applied to this layer because it is probably absorbing tissue fluid from the dentine: it may be important in the maintenance of the 'fit' of the restoration, to compensate for the contraction of the resin on polymerization.

Dehydration shrinkage is still a risk with the resin-modified GICs. This happens very quickly and after a few minutes quite considerable gaps can open up in immature cements. Where failure is seen next to the dentine it is often in the absorption layer, whereas restorations with enamel

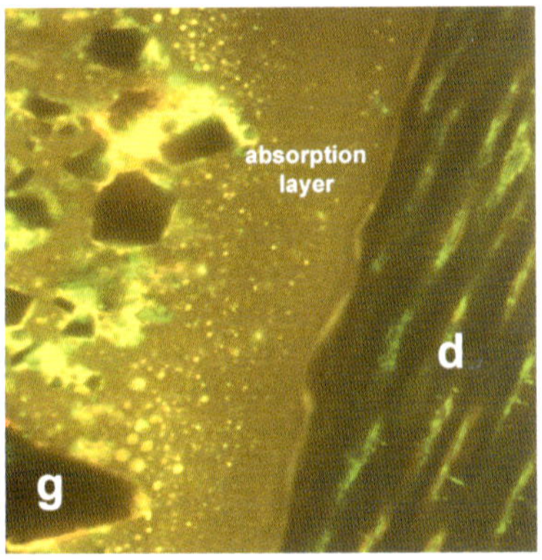

Fig. 6.16 Confocal microscopic image of interface between a resin-modified GIC and dentine. The HEMA in this cement has been labelled with a special dye. There is a non-stained layer between the body of the cement – showing as irregular particles (g) and dots of HEMA – and the dentine on the right (d). This is the *absorption layer*, and there is a very thin hybrid-type layer next to the dentine showing as a yellow line. Field width 75 μm. (Courtesy of Advances in Dental Research.)

margins will often fail with structural cohesive failure of the enamel, in a manner similar to the conventional glass ionomer cements.

The ion exchange that probably occurs at the tooth interface with GICs will certainly give a region which has intermediate properties of the two materials, tooth and cement, and so in those terms it is a hybrid zone. However, the mechanisms involved are undoubtedly more 'subtle', relating more closely to the adsorption and diffusion theories of adhesion referred to earlier than the relatively macroscopic mechanical retention effects seen with resin infiltration.

The polyacid-modified resin composites

The development of the polyacid-modified composites (or compomers) effectively completes the transition from materials which have a water-based setting reaction to those which are almost entirely resin-based. The main alteration to the structure of a resin composite is to use alumino-silicate glasses as fillers with carboxyl groups attached to the resin backbone of the composite. Whilst there is no need to mix the material, the manufacturers consider that slow water uptake allows the acid-base reaction to continue after light activation and polymerization of the resin system. In contrast to the resin composites, these materials are designed to have a degree of water tolerance. In conventional GICs the availability of 'free water' to 'bound water' decreases as the material matures over a period of months. Polyacid-modified composites also show an increase in bound *vs.* free water as the materials mature, giving some evidence that they may have a limited glass ionomer-type setting reaction.

All of the polyacid-modified composites require the use of a separate bonding agent, many of which have been developed to be self-etching and so simple to use.

Bonded amalgam restorations

Historically, amalgam has been used in cavities that are mechanically retentive (as described in Chapter 3). *All* restorations are more likely to survive if they can gain support from surrounding tooth tissue, and bonding techniques can be used to improve the retention of amalgam restorations. There are two approaches to this and both are based on the fact that amalgam is opaque and this prevents light-curing:

1. Place a dentine bonding agent, as for a composite restoration, and light-cure. Then pack the amalgam restoration. This produces a *sealed amalgam restoration*, but any bond between the tooth and the restoration will be minimal. A potential advantage relates to the protection of the tooth from products leaching from the amalgam restoration.
2. Use an auto-polymerizing dentine bonding agent. The bonding agent is placed as a thin layer, normally following mixing of catalyst/base materials, and the amalgam packed into the resin. Excess resin will be displaced and occupy any voids within the amalgam (Fig. 6.17). A *bonded amalgam* will ensue, once the resin has set.

Such bonded amalgam restorations offer many advantages, not least because the alloy restoration shows virtually

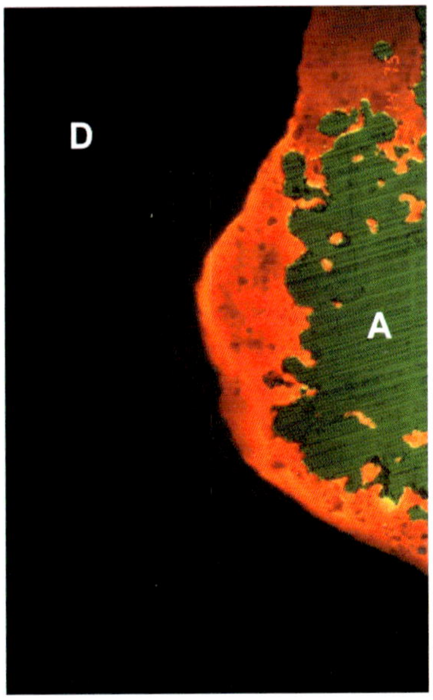

Fig. 6.17 The line angle (corner) between a bonded amalgam restoration and dentine (D). The resin-based cement has been labelled with a fluorescent dye (red) and can be seen to have mixed with the amalgam restoration (A). Field width 300 μm.

no shrinkage, so giving the optimal environment for a successful bond. However, amalgam will expand over time if contaminated by moisture during packing. Bonded restorations are advantageous when amalgam is used as a core material prior to the provision of a crown in the restoration of a badly broken-down tooth, although mechanical retention is usually used as well. Bonded amalgam is useful when repairing fractured amalgam restorations and cusps when the rest of the restoration is sound.

Further reading

Davidson, C. L. and Mjor, I. (1999). *Glass ionomers and their modifications: theory and practice*. Quintessence International, Berlin.

Van Meerbeek, B., Vargas, M., Inoue, S., Yoshika, Y., Peumans, M., Lambrechts, P., *et al.* (2001). Adhesives and cements to promote preservative dentistry. *Operat. Dent.* **6** (Suppl.), 119–44.

Van Noort, X. (2002). *An introduction to dental materials* (2nd edn). Mosby Wolfe.

7

Treatment of pit and fissure caries

Introduction

Fissure sealing
- Indications
- Clinical technique for resin sealers
- Clinical technique for glass ionomer cement sealers

The sealant restoration (or preventive resin restoration)
- Indications
- Clinical technique

Larger posterior composites

Amalgam restorations for pit and fissure caries

improved – for example where patients are mentally or physically disabled – fissures should be sealed. Children with significant medical conditions which put them at risk from the consequences of dental disease should also be offered sealant treatment. These medical conditions include cardiac problems, immunosuppression, bleeding disorders, blood dyscrasias, and metabolic and endocrine problems.

Finally, the tooth to be fissure sealed must be capable of being isolated from salivary contamination since contamination while placing the sealant is the most common cause of failure. At best, salivary contamination will result in the sealant falling off, with no permanent harm. At worst, however, the sealant will be partly retained but leak, so that caries can progress beneath it, safe from salivary protection, fluoride ions, and detection by the dentist. Therefore good isolation from saliva is an essential part of the clinical technique, with a rubber dam being the preferred method.

Clinical technique for resin sealers

Anaesthesia and isolation

If necessary, a little local anaesthetic is infiltrated or topical anaesthetic is applied to avoid discomfort from the rubber dam clamp.

Cleaning

The tooth surface to be etched and sealed may be cleaned with a bristle brush in a handpiece and a pumice and water slurry. Oil-based polishing pastes or those containing fluoride should not be used, as these may interfere with etching. The pumice is washed away using the three-in-one syringe. Some dentists clean the fissure with a high-pressure spray of sodium hydrogen carbonate; this is known as '*air polishing*'. This is similar to '*air abrasion*' as already described in Chapter 5. In this format a high-velocity air stream contains soft sodium bicarbonate powder (baking soda), shrouded by water, and has little cutting effect on intact enamel. The powder is water-soluble and is easily removed after cleaning.

Etching

The tooth is now etched with phosphoric acid (30–50 per cent) (see Chapter 6). The acid etchant is supplied by the manufacturer in the form of a coloured gel. The etchant is applied over the whole occlusal surface extending onto the lingual or buccal surface where grooves require sealing (Fig. 7.1a). Etching the entire occlusal surface avoids the danger of covering an unetched surface with sealant and thus inviting leakage. The acid can be applied with a brush, or alternatively the gel can be placed accurately with a disposable syringe and blunt needle. As soon as the complete

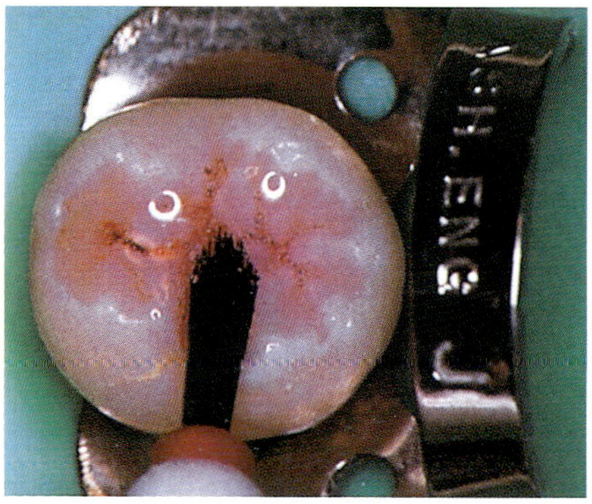

(a)

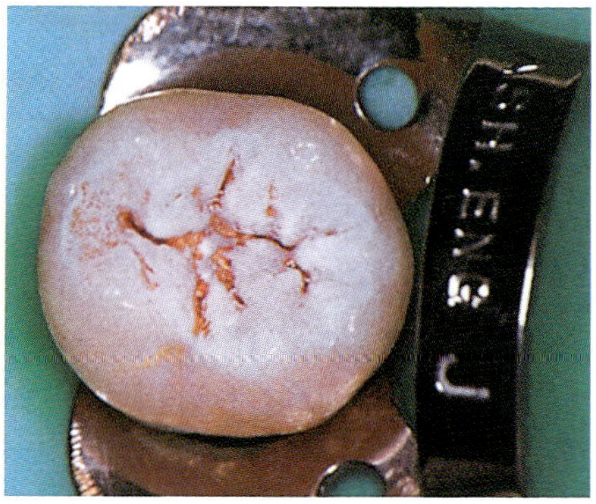

(b)

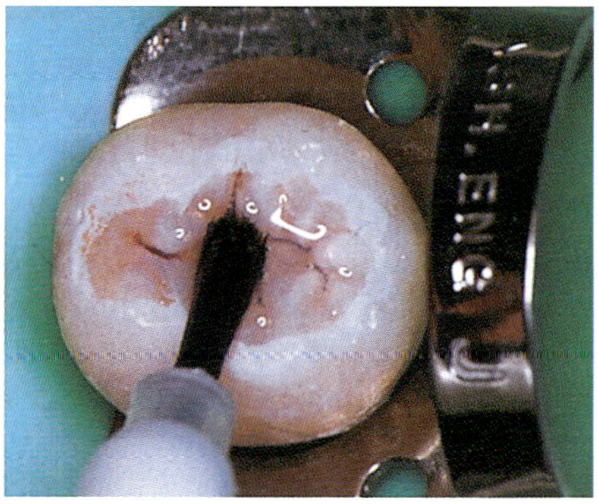

(c)

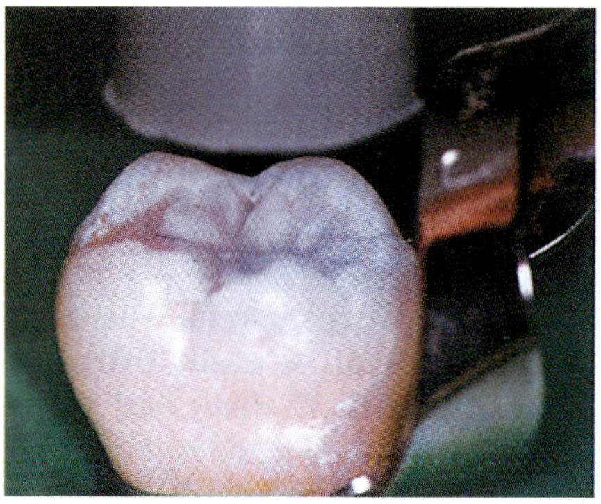

(d)

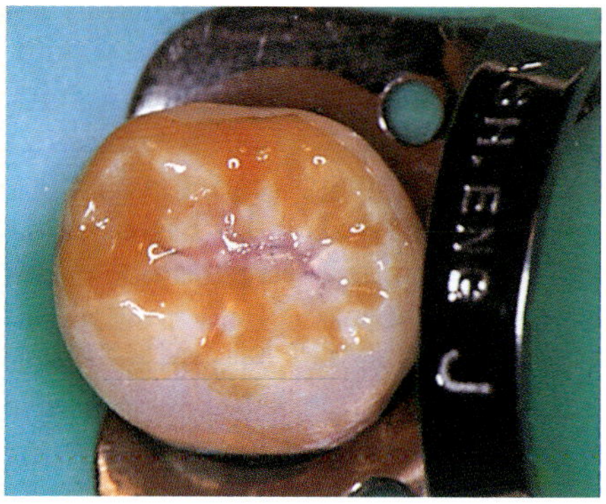

(e)

Fig. 7.1 (a) A brush is used to apply the etchant gel over the occlusal surface of the tooth to be fissure sealed.
(b) Dried etched enamel appears matt, white, and frosty.
(c) The sealant is applied to the etched surface using a small disposable brush or a syringe with a disposable tip.
(d) Light-curing a fissure sealant.
(e) A fluoride-containing varnish is applied to the etched enamel at the periphery of the restoration where it has not been covered with sealant.

area to be etched is covered with acid, the time is noted and the enamel is etched for 15–20 seconds.

Washing

After 20 seconds the acid is washed away. Initially a water jet from the three-in-one syringe is used to remove most of the acid. If a rubber dam is not in place, careful aspiration is important to avoid damage to soft tissue by the acid. After approximately 5 seconds of water, the air button is also pressed, forming a strong water–air spray which should be played over the etched surface for 20–30 seconds. With coloured gels, it is tempting to stop washing when the colour has gone. However, the purpose is not just to remove the surplus acid, but to flush the precipitates out of the newly formed etch pits, and this takes a full 20–30 seconds.

Drying

Many fissure sealants are still based on hydrophobic resins and so a careful drying regime is required. It is good practice to check that the airline is not contaminated by water or oil by blowing it at a clean glass or paper surface. The tooth surface is now thoroughly dried with air from the three-in-one syringe. This drying is most important since any moisture on the etched surface will stop penetration of the hydrophobic resin into the enamel. A minimum of 15 seconds drying is recommended. At this stage the etched area should appear matt, white, and frosty (Fig. 7.1b). With a rubber dam, there should be no danger of salivary contamination of the etched surface. If this does occur, however, it is essential to re-etch the enamel because adherent organic material in saliva will block the pores and it cannot be removed completely, even by vigorous washing.

Applying the sealant

Fissure sealants are supplied both as light-curing and chemically-curing materials. A light-cured resin does not require mixing but a chemically-cured resin has two components which are gently mixed together with a brush.

A sealant is applied to the etched surface using a small disposable brush or applicator supplied by the manufacturer. The sealant is applied to the etched pits and fissures and up the etched cuspal slopes (Fig. 7.1c). If a light-cured material has been chosen, the light should be placed directly over the sealant but should not touch it (Fig. 7.1d). With a molar tooth, if the light source is of a smaller diameter than the tooth it should be directed at the distal part of the occlusal surface for the full curing time recommended by the manufacturer of the resin and then moved mesially for a similar period. Any buccal or palatal groove or pit should be similarly cured with the light source directly over it. Since the polymerizing lights are potentially damaging to the operator's eyes, special eye-protective glasses should be used or the dental nurse should hold a special filter screen in the operator's line of vision (see Fig. 9.8h). Some lights have protective cups which can be placed over the end of the light guide.

Most chemically-cured sealants polymerize in 1–3 minutes and the manufacturer's instructions should be followed.

The outer surface layer of any sealant will not polymerize due to the inhibiting effect of oxygen in the atmosphere. The sealant will therefore always appear to have a greasy film after polymerization. Finally, a fluoride-containing varnish may be applied to the etched enamel at the periphery of the restoration where it has not been covered with sealant (Fig. 7.1e).

Checking the occlusion

The rubber dam is now removed and the occlusion checked with articulating paper. Whilst it is considered acceptable to allow any high spots to be abraded away when unfilled resin fissure sealants are used, with the lightly-filled materials it is wiser to reduce high spots by grinding with a small round diamond stone in a low-speed handpiece.

Clinical technique for glass ionomer cement sealers

The authors would rarely choose a glass ionomer cement for fissure sealing because the scientific evidence on retention and caries prevention has shown these not to be as effective as resin sealants. It is possible that the fluoride in the material may exert a cariostatic effect. However, they are the material of choice on an erupting tooth, where oral hygiene is poor, caries risk is high, and good moisture control is difficult. They should be considered a temporary measure in these circumstances.

The tooth to be sealed is isolated and the fissure is cleaned with 10 per cent polyacrylic acid-conditioning agent, supplied by the manufacturer, for 20 seconds. It is then washed and dried, and the glass ionomer material, mixed to a flowable consistency, is applied along the fissure and firmly burnished into position. Excess material is easily removed with the burnisher (Fig. 7.2). Although glass ionomer will

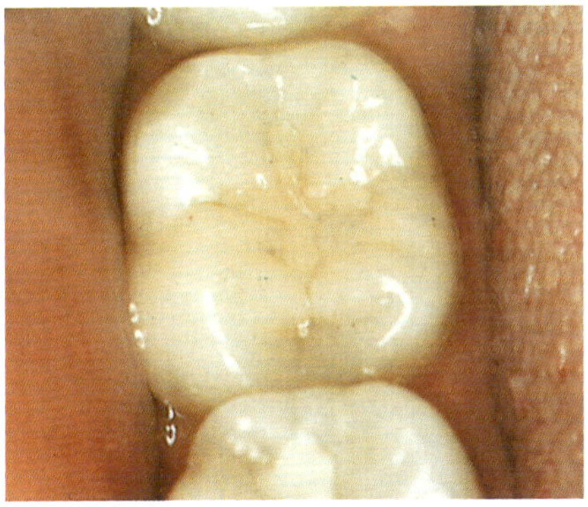

Fig. 7.2 A glass ionomer fissure sealant which has been in place for 14 years. (Reproduced by courtesy of Dr John McLean.)

almost certainly be less well retained than a resin-based system, the material may have a protective effect for high-risk fissures whilst the tooth is at its most vulnerable: in this situation a resin sealant would not work because the tooth may be impossible to isolate satisfactorily.

The sealant restoration (or preventive resin restoration)

Indications

The sealant restoration was born out of the use of pit and fissure sealants. It is a natural extension of the technique where pit and fissure decay is confined to one area in the fissure system. The technique restores the carious area and seals the rest of the fissures. The restoration is indicated where a cavity is present (either a microcavity in the enamel, or a cavity with dentine at its base). The lesion will usually be visible on a bitewing radiograph as an area of radiolucency in the dentine (Fig. 1.26).

Clinical technique

Cavity preparation

Occlusal contacts should be marked with articulating paper prior to preparation so that the dentist can remember where these contacts are. A local anaesthetic is given. A rubber dam is applied and the tooth is thoroughly cleaned as before (Fig. 7.3a). A small, pear-shaped tungsten carbide bur (Jet 330) is used in the air turbine to widen slightly and deepen the fissure and to gain access to caries in dentine.

The air turbine is also used to remove the minimum amount of enamel necessary to gain access to caries (Fig. 7.3b). A small round bur is now used in the low-speed handpiece to remove soft, demineralized dentine, which is often stained, from the enamel–dentine junction. During this process the access cavity may require further enlargement to allow access to caries on the enamel-dentine junction. Thus high- and low-speed handpieces are used alternately so that the cavity is kept as small as possible commensurate with removing the soft dentine from the enamel–dentine junction so that it feels hard when a sharp probe is run along it.

Finally, any soft caries overlying the pulp is removed with either a slowly rotating round bur in the slow-speed handpiece or a sharp excavator (Fig. 7.3c) (see Chapter 3).

Lining and etching

If the cavity is much larger than expected, the deep dentine directly overlying the pulp may be covered with a calcium hydroxide-containing cement (Fig. 7.3d) (see Chapter 3 for a discussion on the use of these cements). A second layer of resin-modified glass ionomer may be placed in a deep cavity to act as a dentine replacement (Fig. 7.3e). The polyacrylic acid conditioning liquid supplied by the manufacturer should be applied to any exposed dentine with a brush. After 10 seconds the cavity is washed and dried and the glass ionomer cement placed. Once this material has set, any glass ionomer material on the enamel walls should be removed with a bur. The enamel walls of the cavity and the occlusal surface of the tooth are now etched with acid (Fig. 7.3f). After 20 seconds this is washed and dried as before (Fig. 7.3g).

Filling the cavity

A composite, designed for use in posterior teeth, is selected. It is supplied with a bonding resin which should be painted on the etched enamel walls and occlusal surface and blown with dry air to form a thin layer, avoiding puddles of material in the cavity. The resin is polymerized with light as before (Fig. 7.3h).

The cavity is now filled with the posterior composite (Fig. 7.3i). These light-cured materials will not cure reliably in depths exceeding 2 mm. Thus, if the cavity is deeper than this (a graduated pocket-measuring probe can be used to check depth), the material must be placed in increments. Each increment is then cured before the next is placed, taking care not to dispense more than is needed because normal light in the surgery will polymerize the unused material. An increment of composite is placed or syringed directly into the cavity and gently nudged into position using a small 'non-stick' instrument. Care should

Fig. 7.3 (*right*) (a) A lower second molar isolated with a rubber dam prior to placing a sealant restoration.
(b) Enamel is removed to gain access to obvious caries.
(c) Soft caries over the pulp is removed.
(d) Exposed dentine is covered with a calcium hydroxide-containing cement: smaller amounts of this type of cement would be used nowadays – simply covering the deepest dentine, close to the pulp.
(e) A second layer of glass ionomer lining may be placed in a deep cavity.
(f) The enamel walls of the cavity and the occlusal surface of the tooth are etched with acid.
(g) Etched enamel after washing and drying.
(h) Bonding resin is applied to the cavity walls and occlusal surface.
(i) The cavity is filled with composite resin. Use of the glass ionomer lining in this tooth allowed the composite to be placed and cured in a single 2 mm increment.
(j) A fissure sealant is applied to the whole occlusal surface.
(k) The occlusion is checked with articulating paper which will locate areas of occlusal contact with a coloured mark.

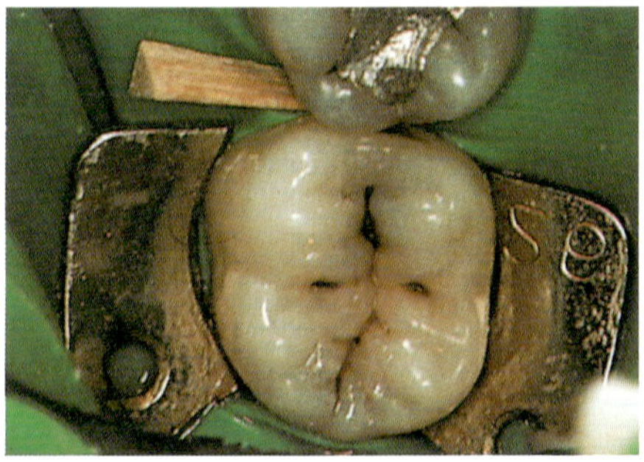

(a)

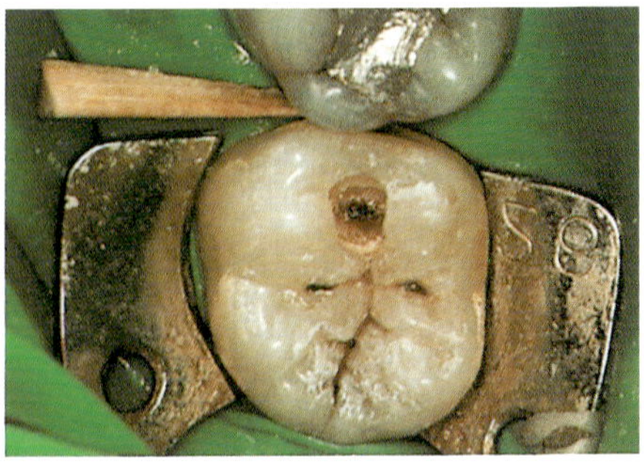

(b)

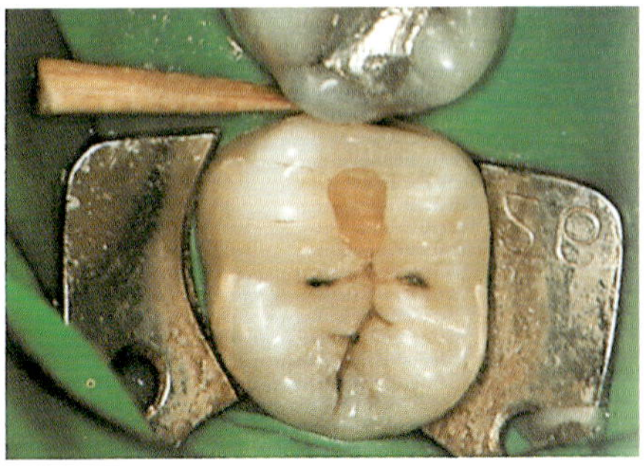

(c)

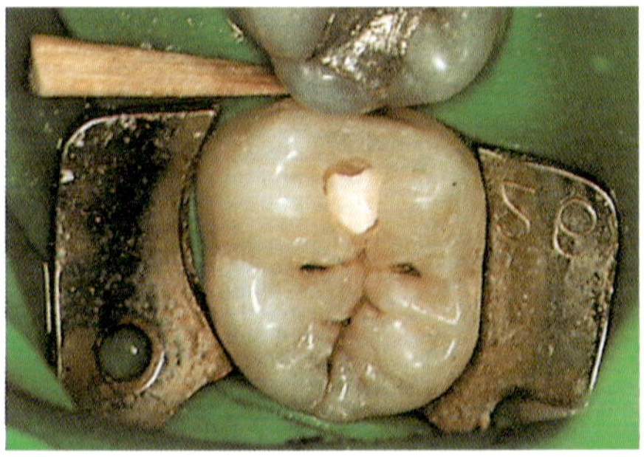

(d)

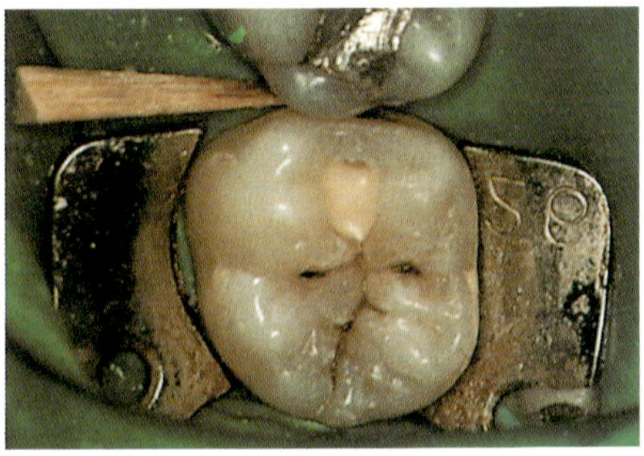

(e)

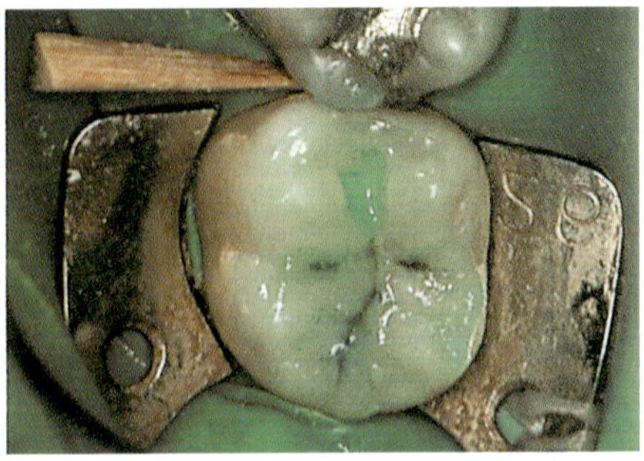

(f)

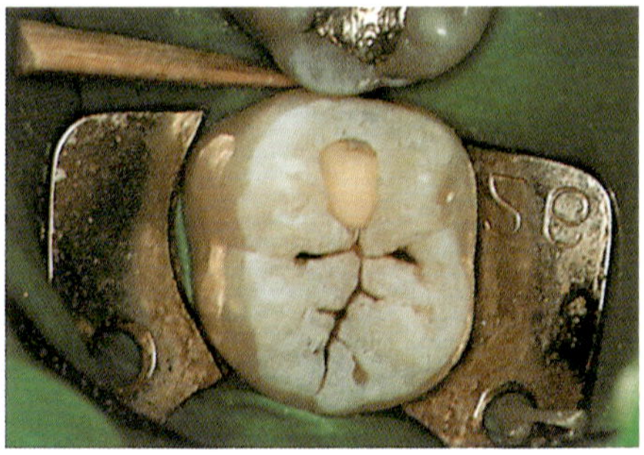

(g)

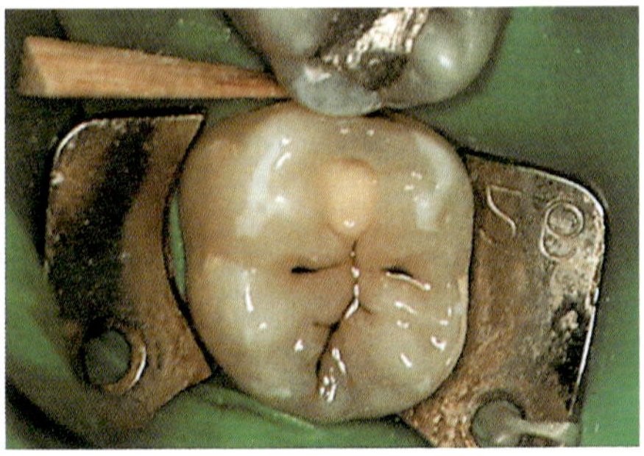

(h)

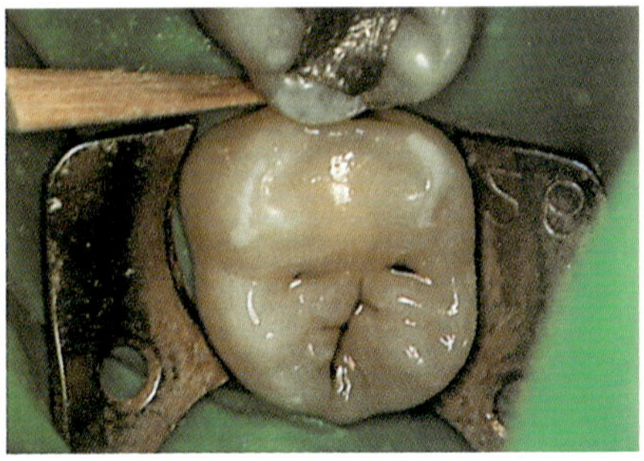

(i)

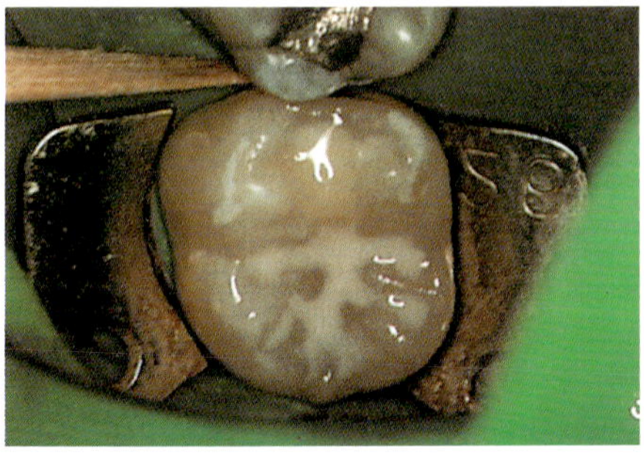

(j)

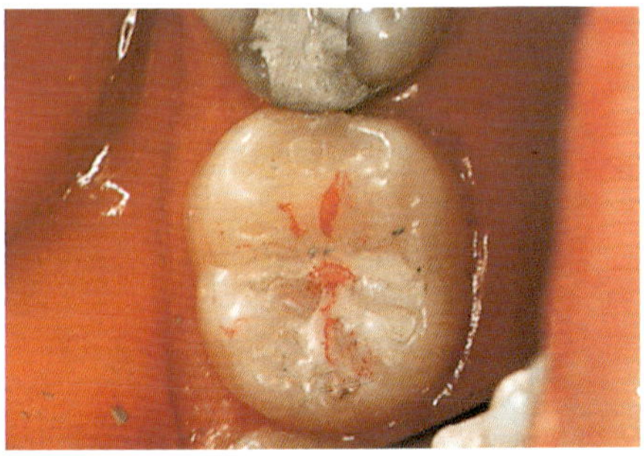

(k)

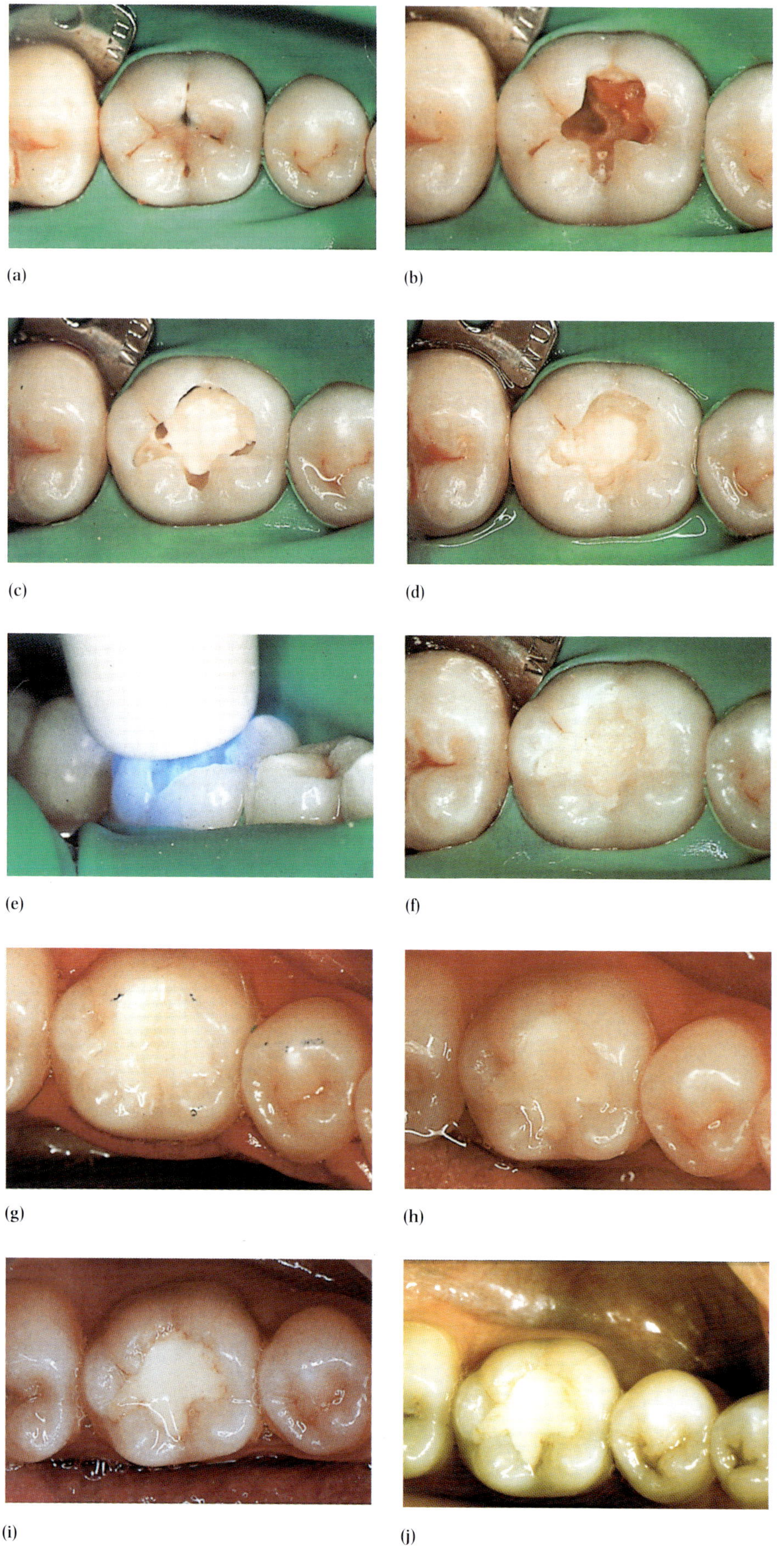
(a) (b) (c) (d) (e) (f) (g) (h) (i) (j)

Fig. 7.4 (a) A large occlusal cavity is present in the lower first molar.
(b) Access to caries begins to reveal the extent of the lesion.
(c) The enamel–dentine junction is made caries-free, soft caries is excavated over the pulp, and a calcium hydroxide-containing cement is placed in the depth of the cavity.
d) Much of the missing dentine is replaced by a second lining of glass ionomer cement. Today this would be brought up to the enamel–dentine junction and only one increment of composite would be required.
(e) An increment of composite being light-cured.
(f) The final increment of composite can now be placed.
(g) The completed restoration.
(h) The restoration after five years.
(i) The restoration after nine years. There is some wear, but the margins are intact and the restoration can still be considered a success. If this wear was thought to be excessive, the surface layer of composite could be removed and the restoration resurfaced with more composite. Such repairs, or maintenance procedures, are not possible with amalgam. Modern composites are likely to be more durable than the materials available when the restoration was placed.
(j) The restoration after 14 years. Additional composite was *not* added as suggested in (i) and there has been no significant change in the last five years. The restoration can now be regarded as stable with a good prognosis.

be taken not to trap air under the material. When the final increment is placed an instrument is used to shape the occlusal surface, restoring cuspal inclines in the larger cavity before light-curing the material. Alternatively, the glass ionomer material is brought up to the enamel–dentine junction to replace all the missing dentine so that only one increment of composite, the thickness of the enamel, is required (Fig. 7.3i).

An alternative to the glass ionomer/composite layered technique is to bond the composite filling materials directly to the etched dentine and enamel. This is called the all-etch technique. The enamel and dentine of the cavity and the enamel of the occlusal surface are etched for 15 seconds and then washed and gently dried. The dentine in particular should not be over-dried (see Chapter 6, pp. 110–12). Now a dentine bonding agent is applied following the exact descriptions of the manufacturer. The bonding agent is polymerized and then the composite is built up in increments as described previously.

Whether the layered technique or the all-etch technique have been used, the remaining fissure system has already been covered by the bonding resin. A layer of fissure sealant is now painted over the entire occlusal surface and polymerized (Fig. 7.3j). Alternatively, composite can be gently agitated with a plastic instrument into the adjacent pits and fissures, and light-cured to act as a heavily-filled pit and fissure sealant.

Finishing the restoration

Excess resin is carefully removed with 12-bladed tungsten carbide finishing burs or with fine diamond composite finishing burs (Fig. 5.20). Once the rubber dam has been removed, the occlusal contacts should be checked with thin articulating paper (Fig. 7.3k). This is placed between the dried teeth and the patient is asked to move the teeth over each other as if eating. Any 'high' spot on the restoration will be located by a mark and can be reduced: the aim is to have the restoration in harmonious occlusion. The restoration can finally be smoothed with aluminium-impregnated rubber points.

Larger posterior composites

It is not uncommon for occlusal caries to undermine the occlusal enamel widely (Figs. 7.4a and b). In the past such restorations have often been restored with amalgam after all the overhanging enamel has been cut away. With posterior composite materials and glass ionomer cements, it is now possible to use these adhesive materials to restore the missing tooth tissue and support the remaining enamel without needing to remove so much of it.

Therefore once soft demineralized dentine has been removed, decisions have to be made about the strength of the remaining tooth tissue. Figure 7.4c shows a large occlusal cavity with a considerable amount of overhanging enamel. This cavity was restored with a calcium hydroxide lining over the deepest pulpal part of the cavity used as an indirect pulp cap followed by a layer of glass ionomer cement to replace much of the missing dentine (Fig. 7.4d). Finally, the enamel walls were acid-etched and the remainder of the tooth restored with a posterior composite which was built up in increments as described previously (Figs. 7.4e–g). The same restoration is shown after 5, 9, and 14 years in Figs. 7.4(h–j).

In these large restorations as much sound tissue should be preserved as possible. Undermined and overhanging enamel can be supported with adhesive posterior composite materials and glass ionomer cements. Where mastication pressure is obvious, a minimum thickness of 2 mm of composite material is required. Where the outline of the preparation is placed beyond the occlusal surface, perhaps because a cusp has fractured or been completely undermined by extensive caries, a bevel should be prepared to optimize the adaptation of the composite to the enamel.

Amalgam restorations for pit and fissure caries

In all the earlier editions of this manual, several pages were devoted to occlusal amalgam restorations. With improved composite and glass ionomer materials and with the increasing evidence of success with these materials from both published evidence and experience, amalgam restorations for pit and fissure caries should now be regarded as obsolete. That is not to say that existing, successful amalgam restorations should be replaced. They should be assessed by the criteria described in Chapter 12 and either left, polished, or replaced as appropriate (Fig. 7.5).

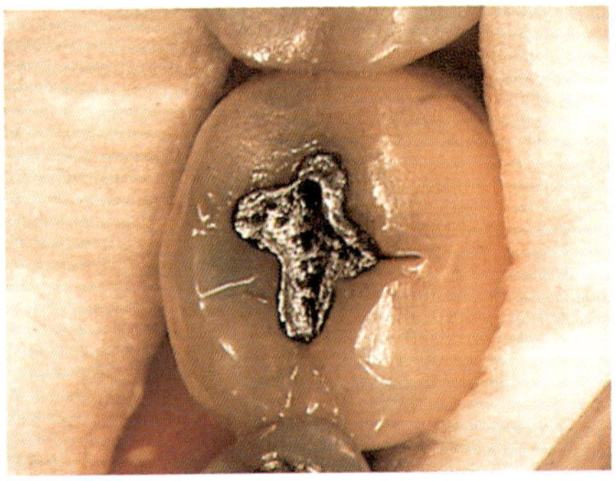

Fig. 7.5 A 25-year-old occlusal amalgam restoration. Although it is pitted and ditched, it is still serviceable.

Further reading

Ekstrand, K. R., Ricketts, D. N. J., and Kidd, E. A. M. (2001). Occlusal caries: pathology, diagnosis, and logical management. *Dent. Update.* **28**, 380–7.

Hassall, D. C. and Mellar, A. C. (2001). The sealant restoration: indications, success, and clinical technique. *Br. Dent. J.* **191**, 358–62.

Shaw, L. (2000). Modern thoughts on fissure sealants. *Dent. Update.* **27**, 370–4.

8

Treatment of approximal caries in posterior teeth

Introduction

Approximal amalgam restorations: access through the marginal ridge

- Pre-operative procedures
- Access to caries and clearing the enamel–dentine junction
- Finishing the enamel margins
- Removing caries over the pulp
- Retention
- Lower premolars
- Lining the cavity
- Applying the matrix band
- Choice of amalgam
- Inserting the amalgam
- Carving and finishing the amalgam
- Polishing

Approximal composite restorations: access through the marginal ridge

- Indications
- Aspects of cavity preparation
- Lining and etching the cavity

- Placing the matrix and restoration
- Finishing the restoration

Approximal 'adhesive' restorations: marginal ridge preserved

- Occlusal approach
- Buccal approach
- Approximal root caries

The mesial–occlusal–distal (MOD) cavity

Problems of the larger cavity

- Pre-operative assessment
- Caries removal
- Designing the restoration
- Choice of restorative material
- Bonded amalgam restorations
- Pin retention for large restorations and cores
- Placing the matrix, packing, carving, and finishing

Treatment of approximal caries in posterior teeth

Introduction

Stagnation areas exist on the approximal surfaces of posterior teeth, cervical to the contact areas, where plaque can form and mature. Unless an interdental cleaning agent such as dental floss is used, this plaque is difficult to remove mechanically and thus caries may develop. In its early stage this lesion is not visible clinically and so good bitewing radiographs are essential for diagnosis (see p. 14).

The management of approximal caries varies according to the state of disease of the surface. As discussed on p. 15, the presence or absence of a cavity is very relevant. Thus, caries confined to the enamel on a bitewing radiograph, where there is unlikely to be a cavity, should be encouraged to arrest. Dietary advice and showing the patient how to floss this particular approximal surface are important. Fluoride in the form of toothpaste or a mouthwash should be used, and in some cases, where patient cooperation is doubtful, chairside application of fluoride by the dentist may also be indicated. The patient should understand that the lesion must be checked again by the dentist both clinically and radiographically, usually in a year.

In contrast, where a cavity is present (establishing this diagnosis is discussed on p. 00), operative treatment is usually indicated, in addition to preventive measures, to restore the integrity of the tooth surface (Fig. 8.1) so that plaque control can be established.

Access to caries may be gained in several ways:

- occlusally, by cutting through the marginal ridge
- occlusally, leaving the marginal ridge intact
- buccally or lingually, leaving the marginal ridge intact
- direct access, which is possible if the adjacent tooth is missing.

Occlusal access through the marginal ridge is the approach that has been used most extensively over the years, with the cavity being filled with amalgam. With the development of adhesive restorative materials (resin composites and glass ionomer cements) specifically for use in posterior teeth, new techniques are being developed and tested for these materials. One possibility is to leave the marginal ridge intact, approaching the caries occlusally, buccally, or lingually and filling the cavity with an adhesive material. This approach is only suited to small approximal lesions where caries has not undermined the marginal ridge to such an extent that it collapses during cavity preparation. The approach should only be used where caries risk is low (e.g. dental students). Clinical evaluation has shown that in many patients these restorations fail due to recurrent caries. However, this is the ideal approach when a large, failed occlusal restoration has to be removed, giving good access to a small approximal lesion.

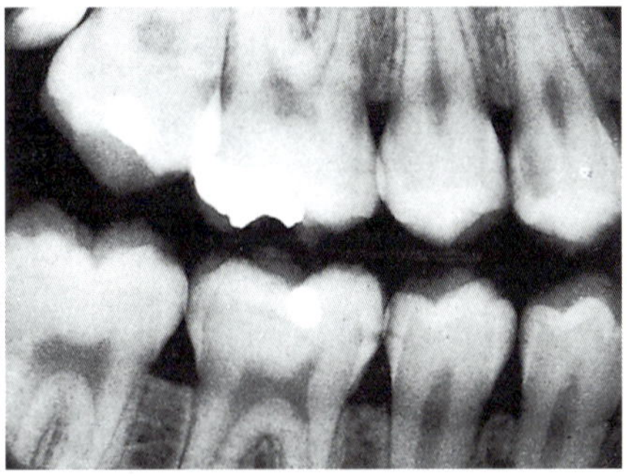

Fig. 8.1 A bitewing radiograph showing a large lesion in dentine on the distal aspect of the upper first premolar. Lesions are also obvious in dentine on the mesial and distal aspects of the lower first molar. All these lesions were managed operatively as well as preventively. In contrast, earlier lesions in the lower first premolar, distal; lower second premolar, mesial and distal; upper second premolar, mesial and distal; and upper first molar, mesial, were not treated operatively.

Each of these operative alternatives will now be considered in greater detail. In addition, techniques for restoring badly broken-down teeth with amalgam will be described.

Approximal amalgam restorations: access through the marginal ridge

Pre-operative procedures

The vitality of the tooth is checked and a local anaesthetic is given if necessary. A rubber dam is applied to the quadrant and a small wooden wedge is inserted interdentally between

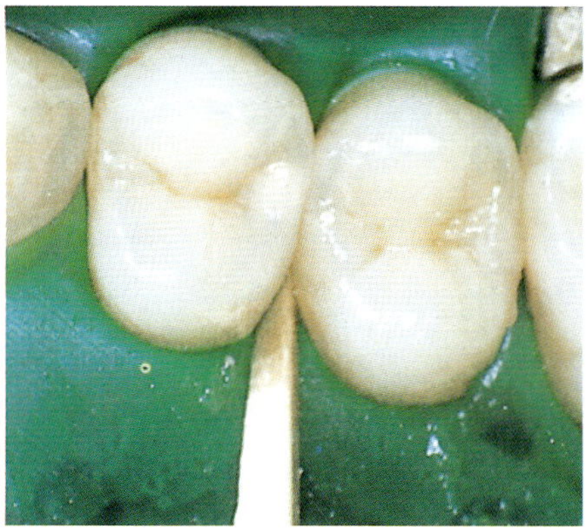

(a)

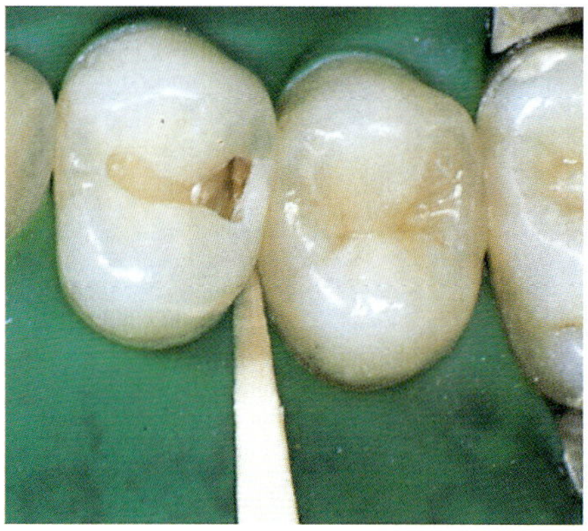

(b)

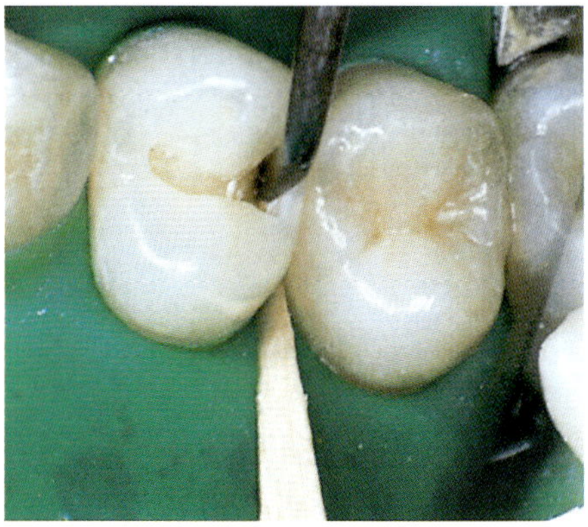

(c)

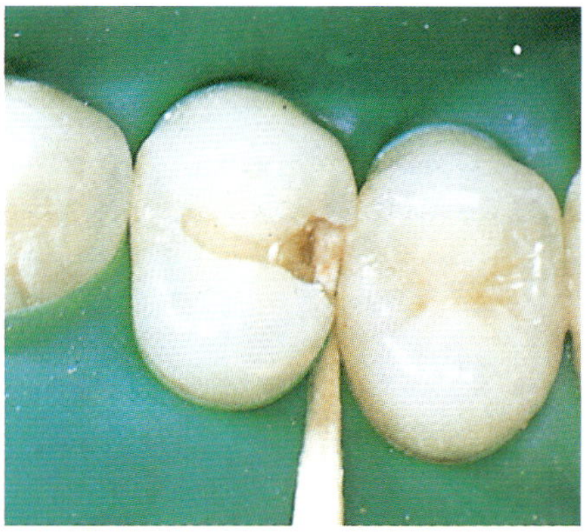

(d)

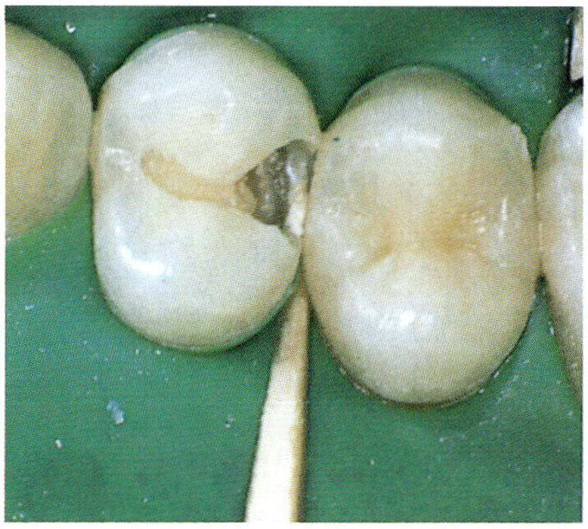

(e)

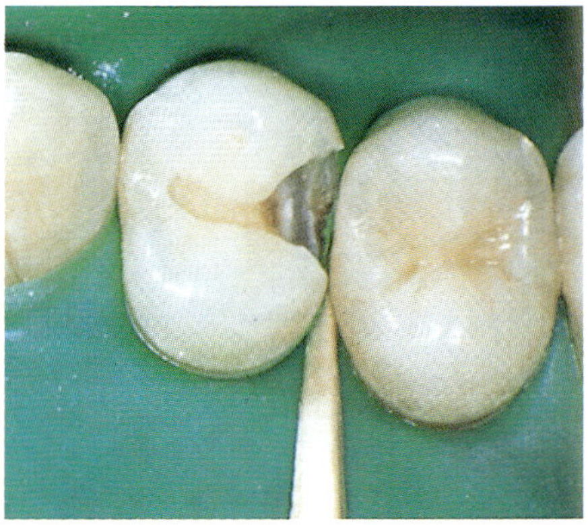

(f)

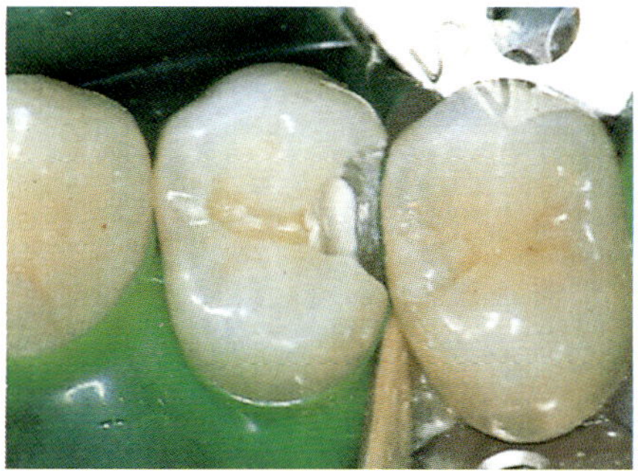

(g)

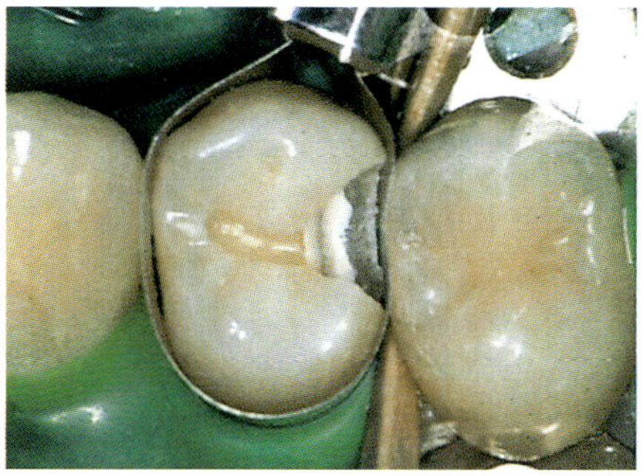

(h)

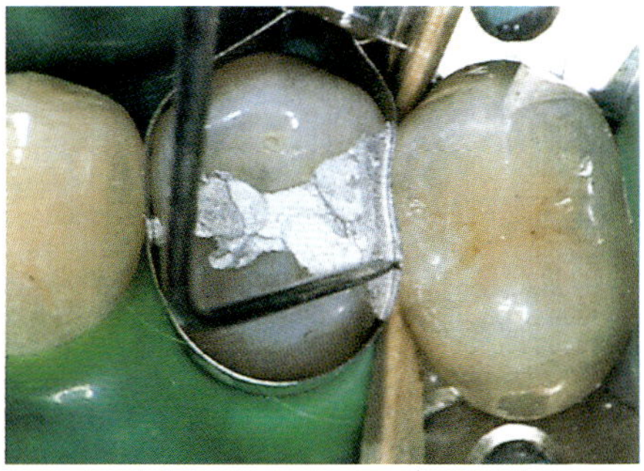

(i)

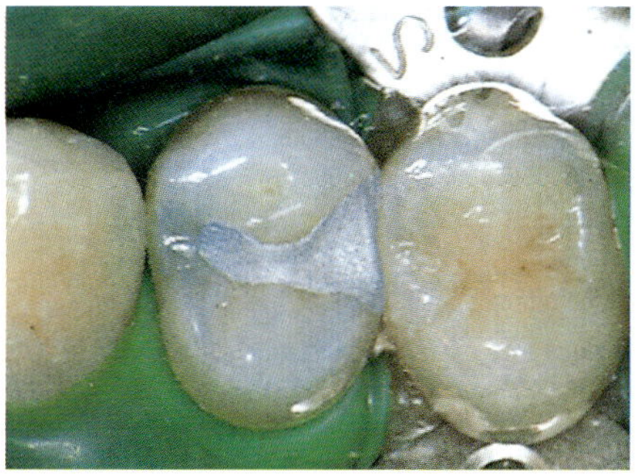

(j)

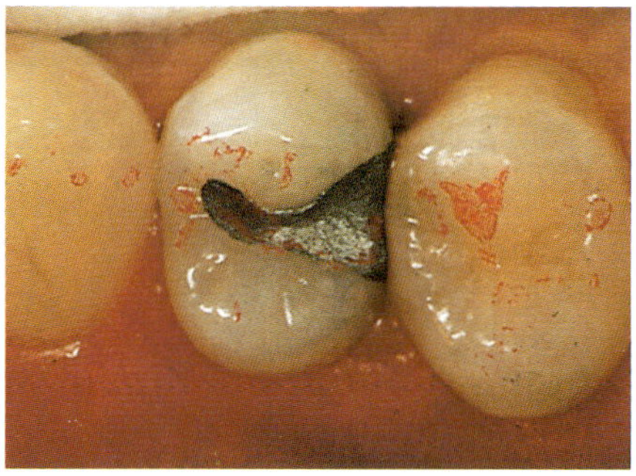

(k)

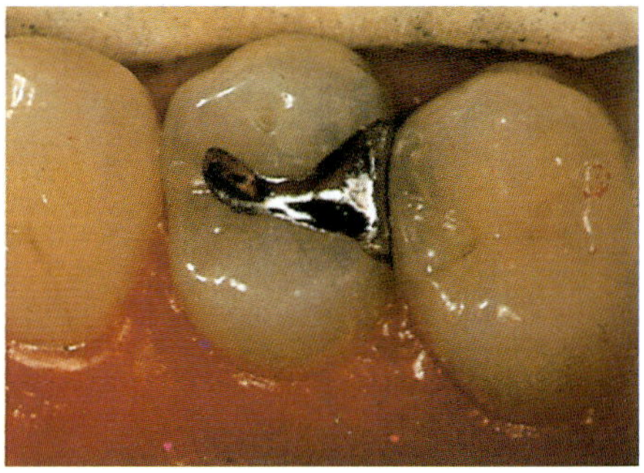

(l)

the carious tooth and the adjacent tooth (Fig. 8.2a). This prevents the rubber from being caught and torn by burs.

Access to caries and clearing the enamel–dentine junction

Access is gained to the carious dentine with a small pear-shaped tungsten carbide bur (e.g. Jet 330) in the air turbine. The bur is placed centrally on the inner aspect of the marginal ridge and angled slightly towards the contact area of the tooth so that it is directed towards the area of affected dentine. The operator will feel the bur suddenly drop into the carious dentine because all resistance to penetration disappears. The cavity is widened slightly bucco-lingually to gain access to the carious dentine beneath. Note that a small sliver of enamel is left at the contact area to prevent accidental damage to the adjacent tooth (Fig. 8.2b). If this precaution is not taken, the risk of damaging the approximal surface of the next tooth is very high and this is a serious, if common, failure of technique. Any occlusal extension to gain access to occlusal caries is conveniently cut at this time. It is important to be conservative of tooth tissue so that the tooth remains as strong as possible and the occlusal forces placed on the amalgam are as small as possible. However, if the tooth is caries-free occlusally, it is not necessary to cut out the fissure.

The sliver of enamel in the region of the contact area can now be fractured out with a small chisel (Fig. 8.2c and d). Subsequently, a round steel bur (the size will vary according to the size of the cavity) is used in the low-speed handpiece to clear caries from the enamel–dentine junction, lingually and cervically (Fig. 8.2e).

Finishing the enamel margins

Any carious or unsupported enamel is now removed. Although the air turbine bur can be used again approximally at this stage, a gingival margin trimmer is often ideal for the purpose. Initially, the instrument is used as a hatchet with a cutting stroke to trim the buccal and lingual aspects of the approximal part of the cavity (Fig. 8.3a). It is then swept round cervically (Fig. 8.3b) where the angulation of the blade at 25° to normal (Fig. 8.3c) removes unsupported enamel at the cervical margin.

The resulting outline of the approximal part of the cavity is thus determined by the extent of the caries, taking the form of a sweeping curve (Fig. 8.3). Since caries begins cervical to the contact area, removal of carious tissue and unsupported enamel will usually leave the cavity margins clear of the adjacent tooth bucally, lingually, and cervically. The resulting margins are thus accessible to instrumentation by the dentist and cleaning by the patient and will not hinder matrix band placement. They can also be checked visually for recurrent caries at subsequent appointments. The margins should not be extended buccally or lingually more than necessary. Wherever caries allows, the gingival margin should be supragingival as subgingival margins encourage plaque accumulation and therefore gingival inflammation and recurrent caries.

This cavity design is conservative of tooth tissue and should minimize damage to adjacent teeth during cavity preparation. However, where the operator is worried about cutting the next tooth, a steel matrix band may be placed around it. Unfortunately, this will not reliably prevent damage to the adjacent tooth and hinders access, which probably explains why few experienced practitioners use it.

The rounded approximal outline facilitates thorough condensation of the amalgam in the gingival area. Using the cervical margin trimmer cervically removes friable flakes of enamel which would otherwise fracture when the matrix band is placed (Fig. 8.2f). Occlusal and approximal parts of the cavity should merge smoothly with each other. Further occlusal extension into the occlusal fissures is only undertaken when caries and/or an existing unsatisfactory occlusal restoration is present.

Removing caries over the pulp

Having established the outline of the cavity and finished the enamel walls, caries over the pulp is removed with a slowly rotating round bur or sharp excavator.

Fig. 8.2 (*left*) (a) The cavity on the distal aspect of the upper first premolar is to be restored. The radiographic appearance of this lesion is seen in Fig. 8.1. A rubber dam is applied and a wooden wedge is inserted interdentally.
(b) A small bur is used to gain access to caries. On the distal aspect, the cavity is widened slightly bucco-lingually, and a small sliver of enamel is left at the contact area.
(c) The sliver of enamel in the contact area is fractured out with a small chisel.
(d) A round steel bur can now be used in the low-speed handpiece to clear caries from the enamel–dentine junction.
(e) The enamel–dentine junction is made caries-free. Carious undermined enamel remains on the cervical floor.
(f) The enamel walls of this cavity have been finished with a cervical margin trimmer. Note the different appearance of the cervical floor when compared with Fig. 8.2(e).
(g) The axial wall of the cavity is lined with a cement containing calcium hydroxide. The occlusal part of the cavity is just into dentine and does not require lining.
(h) A matrix retainer and a curved band are in place. Wedges are positioned buccally and palatally to ensure good cervical adaptation. The band is burnished to contact the adjacent tooth.
(i) The first stage of carving is to adjust the height of the marginal ridge by removing a fillet of amalgam from against the matrix with a sharp probe.
(j) Carving is nearly complete. The rubber dam is now removed so that the occlusion can be checked.
(k) Articulating paper is used to mark areas of occlusal contact.
(l) The completed polished restoration.

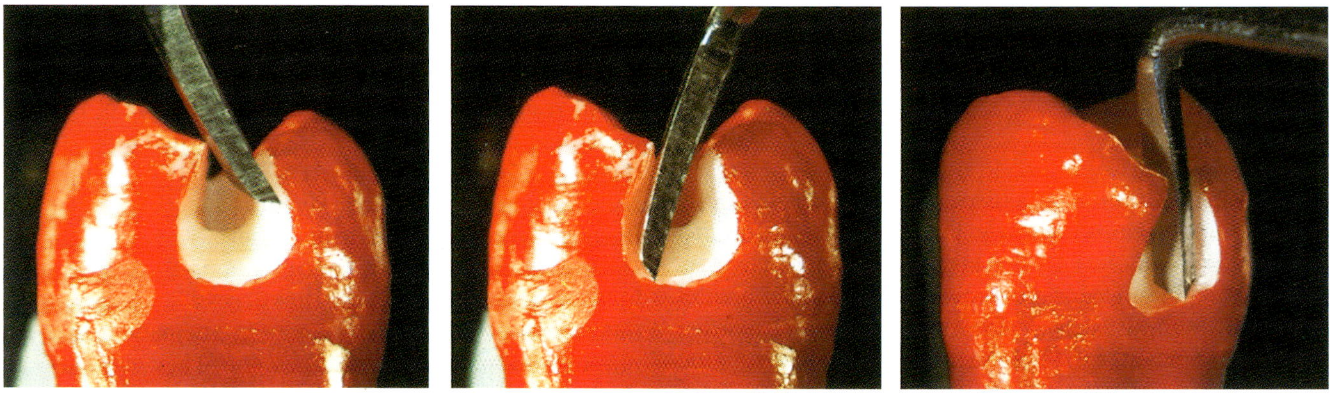

(a) (b) (c)

Fig. 8.3 Use of a gingival margin trimmer on an extracted tooth.
(a) The instrument is initially used as a hatchet with a cutting stroke to trim the buccal and lingual aspects of the cavity.
(b) It is then swept around cervically.
(c) The angulation of the blade, at 25° to normal, should remove grossly unsupported enamel at the cervical margin.

Retention

Since amalgam is not inherently adhesive to enamel and dentine, the cavity must be designed to retain the filling. If the cavity has been prepared as described, it will be undercut and therefore will resist forces tending to dislodge the filling occlusally. However, there is the possibility that the filling may fracture and/or slide out of its cavity towards the adjacent tooth.

Where occlusal caries and/or removal of an old restoration have required occlusal cavity preparation, this is used to hold the approximal part of the restoration in place by making the occlusal part (the 'lock') dovetail-shaped (Fig. 8.2f). However, it is not necessary to cut away further sound tissue occlusally since the approximal part of the cavity can be made self-retentive. This is done by cutting retention grooves in the dentine of the axio-buccal and axio-lingual walls of the box (Fig. 8.4a and b). These are cut with a small round bur.

The use of a round bur to remove caries from the enamel–dentine junction gingivally will usually result in a groove in this area (Fig. 8.5). Thus the curved floor will be inclined slightly inwards and will be at right angles to the long axis of the tooth. In addition to helping to retain

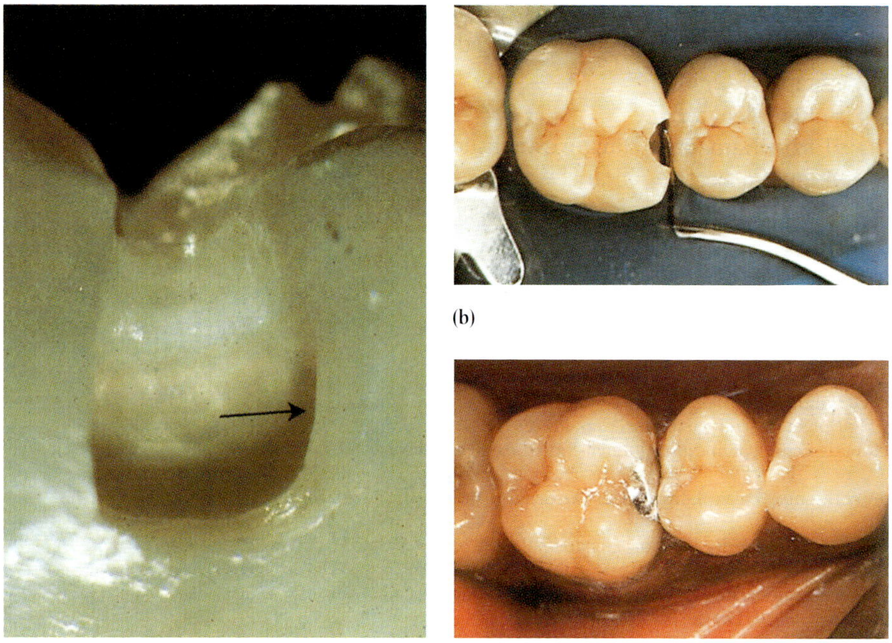

(a) (b) (c)

Fig. 8.4 (a) Retention grooves on an extracted tooth cut with a small round bur in the dentine of axio-buccal and axio-lingual walls. The arrow points to the retention groove on one side of the cavity.
(b) A clinical example.
(c) The restored tooth.
(Fig. 8.4b and c reproduced by courtesy of Dr P. B. Robinson.)

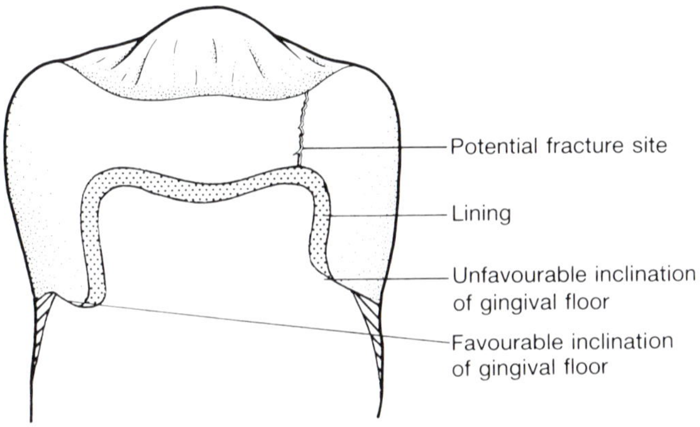

Fig. 8.5 Diagram showing how the use of a round bur to remove caries cervically results in the floor being inclined slightly inwards (the left-hand side of the cavity). This will help to retain the filling and potentially resists the forces of occlusion which would otherwise tend to force the restoration out of the cavity. On the right-hand side of the cavity the gingival floor takes the unfavourable shape of an inclined plane sloping outwards, and so the restoration will tend to fracture. (Reproduced by courtesy of Professor Richard Elderton and Dental Update.)

the filling, this shape potentially resists the forces of occlusion which would otherwise tend to force the restoration out of the cavity (the glacier effect).

Lower premolars

Caries on the approximal surfaces of lower premolar teeth can present difficulties in cavity preparation, particularly in the lower first premolar where the occlusal surface is angled lingually and the occlusal fissure is lingually placed. Where caries necessitates an occlusal extension this should, if possible, be cut at the expense of the buccal cusp, although its position will be dictated by the caries. Angulation of the bur at right angles to the occlusal surface helps to avoid undermining the small lingual cusp. In these teeth, approximal and occlusal parts of the cavity are frequently cut at different angles (Fig. 8.6).

Lining the cavity

This procedure is similar to that described for an occlusal composite preparation except that the axial wall must also be lined. Care should be taken not to block out the retention grooves. The angle between the pulpal floor and the axial wall (pulpo-axial line angle) should be rounded to make the amalgam maximally strong in this area (Figs. 8.2g and 3.8).

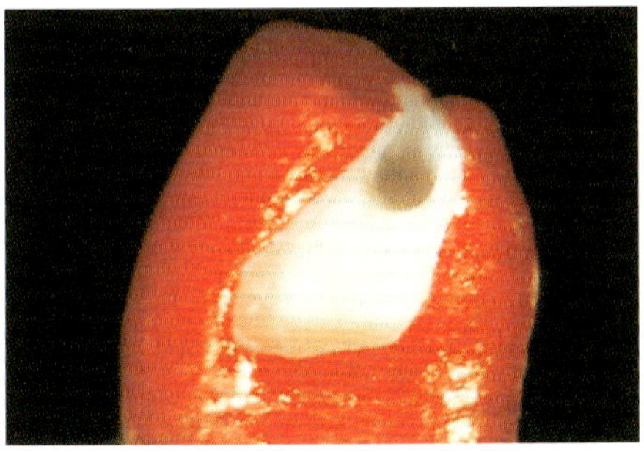

Fig. 8.6 A lower premolar cavity prepared on a carious extracted tooth.

Applying the matrix band

When placing amalgam in the cavity the aim is to restore the contact area and marginal ridge and at the same time have the smoothest possible junction between the restoration and the tooth. However, since the cavity is incompletely enclosed, an extra wall must be provided if amalgam is to be contained and firmly condensed. This extra wall is provided by a metal strip – a matrix band. The functions of the matrix band are as follows:

- to retain the amalgam in the cavity during condensation
- to permit the close adaptation of the amalgam to cervical and axial margins
- to help to restore the contact area and external contour of the crown.

Matrices are of three types:

- The band encircles the tooth and is secured by a retainer on the buccal or, in some cases, the lingual aspect. This is the commonest form and there are many patterns of this type of retainer. In addition, there are many different designs of band – straight, curved, and contoured (Fig. 8.7). The chief advantage of this type is that it can be firmly adapted to the tooth (Fig. 8.2h).
- The band encircles three-quarters of the crown and is retained by jaws impinging into the free embrasure (Fig. 8.8). It is particularly useful where contact points are so tight that it is difficult to place the other types of matrix band.
- This type includes a number of variations in which only a matrix band is used, without a retainer. The matrix strip may be wedged in position, may be retained by a ligature, or may be a complete band tightened by a spring mechanism (Fig. 8.9). It has the advantage that no retainer is needed and is particularly well suited to badly broken-down teeth (see p. 00).

Fig. 8.7 There are many different designs of matrix band. This figure shows examples of straight, curved, and contoured bands.

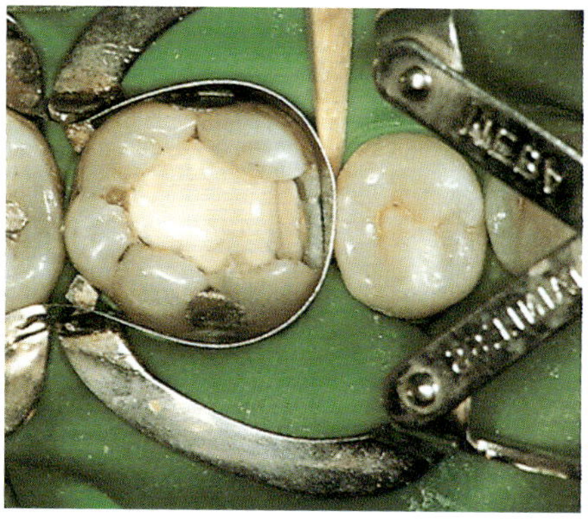

Fig. 8.8 In this design of matrix retainer the band encircles three-quarters of the crown. The matrix band replaces the mesial wall of the cavity. A wedge has been inserted from the lingual side to ensure good cervical adaptation and the band is burnished to contact the adjacent tooth.

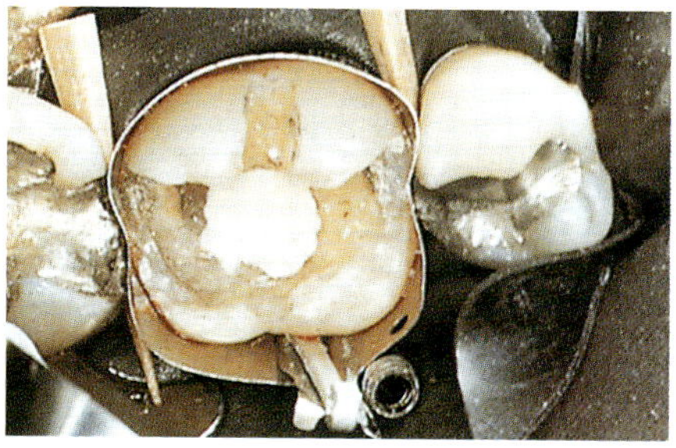

Fig. 8.9 There is no matrix retainer with this design of band. The band is tightened around the tooth by a spring mechanism.

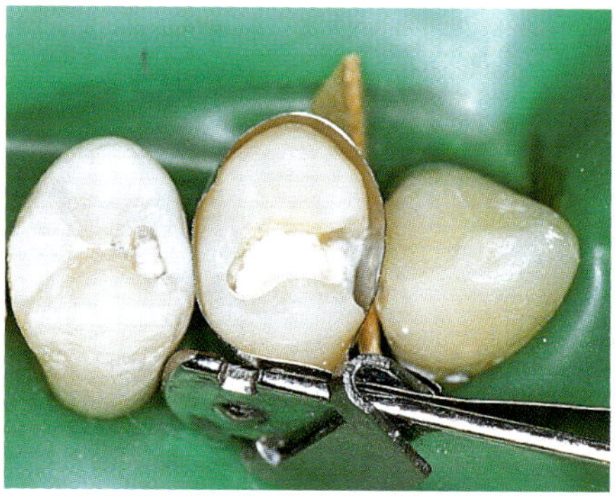

Fig. 8.10 A Siqueland matrix retainer in use. Note the adjustment of the toggle to reduce the circumference of the band cervically. A wooden wedge has also been placed. A gap is present buccally and a second wedge would be useful. However, it is difficult to insert with this matrix retainer because the toggle is in the way.

The most important features of a good matrix are that the band should be thin (about 0.05 mm), smooth and strong, it should be capable of close adaptation, in particular to the cervical margin and finally, it should allow the contact with the adjacent tooth to be restored otherwise food packing will occur. When the matrix band is placed it should be stretched in the contact area by careful burnishing (Figs. 8.2h, 8.8, and 8.9). This is particularly important where a spherical amalgam alloy has been chosen because it is rarely possible to push the contact out during condensation with this type of alloy. The width of the band should allow it to extend 1.0 mm above the marginal ridge to allow for overpacking of the restoration, but it should not be too tall otherwise access is restricted.

The adaptation of the matrix at the cervical margin is very important. The problem is that the occlusal circumference of the tooth is greater than the cervical circumference and access to trim away any excess of amalgam in this area is poor. Curved bands are designed to help solve this problem. An alternative solution is to select a design of matrix retainer which is adjustable, to allow a straight band to be pulled into a truncated cone (Fig. 8.10). As well as this it is also necessary to use a cervical wedge (usually wood) to push the band firmly against the tooth and hold it in position with sufficient force to prevent amalgam escaping between the band and the tooth under packing pressure (Figs. 8.2h, 8.8, and 8.9).

While it should hold the band firmly in position cervically, the wedge should not be of such a height that it prevents the formation of a contact point. Thus the wedge must be triangular in cross-section, with the base of the triangle resting on the gingiva. Since the dimensions of the triangle and space to be filled will vary from tooth to tooth and from mouth to mouth, a variety of sizes of wooden wedge should be available: wooden wedges can be carved and adapted to shape with a scalpel. Another function of the wedge is to separate the teeth slightly so that when it and the matrix are finally removed, the teeth return to their original positions, closing the small space left by the thickness of the matrix band.

The matrix band is gently passed between the contact points so that its lower edges lie just over the cervical margin of the cavity. The band is then tightened and a wedge inserted. The contact area is burnished against the adjacent tooth. When the cavity is wide bucco-lingually, it may be necessary to slacken the matrix band retainer slightly to achieve this. If so, wedging is particularly important to hold the band in place, and wedges should be inserted from both buccal and lingual sides (Fig. 8.2h). This approach may also be useful on the mesial surface of the first upper premolar where the concavity of the canine fossa requires careful wedging.

Before inserting the amalgam, a final check should be made of the following points:

- Is the matrix system stable?
- Does it fit the cervical margin? It should not be possible to insert a probe between the cervical margin and the band. If a small space remains which cannot be eliminated because of a groove in the tooth (e.g. mesially on the upper first premolar teeth), remember where it is and remove excess amalgam in this region as soon as the matrix band is removed (Fig. 8.10).

- Has the band been burnished in the contact area so that the contact point can be restored?
- Is the height of the band sufficient?
- Is the cavity clean and dry?

Choice of amalgam

This is not a textbook of dental materials and reference to such a book is essential at this stage if the student is to understand how to handle the material. Amalgam alloys contain silver, tin, copper, and often zinc. Alloys containing a higher proportion of copper are preferred as they corrode less than the alloys used in the past and show minimal distortion of the set restoration (creep) (see p. 60).

The alloy particles are lathe-cut (irregularly shaped), spherical, or a mixture of the two. It is essential to know which of these alloys is being used because they handle quite differently. Lathe-cut alloys must be firmly condensed into position; they resist packing pressure and are hard work to handle. Spherical alloys, however, can be condensed into a cavity with much less force and larger-diameter instruments may be needed to handle them.

Amalgam alloy is mixed with mercury before being packed into the cavity. The alloy and mercury are supplied in a capsule with alloy at one end and mercury at the other, separated by a diaphragm which is broken just before placing the capsule in the amalgamator (Fig. 8.11). These capsules have the advantage that the manufacturer has placed the optimal quantity of alloy and mercury in the capsules and thus a consistent mix should be assured. They also have the safety advantages that liquid mercury does not need to be stored in bulk in the surgery, reducing the risk of spillage, and as the mixing is carried out in a closed capsule there is less risk of air contamination by mercury vapour.

With all amalgams the manufacturer will recommend the mixing time and this will vary according to the alloy selected. Similarly, the working time of the particular alloy will also have been determined by the manufacturer. Therefore it is possible to select alloys with long or short working times.

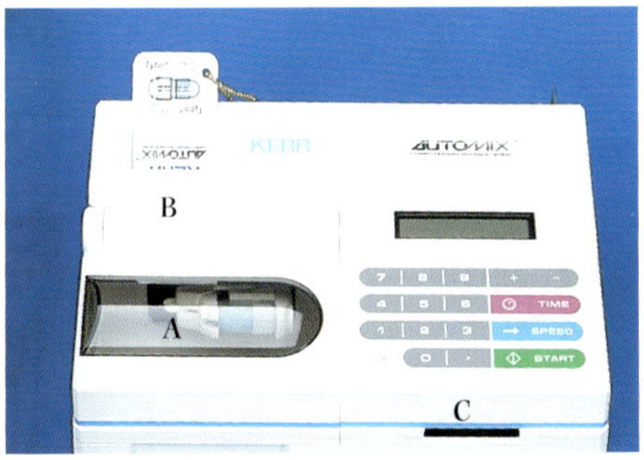

Fig. 8.11 An amalgamator with a capsule of amalgam in position behind a shield (A). The appropriate card is chosen from the rack (B) and inserted into the slot (C). The electronic control is then activated.

Dental schools usually select alloys with long working times for undergraduate use because undergraduates are bound to work slowly at first.

Inserting the amalgam

The mixed alloy is transferred to a suitable container and a small amount is picked up in an amalgam carrier and transferred to the cavity. Sometimes this procedure presents problems because gravity can help the amalgam fall straight out again! The trick is to push the amalgam carrier firmly towards the base of the cavity and keep it in this position while expelling the amalgam.

The condensing instrument of choice is a double-ended plastic instrument with a flat-smooth condensing surface (see Fig. 5.6b). The diameter of the tip must be such that it can be accommodated on the floor of the cavity at its narrowest point, otherwise condensation of the deepest layers of amalgam is impossible.

The first increment of amalgam is directed into the deepest approximal part of the cavity. Great care must be taken to condense the amalgam thoroughly in this critical gingival area. It is helpful to slide the packing instrument from side to side to ensure adaptation of the filling material to the axial walls. Condensation proceeds by pressure on the amalgam mass in the centre of the cavity and then stepping the condenser towards the walls of the cavity and the ends of the fissures. Only when the first increment has been condensed adequately, should the next increment be added. It is wrong to suppose that the earlier layers inserted can later be condensed by heavy pressure in the later stages of packing. Only porosity close to the surface would be eliminated, and voids would remain in the deeper part. In addition, there would be poor union between the increments.

As the amalgam level reaches the cavity margins, packing continues to allow an excess to build up over the ultimate level of the finished restoration.

With a spherical alloy, broader condensing instruments can be used to advantage. This favours quicker condensation and better control of the mass of amalgam. It reduces the tendency to penetrate rather than consolidate the more mobile mass which is characteristic of this type of amalgam. Larger quantities of amalgam can be put in the cavity at one time with these alloys and this is appropriate when packing large cavities.

Carving and finishing the amalgam

Amalgam should not be carved until it is sufficiently firm. Initially, the height of the marginal ridge should be adjusted to that of the next tooth. This is done by removing a fillet of amalgam from against the matrix with a sharp probe (Fig. 8.2i) and then reducing the height of the ridge with a sharp carving instrument (e.g. 1/2 Hollenback). The carver is held so that its blade lies across the margin of the filling, half on tooth and half on amalgam, moving parallel to the margin. In this manner small increments of amalgam are removed, defining the margin of the restoration. In a narrow restoration no attempt should be made to reproduced the natural fissure pattern, but the amalgam can be carved flat to ensure a strong amalgam margin angle. In a larger restoration, cuspal slopes should be carved and fissures may be delineated.

After removing the wedge, the retainer is loosened and removed. The band is first removed from the contact point not being restored. It is then wrapped back against the tooth adjoining the new restoration. From this position it can be lifted in an axial or oblique direction free of the filling; alternatively, one end of the band can be cut off short near the embrasure with scissors and the remaining end pulled through laterally to clear the contact area. Some dentists support the marginal ridge with a pledget of cotton-wool held on the amalgam condenser when removing the band.

Sometimes the marginal ridge is broken off when the matrix band is removed, destroying the occlusal form. This may happen for several reasons: poor cavity preparation, insufficient condensation of the marginal ridge, or inadequate trimming of the ridge before removing the band. It is obviously important to diagnose the cause of the problem before replacing the amalgam so that the same mistake is not repeated.

Once the band is removed, the axial and cervical margins are now accessible. The axial margins are trimmed towards the gingivae with a downward stroke of a sharp carver. The gingival margin should require only the lightest of trimming with a carver inserted into the embrasure, unless an excess has been anticipated (see Fig 8.10, p. 136). A sickle scaler can be a very effective carving instrument in these situations.

Great care should be taken to achieve a smooth and uniform surface whilst the mass is still capable of being carved (Fig. 8.2j). The occlusion should be checked by removing the rubber dam or cotton-wool rolls and asking the patient to place the teeth lightly together. If no abnormality is noted, a light 'rubbing' movement is requested. Sometimes the restoration will feel 'high' to the patient and then a brightly burnished mark will be seen on the amalgam surface, which is otherwise matt in texture. Articulating paper is useful to localize a high spot, particularly in patients who, when anaesthetized, find it difficult to say whether a restoration feels 'high'. The restoration should not be over-carved so that occlusal contacts are lost and the occlusion is left unstable, allowing the tooth to over-erupt (Fig. 8.2k). Finally, the restoration should be smoothed with a tightly-rolled pledget of cotton-wool.

Care is taken to see that all residual fragments of amalgam are removed from the interdental space by dislodging them with a probe and using the water and air spray from a three-in-one syringe.

Polishing

In the past it has been considered essential to polish amalgam restorations to attain a high gloss, thus aiding plaque control and reducing corrosion. However, some studies have shown that polishing may not be essential with the high-copper-content amalgam alloys. Comparison of polished and unpolished high-copper-content alloy restorations after a year of clinical service showed a similar surface finish.

If an amalgam restoration is to be polished, this should not be done until at least 24 hours after it has been placed. The surface should first be inspected to detect any heavily burnished spots which may indicate areas where excessive load is being exerted. Such areas should be reduced with a steel finishing bur which may also be used to run lightly over the whole area. Only the lightest pressure should be necessary as the aim is to smooth the restoration, not remove it from occlusion. The finishing bur is followed by a series of abrasive rubber points (Figs. 5.19 and 8.21), the shapes of which are particularly suited to polishing the fissure surfaces. As in all polishing procedures, success depends upon the use of a light uniform touch and the constant movement of the instrument over the carved surface. A fine finish will only be produced in all (dental) materials if polishing is taken through all the stages recommended by the manufacturer of the polishing system. Jumping from an early stage to a later one will simply produce a surface that is highly polished and deeply scratched. Care should be taken to retain the carving and avoid overheating the amalgam and thus damaging the pulp.

When the surface presents a uniform 'satin' finish, a final polish may be given with a soft cup-shaped brush or rubber cup and a fine abrasive. A proprietary dentifrice or zinc oxide powder moistened with methylated spirit is suitable. The contact area is not polished, but the amalgam cervical to it can be smoothed with a fine abrasive strip.

Approximal composite restorations: access through the marginal ridge

Indications

Many dentists and the UK National Health Service regulations still regard amalgam as the material of choice for approximal restorations. However, it suffers the disadvantages of poor appearance, a lack of adhesion to dental tissues, and no cariostatic properties. Amalgam will obturate a hole, but it will not support enamel and dentine. For these reasons, where appearance is of particular importance, or where enamel and dentine are weakened by caries, a posterior resin composite restoration may well be indicated.

A particular problem exists when composite is used to restore approximal cavities. At the gingival floor of these cavities there is a thin layer of enamel or, if caries has progressed further, the gingival floor may be in dentine. Composite resins shrink as they set (see Chapter 6). This is particularly exacerbated by placing the material in cavities when there are many opposing walls of the cavity that are trying to constrain the polymerization movement of the resin, assuming that a successful bond has been mediated by the adhesive. Either the bond breaks or the tooth breaks. The bond to the enamel of the axial walls will be stronger than the bond to the thin enamel or dentine cervically and so the material may shrink away from the weaker bond. In other words, a space may be created at the cervical margin. The fact that the materials are light-cured actually exacerbates this phenomenon since the composite will polymerize close to the light first of all and material further away from the 'fixed surface' will contract towards the light source, i.e. away from the cervical margin. The larger the cavity, the greater is the potential shrinkage. One solution (as with occlusal restorations) is to fill the bulk of the cavity with glass ionomer cement, sometimes including the whole of the cervical floor, and then restore the occlusal surface with a layer of composite. An alternative is to pack the composite in increments, curing each in turn before placing the next. If there is only one cavity wall remaining, following loss of much of the tooth, then the polymerization stresses imparted by quite large amounts of composite will be small because the cavity configuration is relatively 'open' with a lack of opposing cavity walls. The case for using glass ionomer dentine replacements in these situations is much reduced.

Any adhesive material is very susceptible to blood or saliva contamination while being placed. For this reason, isolation with a rubber dam is advisable. A wooden wedge should be placed interdentally to retract the rubber gingivally, preventing it from being cut with the bur. The wedge will move the teeth apart slightly, which helps to establish a tight contact point when the restoration is placed. This technique is called *pre-wedging*.

Aspects of cavity preparation

The cavity preparation is identical with that described previously (Fig. 8.12a). Access is gained to carious dentine by removing sufficient enamel over it to allow access to the enamel–dentine junction. All caries is removed from the enamel– dentine junction and soft caries excavated over the pulp.

It is principally in the management of the cavity margin that the preparation for receiving a composite may differ from that for filling with amalgam. Two aspects merit discussion:

- What should be done with undermined enamel? Can it be left and supported by composite or must it be removed?
- How should the enamel margins be finished? Should they be bevelled to increase the area available for retention and improve marginal seal, or should they be finished to a butt joint as in the amalgam restoration (Fig. 8.12a)?

There are currently no hard and, fast rules and, more importantly, no clinical evidence as to how to answer either question because insufficient clinical research has been carried out. However, it is probably better to err on the side of a conservative approach and leave, rather than remove, unsupported enamel.

The question of bevelling provokes particular controversy. Some (including the authors) prepare the cavity exactly as if it were to receive an amalgam restoration, as bevelling does not necessarily improve enamel prism orientation for etching/bonding in cavities in posterior teeth. Others place a small bevel occlusally and gingivally and long bevels on the axial enamel walls. This cavity design has been called the adhesive cavity preparation. Before finishing the cavity margins it is wise to check the occlusion with articulating paper to avoid placing composite/tooth margins in areas of high occlusal stress.

Lining and etching the cavity

The rationale for the use of linings has been given in the previous chapter. A lining material containing calcium hydroxide would only be used as an indirect pulp cap in a deep cavity. If a cavity is very large with weakened cusp walls, or there is difficulty in guaranteeing moisture control in the deep cervical regions, then a glass ionomer base replacing the missing dentine and extending to the outer surface of the proximal cavity has a great deal to commend it. The shrinkage stresses imparted by a (relatively) slow-setting conventional GIC restoration are minimal, so allowing recovery of the tooth without the problems of stress imparted by cusp flexure and de-bonding: this may be the case with a large volume of composite shrinking rapidly on light polymerization. Glass ionomer cements are also more moisture tolerant than composite restorations. It is acceptable to place such a material as a *provisional restoration* and then to cut back the GIC at a subsequent visit to allow a harder-wearing composite to be placed. Alternatively, resin-modified glass ionomer cement can be used as a base, if the composite is to be placed at the same visit, as these set more quickly because of their light activation and bond chemically to the overlying adhesive and composite.

Placing the matrix and restoration

Although the resin composites made for use in posterior teeth are viscous, they are still not viscous enough to be positively condensed into the cavity in the same way as amalgam. For this reason, the approximal contour of the final restoration will be dictated by the shape of the matrix. Forming a tight contact area is difficult with these materials.

Pre-wedging, as described on p. 00, is helpful. A thin matrix should be chosen which may be metal or clear mylar strip or pre-contoured metal (Fig. 8.12b) or plastic. Metal has the advantage that it can be firmly burnished against the

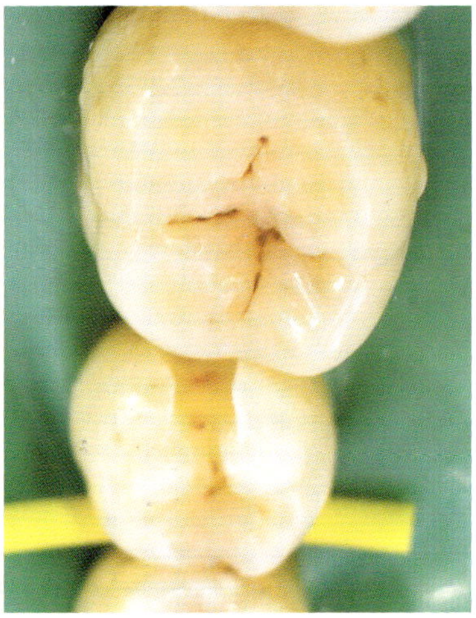

(a)

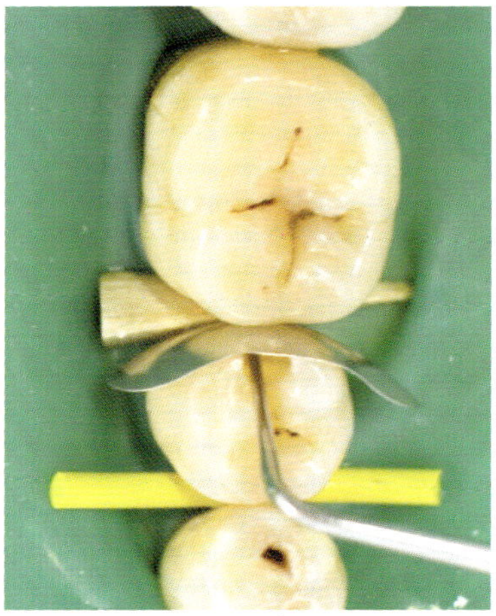

(b)

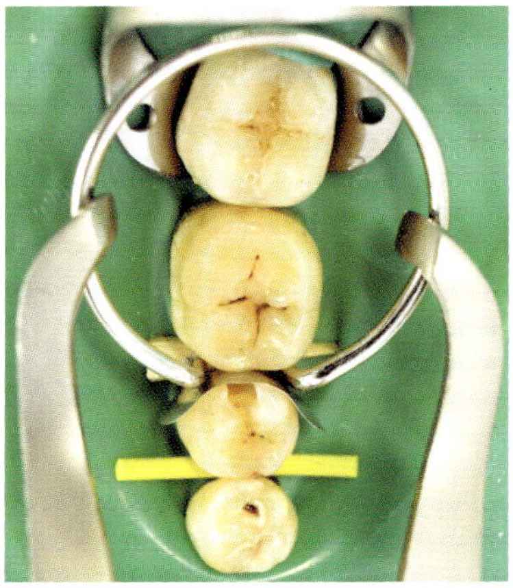

(c)

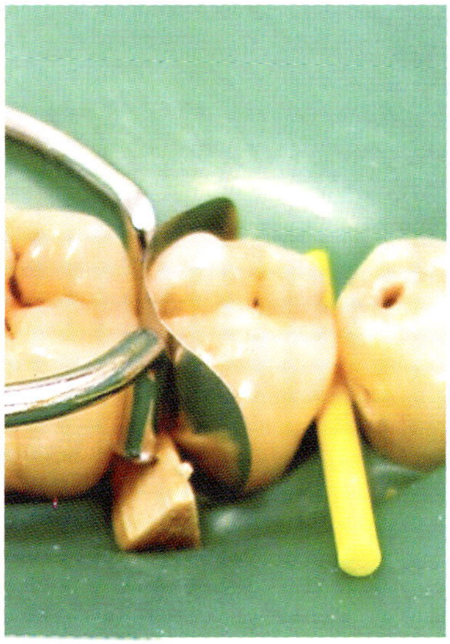

(d)

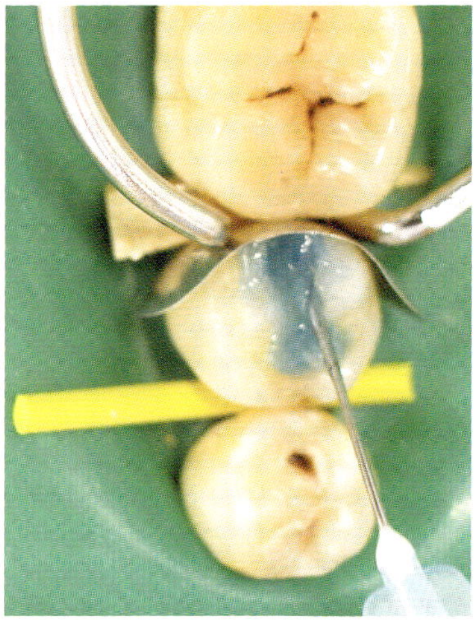

(e)

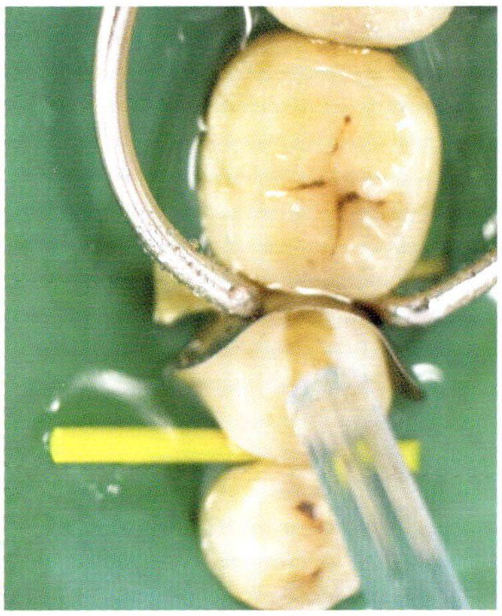

(f)

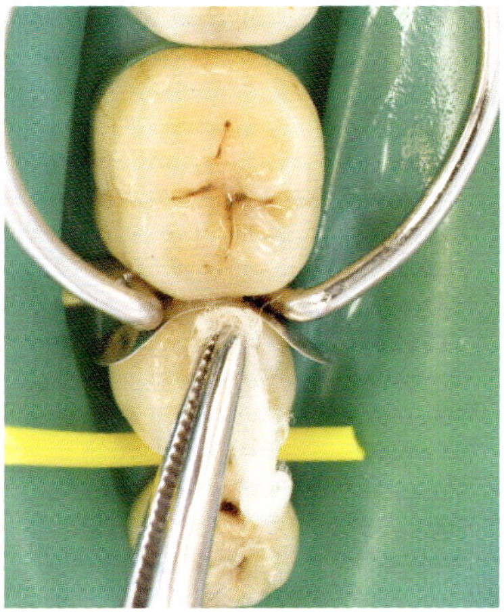

(g)

Fig. 8.12 (*See also pp. 141 and 142*) (a) Cavity prepared in a lower premolar for a posterior composite restoration. Approximal caries and occlusal caries were removed. The occlusal caries was found to be minimal and the cavity was not extended into dentine. Note the flaring of the cavity towards the cervical margin.
(b) A thin, contoured, metal matrix in place. The wedge will encourage adaptation at the cervical margin, but a probe should always be used to check that the band is tightly adapted.
(c) A spring steel ring is used to further stabilize the matrix and encourage tooth separation. These can be applied using rubber dam forceps or a specially made instrument as shown here. The yellow 'widget' helps to keep the rubber dam in place mesially. Strips of the dam or floss could also achieve a similar result.
(d) Side view of matrix holder showing engagement of ring between teeth.
(e) The whole of the cavity is etched with phosphoric acid gel for 20 seconds.
(f) The acid gel is washed away.
(g) Large amounts of water are blown away with an air syringe *without drying the tooth*. Any remaining water is removed from the cavity using a cotton pledget or large endodontic paper point.

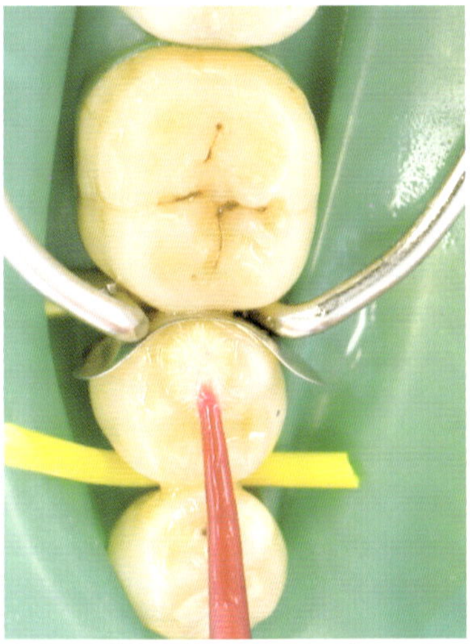

(h)

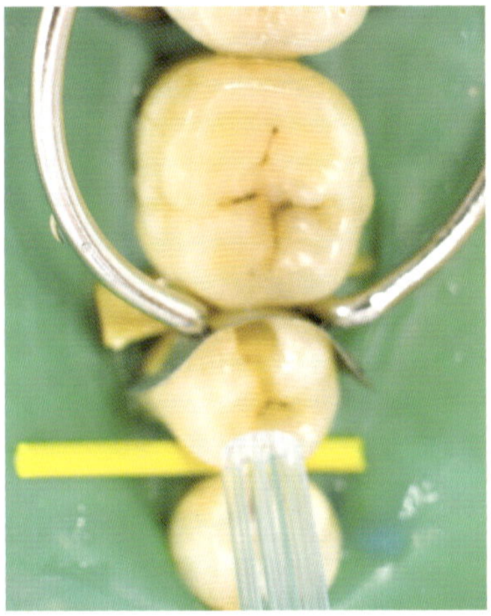

(i)

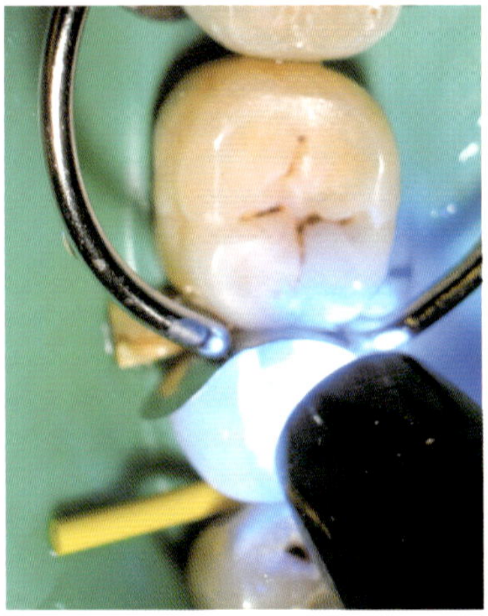

(j)

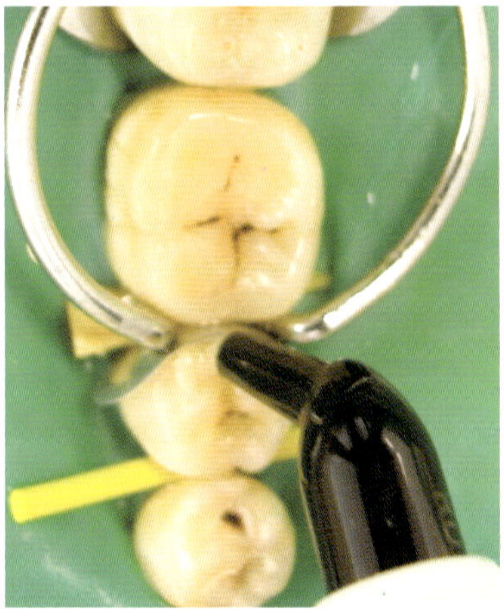

(k)

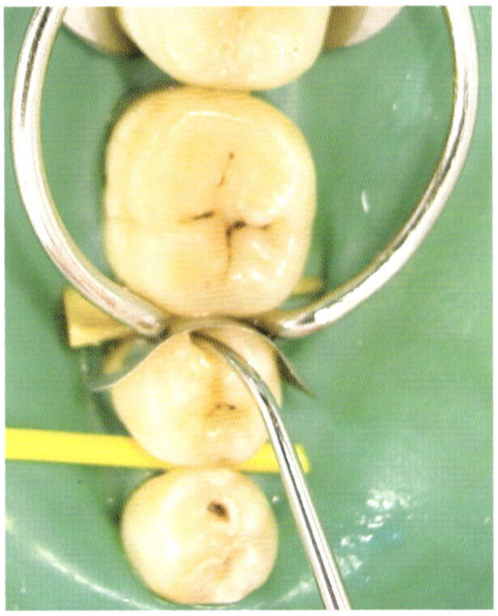

(l)

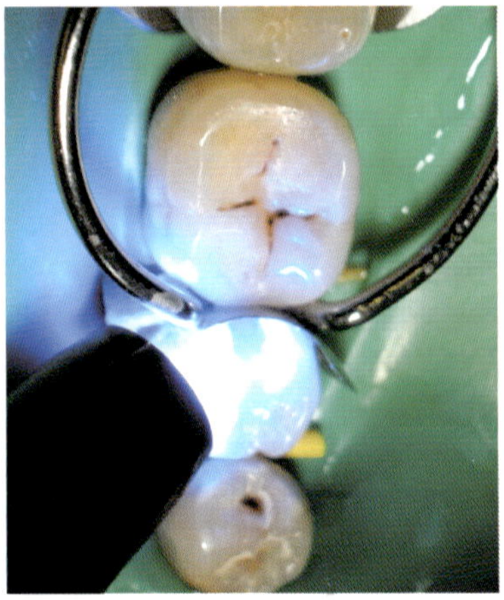

(m)

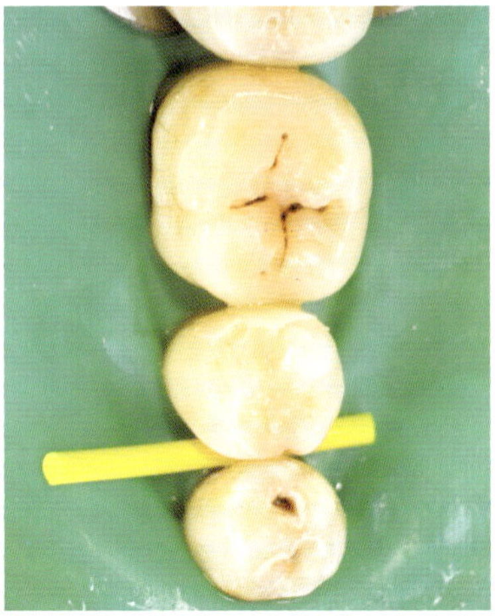

(n)

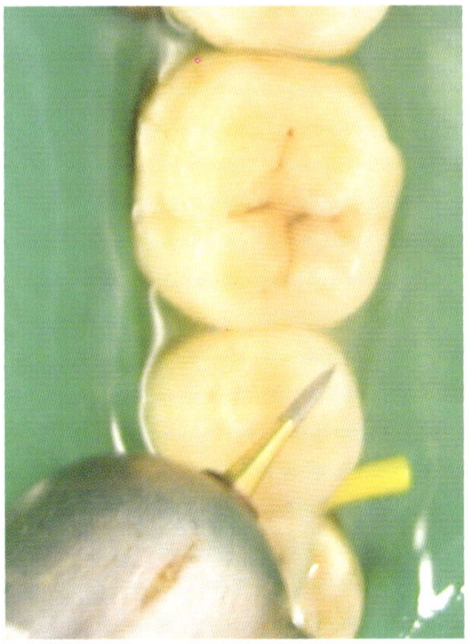

(o)

Fig. 8.12 (*continued*)
(h) The bonding agent is applied (following manufacturer's directions).
(i) Gentle and *complete* solvent evaporation is essential.
(j) The bonding agent is light-cured for 10–20 seconds.
(k) The first portion of composite is placed.
(l) The composite is directed to the floor and one wall of the proximal cavity.
(m) The restoration is cured through the tooth from the same side. This helps to prevent polymerization stress build-up. The second (and any other) increments are then added and cured.
(n) The matrix is removed.
(o) The final increment of composite is contoured as much as possible before it is polymerized. A multi-bladed tungsten carbide finishing bur is used to contour the marginal ridge (note the water spray).

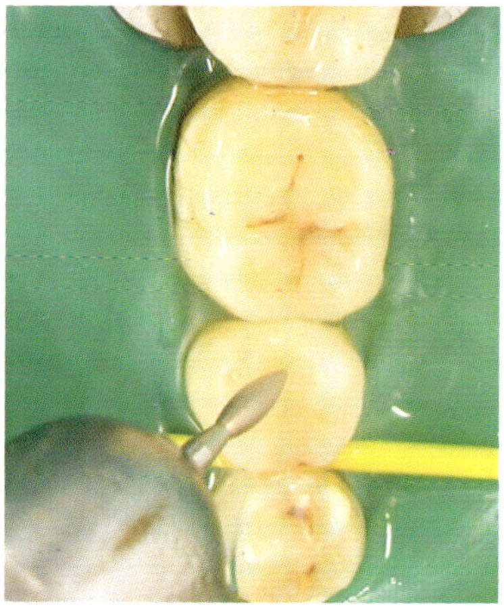

(p)

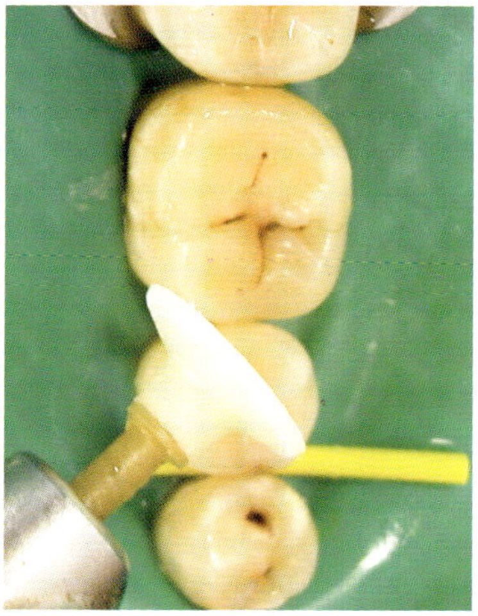

(q)

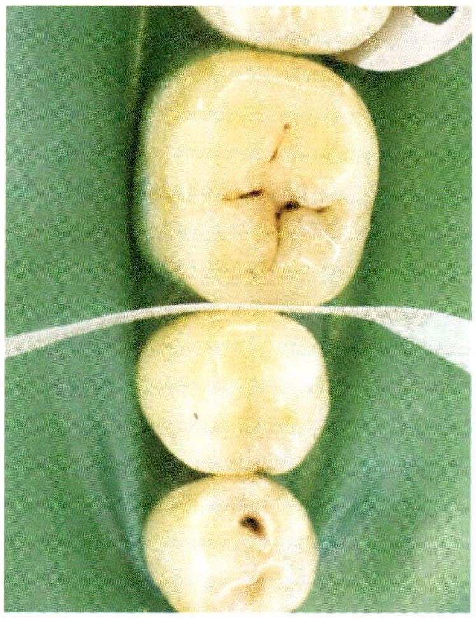

(r)

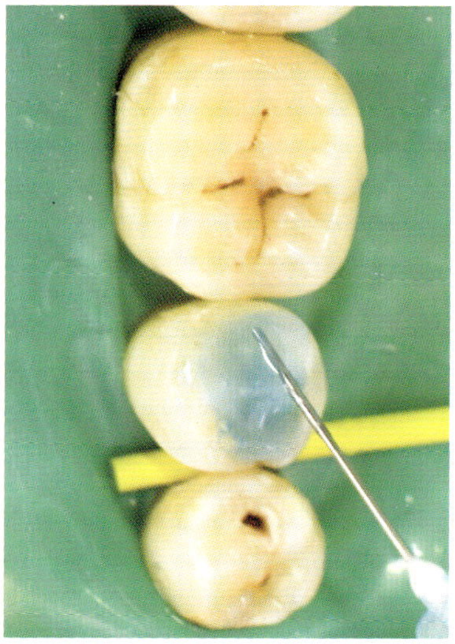

(s)

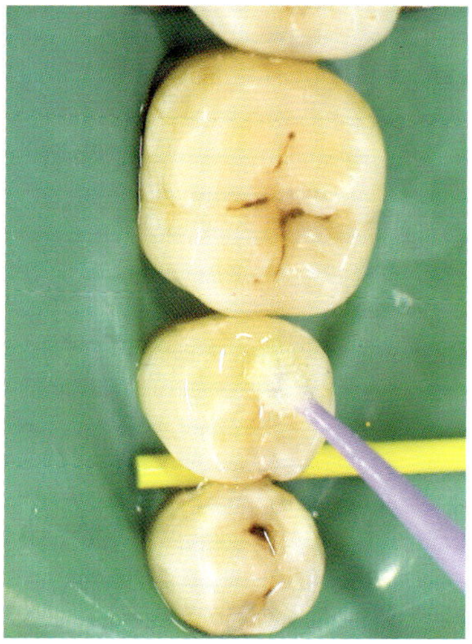

(t)

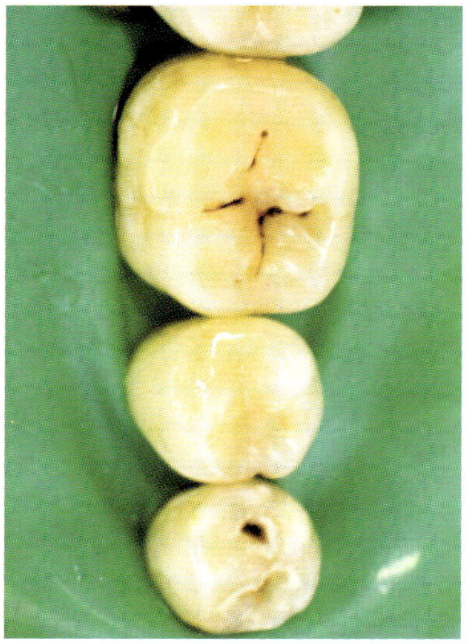

(u)

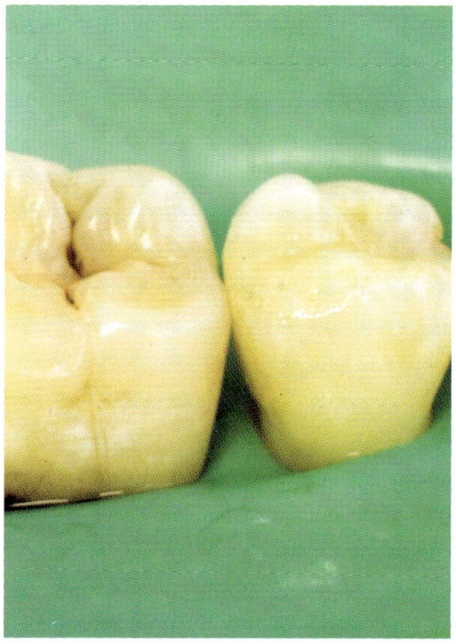

(v)

Fig. 8.12 (*continued*)
(p) A 'rugby ball'-shaped fine diamond is used to contour the occlusal anatomy. All high-speed instruments must be used with water spray.
(q) A flexible, abrasive, impregnated disc is used to smooth the occlusal contours.
(r) The interdental area can be gently polished with suitable abrasive strips.
(s) To seal defective margins, which may show up after polishing, the tooth is re-etched for 15 seconds, washed, and dried as before.
(t) Bonding agent is liberally rubbed over the surface, then air-thinned and any solvent evaporated. It is finally light-cured from all directions.
(u) The completed restoration before removing the rubber dam and checking the occlusion.
(v) Side view showing the rounded proximal contours achievable with soft metal matrices.

adjacent tooth. Mylar strip has the advantage that the curing light can shine through it. When the cavity is small a retainer is not essential, and in a tooth where only one approximal surface is involved in the cavity it is sensible not to pass a band around the tooth. The thickness of the band in the uncut contact area will move the tooth slightly, thus partly negating the pre-wedging effect. Ring-type retainers that engage in the proximal undercuts and potentially spring the teeth apart can help to stabilize a matrix (Fig. 8.12c and d).

Once the band or matrix is in position, it must be firmly wedged cervically (Fig. 8.12b and d). The cavity is now ready for etching (Fig. 8.12e), washing (Fig. 8.12f), removal of excess water (Fig. 8.12g) and the application of the bonding agent and the composite material. The bonding agent is applied to the moist surface (see Chapter 6) with a disposable brush (Fig. 8.12h) and air blown gently to ensure *complete* evaporation of the solvent in the adhesive (Fig. 8.12i). The surface of the tooth should show a shiny adhesive layer. It is particularly important to avoid gingival pooling of the bonding resin as most of the resins are radiolucent and can mimic caries in radiographs. The bonding resin is light-cured (Fig. 8.12j).

The composite is now placed, in increments if necessary, starting at the deepest portion of the cavity (Fig. 8.12k). The material is placed against the floor of the box and one axial wall first (Fig. 8.12l) and then polymerized with light directed from the same side (Fig. 8.12m). This will ensure the proper polymerization of the resin in a very confined area as well as minimizing the polymerization contraction of the resin. A Teflon-coated instrument with smooth rounded ends is a useful packing instrument. If packed incrementally, each increment is light-cured before the next is added. No increment should exceed 2.0–2.5 mm in depth.

As the composite approaches the cavo-surface margin it should be contoured to a reasonable anatomical form, thus minimizing the need for removal of gross excess during finishing (Fig. 8.12n).

Finishing the restoration

With the matrix removed, excess material (Fig. 8.12n) is removed from the occlusal embrasure area with a fine-pointed, multi-bladed tungsten carbide bur (Fig. 8.12o) finishing at high speed with water spray. A fine 'rugby ball'-shaped composite finishing diamond bur can be used to accentuate the occlusal anatomy (Fig. 8.12p). Where possible, a series of flexible, abrasive, impregnated rubber discs or points are used to smooth the restoration (Fig. 8.12q). Finally, the contact point is checked with floss and, if necessary, the interdental area polished with a fine abrasive strip (Fig. 8.12r).

Once the rubber dam is removed, the occlusion should be checked with articulating paper and adjusted as necessary. Final sealing of the margins – 'post-sealing' – can be achieved by re-etching the restoration and margins and reapplying a coat of bonding agent (Fig. 8.12s–v).

Approximal 'adhesive' restorations: marginal ridge preserved

Up to now consideration has been given to cavity preparation where the marginal ridge has been removed to gain access to the carious dentine cervical to it. Since caries has undermined the marginal ridge, this is an obvious approach. However, this access is unnecessarily destructive in small cavities and an approach may be made occlusally or buccally, preserving the marginal ridge (Fig. 8.13a). This approach has been made possible by the adhesive materials (glass ionomer cement and resin composites with bonding agents). Nevertheless, caries should not be treated operatively at any earlier stage to facilitate this approach because an arrested enamel lesion is still preferable to a restoration, however small.

Occlusal approach

Having applied a rubber dam, a small round bur in the air turbine handpiece is used to enter the occlusal side of the marginal ridge, directing the bur diagonally towards the caries (Figs. 8.13b and 3.4). The orifice of the cavity should be wide enough bucco-lingually to obtain adequate visibility and access to the carious dentine beneath. Caries is removed from the enamel–dentine junction with a round bur. The resulting cavity will present two holes in the enamel, one occlusally cut by the dentist and one approximally resulting from caries. It is therefore sometimes called a 'tunnel' cavity or an 'internal' cavity preparation. Airbrasive cutting techniques (Chapter 6) are particularly appropriate for this type of cavity as there is less chance of weakening and cracking the marginal ridge with this type of cutting process. The neighbouring tooth can be protected by the placement of a rubber dam in the interdental area: the energy of the airbrasive particles is absorbed by the rubber.

A thin soft metal matrix, lightly coated with Vaseline on the surface next to the cavity, is contoured and wedged firmly in position (Fig. 8.13b). If the cavity is deep, the dentine nearest the pulp is covered with a thin layer of a proprietary cement containing calcium hydroxide. The polyacrylic acid conditioning agent supplied with the glass ionomer cement should now be applied to the cavity with a brush or small pledget of cotton-wool. After 10 seconds the cavity is thoroughly washed and dried.

A radio-opaque conventional glass ionomer material, produced in capsule form, is mixed, the capsule is inserted into the applicator, and the material is syringed into the cavity (Fig. 8.13c). Excess material is left on the surface and this can be removed, after it has set, with a multi-bladed tung-

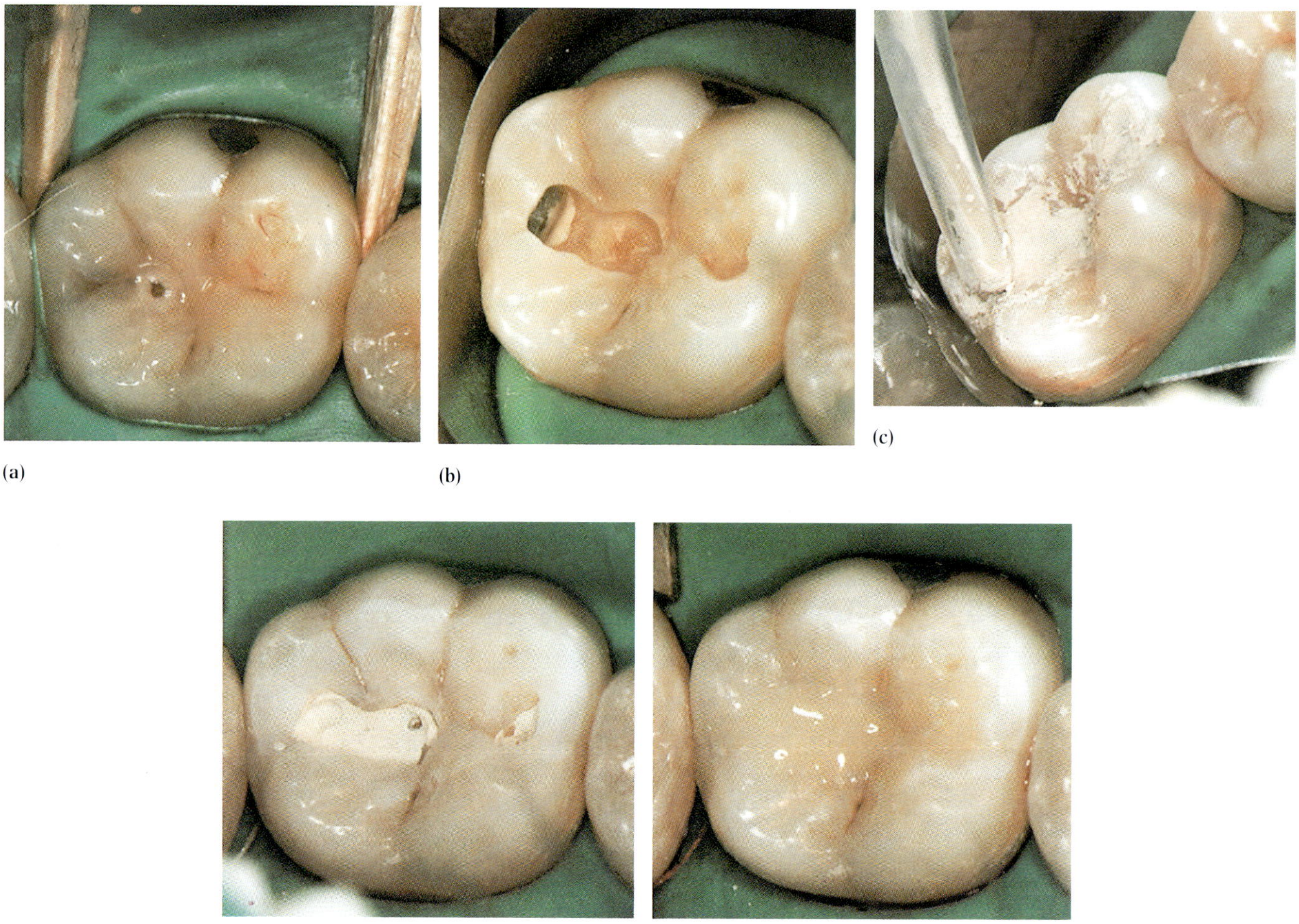

(a) (b) (c) (d) (e)

Fig. 8.13 (a) Clinical examination shows obvious occlusal caries in this lower first molar. A bitewing radiograph (Fig. 8.1) shows approximal lesions, involving dentine.
(b) Occlusal caries has been removed and the cavity extended distally and bucco-lingually to allow a round bur access to the approximal caries. A proprietary cement containing calcium hydroxide has been used to line the deep portion of the cavity, and a thin soft metal matrix has been wedged firmly into position. A similar cavity has been prepared on the mesial aspect of the tooth.
(c) A radio-opaque glass ionomer material is syringed into the cavity, having used the polyacrylic acid conditioning agent supplied with the material.
(d) The occlusal portion of the glass ionomer cement is removed with an airturbine and the enamel walls are acid-etched, washed, and dried.
(e) The occlusal cavities are filled with a light-cured posterior resin composite.

sten carbide bur in the air turbine. Alternatively, a radio-opaque resin-modified glass ionomer cement can be chosen, encapsulated, and syringed in the same manner. The material should be firmly tamped into position to ensure good adaptation within the cavity. The set of this material is initiated by light-curing.

Once the glass ionomer has set, the occlusal portion is removed with the air turbine (Fig. 8.13d). The enamel walls can now be etched and a composite placed in the occlusal surface (Fig. 8.13e).

Buccal approach

This approach is particularly well suited to teeth which are tilted lingually, where an occlusal approach to caries would result in the removal of considerable sound tooth substance, or where mesial or distal tilting has produced an unusual contact area down towards the cement–enamel junction. However, a buccal approach to caries destroys the buccal wall of the cavity, and if the marginal ridge collapses during cavity preparation, retention will be lost. Therefore careful judgement of the strength of the marginal ridge is important before choosing this design. Access to caries is gained with a small round bur in the air turbine and caries is removed from the enamel–dentine junction with a small round bur at slow speed. Since the cavity is not subject to occlusal stress, undermined enamel may be left provided that the dentist can see or feel the enamel–dentine junction with a probe to check that caries is not spreading further (Figs. 8.14 and 3.4).

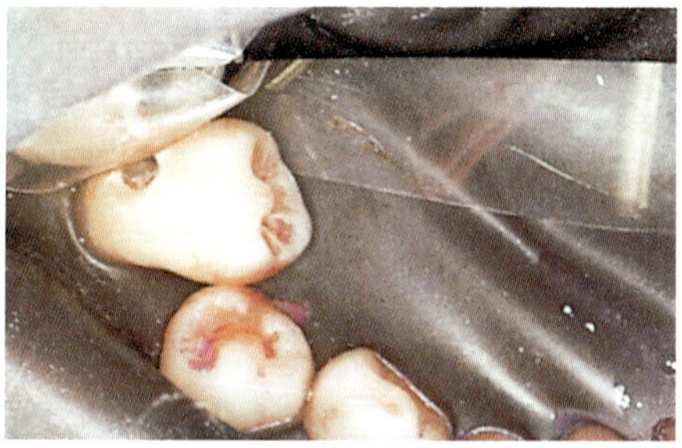

Fig. 8.14 A buccal approach to approximal caries in a lingually-tilted lower premolar. Any occlusal approach would be unnecessarily difficult and destructive of sound tooth tissue in this situation.

The cavity is lined and filled as described in the previous section, except that after insertion of the filling material, the matrix is pulled firmly around the tooth to assist the contouring of the restoration. Where a light-cured material is used, the matrix strip should be made of mylar or polyester so that the light can shine through it to polymerize the filling material. Since the restoration takes no occlusal load, replacement of part of the glass ionomer material by the composite is not usually necessary.

Approximal root caries

Root caries presents some specific operative difficulties relating to access and retention of the restoration. When the lesion is very superficial, it may be possible to smooth and polish the carious area without needing to place a restoration. If the lesion has penetrated more deeply, a restoration will usually be required to aid plaque control and protect the pulp.

Since the caries is on the approximal surface of the root, it would be very destructive to approach it through the marginal ridge. Buccal access is often the most convenient approach although if the lesion were sited more to the lingual side, access from this direction could be preferable. Caries is removed with round burs in the low-speed handpiece until the periphery of the cavity is hard. Where the handpiece head obstructs vision, an excavator with a long shank can be useful because it may be easier to see the caries as it is being removed. Once the periphery of the cavity is judged to be hard, soft dentine caries over the pulpal surface should be removed. Particular care must be taken not to expose the pulp traumatically, since the pulp chamber or root canals are soon reached.

The cavity is filled with a radio-opaque glass ionomer cement. Since this is adhesive to dentine, mechanical retention in the form of an undercut cavity is not required, but the polyacrylic acid conditioning agent supplied with the material should always be used to ensure an optimum bond. An indirect pulp cap using calcium hydroxide cement would be used in a deep cavity.

The mesial–occlusal–distal (MOD) cavity

So far the cavities described have been on one or other approximal surface, with or without the inclusion of the occlusal surface. Therefore the restorations are described as follows:

- mesial
- distal
- mesial–occlusal (MO)
- distal–occlusal (DO).

Commonly, when circumstances favour the initiation of caries, lesions occur on both the mesial and distal surfaces of the same tooth. They can be restored separately by mesial and distal fillings or in some cases by separate MO and DO fillings. This is often done in upper molar teeth, preserving the oblique ridge and thereby more of the strength of the tooth (Fig. 4.18).

However, it is often necessary to join the cavities, producing a mesial–occlusal–distal (MOD) cavity. The preparation does not differ much from the MO or DO cavity except that the natural shape of the cavity makes it easy to produce a retentive design. There is more difficulty in ensuring that the other aspects of the design are right. The approximal boxes should be retentive in their own right so that the occlusal part of the cavity can be kept as narrow as possible commensurate with removing the caries; over-cutting the occlusal part of the cavity is likely to result in cusp fracture at a later date. Bonded restorations may help splint the cusps together, although there is no clinical evidence for this statement (see Chapter 6).

The matrix for an MOD amalgam restoration is similar to an MO or DO except that even more care is needed, since the effect of burnishing the band against one contact point may be to pull it away from the other. The answer is to rely on the wedges to achieve cervical adaptation and slacken the band a little.

Removing the band is also more difficult, but the other stages are similar to the MO or DO restoration.

Problems of the larger cavity

Large restorations may be required either as a result of untreated or recurrent caries or because repeated replacement of restorations has, over a period of years, undermined the strength of the occlusal surface. The principles underlying the restoration of the badly broken-down tooth are the same as those already discussed for smaller restorations. However, these teeth present certain specific difficulties which will now be discussed.

Pre-operative assessment

Changes in the pulp are more likely with large lesions, and a full assessment of the condition of the pulp should be made, including vitality tests, and any necessary root treatment provided before the definitive restoration of the tooth is placed.

Clinical examination will give an idea of the extent of the caries and/or existing restorations and their relationship to the gingival margin. Where caries is well subgingival, periodontal surgery may be required before the tooth is finally restored. This involves reflecting buccal and lingual flaps. The relation of the base of the cavity to the height of the alveolar bone will then be obvious. It may be necessary to remove alveolar bone so that some sound root remains apical to the cavity. The flaps are then sutured so that the base of the cavity will be just supragingival.

The occlusion should be examined in the intercuspal position and in lateral excursions. Problems such as over-eruption of an opposing tooth may then be anticipated. The dentist may elect to re-contour the opposing tooth before restoring the broken-down tooth. Both bitewing and periapical radiographs should be examined. The bitewing radiograph can be used to assess the size of the carious lesion and/or an existing restoration, its proximity to the pulp, and its relationship to the alveolar bone (Fig. 8.15a). The periapical radiograph may reveal a periapical radiolucency (Fig. 8.15b), showing that root canal treatment is required if the tooth is to be saved. The periapical radiograph will also show the number and curvature of roots and root canals and their patency, all of which will be important if root canal treatment is required.

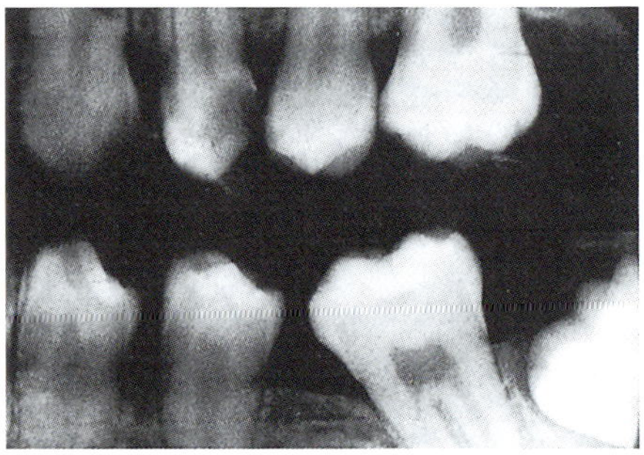

(a)

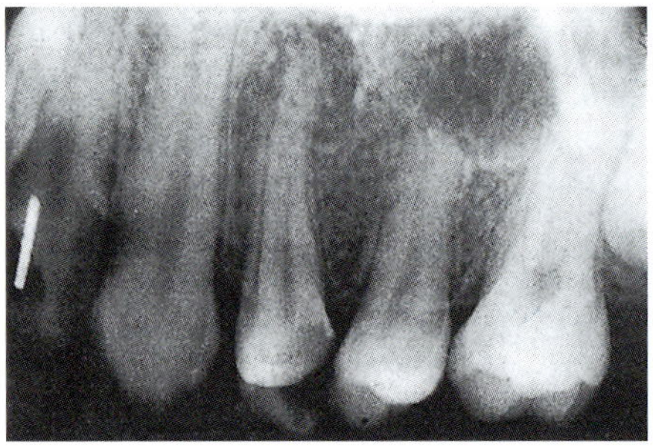

(b)

Fig. 8.15 (a) A bitewing radiograph showing a large distal cavity in the upper first premolar. There is also occlusal caries in the lower molar. (b) A periapical radiograph of the same tooth showing a periapical area.

With a vital pulp, bacterial contamination from saliva should be avoided. A rubber dam should be used and wedges should be placed to retract the rubber and prevent it from being snagged by a bur (Fig. 8.16a).

Caries removal

Access to carious dentine is gained by removing any remaining enamel over it with the air turbine. Old restorations are removed (see p. 00), taking care not to cut away sound tooth substance (Fig. 8.16b). The enamel–dentine junction is made hard with a round bur at low speed. Where enamel undermined by caries prevents access to the enamel–dentine junction, some of the undermined enamel should be removed (Fig. 8.16c).

Finally, caries over the pulp is removed. Since demineralization of dentine precedes bacterial penetration, stained but firm dentine may be left over the pulp where it is thought that its removal might result in pulp exposure. Exposures that are too small to be seen (micro-exposures) may be present in the depth of the cavity and so deep parts of the cavity should always be covered with a proprietary lining containing calcium hydroxide (indirect pulp cap). Where a frank carious exposure is found immediately beneath soft caries, root canal treatment or possibly extraction is indicated because the prognosis for the pulp is poor even if there have been no symptoms. Occasionally, calcium hydroxide is used as a direct pulp cap over a small pulp exposure in a symptomless vital tooth when the exposure results from removing the last bit of firm caries. Exclusion of saliva from the cavity may be important to preserving a healthy vital pulp in these cases. However, root canal treatment is usually required because pulp capping may be followed by chronic pulpitis. Where a radiograph shows that a lesion is close to the pulp in a symptomless, vital tooth, consideration should be given to stepwise excavation as described on p. 64.

Designing the restoration

Thus far, the design of the cavity has been dictated entirely by the extent of the caries and any previous restorations. It is now time to put down the handpiece and think about the eventual restoration.

If root canal treatment is required, this is best carried out through some form of temporary restoration, usually glass ionomer cement. Once root canal treatment is complete, restoration of the crown can be undertaken.

The relationship of the gingival floor of the cavity to the gingival margin must be assessed. Occasionally, caries results in the margin of the restoration being apical to the

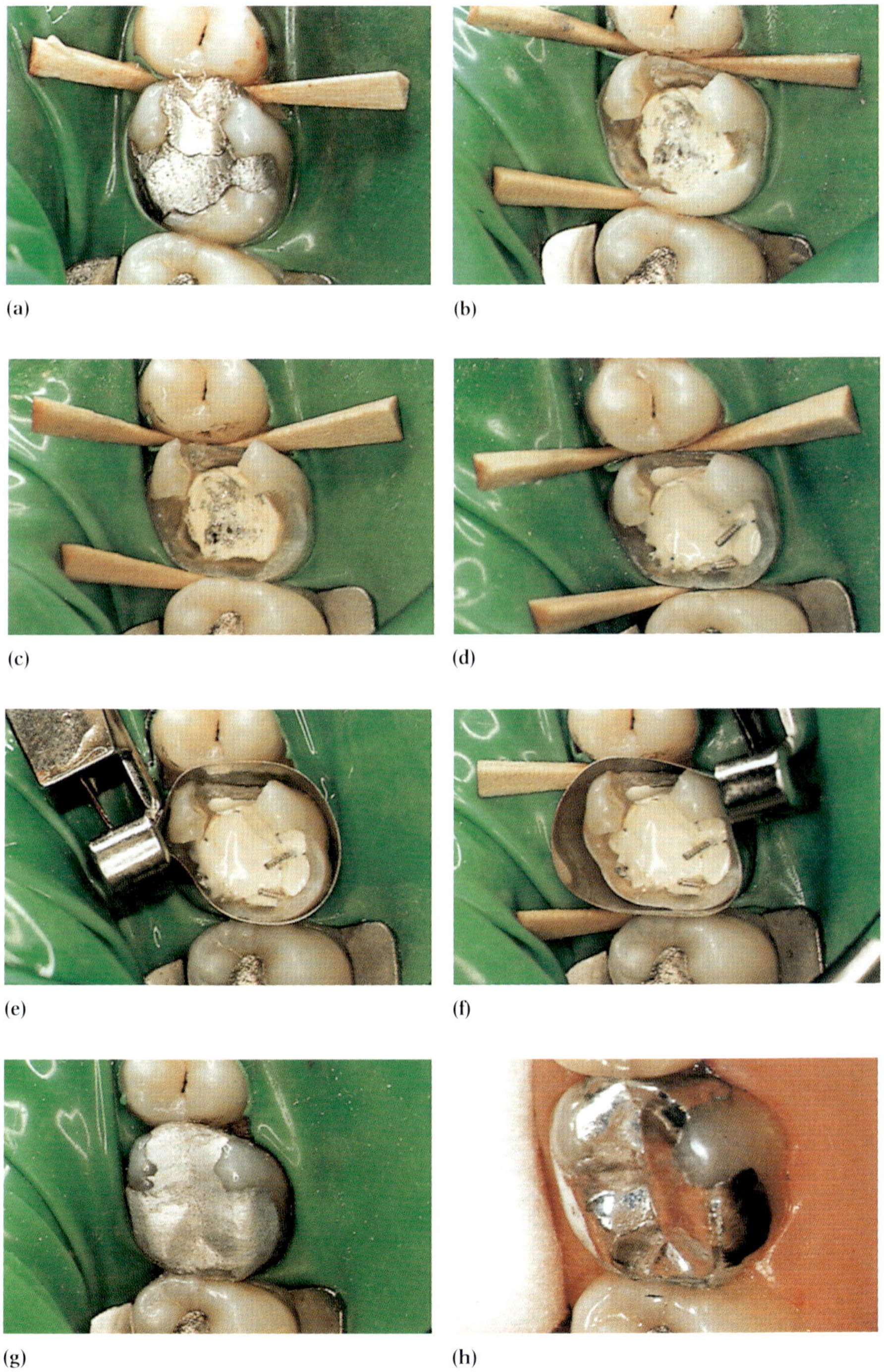

Fig. 8.16 (a) The amalgam in this heavily restored upper first molar is to be replaced. The patient has noticed some discomfort with hot and cold. The tooth is vital and there is no periapical area. A local anaesthetic has been given and a rubber dam placed.
(b) The old restoration is removed. There is caries beneath the enamel–dentine junction distally, but the old lining is left in place because this is a deep cavity and there is no evidence of active caries beneath the lining.
(c) Removal of caries at the enamel–dentine junction distally necessitates removal of overhanging enamel in this area. Loss of this tissue leaves few retentive features in this cavity preparation. For this reason, pins are required.
(d) Three pins are placed to aid retention of the amalgam. They are positioned disto-buccally, disto-palatally, and palatally. The lining is re-covered with fresh material.
(e) A badly placed matrix. There is no room for amalgam between the disto-buccal pin and the matrix band.
(f) The matrix band is reapplied with the retainer lingually. There is now room for amalgam around all the pins and the contact points are burnished. Wedges are in place to prevent an excess of amalgam cervically.
(g) The band is removed and the amalgam carved. The rubber dam must now be removed and the occlusion checked.
(h) At a subsequent visit the amalgam is polished. Note that blue articulating paper has been used to show that this restoration is in occlusion!

crest of the alveolar bone. In these cases, periodontal surgery and removal of some alveolar bone is essential before the tooth can be restored permanently. However, if the margin is just within the gingival crevice, a permanent restoration can be inserted provided that a rubber dam is used to prevent contamination of the filling material with blood, saliva, or crevicular fluid.

Choice of restorative material

The strength of the remaining tooth tissue must be assessed. Undermined enamel in areas of occlusal stress will eventually have to be removed. A decision must be taken as to whether the remaining tooth structure is strong enough to support a restoration, or whether it is weak and must be supported by the restoration. Figure 8.17 shows a first premolar

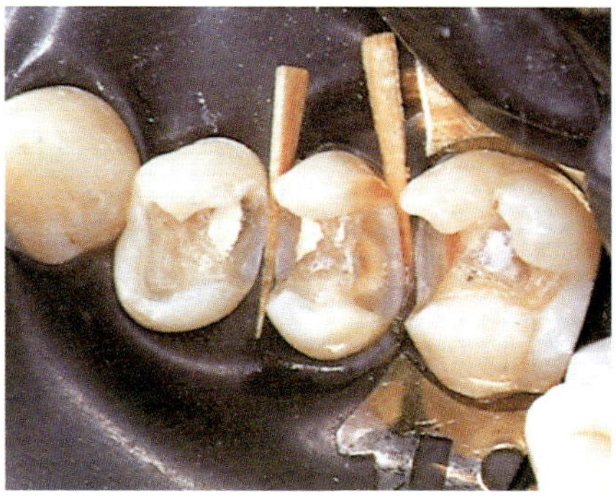

Fig. 8.17 Old amalgam restorations and caries have been removed from three teeth. The first premolar and first molar have cusps judged to be strong enough to support amalgam restorations. However, the cusps of the second premolar are weaker and consideration is given to using cast metal to protect the remaining tooth tissue.

and a molar where the enamel and dentine are strong enough to support amalgam restorations.

However, the cusps of the second premolar have been weakened and, although they are still supported by dentine, they are liable to fracture under occlusal stress. In this tooth, a cast metal restoration should be considered to protect the remaining tooth tissue (see Chapter 11). It is possible to replace or cover weak cusps with amalgam, but an adequate bulk of amalgam (a minimum of 3 mm in height) must be used and this reduction of cusp height produces retention problems.

Figure 7.4 shows an occlusal cavity where the remaining tooth tissue is weak. This cavity, which is completely enclosed in enamel, may best be restored by using adhesive restorative materials which bond to and support the dental tissues. In this case, after placing a proprietary cement containing calcium hydroxide in the deepest parts of the cavity, the missing dentine was replaced with glass ionomer cement. Then a posterior composite was placed after the enamel walls had been acid-etched and bonding resin applied (see Chapter 7). Further possible approaches would be to use composite resin inlays, cured outside the mouth and then cemented, or, alternatively, porcelain inlays (see p. 00).

The following list summarizes the current choice of restorative material and the type of preparation for a badly broken-down posterior tooth:

- amalgam retained by undercuts and other intracoronal retentive features
- amalgam bonded with resins or retained by pins
- posterior composite
- a glass ionomer and posterior composite layered restoration
- a cast metal inlay with cusp protection
- a glass ionomer or composite restoration with a laboratory-processed porcelain or composite resin occlusal surface
- a core of amalgam, retained by pins in a vital tooth or by posts or a Nayyar core in a root-filled tooth, or acid-etch-retained composite core, or glass ionomer core, supporting a crown.

The first five options are considered here; the sixth is a possible option and the final option, the provision of crowns, is beyond the scope of this book.

Bonded amalgam restorations

The principles behind the bonding mechanisms for this type of restoration have been given in Chapter 6. There is a case to be made that all amalgam restorations should be bonded to tooth tissue and this can be made especially strongly when large amalgam cores are acting as a foundation for an overlying cast restoration. The potential advantages of the bonded restoration are the elimination of microbial leakage which may damage the pulp and increased retention of the restoration. The bonding system should only be used in thin layers (Fig. 8.18). It is too early to say if this type of added retention will offer long-term clinical advantages, but fracture of cusps next to non-bonded amalgams and loss of pin-retained restorations are common problems. Clinical trials are needed to compare bonded and conventional restorations. To date there is little clinical evidence for the advantage of the bonded amalgam.

Pin retention for large restorations and cores

Badly broken-down teeth frequently present problems of retention which may be solved by the use of corrosion-resistant pins. This technique imparts considerable stress to the remaining tooth and should only be chosen if other means of retaining a restoration are not possible. Part of the pin is inserted into the dentine while the remainder protrudes into the cavity to be surrounded by the restorative material – often amalgam. Where a large amount of tooth is missing, the number, position, and angle of the pins must be carefully planned. The principle is that it should not be possible to dislodge the restoration in any of the five directions (buccally, lingually, mesially, distally, or occlusally) or at any angle between them. For example, one pin, if it is at an angle to one of the cavity walls, will prevent both occlusal and lateral displacement, but if it cannot be inserted at an angle to a cavity wall, thus creating an undercut, then two pins at an angle to each other will be needed. Often the application of these principles results in one pin being placed for each missing cusp. Thus, where a lingual or buccal wall is missing, two pins might be used. However, one pin per cusp is not a firm rule (Fig. 8.16d). It is a mistake to use more pins than absolutely necessary because they weaken both the tooth and the restoration. However, where a core is being made to support a crown, additional pins may be required to take

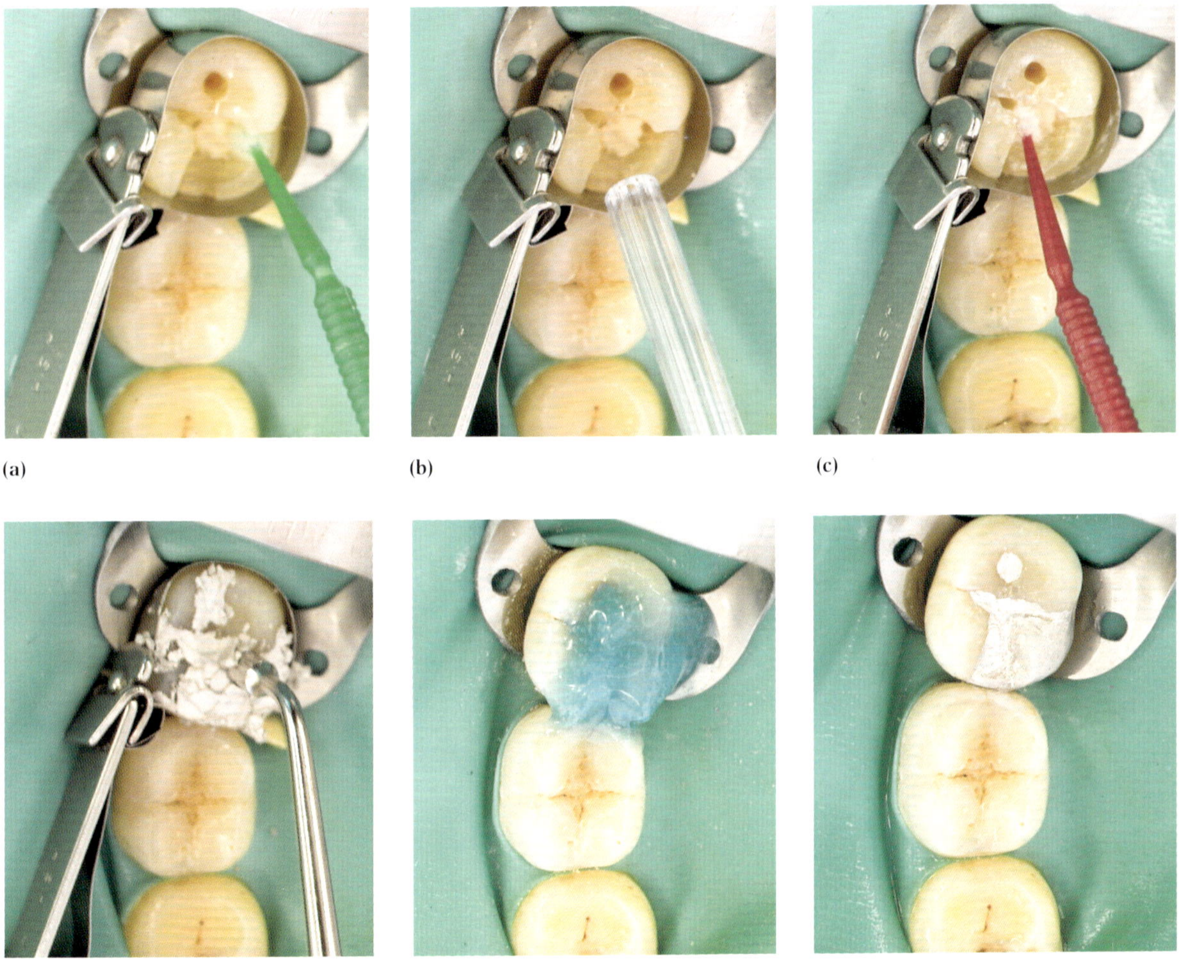

(a) (b) (c)

(d) (e) (f)

Fig. 8.18 (a) Cavity prepared for a bonded amalgam restoration. The mesio-lingual cusp is missing. The extension of the caries into the buccal fissure produces increased retention. A calcium hydroxide cement therapeutic lining has been placed. The self-etching primer is rubbed vigorously into the tooth surface, with plenty of the liquid present. It is left in place for 30 seconds.
(b) The excess primer is either removed with a cotton-wool pledget or blown away. The cavity is thoroughly dried.
(c) A thin film of the adhesive resin-cement is smeared over the cavity surface.
(d) Amalgam is packed rapidly into the unset resin and then carved to the correct contour.
(e) The resin-cement shown is an 'anaerobic adhesive'. This means that it polymerizes when air is excluded. A gel containing a reducing agent is therefore syringed around the margins to cause complete polymerization of the resin-cement. This gel is washed off within a few minutes.
(f) The final restoration.

account of the loss of retention which sometimes results when more tooth is removed in the crown preparation. The operator should mentally superimpose the crown preparation before deciding how many pins are required.

The pinhole should be placed in the greatest bulk of dentine available, but never in the enamel and never at the enamel–dentine junction, as the undermined enamel would break away. Pinholes should be 2–2.5 mm deep, with the diameter ranging from 0.5–0.7 mm according to the make of pin.

Three types of pin have been used historically: cemented pins slightly smaller than the hole prepared for them, smooth friction-retained pins pressed into holes slightly smaller than the pin, and self-tapping threaded pins. The last of these is the most commonly used, convenient, and retentive, and so only this type will be described.

Pin kits are available consisting of a twist drill with a shoulder to control the depth of penetration and a matched, self-tapping, threaded pin (Fig. 8.19). When preparing the pinhole the twist drill must be rotating clockwise, otherwise it will not cut. A low-speed handpiece is used, and it should have good bearings so that the drill does not waver in the head of the handpiece and produce an oversized hole.

The pin must be placed in the dentine and should not perforate either the pulp or the periodontal membrane. When in doubt about the angulation of the pin, it is helpful

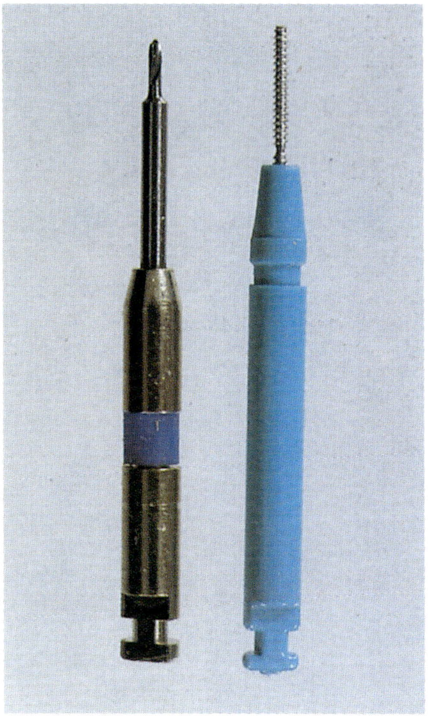

Fig. 8.19 A twist drill with a matched, self-tapping, threaded pin.

to place a flat plastic instrument gently down the outside of the root. A pinhole prepared parallel to this should not perforate either the pulp or the periodontal membrane.

The twist drill is inserted to the shoulder and then removed. The dental nurse should blow away the dentine dust so that the operator can see. The twist drill should never be stalled while cutting the hole because this usually results in breaking the drill. The pin is supplied attached to a disposable latch bur shank, and the low-speed handpiece is used to thread the pin into the hole. It shears at a notch 2–3 mm above the dentine surface.

It is sometimes necessary to shorten the pin with a diamond bur in the air turbine because amalgam 1 mm thick should cover the pin in the finished restoration. Where a crown is to be prepared, the operator should once again mentally superimpose the preparation to ensure that amalgam will remain around the pin after the crown has been prepared. It is sometimes necessary to lean rather than bend the pin inwards to ensure that it will be surrounded by amalgam after crown preparation. Bending pins places great stress on the dentine and may cause microfractures. If a pin is in the way, it is generally preferable to shorten it rather than attempt to put a sharp bend into it.

Occasionally, the pulp may be perforated when a pinhole is being prepared. If this happens, a proprietary cement containing calcium hydroxide should be placed gently down the pinhole with a probe. If symptoms of pulpitis develop or if the pulp becomes necrotic, root canal therapy will be required. If the periodontal membrane is perforated by a pin, it is usually necessary to extend the cavity margin to include the defect. Alternatively, a radio-opaque glass ionomer cement can be used to fill the defect.

Unfortunately, there are many ways in which pins can cause problems during and after the restoration of a broken-down tooth: it is always better to look for alternatives such as adhesive techniques, slots and grooves, and keep the size and number of pins used to the absolute minimum.

Placing the matrix, packing, carving, and finishing

Placing a matrix can be one of the most difficult parts of restoring a badly broken-down tooth. The time taken to achieve a good matrix is well spent, however, because this is critical to the success of the operation.

When placing the matrix it is easy to trap the rubber dam between the matrix band and the tooth. The rubber should be pulled firmly out of the way when placing the band to avoid this. In an attempt to achieve a stable matrix system it is tempting to overtighten the band around the tooth. This may result in a defective contact point or insufficient room for amalgam between the pins and the band (Fig. 8.16e). One way round this problem is to use a matrix system in the form of the band with a tightening screw, but no retainer. The band is sufficiently curved to grip the tooth cervically while flaring out occlusally (Fig. 8.9). An alternative solution to the problem is to use a carefully-wedged conventional matrix retainer and band (Fig. 8.16f), possibly stabilizing it in position with composition.

The matrix band must be slightly higher than the highest cusp to be replaced. It is particularly easy to misjudge this with upper premolar teeth where the cusp tip is well coronal to the marginal ridge.

The help of a dental nurse when placing the amalgam is invaluable. More than one mix of amalgam will be required and a new mix should not be prepared until the operator is ready for it. If this procedure is not observed, the operator will be handling the alloy when it is past its working time. In many dental schools it is currently considered economically unrealistic for dental students to work with a dental nurse at all times. However, when placing a large restoration such assistance is almost mandatory.

Initially, amalgam should be firmly condensed around the pins, taking care to pack amalgam between the pins and the matrix band. The amalgam should cover the pins and finally be overpacked.

Carving is carried out as described previously, with as much as possible being carried out before the matrix band is removed. Before removal the matrix band should be slackened off as much as possible and this should be checked by running a probe around the accessible buccal and lingual parts of the restoration. At the same time, any amalgam that is trapped in the matrix holding/tightening mechanism should be removed, as this can interfere with the easy removal of the band. Once the band is removed, particular care should be taken to ensure that there is no ledge of amalgam cervically (Fig. 8.16g). A sickle scaler pulled along the junction of the amalgam and the tooth is an ideal instrument for removing amalgam. When the rubber dam has been removed, the occlusion is checked with articulating paper and shimstock, and the patient is warned to bite very gently initially. The restoration is finally smoothed with cotton-wool and the patient is asked to avoid chewing hard on that side for a few hours.

The amalgam can be polished at a subsequent appointment (Fig. 8.16h). A carefully-executed pinned amalgam restoration can serve for many years provided that further caries is prevented.

Further reading

McComb, D. (2001). Systematic review of conservative operative management strategies. *J. Dent. Educ.* **65**, 1154–61.

Setcos, J. C., Staninec, M., and Wilson, N. H. F. (1999). The development of resin-bonding for amalgam restorations. *Brit. Dent. J.* **186**, 328–32.

Wassell, R. W., Smart, E. R., and St George, G. (2002). Crowns and other extracoronal restorations: cores for teeth with vital pulps. *Brit. Dent. J.* **192**, 499–509.

9

Treatment of smooth surface caries, erosion–abrasion lesions, and enamel hypoplasia

Treatment of smooth surface caries, erosion–abrasion lesions, and enamel hypoplasia

Smooth surface enamel caries

The buccal pit of lower molar teeth, the palatal groove of upper molars, and the cingulum pits of upper incisor teeth are plaque stagnation areas and are susceptible to caries if the plaque is not regularly disturbed with a fluoride-containing toothpaste in the same way as the occlusal fissures. However, enamel caries occurring elsewhere on the buccal or lingual surfaces is usually a sign of a high caries risk, poor oral hygiene, poor diet, or possibly a dry mouth. These areas are the easiest to keep clean, and caries can be prevented here by good oral hygiene, even in the absence of other preventive measures. This means that when initial enamel lesions occur on the buccal or lingual surfaces, the chances are that there will be extensive caries elsewhere in the mouth and the major emphasis must be on prevention.

With poor oral hygiene, plaque accumulates beneath the maximum bulbosity of the teeth where it is protected to some extent from the action of cheeks and tongue. This may occur in both arches. Therefore smooth surface enamel caries is most common around the necks of the molar and premolar teeth and on the labio-cervical surfaces of the incisors (Fig. 9.1). Caries is rare on the palatal surface of the upper incisor teeth, other than in cingulum pits, and enamel caries is extremely rare on the lingual surface of the lower incisors. It is less common on the labial surface of lower incisors than upper incisors. When there has been a degree of gingival recession, caries often starts at the cement–enamel junction, undermining the enamel.

Where enamel caries is diagnosed at the stage of the white spot lesion, i.e. before cavitation occurs, preventive measures should be used to arrest the lesion. Restoration is indicated only where there is a cavity that hinders plaque control, the pulp is endangered, or the lesion is unsightly. Note that cavitation *per se* is not the indication for a restoration. These lesions are usually cleansable and can be arrested by plaque control alone.

Root caries

Dentine caries on the root of a tooth following gingival recession has a number of characteristics which distinguish it from other types of caries (see Chapter 1, p. 11). It does not need to penetrate enamel and often starts over a large area of the root. It is often circumferential and there may be no distinction between approximal, buccal, and lingual lesions. It is predominantly a disease of older people because gingival recession is more common in this group, but it may occur in younger age groups if roots are exposed. It is sometimes continuous, with caries at the cement–enamel junction undermining the enamel, but does not always spread apically as the gingival margin recedes. New lesions may develop later at the level of the new gingival margin.

Clinically, both active and slowly progressing or arrested lesions can be seen. Active lesions are soft and close to the gingival margin, whereas arrested or slowly progressing lesions are harder and are apparently left abandoned by receding gingival margins in patients with progressive periodontal disease.

Prevention is very important in the management of root caries but may be difficult because it often arises in older people who are having problems in maintaining previously good levels of oral hygiene. In addition, older people are frequently taking medication which depresses salivary flow and this xerostomia makes dental caries more likely. Tranquillizers, antidepressants, antihypertensives, and diuretics all have a xerostomic effect. The feeling of a dry mouth may be alleviated by sucking sweets or taking frequent drinks, many of which are cariogenic. Finally, retirement, bereavement, or illness may result in dietary changes which favour caries.

Early diagnosis is very important so that the dentist can help the patient to find the cause of the root caries and prevent its progression. Plaque control, dietary advice, and topical fluorides are all important in the management of the disease. The aim should be to arrest the lesion so that, over time, a soft area of active root caries becomes hard.

Smoothing and polishing the softened root surface may sometimes assist plaque control and favour lesion arrest. Such areas do not require restorations unless there is an aesthetic problem.

However, a cavitated lesion may endanger the pulp, may be sensitive, and may hinder plaque control. In these cases a restoration is indicated.

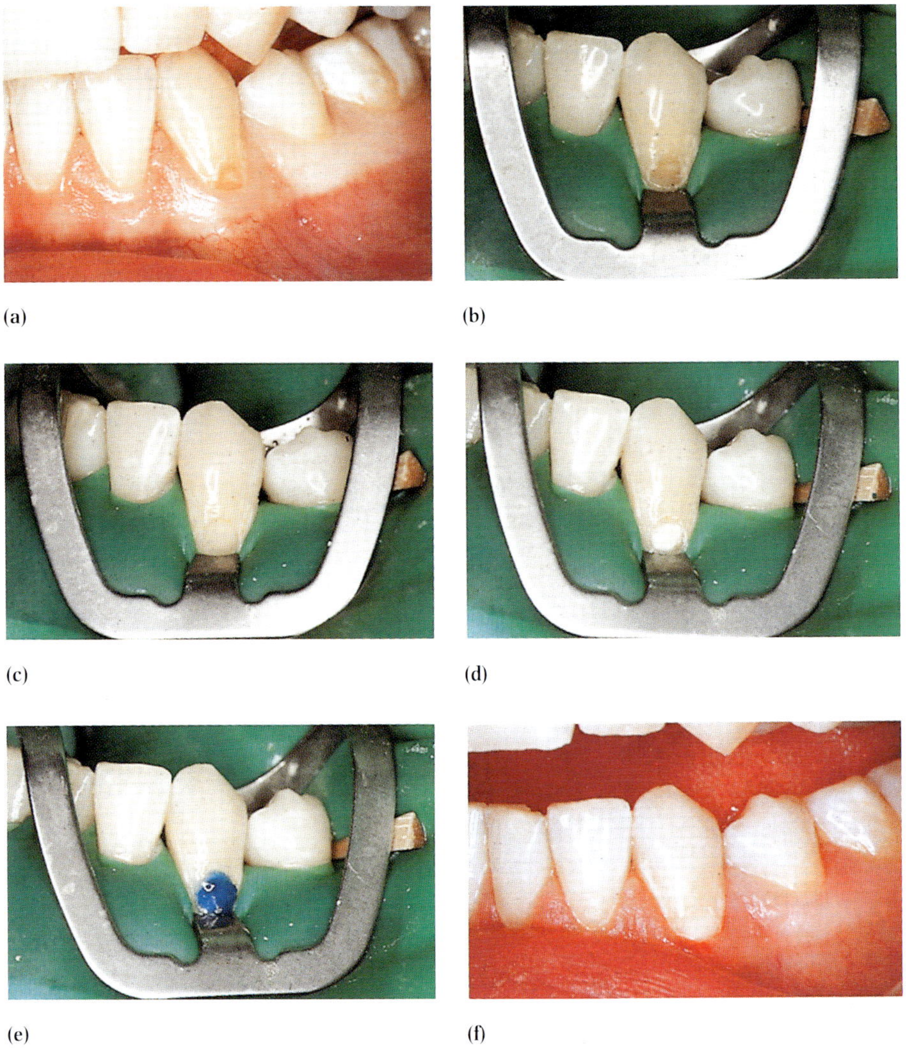

Fig. 9.1 (a) Caries at the gingival margin of the lower canine tooth.
(b) The lesion isolated with a rubber dam using a clamp to retract the gingival margin sufficiently to expose the entire lesion.
(c) Caries has been removed with a steel bur at low speed. There are no natural undercuts but enamel is still present gingivally.
(d) Cavity lined with calcium hydroxide lining material.
(e) Acid-etching gel placed.
(f) The tooth restored with composite immediately after the removal of the rubber dam.

Restoration of free smooth surface carious lesions (both enamel and root caries)

Access to caries

Compared with the lesions described in Chapters 7 and 8, access is much easier. Some lesions affect a wide surface area and problems of access are associated with the surrounding structures rather than the lesions themselves. Access to cervical caries on the buccal surface of upper second and third molars is hindered by the coronoid process of the mandible when the mouth is opened widely. This is a common site for caries because access for the toothbrush is also restricted. A miniature handpiece head and miniature burs may be used, and it is easier to position the head of the handpiece if these lesions are treated with the mouth partly closed.

There is a similar problem with access to the lingual surface of the lower molar teeth when the tongue is large and active. The problem here is mainly to keep a dry field. A rubber dam can be difficult to place. If it is possible to get the rubber dam down below the lesion, it should be placed over teeth right around to the other side of the arch so that the rubber is stretched away from the lingual surface of the tooth to be treated. If it comes straight up from the lingual side of the clamp, it obstructs the handpiece head. If a rub-

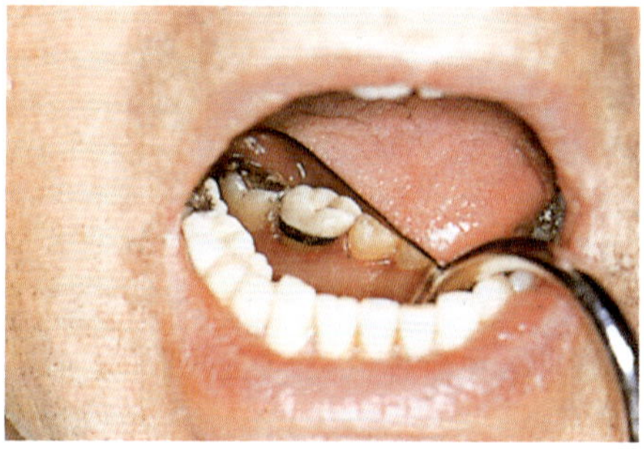

Fig. 9.2 A flanged saliva ejector in place. This retracts and protects the tongue and floor of the mouth. Its polished surface also acts as a mirror and can help the dentist to see.

ber dam cannot be placed, a large flanged saliva ejector can be used to aspirate saliva, retract the tongue, and retract and protect the floor of the mouth (see Figs. 4.8 and 9.2).

Removal of caries

In removing caries from smooth surfaces it is often difficult to know where to start and where to stop. The following will help the decision.

- A white or brown spot lesion can be arrested by preventive means (plaque control; fluoride application in the form of toothpaste, mouth-rinse, or varnish; dietary analysis and advice) and a restoration is not required.
- The rationale for restorative management, in addition to prevention, is to restore the integrity of the tooth surface to aid plaque control, to protect the pulp, and to improve appearance.

Thus, caries removal should start in the area of cavitation and the preparation can often be undertaken with round steel burs in the low-speed handpiece (Figs. 9.1b and c). The white spot lesion will often extend widely around the tooth, sometimes including the approximal surface, but if the area has not cavitated it should not normally be removed.

Similarly, in removing root caries it is often difficult to know where to stop. Large areas of the root surface are often discoloured or softened. Soft dentine should be removed, but hard stained dentine should be left even when it is adjacent to an area which is to be restored. There is a temptation to feel that while one is restoring the tooth it might be as well to tidy up the whole of the affected area, but this is unnecessary and can lead to very large cavities which are difficult, if not impossible, to restore.

When using a round bur to remove carious dentine on the root surface, the bur should be kept at about 45° to the tooth surface because the side of the bur cuts more efficiently than the end. Since these lesions are often circumferential this will mean continually reorientating the head of the handpiece. It is possible to improve control of the handpiece by guiding the head of the handpieces with the left hand (right hand for left-handed operators). It is important to remember not to cut too deeply because the root canal is easily exposed. This is particularly likely in root caries because reparative dentine forms at the pulpal ends of the affected tubules. Since the tubules run cervically in this area, reparative dentine is more apically placed than might be expected.

Another way of removing the soft infected dentine is to scoop it away with excavators. It is gentler for the patient, it is usually painless because the tubules are blocked by sclerotic dentine, and it is self-limiting. Using a bur it is easy to over-cut. A gel, based on sodium hypochlorite-buffered amino acids, can be used to soften the demineralized dentine before using instruments designed to be handled with a scraping action.

Choice of restorative material

Once the caries has been removed there is often a wide shallow cavity with no natural undercuts (Fig. 9.1c). The following restorative materials can be used:

- resin composite, polyacid-modified composite
- glass ionomer cement, resin-modified cement.

When all the walls of the cavity are in enamel an acid-etch-retained composite is a logical choice. Further cavity preparation is not needed unless an additional area is thought necessary for acid-etch retention. In this case, the enamel margins can be bevelled, and this bevelling also has the effect of blending the appearance of the composite restoration into the remainder of the enamel. A resin composite is a particularly good choice where appearance is important, and in this case a material with filler particles below 0.6 μm would be chosen because the smaller filler particles allow the material to be polished and maintain its shine.

The type of composite chosen will depend mainly upon the handling properties required. As an example, some of the composites that are marketed for use in occlusal/proximal cavities are quite viscous and stiff, enabling a certain amount of 'packing' in enclosed cavities. Whilst these materials may have a good appearance and wear well, they are more difficult to apply in thin layers to the open surfaces of more accessible teeth. It is therefore appropriate to select slightly more fluid composites that allow easier sculpting and building. Some of these are also supplied in a greater shade range along with various opacities and translucencies of dentine and enamel to better mimic the appearance of the natural tooth. The shade of the restoration should be selected before treatment as the tooth will become lighter as it dries out. Manufacturers will sometimes provide a model of a tooth built with the composite material(s) or, alternatively, pieces of the same material at various thicknesses. If the requirements for an excellent colour match are very demanding, then a trial shade matching of a small amount

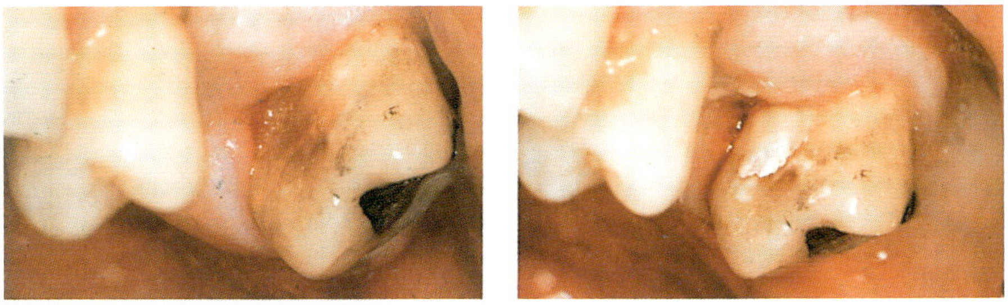

(a) (b)

Fig. 9.3 Restoration of root caries with glass ionomer cement.
(a) The root caries was assessed as active, but the small enamel lesion of the mesial surface was considered to be arrested. Cavity preparation will remove all soft dentine. Hard but stained dentine will be retained and the arrested enamel lesion will not be included in the preparation (see p. 00).
(b) Immediately after restoring with glass ionomer cement. The rubber dam has just been removed. Further finishing will be carried out at a subsequent visit when the glass ionomer cement has fully matured. (Reproduced by courtesy of Mr N. L. Fisher.)

of composite cured – but not bonded – to the tooth may help to decide the shade. Composite materials normally change shade once polymerized.

In root caries the material of choice will depend upon the amount of control that the clinician can apply to the local environment. If the operating field is particularly difficult to keep dry then a glass ionomer cement (Fig. 9.3), or a closely-related material such as a resin-modified glass ionomer cement, would be an appropriate choice. This is because these materials are water-based; they are self-adhesive and release fluoride which may have a cariostatic effect. Composite may not be ideal if there are difficulties in maintaining absolute moisture control – dentine bonding agents are very unforgiving in this respect. Due to their improved moisture tolerance, polyacid-modified composites may be an appropriate choice for these types of cavity.

When restoring a very deep cavity, it is possible to use a resin-modified GIC in a layered technique (see Chapters 7 and 8), and to place both the glass ionomer and the composite materials at the same visit. Initially, the glass ionomer is placed and light-cured. The cavity is now redeveloped in the cement to allow sufficient room for a laminate of composite. Sound enamel walls are exposed to allow use of the acid-etch technique with a resin-based bonding system. Resin-modified GIC contains sufficient free radicals in the resin component to obtain a chemical union with the overlying composite.

Lining

Only deep carious cavities, particularly in young patients, should be lined with a calcium hydroxide lining material (Fig. 9.1d) when it is indicated as a therapeutic material in an indirect or direct pulp cap (see Chapter 3).

Applying the matrix and placing the restoration

Resin composite

The cavity is etched, washed, and dried and the bonding resin is applied. The manufacturer's instructions should be followed carefully with respect to etching and washing times, amount of drying needed, and whether air-thinning of the resin is advised.

Most modern composites, whether marketed for anterior or posterior use, have broadly comparable wear rates and exhibit similar amounts of shrinkage. The composite material must be adequately light-cured. Increments of material should be less than 2 mm thick. The air-inhibited surface layer of composite (see Chapters 4 and 6) will ensure good bonding between one increment and the next, but care must be taken to ensure that there is no contamination by water, blood, saliva, or crevicular fluid between increments.

Most dentists insert these restorations freehand, but if a matrix is required a mylar strip is wrapped around the tooth, passing through both contact points. It is then pulled up against the gingival margin of the preparation contouring the restorative material cervically. A cervical wedge will help to reduce any risk of a cervical overhang and help stabilize the matrix. Any excess is left on the occlusal side of the cavity, and this can be removed once the material has set.

Glass ionomer cement

The dentine conditioning agent supplied with the material (10 per cent polyacrylic acid) should be applied to the cavity for 10 seconds and then the cavity should be thoroughly washed and dried.

Having selected the appropriate shade of glass ionomer cement, the material is mixed and placed in one increment and a matrix may be applied. Once the material has set, the matrix is removed and the filling is immediately protected with a layer of light-cured bonding resin. This prevents both the filling drying out and moisture contamination of the newly set material. At this stage gross excess can be removed with a sharp carving instrument and the margin again covered with a light-cured bonding resin.

When a resin-modified glass ionomer material is chosen and where the set is initiated by light-curing, any matrix

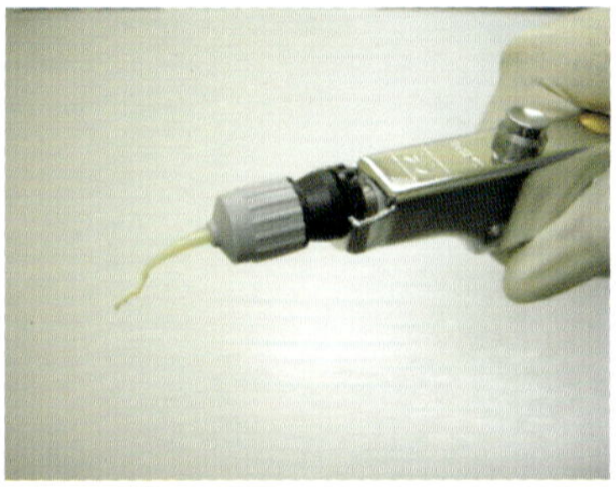

Fig. 9.4 A GIC capsule and gun.

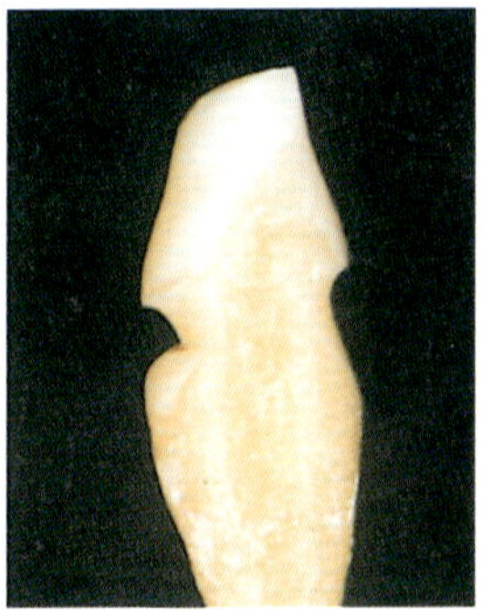

Fig. 9.5 A sharply outlined V-shaped notch in the buccal surface of this extracted lower canine tooth. There is also a similar lingual defect but the aetiology of this is not clear. However, it seems likely that they have some common aetiology and therefore incorrect tooth-brushing alone is unlikely to be the cause.

must allow transmission of light. A capsulated material is easy to handle because the material can be injected directly into the cavity (Fig. 9.4) and the matrix can be adapted. The manufacturer's instructions should be followed with respect to curing time and depth of cure. In deeper cavities incremental build-up will be required, with each increment being light-cured before the next is added. These materials require protection with a layer of light-cured bonding resin to preserve water balance once the matrix is removed. Some glass ionomers are viscous and packable. These are particularly convenient to use for smooth surface restorations. They may be placed and sculpted freehand, without a matrix, but it is helpful to put bonding resin on the packing instrument. This serves two functions; it prevents the cement sticking to the instrument and protects the glass ionomer material. It should be light-cured when the restoration has been contoured.

Finishing

A high polish is particularly important on smooth surface restorations because plaque retention on the surface and around the margins can encourage further caries or gingival inflammation. In addition, the tongue and lips are sensitive to rough surfaces, particularly on the anterior teeth.

Composite restorations can be finished as soon as they have polymerized. Ledges can be removed with a fine, flame-shaped, 12-bladed tungsten carbide bur in the air turbine handpiece, or alternatively diamond composite finishing burs can be used at high or low speed. Great care must be taken not to damage the tooth tissue around the filling. A series of composite finishing discs can then be used, and it is important to complete the process with the very finest of these to ensure that the filling is as smooth as possible. However, unworn natural teeth can have quite a marked texture due to incremental growth lines (perikymata) and these can be reproduced using appropriately oriented grooves. The final polish of this textured surface can be produced using polishing pastes.

Conventional glass ionomer cement restorations should not finally be finished for 24 hours (Fig. 9.3b). However, resin-modified light-cured materials have the advantage that they can be finished immediately. If care has been taken with the use of the matrix, minimal finishing is required. Multi-bladed tungsten carbide or diamond burs can be used at low speed to remove any ledges and the restoration finally smoothed with discs. The filling should be protected with a light-cured bonding resin.

It is difficult to avoid some minor trauma to the gingival margin while placing and finishing a cervical restoration. At a subsequent visit it is important to check that the gingival margin is healthy and that there are no areas of plaque retention.

Erosion–abrasion lesions

These occur predominantly on the buccal and labial surfaces of teeth, but may also occur lingually (see Chapter 1 and Fig. 9.5). They are usually seen in one of two forms: a sharply outlined V-shaped notch (Fig. 1.42b, p. 23) or a saucer-shaped lesion with rounded margins (Figs. 1.42a and 9.6). The V-shaped notches occur at the level of the cement–enamel junction and appear to be more common when there has been a degree of gingival recession. It is assumed that the defect starts primarily in the dentine, but enamel is also lost. Saucer-shaped defects occur anywhere on the buccal or labial surface but mostly at the necks of the teeth. They have a variety of shapes, and one common and unexplained variation is a groove running vertically up the buccal surface of the tooth (Fig. 9.6).

The aetiology of the lesions is unclear, and it has been assumed by some that vigorous tooth-brushing may be relevant although there is little evidence to support this. It is likely that chemical erosion also plays an important role. With this lack of understanding of aetiology it is difficult to prescribe logical treatment. If the aetiology is primarily chemical erosion, the wisdom of restoring the lesion at all must be questioned. The restoration will not prevent further erosion occurring around the margins. Indeed, it is not unreasonable to suggest that the progress of the lesion may be accelerated as a result of chemical action in the deep

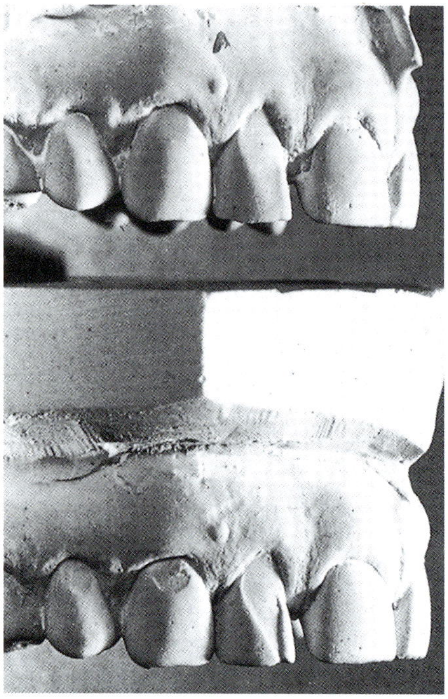

Fig. 9.6 Two study casts from the same patient taken three years apart. The upper cast shows defects starting on the lateral incisor and at the necks of the canine and first premolar teeth. In the lower cast these defects are all much deeper and better defined. The aetiology is unknown.

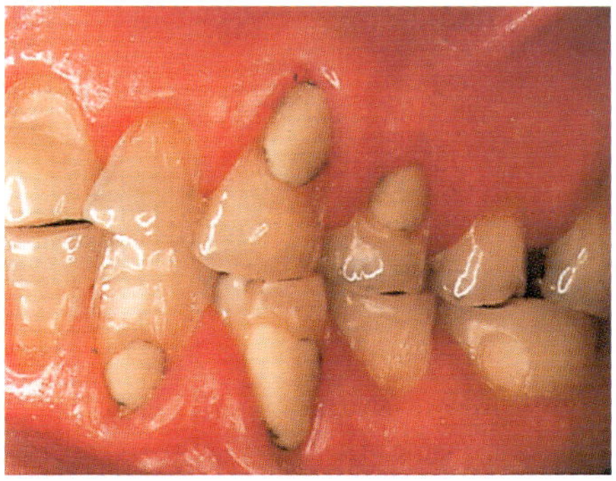

(a)

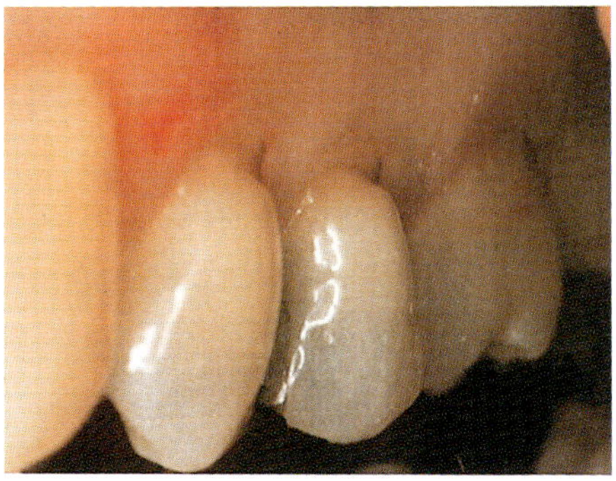

(b)

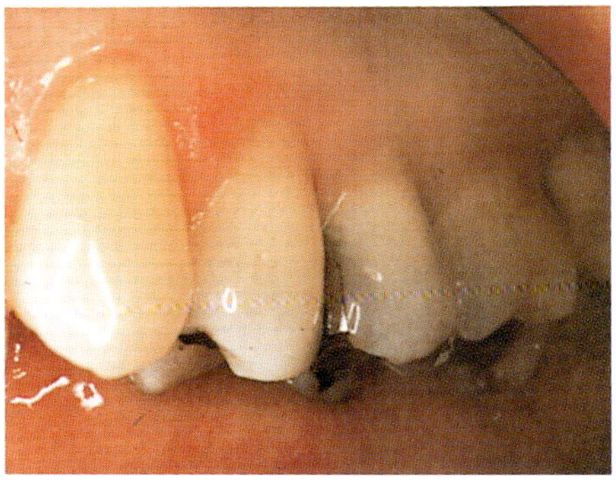

(c)

Fig. 9.7 (a) A number of restorations presumably placed to treat erosion–abrasion cervical lesions. They have been unsuccessful in preventing further tooth wear around the restorations.
(b) Cervical notch-shaped lesions.
(c) The lesions were restored with the layered technique using glass ionomer cement and composite and this photograph was taken three years after the restorations were placed. No further wear has occurred and so it is likely that the aetiology (which was unknown) is no longer present.

narrow fissures around the restoration (Fig. 9.7a). Thus an unrestored wide shallow lesion may be less likely to progress. If the aetiology is not understood, prevention is likely to be ineffective and so the prognosis of many restorations placed in cervical 'erosion–abrasion' lesions is poor.

For these reasons, a carefully considered decision must be made as to whether or not to restore a cervical 'erosion–abrasion' lesion. There are three main reasons for placing a restoration:

- The area is sensitive and the sensitivity cannot be controlled by other means.
- The patient is concerned about the appearance of the lesion or has practical problems, such as food catching in the defect.
- The lesion is continuing to progress, and in particular is deepening, prejudicing the strength of the tooth and/or pulp vitality.

Sensitivity is surprisingly uncommon with the deeper lesions, presumably because of the defence reactions of the pulp–dentine complex, tubular sclerosis within the dentine, and reactionary dentine at the pulpal surface. Early shallower cavities are often more sensitive and yet are not sufficiently deep to restore. In any case restorations do not reliably reduce sensitivity in these cases. Management should be aimed at encouraging more rapid deposition of reactionary dentine and coagulation of the ends of the dentinal processes. This is achieved (sometimes only slowly) by the application of desensitizing toothpastes or varnishes (which contain fluoride) and by fluoride mouth-rinses. Sealing the dentine with a bonding agent has been shown to be successful in some cases.

In the absence of a good reason for restoring the tooth, it is better to leave the lesion alone and continue to monitor it, intervening when one of the conditions above begins to apply. Intervention that is too early is likely to lead to repeated replacement restorations with a reduction rather than an improvement in the long-term prognosis of the tooth.

Choice of restorative material for erosion–abrasion lesions

The choice of material will depend on the known or assumed aetiology. If the aetiology is thought to be primarily erosion and it is decided that a restoration is necessary, either a glass ionomer cement or a dentine bonded composite restoration could be chosen. If abrasion (physical wear) is regarded as the most important cause of the lesion, the restorative material must be capable of withstanding abrasive forces and resin composite is preferred to glass ionomer cement.

At present, the most cost-effective solution is to use composite, and to replace the surface layer from time to time as necessary. In contrast with restorations involving the occlusal surface, wear does not potentially alter the occlusion and so this 'wear and repair' approach is acceptable.

Cavity preparation, lining, and filling

Most erosion–abrasion lesions do not require cavity preparation because tooth wear has produced a shape which can be filled with an adhesive material without further destruction of the tooth. The V-shaped groove is a good example of this (Fig. 9.7b and c). Any carious dentine within the lesion should be excavated or removed with a round bur at low speed.

Deep, sensitive erosion–abrasion lesions may need a therapeutic lining containing calcium hydroxide. Where glass ionomer cement is to be used and no cavity preparation has been necessary, the polyacrylic acid conditioning solution supplied by the manufacturer should be used. This removes pellicle and facilitates the adhesion of the material. It is applied to the cavity on a small pledget of cotton-wool and washed off after 10 seconds.

Matrices and filling techniques are the same as those described for the restoration of carious cavities.

Enamel hypoplasia

In contrast with caries and erosion–abrasion lesions, enamel hypoplasia does not progress. Therefore it is not necessary to restore the tooth in order to treat a disease process, but fillings are sometimes required to improve appearance. For this reason these teeth are usually restored in young patients, and the type of restoration will depend on the extent of the lesion. When the entire surface of several teeth is affected, as in fluorosis, one of the veneering techniques (see Chapter 10) or a crown is used. Composite veneers are described in the next section, porcelain veneers in Chapter 11, and crowns are not included in this book. With localized lesions, a more conservative approach is to prepare a shallow cavity and place a composite restoration (Fig. 9.8).

Summary of the choice of restorative materials for smooth surface lesions

With the developments in adhesive restorative materials, amalgam now has virtually no place in the restoration of the initial smooth surface lesions described in this chapter. The wear resistance and excellent appearance of composites, in conjunction with the improved reliability of adhesives, favour their use where moisture control is good. Glass ionomer cement is the preferred choice in root caries where the local operative environment may be difficult to control.

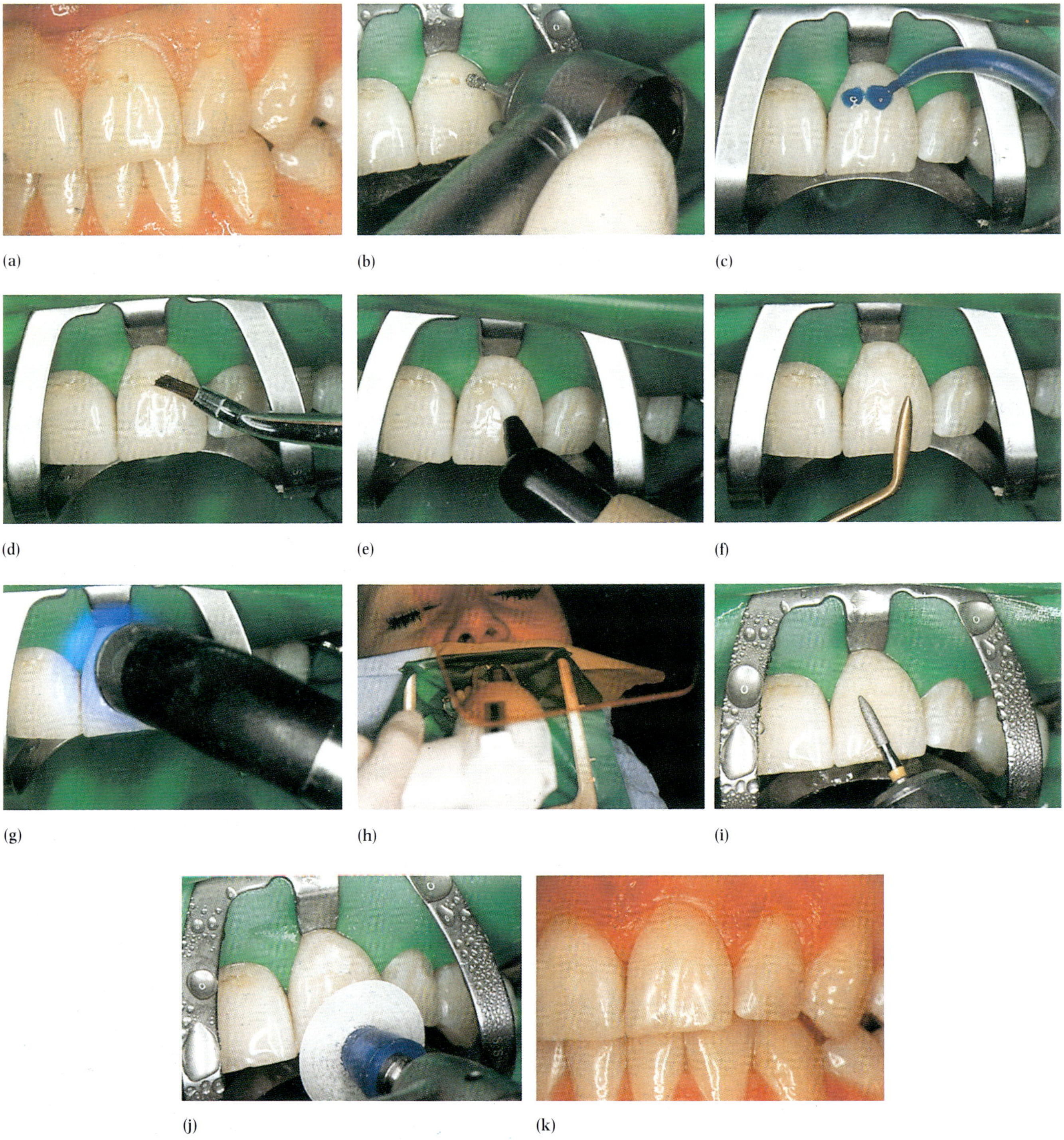

Fig. 9.8 (a) Enamel hypoplasia on the buccal surface of the upper central incisor teeth.
(b) Shallow saucer-shaped cavities being prepared within the enamel using a diamond bur.
(c) Acid-etching gel being applied with a syringe.
(d) The etched surface being coated with bonding resin.
(e) Composite being applied from a capsule in a dispensing gun.
(f) A titanium nitride instrument being used to shape the composite.
(g) The composite being light-cured.
(h) An orange protective shield in place to protect the eyes of the operator and dental nurse.
(i) A fine composite finishing diamond being used to shape the restoration.
(j) A finishing disc mounted on a plastic stub being used in the handpiece.
(k) The completed restoration.

10

Treatment of approximal caries, trauma, developmental disorders, and discoloration in anterior teeth

Conditions affecting anterior teeth which may need restorations
- Approximal caries
- Approximal caries which also involves the incisal edge
- Trauma
- Developmental disorders
- Discoloured teeth
- Tooth wear

Treatment options
- Uses and limitations of anterior composite materials
- Retention of composite to dentine
- Porcelain veneers

Examples of anterior restorations
- Restoration of approximal caries in an anterior tooth
- Composite restorations involving the incisal edge
- Veneering techniques for hypoplastic and discoloured teeth

Bleaching discoloured anterior teeth

Treatment of approximal caries, trauma, developmental disorders, and discoloration in anterior teeth

Conditions affecting anterior teeth which may need restorations

Smooth surface caries, which affects the labial surfaces of anterior teeth but rarely the palatal or lingual surfaces, was dealt with in Chapter 9.

The other conditions affecting anterior teeth are as follows:

- approximal caries
- approximal caries which also involves the incisal edge
- trauma
- developmental disorders
- discoloured teeth
- tooth wear.

Approximal caries

Enamel caries starts on the approximal surface of anterior teeth just gingival to the contact area. It is less common than pit and fissure caries or caries in the approximal surfaces of posterior teeth. This is because the anterior teeth are more accessible for cleaning and the contact area is narrower. Caries may be more likely to occur when the teeth are crowded and overlapping because this increases the difficulty in cleaning between them.

It is difficult to diagnosis early enamel caries at the white spot lesion stage, and so when a patient presents with established caries into dentine in one or more anterior teeth it is possible that the other contact areas have early enamel lesions. For this reason preventive treatment is important, including suitable dietary advice, the use of fluoride supplements (toothpaste, rinses, and varnishes), and teaching the patient to use dental floss interproximally.

Dentine caries can usually be seen by transilluminating the tooth, either with light reflected from the mouth mirror (Fig. 10.1) or by a fibre-optic light (Fig. 1.33). Transillumination is more effective with anterior than posterior teeth because they are thinner. If dentine caries is visible then it is usually too late for a 'prevent and observe' approach; a restoration is needed.

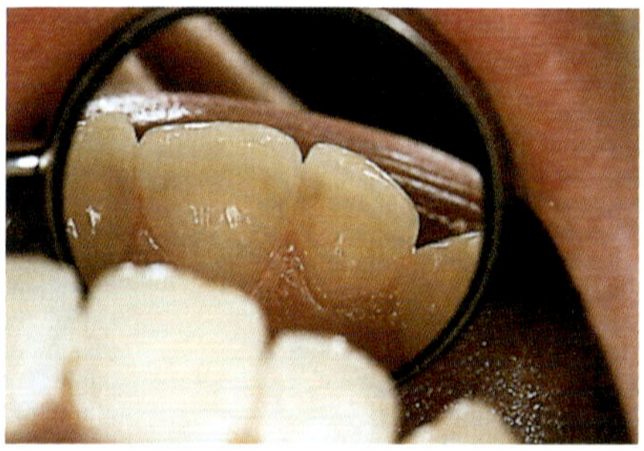

Fig. 10.1 Caries in dentine on the mesial aspect of an upper lateral incisor. The lesion is viewed in the dental mirror and is more obvious because light is passing through the tooth (trans-illumination).

Approximal caries which also involves the incisal edge

A neglected carious lesion, or secondary caries around an approximal restoration, may undermine the enamel of the incisal edge to the point where the corner of the incisor breaks away under occlusal forces. Dentine caries balloons out in all directions from its approximal origin and by the time that it undermines incisal enamel it is often close to, or already affecting, the pulp. The diagnosis of the caries is straightforward, but a vitality test and periapical radiograph are required to access any pulpal involvement and/or spread of infection into the periapical tissues.

Trauma

Accidental damage to teeth has one of the following effects (see Chapter 1):

- fracture of the incisal edge involving enamel only
- fracture involving enamel and dentine
- fracture involving enamel, dentine, and pulp
- root fracture
- cracks in the crown of the tooth without loss of enamel
- no visible damage but damage to the pulp or its blood supply, leading in the long term to pulp necrosis
- partial or complete luxation of the tooth.

The restoration of enamel and dentine fractures will be dealt with here; the other conditions are beyond the scope of this book. A broken incisal corner involving the incisal edge and parts of the approximal surfaces is treated rather similarly to approximal caries which involves the incisal edge.

Developmental disorders

In Chapter 9 small areas of enamel hypoplasia were considered, and the treatment technique described involved preparation of the tooth and the insertion of a shallow restoration. In this chapter, larger areas of hypoplasia or discoloration will be discussed. The techniques described are also suitable for other malformations, including diminutive or peg-shaped teeth.

Discoloured teeth

Several development disorders result in discoloured teeth. However, a common cause of a single discoloured tooth is pulp necrosis, where the breakdown products of haemoglobin discolour the dentine. A bleaching technique to improve the appearance of such teeth will be described in this chapter.

Tooth wear

Smooth surface tooth wear was dealt with in Chapter 9 (p. 00). Tooth wear involving the incisal edges will be discussed here. With modern diets, teeth do not wear appreciably at their approximal surfaces, although this did happen with primitive man.

Treatment options

Composite resin materials came into general use in the late 1960s and early 1970s. This produced a revolution in the restoration of anterior teeth, allowing procedures to be undertaken using the acid-etch retention technique that were impossible with any previous material. Today, with the added versatility of light-curing materials, many anterior teeth which would previously have been treated by crowns or extractions can be restored simply.

Uses and limitations of anterior composite materials

Provided that the occlusion is favourable, virtually the entire crown of an anterior tooth can be built up with composite, at least as a short to medium-term restoration. This means that the majority of teeth with approximal caries, caries or trauma affecting the incisal edge, and many of the developmental disorders can be treated with composite alone. Tooth wear affecting the incisal edges of lower teeth is less successfully treated with composite since it tends to break off.

Composite materials for anterior teeth are available in a variety of shades and in more opaque or more translucent versions. With large restorations it may well be necessary to use more than one shade to produce gradual colour changes across the surface of a tooth to match adjacent teeth (see Chapter 9).

Retention of composite to dentine

Anterior composite material should always be retained to the enamel by the acid-etch technique and intermediate adhesive resin, even if the cavity is naturally undercut. This increases the marginal seal and reduces staining at the margins.

Prior to the use of adhesive techniques the traditional method of retention was by means of retentive grooves and/or pins; the former may naturally be produced in cutting the cavity, the latter are generally best avoided for tooth-coloured adhesive restorations. A pin to support and retain composite replacing a broken incisal corner may produce some discoloration in the composite, whilst their insertion carries some risk to the pulp and does not increase retention as much as a carefully executed bonding technique. The only use for pins with composite restorations is in the treatment of elderly patients where the clinical crown has snapped off and the root canal is completely sclerosed, preventing successful root canal treatment. Pins are completely contraindicated for glass ionomer cements as they increase local stresses in the cement and lead to its premature failure.

Dentine bonding agents have been available for several years and are showing favourable medium to long-term results.

Porcelain veneers

Porcelain veneers are cemented with composite resin to cover all or part of the labial surface of an anterior tooth. Porcelain has been used for crowns for over a century and is a very satisfactory restorative dental material in that it maintains its colour and surface gloss and is compatible with soft tissues.

Indications for porcelain veneers are where one or a number of anterior teeth are discoloured or misshapen in such a way that it is necessary to cover the entire labial surface to disguise the problem and yet the other surfaces are sound. The advantage of porcelain over a composite veneer is that it is more durable in terms of colour and surface gloss, although it is more likely to fracture. The advantage of a porcelain veneer over a crown is that the tooth preparation is more conservative and also, because the palatal surfaces of upper incisor teeth are not prepared, the occlusion is not affected. However, some reduction of the labial surface is usually necessary and so the procedure is not reversible. The restorations are time-consuming and involve laboratory costs which are often as high per tooth as the cost of a crown. If the tooth being covered is very darkly stained, the thin veneer does not sufficiently disguise the colour and so it has to be made more opaque. For these reasons porcelain veneers have by no means replaced crowns and are unlikely to do so. However, they form a useful addition to the operative dentist's techniques. Brief details of the technique for making porcelain veneers are given in Chapter 11 (p. 00).

Examples of anterior restorations

To illustrate the principles of restoring anterior teeth, a number of examples will be described which have wide application in similar situations. There is considerable variety in the design of anterior restorations, and so the concept of an 'ideal' cavity preparation is even less true for anterior teeth than it is for posterior teeth. The approach must always be one of 'problem solving', bearing in mind the basic principles described earlier:

- gain access (if necessary)
- remove caries (if any)
- design the restoration, including its retention, for the restorative material chosen
- complete the preparation
- place the restoration
- finish and monitor.

Restoration of approximal caries in an anterior tooth

Isolation

Many approximal cavities in anterior teeth are close to the gingival margin. This is because caries develops just apical to the contact area and, unless there has been gingival recession, the gingival papilla reaches almost to the contact point. For this reason it is often necessary to retract the gingival papilla in order to avoid the restoration becoming contaminated by blood or gingival exudate. Therefore a rubber dam should be used in most cases, and a wedge or a floss ligature is a convenient way to retract the rubber and the underlying gingival papilla (see p. 85).

Access to the caries

In most caries, access is through the palatal or lingual surface. When the teeth are in good alignment and the thickness of enamel overlying the caries is roughly similar labially and lingually, it is better to leave the sound labial enamel because it will maintain its appearance better than the restoration. In addition, if access is gained from the labial side, leaving only a thin layer of enamel palatally, there is a risk that the palatal enamel may fracture if this area is subject to occlusal forces.

Exceptions to this are where the teeth are overlapping and the caries is much closer to the labial than the palatal or lingual side (Fig. 10.2). A typical approximal lesion in well-aligned teeth is shown in Fig. 10.3a and b and the access cavity is shown in Fig. 10.3c. Access is gained by a small round diamond or tungsten carbide bur using the air turbine, and the same instrument is used to remove carious enamel (Fig. 10.3d).

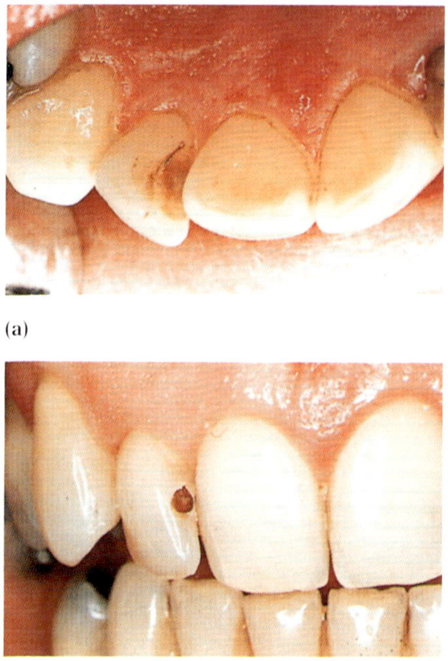

(a)

(b)

Fig. 10.2 (a) Overlapping incisor teeth with caries in the mesial surface of the lateral incisor. Access from the lingual side would be very difficult. (b) Access has been gained from the buccal surface.

Removing the caries

Dentine caries is removed at low speed with a round steel bur (Fig. 10.3e). In this situation, caries in dentine is almost hemispherical in outline. The enamel–dentine junction is cleared first, and then residual caries is removed from the pulpal aspect of the cavity until either it is all removed or a decision is made to leave firm stained dentine close to the pulp. In larger lesions, caries spreading along the enamel–dentine junction leads to decalcified enamel on the inner aspect, although the outer surface is sound. Although this enamel is thin and unsupported by dentine, if it is on the labial surface it is well worth keeping for aesthetic reasons. It also increases retention of the restoration when it is acid-etched on its inner aspect. A caries-free cavity is shown in Fig. 10.3f.

Designing the cavity and producing retention

Often, little more preparation is necessary at this stage. Many small and moderate-sized lesions are naturally undercut. However, sufficient retention for composite is achieved by acid-etching enamel and dentine whether or not undercuts are present, and so it is not necessary to produce an undercut cavity deliberately. Usually there is a sufficiently large area of enamel, often on the inner aspect, for acid-etch retention. In

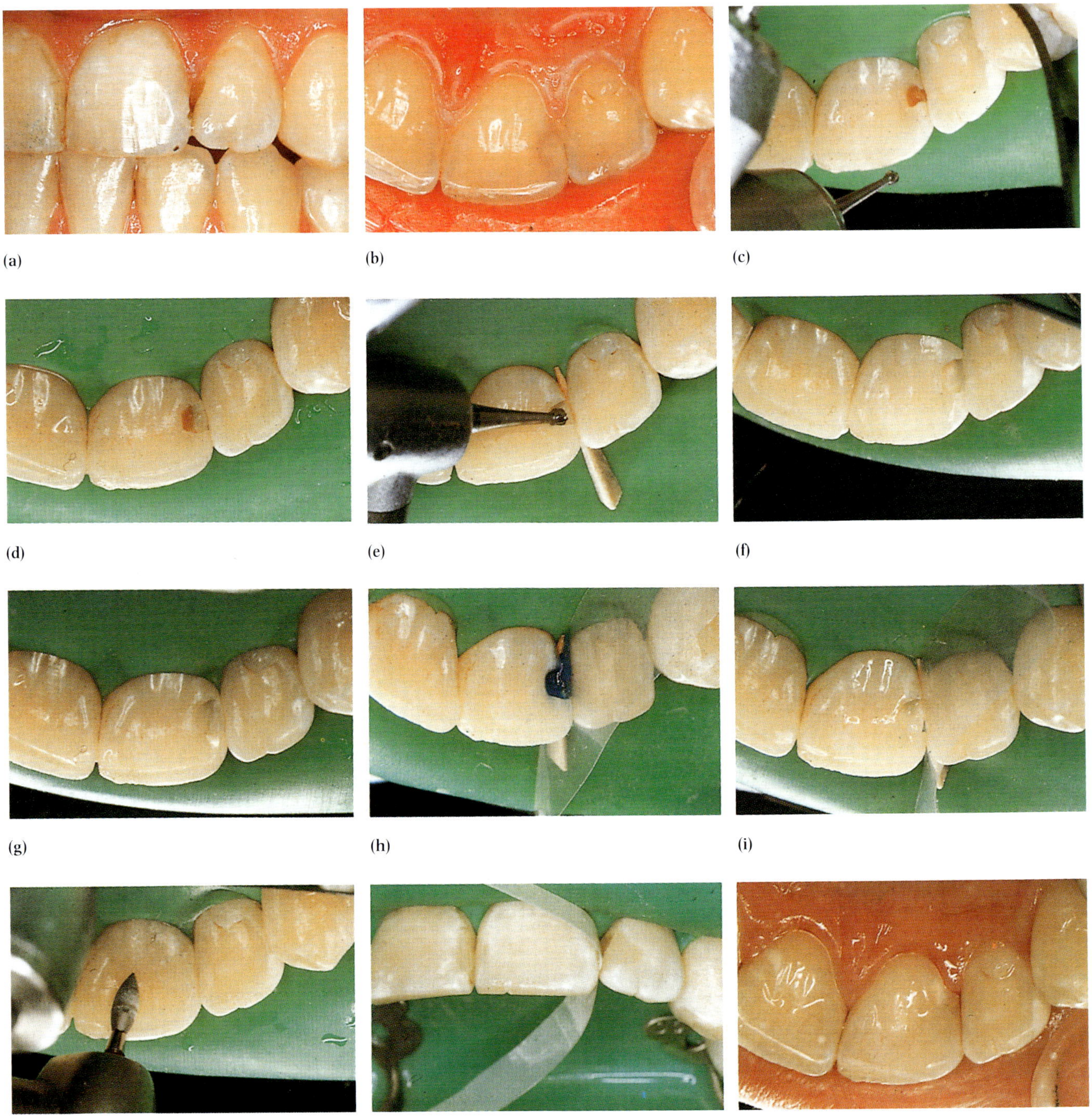

(a) (b) (c) (d) (e) (f) (g) (h) (i) (j) (k) (l)

Fig. 10.3 (a) and (b) A typical approximal lesion in the distal surface of the central incisor in well-aligned teeth.
(c) Access has been gained through the palatal enamel.
(d) The carious enamel has now been removed but there is still caries at the enamel–dentine junction and over the pulp.
(e) A small round steel bur being used at low speed to remove dentine caries.
(f) The cavity is now caries-free.
(g) A glass ionomer cement lining has been placed. Note how well this matches the colour and translucency of natural dentine. This produces a better appearance through thin remaining buccal enamel than opaque lining materials.
(h) Acid-etching gel in place. The matrix strip and wedge are to protect the lateral incisor from being etched as well.
(i) The bonding resin has been applied.
(j) A suitably shaped finishing diamond is used to shape the palatal surface and remove any excess composite.
(k) The final finishing of the cervical margin is carried out with an abrasive strip.
(l) The finished restoration.

the absence of this, some operators cut retentive grooves in the dentine cervically and occlusally with a small round bur at low speed, or bevel the outer aspect of the preparation to increase the enamel surface area for etching and improve the appearance of the tooth–restoration interface.

The main other consideration in designing the cavity is to remove vulnerable enamel which has been thinned out and makes contact with the opposing teeth in the occlusion. 'Unsupported' enamel which does not contact opposing teeth in occlusal movements should be left.

Lining

Approximal carious lesions in anterior teeth are not usually restored until caries is established in dentine. The pulp horn is often close to the base of the caries and a calcium hydroxide lining may be required in the deepest of these cavities. It is applied very carefully on a ball-ended applicator, or alternatively on the back of a suitably sized and shaped excavator (Fig. 10.3g).

Etching

Access to the enamel surfaces to be etched, including the inner aspects of the enamel, is often difficult: one solution to this problem is to use brightly coloured, and therefore clearly visible, etching gel applied with a small disposable nozzle from a syringe or a microbrush. With this technique the gel can be deposited only where it is wanted, without excess (Fig. 10.3h). The enamel of the adjacent tooth should be protected with a mylar matrix strip.

Bonding

The bonding resin is painted onto the etched area, taking care to follow the instructions for the material in use – one should normally be able to see a shiny layer of resin on the cavity surface – to produce a thin even layer (Fig. 10.3i), and the bonding resin is light-cured.

Matrixing and packing

A thin, flexible, transparent matrix strip, which may be straight or curved, is used. The strip should be well adapted to the cervical margin of the cavity and a wedge should be used to adapt the matrix in this area. It is particularly important to avoid creating a ledge cervically since it is difficult to remove an excess from this area. If access has been from the palatal or lingual side, one end of the matrix strip is pulled round to the labial side and held with a finger. The composite is inserted from the palatal or lingual side, the matrix is pulled round, and the composite is light-cured from the palatal or lingual side through the matrix and from the labial side through the thin enamel.

Finishing

If the matrix has been adequate, it should not be necessary to finish the labial or cervical margins. A small cervical ledge can be removed, with difficulty, with a flexible impregnated strip. If there is a large cervical ledge, the filling should usually be replaced. Any excess on the palatal or lingual aspect can be trimmed with one of the following:

- a composite finishing diamond used at high or low speed (Fig. 10.3j)
- a white stone used at low speed
- a multi-bladed tungsten carbide finishing bur in the air turbine.

A final finish is given with a succession of abrasive discs, or, if access is sufficient for them, mounted pumice-impregnated points or abrasive strips (Fig. 10.3k and l).

Composite restorations involving the incisal edge

Cavity preparation

Once the cavity includes the incisal edge, whether it is the result of caries, a previous failed restoration, or trauma, there is no difficulty in gaining access to the lesion and removing any caries that is present (Fig. 10.4a). The problem with the design of these restorations is to achieve adequate retention. For these reasons all the remaining labial enamel should be preserved (Fig. 10.4b). Unsupported enamel at the incisal edge which is in direct contact with the opposing teeth may need to be removed, but even this will usually be kept.

When the lesion is very deep, a calcium hydroxide lining may be placed immediately over the pulp. The 'open' nature of these cavities greatly reduces the problems of polymerization shrinkage of the composite restoration because there are few opposing cavity walls against which stresses can build up. When the lesion is a result of trauma, the dentine and enamel surfaces may be fractured flush with each other and the dentine is not hollowed out as it is with caries. This means that there is not a large internal surface of enamel available for etching, and so with these lesions it is more usual to bevel the external surfaces of the enamel to increase the surface area for retention. It is advantageous to make the bevelled margins irregular in outline so that they do not appear as a straight line: this makes it more difficult for their detection by the onlooker. The dentine surface is used for maximum retention along with extensive use of the enamel.

Matrixing, packing, and finishing

It is possible to trim a cellulose acetate crown form (used to make temporary crowns) to act as a matrix for these restorations, attempting to adapt the margins of the matrix around the entire periphery of the cavity. However, this technique is time-consuming and elaborate and despite all this care it is not possible to adapt all the margins perfectly and insert exactly the right amount of composite; therefore there is always an excess of material to be removed. A simpler technique, which

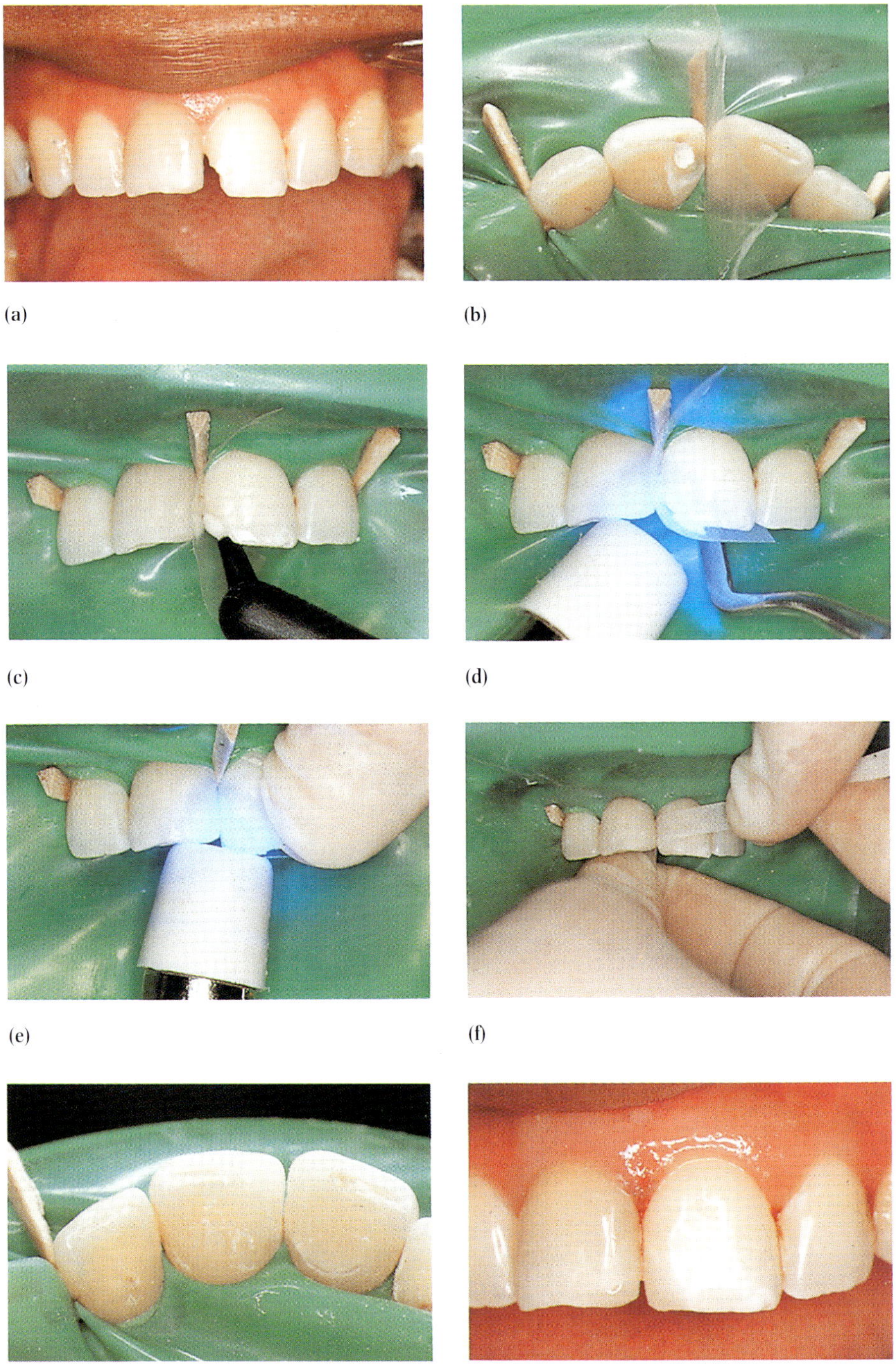

(a) (b) (c) (d) (e) (f) (g) (h)

Fig. 10.4 (a) A lesion involving the incisal edge.
(b) The cavity has been prepared by bevelling the margins. A calcium hydroxide-based lining material has been applied and the enamel etched.
(c) The matrix strip in place and the first increment of composite being applied.
(d) The matrix is adapted with an instrument and the first increment cured.
(e) Further increments are added, holding the matrix with instruments or fingers but ensuring that it is tightly adapted to the cervical margin to reduce excess here. Incisal excess can easily be removed with burs later.
(f) Final finishing of the cervical margin with an abrasive strip.
(g) and (h) The completed restoration. (This restoration was carried out by an undergraduate dental student.)

fulfils the important requirements, is to use a simple mylar strip matrix properly adapted and wedged to the cervical margin interproximally but allowing an excess of material to protrude incisally where it is easy to remove (Fig. 10.4c–e).

Since these restorations are complex to contour and to achieve a realistic appearance, the composite material is sometimes built up in increments; with each increment being light-cured before the next is added. Opaque 'dentine' shades are used first and then a more translucent shade is used for the incisal edge. Either an excess is left incisally, which is trimmed away later, or the last increments are placed without the matrix strip and adapted to shape freehand before curing.

There is usually good access for finishing these restorations with a succession of composite finishing abrasive discs and strips (Fig. 10.4f–h).

Veneering techniques for hypoplastic and discoloured teeth

When the aesthetic problem is such that a restoration inserted into part of the labial surface will not suffice (see Chapter 9, p. 161), there is a choice of three restorative techniques:

- a composite veneer
- a porcelain veneer
- a crown.

Composite veneers

A major advantage of this technique is that it can be used without any preparation of the enamel, other than acid-etching, so that it is an almost entirely reversible procedure. It is atraumatic and there is no need for a local anaesthetic or for the enamel to be cut; therefore it can be undertaken on very young or very nervous patients without great difficulty.

If the tooth is not discoloured at the gingival margin, the composite can be tapered down to a knife-edge finish cervically, leaving a margin that is easy to clean.

A variety of complicated techniques for applying the matrix have been advocated for these restorations, but by far the simplest technique is to build up light-cured composite material freehand on the surface of the tooth, altering the shade as necessary, cervically and incisally. Very thin, Teflon-coated, flat plastic instruments have been designed for this. It is helpful to use a matrix strip between the teeth to avoid the enamel bond or composite becoming attached to the adjacent tooth. However, that is the only matrix that is usually required.

It is often better to place these restorations without a rubber dam. The gingival condition should be healthy before these restorations are placed, and there is no tooth preparation so that there is no risk of gingival bleeding or exudate. Placing the restorations without a rubber dam enables the optimum appearance to be achieved and the restoration can

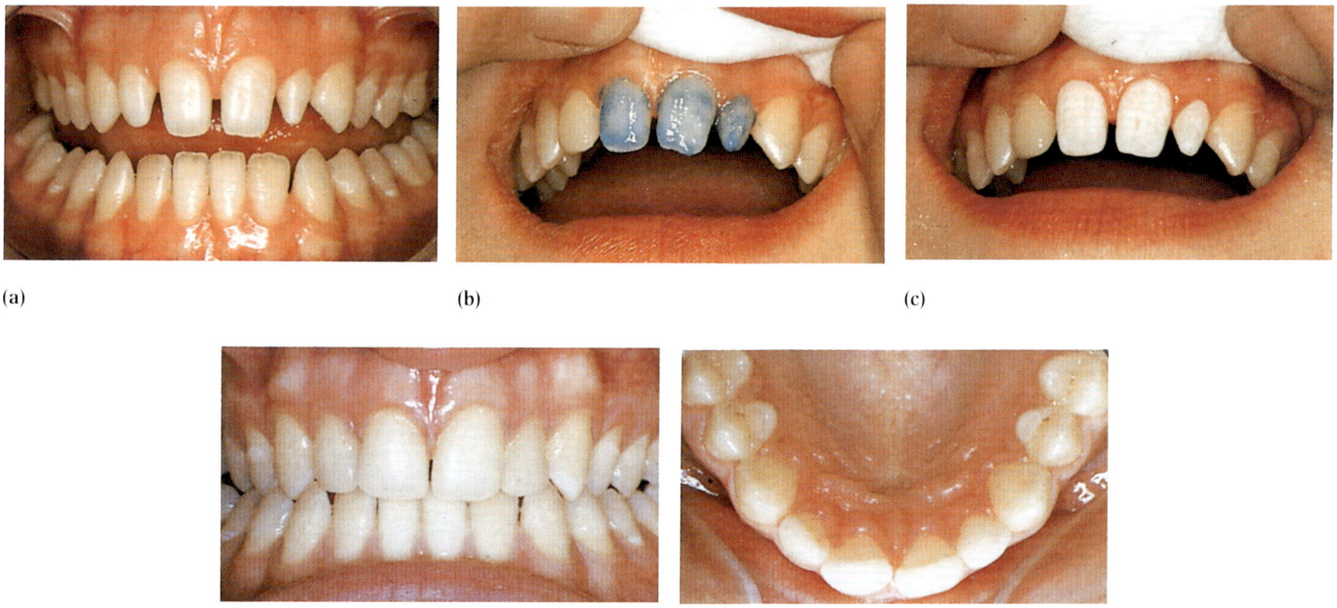

(a) (b) (c) (d) (e)

Fig. 10.5 (a) The upper left lateral incisor is peg-shaped and the central incisors are small and taper towards the incisal edge. The patient was unhappy about the appearance of the spaces.
(b) Acid-etching gel applied to the three incisors. (NB This photograph was taken in 1983 before rubber gloves were worn routinely.)
(c) A well-etched and dried enamel surface, which is the correct procedure if a hydrophobic resin is used to bond the composite to the tooth surface.
(d) and (e) The three composite veneers which have been present for two and a half years at the time that these photographs were taken. There has been some slight dulling of the surface but no discoloration and the appearance is very satisfactory.
(Fig. 10.5a and b by courtesy of Miss K. Warren. Reproduced from *Restorative dentistry* by permission of A. E. Morgan Publications Ltd.)

be contoured to finish just supragingivally so that it can be cleaned.

Finishing is with abrasive discs and, if necessary, with strips interproximally (Fig. 10.5).

With discoloured teeth it is usually necessary to remove some enamel, particularly at the cervical margin. A long, tapered, round-end diamond bur in the air turbine is used for the preparation, which must be done conservatively to avoid penetration of the enamel: this will give a more reliable bond than that achieved with dentine. The enamel may be less than 0.5 mm thick in the cervical region so that particular care is needed to avoid over-cutting and exposing dentine.

For stained teeth there are opaque composite materials which disguise the stain but which leave a rather dead-looking appearance. A better appearance is usually achieved with a porcelain veneer or with a crown but at the cost of more extensive tooth preparation.

Porcelain veneers

In most cases tooth preparation is necessary for porcelain veneers because the veneer cannot be tapered off to a knife-edge cervically without becoming too fragile to handle prior to cementation. Adding a thickness of porcelain cervically without tooth preparation will leave a ledge and a consequent problem with plaque removal. The technique has some similarities to that for inlays in that an impression is taken and the restoration made in the laboratory. Therefore the technique is described and illustrated in Chapter 11 (p. 00).

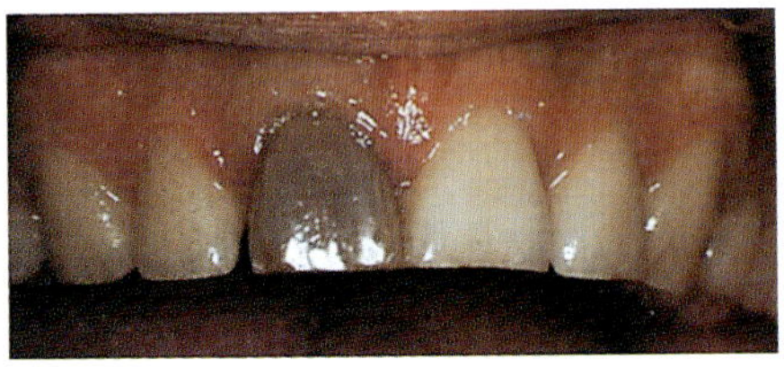

(a)

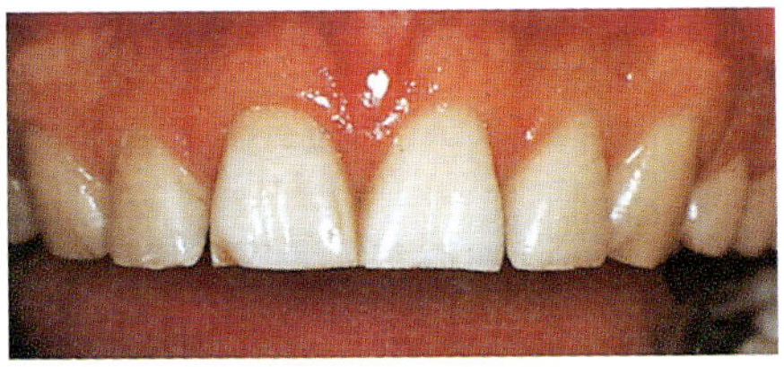

(b)

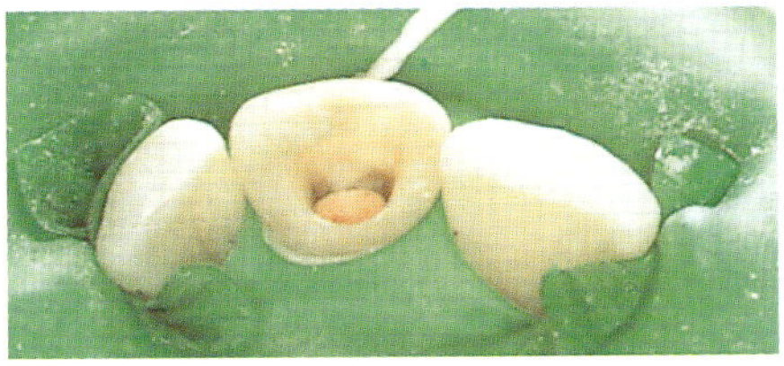

(c)

Fig. 10.6 (a) A very discoloured upper right central incisor. (b) The same tooth after bleaching. (c) The endodontic access cavity must be opened up and the root filling removed to the level of the gingival margin. This allows good access to the dentinal tubules over the entire labial surface and also produces a reasonably thin layer of dentine and enamel to be bleached.

Bleaching discoloured anterior teeth

In some cases it is possible to bleach discoloured anterior teeth rather than veneer or crown them (Fig. 10.6). This is most successful in the case of an individual tooth which is discoloured as a result of haemoglobin breakdown products arising from a necrotic pulp which was not removed promptly enough. Claims have been made for successful bleaching of vital teeth with tetracycline staining or other intrinsic stains, but the results are less predictable and when the stain is not uniform the result is likely to be disappointing.

An individual non-vital tooth discoloured by haemoglobin breakdown products must initially be root filled with an inert material which does not itself discolour the crown (e.g. laterally condensed gutta-percha points with a white sealing paste). The tooth to be bleached must be isolated with a rubber dam. The filling is removed from the access cavity and the access cavity enlarged, removing as much stained dentine as possible without weakening the tooth too much. This leaves a thin uniform layer of dentine through which the bleaching agents can percolate.

The dentine surface is etched for one minute with 30–50 per cent phosphoric acid to remove the smear layer and thus improve its permeability. A pledget of cotton-wool soaked in the bleaching solution is inserted into the access cavity. A strong light (e.g. a composite polymerizing light) or heat is applied to the tooth for two to three minutes to accelerate the bleaching process. After this time the pledget of cotton-wool is removed, the bleaching solution is washed away, and the tooth is inspected. The process may be repeated a number of times until the colour is about right. It is good practice to overbleach the tooth slightly as very commonly some further discoloration of the tooth reappears over a period of weeks after the procedure.

A variety of bleaching solutions have been used. Thirty per cent (or 100 volume) hydrogen peroxide has been the most commonly used and works in most cases. It is sometimes mixed with sodium perborate powder to accelerate the release of oxygen.

Hydrogen peroxide at this concentration is a very irritant material and there is concern (but little evidence) that it may be carcinogenic. For this reason, materials providing more than 0.1 per cent of hydrogen peroxide have been banned in the United Kingdom from use on the external surface of teeth by either dentists or in the 'home bleaching' systems which were available until 1993. The legal position with respect to the use of materials containing more than 0.1 per cent of hydrogen peroxide on the internal surfaces of teeth is not entirely clear, but if it is used it must only be applied with a rubber dam and eye protection in place, and with careful protection of the patient's clothes in case the solution drips off the bottom of the rubber dam while it is being washed away. A layer of Vaseline may be applied to the gingivae before the dam is placed. Good aspiration and plenty of water when washing are necessary. Care must be taken to avoid bleaching solution being drawn around the gingival margin by capillary action and trapped there by the rubber dam.

If the colour of the tooth does not change enough, a mixture of sodium perborate and hydrogen peroxide can be sealed into the access cavity with cotton-wool and a temporary zinc oxide and eugenol dressing. This dressing can be left in place for a week. Cases of external resorption have been reported following bleaching, but it is not always clear whether these are the result of the bleaching or of the trauma or other condition which resulted in the necrotic pulp in the first place.

Once the tooth is bleached the dentine is replaced by a glass ionomer cement restoration. This bonds to the remaining dentine and enamel and strengthens the tooth. The palatal access cavity is then finally restored with composite which is acid-etch retained to the enamel margins and the glass ionomer cement.

Further reading

Fisher, N. L. and Radford, J. R. (1990). Internal bleaching of discoloured teeth. *Dent. Update*. **17**, 110–14.

Greenwall, L. (2001). *Bleaching techniques in restorative dentistry*. Martin Dunitz, London.

11

Indirect cast metal, porcelain, and composite intracoronal restorations

Indirect cast metal, porcelain, and composite intracoronal restorations

Plastic compared with rigid restorations

Most of the restorations described so far have been plastic in the sense that the restorative materials used (amalgam, composite, and glass ionomer cement) have been in a plastic, mouldable state as they were being inserted into the cavity and subsequently set to become rigid. The restorations to be described in this chapter are all constructed outside the mouth from rigid materials and are then cemented into the prepared tooth, which clearly must not be undercut.

The lost wax process

The modern cast restoration was developed by an American dentist, Dr William H. Taggart, who in 1907 described a technique to produce gold castings which fitted prepared teeth with precision. The technique he refined is known as the *lost wax process* and involves making a wax pattern of the restoration which is then invested in a freshly mixed refractory material contained in a metal casting ring. When the investment has set, the whole is heated to a high temperature, causing the wax to burn out, leaving a space. Molten metal or glass–ceramic material is forced into the mould to form a replica of the original wax pattern.

Direct and indirect techniques

In the past there were two methods by which cast metal restorations were made (Fig. 11.1). In the *direct* method the wax was inserted directly into the cavity, carved, removed, invested, and cast. The cast gold inlay was then polished and cemented in the cavity. Sometimes all this was done in one long appointment. However, small cavities suitable for direct gold inlays can be satisfactorily restored with plastic materials, which have other advantages such as being tooth-coloured, and so the direct cast restoration is used very little today. However, because they are so durable some patients still have direct gold inlays (Fig. 11.2).

Indirect cast metal restorations are made in the laboratory. An impression of the cavity and the surrounding area is made in the mouth. From this impression a model of the tooth, a die, is constructed. The wax pattern is formed upon this die, invested, and cast. It is fitted and finished on the die in the laboratory. Thus, only minimal adjustment should be required at the chairside as the majority of the work has been carried out on accurate models in the optimum conditions of the laboratory.

Intracoronal and extracoronal restorations

There is no clear dividing line between intracoronal and extracoronal restorations. A restoration contained within an occlusal cavity is clearly intracoronal, whilst a complete crown is clearly extracoronal; however, between these two extremes there are a number of restorations which are more difficult to categorize. A cast metal inlay which also covers the entire occlusal surface of a posterior tooth is partially intracoronal and partially extracoronal. Traditionally, extracoronal restorations have been considered as complete or partial crowns made of metal or porcelain; however, a composite labial veneer applied to the etched enamel surface must surely be regarded as an extracoronal restoration although it does not fit into the traditional definition.

The restorations to be described here are those which can reasonably be regarded as alternatives to the plastic restorations described earlier and are mostly intracoronal. Complete and partial crowns will not be described as planning for these introduces another set of considerations beyond the scope of this book. Also, many additional clinical and laboratory techniques are necessary, and as these are similar to those used in the construction of bridges it is more logical to consider crowns and bridges together. The restorations to be considered here are as follows:

- indirect cast metal inlays and onlays
- porcelain inlays
- porcelain veneers
- composite inlays.

Materials

Cast metal

The traditional material for inlays is gold. Pure gold (24 carat, 100 per cent, or 1000 fine) is seldom, if ever, used as it is a very soft material. Other metals are added to

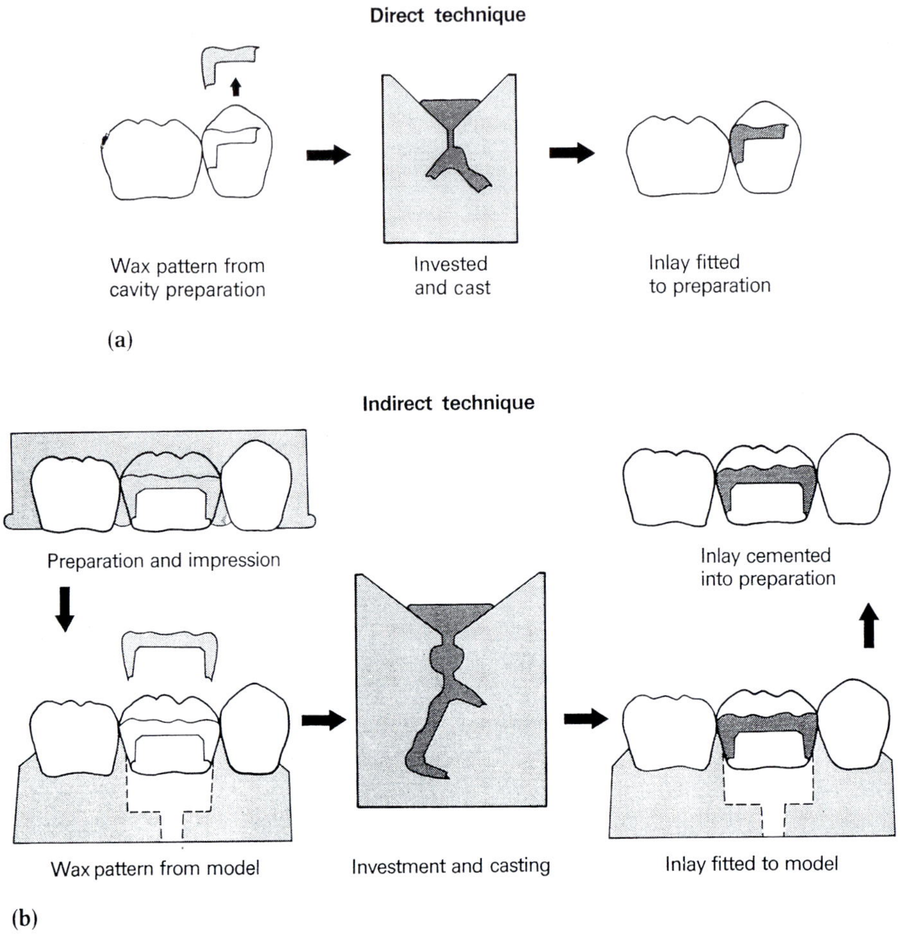

Fig. 11.1 Alternative methods for producing cast metal restorations.

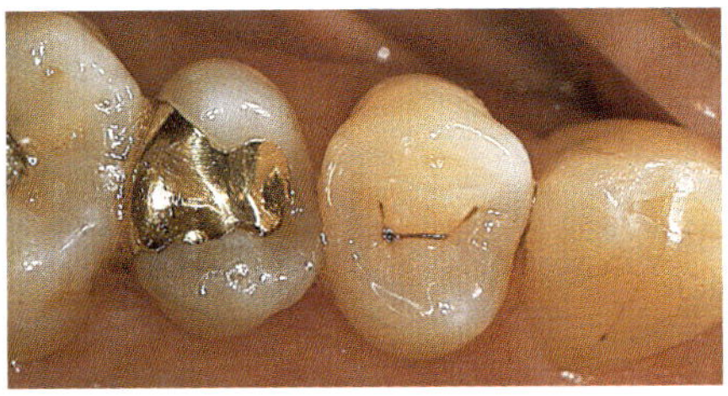

Fig. 11.2 A direct gold inlay made by one of the authors over 30 years ago. By today's standards this is a very large restoration for a small lesion that would today be treated by a much smaller restoration or perhaps none at all, relying instead on preventive measures. However, the tooth and inlay are both in good condition and have an excellent prognosis.

improve the physical properties, and therefore the material used in a traditional 'gold' inlay is in fact a gold alloy. In some cases alloys containing 60 per cent or more of gold are still used and these can reasonably be described as gold alloys. However, the high cost of gold has stimulated development and improvements in other alloys and a vast choice is now available to the clinician and technician. Some alloys which are used for intracoronal restorations contain only 20 per cent or so of gold and so it is misleading to describe these as 'gold' alloys. Other alloys contain no gold at all but are based on a combination of other metals. This is why the term 'cast metal' has been used so far in this chapter.

Despite the improvements in low-gold alloys, they remain more difficult to work with than the traditional high-gold alloys. High-gold alloys should still be used for inlays because the amount of metal used is small and therefore the added cost is relatively insignificant. A textbook on dental materials should be consulted for a detailed comparison of the properties of various types of casting alloys.

Porcelain

Porcelain inlays and veneers are made by one of two completely different techniques. In the first technique, the impression of the tooth is cast in a refractory material which can be heated to very high temperatures without damage. Porcelain powder is mixed to a paste with a liquid and placed into the inlay cavity or onto the labial surface of this refractory model and is then fired in a furnace until the particles of porcelain fuse together. The process is repeated a number of times until the restoration has been built to the required contour and colour. The refractory model is then removed, usually by sand (or glass bead) blasting.

The second method is to cast an ingot of castable glass or ceramic into a mould made by the lost wax technique. This glass restoration is then treated in a ceramming furnace which converts the material to a ceramic which is then surface stained and fired to change its appearance. Both techniques produce a ceramic restoration (commonly, but not really accurately, called porcelain) but the materials have rather different properties. Again, a textbook of dental materials should be consulted for the details of these differences.

Other techniques using computer-aided design/computer-aided manufacture (CAD/CAM) have been developed and are being used increasingly. Further developments look promising, but these processes are beyond the scope of this book.

Advantages and disadvantages of cast metal and porcelain restorations

Strength

Cast metal is stronger in thin sections than amalgam, composite, or glass ionomer cement, and it has a greater ability to resist tensile forces. Thus, it is the material of choice to protect weakened cusps where a metal thickness of 1.0 mm or even less is sufficient compared with a minimum thickness of 3 mm for amalgam. Its strength in thin sections also makes it ideally suited for extracoronal restorations, such as onlays and complete and partial crowns. Preparations for cast metal restorations are usually finished with bevelled or chamfered margins to give a thin edge of metal.

In contrast, porcelain has high compressive strength but low tensile strength. This means that it is relatively brittle in thin sections, at least until it is bonded to the tooth and supported by it. Therefore porcelain restorations should not have bevelled margins, and a minimum thickness is necessary to avoid fracture of the restoration. For a conventional porcelain crown this thickness is about 1.5 mm, but for porcelain veneers which are not subjected to occlusal forces 0.5 mm or less may be sufficient.

Abrasion resistance

Although amalgam is similar to enamel in resisting abrasion, both composite and glass ionomer tend to wear more rapidly than enamel, particularly on the occlusal surface. Cast metal and porcelain are at least as resistant to abrasion as enamel, and indeed there has been some concern that porcelain is *more* resistant so that if a porcelain restoration is opposed by a natural tooth, the natural tooth may wear down more rapidly. This will certainly happen if the glaze on the porcelain is inadequate or has been ground off. With an abrasion cavity at the neck of the tooth, composite or glass ionomer may be inadequate to resist further abrasion and porcelain inlays are sometimes used to overcome this problem (Fig. 11.3).

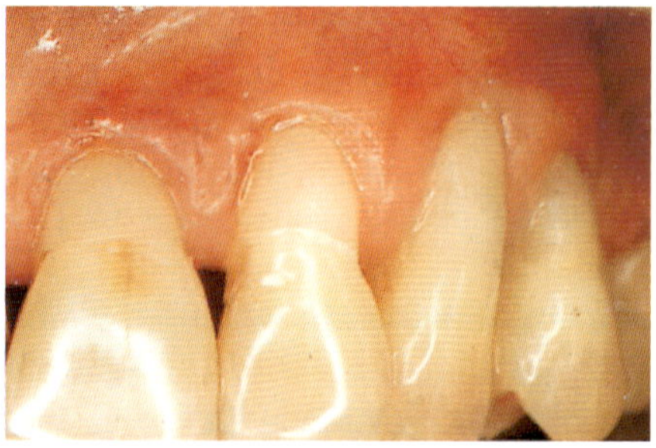

Fig. 11.3 Porcelain inlays used to restore cervical lesions in all four teeth. These porcelain inlays were made by traditional techniques 25 years ago.

Appearance

At one time, when the choice of restorative material was amalgam, gold, or silicate, gold was frequently preferred for aesthetic reasons as it was more attractive than amalgam and did not deteriorate like silicate. Also, in many societies it was regarded as a status symbol to have gold visible in the front or to the side of the mouth. With the introduction of more reliable, tooth-coloured restorative materials 40 years ago, this fashion tended to die away and relatively few patients now ask for visible gold restorations (although fashions do change!).

Porcelain, in contrast, can have a very natural appearance, and in some situations it is the material of choice for this reason. Its appearance, once established, is very durable compared with composite and glass ionomer which sometimes discolour or develop stained margins.

Versatility

Cast metal is a very versatile material. The indirect technique allows it to be shaped accurately in the laboratory to restore occlusal and axial contours and contact areas. Where cast restorations are placed in patients for whom partial dentures are to be made, it is possible to build appropriate guiding planes, rest seats, and reciprocal ledges into the cast restoration at the laboratory stage. If advantage is to be taken of this situation, it is absolutely essential that the partial denture be designed before the cast restoration is made. In addition, cast metal can be soldered and thus contact areas can be added at the fit stage. These alloys are almost unchallenged as the materials of choice for bridges.

Cost

Cost is the major disadvantage of cast metal and porcelain restorations. The reason for the high cost is the amount of time that they take compared with plastic restorations. There is always a laboratory stage and so a minimum of two clinical appointments is necessary, the first to prepare the tooth and take an impression and the second to fit the restoration after it has been made in the laboratory. This extra time taken by the dentist and the technician means that these restorations are inevitably several times more expensive than the equivalent plastic restoration. This extra cost has been seen in the past as giving further status to the restorations, particularly gold inlays. It was assumed that because a gold inlay costs several times more than an amalgam restoration, it must be several times better. This does not automatically follow. Certainly, a gold inlay has some advantages over amalgam in that it does not corrode or discolour the tooth and it is stronger. However, in choosing between the materials a proper cost-effectiveness analysis is needed rather than looking at the cost alone or the effectiveness alone.

Using alloys with less gold (or in some cases none) reduces the cost of the material a little but does not save time, and so the overall cost is still high.

The cement lute

The weak link in any cemented restoration is the cement lute. The margin of even a well-fitting cast metal restoration is some micrometres away from the cavity wall (10-60 μm). Thus, the marginal seal of the restoration is entirely dependent upon the cement lute, whereas the seal of an amalgam restoration is good as corrosion products tend to block the initial microspace. Resin-based adhesives with primers for sticking to gold and non-precious components of a gold alloy allow adhesive cementation of inlays. Time and clinical trials will tell whether or not these offer long-term clinical advantages over the non-adhesive, mechanically-interlocking, rigid cements such as zinc phosphate and glass ionomer cement.

Indications

Bearing these points in mind, the following are the most common indications for each type of restoration although, of course, there will be many variations when the needs of individual patients have been taken into account.

Cast metal inlays

The indirect technique allows a great range of preparation design and the most commonly made cast metal inlays are used to protect the cusps by covering the occlusal surface. These are called either inlays with cuspal protection or onlays. The second most common indication for inlays is as part of a bridge or other appliance replacing missing teeth.

Porcelain inlays

Porcelain inlays were used occasionally in the past (Fig. 11.3) but with the introduction of composite materials they fell into disuse. However, a new generation of materials and techniques has been developed in the last few years and there has been a resurgence in interest in porcelain and composite inlays and onlays (see later).

However, porcelain inlays or onlays have the advantages that they are more natural in appearance than cast metal inlays and are more abrasion-resistant than composite. Therefore they may be appropriate in the occlusal surfaces of posterior teeth when large restorations are needed and appearance is important. They may be used in the buccal surfaces of visible anterior and posterior teeth when abrasion is a problem. They are not as strong as cast metal inlays but when they are bonded to the enamel surfaces of weakened cusps using the acid-etch technique, it is likely that they strengthen the tooth in much the same way as composite or glass ionomer–composite layered restorations. This means that full protection of the occlusal surface of the weakened cusp may not be necessary as it is with cast metal inlays.

Composite inlays

In much the same way as porcelain inlays are prescribed, it is also possible to make indirect inlays from composite material that is polymerized in a die, with the restoration made in the laboratory rather than in the patient's mouth. This avoids the large-volume polymerization shrinkage of the composite in the tooth and is also said to produce a tougher restoration than the direct-placed composites. However, one is still left with the problem of cementation, with relatively greater shrinkage of a low-viscosity cement lute, as is also seen with porcelain inlays.

Porcelain and composite veneers

The general indications for veneering the labial surface of teeth were described in Chapter 10. When a veneer is indicated, the choice of material is between composite and porcelain. Composite has the advantage of being versatile and it can usually be placed without any tooth preparation. This means that the process is largely reversible. The margin can be feathered off at a sharp bevel, producing little change in the contour of the tooth at the cervical margin and interproximally. However, composite tends to wear and sometimes discolours. For these reasons porcelain is sometimes preferred and in most cases the tooth needs to be prepared to accommodate the porcelain veneer, particularly at the margins, since the veneer cannot be finished to such a fine bevel. This means that the process is not reversible. The cost is also high because the veneers have to be made individually in the laboratory and in many cases several teeth need to be treated. Surveys of the success of porcelain veneers have been rather disappointing. Enamel and porcelain have different physical properties so that they respond differently to the stresses and strains of chewing. Over a period of a few years this results in breakdown of the cement lute at the margins and unsightly stains. The stresses can also result in cracks and fractures of porcelain veneers. With the improvement of direct-placed composite materials and dentists' greater experience in using them, composite veneers are now usually preferred to porcelain.

Preparations and clinical techniques

Indirect cast metal inlay

Preparation for a mesial–occlusal–distal (MOD) inlay with cuspal protection

This is the most common type of inlay still made. The preparation follows the general principles of cavity preparation and design described in Chapter 3. These principles are applied in rather different ways to take account of the properties of the materials being used, but remain essentially the same as for plastic restorations:

- gain access to the caries or remove the old restoration
- remove caries
- put the handpiece down and think.

The decision to make an inlay should be reconsidered at this stage, and if the decision is confirmed details of the design should be planned:

- prepare the cavity to be retentive and resistant
- prepare cuspal coverage and check for adequate occlusal clearance in all excursions of the mandible
- check for undercuts
- prepare finishing lines
- line the cavity.

RETENTION FOR INLAY CAVITIES

The general principles of retention were described in Chapter 3. Retention is achieved by preparing opposing walls as near parallel to each other as is practical (see Fig. 3.7), but without undercuts. This allows a single path of insertion from an occlusal direction, and is most conveniently achieved by cutting the preparation with a straight-cut, taper-fissure tungsten carbide bur in the air turbine. To achieve near-parallel walls the bur should be realigned very slightly when transferring from the buccal to the lingual side of the cavity. Theoretically, the angle between the walls of the cavity should be 7–10°, but this is almost impossible to achieve clinically, and measurements of preparation tapers undertaken for large numbers of clinical preparations show an average taper of about 20°. This is clinically acceptable, and in any case the actual angle is irrelevant as no attempt is made to measure it clinically. Loss of retention in other directions is prevented by the presence of cusps and by occlusal locks in much the same way as amalgam restorations are retained.

(a)

(b)

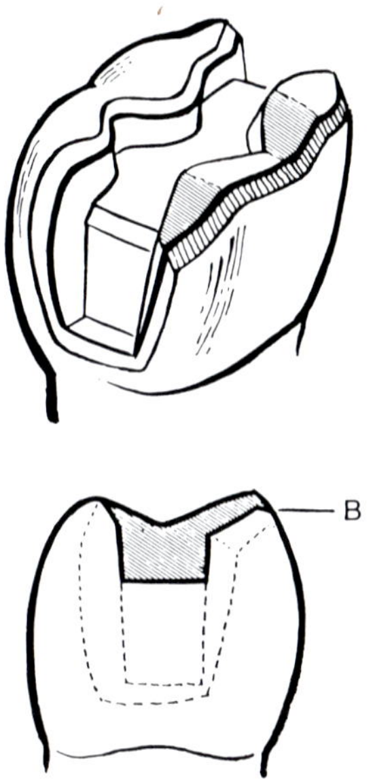

Fig. 11.4 (a) A typical design for a MOD inlay with cuspal protection for one wall of the tooth.
(b) A cross-sectional view. The reverse bevel (B) produces an acute metal margin.

CUSPAL COVERAGE

The important aspect of the design and the main reason for choosing this type of restoration is to prevent the weakened cusps from breaking under occlusal pressures. To do this, the weakened cusps are reduced in height in a direction parallel to the slope of the cusp. The amount of reduction will depend on the circumstances but should not be less than 0.5 mm. In some cases it will need to be more (up to 1.5 mm), particularly when the cusp being protected is in contact in lateral movements of the mandible (a functional cusp) and therefore is vulnerable to lateral forces. In addition, the metal may wear and become thinner over a period of years. A typical design is shown in Fig. 11.4.

CHECKING FOR UNDERCUTS

The cavity must be free from undercuts so that it is possible to see all the line angles and corners of the cavity at once. This can be checked by looking into the cavity, either directly or with a mirror (preferably one which is surface-reflecting) in the line of withdrawal of the inlay. Without the operator moving their head, a probe is passed along all the line angles and into all the corners of the cavity. If the point of the probe is lost from view, it will have entered an undercut. It is undoubtedly easier to look for undercuts with one eye shut in order not to be misled by binocular vision. In the MOD cavity, particular care should be taken to ensure that the boxes are not undercut with respect to one another. Any undercut must be eliminated, either by further preparation of the tooth or, if it is well supported by dentine, by blocking out with glass ionomer cement.

FINISHING LINES

Some form of bevel or chamfer is the finishing line of choice for intracoronal cast restorations. Their use gives a cavo-surface angle of approximately 135° and a gold margin angle of 45°. When the inlay is fitted, this thin gold margin can be burnished onto the enamel.

Any functional cusp can be finished with a chamfer finishing line, bringing the margin of the gold away from the area of occlusal stress. This is cut with a tungsten carbide chamfer finishing bur used in the air turbine. On non-functional cusps a reverse bevel should be cut with the air turbine using a tungsten carbide finishing bur (Fig. 11.4).

With large boxes, bevels should be placed along the axial walls of the box and at the cervical margin. This is difficult but can be achieved with care using a straight-cut tapered tungsten carbide bur in a 1:4 ratio speed-increasing handpiece. This bevel must be large if it is to avoid creating undercuts beneath the maximum bulbosity of the tooth. Care should be taken to merge these bevels with the occlusal bevels. The cervical margin bevel can be cut with a pointed, flame-shaped composite finishing diamond (Fig. 11.5a and b).

CAVITY LINING

In a deep cavity a sublining of a proprietary cement containing calcium hydroxide may be used. A second lining material should then be placed to line out any undercuts, flatten the occlusal floor and pulpal walls, and provide thermal insulation for the pulp. Glass ionomer cement is the optimum material for this structural lining because it is adhesive to dentine. It is often easiest to place a small excess of the material and, once it has set, cut it back to achieve a smooth and precise lining; every wrinkle is a possible source of error as it is reproduced in the impression, the die, the wax, and the metal. The pulpo-axial line angle should be bevelled. If it is left sharp it will be reproduced in the investment, a relatively weak material, which may be fractured as the molten alloy rushes past it during the casting procedure.

Impressions

An impression of the cavity and the full arch of teeth is taken in an elastomeric impression material (Fig. 11.5c). The dentist may choose to use one of two groups of these materials: the polyethers or silicones. A textbook of dental materials should be consulted for the chemical composition of the materials and the manufacturer's instructions should be read concerning the handling of the chosen material.

An impression of the opposing arch is taken, usually in alginate. An important feature of this impression is that the occlusal surface of the teeth should be recorded without air bubbles so that the opposing models can be articulated accurately.

An interocclusal record will not be needed where there are sufficient occluding teeth. However, if there is any doubt about the occlusion, a suitable interocclusal record is taken in the intercuspal position.

THE SPECIAL TRAY

A special tray is recommended with several, but not all, the elastomeric impression materials. The tray supports the material around the teeth; this means that less impression materi-

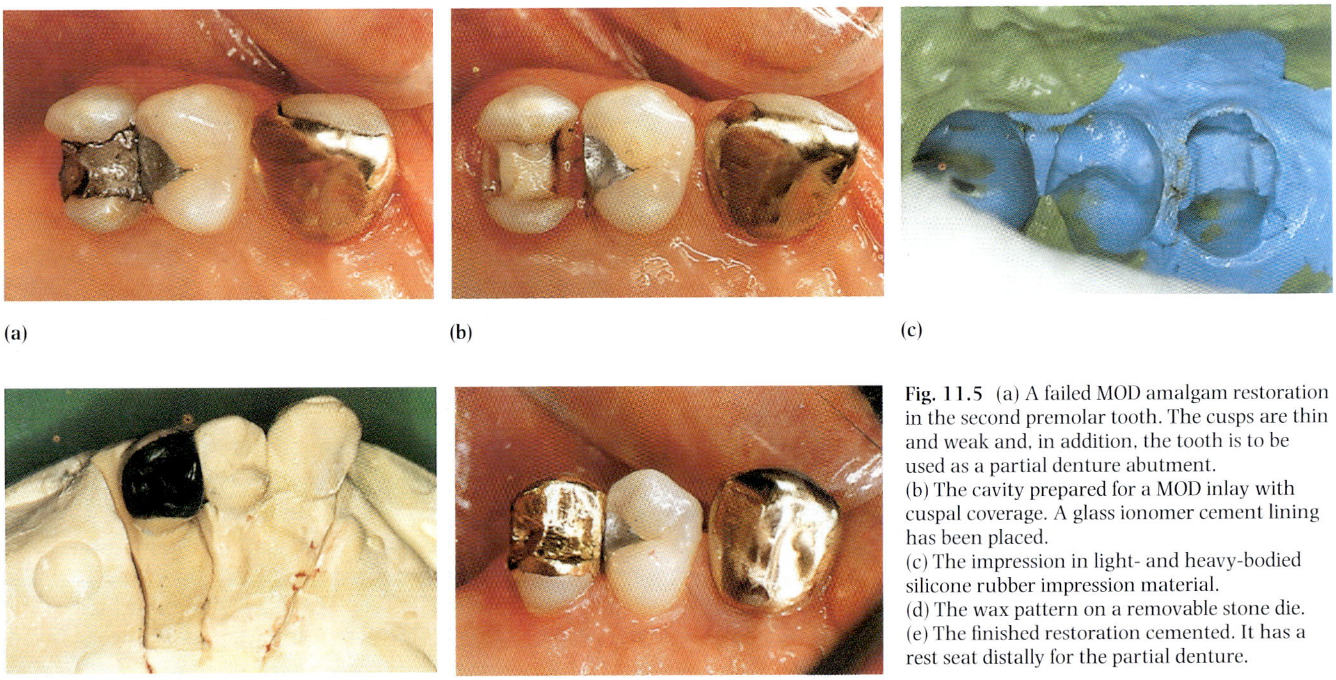

(a) (b) (c) (d) (e)

Fig. 11.5 (a) A failed MOD amalgam restoration in the second premolar tooth. The cusps are thin and weak and, in addition, the tooth is to be used as a partial denture abutment.
(b) The cavity prepared for a MOD inlay with cuspal coverage. A glass ionomer cement lining has been placed.
(c) The impression in light- and heavy-bodied silicone rubber impression material.
(d) The wax pattern on a removable stone die.
(e) The finished restoration cemented. It has a rest seat distally for the partial denture.

al is used and ensures a consistent thickness of material. This may be relevant to the dimensional stability of the material.

When required, a special tray is made of acrylic resin on a study model. The tray should cover all the teeth in the arch and is extended 2 mm beyond the gingival margins. The tray is spaced over the teeth by 1–3 mm but contacts three or four teeth around the arch so that it can be seated accurately without touching the prepared tooth.

The correct adhesive for the impression material should be painted on the inside of the tray and around the margins and allowed to dry before the impression is taken.

ISOLATING THE TOOTH: GINGIVAL RETRACTION

The elastomeric impression materials are hydrophobic and so the prepared tooth surface must be dry. The tooth is isolated with cotton-wool rolls and a saliva ejector is placed in the mouth. Careful management of the gingival tissues is the key to taking good impressions, since any gingival exudate or bleeding will prevent the material from flowing over the prepared tooth surface. It is essential that the gingival tissues are healthy before the preparation is started. When the preparation margin extends to or beneath the gingival margin, it is necessary to retract the gingival margin before taking the impression so that an accurate impression of the margin can be recorded.

A suitable gingival retraction cord impregnated with styptic, such as aluminium chloride, or a vasoconstrictor, such as adrenalin, is chosen. The latter would not be used in patients with cardiovascular problems or those taking tricyclic antidepressants because the adrenalin is readily absorbed. The cord is gently pressed into the gingival crevice with a flat plastic instrument. It is left for a minute or two before the impression is taken.

TAKING THE IMPRESSION

The impression materials are mixed thoroughly, usually in an automix gun system, according to the manufacturer's instructions. The retraction cord is removed and a low-viscosity impression material is syringed into the preparation and around the tooth. A heavier-viscosity material or putty mix (the putty materials obviate the need for a special tray) is placed in the impression tray and the tray is seated over the unset low-viscosity material. This helps to adapt it into all the areas of the preparation and into the gingival crevice. The impression is supported while it sets and is then removed from the mouth.

EXAMINING THE IMPRESSION

The impression of the prepared tooth should be examined in detail to check that the entire margin is visible and that there are no voids caused by air entrapment. The detail of the occlusal surface of the entire impression should also be checked because voids caused by air bubbles will subsequently fill with plaster and prevent accurate occlusion of the models (Fig. 11.5c).

The temporary inlay

While the cast inlay is being constructed, an accurate temporary restoration is needed for the following reasons:

- to protect the pulp
- to prevent ingrowth of gingival tissues
- to prevent alteration of occlusal and approximal contacts
- to prevent fracture of weakened cusps
- to restore appearance and comfort.

A durable inlay is required that can be cemented with a temporary luting material but is easily removed at a subsequent visit. One of the temporary crown and bridge materials is conveniently made into a temporary inlay.

The cavity is lightly lubricated with Vaseline and a matrix band is fitted to the tooth. The band is burnished to obtain accurate approximal contacts, and wedges are placed to ensure good cervical adaptation. The resin is mixed and when it has a putty consistency it is firmly placed into the band. Alternatively the inlay can be made freehand, without a band, which will produce more excess resin, but this can easily be removed by trimming out of the mouth.

As the resin sets it loses its plasticity and the temporary inlay can now be removed. It should be replaced gently and withdrawn a number of times until it has set. Excess resin is now trimmed off the inlay outside the mouth with a bur or stone in a laboratory handpiece. Finally, the inlay is inserted and the occlusion is checked with articulating paper and adjusted until it is correct in intercuspal position and in lateral excursions. The temporary inlay is finally smoothed with a rubber wheel before cementing it with a zinc oxide and eugenol temporary luting cement (or eugenol-free cement if a composite luting system is to be used). Once the cement has set, excess is removed with a probe.

Laboratory stages

The laboratory procedures will not be described in detail. Basically, the working impression is cast in a hard artificial stone incorporating tapered pins or other devices to allow the model of the prepared tooth to be sawn out of the rest of the model in such a way that it can be reinserted in the same position. This is the die. The wax pattern is made on the lubricated die and, because the die can be removed from the master model, accurate adaptation of proximal gingival margins, contact points, etc. is possible (Fig. 11.5d). The wax pattern is then sprued, usually with wax or plastic, and cast. The sprue and pattern are sealed onto a cone-shaped form; this is covered by a casting ring and investment material is poured into the other end of the ring and allowed to set. The ring is then heated in a furnace until the wax melts, including the wax or plastic sprue, and evaporates and then molten metal is cast into the cone-shaped end of the ring and allowed to set. When still hot the ring is dropped into water and the investment cracks and can easily be removed. The sprue is removed and the inlay polished in the laboratory before returning to the surgery.

The occlusion is checked while the wax pattern is being made and during polishing by articulating the working model with the opposing model. This can be done by hand, but it is very much better to articulate the casts in a simple articulator. The advantage is that with handheld models the majority of teeth will come together even if the wax pattern or inlay is proud. However, with articulated models a high contact on the pattern will keep the other teeth apart and the occlusal discrepancy will be more obvious.

The second clinical visit

Before the patient arrives, the fit of the casting on the die should be checked and the fit surface examined for small excesses that could prevent the restoration from seating.

REMOVING THE TEMPORARY INLAY

It may not be convenient to use a rubber dam when fitting a cuspal coverage restoration because the occlusion must be checked carefully. Care must be taken to ensure that the inlay is not swallowed or inhaled. One possibility is to work with the patient sitting up, another is to place a gauze square in the mouth to isolate the throat. However, this may mask the patient's cough reflex. A scaler is used to remove the temporary inlay and all traces of temporary cement are gently removed with a probe.

TRYING IN THE CASTING

Seat the casting and check the margins with a sharp probe for deficiencies or ledges. If the casting will not seat, look for causes in the following sequence:

- Debris or temporary cement still in the preparation.
- Gingival overgrowth into the preparation.
- An overbuilt proximal contour. This can be detected with dental floss. Stabilize the restoration with a finger and attempt to floss the contact. A shiny facet on the contact may indicate where metal should be removed with a green stone or small sandpaper disc. Where it is difficult to detect exactly where to disc, paint the contact area with a thin layer of graphite and water or use a proprietary spray developed for this purpose; dry the contact and insert the restoration. On removing the restoration the precise contact point will show as an area of metal where the graphite or spray has rubbed off. Metal should be removed from the contact until floss will just pass.
- If the restoration will not seat, distortion of the wax pattern or the impression is the likely cause. The fit surface of the casting should be carefully re-examined using magnification to see if there are any shiny areas which might give an indication of the site of an undetected blob on the casting. The preparation should then be re-examined for undercuts that could have caused the distortion. It is obviously preferable to avoid this situation as it is time-wasting and expensive.

If the marginal fit is good but the contact point is inadequate, this can be re-established by adding metal solder at the appropriate region.

Once the casting is seated the occlusion should be checked in all excursions of the mandible. Articulating paper should be used to show initial contacts. When the occlusion has been adjusted the inlay should be removed, smoothed, and polished.

Finally, before cementation, the margins of the restoration should be burnished to the enamel. This can be done with hand instruments or rotating burnishers. The instrument should always be worked from the gold to the tooth.

CEMENTING THE RESTORATION

The inlay can be cemented with glass ionomer, zinc phosphate, or resin-based cement. In either case the quadrant must be carefully isolated and dried, and the cement mixed according to the manufacturer's instructions.

Zinc phosphate cement is mixed slowly to a creamy consistency. Glass ionomer cement is mixed rapidly to a slightly more viscous consistency. The consistency of resin-based lutes will be predetermined as they are usually paste–paste mixing systems. The cavity is filled with cement, using a flat plastic instrument, and the casting seated rapidly and firmly. The patient is asked to close firmly on a cotton-wool roll to apply a steady pressure while the cement sets. With the classical cement systems excess should only be removed when the mix is completely set, taking particular care not to leave any flash of cement at the gingival margin (Fig. 11.5e). In the case of the resin-based systems excess should be removed with a small brush, once the restoration has been tacked into place with a short (10 second) cure with the polymerization light on the occlusal aspect. Once all of the excess has been removed, perhaps using dental tape interproximally, then the rest of the margins are light-cured. These luting composites will also have a self-polymerizing mechanism so that the material is fully set below surfaces that are impenetrable to the blue light.

Porcelain inlay

Modern porcelain inlays or onlays have an etched or at least a roughened fit surface. They are cemented with a composite luting cement to etched enamel and dentine or to a glass ionomer base. Thus, the retentive design of the cavity is less important than it is for a conventional cast metal inlay. There is still the need to remove caries and previous restorations, but in many cases a thick base of glass ionomer is placed, sometimes over a calcium hydroxide lining, serving

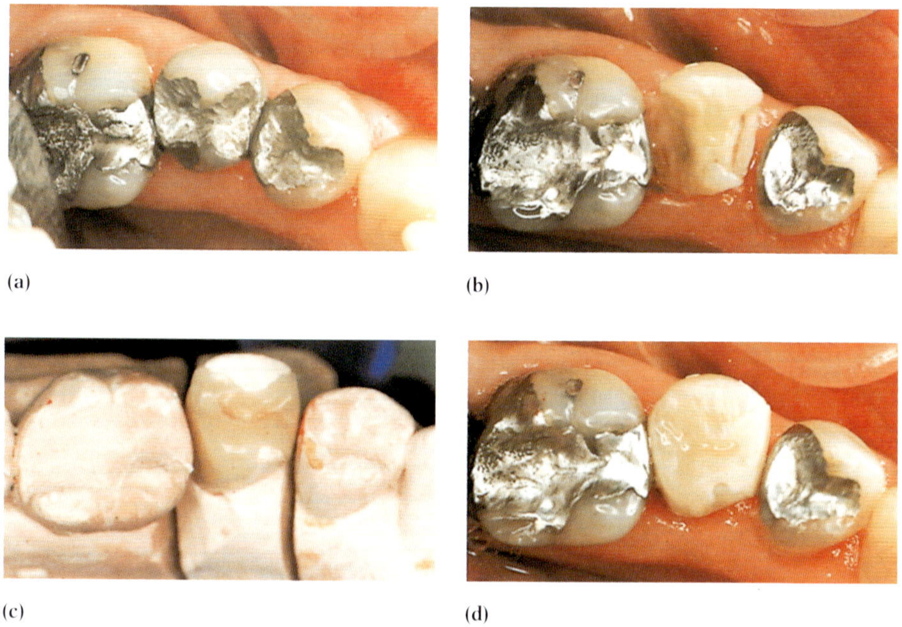

Fig. 11.6 (a) An MOD amalgam restoration in the lower second premolar tooth. Part of the lingual cusp has fractured off.
(b) The tooth prepared for a MOD porcelain inlay. A glass ionomer lining has been placed.
(c) The completed porcelain inlay on the die. This inlay was made in the laboratory on a refractory die and fired in the furnace.
(d) The porcelain inlay cemented in place. Note that the buccal margin of the restoration would be visible from the front of the mouth. This would have a better appearance in porcelain than in amalgam or gold.

the purpose of bonding together and strengthening the dentine remaining in the cusps. The porcelain inlay or onlay is primarily there to provide an occlusal layer which is resistant to abrasion and attrition.

The principles of the cavity design are that sufficient tooth or glass ionomer surface should be present for bonding and that the margins should not be bevelled.

Figures 11.6 and 11.7 show typical preparations and restorations. The impression technique is the same as for indirect cast metal inlays and the alternative laboratory techniques, which are beyond the scope of this book, are briefly outlined on p. 183.

Special luting composite resins are used for cementation. The inlay is returned from the laboratory with the surface etched with hydrofluoric acid or simply left rough as a result of removing the refractory die by sandblasting. The tooth is isolated with a rubber dam, the temporary inlay is removed, and the enamel, dentine, and any glass ionomer cement which forms part of the preparation are etched, washed, and dried to the required degree as given

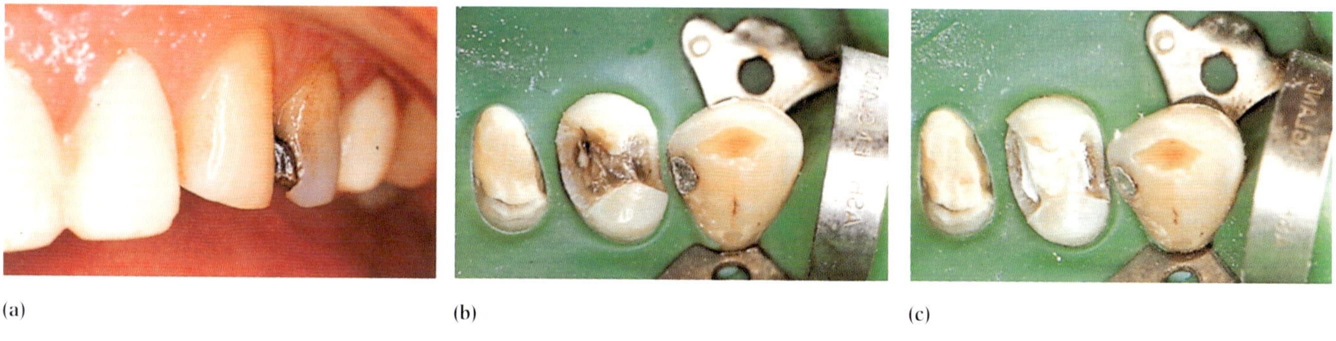

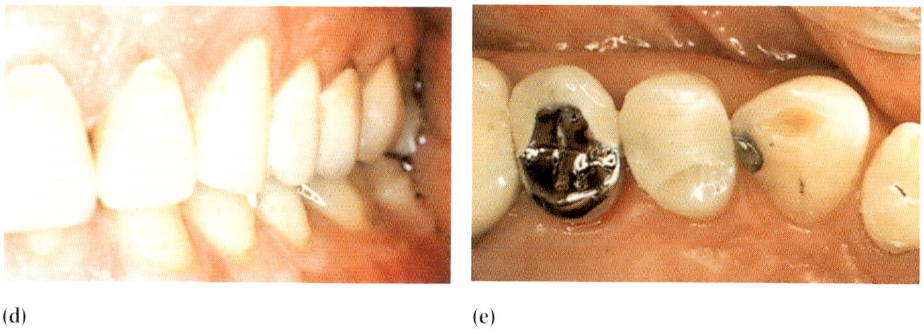

Fig. 11.7 (a) The unsatisfactory appearance of the first premolar tooth is due to the failed amalgam and the discoloration of the buccal cusp by the amalgam.
(b) The tooth has been prepared for an MOD porcelain inlay. The second premolar has also been prepared for a crown.
(c) A glass ionomer lining has been placed.
(d) The completed porcelain inlay improves the appearance of the buccal surface.
(e) The occlusal view. This inlay was made by one of the CAD/CAM techniques referred to on p. 179.

by the manufacturer's instructions. The luting resin is then applied according to the manufacturer's directions. With some luting cements the setting reaction is triggered by the application of a curing light, and the setting reaction then continues chemically. It is easier to remove excess cement before it finally sets. Once the cement is hard the rubber dam is removed and the occlusion checked with articulating paper and adjusted with fine diamond burs. Adjusted surfaces can be polished with composite finishing discs or with rubber wheels and points specifically designed for polishing porcelain.

Porcelain veneer

In most cases some tooth preparation will be necessary in order to accommodate the thickness of a porcelain veneer without making the tooth too bulky. Occasionally, the patient has had previous acrylic or composite veneers which have been added to the surface of the tooth and is therefore already accustomed to the appearance or greater bulk. In these cases little or no preparation of the enamel may be necessary once the existing veneers are removed. If preparation is required, a chamfer is produced at the gingival margin without penetrating the enamel. As the enamel tapers down to nothing at the cement–enamel junction, only a fraction can be removed before exposure of dentine. Enamel is also removed from the remainder of the buccal surface and into the contact area without going right through to the lingual side. The approximal finishing line is important. If it is left too far labially, it will show and eventually stain; if it is taken too far lingually, it will increase the difficulty of cleaning the junction and there is an increased risk of caries developing. The incisal edge may be left unprepared, or the incisal-buccal edge may be rounded off so that the veneer extends over it.

Impression techniques are again similar to the indirect cast metal inlay, although occlusal records are less important because these restorations should not be made where there is substantial occlusal contact on the restoration. An additional stage is the selection of the correct colour of porcelain using an appropriate shade guide. Temporary restorations are not usually needed. Again, the laboratory stages are outside the scope of this book.

In bonding the finished veneer it is important to achieve the correct colour. As well as choosing the correct porcelain shade, this can be done by trying in the veneer using a non-setting trial cement which is available in a variety of shades. With thin porcelain veneers the colour of the cement has a considerable influence over the appearance of the final restoration.

Once the correct shade of cement has been chosen, the tooth and facing are washed and dried and the tooth is isolated and etched. The same shade of setting cement, usually a lightly-filled, resin-based cement, is then applied to the facing and the facing is seated. The excess cement is removed and the cement is allowed to set. Most cements are initiated by a curing light.

Once any final adjustments have been made and the margins have been checked, the patient must be shown how to brush and floss to maintain the margins of the facing as plaque-free as possible, thus avoiding approximal caries and gingival inflammation (Figs. 11.8 and 11.9). Composite veneers were described and illustrated in Chapter 10.

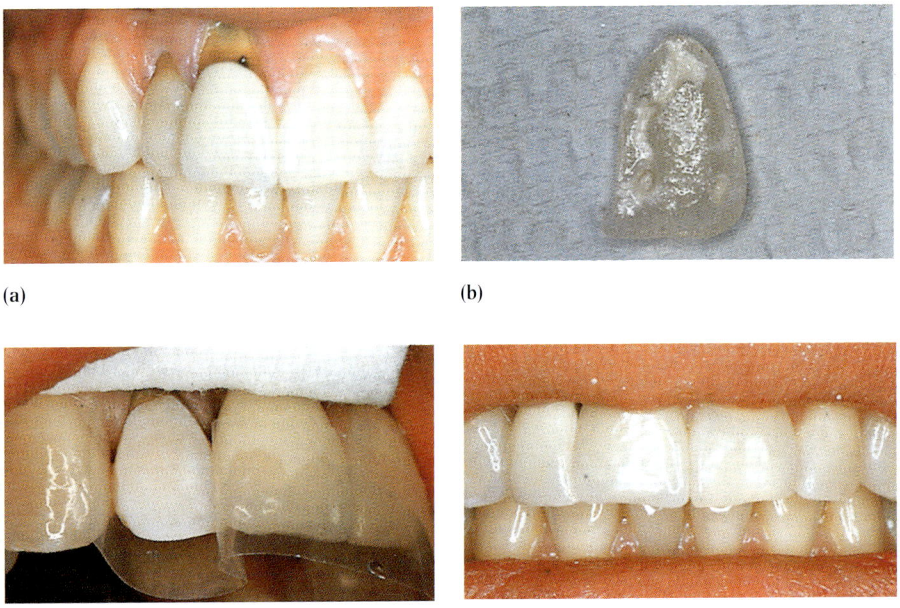

(a) (b) (c) (d)

Fig. 11.8 (a) An instanding discoloured upper lateral incisor tooth. The tooth is not vital and has been apicected, as has the central incisor. The central incisor already has a crown and a discoloured exposed root surface. However, ths does not show during normal speech and smiling.
(b) The porcelain veneer. Note the translucency.
(c) The etched enamel surface. Note that this tooth did not need any preparation as one of the purposes was to build out the contour of the tooth.
(d) The completed porcelain veneer.

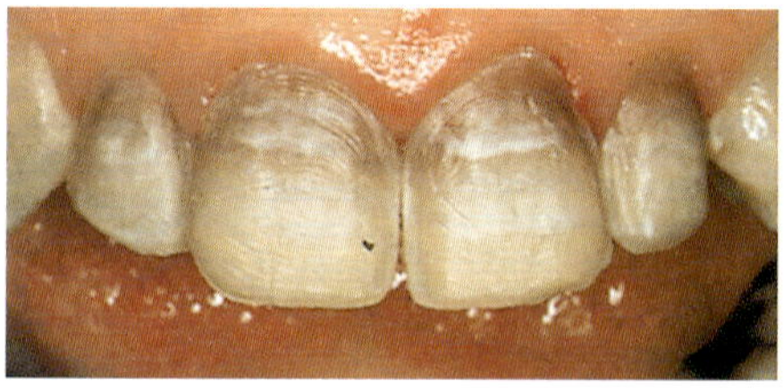

(a)

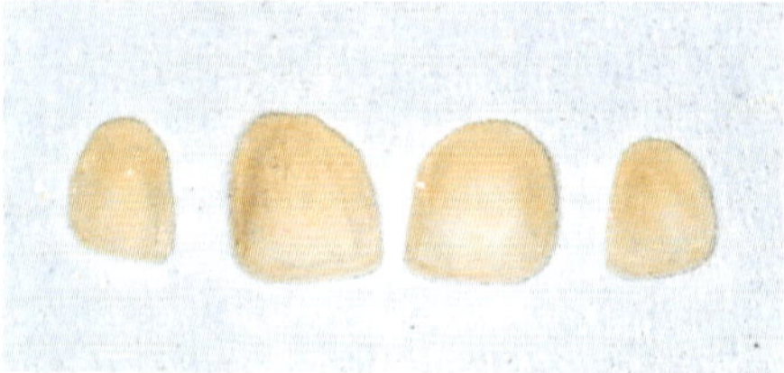

(b)

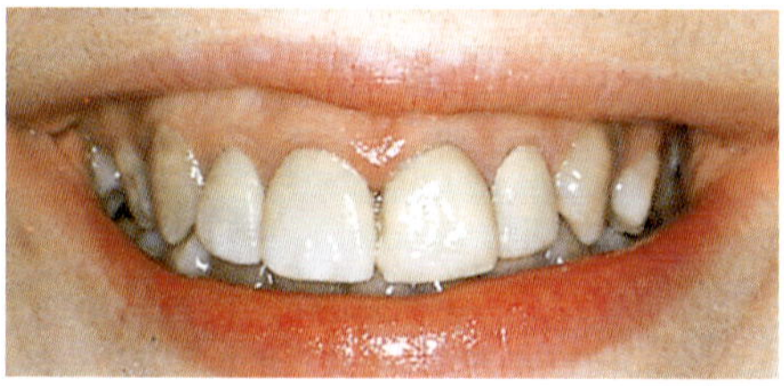

(c)

Fig. 11.9 (a) Tetracycline-stained teeth which had been treated with acrylic veneers several years ago. The margins of the veneers had begun to break down, making it difficult for the patient to clean and producing the gingival inflammation which can be seen. These teeth have now been prepared for porcelain veneers.
(b) Porcelain veneers made on refractory dies. Note that they are opaque to disguise the underlying colour of the teeth.
(c) The completed porcelain veneers.

Further reading

McLean, J. W. (1988). Ceramics in clinical dentistry. *Br. Dent. J.* **164**, 187–94.

Van Noort, R. (2002). *An introduction to dental materials* (2nd edn). Mosby Wolfe, London.

PART III

MONITORING AND MAINTENANCE

12

The long-term management of patients with restored dentitions

The long-term management of patients with restored dentitions

Introduction

Dental care involves more than the treatment of the consequences of disease. It concerns preventing disease, repair when necessary, and monitoring the restored state to ensure that health is maintained. Artificial restorations need to be checked regularly and occasionally repaired or replaced.

The dentist who has not seen his or her work fail over the years is myopic, peripatetic, or very young. It is appropriate to be critical about one's own operative work, continually seeking ways to improve. However, it is important not to be unfairly critical of the work of others, if only because we do not know the circumstances in which the restoration was done. Such criticism often betrays inexperience or arrogance. It is salutary to replace a restoration that has been condemned as faulty, only to produce a new restoration with just as many, if not more, faults. Preclinical operative dentistry is difficult, but when the manikin turns into a real person with fears, aspirations, and a small wet wriggling mouth, the difficulties are compounded.

An interesting picture has emerged from the latest UK Adult Dental Health Survey, carried out in 1998. Almost one in three young adults (16–24 years) have no fillings. Those who have most filled teeth are people aged 35 years and over. Women have more fillings than men. People from non-manual backgrounds and those reporting regular dental attendance have more fillings than those from skilled backgrounds and those who do not attend regularly. This big difference in the dental condition of younger *vs.* older people in the UK is partly due to delayed caries progression following the introduction of fluoride toothpaste about 25 years ago.

This means that there are, very broadly, three groups of adult patients:

- young people with no caries or fillings (hopefully including most dental students) who need to be helped to maintain this state
- both young and older people who do have some caries and/or recent restorations and who need to be treated as described in earlier chapters, with a very high priority given to prevention
- people, mostly older, who have a number of restorations but who have no active dental disease and have not needed any more restorations for several years (e.g. two of the authors of this book). This chapter is mostly about this group.

How long do restorations last?

A number of surveys have been carried out in general dental practice on the longevity of restorations. In these studies general dental practitioners have been asked to record, by reference to their patients' notes, the age of the restorations they have decided should be replaced. Many practitioners, from many practices, from several countries have been involved in these studies. The results are expressed as the median age of replaced restorations. This means the survival time of 50 per cent of the restorations.

The studies have been carried out over several years and, encouragingly, the median age of replaced restorations has been shown to increase over the last 20–30 years, especially for composite restorations. This is likely to reflect improvements in the material itself. The decline in caries prevalence and incidence over the last 30 years is also likely to be relevant, particularly because recurrent caries was the main reason for replacement of all types of restorations; generally more than 50 per cent of all replacements. The diagnostic criteria for what constitutes failure may also have changed over this time.

The most recent data on the age of restorations at the time of replacement indicates the median age to be 10 years for amalgam, 8 years for composite, 3 years for glass ionomer, and about 18–20 years for cast gold restorations. These figures are of some interest when comparing one material with another. For instance they indicate glass ionomer materials may not last as long as composite resin.

However, they do not help advise a patient how long a restoration will last in their mouth. This will depend on factors such as:

- their disease status
- the material used

- the size of the cavity
- the skill of the dentist.

In the collective experience of the authors, amalgam restorations last from 9 minutes to 90 years! The 9 minutes was a patient dismissed with a 'high' restoration who broke it while putting his coat on in the waiting room. The 90 years was a lady of 98 years, who had an occlusal amalgam placed in a lower first molar when she was a child.

The longevity of restorations is dependent on a number of factors, including:

- The caries risk status of the patient.
- The age of the patient. When adolescents and adults are compared restorations last longer in adults. This may reflect the susceptibility to caries of younger people.
- The type and size of restorations. Small restorations last longer than large ones.
- The restorative material.
- The diagnostic criteria of the dentist. This is particularly important with respect to recurrent caries because this is the most common reason dentists give for replacing restorations.
- The age of the dentist. Young dentists replace more restorations than older dentists.
- Whether the dentist is reviewing their own work or that of another dentist. Changing dentist puts a patient 'at risk' of the diagnosis of failed restorations.

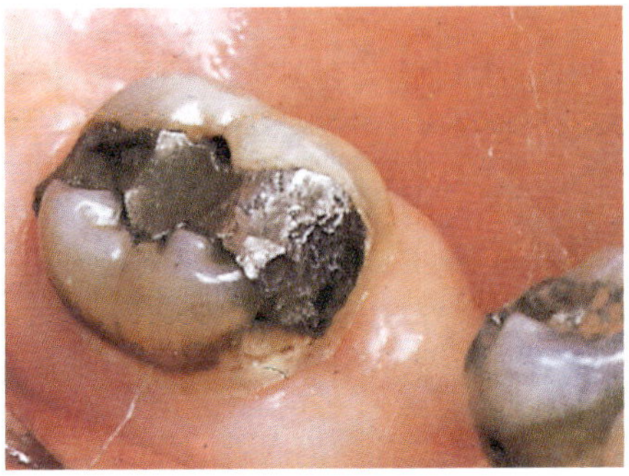

Fig. 12.1 A cavitated carious lesion is present at the cervical margin of the restoration in this molar.

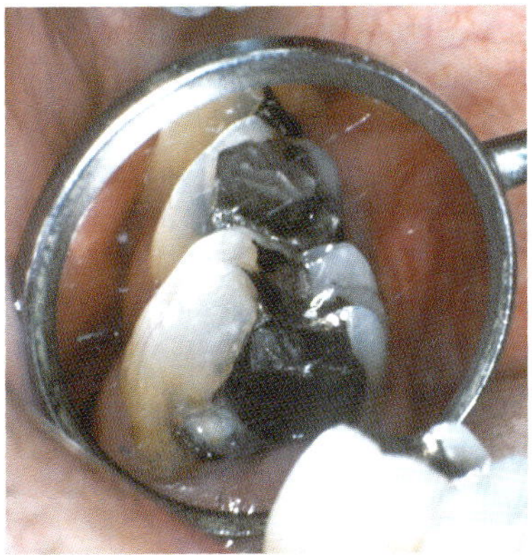

Fig. 12.2 Active secondary caries on a root surface next to an amalgam restoration.

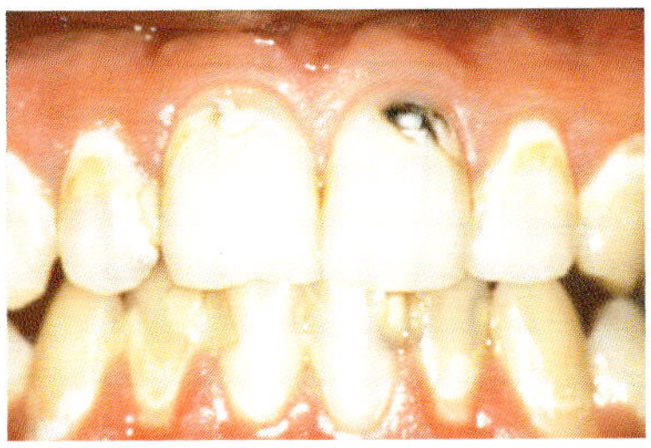

Fig. 12.3 Arrested secondary caries at the margin of the restorations on the labial surface of the upper central incisors.

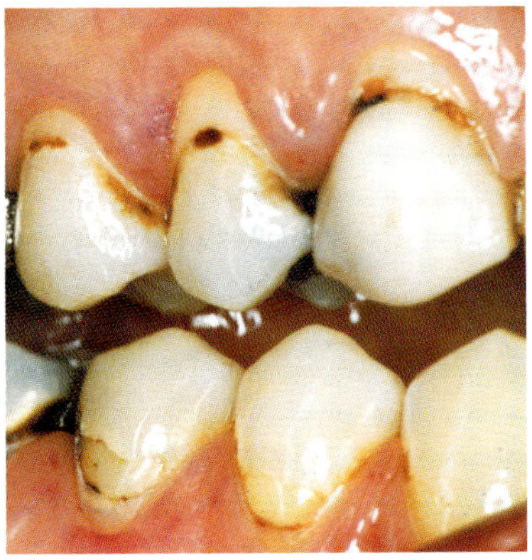

Fig. 12.4 Arrested secondary caries on a root surface next to a veneer restoration on the upper canine.

The ways in which restorations fail

Restorations commonly fail in one of two ways: new disease or technical failure. This failure may be minor, requiring only monitoring or repair, or it may necessitate replacement of the restoration.

New disease

Caries

Placing a restoration in a tooth does not confer immunity on the tooth, and new disease may occur either around a restoration or on another aspect of the tooth (Figs. 12.1 and 12.2).

New decay at the margin of a restoration is called *secondary* or *recurrent caries* and the term recurrent caries will be used in the remainder of this chapter. This *clinical* diagnosis is of enormous importance because it is the most common reason for replacement of restorations. In recent years clinical studies have taught us much about this diagnosis. The relevant points may be summarized as follows:

- Recurrent caries is primary caries at the margin of a filling.
- As with primary caries, lesions may be active (Figs. 12.1 and 12.2) or arrested (Figs. 12.3 and 12.4).

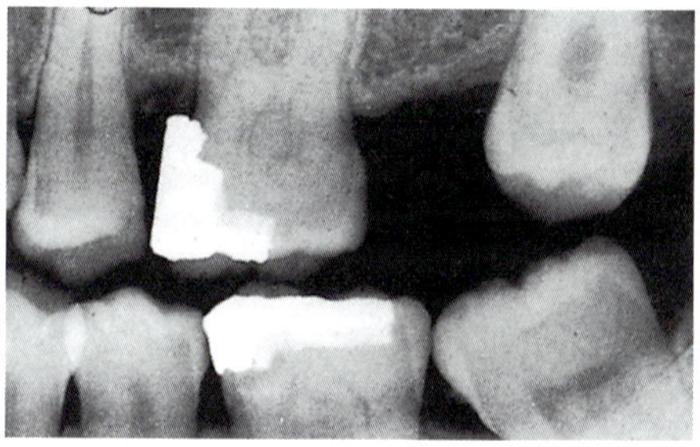

Fig. 12.5 Caries is present beneath the restoration in the lower first molar. There is a large ledge of amalgam present on the mesial aspect of the upper first. This is a plaque trap and is probably responsible for the periodontal and mesial bone loss as well as the caries.

This distinction is important because arrested lesions do not require treatment, unless there is a problem of appearance.

- It occurs in areas of plaque stagnation and for this reason it is most often seen cervically, particularly where a poorly placed restoration precludes adequate plaque removal (Fig. 12.5).
- It can be diagnosed visually (Figs. 12.1–12.4) or on radiographs. A bitewing radiograph is particularly useful (Figs. 12.5 and 12.6) to see approximal, cervical lesions but in order to differentiate the filling from the lesion, the restoration must be radio-opaque (Fig. 12.7).
- Stain around a filling is not synonymous with recurrent caries provided the margin of the restoration is intact (Figs. 12.8–12.11).
- Ditching around amalgam restorations (Fig. 12.12a) is not indicative of recurrent caries. These restorations do not need to be replaced. Ditching is usually seen occlusally where plaque removal is relatively easy, but recurrent caries occurs cervically where plaque can stagnate. Large discrepancies between a filling and a tooth may make it difficult for the patient to clean (Fig. 12.12b) and replacement may be wise to facilitate plaque control. Figure 12.12c shows a composite restoration which has fractured. This invites plaque stagnation and the restoration should be repaired (Fig. 12.12d).

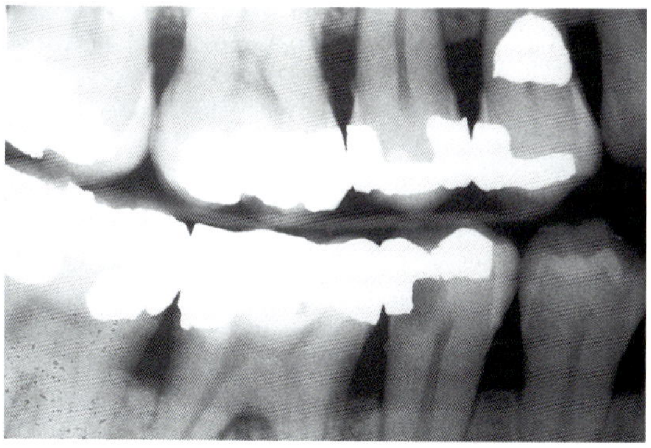

Fig. 12.6 A bitewing radiograph showing secondary caries at the margin of the lower right second premolar. Note the lesion at the margin of the tooth spreading towards the pulp.

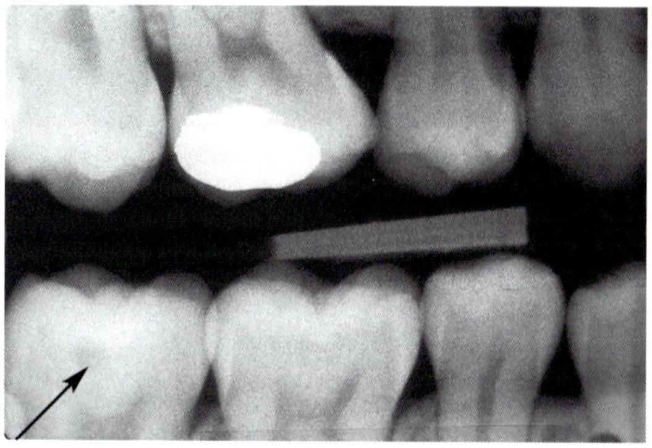

Fig. 12.7 A bitewing radiograph. A radiolucent area is present on the lower second molar. This could be caries, a restoration which is not radio-opaque, or both. In fact it was a radiolucent, tooth-coloured restoration.

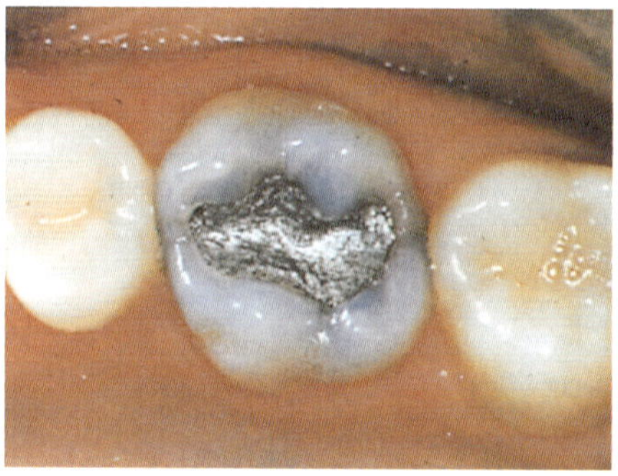

Fig. 12.8 The enamel around the amalgam in the upper first molar is discoloured. This discoloration could be due to caries or corrosion of the amalgam. Since the discoloured area is so extensive it is likely to indicate caries, which is likely to be residual (the dentist left it in the first place). If it was recurrent (new caries), a new lesion would be present next to the filling.

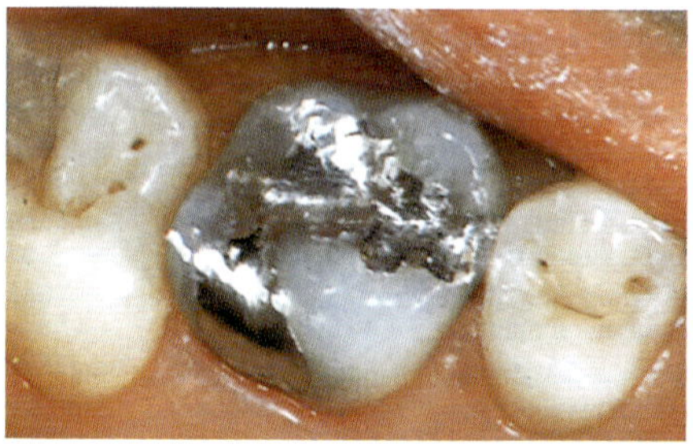

Fig. 12.9 A new amalgam restoration. Note how the amalgam discolours the tooth. In a few years time it may be difficult for another dentist to judge whether this discoloration represents the amalgam, corrosion products, or caries. (Compare with Fig. 12.8.)

WHY DOES RECURRENT CARIES SO OFTEN OCCUR GINGIVALLY?

This question is worth considering because if one can define why an adverse event occurs, one is on the way to preventing

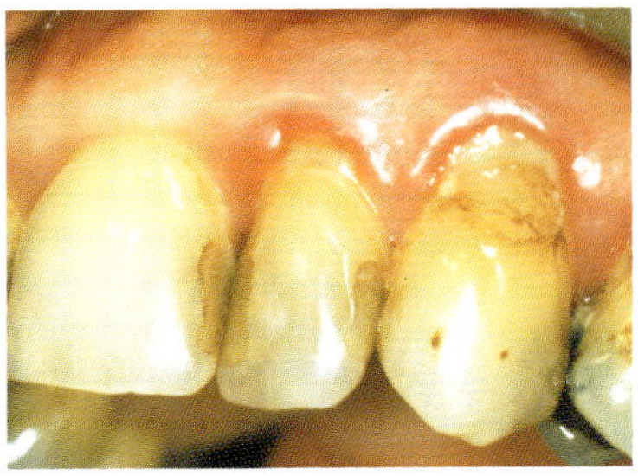

Fig. 12.10 Stain around the margins of composite restorations in the upper anterior teeth. This appearance may indicate leakage of fluid around the restoration or carious lesions developing at the filling margins. However, there is no evidence that this will either start *de novo*, or reactivate lesions in dentine *beneath* the restorations. These fillings may be replaced because appearance is a problem. Notice plaque stagnation and gingival inflammation. Oral hygiene instruction will be very important in this case.

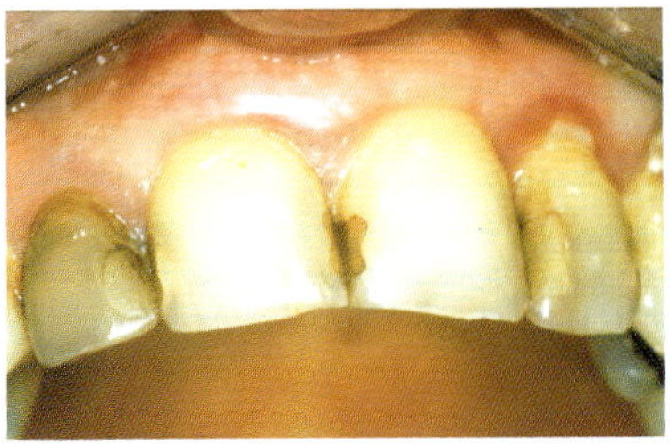

Fig. 12.11 Undermining stain around a tooth-coloured restoration on the distal aspect of the upper right central incisor. This is likely to be residual caries (the dentist left it when the tooth was restored). If the filling is not a perfect seal these areas of residual demineralized dentine may take up stain from the mouth. There is no evidence such areas represent active secondary caries. The restoration does not need to be replaced unless appearance is a problem. The upper right lateral incisor is dark because it is non-vital.

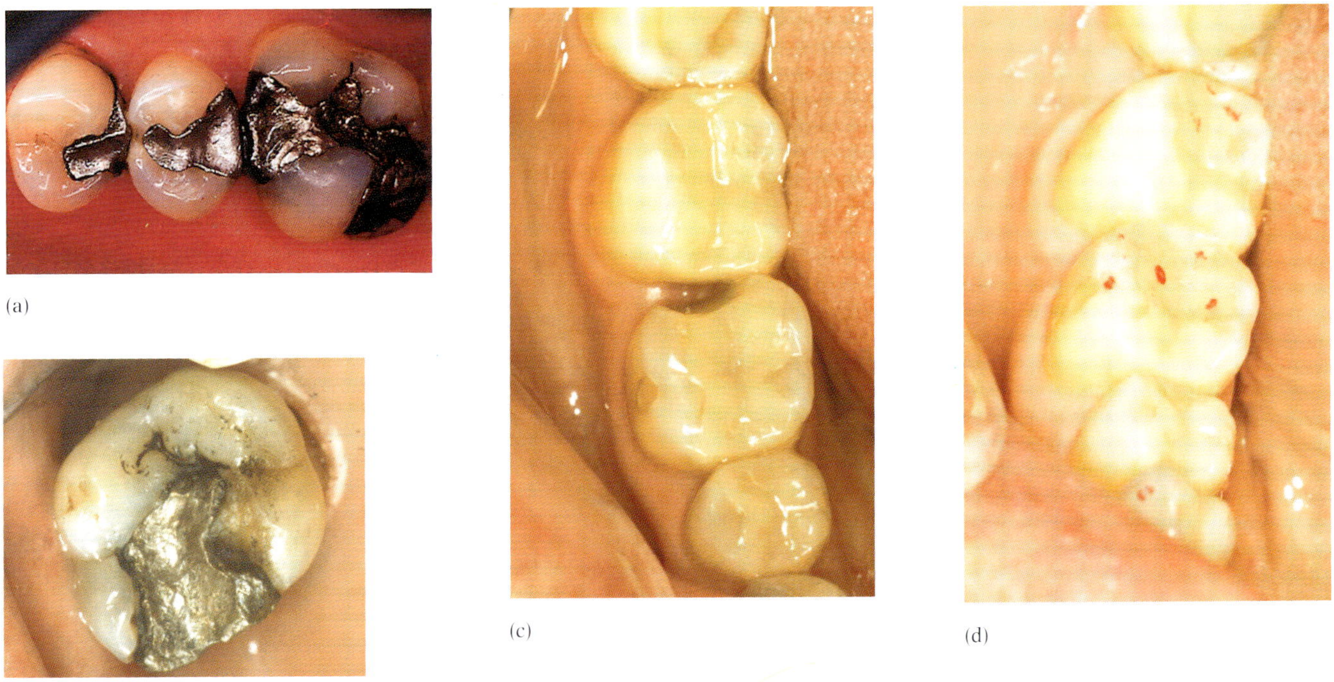

(a) (b) (c) (d)

Fig. 12.12 (a) Ditched amalgam restorations.
(b) In this tooth the marginal defects are wide enough in places to admit the tip of the periodontal probe. This restoration is difficult for the patient to clean and replacing it would facilitate plaque control.
(c) The composite inlay restoration in this molar has a marginal ridge fracture in one area only.
(d) The restoration has been repaired by gritblasting ('air abrasion') the defect and bonding new composite material to the roughened surface, using a silanating agent followed by a bonding agent. The red marks show the opposing occlusion.

it. *Mechanical tooth-cleaning can miss cervical areas*, particularly on an approximal tooth surface where only an interdental cleaning aid (e.g. floss, interdental brushes) will remove plaque. Root surfaces are also easy to miss, particularly close to the gingival margin. This means that reinforcement of oral hygiene instructions, especially focusing on the gingival part of restorations, should be an integral part of operative dentistry.

Aspects of good *clinical technique* are difficult to achieve in cervical areas. These include:

- moisture control because of the proximity of the gingival margin
- good adaptation of the filling to the tooth with neither a negative nor a positive (Fig. 12.5) ledge

- a cavo-surface margin without voids and porosities. It is critical to condense amalgam firmly into the corners of the 'box' in an approximal restoration. Similarly, a composite filling must not be left short in this area.

Finally, the *properties of the restorative materials* themselves may mitigate against good cervical adaptation. One good example of this is the shrinkage of the resin-based restorative materials on polymerization.

Laboratory study seemed to show that the fluoride-containing restorative materials, such as glass ionomer cement, might prevent recurrent caries at the margin of these fillings. Disappointingly, the clinical reality has not lived up to the laboratory promise. It appears that practitioners replace just as many glass ionomer restorations as composites because of a diagnosis of recurrent caries.

Tooth wear

Placing restorations does not prevent tooth wear occurring either around a restoration or on another aspect of the tooth (Fig. 12.13). For this reason with tooth wear, as well as with caries, it is very important to diagnose the cause of the disease and attempt to institute preventive measures.

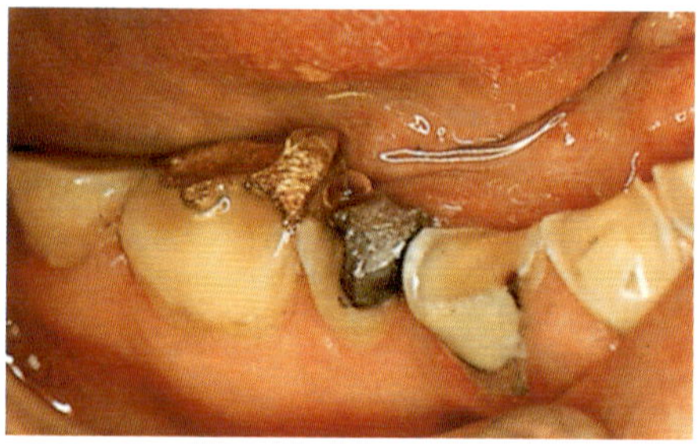

Fig. 12.13 There has been further tooth wear around the amalgam and gold restorations which are now 'proud' of the original tooth surface.

Pulpal problems

Heavily-restored teeth are liable to pulpal inflammation. The pulp of a carious tooth which was vital at the time of restoration may still undergo necrosis as a result of either the original disease or damage from the operative procedures to restore it. Toxins from the necrotic pulp result in inflammation of the periapical tissues and radiographic change (Fig. 12.14). Thus teeth with necrotic pulps should be root filled to prevent infection.

Trauma

Similarly, restoration of traumatized teeth will not prevent further trauma, although the use of a soft vinyl mouth-guard (gum shield) in those playing contact sports helps to prevent further injury. These can be made on study models, using a vacuum moulding machine and a sheet of soft plastic (Fig. 12.15), or by more sophisticated (and expensive) means, producing a better fit and better occlusion with the opposing teeth.

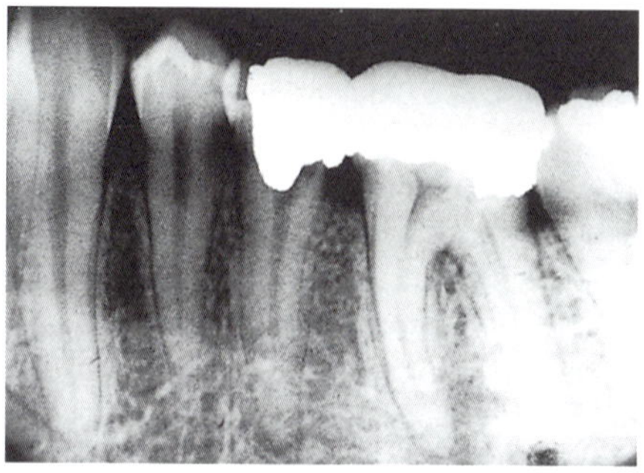

Fig. 12.14 A periapical radiograph of a heavily-restored lower second premolar. A periapical area is present and the tooth does not respond to an electric pulp test.

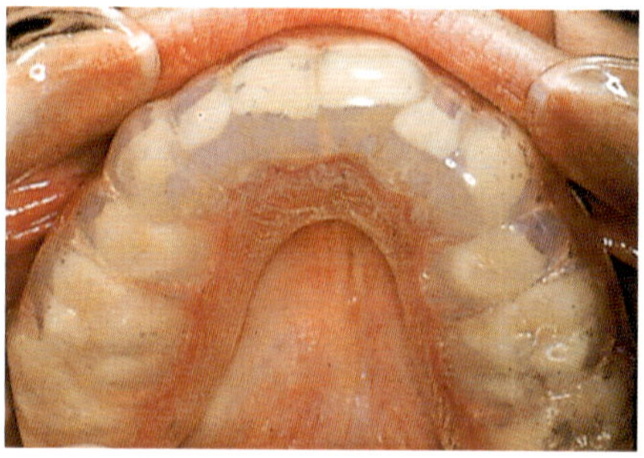

Fig. 12.15 A soft vinyl mouth-guard.

Periodontal disease

Operative dentistry may also 'fail' for periodontal reasons. The tooth in Fig. 12.16 had been well restored recently, but periodontal disease and bone loss have now progressed to the stage where the tooth has to be extracted for the patient's comfort. This emphasizes that each examination of the dentition must include a thorough periodontal examination.

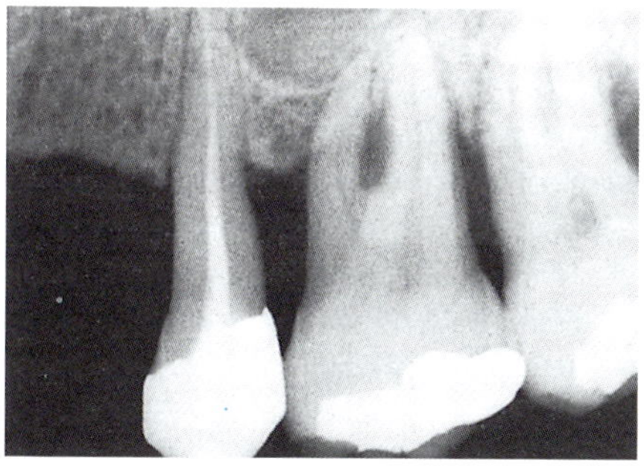

Fig. 12.16 A periapical radiograph of a well-restored upper first molar which was excessively mobile due to bone loss caused by periodontal disease.

Technical failure

There are several technical reasons why restorations may be judged to have failed.

Fractured restorations

Fractured restorations are important, particularly those where the fractured pieces remain in place (Fig. 12.17) since this invites recurrent caries. The loose restoration allows plaque stagnation around and beneath it. Frequently, however, part of the fractured restoration is lost. The tooth may be symptomless or the patient may notice sensitivity to hot and cold, food packing, or a sharp edge with the tongue. Wherever a fractured restoration is to be replaced it is important to determine why the restoration has fractured. There is often a fault in the cavity preparation, such as too thin a restoration in a high-stress-bearing area, or the occlusion may have been incorrectly adjusted, and such errors must be corrected if the new restoration is to last.

Marginal breakdown

A particular problem with amalgam restorations is the phenomenon of marginal breakdown or fracture which is often referred to as *ditching* (Fig. 12.12a). As early as 1895, G. V. Black noted this appearance and attributed it to deformation of the filling material under the stress of mastication. Recent research has confirmed this observation and has shown that the amalgam alloys with the lowest creep rate have the lowest incidence of marginal breakdown. Modern alloys with a higher copper content show a significant reduction in creep in comparison with previous alloys and are more resistant to corrosion. Since it has also been suggested that the mechanism of marginal fracture is related to corrosion, alloys with a high copper content are likely to show improved marginal adaptation, and clinical trials have confirmed this. However, ditching may be reduced by attention to detail in cavity preparation. The amalgam–margin angle must exceed 70° (see p. 60) since angles less than this are prone to fracture. As already explained, ditching is not synonymous with recurrent caries. Unless there is plaque stagnation, ditching does not necessarily result in recurrent caries. Gaps between the restoration and the tooth that are large enough to admit the end of a periodontal probe (Fig. 12.12b) may well trap plaque and be difficult for the patient to clean. These, and even larger defects, are quite capable of being repaired (Fig. 12.12c and d).

While ditching is the main cause of marginal breakdown with amalgam restorations, cast restorations which are short of the margin were almost certainly 'short' when originally fitted since cast gold or other metal does not deteriorate in this way. Immediately after cementation the gap between the casting and tooth would have been filled with cement. However, cements dissolve slowly in the oral fluids, and this may result in a space developing between the restoration and the tooth over a period.

Tooth fracture

Unfortunately, tooth fracture, especially loss of a cusp, is common (Fig. 12.18). Fractured cusps have often been

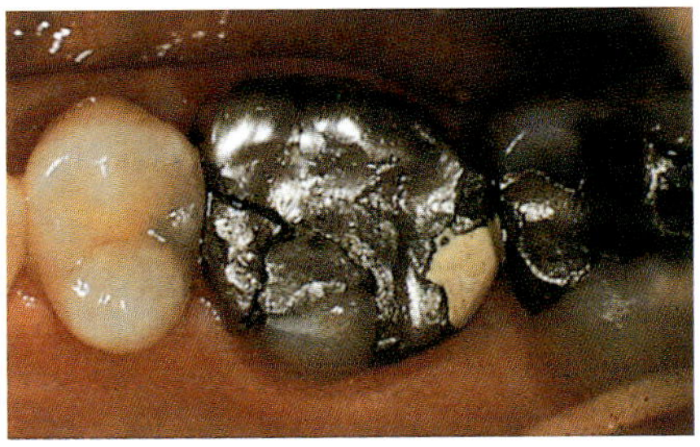

(a)

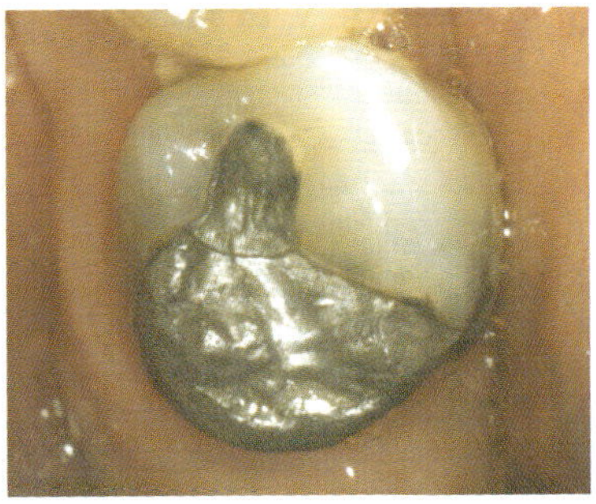

(b)

Fig. 12.17 (a) A large amalgam restoration is present in the upper first molar. A distal part of the restoration fractured and was lost. A temporary zinc oxide and eugenol dressing is in place. The amalgam is also fractured mesially, with the fractured piece remaining in place. This invites recurrent caries in this tooth. A distal carious lesion can be seen in the premolar, shining up through the marginal ridge.
(b) A fractured amalgam restoration. This restoration should be replaced.

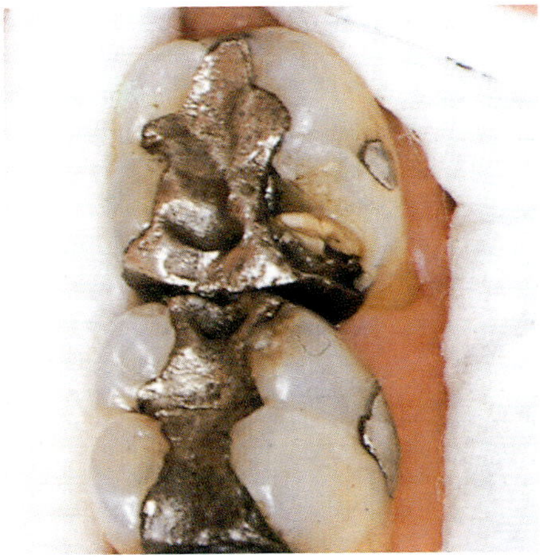

Fig. 12.18 Part of the mesio-buccal cusp of the lower second molar has fractured adjacent to an amalgam restoration.

weakened by cavity preparations for large amalgam restorations but this is not invariably the case. It is difficult to know which weakened cusps are liable to fracture and should be protected with cuspal coverage cast restorations or by adhesive intracoronal restorations, although examination of the occlusion will help.

It is not only caries that is to blame for cusp fracture. It is only too easy to over-cut cavities with the airturbine. It is sometimes necessary to replace restorations a number of times over the years, and research has shown that without sufficient care occlusal cavities are often enlarged by an average of 0.6 mm in width each time that a restoration is replaced and thus, after a number of replacements, there is simply no tooth left.

DIAGNOSIS OF CRACKED CUSPS

The diagnosis of cusp fracture is easy when the cusp has fallen off (Fig. 12.18). Before this actually happens, however, the patient may experience pain but often finds it remarkably difficult to locate this to a particular tooth. The patient will frequently complain of sensitivity to hot and cold and discomfort on biting. Even on clinical examination it is often difficult to pinpoint which tooth is causing the pain, but a fibre-optic light or disclosing solution may assist the diagnosis by making the crack easier to see. Lateral pressure on the suspect cusp may also help by producing a sensitivity that mirrors the patient's symptoms. Often the pain occurs when the pressure is released.

Defective contours

A *defective contact point* is often an immediate cause of failure of a new restoration (Fig. 12.19), and the patient may return to the surgery complaining of food packing.

In contrast, *overhanging margins*, which are particularly likely to occur approximally at the gingival margin as a result of poor matrix technique, are only noticed by fastidious flossers. This failure is often not noticed by patient and dentist until new bitewing radiographs are taken, and then the overhang is only too obvious (Fig. 12.20). Since overhanging margins are difficult to clean, they encourage plaque stagnation and therefore periodontal disease and caries.

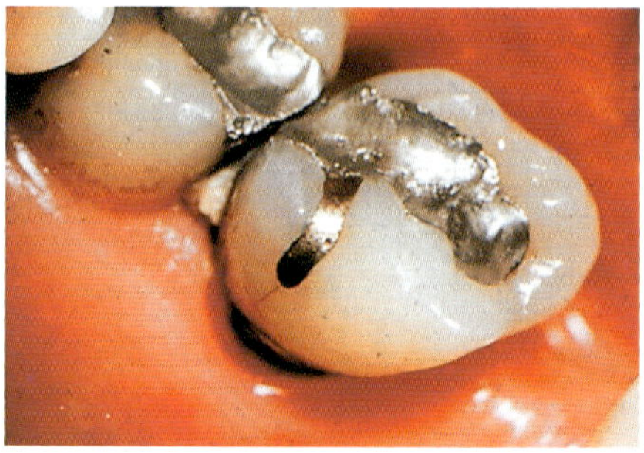

Fig. 12.19 A defective contact allowing food packing. The likely cause in this instance is mesial movement of the upper first molar following extraction of the upper second premolar.

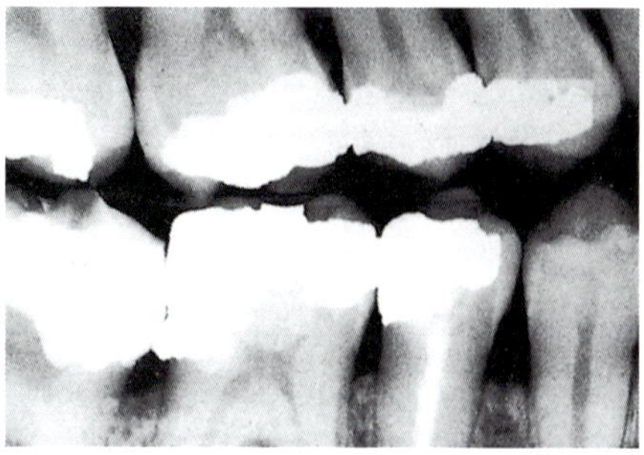

Fig. 12.20 This bitewing radiograph shows a large overhang on the distal aspect of the lower first molar. There is evidence of some distal bone loss which is probably a consequence of plaque stagnation around the overhanging restoration and subsequent periodontal disease.

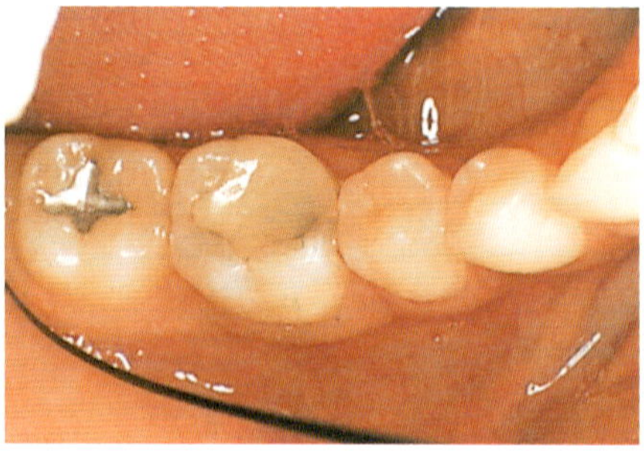

Fig. 12.21 Occlusal wear and marginal staining of the posterior composite in the lower first molar.

Occlusal wear is well resisted by gold and amalgam but was a frequent cause of failure in the first generation of posterior composites (Fig. 12.21). The newer materials described in this book are better in this respect.

Appearance

Where the appearance of a restoration is important, deterioration in the colour match of the restoration with the tooth is an important cause of failure, often noticed by the patient as well as the dentist (Figs. 12.10, 12.11, and 12.22). This problem is most common with the tooth-coloured restorative materials but can occur with amalgam restorations, where corrosion products may progressively discolour the rest of the tooth (Fig. 12.23). Residual caries (caries that was left during cavity preparation) can pick up stain from the mouth (Figs. 12.8 and 12.11). This appearance does not indicate active, recurrent (new) caries provided the margin of the restoration is intact. Recurrent caries presents as new caries at the margin of the filling, not as stain beneath a filling.

Failure of retention

A complete failure of retention is where the restoration is either lost or loose in the cavity. The latter invites recurrent caries (Fig. 12.24).

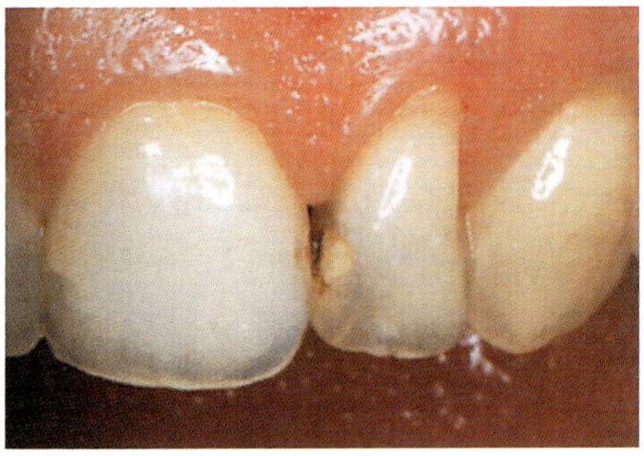

Fig. 12.22 A discoloured anterior composite on the mesial aspect of the upper left lateral incisor. The patient requested that this restoration should be replaced to improve its appearance.

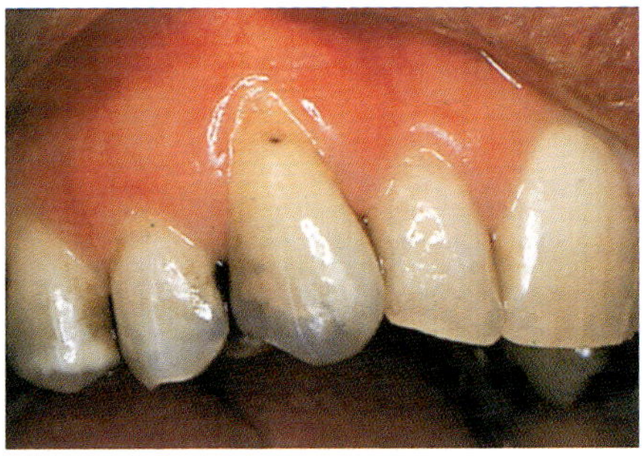

Fig. 12.23 Corrosion products around the amalgam on the distal surface of the upper right canine. The crown is discoloured and the patient is concerned by the appearance.

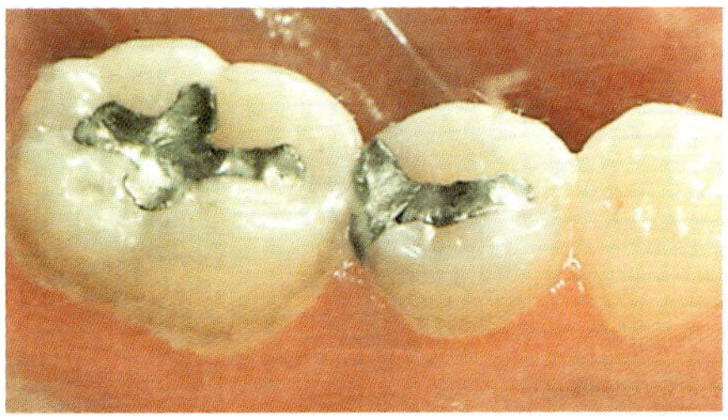

Fig. 12.24 The amalgam restoration in the lower premolar has fractured. The pieces are in place, the tooth is symptomless, and the patient is unaware that anything is wrong. The restoration should be replaced since this invites recurrent caries.

Acceptable and unacceptable deterioration or failure

Research has shown that wide variation occurs between dentists in deciding which restorations have failed and should be replaced. The diagnosis of recurrent caries (the commonest reason given by dentists for a decision to replace a restoration) in particular has caused confusion, although in recent years evidence from clinical research has helped to define the criteria that are given on pp. 194 and 195. Unfortunately, the reasons for failure given by clinicians are subjective and very variable. These are uncomfortable findings which have disturbed the profession, but they are not altogether surprising. Dental students will probably not be surprised because they become used to variation in diagnosis and treatment planning among their teachers. The perspicacious dental student will realize that a treatment plan may have more to do with the attitude of the teacher with respect to when to restore caries or replace a restoration than the amount of disease with which the patient presents. This variation is inevitable when many factors, some of them poorly understood, are involved, and where additional research findings and clinical experience influence dentists at different rates.

Bias will also be contained within these pages. Many textbooks of operative dentistry do not address these questions which, in view of the confusion which exists within the profession, is understandable. However, since so much of operative dentistry is the replacement of restorations that are judged to have failed, it is unacceptable not to give guidance.

The patient's perception of the problem

The patient's opinion can and should influence the dentist's advice. The patient shown in Fig. 12.22 was unhappy with the appearance of the composite restoration; therefore this restoration, which was otherwise acceptable, was replaced. Some patients would be prepared to accept this appearance.

Similarly, the fractured cusp shown in Fig. 12.18 caused discomfort, as did the food packing occasioned by the defective contact seen in Fig. 12.19. In each case these restorations were replaced. The patient requested a tooth-coloured crown to deal with the staining around the amalgam in Fig. 12.23. Since considerable further destruction of the tooth would have been needed, this was not considered to be in the patient's best interest, and after discussion with the patient it was agreed that the amalgam should be replaced by a posterior composite.

Sometimes dentist and patient do not reach agreement because the dentist cannot accept that the patient's request is in their best interest. When this happens, they should agree to differ and part company. On no account should a dentist be persuaded to carry out treatment which they believe to be ill-advised. Not only is this unethical, but it is cases like this that subsequently may go wrong and can result in litigation. A patient's request to replace all their amalgam restorations with tooth-coloured fillings is a good example of this. The dentist may consider that research evidence indicates that large restorations would not serve as well if composite was used instead of amalgam (see p. 61 for a discussion of the toxicity of mercury in amalgam and the risks of an allergic response).

The dentist's assessment of the effect of technical failure

The patient is often unaware of technical failure. The fractured restorations in Fig. 12.17b and the loose restoration in Fig. 12.24 were causing no symptoms but both were replaced because of the danger of development of recurrent caries. However, Fig. 12.25 shows an occlusal amalgam

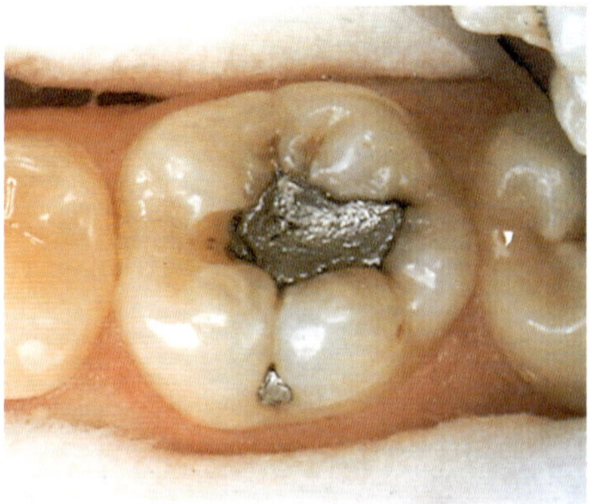

Fig. 12.25 An occlusal restoration is present in the lower first molar. The mesial portion of the amalgam has fractured, probably because the cavity is very shallow. Since the area is caries-free, easy to clean, and symptomless, this restoration does not have to be replaced yet. It would probably have been better to restore this tooth initially with a sealant restoration. If the amalgam does eventually have to be replaced, it would be advisable to consider replacing it with a sealant restoration. The fissures on the lingual side of the occlusal surface (top of the picture) are already stained, suggesting early caries at the base of the fissures.

with one small part fractured away. The cavity is very shallow (probably the cause of the fracture), easy to clean, and symptomless. Such a restoration might be left since its replacement with amalgam would result in the destruction of further sound tooth substance. However, a sealant restoration could be considered.

The ditched restorations shown in Fig. 12.12a also should not be replaced automatically. Ditched restorations should be accepted and put under review. This approach is particularly applicable in mouths which are not caries-prone. Replacement restorations frequently contain the same in-built errors as their predecessors. However, where a margin is severely ditched, so that it will admit the tip of a periodontal probe, plaque accumulation and therefore caries is encouraged. In this case it may be logical to repair only that part of the restoration, concentrating on improving it. If amalgam is used for the repair, a small retentive cavity is prepared. Alternatively, a composite can be used, in which case the ditched crevice is prepared as for a composite restoration.

Unfortunately, it is common to see ledges on amalgam restorations on bitewing radiographs. These ledges usually cause plaque accumulation and gingival inflammation. Bleeding on gentle probing with a pocket measuring probe is evidence of this inflammation. Usually the ledge should be removed (see p. 204) or the restoration replaced to aid plaque control.

Monitoring techniques: recall and reassessment

Monitoring dental health or restored health is one of the most important aspects of dental care. A course of treatment involving operative dentistry does not end once restorations have been completed. The aim of the initial course of treatment is to determine the level of dental disease, to find the cause, to arrest it by preventive means, and to provide restorations as required. However, these restorations do not themselves prevent further disease, but by restoring the integrity of the tooth surface they aid plaque control. This is why high-quality restorative dentistry is worth the effort, and shoddy work can be detrimental by encouraging plaque accumulation. However, it is the patient's efforts to improve plaque control, to control diet, and to apply other preventive measures which are of prime importance. It is patients who primarily control caries, not dentists.

Why then is it necessary to see patients again when all that appears to be required is compliance with simple preventive measures? To answer this, an analogy with the well-known relationship between smoking and lung cancer helps. Since this knowledge does not stop everyone smoking, why should the relationship between the frequency of sugar intake and caries modify a patient's diet? Patients vary both in their susceptibility to the disease and in the lengths to which they are prepared to go to prevent it. However, preventive advice may be more readily accepted if it is regularly reinforced. Thus dentists recall their patients to repeat and modify any relevant preventive advice, to detect any new disease sufficiently early for preventive measures to arrest it, and to detect and repair technical failure. In addition, early disease is monitored to see whether preventive measures are being effective. This applies equally to caries, tooth wear, and periodontal disease.

Frequency of recall

How frequently should patients be seen for reassessment? This depends partly on the susceptibility of the individual to the various dental diseases and the success or otherwise of their preventive efforts; there is no general rule that can be applied to all. However, it is useful to have some guidance.

All patients should have been placed into a caries risk category, either high or low, with all others (this is likely to be the majority) designated as medium risk (see p. 16). High-risk patients should be reviewed at three-monthly intervals. Medium-risk patients should return for review after one year and longer periods may be appropriate for low-risk patients. Dentists should be in the low-risk group with the knowledge and motivation to prevent dental disease.

The patient's age and the natural history of the disease should also be considered. Teeth are most susceptible to occlusal enamel caries as they erupt. Frequent recall to check oral hygiene is appropriate with some children, with fissure sealants being placed if good oral hygiene is not established.

As far as tooth wear is concerned, a six-month or annual recall is usually appropriate where wear is excessive for the patient's age.

The recall assessment

The recall visit follows a pattern similar to the initial assessment described in Chapter 2. The history will concentrate on what has happened since dentist and patient last met. For instance, it is important to recheck the medical history carefully, but questions about past dental history need not be asked again except to check that no other dental treatment has been provided in the interim. When the clinical examination is carried out, particular attention is paid to areas noted as important or specifically requiring monitoring. Thus, where suspect restorations or early carious lesions have been put on probation, a careful check of these is required (Fig. 12.26).

The vitality of heavily-restored teeth should be checked, paying particular attention to those where direct or indirect pulp caps were placed at the last visit.

Study casts are of particular assistance in monitoring the rate of tooth wear (Fig. 12.27). It is easier to compare two sets of casts than original casts with the current clinical picture.

The recall visit is in many ways one of the particular pleasures of the profession. When dentist and patient first meet they know very little about each other, but as the years pass they became better acquainted. Both dentist and patient often come to expect what will happen at the recall visit; perhaps a check that all is well and catching up on a year's news of family and work events. However, there is a trap here for the unwary professional. It is all too easy to assume that the mouth is stable or to perform a perfunctory examination, perhaps missing signs of early root caries, bleeding on probing in some areas, a sinus discharging over a non-vital tooth, or even an early malignancy. Attention to detail is vital.

If, as a result of proper history, examination, and special tests, treatment is required, the dentist should differentiate between that caused by essentially preventable disease and that occasioned by mechanical, aesthetic, or functional defects. The former require the patient's active cooperation in further preventive action.

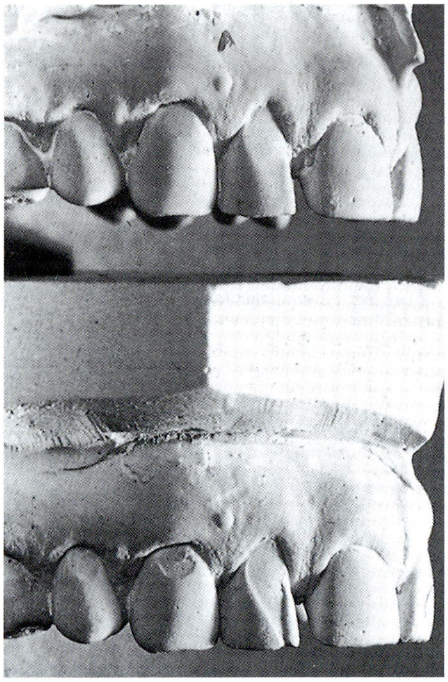

Fig. 12.27 Two study casts showing progressive tooth wear. There was a three-year interval between the two impressions.

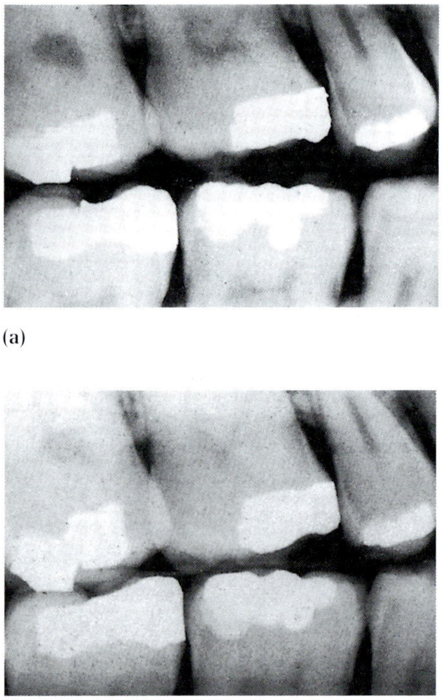

(a)

(b)

Fig. 12.26 (a) A bitewing radiograph showing an early distal carious lesion on the upper second premolar. Preventive advice was given and the rough amalgam on the mesial aspect of the upper first molar was smoothed with a linen strip to aid plaque control and flossing by the patient. A new radiograph was taken after six months to check that the lesion had not progressed.
(b) A bitewing radiograph of the same area taken 18 months later. The carious lesion has apparently arrested.

Techniques for removal, adjustment, and repair

Up to now the operative part of this text has considered cavity designs unfettered by the presence of old restorations. Some mouths are already restored, and dentists currently spend more time replacing existing unsatisfactory restorations than treating new carious lesions.

Amalgam

Amalgam is a relatively easy restorative material to remove. An appropriate size and shape of Beaver bur (see p. 98) is

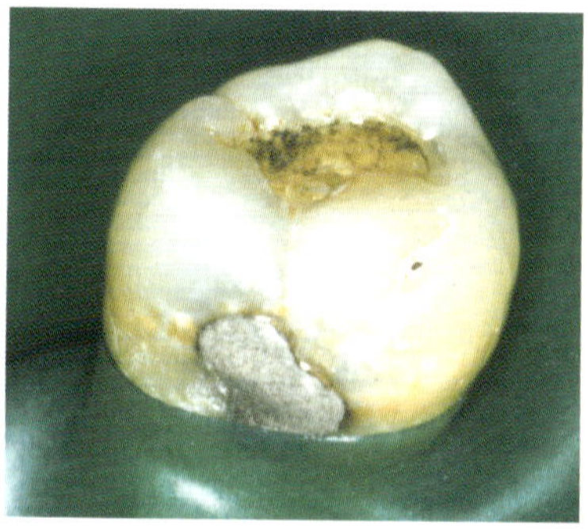

Fig. 12.28 Corrosion products from the amalgam have discoloured the cavity walls. The tissue is hard and should not be needlessly sacrificed to produce a 'clean' margin.

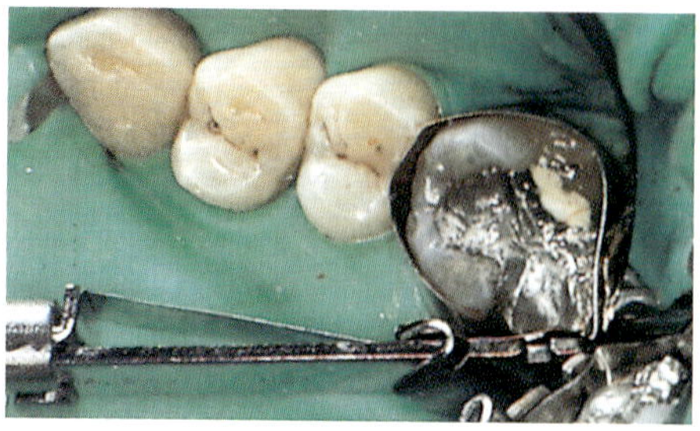

Fig. 12.29 A large pinned amalgam restoration (two pins) was present in this upper first molar. The disto-buccal cusp fractured. The original amalgam is satisfactory and if it is removed two good pin sites will be lost. For this reason a third pin has been inserted and the amalgam will be repaired to serve as the base for a complete gold crown.

used in the air turbine, and is inserted into the middle of the restoration and moved towards the cavity walls. The restoration can generally be removed with this bur but small fragments of amalgam may be left attached to the cavity walls and over the pulp; these are then broken away from the wall or floor with an excavator or probe. Removing amalgam in this way avoids unnecessary over-cutting of the cavity. No attempt should be made to 'freshen up' the margins. The cavity walls will often be discoloured (Fig. 12.28) by corrosion products from the amalgam filling. Both the enamel and dentine may be discoloured and this tissue should not be removed unless it is soft. Soft dentine may represent *residual caries* that a previous dentist left in place. This is usually hard and dry. It may be removed with an excavator although it is minimally infected and this is not essential. *Recurrent caries* presents as primary caries around the filling margin and the soft infected dentine should be removed. Thus the cavity should only be extended where caries dictates, where it has proved to be unretentive, or where the margin requires modification for other reasons such as chipped enamel or incorrect cavo-surface angle. Old lining material need not be removed unless caries has spread underneath it or the patient has symptoms of pulpitis and the operator wishes to look for an exposure.

It is often possible to repair an amalgam restoration, and this can be preferable to its complete removal where a single area requires extension or replacement. In these circumstances, removal and replacement of the entire restoration may introduce new faults. However, a decision to repair rather than replace a restoration should always be reviewed during the repair.

Where new disease on another aspect of the tooth necessitates extension of a restoration, consideration should always be given to retaining part of the original filling. Exactly the same argument applies to restorations where part of the tooth fractures away. The original restoration may well be retained and a new cavity designed alongside and within it (Fig. 12.29). However, there is a need for some mechanical retention (such as a lock) between the new and the old filling and/or a bonded amalgam technique (see p. 148). This technique can be particularly useful where pins are present in the original restoration. It is very difficult to remove such a restoration leaving the pins intact. If the pins are cut off when the restoration is removed, new pin sites will have to be found and this is difficult and risky for the pulp and periodontal ligament.

The possibility of replacing failed amalgam restorations with composite or glass ionomer–composite layered restorations should be considered. For example, they should be considered for the replacement of the restorations shown in Fig. 12.25, the first premolar in Fig. 12.12a, and the canine in Fig. 12.23 (where it was in fact used). Composite could also be used for the premolar in Fig. 12.24, particularly if the cause of the amalgam fracture was that the cavity was too shallow. In this instance a composite could be placed without deepening the cavity, whereas this would be necessary for a replacement amalgam.

Composite and glass ionomer cement

Tooth-coloured filling materials are much more difficult to remove than amalgam because the colour of the composite or glass ionomer cement is almost impossible to distinguish from the tooth when under the water spray. Use of an air turbine is again obligatory and small tungsten carbide or diamond burs may be chosen. The technique is similar to that with amalgam except for the following:

- The materials should never be chipped away from the enamel or dentine walls because these materials are adhesive and the forces are likely to fracture the enamel at the cavity margins.
- The operator should stop frequently and the dental nurse should dry the tooth. A colour difference between tooth and composite will now be easier to see.

Repair of these materials is an accepted technique as the new filling bonds to the old with adequate strength in some clinical situations. Such repairs can be particularly well executed by the use of airbrasion to remove the surface and defective areas of the old restorations (Fig. 12.12c and d).

The rough surface is excellent for giving a mechanically rough surface for bonding. Where new material is to be added to old, it is important to cut some of the old material away to produce a clean surface for bonding. Where a restoration is subject to occlusal stress it is usually better to replace it.

Cast metal and ceramic restorations

These restorations can be time-consuming and tedious to remove. An appropriate size of Beaver bur in an air turbine handpiece is the instrument of choice for cutting cast metal, and diamond burs should be used for ceramic restorations. It may be possible to divide the restoration and then use a stiff instrument, such as a Mitchell's trimmer, to flex the metal towards the cut and break the cement seal, allowing the pieces to be removed individually. If the crown has been bonded to the tooth preparation using a resin bonding system then its removal will be a very slow process and somewhat tedious. Great care should be taken not to fracture the tooth when removing an intracoronal restoration.

A small localized marginal discrepancy in an inlay caused either by an area of new decay or a lack of fit of the original restoration can be repaired by preparing a cavity adjacent to the inlay and restoring it with glass ionomer cement or composite.

Removal of ledges

It is very easy to produce a ledge of restorative material overhanging the gingival margin cervically: careful use of matrices, wedging, and early carving of this critical area will help to avoid this fault. Despite care, ledges may sometimes be created and discovered on a subsequent bitewing radiograph (Fig. 12.20). Alternatively, the error may present as bleeding of the gingiva on probing as a result of plaque stagnation.

Buccal and lingual ledges are relatively easy to remove with fine tapered tungsten carbide or diamond finishing burs (see p. 99) but since these also cut the tooth easily, great care must be taken. Proximal ledges on tooth-coloured restorative materials can often be removed with abrasive strips, although where such ledges are large it may be less traumatic to the gingival margin and quicker to remove and replace the entire restoration or part of it.

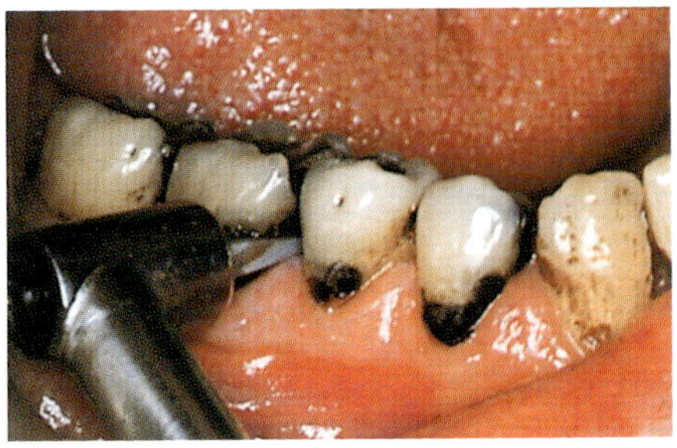

Fig. 12.30 An Eva handpiece being used to remove a ledge on the mesial aspect of the lower first molar.

Proximal ledges on amalgam restorations can be more difficult to remove. Sometimes the ledge is accessible to trimming with a flame-shaped steel finishing bur or metal abrasive strip. Alternatively, a special handpiece (Eva), designed specifically for the task, can be used (Fig. 12.30). This has a reciprocating (in-and-out) movement rather than revolving action. Small triangular wedge-shaped points, coated with abrasive on one side, are used in the handpiece to grind away the ledge. However, even when this is successful the remaining amalgam is often porous because it was not properly retained and condensed when it was being packed, and so, with extensive ledges, particular attention should be paid to wedging and trimming when the restoration is being replaced.

Further reading

Mjör, I. A. (1993). Repair versus replacement of failed restorations. *Int. Dent. J.* **43**, 466–72.

Mjör, I. A. (2000). The age of restorations at replacement in permanent teeth in general dental practice. *Acta. Odontol. Scand.* **58**, 97–101.

Mjör, I. A., Moorhead, J. E., and Dahl, J. E. (2000). Reasons for replacement of restorations in permanent teeth in general dental practice. *Int. Dent. J.* **50**, 361–6.

Mjör, I. A. and Toffenetti, F. (2000). Secondary caries: a literature review with case reports. *Quintessence Int.* **31**, 165–79.

Pine, C. M., Pitts, N. B., Steele, J. G., Nunn, J. N., and Treasure, E. (2001). Dental restorations in adults in the UK in 1998 and implications for the future. *Br. Dent. J.* **190**, 4–8.

Index